Spanish Chemical
&
Pharmaceutical
Glossary

Spanish Chemical
&
Pharmaceutical
Glossary

Dr. Hilda M. Zayas

SCHREIBER PUBLISHING
Rockville, Maryland

Spanish Chemical & Pharmaceutical Glossary
Hilda M. Zayas

Published by:

Schreiber Publishing
Post Office Box 4193
Rockville, MD 20849 USA

800-296-1961
SchreiberLanguage.com

Library of Congress Cataloging-in-Publication Data

Zayas, Hilda M.
  Spanish chemical and pharmaceutical glossary / Hilda M. Zayas
    p. cm.
  ISBN 978-0-88400-315-1
1.   Chemistry-Dictionaries. 2. Pharmacy--Dictionaries. 3.
Drugs--Dictionaries. 4. English language--Dictionaries--Spanish. I. Title.

QD5.Z39 2005
540'. 03--dc22

2005010958

PREFACE

There has always been a need for a Spanish - English glossary that includes the most important and frequently used chemical and pharmaceutical terms. It is my hope that this glossary satisfies this need and that it will serve as a valuable tool for translators, scientists, and everyone with an interest in this field.

Throughout my career, I have translated volumes of chemical and pharmaceutical material from English into Spanish. Finding just the right word or phrase to express the equivalent English meaning sometimes presented quite a challenge, especially without the appropriate reference tool. This has motivated me to author this glossary, the objective of which is to provide a precise Spanish translation for such scientific English terms.

This glossary has been rigorously alphabetized in order to facilitate the location of appropriate references. Please note, however, that Latin prefixes (cis, trans, sec, terc, vec), Greek prefixes (α, ß, ϒ, meta, orto, para, uns, sim), and position indicators (N- ; 1,4- etc.) have not been taken into consideration for alphabetizing.

PREFACIO

Siempre ha existido la necesidad de un glosario en inglés y castellano en el que figuraran los términos más importantes y de uso frecuente en química y farmacia. Es mi deseo que este glosario satisfaga esa necesidad y sirva de ayuda a traductores, investigadores y todos los que estén interesados en esta área.

A lo largo de mi carrera he traducido frecuentemente material químico y farmacéutico al castellano, encontrando a veces dificultades en hallar la palabra o frase correcta para expresar el término equivalente en inglés, particularmente al no contar con referencias apropiadas, lo que me llevó a preparar este glosario cuyo objetivo principal fuese dar una traducción precisa en castellano de cada término en inglés.

En este glosario, las palabras siguen un orden alfabético riguroso para facilitar su localización, pero los prefijos latinos (cis, trans, sec, terc, vec.), griegos (α, ß, ϒ, meta, orto, para, uns o unsim, sim) y los indicadores de posición (N- ; 1,4-, etc.) no se han tomado en cuenta en dicha alfabetización.

ACKNOWLEGMENTS

My most heartfelt gratitude goes to D.Vilma Vosskaemper of Scientific Spanish Translation. Her assistance in the editing of this glossary, as well as her constant support and advice, made this project possible.

June 26, 2005   Dr. Hilda M. Zayas

AGRADECIMIENTO

Mi más sincero agradecimiento va a D. Vilma Vosskaemper (Scientific Spanish Translations), por su asistencia en la preparación de este glosario, así como por sus consejos y apoyo en todo momento.

ABOUT THE AUTHOR

The author, Dr. Hilda M. Zayas, was born in Camagüey, Cuba in 1925. She lived in Camagüey until she relocated to attend the University of Havana, where she received a Doctor of Pharmacy degree in 1948. After graduation, Dr. Zayas worked as a registered pharmacist until 1958, when she opened her own pharmacy in Havana.

The unfortunate events that ocurred in Cuba in the late 1950's and early 1960's caused an abrupt change in direction for Dr. Zayas. Leaving her thriving business behind, she and her familiy immigrated to the United States in 1961, settling in northern New Jersey.

Dr. Zayas was able to obtain employment with a major New Jersey based pharmaceutical manufacturer in late 1961. Falling back on her formal training, she worked as a research scientist in the manufacturer's Physical Chemistry Department, where she played an instrumental role in the development and testing of several new and very sucessful medications.

After 11 years as a research scientist, Dr. Zayas left the laboratory in 1972 and moved into the International Regulatory Affairs department, where she specialized in product registrations in Europe and Latin America. Many of the same products she helped develop in the laboratory were now her responsibility to present to foreign regulatory agencies for marketing and distribution approvals. Her lab and research experience proved invaluable in presenting the necessary scientific and study data. It was during this period that she utilized her scientific knowledge and her command of the Spanish language to translate thousands of scientific documents, conveying the required data properly to foreign governments.

Dr. Zayas has since retired from an active role in the pharmaceutical industry and currently serves as a freelance scientific and chemical translator. She still resides in the United States, but in the warmer climate of South Florida. This glossary is her first publication.

ACERCA DE LA AUTORA

La autora, Dra. Hilda M. Zayas, nació en Camagüey, Cuba en 1925. Vivió en Camagüey hasta que se mudó a la Habana para asistir a la Universidad donde obtuvo el Doctorado en Farmacia en el año 1948. Después de graduada, la Dra Zayas ejerció su profesión hasta el año 1958, en el que abrió su propia farmacia en La Habana.

Los sucesos desafortunados, de finales de los años 50 y principio de los 60, causaron un repentino cambio en la vida de la Dra. Zayas. Dejando atrás un negocio próspero, ella y su familia emigraron a los Estados Unidos en el año 1961 y se radicaron en el norte de Nueva Jersey.

La Dra. Zayas obtuvo empleo con una compañía farmacéutica importante de Nueva Jersey a finales de 1961. Capitalizando en su formación previa, trabajó como Investigadora Científica en el Departamento de Física y Química, donde desempeñó un papel importante en el desarrollo y análisis de varios medicamentos nuevos y de gran éxito.

Después de 11 años en esta posición, la Dra. Zayas dejó el laboratorio en el año 1972 pasando al departamento de Asuntos Reglamentarios Internacionales, donde se especializó en el registro de productos farmacéuticos en Europa y América Latina. Muchos de los mismos productos que había ayudado a elaborar en el laboratorio pasaron ahora a ser responsabilidad suya para presentarlos a agencias reglamentarias de otros paises para solicitar aprobación mercadotécnica y para distribución. La experiencia adquirida en el laboratorio y en las investigaciones, fueron de un valor incalculable en presentar los datos científicos necesarios. Fue durante esta época en que la Dra. Zayas utilizó sus conocimientos científicos y su dominio de la lengua castellana para traducir gran número de documentos científicos y transmitir, en forma apropiada, los datos exigidos por los diversos gobiernos.

La Dra. Zayas se ha jubilado de su papel activo en la industria farmacéutica y en la actualidad trajaba por su cuenta como traductora de documentos científicos y químicos. Todavía reside en los Estados Unidos pero en los climas más cálidos del sur de la Florida. Este glosario es su primera publicación.

A

AAMX.
abreviatura de
acetoacetil-meta-xilidida
abaca
abacá (cáñamo de
Manila)
abacus
ábaco
abamectin
abamectina
abate, to
disminuir, abatir
ABC salt
sal de ABC (sal sódica
del ácido 3',4"-azobis-
4-difenilcarboxílico)
abciximab
abciximab
aberration
aberración
abherent
antiadherente
abies siberica oil
aceite de *Abies siberica*
abietate
abietato
abietic acid
ácido abiético
abietic anhydride
anhídrido abiético
abietinic acid
ácido abietínico
abikoviromycin
abicoviromicina
A-bomb
bomba atómica
abradant
abrasivo
abrade, to
raer, gastar
abrasion
abrasión
abrasive
abrasivo
abridge, to
abreviar
abrin
abrín
abrine
abrina
abrupt
brusco
abscisic acid
ácido abscísico

abscisin
abscisina
absciss, abscissa
abscisa
absent
ausente
absinthe oil
esencia (aceite) de
absenta
absinthin
absentina
absinthium
absenta, ajenjo
absolute
absoluto
absolute alcohol
alcohol absoluto
absolute density
densidad absoluta
absolute humidity
humedad absoluta
absolute temperature
temperatura absoluta
absolute zero
cero absoluto
absolutely
absolutamente
absorb, to
absorber
absorbance
absorbancia
absorbate
absorbato, producto de
la absorción
absorbency
absorbencia
absorbent
absorbente
absorbent charcoal
carbón absorbente
absorbent clay
arcilla absorbente
absorber
absorbedor, torre de
absorción
absorbing
absorbente
absorption
absorción, absorbencia
absorption band
banda de absorción
absorption coefficient
coeficiente de
absorción

absorption oil
aceite de absorción
absorption spectrum
espectro de absorción
absorption spectroscopy
espectroscopía de
absorción
absorption tower
torre de absorción
absorptive
absorbente
absorptivity
absorbencia, capacidad
de absorción
ABS resin
(acrylonitrilebutadiene-
styrene resin)
resina de ABS
(resina de acrilonitrilo,
butadieno y estireno)
abstract
resumen
abstract, to
extraer, resumir
abstraction
abstracción
abundance
abundancia
abundance ratio,
isotopic
proporción de
abundancia isotópica
abundant
abundante
acacetin
acacetina
acacia
acacia
acacic acid
ácido acácico
acaprazine
acapracina, acaprazina
acarbose
acarbosa
acaricide
acaricida
accelerate, to
acelerar
accelerated aging test
prueba de añejamiento
(envejecimiento)
acelerado
acceleration
aceleración

accelerator
acelerador
acceptable risk
riesgo aceptable
acceptance
aceptación, recepción,
captura
acceptor
aceptor
access
acceso
accessibility
accesibilidad
accessible
accesible
accesories
accesorios
acclimatization
aclimatación
account, to
interpretar
account for, to
dar cuenta de
accretion
aumento,
acrecentamiento
accumulation
acumulación
accumulation point
punto de acumulación
accuracy
precisión, exactitud
accuracy of
measurement
exactitud de la medida,
precisión de las
medidas
accuracy of readings
exactitud de las
lecturas
accurate
exacto, preciso
acebrochol
acebrocol
aceburic acid
ácido acebúrico
acebutolol
acetobutolol
acecarbromal
acecarbromal
acecainide
acecainida
aceclidine
aceclidina

aceclofenac
aceclofenaco
acedapsone
acedapsona
acediasulfone
acediasulfona
acediasulfone sodium
acediasulfona sódica
acedoben
acedobén
acefurtiamine
acefurtiamina
acefylline
acefilina
acefylline clofibrol
clofibrol acefilínico
acefylline piperazine
piperacina acefilínica,
piperazina acefilínica
aceglatone
aceglatona
aceglutamide
aceglutamida
acelazotamide
acelazotamida
acemetacin
acemetacina
acenaphthene
acenafteno
1,2-acenaphthenedione
1,2-acenaftendiona
acenaphthenequinone
acenaftenquinona
acenocoumarin
acenocumarina
acenocoumarol
acenocumarol
aceperone
aceperona
acephate
acefato
acepromazine
acepromacina,
acepromazina
aceprometazine
aceprometazina,
aceprometazina
acequinoline
acequinolina
acerin
acerina
acerola
acerola
acesulfame
acesulfamo
acetadol
acetadol
acetal
acetal

acetal resin
resina acetálica, resina
de acetal
acetaldehyde
acetaldehído
acetaldehyde ammonia
acetaldehído
amónico
acetaldehyde
cyanohydrin
acetaldehído
cianhidrínico
acetaldehyde sodium
bisulfite
acetaldehído de
bisulfito de sodio
acetaldol
acetaldol
acetaldoxime
acetaldoxima
acetalising
acetalización
acetamide
acetamida
acetamidine
hydrochloride
clorhidrato de
acetamidina
acetamido
acetamido
3-acetamido-5-
aminobenzoic acid
ácido 3-acetamido-5-
aminobenzoico
5-acetamido-8-amino-
2-naphthalenesulfonic
acid
ácido 5-acetamido-8-
amino-2-
naftalensulfónico
8-acetamido-5-amino-
2-naphthalenesulfonic
acid
ácido 8-acetamido-
5-amino-2-naftalen-
sulfónico
p-acetamidobenzene-
sulfonyl chloride
cloruro de
p-acetamidobencen-
sulfonilo
•-acetamidocaproic
acid
ácido •-acetamido-
caproico
acetamidocyanoacetic
ester
éster acetamido-
cianoacético

acetamidoeugenol
acetamidoeugenol
3-acetamido-4-
hydroxybenzene-
arsonic acid
ácido 3-acetamido-4-
hidroxibencenarsónico
8-acetamido-2-
naphtalensulfonic
acid magnesium salt
sal de magnesio del
ácido 8-acetamido 2-
naftalensulfónico
acetaminophen
acetaminofeno,
acetaminofén
p-acetaminophenol
p-acetaminofenol,
acetaminofeno
acetaminosalol
acetaminosalol
acetanilide
acetanilida
acetanisidine
acetanisidina
acetanisole
acetanisol
acetarsol
acetarsol
acetarsone
acetarsona
acetate
acetato
acetate dye
colorante de acetato
acetate fiber
fibra de acetato
acetate fiber, saponified
fibra de acetato
saponificada
acetate film
película de acetato
acetate of lime
acetato de cal
acetate process
proceso de acetato
acetazolamide
acetazolamida
acetergamine
acetergamina
acetiamine
acetiamina
acetic acid
ácido acético
acetic acid amine
amina del ácido
acético
acetic acid glacial
ácido acético glacial

acetic aldehyde
aldehído acético
acetic anhydride
anhídrido acético
acetic ester
éster acético
acetic ether
éter acético
acetic fermentation
fermentación acética
acetic oxide
óxido acético
acetification
acetificación
acetify
acetificar
acetimeter,
acetometer
acetímetro
acetimidoquinone
acetimidoquinona
acetin
acetina
acetiromate
acetiromato
acetoacetanilide
acetoacetanilida
acetoacet-o-anisidide
acetoacetil-o-anisidida
acetoacet-o-chloranilide
acetoacetil-o-
cloranilida
acetoacet-p-
chloranilide
acetoacetil-p-
cloranilida
acetoacetic acid
ácido acetoacético,
ácido acetilacético
acetoacetic ester
éster acetoacético
acetoacet-toluidine
acetoacetiltoluidina
acetoacet-m-xylidide
acetoacetil-m-xilidida
acetoaminofluorene
acetoaminofluoreno
p-acetoanisole
p-acetoanisol
acetobromglucose
acetobromoglucosa
acetoglyceride
acetoglicérido
acetohexamide
acetohexamida
acetohydroxamic acid
ácido acetohidroxámico
acetoin
acetoína

acetol
acetol
acetoluidide
acetoluidida
acetolysis
acetólisis
acetomeroctol
acetomeroctol
acetone
acetona
acetone cyanohydrin
cianhidrina acetónica
acetone oils
aceites acetónicos
acetone oxime
oxima acetónica
acetone semicarbazone
semicarbazona
acetónica
acetone sodium
bisulfite
bisulfito sódico de
acetona
acetonecarboxylic acid
ácido aceton-
carboxílico
acetonedicarboxylic
acid
ácido acetondi-
carboxílico
acetonitrile
acetonitrilo
acetonyl alcohol
alcohol acetonílico
acetonylacetone
acetonilacetona
3-(α -acetonylbenzyl) -
4-hydroxycoumarin
3-(α-acetonilbencil)-4-
hidroxicumarina
3-(α-acetonylfurfuryl)-
4-hydroxycoumarin
3-(α-acetonilfurfuril)-
4-hidroxicumarina
3-(α-acetonylnitro-
benzyl)-4-hydroxy-
coumarin
3-(α-acetonilnitro-
bencil)-4-hidroxi-
cumarina
acetophenazine
acetofenacina,
acetofenazina
acetophenetidin
acetofenetidina
acetophenone
acetofenona
acetophenone oxime
oxima acetofenónica

acetophenone acetone
acetofenonacetona
acetophenone-p-
phenetidine
acetofenona-p-
fenetidina
acetorphine
acetorfina
acetose, acetous
acetoso, acedo
acetostearin
acetoestearina
acetosulfone sodium
acetosulfona sódica
acetotoluide
acetotoluida
acetoxime
acetoxima
acetoxolone
acetoxolona
o-acetoxybenzoic acid
ácido o-acetoxi-
benzoico
acetoxylation
acetoxilación
4-(p-acetoxyphenyl)-2-
butanone
4-(p-acetoxifenil)-2-
butanona
21-acetoxy-
pregnenolone
21-acetoxi-
pregnenolona
acetozone
acetozona
acetrizoate sodium
acetrizoato de sodio
acetryptine
acetriptina
aceturate
aceturato
aceturic acid
ácido acetúrico
acetyl
acetilo
acetyl benzoyl
peroxide
peróxido de
acetilbenzoílo
acetyl bromide
bromuro de acetilo
acetyl carbamide
acetilcarbamida,
carbamida acética
acetyl carbinol
acetilcarbinol, carbinol
acetílico
acetyl chloride
cloruro acetílico

acetyl eugenol
acetileugenol, eugenol
acetílico
acetyl iodide
yoduro acetílico
acetyl ketene
acetilceteno
acetyl nitrate
nitrato acetílico
acetyl oxide
óxido acetílico
acetyl peroxide
peróxido acetílico
acetyl phenol
acetilfenol, fenol
acetílico
4-acetyl resorcinol
4-acetil resorcinol
acetyl sulfamethoxy-
pyrazine
acetilsulfametoxi-
piracina,
acetilsulfametoxi-
pirazina
acetyl sulfisoxazole
acetilsulfisoxazol
acetyl triallyl citrate
citrato de acetiltrialilo
acetyl tributyl citrate
citrato de acetiltributilo
acetyl triethyl citrate
citrato de
acetiltrietilo
acetyl valeryl
acetilvalerilo
acetyl value
valor acetilo
acetylacetanilide
acetilacetanilida,
acetanilida acetílica
acetylacetic acid
ácido acetilacético
acetylacetonate bis
(ethylene) rhodium
acetilacetonato
bis(etileno) de rodio
acetylacetonate
dicarbonyl rhodium
acetilacetonato
dicarbonílico de rodio
acetylacetone
acetilacetona, acetona
acetílica
acetylate
acetilato
acetylate, to
acetilar
acetylation
acetilación

acetylator
acetilador
acetylamino
acetilamino
acetylaminoacetic acid
ácido
acetilaminoacético
p-acetylamino-
benzenesulfonyl
chloride
cloruro de p-acetil-
aminobencensulfonilo
o-acetylaminobenzoic
acid
ácido o-acetilamino-
benzoico
acetylamino
hydroxy phenyl-
arsonic acid
ácido acetilamino-
hidroxifenil arsónico
p-acetylaminophenol
p-acetilaminofenol
p-acetylaminophenyl
salicylate
salicilato de
p-acetilaminofenilo
p-acetylanisole
p-acetilanisol
N-acetylanthranilic
acid
ácido N-acetil-
antranílico
acetylation
acetilación
acetylbenzene
acetilbenceno
N-acetyl-N-
bromodietylacetyl urea
urea N-acetil-N-
bromodietilacetílica
α-acetylbutyrolactone
α-acetilbutirolactona
acetylcarbromal
acetilcarbromal,
carbromal acetílico
acetylcarnitine
acetilcarnitina,
carnitina acética
acetylcholine
acetilcolina
acetylcholine
bromide
bromuro de
acetilcolina
acetylcholine chloride
cloruro de acetilcolina
acetylcholinesterase
acetilcolinesterasa

3

acetylcysteine
acetilcisteína
acetyldigitoxin(e)
acetildigitoxina
acetylene
acetileno
acetylene black
negro de acetileno, negro
de humo de acetileno
acetylene dibromide
dibromuro de acetileno
acetylene dichloride
dicloruro de acetileno
acetylene hydrocarbon
hidrocarburo de
acetileno
acetylene polymer
polímero de acetileno
acetylene tetrabromide
tetrabromuro de
acetileno
acetylene tetrachloride
tetracloruro de
acetileno
acetylene torch
soplete oxiacetilénico
acetyleneurea
acetilenurea, urea
acetilénica
acetylenogen
acetilenógeno
**N-acetylethanol-
amine**
N-acetiletanolamina,
etanolamina N-acetílica
**acetylethanoltrimethyl
ammonium hydroxyde**
hidróxido de
acetiletanoltrimetil
amonio
acetylferrocene
acetilferroceno,
ferroceno acetílico
acetylformic acid
ácido acetilfórmico
N-acetylglycine
N-acetilglicina
acetylide
acetiluro
acetylisoeugenol
acetilisoeugenol,
isoeugenol acetílico
**acetylleucine mono-
ethanolamine**
monoetanolamina
acetilleucínica
acetylmethadol
acetilmetadol, metadol
acetílico

acetylmethionine
acetilmetionina,
metionina acetílica
**5-acetyl-2-methoxy-
benzaldehyde**
2-metoxibenzaldehído
5-acetílico
acetylmethylcarbinol
acetilmetilcarbinol,
carbinol acetil-
metílico
N-acetylpenicillamine
N-acetilpenicilamina
acetylphenetidin
acetilfenetidina
acetylpheneturide
acetilfeneturida
**N-acetyl-p-phenylene-
diamine**
N-acetil-p-fenilen-
diamina
acetylpropionic acid
ácido
acetilpropiónico
acetylpropionyl
acetilpropionilo
acetylsalicylic acid
ácido acetilsalicílico
N-acetylsulfanilamide
N-acetilsulfanilamida
acetylsulfanilic acid
ácido acetilsulfanílico
**N-acetylsulfanilyl
chloride**
cloruro de N-
acetilsulfanililo
acetyltannic acid
ácido acetiltánico,
acetato de tanilo
2-acetylthiophene
2-acetiltiofeno
acetyl-o-toluidine
acetil-o-toluidina
acetyl-p-toluidine
acetil-p-toluidina
**acetyl-tri-2-ethylhexyl
citrate**
citrato de acetil-tri-2-
etilhexilo
N-acetyltryptophan
N-acetiltriptófano
acetylurea
acetilurea
acevaltrate
acevaltrato
acexamic acid
ácido acexámico
achromatic
acromático

achromatism
acromatismo
aciclovir
aciclovir
acicular
acicular
acid
ácido
1,2,4-acid
ácido-1,2,4
acid alkylation
alquilación ácida
acid amide
amida ácida
acid ammonium sulfate
sulfato ácido de
amonio
**acid ammonium
tartrate**
tartrato ácido de
amonio
acid anhydride
anhídrido ácido
acid bath
baño ácido
acid black 2
negro ácido 2
acid butyl phosphate
fosfato butílico ácido
acid calcium phosphate
fosfato ácido de calcio
acid chlorides
cloruros ácidos
acid dye
colorante ácido
acid ethyl sulfate
sulfato ácido de etilo
acid fungal protease
proteasa micótica ácida
acid, fatty
ácido graso
acid free
libre de ácido, sin ácido
acid fuchsin
fucsina ácida
acid glaucine blue
azul ácido de glaucina
acid, hard
ácido fuerte
acid inhibitor
inhibidor de ácido
acid lining
revestimiento ácido
acid magenta
fucsina ácida, magenta
ácida
acid magnesium citrate
citrato ácido de
magnesio

**acid magnesium
phosphate**
fosfato ácido de
magnesio
acid methyl sulfate
sulfato ácido de metilo
acid number
número ácido, valor
ácido
acid phosphatase
fosfatasa ácida
acid phosphate
fosfato ácido
acid potassium oxalate
oxalato ácido de
potasio
acid potassium sulfate
sulfato ácido de
potasio
acid precipitation
precipitación ácida
acid proof
a prueba de ácidos
acid radical
radical ácido
acid rain
lluvia ácida
acid resistant
antiácido, resistente al
ácido
acid salt
sal ácida
acid sludges
sedimentos ácidos
acid, soft
ácido débil
acid soluble
soluble en ácido
acid treatment
tratamiento ácido
acid value
valor ácido
acid violet 7b
violeta ácida 7b
acid washed
lavado al ácido
acid yellow
amarillo ácido
acidaffin
acidafina
acidic
ácido, acidógeno
acidic oxide
óxido ácido
acidification
acidificación
acidifier
(sustancia)
acidificante

4

acidify, to
acidificar
acidimeter
acidímetro
acidimetry
acidimetría
acidity
acidez
acidulant
acidulante
acidulate, to
acidular, aumentar la
acidez, acidificar
acifluorfen
acifluorfeno
acipimox
acipimox
acivicin
acivicina
acitretin
acitretina
aclacinomycine
aclacinomicina
aclantate
aclantato
aclarubicin
aclarrubicina
aclatonium
napadisilate
napadisilato de
aclatonio
aclimatization
aclimatización
acoin
acoína
aconiazide
aconiazida
aconine
aconina
aconite
acónito
aconitic acid
ácido aconítico
aconitine
aconitina
aconitine, amorphous
aconitina amorfa
aconitum ferox
acónito indio
acoxatrine
acoxatrina
acraldehyde
acraldehído
acranil
acranilo
acrid
acre, agrio, corrosivo
acridine
acridina

acridine orange
naranja de acridina
acridine yellow
amarillo de acridina
acridorex
acridorex
acriflavine
acriflavina
acriflavinium
chloride
cloruro de acriflavinio
acrihellin
acrihelina
acrisorcin
acrisorcina
acrivastine
acrivastina
acrocinonide
acrocinonida
acroleic acid
ácido acroleico
acrolein
acroleína
acrolein dimer
dímero de acroleína
acrolein resins
resinas acroleínicas
acronine
acronina
acrylaldehyde
aldehído acrílico
acrylamide
acrilamida
stacking gel solution
solución de apilado de
gel de acrilamida
acrylate
acrilato
acrylate resins
resinas de acrilatos
acrylic
acrílico
acrylic acid
ácido acrílico
acrylic aldehyde
aldehído acrílico
acrylic fiber
fibra acrílica
acrylic resin
resina acrílica
acrylic rubber
caucho acrílico
acrylonitrile
acrilonitrilo,
propenonitrilo, cianuro
vinílico
acrylonitrile-butadiene
rubber
caucho de acrilonitrilo

y butadieno
acrylonitrile dimer
dímero de acrilonitrilo
acryloyl chloride
cloruro de aciloílo
ACS (American
Chemical Society)
ACS (Sociedad de
Químicos
Estadounidenses)
actagardin
actagardina
actaplanin
actaplanina
ACTH
ACTH, corticotropina,
hormona
adrenocorticotrófica
actin
actina
actinic
actínico
actinic ray
rayo actínico
actinide series
serie de los
actínidos
actinides
actínidos
actinism
actinismo
actinium
actinio
actinium series
familia del actinio
actinobolin
actinobolina
actinodaphnine
actinodafnina
actinomycetin
actinomicetina
actinomycin
actinomicina
actinon
actinón
actinoquinol
actinoquinol
actinorhodine
actinorrodina
action
acción
actiphenol
actifenol
activate, to
activar
activated
activado
activated alumina
alúmina activada

activated charcoal
carbón activado
activated molecule
molécula activada
activated sludge
sedimento activado
activation
activación
activation analysis
análisis por activación
activation energy
energía de activación
activator
activador
active
activo
active amyl alcohol
alcohol amílico activo
active carbon
carbón activado
active coat pellet
gránulo de
recubrimiento activo
activine
activina
activity
actividad
activity chemical
agente químico
activo
activity coefficient
coeficiente de
actividad
activity series
serie de actividad
actodigin
actodigina
actoll
actato de plata
actual value
valor real
actuate, to
accionar
actuator
accionador
acute
agudo
acute angle
ángulo agudo
acyclic
acíclico
acyclovir
aciclovir
acyclovir sodium
aciclovir sódico
acyl
acilo
acylate, to
acilar

5

acylation
acilación
1-adamantanamine hydrochloride
clorhidrato de 1-adamantanamina
adamantane
adamantano
adamexine
adamexina
adamsite
adamsita, difenil-aminocloroarzina, cloruro de fernasarzina
adapalene
adapaleno
adapt, to
adaptar
add
sumar, agregar, añadir
add up, to
agregar
addendum
apéndice, adenda, agregado
addition
adición, suma, agregado
addition compound
compuesto agregado
additional
adicional
additional patent
patente adicional
addition polymer
polímero de adición
additive
aditivo
adduct
aducto
adduct (inclusion complex)
aducto (complejo de inclusión)
adenine
adenina
adenocorticotropic hormone
hormona adenocorticotrófica
A-denopterin
A-denopterín
adenosine
adenosina
adenosine diphosphate
difosfato de adenosina
adenosine monophos-phate

monofosfato de adenosina
adenosine phosphate
fosfato de adenosina
adenosine triphosphate
trifosfato de adenosina
S-adenosylmethionine
S-adenosilmetionina
3'-adenylic acid
ácido 3'-adenílico
5'-adenylic acid
ácido 5'-adenílico
adequacy
pertinencia
adherence
adherencia
adhere, to
adherir
adherent
adherente
adhesion
adhesión
adhesive
adhesivo
adhesive, high temperature
adhesivo de alta tempertura
adhesive, hot-melt
adhesivo de fusión en caliente
adhesive, rubber-based
adhesivo a base de caucho
adhesiveness
adherencia
adiabatic
adiabático
adiabatic expansion
expansión adiabática
adiabatic index
índice adiabático
adiabatic process
proceso adiabático
adicillin(e)
adicilina
adinazolam
adinazolán, adinazolam
adiphenine
adifenina
adiphenine hydrochloride
clorhidrato de adifenina
adipic acid
ácido adípico
adipiodone
adipiodona

adiponitrile
adiponitrilo
adipsin
adipsina
aditeren(e)
aditereno
adjacent
adyacente
adjoining
adyacente, contiguo,
adjunto
adjunct
auxiliar
adjust, to
ajustar
adjustable
ajustable, regulable
adjusting ring
anillo de ajuste
adjustment
ajuste
adjuvant
adyuvante
Adkins catalyst
catalizador de Adkins
Adkins-Peterson reaction
reacción de Adkins y Peterson
adlumidine
adlumidina
adlumine
adlumina
admiralty metal
aleación de cobre (71%), cinc (28%) y estaño (1%)
admix, to
mezclar
admixtion
mezcla
admixture
mezcla
adocain
adocaína
adonitol
adonitol
adonitoxin
adonitoxina
adrafinil
adrafinilo
adrenal cortical extract
extracto corticosuprarrenal
adrenaline
adrenalina, epinefrina
adrenalone
adrenalona

adrenochrome
adrenocromo
adrenocorticotropic hormone
hormona adrenocorticotrópica
adrenoglomerulotropin
adrenoglomerulotropina
adrenol acetate
acetato de adrenol
adrenolutin
adrenolutina
adrenosterone
adrenosterona
adsorb, to
adsorber
adsorbate
adsorbato
adsorbed
adsorbido
adsorbent
adsorbente
adsorbing
adsorción, adsorbente
adsorption
adsorción
adsorption agent
agente de adsorción
adsorption chromatography
cromatografía de adsorción
adsorption column
columna de adsorción
adsorption indicator
indicador de adsorción
adulterate, to
adulterar
adulteration
adulteración
advance, to
progresar, adelantar
advantage factor
factor de irradiación óptima
adventitious
fortuito, accidental
aerate, to
airear, ventilar
aeration
aireación, ventilación
aerobes
aerobios
aerobic
aeróbico
aerogel
aerogel
aerosol
aerosol

aerozine
aerocina,
aerozina
affinin
afinina
affinity
afinidad
aflatoxine
aflatoxina
afloqualone
aflocualona
after-chromed dye
colorantes cromados
ulteriormente
after effect
efecto secundario
after glow
fosforescencia,
posluminiscencia
afterheat
calor residual
afurolol
afurolol
against
en función de,
comparado con
agar
agar
agaric
agárico
agaricic acid
ácido agarícico
agaritine
agaritina
agate
ágata
agate mortar
mortero de ágata
age
edad
age hardening
endurecimiento por
envejecimiento
agent
agente
agent, gelling
gelificante
agent orange
agente naranja
age-resister
antienvejecedor
agglomerate
aglomerado
agglomerate, to
aglomerar
agglomeration
aglomeración
agglutinant
aglutinante

agglutinate, to
aglutinar
agglutination
aglutinación
agglutinative
aglutinante
aggregate
agregado, aglomerado
aggregation
agregación, agregado
aggresive
agresivo
aging
envejecimiento,
añejamiento,
maduración
aging test
prueba de
envejecimiento
agitate, to
agitar
agitation
agitación
agitator
agitador
aglucone
aglucona
aglycone
aglicona
agmatine
agmatina
agricultural chemical
producto químico para
la agricultura
agroclavine
agroclavina
agrocybin
agrocibina
AHF unit
FAH (factor
antihemofílico), unidad
ahistan
ahistano
air
aire
air, to
airear, ventilar
air admission
entrada, admisión de aire
air bubble
burbuja de aire
air classification
clasificación por aire,
separación por
contracorriente de aire
air dried
secado al aire
air free
sin aire

air flotation
elutriación, separación
por contracorriente de
aire
air gas
gas de aire, gas
carburado
air inlet
entrada de aire
air nozzle
boquilla de aire
air pressure
presión atmosférica,
presión de aire
air pollution
contaminación del
aire
air pump
bomba de aire
air stream
corriente de aire
air tight
hermético
air void
sin aire, vacío de aire
aired
aireado,
ventilado
ajacine
ajacina
ajaconine
ajaconina
ajmaline
ajmalina
ajoene
ajoeno
ajowan oil
aceite de semillas de
ajowan
ajugarine
ajugarina
aklomide
aclomida
akuammicine
acuamicina
akuammine
acuamina
alabaster
alabastro
alacepril
alaceprilo
alachlor
alacloro
alafosfalin
alafosfalina
alanine
alanina
alanosine
alanosina

alantolactone
alantolactona
alanylhistidine
alanilhistidina
alaproclate
alaproclato
alaskite
alasquita
alazanine triclofenate
triclofenato de
alazanina
alazopeptin
alazopeptina
albaspidin
albaspidina
albedo
albedo
albendazole
albendazol
albertite
albertita
albizziin
albiciína
albofungin
albofungina
albomycin
albomicina
alborixin
alborrixina
albumen
albumen
albumin
albúmina
albumin, blood
albúmina sanguínea
albumin, egg
albúmina de huevo
albumin, milk
albúmina láctea
albumin, serum
(normal human)
albúmina sérica
(humana normal)
albumin tannate
tanato de albúmina
albuminometer
albuminómetro
albuminous
albuminoso
albumose
albumosa
albuterol
albuterol
albuterol sulfate
sulfato de albuterol
albutoin
albutoína
alcaloids
alcaloides

alchemy
alquimia
alcian blue
azul alciano
alclofenac
alclofenac, alclofenaco
alclometasone
alclometasona
alcloxa
alcloxa
Alcoa process
proceso Alcoa
alcohol
alcohol
alcohol, absolute
alcohol absoluto
alcohol acids
hidroxiácidos
alcohol dehydrogenase
deshidrogenasa
alcohólica
alcohol, denatured
alcohol desnaturalizado
alcohol, grain
alcohol de granos
alcohol, industrial
alcohol industrial
alcoholate
alcoholato
alcoholic fermentation
fermentación
alcohólica
alcoholic solution
solución alcohólica
alcoholic strength
grado alcohólico
alcohol, wood
alcohol de madera,
alcohol metílico
alcoholometer
alcoholímetro
alcoholysis
alcohólisis
alcuronium
alcuronio
alcuronium chloride
cloruro de alcuronio
aldehyde
aldehído
aldehyde acids
ácidos aldehídicos
aldehydine
aldehidina
aldesulfone sodium
aldesulfona sódica
aldicarb
aldicarb
aldioxa
aldioxa

aldol
aldol
aldol condensation
condensación
aldólica
aldolase
aldolasa
aldo-α-naphthylamine
condensate
condensado de aldo-α-
naftilamina
aldose
aldosa
aldosterone
aldosterona
aldoxime
aldoxima
aldramate sulfate
sulfato de aldramato
aldrin
aldrina
alembic
alambique
alendronate sodium
alendronato sódico
alepride
aleprida
aletris
aletris
aleuritic acid
ácido aleurítico
alexidine
alexidina
alexitol sodium
alexitol sódico
alfacalcidol
alfacalcidol
alfadolone
alfadolona
alfadolone acetate
acetato de alfadolona
alfaprostol
alfaprostol
alfaxalone
alfaxalona
alfentanil
alfentanilo
alfetamine
alfetamina
alfin
alfina
alfin catalyst
catalizador de alfina
alfuzosin
alfuzosina
alga
alga
algae
algas

Algar-Flynn-Oyamada
reaction
reacción de Algar,
Flynn y Oyamada
algeldrate
algeldrato
algestone
algestona
algestone acetophenide
acetofenida algestónica
algicide
algicida
algin
algina
alginate
alginato
alginic acid
ácido algínico
alglucerase
alglucerasa
alibendol
alibendol
aliconazole
aliconazol
alicyclic
alicíclico
aliflurane
aliflurano
alimadol
alimadol
alimemazine
alimemacina,
alimemazina
alinidine
alinidina
alipamide
alipamida
aliphatic
alifático
aliphatic chemicals
agentes alifáticos
aliphatic compound
compuesto alifático
aliphatic hydrocarbons
hidrocarburos alifáticos
aliphatic series
serie alifática
aliquot
alícuota
alitame
alitama
alizapride
alizaprida
alizarin(e)
alizarina
alizarin assistant
auxiliar de alizarina
alizarin blue
azul de alizarina

alizarin bordeux
alizarina de Burdeos
alizarin brown
marrón de alizarina
alizarin cardinal
cardenal de alizarina
alizarin cyanine green G
cianina verde G de
alizarina
alizarin cyanine R
cianina R de alizarina
alizarin dye
colorante de alizarina
alizarin irisol R
irisol R de alizarina
alizarin orange
anaranjado de
alizarina
alizarin red
rojo de alizarina
alizarin yellow
amarillo de alizarina
alkadiene
alcadieno
alkalescent
alcalescente, alcalino
alkali
álcali
alkali amide
amida alcalina
alkali blue
azul alcalino
alkali cellulose
celulosa alcalina
alkali lake
laca alcalina
alkali liquour
solución alcalina
alkali metals
metales alcalinos
alkali proof
resistente a los álcalis
alkali test
prueba de álcali
alkali wash
lavado alcalino
alkalimeter
alcalímetro
alkalimetric
alcalimétrico
alkalimetry
alcalimetría
alkaline
alcalino
alkaline earths
tierras alcalinas,
alcalinotérreo
alkaline earth metals
metales alcalinotérreos

alkaline reaction
reacción alcalina
alkaline solution
solución alcalina
alkaline water
agua alcalina
alkalinity
alcalinidad
alkalinous
alcalino
alkalization
alcalinización
alkalize
alcalinizar
alkaloid
alcaloide
alkaloidal
alcaloideo
alkanes
alcanos
alkanesulfonic acid,
mixed
ácido alcansulfónico
mixto
alkanet
onoquiles, ancusa
alkannin
alcanina
alkanolamine
alcanolamina
alkenes
alquenos
alkofanone
alcofanona
alkoside
alcósido, alcoholato
alkoxide
alcóxido, alcoholato
alkoxilate
alcoxilato
alkoxyaluminium
hydrides
hidruros de
alcoxialuminio
alkoxyl
alcohóxilo, alcoxilo
alkyd resin
resina alquídica
alkyl
alquilo
alkyl chloride
cloruro de alquilo,
cloruro alquílico
alkyl halide
aluro alquílico
alkylarylpolyethylene
glycol ether
éter alquilarílico de
glicol polietilénico

alkylaryl sulfonate
sulfonato de alquilarilo
alkylate
alquilato
alkylation
alquilación
alkylbenzene
alquilbenceno
alkylbenzene sulfonate
sulfonato de
alquilbenceno
alkyldimethylbenzyl
ammonium chloride
cloruro de alquildi-
metilbencilamonio
alkylfluorophosphate
fluorofosfato alquílico
alkylamine
alquilamina
alkylene
alquileno
alkylidene
alquilideno
alkylmagnesium
alquilmagnesio
alkylolamine
alquilolamina
alkyloxide
óxido de alquilo,
alcoholato
alkylphenol resin
resina
alquilfenólica
alkylsulfonate
alquilsulfonato,
sulfonato alquílico
alkylsulfonic acid
ácido alquilsulfónico
alkyne
alquino
Allan-Robinson
reaction
reacción de Allan y
Robinson
allantoin
alantoína
allele
alelo
allelopathic chemical
producto químico
alelopático
allene
aleno
allenolic acid
ácido alenólico
allergen
alergeno
allethrin
aletrina, aletrín

alletorphine
aletorfina
allicin
alicina
allidochlor
alidocloro
alligatoring
cuarteado,
resquebrajamiento,
exfoliación
alliin
aliína
allo-
alo-
allobarbital
alobarbital
allocholesterol
alocolesterol
alloclamide
aloclamida
allocryptopine
alocriptopina
allocupreide sodium
alocupreido sódico
allomaleic acid
ácido alomaleico
allomerism
alomería
allomethadione
alometadiona
allomorphism
alomorfismo
alloocimene
aloocimeno
allophanamide
alofanamida
allophanate
alofanato
allopregnane
alopregnano
allopurinol
alopurinol
allose
alosa
allotetrahydro-
cortisone
alotetrahidrocortisona
allothreonine
alotreonina
allotrope
forma alotrópica
allotropic
alotrópico
allotropism, allotropy
alotropía, alotropismo
alloxan
aloxana
alloxantin
aloxantina

alloy
aleación
alloy, to
alear
alloy, fusible
aleación fusible
alloy steel
acero aleado
all-purpose
universal, de uso
múltiple
allyl
alilo
allyl acrylate
acrilato de alilo,
acrilato alílico
allyl alcohol
alcohol alílico
allyl bromide
bromuro de alilo,
bromuro alílico
allyl caproate
caproato de alilo,
caproato alílico
allyl carbamate
carbamato de alilo,
carbamato alílico
allyl chloride
cloruro de alilo,
cloruro alílico
allyl chlorocarbonate
clorocarbonato de alilo,
clorocarbonato alílico
allyl chloroformate
cloroformiato de alilo,
cloroformiato alílico
allyl cyanide
cianuro de alilo,
cianuro alílico,
vinilacetonitrilo
allyl diglycol
carbonate
carbonato de
alildiglicol
allyl ether
éter alílico
allyl ethyl ether
éter alil etílico
allyl glycidyl ether
éter alil glicidílico
allyl hexanoate
hexanoato de alilo,
hexanoato alílico
allyl iodide
yoduro de alilo, yoduro
alílico
allyl isocyanate
isocianato de alilo,
isocianato alílico

allyl isopropyl-
malonylurea
alilisopropil-
malonilurea,
malonilurea
alilisopropílica
allyl isothiocyanate
isotiocianato de alilo,
isotiocianato alílico
allyl mercaptan
mercaptano alílico
allyl methacrylate
metacrilato de alilo,
metacrilato alílico
allyl pelargonate
pelargonato de alilo,
pelargonato alílico
allyl resin
resina alílica
allyl sulfide
sulfuro de alilo, sulfuro
alílico, éter tioalílico
allyl sulphide
sulfuro de alilo, sulfuro
alílico
allyl thiol
aliltiol
4-allyl veratrole
4-alil veratrol
allylacetone
alilacetona
allylamine
alilamina
4-allyl-1,2-dimetoxy-
benzene
4-alil-1,2-dimetoxi-
benceno
allylene
alileno
allylestrenol
alilestrenol
2-allyl-2-ethyl-1,3-
propanediol
2-alil-2-etil-1,3-
propandiol
1-allyl-4-hydroxy-
benzene
1-alil-4-hidroxi-
benceno
1-N-allyl-3-hydroxy-
morphinan bitartrate
bitartrato de 1-N-
alil-3-hidroxi-
morfinano
allylic
alílico
allylic
rearrangements
reordenaciones alílicas

allyl-α-ionone
alil-α-ionona
5-allyl-5-isobutyl-
barbituric acid
ácido 5-alil-5-
isobutilbarbitúrico
5-allyl-5-(1-methyl-
butyl) barbituric acid
ácido 5-alil-5-(1-
metilbutil) barbitúrico
4-allyl-1,2-methylene-
dioxybenzene
4-alil-1,2-metilen-
dioxibenceno
4-allyl-2-methoxy-
phenol
4-alil-2-metoxifenol
p-allylphenol
p-alilfenol
allylprodine
alilprodina
allylpropyl disulfide
disulfuro de alilpropilo,
disulfuro alilpropílico
allylthiourea
aliltiourea
allyltrichlorosilane
aliltriclorosilano
allylurea
alilurea
almadrate sulfate
sulfato de almadrato
almagate
almagato
almasilate
almasilato
almecillin
almecilina
almestrone
almestrona
alminoprofen
alminoprofeno
almitrine
almitrina
almond, bitter
almendra amarga
almond oil, bitter
esencia (aceite) de
almendra amarga
almond, sweet
almendra dulce
alnico
alnico
aloe
áloe
aloin
aloína
alonimid
alonimida

aloxidone
aloxidona
aloxiprin
aloxiprina
alozafone
alozafona
alpertine
alpertina
alpha
alfa
alpha particle
partícula alfa
alpha-cellulose
celulosa alfa
alphacetylmethadol
alfacetilmetadol
alphameprodine
alfameprodina
alphamethadol
alfametadol
alphamethyl-
naphthalene
alfametilnaftaleno
alphaprodine
alfaprodina
alpiropride
alpiroprida
alprazolam
alprazolán, alprazolam
alprenolol
alprenolol
alprostadil
alprostadil
alrestatin
alrestatina
alsactide
alsactida
alstonidine
alstonidina
alstonine
alstonina
althea
altea
altheine
alteína
althiazide
altiazida
altizide
altizida
altrenogest
altrenogest
altretamine
altretamina
altrose
altrosa
alum
alumbre
alum burnt
alumbre quemado

alum chrome
alumbre crómico
alumina
alúmina, óxido de
aluminio
alumina, activated
alúmina activada,
óxido de aluminio
activado
alumina fused
alúmina fundida, óxido
de aluminio fundido
alumina gel
gel de alúmina, gel de
óxido de aluminio
alumina trihydrate
alúmina trihidratada,
óxido de aluminio
trihidratado
aluminate
aluminato
aluminite
aluminita, tierra de
Hall
aluminium
aluminio
aluminon
aluminón
aluminosilicate
aluminosilicato
aluminothermics
aluminotermia
aluminum
aluminio
aluminum acetate
acetato de aluminio
aluminum acetate
solution
solución de acetato de
aluminio, solución de
Burow
aluminum
acetotartrate
acetotartrato de
aluminio
aluminum
acetylacetonate
acetilacetonato de
aluminio
aluminum alloy
aleación de aluminio
aluminun ammonium
chloride
cloruro de aluminio y
amonio
aluminum ammonium
sulfate
sulfato doble de
aluminio y amonio

10

aluminum amylate
amilato de aluminio
aluminum anodized
aluminio anodizado
aluminum antimonide
antimoniuro de aluminio
aluminum arsenide
arseniuro de aluminio
aluminum benzoate
benzoato de aluminio
aluminum bis(acetylsalicylate)
bis(acetilsalicilato) de aluminio
aluminum borate
borato de aluminio
aluminum boride
boruro de aluminio
aluminum boroformate
boroformiato de aluminio
aluminum borohydride
borhidruro de aluminio
aluminum brass
latón de aluminio
aluminum bromide
bromuro de aluminio
aluminum bronze
bronce de aluminio, aleación de aluminio y bronce
aluminum n-butoxide
n-butóxido de aluminio
aluminum calcium hydride
hidruro de aluminio y calcio
aluminum carbide
carburo de aluminio
aluminum carbonate
carbonato de aluminio
aluminum cesium sulfate
sulfato de aluminio y cesio
aluminum chlorate
clorato de aluminio
aluminum chloride, anhydrous
cloruro de aluminio anhidro
aluminum chloride, hydrate
cloruro de aluminio hidratado

aluminum chlorohydrate
clorhidrato de aluminio
aluminum clofibrate
clofibrato de aluminio
aluminum diacetate
diacetato de aluminio
aluminum diethyl monochloride
monocloruro dietílico de aluminio
aluminum diformate
diformiato de aluminio
aluminum distearate
diestearato de aluminio
aluminum ethoxide
etóxido de aluminio
aluminum ethylate
etilato de aluminio
aluminum ethylhexoate
etilhexoato de aluminio
aluminum ferrosilicon
ferrosilicio alumínico
aluminum fluoride, anhydrous
fluoruro de aluminio anhidro
aluminum fluoride, hydrate
floruro de aluminio hidratado
aluminum fluosilicate
fluosilicato de aluminio
aluminum foil
hoja de aluminio, papel de aluminio
aluminum formate
formiato de aluminio
aluminum formate, basic
formiato básico de aluminio
aluminum formate, normal
formiato normal de aluminio
aluminum formoacetate
formoacetato de aluminio
aluminum hexafluorosilicate
hexafluorosilicato de aluminio

aluminum hydrate
hidrato de aluminio
aluminum hydride
hidruro de aluminio
aluminium hydroxide
hidróxido de aluminio
aluminum hydroxide, anhydrous
hidróxido de aluminio anhidro
aluminum hydroxide gel
gel de hidróxido de aluminio
aluminum hydroxystearate
hidroxiestearato de aluminio
aluminum hypophosphite
hipofosfito de aluminio
aluminum iodide
yoduro de aluminio
aluminum iron
ferroaluminio
aluminum isopropoxide
isopropóxido de aluminio
aluminum isopropylate
isopropilato de aluminio
aluminum lactate
lactato de aluminio
aluminum lithium hydride
hidruro de aluminio y litio
aluminum magnesium silicate
silicato de aluminio y magnesio
aluminum metaphosphate
metafosfato de aluminio
aluminum monobasic stearate
estearato de aluminio monobásico
aluminum monopalmitate
monopalmitato de aluminio
aluminum monostearate
monoestearato de aluminio

aluminum naphthenate
naftenato de aluminio
aluminum ß-napthol-disulfonate
ß-naftoldisulfonato de aluminio
aluminum nicotinate
nicotinato de aluminio
aluminum nitrate
nitrato de aluminio
aluminum nitride
nitruro de aluminio
aluminum octoate
octoato de aluminio
aluminun oleate
oleato de aluminio
aluminum ortophosphate
ortofosfato de aluminio
aluminum oxalate
oxalato de aluminio
aluminum oxide
óxido de aluminio
aluminum oxide, hydrated
óxido de aluminio hidratado
aluminum oxide, hydrous
óxido de aluminio hidratado
aluminum palmitate
palmitato de aluminio
aluminum paste
pasta de aluminio
aluminum phenosulfonate
fenosulfonato de aluminio
aluminum phosphate
fosfato de aluminio
aluminum phosphide
fosfuro de aluminio
aluminum picrate
picrato de aluminio
aluminum potassium sulfate
sulfato de aluminio y potasio
aluminum resinate
resinato de aluminio
aluminum rubidium sulfate
sulfato de aluminio y rubidio
aluminum salicylate
salicilato de aluminio
aluminum selenide
seleniuro de aluminio

aluminum silicate
silicato de aluminio
aluminum silico-
fluoride
silicofluoruro de
aluminio
aluminum soap
jabón de aluminio
aluminum sodium
chloride
cloruro de aluminio y
sodio
aluminun sodium
sulfate
sulfato de aluminio y
sodio
aluminum stearate
estearato de aluminio
aluminum subacetate
subacetato de
aluminio
aluminum sulfate
sulfato de aluminio
aluminum sulfide
sulfuro de aluminio
aluminum
sulfocarbonate
sulfocarbonato de
aluminio
aluminum sulfocyanide
sulfocianuro de
aluminio
aluminum tartrate
tartrato de aluminio
aluminum thiocyanate
tiocianato de aluminio
aluminum triformate
triformiato de aluminio
aluminum
triricinoleate
trirricinoleato de
aluminio
aluminum tristearate
triestearato de
aluminio
aluminum zinc sulfate
sulfato de aluminio y
cinc
alum, papermaker
alumbre de los
papeleros
alum, pearl
sulfato de aluminio
alum, pickle
alumbre de curtido
alum, porous
alumbre poroso
alum, potash
alumbre de potasa

alum, rubidium
alumbre rubídico
alunite
alunita
alusulf
alusulfo
alverine
alverina
amadinone
amadinona
amafolone
amafolona
amalgam
amalgama
amanitin
amanitina
amanozine
amanocina, amanozina
amantadine
amantadina
amantadine hydro-
chloride
clorhidrato de
amantadina
amantanium bromide
bromuro de amantanio
amantocillin
amantocilina
amaranth
amaranto
amarogentin
amarogentina
amarolide
amarolida
amatol
amatol
ambazone
ambazona
ambenonium
chloride
cloruro de ambenonio
ambenoxan
ambenoxano
amber
ámbar, succinita
amber oil
aceite de cárabe
ambergris
ámbar gris, ambargris
ambicromil
ambicromil
ambient temperature
temperatura ambiente
amblygonite
ambiglonita
ambomycin
ambomicina
ambrettolide
ambretólido

ambrosin
ambrosina
ambroxol
ambroxol
ambruticin
ambruticino
ambucaine
ambucaína
ambucetamide
ambucetamida
ambuphylline
ambufilina
ambuside
ambusida
ambutonium bromide
bromuro de ambutonio
amcinafal
ancinafal
amcinafide
ancinafida
amcinonide
amcinonida
amdinocillin
andinocilina,
mecilinamo
amdinocillin pivoxil
andinocilina
pivoxílica
amedalin
amedalina
americium
americio
ametantrone
ametantrona
amethopterin
ametopterina
ametryn
ametrina
amezepine
amecepina
amezinium methyl
sulfate
metilsulfato de
amecinio, sulfato
metílico de amecinio
amfebutamone
anfebutamona
amfecloral
anfecloral
amfenac
anfenaco, amfenaco
amfepentorex
anfepentorex
amfepramone
anfepramona
amfetaminil
anfetaminil
amfomicyn
anfomicina

amfonelic acid
ácido anfonélico
amianthus
amianto, asbesto
amiben
amibeno
amicarbalide
amicarbalida
amicetin
amicetina
amicibone
amicibona
amicicline
amiciclina
amicoumarine A
amicumarina A
amicroscopic
amicroscópico
amidantel
amidantel
amidapsone
amidapsona
amide
amida
amidephrine
amidefrina
amidines
amidinas
amidinomycin
amidinomicina
4-amidino-1-
(nitrosamino amidino)-
1-tetrazene
4-amidino-1-
(nitrosamino amidino)-
1-tetraceno
amido
amido
amido naphtol
red 6B
rojo amidonaftol 6B
amidochlor
amidocloro
amidol
amidol
amidomycin
amidomicina
amidopropylamine
oxide
óxido de
amidopropilamina
amifloverine
amifloverina
amifloxacin
amifloxacina
amifostine
amifostina
amikacin
amicacina, amikacina

amilomer
amilómero
amiloride
amilorida
amiloride hydro-
chloride
clorhidrato de
amilorida
aminacrine
aminacrina
aminacrine hydro-
chloride
clorhidrato de
aminacrina
amination
aminación
amindocate
amindocato
amine
amina
amine absorption
process
método de absorción
por aminas
amineptine
amineptina
aminic
amínico
aminimide
aminimida
aminitrozole
aminitrozol
amino alcohol
aminoalcohol, alcohol
amínico
amino acid
aminoácido
amino acid oxidase
aminoácido oxidasa
p-aminoacetanilide
p-aminoacetanilida
aminoacetic acid
ácido aminoacético
aminoacetonitrile
aminoacetonitrilo
aminoacetophenetidine
hydrochloride
clorhidrato
de aminoaceto
fenetidina
aminoacetophenone
aminoacetofenona
aminoacridine
aminoacridina
α-aminoadipic acid
ácido α-aminoadípico
aminoaldehyde
aminoaldehído,
aldehído amínico

aminoamylene glycol
aminoamilénglicol,
glicol
aminoamilénico
5-amino-2-
anilinobenzene
sulfonic acid
ácido 5-amino-2-
anilinobencen-
sulfónico
aminoanisole
aminoanisol
aminoanthraquinone
aminoantraquinona
1-amino-
anthraquinone-2-
carboxylic acid
ácido 1-amino-
antraquinona-2-
carboxílico
aminoantipyrine
aminoantipirina
aminoazobenzene
aminoazobenceno
4-aminoazobenzene-
3,4'-disulfonic acid
ácido 4-amino-
azobenceno-
3,4'-disulfónico
p-aminoazobenzene
hydrochloride
clorhidrato de p-
aminoazobenceno
aminoazobenzene-
monosulfonic acid
ácido aminoazo-
bencenmono-
sulfónico
aminoazobenzene-
sulfonic acid
ácido aminoazo-
bencensulfónico
o-aminoazotoluene
o-aminoazotolueno,
toluazotoluidina
aminobenzene
aminobenceno
p-aminobenzene-
arsonic acid
ácido p-aminobencen-
arsónico
2-amino-p-benzene-
disulfonic acid
ácido 2-amino-p-
bencendisulfónico
4-amino-m-benzene-
disulfonic acid
ácido 4-amino-m-
bencendisulfónico

aminobenzene-
sulphonic acid
ácido aminobencen-
sulfónico
aminobenzoate
potassium
aminobenzoato de
potasio
aminobenzoic acid
ácido aminobenzoico
aminobenzothiazole
aminobenzotiazol
aminobenzotrifluoride
aminobenzotrifluoruro
o-aminobenzoyl-
formic anhydride
anhídrido o-amino-
benzoilfórmico
N-(p-aminobenzoyl)
glutamic acid
ácido N-(p-amino-
benzoil)glutámico
N-(p-aminobenzoyl)
glycine
N-(p-aminobenzoil)
glicina
α-(α-aminobenzyl)
alcohol
alcohol α-(α-
aminobencílico)
p-aminobenzyldi-
ethylamine
p-aminobencil-
dietilamina
aminobenzyldimethyl
amine
aminobencildimetil-
amina
o-aminobiphenyl
o-aminobifenilo
aminobutane
aminobutano
aminobutanoic acid
ácido aminobutanoico
2-amino-1-butanol
2-amino-1-butanol
aminobutyric acid
ácido aminobutírico
aminocaproic acid
ácido aminocaproico
aminocaproic lactam
lactama
aminocaproica
aminocarb
aminocarb
7-amino-
cephalosporanic acid
ácido 7-amino-
cefalosporánico

aminochlorobenzene
aminoclorobenceno
4-amino-4'-chloro-
diphenyl
4-amino-4'-
clorodifenilo
2-amino-4-
chlorophenol
2-amino-4-
clorofenol
2-amino-4-
chlorotoluene
2-amino-4-
clorotolueno
4-amino-2-chloro-
toluene-5-sulfonic
acid
ácido 4-amino-2-
clorotolueno-5-
sulfónico
2-amino-5-chloro-
pyridine
2-amino-5-
cloropiridina
aminochlor-
tenoxazin
aminoclortenoxacina
m-amino-p-cresol
methyl ether
éter metílico de m-
amino p-cresol
aminochromes
aminocromos
aminocyclohexane
aminociclohexano
aminodehydrogenase
aminodeshidrogenasa
3-amino-2,5-dichloro-
benzoic acid
ácido 3-amino-2,5-
diclorobenzoico
2-amino-4,6-
dichlorophenol
2-amino-4,6-
diclorofenol
p-aminodiethylanilide
hydrochloride
clorhidrato de p-
aminodietilanilida
p-aminodiethylaniline
p-aminodietilanilina
2-amino-4,6-di-
hydroxypteridine
2-amino-4,6-
dihidroxipteridina
di-p-aminodimethoxy-
diphenyl
di-p-aminodimetoxi-
difenilo

13

p-aminodimethyl-
aniline
p-aminodimetil-
anilina
p-aminodimethyl-
benzene
p-aminodimetil-
benceno
1-amino-2,3-dimethyl-
benzene
1-amino-2,3-
dimetilbenceno
4-amino-1,5-
dimethyl- 2-phenyl-
3-pyrazolone
4-amino-1,5-dimetil-2-
fenil-3-pirazolona
2-aminodimethyl-
pyridine
2-aminodimetil-
piridina
2-aminodinitrophenol
2-aminodinitrofenol
p-aminodiphenyl
p-aminodifenilo
aminodiphenylamina
aminodifenilamina
4-aminodiphenyl-
amine-2-sulfonic acid
ácido 4-amino-
difenilamina-2-
sulfónico
2-amino-1,2-diphenyl-
ethanol
2-amino-1,2-
difeniletanol
aminodithioformic
acid
ácido aminoditio-
fórmico
aminoethane
aminoetano
2-aminoethane-
sulfonic acid
ácido 2-aminoetan-
sulfónico
2-aminoethanethiol
2-aminoetantiol
aminoethanol
aminoetanol
6,9-amino-2-ethoxy-
acridine lactate
monohydrate
lactato de 6,9-
amino-2-etoxiacridina
monohidratado
2-(2-aminoethoxy)
ethanol
2-(2-aminoetoxi) etanol

aminoethoxyvinyl-
glycine
aminoetoxivinilglicina
aminoethyl nitrate
nitrato de aminoetilo
1-[(2-aminoethyl)
amino]-2-propanol
1-[(2-aminoetil)
amino]-2-propanol
2-amino-2-ethyl-1,3-
propanediol
2-amino-2-etil-1,3-
propandiol
aminoethylethanol-
amine
aminoetiletanolamina
4-aminoethyl-
glyoxaline
4-aminoetilglioxalina
α-(1-aminoethyl)-m-
hydroxybenzyl alcohol
bitartrate
bitartrato de alcohol
α-(1-aminoetil)-m-
hidroxibencílico
4-(2-aminoethyl)
imidazole
4-(2-aminoetil)
imidazol
ß-aminoethyliso-
thiourea dihydro-
bromide
dibromhidrato de ß-
aminoetilisotiourea
p-ß-aminoethylphenol
p-ß-aminoetilfenol
N-aminoethyl-
piperazine
N-aminoetilpiperazina
2-aminoethylsulfuric
acid
ácido 2-aminoetil-
sulfúrico
2-(2-aminoethyl)-2-
thiopseudourea
dihydrobromide
dibromhidrato de 2-
(2-aminoetil)-2-
tiopseudourea
3-amino-α-ethyl-2,4,6-
triiodohydrocinnamic
acid
ácido 3-amino-α-
etil-2,4,6-triyodo
hidrocinámico
ß-aminoflavo-
purpurine
ß-aminoflavo-
purpurina

4-aminofolic acid
ácido 4-aminofólico
aminoform
aminoformo
amino-G acid
ácido amino-G
α-aminoglutaric acid
ácido α-amino-
glutárico
aminoglutethimide
aminoglutetimida
aminoguanidine
aminoguanidina
amino-4-guanido-
valeric acid
ácido amino-4-
guanidovalérico
aminohexamethylene-
imine
aminohexametilen-
imina
2-aminohexanoic acid
ácido 2-amino-
hexanoico
6-aminohexanoic acid
ácido 6-amino-
hexanoico
p-amino-hippuric acid
ácido p-amino-
hipúrico
aminohydroxybenzoic
acid
ácido aminohidroxi-
benzoico
α-amino-ß-hydroxy-
butyric acid
ácido α-amino-ß-
hidroxibutírico
2-amino-2-hydroxy-
methyl-1,3-
propanediol
2-amino-2-
hidroximetil-1,3-
propandiol
α-amino-ß-hydroxy-
propionic acid
ácido α-amino-ß-
hidroxipropiónico
α-amino-ß-imidazole-
propionic acid
ácido α-amino-ß-
imidazolpropiónico
α-aminoisobutyric acid
ácido α-amino-
isobutírico
α-aminoisocaproic
acid
ácido α-amino-
isocaproico

α-aminoisovaleric
acid
ácido α-amino-
isovalérico
amino-J acid
ácido amino-J
amino-ketones
aminocetonas
aminolevulinic acid
ácido amino-
levulínico
2-amino-6-mercapto-
purine
2-amino-6-
mercaptopurina
aminomercuric
chloride
cloruro
aminomercúrico
aminomethane
aminometano
aminometradine
aminometradina
3-amino-4-methoxy-
benzanilide
3-amino-4-
metoxibenzanilida
1-amino-2-methoxy-5-
methylbenzene
1-amino-2-metoxi-5-
metilbenceno
m-(4-amino-3-
methoxyphenylazo)-
benzenesulfonic acid
ácido m-(4-amino-3-
metoxifenilazo)
bencensulfónico
p-aminomethyl-
benzene sulfonamide
hydrochloride
clorhidrato de
p-aminometilbencen
sulfonamida
1-α-(aminomethyl)-3,4-
dihydroxybenzyl
alcohol
alcohol 1-α-
(aminometil)-3,4-
dihidroxibencílico
4-amino-4'-methyl-
diphenylamine-2-
sulfonic acid
ácido 4-amino-4'-
metildifenilamino-2
sulfónico
4-amino-10-methyl-
folic acid
ácido 4-amino-10-
metilfólico

4-aminomethyl-1-naphtol
4-aminometil-1-naftol
3-amino-5-methylisoxasole
3-amino-5-metilisoxasol
2-amino-3-methylpentanoic acid
ácido 2-amino-3-metilpentanoico
ß-amino-α-methylphenethyl alcohol
alcohol ß-amino-α-metilfenetílico
2-amino-2-methyl-1,3-propanediol
2-amino-2-metil-1,3-propandiol
2-amino-2-methyl-1-propanol
2-amino-2-metil-1-propanol
2-amino-3-methylpyridine
2-amino-3-metilpiridina
2-amino-4-(methylthio)butyric acid
ácido 2-amino-4-(metiltio)butírico
2-amino-4-methylthiazole
2-amino-4-metiltiazol
α-amino-ß-methylvaleric acid
ácido α-amino-ß-metilvalérico
α-amino-τ-methylvaleric acid
ácido α-amino-τ-metilvalérico
aminometradine
aminometradina
3-amino-1,5-naphthalenedisulfonic acid
ácido 3-amino-1,5-naftalendisulfónico
1-aminonaphthalene-4-sulfonic acid
ácido 1-amino-naftalen-4-sulfónico
2-amino-1-naphthalenesulfonic acid
ácido 2-amino-1-naftalensulfónico
8-amino-1,3,6-

naphthalenetrisulfonic acid
ácido 8-amino-1,3,6-naftalentrisulfónico
3-amino-2-naphthoic acid
ácido 3-amino-2-naftoico
4-amino-1-naphthol
4-amino-1-naftol
1-amino-8-naphthol-3,5 disulfonic acid
ácido 1-amino-8-naftol-3,5-disulfónico
1-amino-2-naphthol-4-sulfonic acid
ácido 1-amino-2-naftol-4-sulfónico
6-aminonicotinic acid
ácido 6-amino-nicotínico
2-amino-5-nitro-thiazole
2-amino-5-nitrotiazol
aminonaphtol monosulfonic acid
ácido aminonaftol-monosulfónico
amino oxidase
aminoxidasa
2-amino-6-oxypurine
2-amino-6-oxipurina
aminoparathion
aminoparatión
6-aminopenicillanic acid
ácido 6-amino-penicilánico
aminopentamide
aminopentamida
aminopentane
aminopentano
aminophenazone
aminofenazona
aminophenazone cyclamate
ciclamato de aminofenazona
aminophenetole
aminofenetol
(o-m-p) aminophenol
(o-m-p) aminofenol
4-amino-1-phenol-2,6-disulfonic acid
ácido 4-amino-1-fenol-2,6-disulfónico
2-amino-1-phenol-4-sulfonic acid
ácido 2-amino-1-fenol-4-sulfónico

o-aminophenol-p-sulfonic acid
ácido o-aminofenol-p-sulfónico
p-aminophenol hydrochloride
clorhidrato de p-aminofenol
o-aminophenol-methylether
o-aminofenolmetiléter
6-(D-α-aminophenylacetamido) penicillanic acid
ácido 6-(D-α-aminofenilacetamido) penicilánico
p-aminophenylacetic acid
ácido p-aminofenilacético
p-aminophenylarsonic acid
ácido p-aminofenil-arsónico
p-aminophenylboronic acid hemisulfate
hemisulfato de ácido p-aminofenilborónico
4-amino-3-phenyl-butyric acid
ácido 4-amino-3-fenilbutírico
1-amino-2-phenyl-ethane
1-amino-2-feniletano
o-aminophenyl-glyoxalic acid
ácido o-aminofenil-glioxálico
o-aminophenyl-glyoxalic lactim
lactima o-amino-fenilglioxálica,
lactonimina o-aminofenilglioxálica
p-aminophenyl-mercaptoacetic acid
ácido p-aminofenil-mercaptoacético
2-(p-aminophenyl)-6-methylbenzothiazole
2-(p-aminofenil)-6-metilbenzotiazol
m-aminophenyl methyl carbinol
m-aminofenil metilcarbinol

1-(m-aminophenyl)-3-methyl-5-pirazolone
1-(m-aminofenil)-3-metil-5-pirazolona
α-amino-ß-phenyl-propionic acid
ácido α-amino-ß-fenilpropiónico
aminophylline
aminofilina
aminopicoline
aminopicolina
aminoplast
aminoplástico, plástico amínico
aminoplast resin
resina aminoplástica
aminopromazine
aminopromacina, aminopromazina
2-aminopropane
2-aminopropano
2-aminopropanoic acid
ácido 2-amino-propanoico
1-amino-2-propanol
1-amino-2-propanol
3-aminopropionitrile
3-aminopropionitrilo
p-aminopropio-phenone
p-aminopropiofenona
2-aminopropyl alcohol
alcohol 2-aminopropílico
N-aminopropyl-morpholine
N-aminopropil-morfolina
aminopropylon
aminopropilona
p-(aminopropyl) phenol
p-(aminopropil) fenol
γ-aminopropyl-triethoxysilane
γ-aminopropil-trietoxisilano
γ-aminopropyl-trimethoxysilane
γ-aminopropil-trimetoxisilano
aminopterin
aminopterina
aminopterin sodium
aminopterina sódica
6-aminopurine
6-aminopurina

2-aminopyridine
2-aminopiridina
aminopyrine
aminopirina
aminoquinol
aminoquinol
aminoquinuride
aminoquinurida
aminorex
aminorex
4-aminosalicylic
acid
ácido 4-amino-
salicílico
α-aminosuccinamic
acid
ácido α-amino-
succinámico
aminosuccinic acid
ácido amino-
succínico
4-amino-2-sulfobenzoic
acid
ácido 4-amino-2-
sulfobenzoico
4-amino-3-sulfonic
acid
ácido 4-amino 3-
sulfónico
aminoteroylglutamic
acid
ácido amino-
teroilglutámico
2-aminothiazole
2-aminotiazol, 2-
tiazolamina
α-amino-ß-thiol-
propionic acid
ácido α-amino-ß-
tiolpropiónico
aminothiourea
aminotiourea
m-aminotoluene
m-aminotolueno
6-amino-s-triazine-
2,4-diol
6-amino-s-triazin-2,4-
diol
3-amino-1,2,4-
triazole
3-amino-1,2,4-triazol
4-amino-3,5,6-tri-
chloropicolinic acid
ácido 4-amino-3,5,6-
tricloropicolínico
2-amino-1,1,3-tri-
cyanopropene
2-amino-1,1,3-
tricianopropeno

3-(3-amino-2,4,6-
triiodophenyl)-2-
ethylpropanoic
acid
ácido 3-(3-amino-
2,4,6-triyodofenil)-2-
etilpropanoico
aminourea
hydrochloride
clorhidrato de
aminourea
aminoxylene
aminoxileno
aminoxylol
aminoxilol
aminoxytriphene
aminoxitrifeno
amiodarone
amiodarona
amiperone
amiperona
amiphenazole
amifenazol
amipizone
amipizona
amiprilose
amiprilosa
amiquinsin
amiquinsina
amisometradine
amisometradina
amisulpride
amisulprida
amiterol
amiterol
amitriptyline
amitriptilina
amitrole
amitrol
amixetrine
amixetrina
amlexanox
anlexanox
amlodipine besylate
besilato de
anlodipina
ammelide
amelida
ammeline
amelina
ammeter
amperímetro
ammine
amina
ammonia
amoníaco
ammonia,
anhydrous
amoníaco anhidro

ammonia, aromatic
spirits of
alcoholes aromáticos
de amoníaco
ammonia gas
gas amoníaco
ammonia leaching
lixiviación al amoníaco
ammonia liquor
agua amoniacal
ammonia nitrogen
nitrógeno amoniacal
ammonia solution
solución amoniacal
ammonia soda process
método de la sosa
amoniacal
ammonia water
agua amoniacal
ammonicate
amoniacato
ammoniated
amoniacal
ammoniated mercury
chloride
cloruro mercúrico
amoniacal
ammoniated
ruthenium oxychloride
oxicloruro de rutenio
amoniacal
ammoniated super-
phosphate
superfosfato amoniacal
ammonium
amonio
ammonium acetate
acetato de amonio
ammonium acid
carbonate
carbonato ácido de
amonio
ammonium acid
fluoride
fluoruro ácido de
amonio
ammonium acid
phosphate
fosfato ácido de
amonio
ammonium alginate
alginato de amonio
ammonium alum
alumbre amoniacal,
alumbre amónico
ammonium aluminum
chloride
cloruro amónico
alumínico

ammonium amalgam
amalgama de amonio
ammonium arsenate
arseniato de amonio
ammonium aurin
tricarboxylate
tricarboxilato aurínico
de amonio
ammonium
benzenesulfonate
bencensulfonato de
amonio
ammonium benzoate
benzoato de amonio
ammonium biborate
biborato de amonio
ammonium
bicarbonate
bicarbonato de amonio
amonium bichromate
bicromato de amonio
ammonium bifluoride
bifluoruro de amonio
ammonium bimalate
bimalato de amonio
ammonium binoxalate
binoxalato de amonio
ammonium biphosphate
bifosfato de amonio
ammonium bisulfide
bisulfuro de amonio
ammonium bisulfite
bisulfito de amonio
ammonium bitartrate
bitartrato de amonio
amonium borate
borato de amonio
ammonium bromide
bromuro de amonio
ammonium cadmium
bromide
bromuro amónico
cádmico
ammonium caprylate
caprilato de amonio
ammonium carbamate
carbamato de amonio
ammonium
carbazotate
carbazotato de amonio
ammonium carbonate
carbonato de amonio
ammonium ceric
nitrate
nitrato cérico amónico
ammonium chlorate
clorato de amonio
ammonium chloride
cloruro de amonio

16

ammonium chloroosmate
clorosmiato de amonio

ammonium chloroplatinate
cloroplatinato de amonio

ammonium chloroplatinite
cloroplatinito de amonio

ammonium chromate
cromato de amonio

ammonium chrome alum
alumbre amónico crómico

ammonium chromium sulfate
sulfato amónico crómico

ammonium citrate, dibasic
citrato de amonio dibásico

ammonium cobaltous phosphate
fosfato cobaltoso amónico

ammonium cobaltous sulfate
sulfato cobaltoso amónico

ammonium cupric chloride
cloruro cúprico amoniacal

ammonium cupric sulfate
sulfato cúprico amoniacal

ammonium decaborate
decaborato de amonio

ammonium dichromate
dicromato de amonio

ammonium dihydrogen phosphate
dihidrofosfato de amonio

ammonium dimethyl-dithiocarbamate
dimetilditiocarbamato de amonio

ammonium dinitro-o-cresolate
dinitro-o-cresolato de amonio

ammonium dithiocar-bamate
ditiocarbamato de amonio

ammonium ferric citrate
citrato férrico de amonio

ammonium ferric chromate
cromato férrico de amonio

ammonium ferric oxalate
oxalato férrico de amonio

ammonium ferric sulfate
sulfato férrico de amonio

ammonium ferricyanide
ferricianuro de amonio

ammonium ferrocyanide
ferrocianuro de amonio

ammonium ferrous fluoride
fluoruro ferroso de amonio

ammonium fluoride
fluoruro de amonio

ammonium fluosilicate
fluosilicato de amonio

ammonium formate
formiato de amonio

ammonium gluconate
gluconato de amonio

ammoniun glutamate
glutamato de amonio

ammonium hexa-chloroosmate
hexaclorosmiato de amonio

ammonium hexachloroplatinate
hexacloroplatinato de amonio

ammonium hexa-fluoroaluminate
hexafluoroaluminato de amonio

ammonium hexa-fluorogallate
hexafluorogalato de amonio

ammonium hexafluoro-germanate
hexafluorogermanato de amonio

ammoniumhexa-fluorophosphate
hexafluorofosfato de amonio

ammonium hexafluorosilicate
hexafluorosilicato de amonio

ammonium hexanitratecerate
hexanitratocerato de amonio

ammonium hydrate
hidrato de amonio

ammonium hydrogen carbonate
carbonato ácido de amonio

ammonium hydrogen fluoride
fluoruro ácido de amonio, hidrofluoruro de amonio

ammonium hydrogen sulfate
sulfato ácido de amonio

ammonium hydroxide
hidróxido de amonio

ammonium hydrosulfide
hidrosulfuro de amonio

ammonium hypochlorite
hipoclorito de amonio

ammonium hypophosphite
hipofosfito de amonio

ammonium hyposulfite
hiposulfito de amonio

ammonium icthosulfonate
ictosulfonato de amonio

ammonium iodate
yodato de amonio

ammonium iodide
yoduro de amonio

ammonium iron tartrate
tartrato de amonio y hierro

ammonium lactate
lactato de amonio

ammonium laurate, anhydrous
laurato de amonio anhidro

ammonium lignin sulfonate
sulfonato de amonio y lignina

ammonium linoleate
linoleato de amonio

ammonium magnesium chloride
cloruro de amonio y magnesio

ammonium mandelate
mandelato de amonio

ammonium metaborate
metaborato de amonio

ammonium metatungstate
metatungstato de amonio

ammonium metavanadate
metavanadato de amonio

ammonium molybdate
molibdato de amonio

ammonium 12-molybdophosphate
12-molibdofosfato de amonio

ammonium 12-molybdosilicate
12-molibdosilicato de amonio

ammonium muriate
muriato de amonio

ammonium nickel chloride
cloruro de amonio y níquel

ammonium nickel sulfate
sulfato de amonio y níquel

ammonium nitrate
nitrato de amonio

ammonium nitrate-carbonate mixtures
mezclas de nitrato y carbonato de amonio

ammonium nitroferricyanide
nitroferricianuro de amonio

ammonium oleate
oleato de amonio

ammonium osmium chloride
cloruro de amonio y osmio, clorosmiato de amonio

ammonium oxalate
oxalato de amonio
ammonium p-tungstate
p-tungstato de amonio
ammonium palmitate
palmitato de amonio
ammonium pentaborate
pentaborato de amonio
ammonium pentachlorozincate
pentaclorocincato de amonio
ammonium perchlorate
perclorato de amonio
ammonium permanganate
permanganato de amonio
ammonium peroxydisulfate
peroxidisulfato de amonio
ammonium perrhenate
perrenato de amonio
ammonium persulfate
persulfato de amonio
ammonium phosphate, di-, hemi-, monobasic
fosfato de amonio di, hemi, monobásico
ammonium phosphite
fosfito de amonio
ammonium phosphomolybdate
fosfomolibdato de amonio
ammonium phosphotungstate
fosfotungstato de amonio
ammonium phosphowolframate
fosfowolframato de amonio
ammonium picrate
picrato de amonio
ammonium picronitrate
picronitrato de amonio
ammonium platinic chloride
cloruro platínico de amonio
ammonium platinous chloride
cloruro platinoso de amonio

ammonium polymannuronate
polimanuronato de amonio
ammonium polyphosphate
polifosfato de amonio
ammonium polysulfide
polisulfuro de amonio
ammonium reineckate
sal de Reinecke
ammonium ricinoleate
ricinoleato de amonio
ammonium saccharin
sacarina amónica
ammonium salicylate
salicilato de amonio
ammonium salt
sal de amonio
ammonium selenate
seleniato de amonio
ammonium selenite
selenito de amonio
ammonium sesquicarbonate
sesquicarbonato de amonio
ammonium silicofluoride
silicofluoruro de amonio
ammonium silicomolybdate
silicomolibdato de amonio
ammonium soap
jabón amoniacal
ammonium sodium phosphate
fosfato de amonio y sodio
ammonium stearate
estearato de amonio
ammonium sulfamate
sulfamato de amonio
ammonium sulfate
sulfato de amonio
ammonium sulfate nitrate
nitrosulfato de amonio
ammonium sulfide
sulfuro de amonio
ammonium sulfide solution
solución de sulfuro de amonio
ammonium sulfite
sulfito de amonio

ammonium sulfocyanate
sulfocianato de amonio
ammonium sulfocyanide
sulfocianuro de amonio
ammonium sulfonate
sulfonato de amonio
ammonium sulforicinoleate
sulforricinoleato de amonio
ammonium tartrate
tartrato de amonio
ammonium tetrachloroaluminate
tetracloroaluminato de amonio
ammonium tetrachlorozincate
tetraclorocincato de amonio
ammonium tetrathiocyanodiammonochromate
tetratiociandiamonocromato de amonio
ammonium tetrathiotungstate
tetratiotungstato de amonio
ammonium thiocyanate
tiocianato de amonio
ammonium thioglycolate
tioglicolato de amonio
ammonium thiosulfate
tiosulfato de amonio
ammonium titanium oxalate
oxalato de amonio y titanio
ammonium tungstate
tungstato de amonio
ammonium uranate
uranato de amonio
ammonium uranium carbonate
carbonato de amonio y uranio
ammonium uranium fluoride
fluoruro de amonio y uranio
ammonium valerate
valerato de amonio

ammonium vanadate
vanadato de amonio
ammonium wolframate
wolframato de amonio
ammonium zinc phosphate
fosfato amónico cíncico, fosfato de amonio y cinc
ammonium zirconifluoride
circonifluoruro de amonio
ammonium zirconyl carbonate
carbonato circonílico de amonio
ammonization
amonización
amobarbital
amobarbital
amodiaquin(e)
amodiaquina
amodiaquin hydrochloride
clorhidrato de amodiaquina
amogastrin
amogastrina
amolanone
amolanona
amoproxan
amoproxano
amopyroquine
amopiroquina
amorolfine
amorolfina
amorphic
amorfo
amorphous
amorfo
amorphous carbon
carbon amorfo
amoscanate
amoscanato
amosite
amosita
amosulalol
amosulalol
amotriphene
amotrifeno
amoxapine
amoxapina
amoxecaine
amoxecaína
amoxicillin
amoxicilina

amoxydramine camsilate
cansilato de amoxidramina

ampelopsin
ampelopsina

amperage
amperaje

ampere
amperio

amperozide
amperozida

amphecloral
anfecloral

amphenidone
anfenidona

amphenone B
anfenona B

amphetamine
anfetamina

amphetaminil
anfetaminilo

amphibole
anfibol

amphiphilic
anfifílico

ampholyte
anfolito

ampholytic detergens
detergentes anfolíticos

amphomycin
anfomicina

amphotalide
anfotalida

amphoteric
anfótero, anfotérico

amphotericin B
anfotericina B

ampicillin
ampicilina

amplifier
amplificador

ampligen
amplígeno

ampoule
ampolla, ampolleta

amprolium
amprolio

amprotropine phosphate
fosfato de amprotropina

ampule
ampolla, ampolleta

ampyrimine
ampirimina

ampyrone
ampirona

amquinate
anquinato

amrinone
anrinona

amsacrine
ansacrina

amsonic acid
ácido ansónico

amsonate
ansonato

AMU (atomic mass unit)
UMA (unidad de masa atómica)

amygdalic acid
ácido amigdálico

amygdalin
amigdalina

amyl
amilo

amyl acetate
acetato de amilo

amyl acetic ester
éster amilacético

amyl acetic ether
éter amilacético

amyl acid phosphate
fosfato ácido de amilo

amyl alcohol
alcohol amílico

n-sec-amyl alcohol
alcohol n-amílico secundario

tert-amyl alcohol
alcohol amílico terciario

amyl aldehyde
aldehído amílico

amyl benzoate
benzoato de amilo, benzoato amílico

amyl bromide
bromuro de amilo, bromuro amílico

amyl butyrate
butirato de amilo, butirato amílico

amyl caproate
caproato de amilo, caproato amílico

amyl carbamate
carbamato de amilo, carbamato amílico

amyl carbinol
amilcarbinol

n-amyl chloride
cloruro de n-amilo, cloruro n-amílico

amyl cinnamate
cinamato de amilo, cinamato amílico

amyl ether
éter amílico

amyl formate
formiato de amilo, formiato amílico

n-amyl furoato
furoato de n-amilo, furoato n-amílico

amyl hydrate
hidrato de amilo, hidrato amílico

amyl hydride
hidruro de amilo, hidruro amílico

amyl isovalerate
isovalerato de amilo, isovalerato amílico

amyl lactate
lactato de amilo, lactato amílico

amyl laurate
laurato de amilo, laurato amílico

amyl mercaptan
amilmercaptano

amyl nitrate
nitrato de amilo, nitrato amílico

amyl nitrite
nitrito de amilo, nitrito amílico

amyl hydrosulfide
hidrosulfuro de amilo, hidrosulfuro amílico

amyl propionate
propionato de amilo, propionato amílico

amyl pyromucate
piromucato de amilo, piromucato amílico

amyl salicylate
salicilato de amilo, salicilato amílico

amyl sulfide
sulfuro de amilo, sulfuro amílico

amyl valerate
valerianato de amilo, valerianato amílico

amyl carbamate
carbamato de amilo, carbamato amílico

amyl valerianate
valerianato de amilo, valerianato amílico

amylaceous
amiláceo

n-amylamine
n-amilamina

sec-amylamine
sec-amilamina, amilamina secundaria

amylase
amilasa

n-amylbenzene
n-amilbenceno

sec-amylbenzene
sec-amilbenceno, amilbenceno secundario

α-amylcinnamic alcohol
alcohol α-amilcinámico

α-amylcinnamic aldehyde
aldehído α-amilcinámico

6-n-amyl-m-cresol
6-n-amilo-m-cresol

amyl-p-dimethyl-aminobenzoate
p-dimetilamino-benzoato de amilo

amylene
amileno, penteno

amylene dichloride
dicloruro de amileno

amylene hydrate
hidrato de amileno, amileno hidratado

amylene-oxide ring
anillo de óxido amilénico

amylic
amílico

amylocaine hydrocloride
clorhidrato de amilocaína

amylodextrin
amilodextrina

amyloglucosidase
amiloglucosidasa

amyloid
amiloide

amylolysis
amilólisis

amylolytic enzymes
enzimas amilolíticas

amylon
almidón

amylopectin
amilopectina

amylopsin
amilopsina

amylose
amilosa
amylpenicillin sodium
amilpenicilina sódica
o-sec-amylphenol
o-sec-amilfenol
p-tert-amylphenol
p-terc-amilfenol
p-tert-amylphenyl
acetate
acetato de p-terc-
amilfenilo
amyltrichlorosilane
amiltriclorosilano
amylum
almidón
(α),(ß)-amyrin
(α),(ß)-amirina
anabasine
anabasina
anabsinthin
anabsintina
anacardic
anacárdico
anacardic acid
ácido anacárdico
anacardium gum
goma de anacardo
anaerobes
anaerobios
anaerobic
anaeróbico, anaerobio
anaerobic resins
resinas anaeróbicas,
resinas anaerobias
anagestone
anagestona
anagrelide
anagrelida
anagrelide hydro-
chloride
clorhidrato de
anagrelida
anagyrine
anagirina
analcite
analcita
analgen
analgeno
analogous
análogo
analogy
analogía
analizer
analizador
analysis
análisis
analyst
analista, laboratorista

analyte
analito, agente,
muestra o espécimen
analizado
analytic
analítico
analytical
analítico
analytical balance
balanza analítica
analytical chemistry
química analítica
analytical error
error analítico
analytical laboratory
laboratorio analítico
analytically pure
pureza analítica,
analíticamente puro
analyze
analizar
anaphylaxis
anafilaxis
anastrozole
anastrozol
anatabina
anatabina
anatase
anatasa
anazocine
anazocina
anazolene sodium
anazoleno sódico
ancarolol
ancarolol
ancitabine
ancitabina
ancrod
ancrodo
ancymidol
ancimidol
andalusite
andalucita
androgen
andrógeno
andrographolide
andrografólido
androisoxazole
androisoxazol
androstane
androstano
androstanolone
androstanolona
androstenediol
androstendiol
androsterone
androsterona
anemometer
anemómetro

anemonin
anemonina
anesthesia ether
éter anestésico
anesthetic
anestésico
anethole
anetol
angelic acid
ácido angélico
angelica
angélica
angelica oil
esencia (aceite) de
angélica
angelsite
angelsita
angiotensin
angiotensina
angiotensinamide
angiotensinamida
angiotonin
angiotonina
angle
ángulo
angostura bark
corteza de angostura
angstrom unit
unidad angstrom
angular deviation
desviación angular
anhalamine
analamina
anhalonidine
analonidina
anhalonine
analonina
anhydride
anhídrido
anhydrite
anhidrita, yeso
anhydroenneaheptitol
anhidroeneaheptitol
anhydrous
anhidro
anhydrous aluminum
chloride
cloruro de aluminio
anhidro
anhydrous ammonia
amoníaco anhidro
anhydrous ether
éter anhidro
anhydrous hydrogen
fluoride
ácido fluorhídrico
anhidro
anhydrous lime
cal anhidra

anhydrous salt
sal anhidra
anidex
anidex
anidoxime
anidoxima
anilamate
anilamato
anilazine
anilacina, anilazina
anileridine
anileridina
aniline
anilina
aniline acetate
acetato de anilina
aniline black
negro de anilina
aniline chloride
cloruro de anilina
aniline dye
colorante de anilina,
colorante azoico
aniline hydrochloride
clorhidrato de anilina
aniline ink
tinta de anilina
aniline point
punto de anilina
aniline red
rojo de anilina
aniline salt
sal de anilina,
clorhidrato de anilina
aniline yellow
amarillo de anilina
aniline-2,4-disulfonic
acid
ácido anilina-2,4-
disulfónico
anilinephthalein
anilinftaleína
p-anilinesulfonic acid
ácido p-anilin-
sulfónico
1-anilino-4-hydroxy-
anthraquinone
1-anilino-4-
hidroxiantraquinona
6-anilino-1-naphtol-3-
sulfonic acid
ácido 6-anilino-1-
naftol-3-sulfónico
anilinophenol
anilinofenol
anilopam
anilopán, anilopam
animal black
negro animal

animal charcoal
carbón animal, negro
animal
animal diastase
diastasa animal
animal fat
grasa animal
animal oil
aceite animal
animal starch
almidón animal
anion
anión
anion exchanger
permutador de aniones
anionic
aniónico
aniracetam
aniracetán, aniracetam
anisacril
anisacrilo
anisaldehyde
anisaldehído
anise
anís
anise oil
esencia (aceite) de anís
anise seed oil, aniseed oil
aceite de anís, aceite de semillas de anís
anisic acid
ácido anísico
anisic alcohol
alcohol anísico
anisic aldehyde
aldehído anísico
anisidine
anisidina
anisindione
anisindiona
anisol, anisole
anisol
anisomycin
anisomicina
anisopirol
anisopirol
anisotropic
anisótropo, anisotrópico
anisotropine methylbromide
metilbromuro de anisotropina
anisotropy
anisotropía, anisotropismo
anisoyl chloride
cloruro de anisoílo

anistreplase
anistreplasa
anisyl acetate
acetato de anisilo
anisyl alcohol
alcohol anisílico
anisylacetone
anisilacetona
p-anisylchlorodiphenilmethane
p-anisilclorodifenilmetano
2-p-anisyl-1,3-indandione
2-p-anisil-1,3-indandiona
anitrazafen
anitrazafeno
annatto
anato
annealing
recocido
annotinine
anotinina
anode
ánodo
anode solution
solución anódica
anode mud
fango anódico
anodic
anódico
anodic (anodized) coating
revestimiento anódico (anodizado)
anodical
anódico
anodizing
anodización
p-anol
p-anol
anomalous water
agua anómala
anomer
anómero
anserine
anserina
antabuse
antabús, antabuse,
antacid
antiácido, antácido
antafenite
antafenita
antagonistic
antagónico
antagonist, structural
antagonista estructural

antazoline
antazolina
antazonite
antazonita
antelmycim
antelmicina
anthelmintic
vermífugo, antihelmíntico
antheridiol
anteridiol
anthiolimine
antiolimina
anthocyanin
antocianina
anthophyllite
antofilita
anthracene
antraceno
anthracene oil
aceite de antraceno
anthracene red
rojo de antraceno
anthracene yellow
amarillo de antraceno
1,8,9-anthracenetriol
1,8,9-antracenotriol
anthracite
antracita
anthragallic acid
ácido antragálico
anthragallol
antragalol
anthralin
antralina
anthramycin
antramicina
anthranilic acid
ácido antranílico
anthranol
antranol
anthranone
antranona
anthrapurpurin
antrapurpurina
anthraquinone
antraquinona
anthraquinone-1,5-disulfonic acid
ácido antraquinona 1,5-disulfónico
anthraquinone dye
colorante de antraquinona
anthrarobin
antrarrobina
anthrarufin
antrarrufina

anthrimide
antrimida
anthrone
antrona
antianxiety agent
agente ansiolítico
antiarin
antiarina
antibiotic
antibiótico
antibiotic ointment
ungüento antibiótico
antibiotic sensitivity discs
discos para antibiogramas
antibiotic resistant
resistente a los antibióticos
antibody
anticuerpo
anticaking agent
agente antiaglutinante
anticatalyst
anticatalizador
anticathode
anticátodo
antichlor
anticloro, tiosulfato sódico
anticholinesterase
anticolinesterasa
anticolinergic
anticolinérgico
anticlockwise rotation
rotación izquierda
anticoagulant
anticoagulante
anticorrosive
anticorrosivo
antidepressant
antidepresivo
antidote
antídoto
antiemetic
antiemético
antienite
antienita
antienzyme
antienzima
antiferment
antifermento
antifertility agent
agente anticonceptivo
antifoam
antiespumante
antifreeze
anticongelante

21

antifroth
antiespumante
antigelling agent
agente antigelificante
antigens
antígenos
antigen-antibody
antígeno-anticuerpo
antiglobulin
antiglobulina
antihistamine
antihistamina
antihypertensive agent
agente antihipertensivo
antiinflammatory agent
agente antinflamatorio
antiknock agent
agente antidetonante
antilogarithm
antilogaritmo
antilymphocytic serum
suero antilinfocítico
antimalarial agent
agente antipalúdico
antimetabolite
antimetabolito
antimicrobial preservative effectiveness test
prueba de eficacia del conservador antimicrobiano
antimonial
antimonial
antimoniate
antimoniato
antimonic
antimónico
antimonic acid
ácido antimónico
antimonic anhydride
anhídrido antimónico
antimonide
antimoniuro
antimonious, antimonous
antimonioso
antimonous sulfide
sulfuro antimonioso
antimonite
antimonita
antimony
antimonio
antimony black
negro de antimonio
antimony bloom
óxido de antimonio

antimony bromide
bromuro de antimonio
antimony caustic
antimonio cáustico
antimony chloride
cloruro de antimonio
antimony chloride oxide
oxicloruro de antimonio, cloruro básico de antimonio
antimony dichlorotrifluoride
diclorotrifluoruro de antimonio
antimony fluoride
fluoruro de antimonio
antimony hydride
hidruro de antimonio
antimony iodide
yoduro de antimonio
antimony lactate
lactato de antimonio
antimony needles
agujas de antimonio
antimony orange
anaranjado de antimonio, pentasulfuro de antimonio
antimony oxide
óxido de antimonio
antimony oxychloride
cloruro básico de antimonio, oxicloruro de antimonio
antimony pentachloride
pentacloruro de antimonio
antimony pentafluoride
pentafluoruro de antimonio
antimony pentasulfide
pentasulfuro de antimonio
antimony pentoxide
pentóxido de antimonio
antimony perchloride
percloruro de antimonio
antimony persulfide
persulfuro de antimonio
antimony potassium oxalate
oxalato de antimonio y potasio

antimony potassium tartrate
tartrato de antimonio y potasio
antimony red
rojo de antimonio
antimony salt
sal de antimonio
antimony sodiate
antimoniato de sodio
antimony sodium gluconate
gluconato de antimonio y sodio
antimony sodium tartrate
tartrato de antimonio y sodio
antimony sodium thioglycollate
tioglicolato de antimonio y sodio
antimony sulfate
sulfato de antimonio
antimony sulfide
sulfuro de antimonio
antimony sulfide golden
sulfuro dorado de antimonio
antimony thioglycollamide
tioglicolamida de antimonio
antimony tribromide
tribromuro de antimonio
antimony trichloride
tricloruro de antimonio
antimony trifluoride
trifluoruro de antimonio
antimony triiodide
triyoduro de antimonio
antimony trioxide
trióxido de antimonio
antimony triselenide
triseleniuro de antimonio
antimony trisulfate
trisulfato de antimonio
antimony trisulfide
trisulfuro de antimonio
antimony white
blanco de antimonio, trióxido de antimonio
antimonyl
antimonilo
antimonyl chloride
cloruro de antimonilo

antimycin A
antimicina A
antineutron
antineutrón
antineoplastic
antineoplásico
antioxidant
antioxidante
antiozonant
antiozono
antiparticle
antipartícula
antiperspirant
antisudorante
antipodal
antípoda
antiproton
antiprotón
antipyretic
antipirético
antipyrine
antipirina
antipyrine salicylate
salicilato de antipirina
antireticular cytotoxic serum
suero citotóxico antirreticular
antirheumatic
antirreumático
antirust
antioxidante, anticorrosivo
antiscorbutic
antiescorbútico
antiseptic
antiséptico
antispasmodic
antiespasmódico
antistatic agent
agente antiestático
antithrombin
antitrombina
antitoxin
antitoxina
antitussive
antitusivo
antiviral activity
actividad antiviral
antivirin AV
antivirina AV
antizymotic
antifermento
antrafenine
antrafenina
antramycin
antramicina
APAP
acetaminofeno

apalcillin
apalcilina
apamin
apamina
apatite
apatita
apazone
apazona
apex
vértice, ápice
aphidicolin
afidicolina
aphlogistic
aflogístico
apholate
afolato
aphrodine
afrodina
aphylline
afilina
apicycline
apiciclina
apigenin
apigenina
apigetrin
apigetrina
apiin
apiína
apiole
apiol
apiose
apiosa
apoatropine
apoatropina
apocarotenal
apocarotenal
apocodeine
apocodeína
apocynin
apocinina
apo-ß-
erythroidine
apo-ß-eritroidina
apomorphine
apomorfina
apoquinine
apoquinina
aporeine
aporeína
apparatus
aparato, equipo
apparent density
densidad aparente
apparent viscosity
viscosidad aparente
appearance
aspecto
apple acid
ácido málico

apple essence
valerianato de amilo,
esencia de manzana
apple oil
valerianato de amilo,
aceite de manzana
applied research
investigación aplicada
appraise
evaluar
approach
enfoque,
abordaje
approchable
accesible
approval
aprobación
approved
aprobado
approximate calcula-
tion
cálculo aproximado
approximate formula
fórmula aproximada
approximate value
valor aproximado
approximation
aproximación
apraclonidine
apraclonidina
apramycin
apramicina
apricot kernel oil
aceite de huesos de
albaricoque
aprindine
aprindina
aprobarbital
aprobarbital
aprofene
aprofeno
apronalide
apronalida
aprotic solvent
disolvente aprótico
aprotinin
aprotinina
aptocaine
aptocaína
apyrase
apirasa
aqua
agua, solución
acuosa
aqua ammonia
agua amoniacal
aqua fortis
agua fuerte, ácido
nítrico

aqua pura
agua destilada
aqua regia
agua regia, ácido
nítrico
aqueous
acuoso
aqueos phase
fase acuosa
aquocobalamine
acuocobalamina
arabic gum
goma arábiga
arabinogalactan
arabinogalactano
arabinose
arabinosa
arabitol
arabitol
D-araboflavin
D-araboflavina
arbutamine
hydrochloride
clorhidrato de
arbutamina
arachidic acid
ácido araquídico
arachidonic acid
ácido araquidónico
arachidyl alcohol
alcohol araquidílico
arachin, arachina
araquina
arachis oil
aceite de maní, aceite
de cacahuete
aragonite
aragonita
aragonite needles
agujas de aragonita
aralia
aralia
aralkonium
chloride
cloruro de aralconio
aralkyl
aralquilo
aramid
aramida
aranotin
aranotina
araroba
araroba, angelín
arbaprostil
arbaprostilo
arbekacin
arbecacina, arbekacina
arborescin
arborescina

arbutin
arbutina
archaeometry
arqueometría
arecaidine
arecaidina
arecoline
arecolina
arfalasin
arfalasina
arfendazam
arfendazán, arfendazam
argatroban
argatrobano
argentite
argentita, arginosa
argentum
plata
arginase
arginasa
arginine
arginina
arginine glutamate
glutamato de arginina
argol
argol
argon
argón
argipressin
argipresina
argiprestocin
argiprestocina
aricine
aricina
arildone
arildona
aristate
aristato
aristolochic acid
ácido aristolóquico
aristochin, aristoquin
aristoquina, carbonato
de quinina
arkose
arcosa
armepavine
armepavina
Armstrong' acid
ácido de Armstrong
arnica
árnica
arogenic acid
ácido arogénico
aromatic
aromático
aromatic aldehyde
aldehído aromático
aromatic hydrocarbon
hidrocarburo aromático

aromaticity
aromaticidad
aromatization
aromatización
arprinocid
arprinocida
arsacetin
arsacetina
arsenamide
arsenamida
arsanilic acid
ácido arsanílico
arsenate
arseniato
arsenic
arsénico
arsenic acid
ácido arsénico
arsenic disulfide
disulfuro de arsénico
arsenic hemiselenide
hemiseleniuro de
arsénico
arsenic pentafluoride
pentafluoruro de
arsénico
arsenic pentaselenide
pentaseleniuro de
arsénico
arsenic pentasulfide
pentasulfuro de
arsénico
arsenic pentoxide
pentóxido de arsénico
arsenic tribromide
tribromuro de arsénico
arsenic trichloride
tricloruro de arsénico
arsenic trifluoride
trifluoruro de arsénico
arsenic triiodide
triyoduro de arsénico
arsenic trioxide
trióxido de arsénico
arsenic triselenide
triseleniuro de
arsénico
arsenic trisulfide
trisulfuro de arsénico
arsenic anhydride
anhídrido arsénico
arsenic bisulphide
bisulfuro de arsénico
arsenic, black
negro de arsénico
arsenic bromide
bromuro de arsénico
arsenic chloride
cloruro de arsénico

arsenic disulfide
disulfuro de arsénico
arsenic hydride
hidruro de arsénico
arsenic iodide
yoduro de arsénico
arsenic monosulfide
monosulfuro de
arsénico
arsenic oxide
óxido de arsénico
arsenic pentafluoride
pentafluoruro de
arsénico
arsenic pentasulfide
pentasulfuro de
arsénico
arsenic pentoxide
pentóxido de arsénico
arsenic red
rojo de arsénico
arsenic sesquioxide
sesquióxido de
arsénico
arsenic sulfide
sulfuro de arsénico
arsenic tersulfide
tersulfuro de arsénico
arsenic thioarsenate
tioarseniato de arsénico
arsenic tribromide
tribromuro de arsénico
arsenic trichloride
tricloruro de arsénico
arsenic trifluoride
trifloruro de arsénico
arsenic triiodide
triyoduro de arsénico
arsenic trioxide
trióxido de arsénico
arsenic triselenide
triseleniuro de arsénico
arsenic trisulfide
trisulfuro de arsénico
arsenic white
blanco de arsénico
arsenical
arsenical
arsenical liquid
licor arsenical
arsenical nickel
níquel arsenical
arsenical poisoning
envenenamiento con
arsénico
arsenide
arseniuro
arseniferous
arsenífero

arsenious acid
ácido arsenioso
arsenious anhydride
anhídrido arsenioso
arsenious bromide
bromuro arsenioso
arsenious chloride
cloruro arsenioso
arsenious iodide
yoduro arsenioso
arsenious oxide
óxido arsenioso
arsenious sulfide
sulfuro arsenioso
arsenoacetic acid
ácido arsenoacético
arsenobenzene
arsenobenceno
arsine
arsina
arsphenamine
arsfenamina
arsthinol
arstinol
1-arterenol
1-arterenol
artificial cinnabar
cinabrio artificial
artemisin
artemisina
artemisinin
artemisinina
artesunate
artesunato
articaine
articaína
aryl
arilo
aryl compound
compuesto arílico
aryl halide
haluro de arilo,
haluro
arílico
arylalkyl
arilalquilo
arylate
arilato
asafetida, asafoetida
asafétida
asaprol
asaprol
asarinin
asarinina
asarone
asarona
asarum oil
esencia (aceite) de
dragontea, serpentaria

asbestine
asbestina
asbestos
amianto, asbestos
ascaridole
ascaridol
ascorbic acid
ácido ascóbico
ascorbic acid
oxidase
oxidasa de ácido
ascórbico
ascorbigen
ascorbígeno
ascorbyl palmitate
palmitato de ascorbilo,
palmitato ascorbílico
aseptic
aséptico
ash
ceniza
ash, to
incinerar
asiaticoside
asiaticósido
asocainol
asocainol
asparagic acid
ácido asparágico
asparaginase
asparaginasa
asparagine
asparagina
asparaginic acid
ácido asparagínico
1-L-asparaginyl-5-L-
valyl angiotensin
octapeptide
octapéptido de 1-L-
asparaginil-5-L-valil
angiotensina
aspartame
aspartamo
aspartamic acid
ácido aspartámico
aspartamide
aspartamida
aspartic acid
ácido aspártico
aspartocin
aspartocina
aspergillic acid
ácido aspergílico
aspergillin
aspergilina
asperlicin
asperlicina
asphalt
asfalto

asphalt blown	**astatine**	**atomic number**	**AUFS**
asfalto soplado	astatina, astatinio	número atómico	Unidades de
asphalt, cut-back	**astaxanthin**	**atomic theory**	absorbancia de la
asfalto diluido	astaxantina	teoría atómica	escala completa
asphaltene	**astemizole**	**atomic volume**	(AUFS)
asfalteno	astemizol	volumen atómico	**auramine**
asphyxiant gas	**astringent**	**atomic weight**	auramina
gas asfixiante	astringente	peso atómico	**auranofin**
aspidin	**astrochemistry**	**atomicity**	auranofina
aspidina	astroquímica	atomicidad	**aurantiogliocladin**
aspidinol	**astromycin**	**atorvastatin**	aurantiogliocladina
aspidinol	astromicina	atorvastatina	**aureolin**
aspidosperma	**asymmetrical**	**atorvastatin calcium**	aureolina
aspidosperma,	asimétrico	atorvastanina cálcica	**aureothin**
quebracho	**asymmetry**	**atovaquone**	aureotina
aspidospermine	asimetría	atovacuona	**aureothricin**
aspidospermina	**atactic**	**atractyloside**	aureotricina
aspoxicillin	atáctico	atractilosida	**auric**
aspoxicilina	**atenolol**	**atracurium besylate**	áurico, de oro
aspirator	atenolol	besilato de atracurio	**auric and aureous**
aspirador	**athamantin**	**atranorin**	**compounds**
aspirin	atamantina	atranorina	compuestos áuricos y
aspirina	**atisine**	**atrazine**	aurosos
assay	atisina, antorina	atracina, atrazina	**aurin**
ensayo, prueba, análisis	**atmosphere**	**atrial natriuretic factor**	aurina
assay, to	atmósfera	factor natriurético	**aurodox**
ensayar, analizar	**atmosphere, controlled**	auricular	aurodox
assay balance	atmósfera controlada	**atrolactamide**	**aurothioglucose**
balanza de ensayos	**atmospheric**	atrolactamida	aurotioglucosa
assemble	atmosférico	**atrolactic acid**	**aurothioglycanide**
ensamblar, montar,	**atmospheric pressure**	ácido atroláctico	aurotioglucanuro
armar	presión atmosférica	**atromepine**	**aurum**
assembly	**atmospheric pollution**	atromepina	oro
conjunto	contaminación	**atropamine**	**austenite**
assess	atmosférica	atropamina	austenita
evaluar	**atolide**	**atropic acid**	**austenitic alloys**
assign	atolida	ácido atrópico	aleaciones
asignar	**atom**	**atropine**	austeníticas
assimilation	átomo	atropina	**autocatalysis**
asimilación	**atom gram**	**atropine methonitrate**	autocatálisis
assistant	átomo gramo	metonitrato de	**autoclave**
auxiliar, asistente	**atomic**	atropina	autoclave
association	atómico	**atropine oxide**	**autoclaved, to**
asociación	**atomic absorption**	óxido de atropina	someter a autoclave,
assortment	**spectroscopy**	**atropine sulfate**	poner en autoclave
surtido	espectroscopía de	sulfato de atropina	**autoignition point**
assume, to	absorción atómica	**attapulgite**	punto de autoignición
suponer	**atomic bomb**	atapulguita	**autolysis**
assumed	bomba atómica	**attacin**	autólisis
hipotético,	**atomic bond**	atacina	**automated spray**
supuesto	enlace atómico	**attar of roses**	**coater**
assumption	**atomic charge**	attar de rosas, esencia	revestidor automático a
hipótesis	carga atómica	de rosas	rocío
assure	**atomic energy**	**attenuation**	**automatic control**
garantizar, asegurar	energía atómica	atenuación	control automático
A-stage resin	**atomic hydrogen**	**attrition mill**	**autosampler**
resina de fase A	**welding**	molino de frotación	equipo automático de
astacin	soldadura oxhídrica	**aucubin**	obtención de muestras,
astacina	con hidrógeno atómico	aucubina	sacamuestra automático

autooxidation
autoxidación
auxiliary
auxiliar
auxin
auxina
auxochrome
auxocromo
aviation gasoline
gasolina de aviación
avidin
avidina
avilamycin
avilamicina
avocado oil
aceite de aguacate
Avogadro's law
ley de Avogadro
avoparcin
avoparcina
A.W.U. (atomic weight unit)
U.P.A. (unidad de peso atómico)
axial
axial
axis
eje
axis of rotation
eje de rotación
3-azabicyclo-(3,2,2)-nonane
3-azabiciclo-(3,2,2)-nonano
azabon
azabón
azabuperone
azabuperona
azacitidine
azacitidina
azaclorzine
azaclorcina, azaclorzina
azaconazole
azaconazol
azacosterol
azacosterol
azacyclonol hydrochloride
clorhidrato de azaciclonol
azafrin
azafrina
azaftozine
azaftocina, azaftozina

8-azaguanine
8-azaguanina
azalomycin
azalomicina
azamethonium bromide
bromuro de azametonio
azanator
azanator
azanidazole
azanidazol
azaperone
azaperona
azaprocin
azaprocino
azapropazone
azapropazona
azaquinzole
azaquinzol
azaribine
azaribina
azaserine
azaserina
azaspirium chloride
cloruro de azaspirio
azastene
azasteno
azatadine
azatadina
azatadine maleate
maleato de azatadina
azatepa
azatepa
azathioprine
azatioprina
azathymine
azatimina
6-azauridine
6-azauridina, ribósido de s-triazina-3,5-(2H, 4H)diona
azelaic acid
ácido acelaico
azelaoyl chloride
cloruro de acelaoílo
azelastine
acelastina
azeotrope
aceótropo
azeotropic distillation
destilación aceotrópica

azeotropic mixture
mezcla aceotrópica
azepexole
acepexol
azepindole
acepindol
2-azetidinecarboxylic acid
ácido 2-acetidin-carboxílico
azidamfenicol
acidanfenicol
azide
azida
azidocillin
acidocilina
azimexone
acimexona
aziminobenzene
aciminobenceno
azine
azina
azine dye
colorante acínico
azinphos
azinfós
azinphos methyl
metilazinfós
azintamide
acintamida
azipramine
acipramina
aziridine
aciridina
1-aziridineethanol
1-aciridinetanol
azithromycin
acitromicina
azlocillin
azlocilina
azlon
azlón
azo compound
compuesto azoico
azo dye
colorante azoico
azo yellow
amarillo azoico
azobenzene
azobenceno
azobenzene-p-sulfonic acid
ácido azobencen-p-sulfónico

4,4'-azobis-(4-cyanovaleric acid)
ácido 4,4'-azobis-(4-cianovalérico)
1,1-azobisformamide
1,1-azobisformamida
azobisdimethyl-valeronitrile
azobisdimetil-valeronitrilo
azobisisobutyronitrile
azobisisobutironitrilo
azocyclic
azocíclico
azodicarbonamide
azodicarbonamida
azodine
azodina
azogue
mercurio, azogue
azoic
azoico
azole
azol
azolitmin
azolitmina
azomycin
azomicina
azophenylene
azofenileno
azosemide
azosemida
azosulfamide
azosulfamida
azote
azoe, nitrógeno
azotic acid
ácido azoico
azotic
azoico, nitrogenado
azotomycin
azotomocina
azoxybenzene
azoxibenceno
azoxytoluidine
azoxitoluidina
aztreonam
aztreonán
azulene
azuleno
azure blue
azul celeste, azul azurado

B

babassu oil
aceite de babasú
Babbitt metal
metal de Babbitt
Babcock test
prueba de Babcock
bacampicillin
bacampicilina
bacampicillin
hydrochloride
clorhidrato de
bacampicilina
bacilus
bacilo
bacilysin
bacilisina
bacimethrin
bacimetrina
bacitracin
bacitracina
bacitracin methylene
disalycilate
disalicilato metilénico
de bacitracina
back
atrás, revés
back reaction
reacción inversa
back extract
retroextraer
back titration
titulación de
verificación,
retrotitulación
backflow
reflujo
backflow condenser
condensador de reflujo
background
antecedente, fondo
backing material
material de respaldo,
material de refuerzo
backlash
reacción violenta,
reacción contraria
baclofen
baclofeno
bacmecillinam
bacmecilinamo
bacteria
bacteria, bacterias
bactericidal
bactericida

bactericide
bactericida
bacteriological
bacteriológico
bacteriology
bacteriología
bacteriophage
bacteriófago
bacteriostat
bacteriostático
bacterium
bacteria
baddeleyite
badeleyita
Badische acid
ácido de Badische
Baekeland (Bakelite)
process
proceso de Baekeland
(baquelita)
Baeyer-Drewson indigo
synthesis
síntesis de índigo de
Baeyer y Drewson
Baeyer-Villiger
reactions
reacciones de Baeyer y
Villiger
baffle
deflector, pantalla,
tabique
bag
saco, bolsa
bagasse
bagazo
bagfilter
filtro de bolsa
baghouse
cámara de filtros de
bolsas, instalación de
filtrado
baicalein
baicaleína
bait
carnada, cebo
bakankosin
bacancosina
bake, to
hornear
bakelite
baquelita
baking powder
polvo de hornear,
levadura en polvo

balance
balanza; equilibrar
balance arm
brazo de balanza
balata
balata, balatá
Bally-Scholl synthesis
síntesis de Bally y
Scholl
balm oil
esencia (aceite) de
melisa, toronjil;
ungüento dulce, melisa
balsam
bálsamo
balsam Canada
bálsamo del Canadá
balsam gurjun
bálsamo de gurjún
balsam Mecca
bálsamo de la Meca
balsam Peru
bálsamo del Perú
balsam tolu
bálsamo de tolú
balsam traumatic
bálsamo para trauma
bambermycins
bambermicinas
bamboo
bambú
bambuterol
bambuterol
bamethan
bametán
bamifylline
bamifilina
bamipine
bamipina
baminidazole
baminidazol
banana oil
aceite de plátano,
acetato de amilo
baptigenin
baptigenina
baptisia
baptisia
barban
barbán
barbasco
barbasco
barberry bark
corteza de berbero

barberite
barberita
barbexaclone
barbexaclona
barbital
barbital
barbital sodium
barbital sódico
barbiturate
barbiturato
barbituric acid
ácido barbitúrico
Barden clay
arcilla Barden
Bardhan-Sengupta
phenanthrene synthesis
síntesis de fenantrenos
de Bardhan y Sengupta
barite
barita
barium
bario
barium acetate
acetato de bario
barium aluminate
aluminato de bario
barium azide
azida bárica
barium benzene-
sulfonate
sulfonato bencénico de
bario, bencensulfonato
de bario
barium bioxide
bióxido de bario
barium borotungstate
borotungstato de bario
barium borowolframate
borowolframato de
bario
barium bromate
bromato de bario
barium bromide
bromuro de bario
barium carbonate
carbonato de bario
barium chlorate
clorato de bario
barium chloride
cloruro de bario
barium chromate
cromato de bario
barium citrate
citrato de bario

barium cyanide
cianuro de bario
barium cyanoplatinite
cianoplatinito de bario
barium dichromate
dicromato de bario
barium dioxide
dióxido de bario
barium diphenylamine
sulfonate
difenilaminsulfonato
de bario
barium di-o-phosphate
di-o-fosfato de bario
barium dithionate
ditionato de bario
barium diuranate
diuranato de bario
barium ethylsulfate
sulfato etílico de bario,
etilsulfato de bario
barium ferrite
ferrita de bario
barium ferrocyanide
ferrocianuro de bario
barium fluoride
fluoruro de bario
barium fluorosilicate
fluorosilicato de bario
barium formate
formiato de bario
barium fructose
diphosphate
difosfato de fructosa y
bario
barium hexafluoro-
germanate
hexafluorogermanato
de bario
barium
hexafluorosilicate
hexafluorosilicato de
bario
barium hydrate
hidrato de bario
barium hydrosulfide
sulfhidrato de bario
barium hydroxide
anhydrous
hidróxido de bario
anhidro
barium hydroxide,
mono-, octa-,
pentahydrate
hidróxido de bario
mono, octa,
pentahidratado
barium hypophosphite
hipofosfito de bario

barium hyposulfite
hiposulfito de bario
barium iodate
yodato de bario
barium iodide
yoduro de bario
barium manganate
manganato de bario
barium mercury
bromide
bromuro de bario y
mercurio
barium mercury iodide
yoduro de bario y
mercurio
barium meta-
phosphate
metafosfato de bario
barium metasilicate
metasilicato de bario
barium molybdate
molibdato de bario
barium monohydrate
bario monohidratado,
monohidrato de bario
barium monosulfide
monosulfuro de bario
barium monoxide
monóxido de bario
barium nitrate
nitrato de bario
barium nitrite
nitrito de bario
barium oxalate
oxalato de bario
barium oxide
óxido de bario
barium perchlorate
perclorato de bario
barium permanganate
permanganato de bario
barium peroxide
peróxido de bario
barium phosphate,
dibasic
fosfato de bario
dibásico, fosfato de
bario secundario
barium phospho-
silicate
fosfosilicato de bario
barium platinum
cyanide
cianuro de bario y
platino
barium potassium
chromate pigment
pigmento de cromato
de bario y potasio

barium protoxide
protóxido de bario
barium pyrophosphate
pirofosfato de bario
barium selenide
seleniuro de bario
barium silicate
silicato de bario
barium silicide
siliciuro de bario
barium silicofluoride
silicofluoruro de bario
barium sodium
niobate
niobato de bario y
sodio
barium stannate
estannato de bario
barium stearate
estearato de bario
barium sulfate
sulfato de bario
barium sulfide
sulfuro de bario
barium sulfite
sulfito de bario
barium sulfocyanide
sulfocianuro de bario
barium superoxide
superóxido de bario
barium tartrate
tartrato de bario
barium thiocyanate
tiocianato de bario
barium thiosulfate
tiosulfato de bario
barium titanate
titanato de bario
barium tungstate
tungstato de bario
barium uranium
oxide
óxido de bario y uranio
barium white
blanco de bario
barium wolframate
wolframato de bario
barium zirconate
circoniato de bario
barium zirconium
silicate
silicato de bario y
circonio
bark
corteza
barley
cebada
barn
barnio

Barnett acetylation
method
método de acetilación
de Barnett
barometer
barómetro
barometric pressure
presión barométrica
barrel finishing
acabado en barril
barrier, moisture
barrera contra la
humedad
barthrin
bartrina
Barton reaction
reacción de Barton
Bart reaction
reacción de Bart
baryta, calcined
barita calcinada
baryta caustic
barita cáustica
baryta water
agua de barita
baryta yellow
amarillo de barita
barytes
baritas
basalt
basalto
basal metabolism
metabolismo basal
base
base
based on
a base de
baseline
valor basal, valor
inicial
baseline resolution
resolución basal
basic
básico, alcalino
basic aluminum
carbonate gel
gel básico de carbonato
de aluminio
basic cupric chromate
cromato cúprico básico
basic dichromate
dicromato básico
basic ferric acetate
acetato de hierro básico
basic fuchsin
fucsina básica
basic lead carbonate
carbonato de plomo
básico

28

basic lining
recubrimiento básico
basic manganese
chromate
cromato de manganeso
básico
basic metal
metal alcalino, metal
básico
basic nitrate
nitrato alcalino, nitrato
básico
basic oxide
óxido alcalino, óxido
básico
basic patent
patente original
basic research
investigación original
basic salt
sal alcalina, sal básica
basic slag
escoria alcalina,
escoria básica
basic stain
colorante alcalino,
colorante básico
basicity
alcalinidad
basil oil
esencia (aceite) de
albahaca
basis
base
basswood
tilo americano
bastnasite
bastnasita
batch
lote, tanda
batch distillation
destilación
intermitente, destilación
en etapas, destilación
por lote
batch process
proceso intermitente,
proceso en etapas,
proceso por lotes
batch production
producción por lotes
batching
producir el lote
batilol
batilol
bating
maceración
batrachotoxin
batracotoxina

batrachotoxinin A
batracotoxinina A
batroxobin
batroxobina
battery
batería, pila eléctrica,
acumulador, serie (de
pruebas)
batyl alcohol
alcohol batílico
Baudisch reaction
reacción de
Baudisch
Baumé scale
escala de Baumé
bauxite
bauxita
bayberry bark
corteza de arrayán
bayberry wax
cera de arrayán
Bayer's acid
ácido de Bayer
Bayer process
método de Bayer
bay oil
esencia (aceite) de
laurel
bay rum
ron de laurel
BCG
abreviatura de
Bacillus Calmette-
Guérin
bead
cuenta, perla
beaker
vaso de precipitados
beam
haz, rayo
bebeerine
bebirina
bebeeru bark
corteza de bibirú
becanthone
becantona
Bechamp reaction
reacción de
Bechamp
Beckmann
rearrangement
transposición de
Beckmann
beclamide
beclamida
beclobrate
beclobrato
beclomethasone
beclometasona

beclomethasone
dipropionate
dipropionato de
beclometasona
beclotiamine
beclotiamina
beerstone
caliza no oolítica
(piedra porosa)
beeswax
cera de abejas
beet molasses
melaza de remolacha
beet sugar
azúcar de remolacha
befunolol
befunolol
befuraline
befuralina
behenic acid
ácido behénico
behenone
behenona
behenyl alcohol
alcohol behenílico
bekanamycin
becanamicina
belarizine
belaricina, belarizina
belladonna
belladona
belladonnine
belladonina
beloxamide
beloxamida
bemegride
bemegrida
bemetizide
bemetizida
benactyzine
benacticina
benafentrine
benafentrina
benalaxyl
benalaxil
benapryzine
benapricina
benazepril
hydrochloride
clorhidrato de
benacepril
Bence-Jones
proteins
proteínas de Bence y
Jones
bencisteine
bencisteína
benclonidine
benclonidina

bencyclane
benciclano
bendazac
bendazac
bendazol
bendazol
benderizine
bendericina,
benderizina
bending strength
resistencia a la flexión
bending test
prueba de flexión
bendiocarb
bendiocarb
bendroflumethiazide
bendroflumetiazida
Benedict solution
solución de Benedict
beneficiation
beneficio
benefin
benefina
benethamine penicillin
penicilina
benetamínica
benexate
hydrochloride
clorhidrato de benexato
benfluralin
benfluralina
benfluorex
benfluorex
benfosformine
benfosformina
benfotiamine
benfotiamina
benfuracarb
benfuracarb
benfurodil
hemisuccinate
hemisuccinato de
benfurodilo
benhepazone
benhepazona
Benjamin gum
goma de Benjamín
benmoxine
benmoxina
benolizime
benolicima
benomyl
benomilo
benorylate
benorilato
benorterone
benorterona
benoxafos
benoxafós

benoxaprofen
benoxaprofeno
benoxinate
benoxinato
benoxinate
hydrochloride
clorhidrato de
benoxinato
benpenolisin
benpenolisina
benperidol
benperidol
benproperine
benproperina
benrixate
benrixato
bensalan
bensalano
benserazide
benserazida
bensuldazic acid
ácido bensuldácico
bensulide
bensulida
bentazepam
bentacepán
bentazon
bentazona
bentemazole
bentemazol
benthos
bentós
bentiamine
bentiamina
bentipimine
bentipimina
bentiromide
bentiromida
bentonite
bentonita
benurestat
benurestato
benzal
benzal
benzal chloride
cloruro de benzal
benzalacetona
benzalacetona
benzalazine
benzalacina,
benzalazina
ß-benzalbutyramide
ß-benzalbutiramida
benzaldehyde
benzaldehído
benzaldehyde
cyanohydrin
cianohidrina
benzaldehídica

benzaldehyde green
verde de benzaldehído
o-benzaldehyde
malonitrile
malonitrilo de o-
benzaldehído
benzalkonium chloride
cloruro de benzalconio
benzamide
benzamida
benzaminoacetic acid
ácido benzamino-
acético
benzanilide
benzanilida
benzanthracene
benzantraceno
benzanthrone
benzantrona
benzaprinoxide
benzaprinoxida
benzarone
benzarona
benzathine
benzatina
benzathine
benzylpenicillin
bencilpenicilina
benzatínica
benzathrone
benzatrona
benzatropine
benzatropina
benzazimide
benzacimida
benzbromarone
benzobromarona
benzene
benceno
benzene azoimide
azoimida bencénica
benzene dibromide
dibromuro bencénico
m-benzene disulfonic
acid
ácido disulfónico m-
bencénico, ácido m-
bencendisulfónico
benzene hexachloride
hexacloruro de
benceno
benzene hydrocarbons
hidrocarburos
bencénicos
benzene nucleus
anillo bencénico,
núcleo bencénico
benzene ring
anillo bencénico

benzenearsonic acid
ácido bencenarsónico
benzeneazoanilide
azoanilida bencénica,
bencenazoanilida
benzeneazobenzene
azobenceno bencénico,
bencenazobenceno
benzeneazo-p-
benzeneazo-ß-naphthol
bencenazo-p-
bencenazo-ß-naftol
benzeneboronic acid
ácido borobencénico,
ácido bencenborónico
benzenecarboxilic acid
ácido carboxil
bencénico, ácido
bencencarboxílico
benzenediazonium
chloride
cloruro de
bencendiazonio
benzene-o-dicarboxilic
acid
ácido bencen-o-
dicarboxílico
1,2-benzenedi-
carboxylic anhydride-
4-formyl chloride
cloruro de 4-formil-
anhídrido de 1,2-
bencendicarboxilo
benzenemonosulfonic
acid
ácido monosulfon-
bencénico,
ácido bencenmono-
sulfónico
benzenephosphinic
acid
ácido bencenfosfínico
benzenephosphonic
acid
ácido bencenfosfónico
benzenephosphorus
dichloride
dicloruro
bencenfosforoso
benzenephosphorus
oxydichloride
dicloruro básico
bencenfosforoso
benzenestibonic acid
ácido bencenestibónico
benzenesulfone
chloride
cloruro de
benzensulfona

benzenesulfonic acid
ácido bencensulfónico
benzenesulfonic
anhydride
anhídrido
bencensulfónico
benzenesulfonic
chloride
cloruro bencensulfónico
benzenesulfonyl
chloride
cloruro de
bencensulfonilo
benzene-1,3,5-
tricarboxylic acid
chloride
cloruro ácido benceno-
1,3,5-tricarboxílico
benzenetriol
bencenotriol
benzenoid
bencenoide
benzenyl trichloride
tricloruro de bencenilo,
tricloruro bencenílico
benzestrol
bencestrol
benzethidine
bencetidina
benzethonium chloride
cloruro de bencetonio
benzetimide
bencetimida
benzhydrol
bencidrol,
difenilcarbinol
benzhydrylamine
bencidrilamina
benzhydryl bromide
bromuro de bencidrilo
benzhydryl chloride
cloruro de bencidrilo
2-(benzhydryloxy)-,N-N
dimethylethylamine
hydrochloride
clorhidrato de 2-
(bencidriloxi)-N,N-
dimetiletilamina
benzidine
bencidina
benzidine dicarboxylic
acid
ácido bencidin-
dicarboxílico
benzidine dye
colorante de bencidina
benzidine orange
anaranjado de
bencidina

benzidine
rearrangement
transposición de la
bencidina
benzidine sulfate
sulfato de bencidina
benzidine yellow
amarillo de bencidina
benzil
bencilo
benzil dioxime
dioxima bencílica
benzilic acid
ácido bencílico
**benzilic acid
rearrangement**
transposición del ácido
bencílico
benzilonium bromide
bromuro de bencilonio
benzimidazole
bencimidazol
benzimidazolethiol
bencimidazoltiol
benzine
bencina
benzindopyrine
bencindopirina
benziodarone
benciodarona
benzmalecene
benzomaleceno
benznidazole
benzonidazol
benzo azurine G
benzoazurina G
benzobarbital
benzobarbital
benzocaine
benzocaína
benzoclidine
benzoclidina
benzoctamine
benzoctamina
benzodepa
benzodepa
benzodihydropyrone
dihidropirona
bencénica,
benzodihidropirona
**benzododecinium
chloride**
cloruro de
benzododecinio
benzofuran
benzofurano
benzoglycolic acid
ácido glicol bencénico,
ácido benzoglicólico

benzoguanamine
benzoguanamina
benzohydrol
benzohidrol
benzoic acid
ácido benzoico
benzoic aldehyde
aldehído benzoico
benzoic anhydride
anhídrido benzoico
benzoic ether
éter benzoico
benzoic trichloride
tricloruro benzoico
benzoin
benzoína
benzoin gum
goma de benzoína
α-benzoin oxime
α-benzoinoxima
benzoin resin
resina de benjuí
benzol
benzol, benceno
benzol sulfamide
sulfamida
bencénica
benzol sulfochloride
sulfocloruro de
benceno
benzomorphan
benzomorfano
benzonatate
benzonatato
benzonitrile
benzonitrilo
benzophenol
benzofenol
benzophenone
benzofenona
benzophenone oxide
óxido de
benzofenona
**3,3',4,4'-benzophenone
tetracarboxylic
dianhydride**
dianhídrido
tetracarboxílico de
3,3',4,4'-benzofenona
benzopinacol
benzopinacol
benzopurpurine 4B
benzopurpurina 4B
benzopyran
benzopirano
benzopyrene
benzopireno
benzopyrone
benzopirona

**benzopyrronium
bromide**
bromuro de
benzopirronio
benzoquinoline
benzoquinolina
benzoquinone
benzoquinona
**benzoquinonium
chloride**
cloruro de
benzoquinonio
benzoresorcinol
benzorresorcinol
benzosulfimide
benzosulfimida
benzothiazole
benzotiazol
**benzothiazolyl
disulfide**
disulfuro de
benzotiazolilo
**benzothiazyl-2-
cyclohexylsulfenamide**
2-ciclohexil-
sulfenamida
de benzotiacilo
**2-benzothiazyl-N,N-
diethylthiocarbamyl
sulfide**
sulfuro de 2-benzotiacil-
N,N-dietiltiocarbamilo
benzothiazyl disulfide
disulfuro de
benzotiacilo
benzotriazole
benzotriazol
benzotrichloride
tricloruro bencénico,
benzotricloruro,
tricloruro de tolueno
benzotrifluoride
trifluoruro bencénico,
benzotrifluoruro,
trifluoruro de tolueno
benzoxiquine
benzoxiquina,
benzoxilina
benzoxonium chloride
cloruro de benzoxonio
benzoyl
benzoílo
benzoyl chloride
cloruro de benzoílo
benzoyl fluoride
fluoruro de benzoílo
benzoyl isothiocyanate
isotiocianato de
benzoílo

benzoyl peroxide
peróxido de benzoílo
**trans-ß-benzoylacrylic
acid**
ácido trans-ß-
benzoilacrílico
N-benzoyl-L(+)-alanine
N-benzoíl-L(+)-alanina
benzoylamide
amida benzoílica,
benzoilamida
**benzoylaminoacetic
acid**
ácido acético
benzoilamínico,
ácido benzoil-
aminoacético
benzoylanilide
benzoilanilida,
anilida benzoílica
**benzoyl-2,5-diethoxy-
aniline**
2,5-dietoxianilina
benzoílica, benzoíl-2,5-
dietoxianilina
benzoylecgonine
ecgonina benzoílica,
benzoilecgonina
benzoylferrocene
ferroceno benzoílico,
benzoilferroceno
benzoylglycin
glicina benzoílica,
benzoilglicina
benzoylglycocoll
glicocola benzoílica,
benzoilglicocola
benzoylphenyl carbinol
carbinolbenzoilfenílico,
benzoilfenilcarbinol
2-benzoylpyridine
2-benzoilpiridina
benzoylsulfonic imide
imida benzoilsulfónica
benzozone
benzozona
1,2-benzphenanthrene
1,2-benzofenantreno
benzphetamine
benzofetamina
benzpiperylon
benzopiperilona
benzpyrene
benzopireno
benzpyrinium bromide
bromuro de
benzopirinio
benzquercin
benzoquercina

benzquinamide
benzoquinamida
benzthiazide
benzotiazida
benztropine mesylate
mesilato de
benzotropina
benzydamine
bencidamina
benzyl
bencilo
benzyl abietate
abietato bencílico,
abietato de bencilo
benzyl acetate
acetato bencílico,
acetato de bencilo
benzyl alcohol
alcohol bencílico
benzyl benzoate
benzoato bencílico,
benzoato de bencilo
benzyl bromide
bromuro bencílico,
bromuro de bencilo
benzyl butirate
butirato bencílico,
butirato de bencilo
benzyl butyl phthalate
ftalato bencilbutílico,
ftalato de bencilbutilo
benzyl carbinol
carbinol bencílico,
bencilcarbinol
benzyl chloride
cloruro bencílico,
cloruro de bencilo
**benzyl chloro-
carbonate**
clorocarbonato de
bencilo
benzyl chloroformate
cloroformiato de
bencilo
benzyl cinnamate
cinamato de bencilo
benzyl cyanide
cianuro bencílico,
cianuro de bencilo
benzyl dichloride
dicloruro bencílico,
dicloruro de bencilo
benzyl ether
éter bencílico
benzyl ethyl ether
éter etilbencílico
benzyl fluoride
fluoruro bencílico,
fluoruro de bencilo

benzyl formate
formiato de bencilo
benzyl fumarate
fumarato de bencilo
benzyl iodide
yoduro bencílico,
yoduro de bencilo
benzyl isoamyl ether
éter bencilisoamílico
benzyl isobutyl ketone
cetona
bencilisobutílica,
bencilisobutilcetona
benzyl isoeugenol
isoeugenol bencílico,
bencilisoeugenol
benzyl isothiocyanate
isotiocianato bencílico,
isotiocianato de
bencilo
benzyl mercaptan
mercaptano bencílico,
bencilmercaptano
benzyl methyl ether
éter metilbencílico
benzyl pelargonate
pelargonato de
bencilo
benzyl propionate
propionato de bencilo
benzyl salicylate
salicilato de bencilo
benzyl succinate
succinato de bencilo
benzyl sulfide
sulfuro de bencilo
benzyl thiol
tiol bencílico,
benciltiol
benzylamine
bencilamina
**N-benzyl-p-
aminophenol**
N-bencil-p-aminofenol
**2-benzylamino-1-
propanol**
2-bencilamino-1-
propanol
benzylaniline
anilina bencílica,
bencilanilina,
bencilfenilamina
benzylbenzene
benceno bencílico,
bencilbenceno
**o-benzyl-p-
chlorophenol**
o-bencil-p-clorofenol,
clorofeno, septifeno

**N-benzyldiethanol-
amine**
N-bencildietanol-
amina
**N-benzyldimethyl-
amine**
N-bencildimetilamina
N-benzylethanolamine
N-benciletanolamina
benzylethylsalicylate
etilsalicilato de
bencilo
**benzylhexadecyl-
dimethylammonium
chloride**
cloruro de amonio
bencilhexadecil-
dimetílico, cloruro de
bencilhexadecil-
dimetilamonio
**benzylhydrochloro-
thiazide**
hidroclorotiazida
bencílica,
bencilhidrocloro-
tiazida
benzylhydroquinone
hidroquinona bencílica,
bencilhidroquinona
benzylidene azine
acina bencilidénica,
bencilidenacina, azina
bencilidénica,
bencilidenazina
benzylidene chloride
cloruro de
bencilideno
benzylideneacetone
acetona bencilidénica,
bencilidenacetona
benzylideneaniline
anilina bencilidénica,
bencilidenanilina
**2-benzylidene-1-
heptanol**
2-bencilidén-1-
heptanol
**N-benzylisopropyl-
amine**
isopropilamina N-
bencílica, N-bencil-
isopropilamina
**3-benzyl-4-methyl
umbelliferone**
3-bencil-4
metilumbeliferona
benzylmethylamine
metilamina bencílica,
bencilmetilamina

**N-benzyl-N,N-methyl-
ethanolamine**
N-bencil-N,N-
metiletanolamina
benzylmorphine
morfina bencílica,
bencilmorfina
**benzylnicotinium
chloride**
cloruro de
bencilnicotinio
p-benzyloxyphenol
p-benciloxifenol
benzylpenicillinic acid
ácido bencil-
penicilínico
**benzylpenicillin
sodium**
bencilpenicilina
sódica
o-benzylphenol
o-bencilfenol
p-benzylphenol
p-bencilfenol
benzylphenyl ketone
cetona bencilfenílica,
bencilfenilcetona
benzylphenylacetate
fenilacetato
bencílico
benzylphenylamine
bencilfenilamina,
bencilanilina
benzylpyridine
bencilpiridina
**bephenium hydroxy-
benzylsulfamide**
sulfamida bencílica,
bencilsulfamida
**p-(benzylsulfon-
amido)benzoic acid**
ácido p-
(bencilsulfonamido)
benzoico
**benzylthionium
chloride**
cloruro de benciltionio
2-benzyl-6-thiouracil
2-bencil-6-tiouracilo
**S-benzylthiuronium
chloride**
cloruro de S-
benciltiuronio
**benzyltrimethyl-
ammonium chloride**
cloruro de amonio
benciltrimetílico,
cloruro de
benciltrimetilamonio

benzyltrimethyl-
ammonium hexafluoro-
phosphate
hexafluorofosfato de
amonio benciltri-
metílico, hexafluor-
fosfato de bencil-
trimetilamonio
benzyltrimethyl-
ammonium methoxide
metóxido de amonio
benciltrimetílico,
metóxido de bencil-
trimetilamonio
benztropine mesylate
mesilato de
benzotropina
benzylurea
urea bencílica,
bencilurea
benzyne
bencina
bephenium
befenio
bephenium hydroxy-
naphthoate
hidroxinaftoato de
befenio
bepiastine
bepiastina
bepridil
bepridil
berbamine
berbamina
berberine
berberina,
umbelatina
berberine sulfate
sulfato de berberina,
sulfato de umbelatina
berberis
berberís
berbine
berbina
bergamot oil
esencia (aceite) de
bergamota
bergapten(e)
bergapteno
bergenin
bergenina
Bergmann tube
tubo de Bergmann
Bergius process
proceso de Bergius
beri-beri
beriberi
berkelium
berkelio, berquelio

Berlin blue
azul de Berlín
Berlin red
rojo de Berlín
bertholite
bertolita
berninamycin
berninamicina
beryl
berilo
beryllia
berilia, óxido de berilio
beryllides
beriluros
beryllium
berilio
beryllium acetate
acetato de berilio
beryllium acetyl-
acetonate
acetonato acetílico de
berilio, acetilacetonato
de berilio
beryllium borohydride
borohidruro de berilio
beryllium bromide
bromuro de berilio
beryllium bronze
bronce de berilio
berylium carbide
carburo de berilio
berylium carbonate
carbonato de berilio
berylium chloride
cloruro de berilio
beryllium copper
cobre de berilio
beryllium fluoride
fluoruro de berilio
beryllium formate
formiato de berilio
beryllium gold
oro con (5%) de
berilio
beryllium hydrate
hidrato de berilio
beryllium hydride
hidruro de berilio
beryllium hydroxide
hidróxido de berilio
beryllium iodide
yoduro de berilio
beryllium
metaphosphate
metafosfato de berilio
beryllium nitrate
nitrato de berilio
beryllium nitride
nitruro de berilio

beryllium oxide
óxido de berilio
beryllium perchlorate
perclorato de berilio
beryllium potassium
fluoride
fluoruro de berilio y
potasio
beryllium potassium
sulfate
sulfato de berilio y
potasio
beryllium selenate
seleniato de berilio
beryllium silicate
silicato de berilio
beryllium sodium
fluoride
fluoruro de berilio y
sodio
beryllium sulfate
sulfato de berilio
berythromycin
beritromicina
Berzelius beaker
vaso de precipitados de
Berzelius, vaso de
precipitados alto
besilate
besilato
bestrabucil
bestrabucilo
besunide
besunida
beta-
beta-
beta battery
batería beta
betacarotene
beta-caroteno,
betacaroteno
betacetilmethadol
betacetilmetadol
betahistine
betahistina
betaine
betaína
betaine hydrochloride
clorhidrato de betaína
betaine phosphate
fosfato de betaína
betalactam
betalactámico
betameprodine
betameprodina
betamethadol
betametadol
betamethasone
betametasona

betamethasone
acibutate
acibutato de
betametasona
betamethasone
dipropionate
dipropionato de
betametasona
betamethasone
valerate
valerato de
betametasona
betamicin
betamicina
betanidine
betanidina
beta particle
partícula beta
betaprodine
betaprodina
beta rays
rayos beta
betasine
betasina
betatron
betatrón
betaxolol
betaxolol
betazole
betazol
betazole hydrochloride
clorhidrato de betazol
betel
betel
bethanechol chloride
cloruro de betanecol
bethanidine
betanidina
betonicine
betonicina
betoxycaine
betoxicaína
Bettendorf's reagent
reactivo de Bettendorf
Betterton-Kroll
process
proceso de Betterton
Kroll
Betti reaction
reacción de Betti
Betts process
proceso de Betts
betula
bétula
betula oil
esencia (aceite) de
bétula
betulin
betulín

betylium tosylate
tosilato de betilio
bevantolol
bevantolol
beveled edge
borde biselado
bevonium methyl
sulfate
metilsulfato de bevonio
bezafibrate
bezafibrato
bezitramide
becitramida
BF$_3$-ether complex
complejo de éter-BF$_3$
(eterato de trifluoruro
de boro)
BF$_3$-MEA
BF$_3$-MEA (trifluoruro
de boro y
monoetilamina)
BF-MEOH
BF$_3$-MEOH
(trifluoruro de boro y
metanol)
BHA
HAB (hidroxianisol
butilado)
BHT
HTB (hidroxitolueno
butilado)
bialamicol
bialamicol
bialamicol
hydrochloride
clorhidrato de
bialamicol
bias
sesgo, parcialidad
bibenzonium bromide
bromuro de bibenzonio
bibenzyl
bibencilo
bibrocathol
bibrocatol
bicarbonate
bicarbonato
bicalcium phosphate
fosfato bicálcico
bicalutamide
bicalutamida
bichloride
bicloruro
bichromate
bicromato
bicifadine
bicifadina
bicine
bicina

biclofibrate
biclofibrato
biclothymol
biclotimol
biconvex
biconvexo
bicozamycin
bicozamicina
bicuculline
bicuculina
bicyclic
bicíclico
bicyclo(2,2,1)hept-5-
ene-2-methylol
biciclo(2,2,1)hept-5-
eno-2-metilol
bicyclohexyl
biciclohexilo
bidimazium iodide
yoduro de bidimacio
bietamiverine
bietamiverina
bietanautine
bietanautina
bietaserpine
bietaserpina
bifemelane
bifemelano
bifenox
bifenox
bifenthrin
bifentrín
bifidus factor
factor bífido
bifluranol
bifluranol
bifonazole
bifonazol
biformin
biformina
Biginelli reaction
reacción de
Biginelli
biguanide
biguanida
bikhaconitine
bicaconitina
bile acid
ácido biliar
bilirubin
bilirrubina
biliverdine
biliverdina
bimetal
bimetal
binapacryl
binapacrilo
binary
binario

binary compound
compuesto binario
binary system
sistema binario
bind
unir, conjugar,
aglutinar
binder
aglutinante
binder (note book)
anotador
binding
conjugante,
conjugación,
aglutinación
binding agent
agente aglutinante,
agente conjugante
binding energy
energía de enlace,
energía de conjugación,
energía de
aglutinación
binedaline
binedalina
binifibrate
binifibrato
biniramycin
binirramicina
binodaline
binodalina
binuclear
binucleado, binuclear
bioavailability
biodisponibilidad
bioburden
biocarga, carga
biológica
biochemical oxygen
demand
demanda biológica de
oxígeno
biochemistry
bioquímica, química
biológica
biocide
biocida
biocolloid
biocoloide, coloide
biológico
biocomputer
biocomputadora,
computadora
biomédica
bioconversion
bioconversión,
conversión biológica
biocytin
biocitina

biodegradability
biodegradación,
degradación biológica
bioelectrochemistry
bioelectroquímica,
electroquímica
biológica
bioengineering
bioingeniería,
ingeniería biomédica
bioethics
bioética, ética
biomédica
bioflavonoid
bioflavonoide
biogas
gas biológico, biogas
biogeochemistry
biogeoquímica,
geoquímica biológica
biogenesis
biogenia
biogénesis
biogenetics
biogénico,
biogenético
biogenic sediment
sedimento biógeno
sedimento biogénico
biohazard
peligro biológico,
biopeligro
bioinorganic
chemistry
química bioinorgánica
biological oxidation
oxidación biológica
biological oxygen
demand
demanda biológica de
oxígeno
bioluminescence
bioluminiscencia
biomass
biomasa, masa
biológica
biomaterial
material biológico,
biomaterial
biomimetic chemistry
química biomimética
biophyl
biófilo
biophysibility
viabilidad biológica
biopolymer
biopolímero
biopterin
biopterina

34

bioresmethrin
biorresmetrina
biosynthesis
biosíntesis, síntesis
biológica
biota
biota
biotechnology
biotecnología
biotin
biotina
N-biotinyl-L-lysine
N-biotinil-L-lisina
biotite
biotita
biperiden
biperidén, biperideno
biperiden lactate
lactato de biperiden,
lactato de biperideno
biphenamine
bifenamina
biphenyl
bifenilo
p-biphenylamine
p-bifenilamina
2,4'-biphenyldiamine
2,4'-bifenildiamina
bipiperidyl mustard
mostaza
bipiperidílica
bipolar
bipolar
Birch reduction
reducción de Birch
birch tar oil
aceite de alquitrán de
abedul
birefringent
birrefringente
bisabolol
bisabolol
**N,N-bisacetoxyethyl-
amine**
N,N-bisacetoxietil-
amina
**2,2-bis(acetoxymethyl)
propyl acetate**
acetato de 2,2-
bis(acetoximetil)
propilo
bisacodyl
bisacodilo
bisamides
bisamidas
**bis(2-aminoethyl)
sulfide**
sulfuro de bis (2-
aminoetilo)

**N,N-bis(3-
aminopropyl)
methylamine**
N,N-bis(3-
aminopropil)
metilamina
**bis(4-amino-1-
anthraquinonyl)-
amine**
bis(4-amino-1-
antraquinonil) amina
bisantrene
bisantreno
bisbendazole
bisbendazol
bisbentiamine
bisbentiamina
**1,3-bis(2-benzo-
thiazolylmercapto-
methyl) urea**
1,3-bis(2-benzotiazolil-
mercaptometil) urea
**p-bis(2-(5-p-biphenyl-
oxazolyl)benzene**
p-bis(2-(5-p-bifenil-
oxazolilo) benceno
**2,2-bis(p-bromo-
phenyl)-1,1,1-
trichloroethane**
2,2-bis(p-bromofenil)-
1,1,1-tricloroetano
**bis(tert-butylperoxy)-
2,5-dimethylhexane**
bis(terc-butilperoxi)-
2,5-dimetilhexano
**Bischler-Mohlau indole
synthesis**
síntesis del indol de
Bischler Mohlau
**bis(2-chloroethoxy)
methane**
bis(2-cloroetoxi)
metano
**4-[p-[bis(2-chloro-
ethyl)amino]phenyl]
butyric acid**
ácido 4-[p-[bis(2-
cloroetil)amino]-
fenil]butírico
**5-[bis(2-chloroethyl)
amino]uracil**
5-[bis(2-cloroetil)
amino]uracilo
**bis(2-chloroethyl)
ether**
bis(2-cloroetil)éter
**bis(chloromethyl)
ether**
bis(clorometil) éter

**1,1'-bischloro-
mercuriferrocene**
1,1'-biscloro-
mercuriferroceno
**3,3-bis(chloromethyl)
oxetane**
3,3-bis(clorometil)
oxetano
**bis(p-chlorophenoxy)
methane**
bis(p-clorofenoxi)
metano
**2,2-bis(p-chloro-
phenyl)-1,1-
dichlorethane**
2,2-bis(p-clorofenil)-
1,1-dicloroetano
**1,1-bis(p-chloro-
phenyl)ethanol**
1,1-bis(p-cloro-
fenil)etanol
**1,1-bis(p-chloro-
phenyl)-2,2,2-
trichlorethane**
1,1-bis(p-clorofenil)-
2,2,2-tricloroetano
**bis-cyclopenta-
dienyliron**
bis-ciclopenta-
dienilhierro
**bisdequalinium
chloride**
cloruro de
bisdecualineo
**bis(2,6-diethylphenyl)
carbodiimide**
bis(2,6-dietilfenil)
carbodiimida
**bis(p-dimethylamino-
benzylidene)benzidine**
bis(p-dimetilamino-
bencilideno)bencidina
**2,6-bis(dimethyl-
aminomethyl)-
cyclohexanone**
2,6-bis(dimetil-
aminometil)-
ciclohexanona
**2,6-bis(dimethyl-
aminomethyl)
cyclohexanone
dihydrochloride**
diclorhidrato de 2,6-
bis(dimetilamino-
metil) ciclohexanona
**bis(1,3-dimethyl-
butyl)amine**
bis(1,3-dimetilbutil)
amina

**1,3-bis ethylamino-
butane**
1,3-bis etilamino-
butano
**N,N'-bis(1,4-
dimethylpentyl)-p-
phenylene
diamine**
N,N'-bis(1,4-
dimetilpentil)-p-
fenilendiamina
**bis(1,2-dimethyl-
propyl)borane**
bis(1,2-dimetil-
propil)borano
**bis(2-ethylhexyl)
phthalate**
ftalato de bis(2-
etilhexilo)
**bis(2-ethylhexyl)
sebacate**
sebacato de
bis(2-etilhexilo)
**N,N-bis(1-ethyl-3-
methylpentyl)-p-
phenylene
diamine**
N,N-bis(1-etil-3-
metilpentil)-p-
fenilendiamina
**2,2-bis(p-ethylphenyl)
1,1-dichloroethane**
2,2-bis(p-etilfenil)-1,1-
dicloroetano
bisethylxanthogen
bisetilxantógeno
bisfenazone
bisfenazona
**1,3-bis(3-glycidoxy-
propyl)
tetramethyldisiloxane**
1,3-bis(3-glicidoxi-
propil)tetrametil-
disiloxano
bishydroxycoumarin
bishidroxicumarina
**bis(1-hydroxycyclo-
hexyl) peroxide**
peróxido de bis(1-
hidroxiciclohexilo)
**N,N-bis(2-hydroxy-
ethyl) alkilamine**
N,N-bis(2-hidroxi-
etil)alquilamina
**bis(hydroxyethyl)
butydienol
ether**
éter bis(hidroxietil)
butidienólico

bis(hydroxyethyl) cocoamine oxide
óxido de bis(hidroxietil) cocoamina

N,N-bis(hydroxyethyl)oleamide
N,N-bis(hidroxietil) oleamida

ß-bishydroxyethyl sulfide
sulfuro de ß-bishidroxietilo

1,3-bishydroxymethyl urea
urea 1,3-bishidroximetílica; 1,3-bis-hidroximetilurea

4,4-bis(4-hydroxyphenyl)pentanoic acid
ácido 4,4-bis(4-hidroxifenil) pentanoico

bishydroxyphenyl sulfone
sulfona bishidroxifenílica

1,4-bis(2-hidroxypropyl)-2-methylpiperazine
1,4-bis(2-hidroxipropil)-2-metilpiperacina, 1,4-bis(2-hidroxipropil)-2-metilpiperazina

bis-intercalator
bis-intercalador

2,4-bis(isopropylamino)-6-methoxy-s-triazine
2,4-bis(isopropil-amino)-6-metoxi-s-triazina

bis-ketotriazine
bis-cetotriazina

Bismarck Brown R
marrón Bismarck R

Bismarck Brown Y
marrón Bismarck Y

bis(2-methoxyethoxy) ethyl ether
éter bis(2-metoxietoxi)etílico

bis(1-methylamyl) sodium sulfosuccinate
sulfosuccinato bis(1-metilamil) sódico

N,N-bis(1-methylheptyl)-p-phenylene diamine
N,N-bis(1-metil-heptil)-p-fenilendiamina

1,4-bis(2-(4-methyl-5-phenyloxazolyl) benzene
1,4-bis(2-(4-metil-5-feniloxazolil) benceno

bis[methylthio] methane
bis[metiltío]metano

bismite
bismita

bismuth
bismuto

bismuth aluminate
aluminato de bismuto

bismuth ammonium citrate
citrato de bismuto y amonio

bismuth antimonide
antimoniuro de bismuto

bismuth bromide
bromuro de bismuto

bismuth bromide oxide
óxido de bromuro de bismuto

bismuth butylthiolaurate
butiltiolaurato de bismuto

bismuth carbonate basic
carbonato básico de bismuto

bismuth chloride
cloruro de bismuto

bismuth chloride basic
cloruro básico de bismuto

bismuth chloride oxide
cloruro básico de bismuto

bismuth chromate
cromato de bismuto

bismuth citrate
citrato de bismuto

bismuth dimethyl-dithiocarbamate
ditiocarbamato dimetílico de bismuto

bismuth ethyl camphorate
alcanforato etílico de bismuto

bismuth ethyl chloride
cloruro etílico de bismuto

bismuth fluoride
fluoruro de bismuto

bismuth gallate basic
galato básico de bismuto

bismuth glance
bismuto vítreo

bismuth hydrate
hidrato de bismuto

bismuth hydroxide
hidróxido de bismuto

bismuth iodide
yoduro de bismuto

bismuth iodide oxide
yoduro básico de bismuto

bismuth iodosubgallate
yodosubgalato de bismuto

bismuth-ß-naphtol
bismuto-ß-naftol

bismuth nitrate
nitrato de bismuto

bismuth nitrate basic
nitrato básico de bismuto

bismuth oleate
oleato de bismuto

bismuth oxalate
oxalato de bismuto

bismuth oxide
óxido de bismuto

bismuth oxide hydrated
óxido de bismuto hidratado

bismuth oxybromide
bromuro básico de bismuto

bismuth oxycarbonate
carbonato básico de bismuto

bismuth oxychloride
cloruro básico de bismuto

bismuth oxyhydrate
hidrato básico de bismuto

bismuth oxynitrate
nitrato básico de bismuto

bismuth pentafluoride
pentafluoruro de bismuto

bismuth pentoxide
pentóxido de bismuto

bismuth phenate
fenato de bismuto

bismuth phenol-sulfonate
sulfonato fenólico de bismuto, fenolsulfonato de bismuto

bismuth phenylate
fenilato de bismuto

bismuth phosphate
fosfato de bismuto

bismuth potassium iodide
yoduro de bismuto y potasio

bismuth potassium tartrate
tartrato de bismuto y potasio

bismuth pyrogallate
pirogalato de bismuto

bismuth salicylate basic
salicilato básico de bismuto

bismuth selenide
seleniuro de bismuto

bismuth sodium iodide
yoduro de bismuto y sodio

bismuth sodium tartrate
tartrato de bismuto y sodio

bismuth sodium triglycollamate
triglicolamato de bismuto y sodio

bismuth stannate
estannato de bismuto

bismuth subacetate
subacetato de bismuto

bismuth subcarbonate
subcarbonato de bismuto

bismuth subchloride
subcloruro de bismuto

bismuth subgallate
subgalato de bismuto

bismuth subnitrate
subnitrato de bismuto

bismuth subsalicylate
subsalicilato de bismuto

bismuth sulfate
sulfato de bismuto
bismuth sulfide
sulfuro de bismuto
bismuth sulfo-
carbolate
sulfocarbolato de
bismuto
bismuth tannate
tanato de bismuto
bismuth tartrate
tartrato de bismuto
bismuth telluride
telururo de bismuto
bismuth tetraoxide
tetraóxido de bismuto
bismuth tribromide
tribromuro de bismuto
bismuth tribromo-
phenate
tribromofenato de
bismuto
bismuth trichloride
tricloruro de bismuto
bismuth trihydrate
trihidrato de bismuto
bismuth
trihydroxide
trihidróxido de
bismuto
bismuth triiodide
triyoduro de bismuto
bismuth trinitrate
trinitrato de bismuto
bismuth trioxide
trióxido de bismuto
bismuth trisulfide
trisulfuro de bismuto
bismuth tritelluride
tritelururo de bismuto
bismuth valerate
basic
valerato básico de
bismuto
bismuth yellow
amarillo de
bismuto
bismuth zirconate
circonato de bismuto
bismuthate
bismutato
bismuthine
bismutina
bismuthinite
bismutinita
bis(1-naphtylmethyl)
amine
bis(1-naftilmetil)
amina

p-bis[2-(5-α-naphthyl-
oxazolyl)]benzene
p-bis[2-(5-α-naftil-
oxazolil)]benceno
bis(3-nitrophenyl)
disulfide
disulfuro de bis(3-
nitrofenilo)
bisobrin
bisobrina
bisoprolol
bisoprolol
bisoprolol fumarate
fumarato de bisoprolol
bisoxatin
bisoxatina
bisoxatin acetate
acetato de bisoxatina
bisphenol A
bisfenol A
1,4-bis-2-(5-phenyl-
oxazoyl)benzene
1,4-bis-2-(5-fenil-
oxazoíl)benceno
bis(tetrachloro-
ethyl)disulfide
disulfuro de
bis(tetracloretilo)
bis(tribromophenoxy)
ethane
bis(tribromofenoxi)
etano
bis(tri-n-butyltin)oxide
óxido de bis(tri-n-
butilestaño)
bis(trichloromethyl)
benzene
bis(triclorometil)
benceno
bis(trichlorosilyl)
ethane
bis(triclorsilil)etano
bistridecylphthalate
ftalato de
bistridecilo
bis(trimethylsilyl)
trifluoro acetamide
bis(trimetilsilil)
trifluoroacetamida
bitertanol
bitertanol
bithionol
bitionol
bitipazone
bitipazona
bitolterol
bitolterol
bitolterol mesylate
mesilato de bitolterol

4,4'-bi-o-tolylenedi-
isocyanate
diisocianato de 4,4'-bi-
o-tolileno
bitoscanate
bitoscanato
bitter
amargo
bitter almond oil
esencia (aceite) de
almendras amargas
bittern
aguas madres (salinas),
composición amarga
para adulterar la
cerveza
bitumen
asfalto, alquitrán, betún
bituminous coal
carbón bituminoso
biuret
biuret (carbamilurea)
biuretamidine sulfate
sulfato de
biuretamidina
biuret reaction
reacción de biuret
bivalence
bivalencia
bivalent
bivalente
bixin
bixina, bija
black
negro
black, aniline
negro de anilina
black antimony
negro de antimonio
black ash
ceniza negra, sosa bruta
black body
cuerpo negro
black bone
negro de hueso
black cyanide
cianuro negro
black lead
plomo negro, grafito
black liquor
licor negro
black oil
aceite negro
black phosphorus
fósforo negro
black plate
lámina negra
black platinum
negro de platino

blank
blanco, en blanco,
virgen
blank test
ensayo en blanco
blasticidin S
blasticidina S
bleach
blanqueo
bleaching assistant
auxiliar de
blanqueo
bleach liquid
líquido
blanqueador
bleed
sangrado
blend
combinación, mezcla
blend, to
mezclar
bleomycin
bleomicina
bleomycin sulfate
sulfato de
bleomicina
blister copper
cobre bruto, cobre sin
refinar, cobre negro
blister gas
gas vesicante
blister packs
envases vesiculares,
envases en
burbujas
blister packaging
envasado vesicular,
envasado en
burbujas
blistering
burbujeo,
vesiculación
block
bloque
blood
sangre
bloom
proliferación,
multiplicación,
floración,
blotting
secado (con papel
secante)
blotting paper
papel secante
blowing agent
agente soplante
blue
azul

blue copperas
sulfato de cobre, vitriolo azul, caparrosa azul

blue gas
gas azul, vapor de petróleo a alta presión

blue lead
plomo metálico, plomo azul

blue verdigris
verdín azul, cardenillo azul

blue vitriol
sulfato de cobre hidratado, vitriolo azul, caparrosa azul

bluensomycin
bluensomicina

BOD
DBO (demanda biológica de oxígeno)

Bodroux reaction
reacción de Bodroux

bofumustine
bofumustina

boghead coal
carbón bituminoso sapropélico, carbón algal

boil
ebullición

boil down, to
concentrar por ebullición

boil off, to
extraer por ebullición

boil, to
hervir, llevar a ebullición, mantener en ebullición

boiled oil
aceite cocido

boiler
caldera

boiling point
punto de ebullición

boiler range
zona de ebullición, intervalo de ebullición

boiling stones
piedras para ebullición

boiling water
agua hirviendo

bolandiol
bolandiol

bolasterone
bolasterona

bolazine
bolacina, bolazina

boldenone
boldenona

boldine
boldina

boldo
boldo

bole, Armenian
arcilla roja de Armenia

bolenol
bolenol

bolmantalate
bolmantalato

bomb
bomba

bombardment
bombardeo

bombardment, nuclear
bombardeo nuclear

bombesin
bombesina

bometolol
bometolol

bond
unión, enlace, conjugación, vinculación

bond, chemical
enlace químico

bond clay
arcilla aglutinante

bond cleavage
ruptura del enlace, ruptura de la unión

bond direction
dirección de la unión

bonding additive
aditivo adherente, aditivo de adhesión

bonding electron
electrón de enlace

bonding strength
potencia de la unión, poder aglutinante

bone
hueso

bone ash
ceniza de hueso

bone black
negro de hueso

bone china
porcelana fosfatada

bone glue
oseína, osteocola, cola de hueso

bone meal
harina de huesos, abono de huesos

bone oil
aceite de huesos, aceite animal, aceite de Dippel

bone phosphate
fosfato de huesos

bone seeker
osteófilo, osteotrópico

bone tallow
sebo de huesos

bongkrekic acid
ácido bongkrékico

BON maroon
BON granate (abreviatura del ácido ß-oxinaftoico)

BON red
BON rojo

Boord olefin synthesis
síntesis de olefinas de Boord

bopindolol
bopindolol

boracic acid
ácido bórico

borane
borano

borate
borato

borax
bórax, borato de sodio

borax anhydrous
bórax anhidro

borax pentahydrate
bórax pentahidratado

borazole
borazol

borazon
borazón

boric acid
ácido bórico

o-boric acid
ácido o-bórico

boric acid ester
éster de ácido bórico

boric anhydride
anhídrido bórico

boric oxide
óxido bórico

boride
boruro

bornane
bornano, canfano

bornaprine
bornaprina

bornaprolol
bornaprolol

bornelone
bornelona

borneol
borneol

bornite
bornita

bornyl acetate
acetato de bornilo

bornyl alcohol
alcohol bornílico

d-bornyl α-bromoisovalerate
α-bromoisovalerato de d-bornilo

bornyl formate
formiato de bornilo

bornyl isovalerate
isovalerato de bornilo

boroethane
boroetano

boromycin
boromicina

boron
boro

boron B
boro B

boron alloy
aleación de boro

boron bromide
bromuro de boro

boron carbide
carburo de boro

boron chloride
cloruro de boro

boron fiber
fibra de boro

boron fluoride
fluoruro de boro

boron fuel
combustible de boro

boron hydride
hidruro de boro

boron monoxide
monóxido de boro

boron nitride
nitruro de boro

boron nitride fiber
fibra de nitruro de boro

boron nitride pyrolytic
nitruro pirolítico de boro

boron oxide
óxido de boro

boron phosphate
fosfato de boro

boron phosphide
fosfuro de boro

boron steel
acero al boro

boron superphosphate
superfosfato de boro
boron tribromide
tribromuro de boro
boron trichloride
tricloruro de boro
boron trifluoride
trifluoruro de boro
boron trifluoride
etherate
eterato de trifluoruro
de boro
boron trifluoride-
methanol
trifluoruro de boro y
metanol
boron trifluoride
monethylamide
monetilamida de
trifluoruro de boro
borophosphoric acid
ácido borofosfórico
borosilicate glass
vidrio de
borosilicato
borotungstic acid
ácido borotúngstico
Bosh-Meiser urea
process
proceso de urea de
Bosh Meiser
bostrycoidin
bostricoidina
ß-boswellic acid
ácido ß-boswélico
bottom (capsule)
cartucho
bottromycin
botromicina
bound (biochemistry)
conjugado
bound electron
electrón ligado,
electrón capturado
bound water
agua ligada, agua
capturada
bournonite
bournonita,
sulfoantimoniuro de
cobre y plomo
Bouveault-Blanc
reduction
reducción de
Bouveault Blanc
bowl
tazón, cuenco
boxidine
boxidina

Boyle's law
ley de Boyle
bracket
agrupar, rodear,
intercalar
brackish water
aguas salobres
Bradsher reaction
reacción de Bradsher
brallobarbital
bralobarbital
branched chain
cadena ramificada
branched chain
hydrocarbon
hidrocarburo con
cadena ramificada
brand
marca
branding ink
tinta de marcar
brand name
nombre comercial,
nombre industrial
brandy
brandy, coñac
bran oil
aceite de salvado
brasilin
brasilina
brass
latón, bronce
brassidic acid
ácido brasídico
brassinolide
brasinólido
braunite
braunita
brayera
brayera, couso, cuso
B-rays
rayos beta
Brazil wax
cera del Brasil
brazilin
brasilina
breadth
ancho
breeze
polvo de coque, cisco
de coque
brefeldin A
brefeldina A
bremazocine
bremazocina
bretonite
bretonita
bretylium tosilate
tosilato de bretilio

brevetoxins
brevetoxinas
brewing
fermentación
Brewster process
proceso de Brewster
brick clay
arcilla para ladrillos
brick, refractory
ladrillo refractario
bridge
puente
brigth
brillante
brightener
abrillantador
brilliant blue FCF
azul FCF brillante
brilliant crocein
croceína brillante
brilliant green
verde brillante
brilliant green agar
agar verde brillante
brilliant scarlet
yoduro mercúrico
brilliant yellow
curcumina, amarillo
brillante
brim
borde
brimonidine tartrate
tartrato de
brimonidina
brimstone
piedra de azufre, azufre
nativo
brinase
brinasa
brindoxime
brindoxima
brine
salmuera, saladar
bring, to
traer, llevar
British thermal unit
unidad térmica
británica (B.T.U. o
b.t.u.)
brittle
frágil, quebradizo
brittle point
punto de fragilidad
brittleness
fragilidad
broclepride
brocleprida
brocresine
brocresina

brodimoprin
brodimoprina
Broenner acid
ácido de Broenner
brofezil
brofecilo
brofoxine
brofoxina
bromacil
bromacilo
bromacrylide
bromacrílido
bromadiolone
bromadiolona
bromal
bromal,
tribromacetaldehído
bromal hydrate
hidrato de bromal
bromamide
bromamida
bromate
bromato
bromazepam
bromacepán,
bromazepam
bromazine
bromacina, bromazina
bromchlorenone
bromoclorenona
bromcresol green
verde de bromocresol
bromcresol purple
púrpura de bromocresol
bromebric acid
ácido brómébrico
bromelain
bromelaína
bromelin
bromelina
bromeosin
bromeosina
bromethalin
brometalina
brometenamine
brometenamina
bromhexine
bromhexina
bromhydric acid
ácido
bromhídrico
bromic acid
ácido brómico
bromide
bromuro
bromide number
índice de bromuro
brominate, to
bromar

brominated camphor
alcanfor bromado
bromination
bromación
bromindione
bromindiona
bromine
bromo
bromine azide
azida de bromo
bromine chloride
cloruro de bromo
bromine cyanide
cianuro de bromo
bromine iodide
yoduro de bromo
bromine number
índice de bromo,
número de bromo
bromine pentafluoride
pentafluoruro de bromo
bromine trifluoride
trifluoruro de bromo
bromine value
índice de bromo, valor de bromo
bromine water
agua bromada, agua de bromo
brominize, to
bromar
brominolysis
brominólisis
bromisoval
bromisoval
bromisovalum
bromisovalo
bromite
bromita, bromito
N-bromoacetamide
N-bromacetamida
bromoacetanilide
bromacetanilida
bromoacetic acid
ácido bromacético
bromoacetone
bromacetona
bromoacetone cyanohydrin
cianohidrina de bromacetona
bromoacetophenone
bromacetofenona
5-(2-bromoallyl)-5-sec-butyl barbituric acid
ácido 5-(2-bromalil)-5-sec-butilbarbitúrico

bromoallylene
bromalileno
4-bromoaniline
4-bromanilina
5-bromoanthranilic acid
ácido 5-bromantranílico
bromoauric acid
ácido bromáurico
p-bromoaniline
p-bromanilina
p-bromobenzaldehyde
p-bromobenzaldehído
bromobenzene
bromobenceno
p-bromobenzene acid
ácido p-bromobencénico
p-bromobenzenesulfonic acid
ácido p-bromobencensulfónico
p-bromobenzenesulfonyl chloride
cloruro de p-bromobencensulfonilo
p-bromobenzoic acid
ácido p-bromobenzoico
p-bromobenzyl bromide
bromuro de p-bromobencilo
p-bromobenzyl chloride
cloruro de p-bromobencilo
p-bromobenzyl chloroformate
cloroformiato de p-bromobencilo
α-bromobenzylcyanide
cianuro de α-bromobencilo
o-bromobenzylcyanide
cianuro de o-bromobencilo
1-bromobutane
1-bromobutano
5-bromo-3-sec-butyl-6-methyluracil
5-bromo-3-sec-butil-6-metiluracilo
α-bromobutyric acid
ácido α-bromobutírico
bromocarnallite
bromocarnalita

3-bromo-d-camphor
3-bromo-d-alcanfor
α-bromo-n-caproic acid
ácido α-bromo-n-caproico
3-bromo-1-chloro-5,6-dimethylhydanthoin
3-bromo-1-cloro-5,6-dimetilhidantoína
sym-bromochloroethane
sim-bromocloroetano
bromochloromethane
bromoclorometano
1-bromo-3-chloropropane
1-bromo-3-cloropropano
2-bromo-2-chloro-1,1,1-trifluoroethane
2-bromo-2-cloro-1,1,1-trifluoroetano
bromociclen
bromocicleno
bromocresol green
verde de bromocresol
bromocriptine
bromocriptina
bromocriptine mesylate
mesilato de bromocriptina
2-bromo-α-cyanotoluene
2-bromo-α-cianotolueno
bromocyclopentane
bromociclopentano
bromodiethylacetylurea
urea bromodietil acetílica, bromodietilacetilurea
bromodiphenhydramine
bromodifenhidramina
1-bromododecane
1-bromododecano
bromoethane
brometano
2-bromoethyl alcohol
alcohol 2-brometílico
bromoethyl chlorosulfonate
clorosulfonato de brometilo

2-bromoethylamine hydrobromide
bromhidrato de 2-brometilamina
bromofenofos
bromofenofós
p-bromofluorobenzene
p-bromofluorobenceno
bromoform
bromoformo, tribromometano
bromofos
bromofós
1-bromohexane
1-bromohexano
α-bromoisobutyric acid
ácido α-bromisobutírico
α-bromoisovaleric acid
ácido α-bromisovalérico
2-bromoisovalerylurea
urea 2-bromisovalerílica, 2-bromisovalerilurea
bromol
bromol, 2,4,6-tribromofenol
bromolysergide
bromolisergida
p-bromomandelic acid
ácido p-bromomandélico
bromomethane
bromometano
bromomethylethylketone
cetona bromometiletílica, bromometiletilcetona
α-bromonaphthalene
α-bromonaftaleno
1-bromo-2-naphthol
1-bromo-2-naftol
2-bromopentane
2-bromopentano
p-bromophenacyl bromide
bromuro de p-bromfenacilo
bromopheniramine maleate
maleato de bromofeniramina
p-bromophenol
p-bromofenol

bromophenol blue
azul de bromofenol
o-bromophenyl-
acetonitrile
acetonitrilo o-
bromofenílico, o-
bromofenilaceto-
nitrilo
p-bromophenyl-
hydrazine
hidracina p-
bromofenílica, p-
bromofenilhidracina,
hidrazina p-
bromofenílica, p-
bromofenilhidrazina
p-bromophenyl-
isocyanate
isocianato p-
bromofenílico,
p-bromofeniliso-
cianato
2-bromo-4-
phenylphenol
2-bromo-4-fenilfenol
bromophos
bromofós
bromophosgene
bromofosgeno
bromopicrin
bromopicrina
bromopride
bromoprida
3-bromopropene
3-bromopropeno
α-bromopropionic acid
ácido α-bromo-
propiónico
bromopropylate
propilato de bromo,
bromopropilato
3-bromo-1-propyne
3-bromo-1-propino
2-bromopyridine
2-bromopiridina
bromosalicylchlor-
anilide
cloranilida
bromosalicílica,
bromosalicil-
cloranilida
5-bromosalicyl-
hydroxamic acid
ácido 5-bromosalicil
hidroxámico
bromosalicylic acid
acetate
acetato de ácido
bromosalicílico

bromosaligenin
bromosaligenina
ß-bromostyrene
ß-bromoestireno
bromosuccinic acid
ácido bromosuccínico
N-bromosuccinimide
N-bromosuccinimida
4-bromothiophenol
4-bromotiofenol
bromothymol blue
azul de bromotimol
α-bromotoluene
α-bromotolueno
p-bromotoluene
p-bromotolueno
bromotrichloro-
methane
bromotriclorometano
bromotrifluoro-
ethylene
bromotrifluoroetileno
bromotrifluoro-
methane
bromotrifluorometano
5-bromouracil
5-bromouracilo
bromoxanide
bromoxanida
bromoxynil
bromoxinilo
bromperidol
bromperidol
brompheniramine
bromofeniramina
brompheniramine
maleate
maleato de
bromofeniramina
bromphenol blue
azul de bromofenol
bromthymol blue
azul de bromotimol
p-bromtripelenamine
p-bromotripelenamina
bronopol
bronopol
bronze
bronce, latón
bronze blue
azul bronceado
bronze orange
anaranjado bronceado
bronzing
broncear
bronzing liquid
líquido bronceador
broparestrol
broparestrol

broperamole
broperamol
broquinaldol
broquinaldol
brosotamide
brosotamida
brosuximide
brosuximida
brosylate ester
éster de brosilato
broth
caldo, caldo de cultivo
brotianide
brotianida
brotizolam
brotizolán, brotizolam
brovanexine
brovanexina
brovincamine
brovincamina
brown
marrón
Brownian movement
movimiento
browniano
broxaldine
broxaldina
broxuridine
broxuridina
broxyquinoline
broxiquinolina
bruceantin
bruceantina
brucine
brucina
brucite
brucita
bryonia
brionia
B-stage resin
resina de fase B, resina
termosólida blanca y
maleable
bubble
burbuja
bubble, to
burbujear
bucainide
bucainida
bucetin
bucetina
buchu
buchú, bucú
bucillamine
bucilamina
bucindolol
bucindolol
bucladesine
bucladesina

buclizine
buclicina, buclizina
buclizine hydrochloride
clorhidrato de
buclicina
buclosamide
buclosamida
bucloxic acid
ácido buclóxico
bucket elevator
montacargas de
cubetas, elevador de
cangilones
bucolome
bucolomo
bucrylate
bucrilato
bucumolol
bucumolol
budesonide
budesonida
budipine
budipina
budralazine
budralacina,
budralazina
bufalin
bufalina
bufenadrine
bufenadrina
bufencarb
bufencarb,
metalcamato
bufeniode
bufeniodo,
diyodobufenida,
Diastal
bufetolol
bufetolol
bufexamac
bufexamaco
bufezolac
bufezolaco
buffalo yellow
amarillo búfalo
buffer
tampón
buffer solution
solución tampón
buffer system
sistema tampón
buflomedil
buflomedilo
bufogenin
bufogenina
bufogenin B
bufogenina B
buformin
buformina

41

bufotalin
bufotalina
bufotenine
bufotenina
bufotoxin
bufotoxina
bufrolin
bufrolino
bufuralol
bufuralol
build up pressure
aumento de la presión
building up process
proceso de síntesis
bulbocapnine
bulbocapnina
bulk agent
agente de relleno
bulk density
densidad a granel
bumadizon(e)
bumadizona
bumecaine
bumecaína
bumepidil
bumepidilo
bumetanide
bumetanida
bumetrizole
bumetrizol
bunaftine
bunaftina
bunamidine
bunamidina
bunamiodyl
bunamiodilo
bunapsilate
bunapsilato
buna rubbers
bunas, cauchos
sintéticos
bunazosin
bunazosina
bungarotoxins
bungarotoxinas
bunitrolol
bunitrolol
bunolol
bunolol
Bunsen burner
mechero de Bunsen
buparvaquone
buparvacuona
buphanamine
bufanamina
buphanitine
bufanitina
buphenine
bufenina

bupicomide
bupicomida
bupirimate
bupirimato
bupivacaine
bupivacaína
bupranolol
bupranolol
buprenorphine
buprenorfina
buprofen
buprofeno
bupropion
bupropiona
buquineran
buquinerán
buquinolate
buquinolato
buramate
buramato
burette
bureta
Burgundy mixture
soda de Burdeos,
mezcla de la Borgoña
burlap
arpillera, tela de yute
burnable poison
veneno combustible
burn, to
quemar, incinerar
burner
mechero, quemador
burning
combustión
burnt lime
óxido de calcio, cal
quemada
burnt sienna
siena tostado
burnt umber
ocre oscuro
burodiline
burodilina
Burow´s solution
solución de Burow,
solución de acetato de
albúmina y ácido
acético glacial
buserelin
buserelina
buspirone
buspirona
busulfan
busulfán
butabarbital sodium
butabarbital sódico
butacaine
butacaína

butacaine sulfate
sulfato de butacaína
butacetin
butacetina
butachlor
butacloro
butaclamol
butaclamol
butadiazamide
butadiazamida
1,3-butadiene
1,3-butadieno,
viniletileno
butadiene
butadieno
butadiene-acrylo-
nitrile copolymer
copolímero de
butadieno y
acrilonitrilo
butafosfan
butafosfán
butalamine
butalamina
butalbital
butalbital, alibarbital
butaldehyde
butaldehído
butallylonal
butalilonal
butamben
butambeno
butamirate
butamirato
butamisole
butamisol
butamoxane
butamoxano
butanal
butanal
butane
butano
butanedial
butanodial
1,4-butanedicarboxilic
acid
ácido 1,4-butan-
dicarboxílico
butanedioic anhydride
anhídrido butandioico
1,3-butanediol
1,3-butanodiol
butanediolamine
butandiolamina
butanedione
butandiona
2,3-butanedione oxyme
thiosemicarbazone
tiosemicarbazona

de 2,3 butan-
dionoxima
butane dioxyme
butandioxima
butanenitrile
butanonitrilo
1-butanethiol
1-butanotiol
1,2,4-butanetriol
1,2,4-butanotriol
butanilicaine
butanilicaína
butanixin
butanixina
butanoic acid
ácido butanoico
1-butanol
1-butanol
2-butanol acetate
acetato de 2-butanol
2-butanone
2-butanona
butanoyl chloride
cloruro de butanoílo
butaperazine
butaperacina,
butaperazina
butaverine
butaverina
butaxamine
butaxamina
butazolamide
butazolamida
butedronic acid
ácido butedrónico
butenafine
hydrochlorhide
clorhidrato de
butenafina
2-butenal
2-butenal
butene-1
buteno-1
cis-butene-2
cis-buteno-2
trans-butene-2
trans-buteno-2
trans-butenedioic acid
ácido trans-butendioico
2-butene-1,3-diol
2-buteno-1,3-diol
3-butenenitrile
3-butenonitrilo
butenes
butenos
butenoic acid
ácido butenoico
3-buten-2-one
3-buten-2-ona

buterizine
butericina, buterizina
butesin
butesina
butethal
butetal
butethamate
butetamato
butethamine
butetamina
butethamine hydrocloride
clorhidrato de butetamina
buthalital sodium
butalital sódico
buthiazide
butiazida
buthiobate
butiobato
butibufen
butibufeno
butidrine
butidrina
butidrine hydrochloride
chlorhidrato de butidrina
butikacin
buticacina
butilfenin
butilfenina
butinoline
butinolina
butirosin
butirosina
butixirate
butixirato
butizide
butizida
butobendine
butobendino
butoconazole
butoconazol
butocrolol
butocrolol
butoctamide
butoctamida
butofilolol
butofilolol
butonate
butonato
butopamine
butopamina
butopiprine
butopiprina
butoprozine
butoprocina,
butoprozina

butopyrammonium iodide
yoduro de butopiramonio
butopyronoxol
butopironoxol
butopyronoxyl
butopironoxilo
butorphanol
butorfanol
butorphanol tartrate
tartrato de butorfanol
butoxycaine
butoxicaína
2-butoxyethanol
2-butoxietanol
2-(2-butoxyethoxy)-ethyl thiocyanate
tiocianato de 2-(2-butoxietoxi)etilo
1-butoxyethoxy-2-propanol
1-butoxietoxi-2-propanol
butoxyethyl laurate
laurato de butoxietilo
butoxyethyl oleate
oleato de butoxietilo
butoxyethyl stearate
estearato de butoxietilo
butoxylate
butoxilato
p-butoxyphenol
p-butoxifenol
butoxy polypropylene glycol
glicol butoxipoli-propilénico, butoxipolipropilen-glicol
n-butoxypropanol
n-butoxipropanol
ß-butoxy-ß'-thio-cyanodiethyl ether
éter ß-butoxi-ß'-tiocianodietílico, ß-butoxi-ß'-tiociano-dietiléter
butoxytriglycol
butoxitriglicol
butralin
butralina
butriptyline
butriptilina
butropium bromide
bromuro de butropio
butter cup yellow
amarillo ranúnculo, amarillo botón de oro

butterfat
grasa de leche
butter yellow
dimetilaminobenzol, amarillo mantequilla
butyl
butilo
n-butyl acetate
acetato de n-butilo
sec-butyl acetate
acetato de sec-butilo
tert-butyl acetate
acetato de terc-butilo
butyl acetoacetate
acetoacetato de butilo
butyl acetoxystearate
acetoxiestearato de butilo
butyl acetyl ricinoleate
acetilrricinoleato de butilo
n-butyl acid phosphate
fosfato ácido de n-butilo
n-butyl acrylate
acrilato n-butílico
tert-butyl acrylate
acrilato terc-butílico
n-butyl alcohol
alcohol n-butílico
sec-butyl alcohol
alcohol sec-butílico
tert-butyl alcohol
alcohol terc-butílico, 3,4,5-trimetoxi-fenetilamina
n-butyl aldehyde
aldehído n-butílico
butyl aminobenzoate
aminobenzoato butílico
butyl anthranilate
antranilato de butilo
butyl benzoate
benzoato de butilo
butyl benzyl phthalate
ftalato butilbencílico
butyl benzyl sebacate
sebacato butilbencílico
butyl borate
borato de butilo
n-butyl bromide
bromuro n-butílico
sec-butyl bromide
bromuro sec-butílico
butyl butanoate
butanoato butílico
n-butyl butyrate
butirato n-butílico

n-butyl carbinol
n-butilcarbinol
sec-butyl carbinol
sec-butilcarbinol
n-butyl carbonate
carbonato de n-butilo
butyl chloral hydrate
hidrato de cloral butílico, hidrato de butilcloral
n-butyl chloride
cloruro n-butílico
sec-butyl chloride
cloruro sec-butílico
tert-butyl chloro-acetate
cloroacetato terc-butílico
tert-butyl chromate
cromato terc-butílico
butyl citrate
citrato butílico
butyl crotonate
crotonato de butilo
butyl cyclohexyl phthalate
ciclohexilftalato butílico
butyl decyl phthalate
decilftalato butílico
butyl dichloro-phenoxyacetate
diclorofenoxiacetato de butilo
n-butyl diethanol-amide
n-butildietanolamida
n-butyl diethyl malonate
dietilmalonato n-butílico
butyl diglycol carbonate
carbonato de butilo diglicólico
butyl diglyme
diglima butílica
butyl dodecanoate
dodecanoato de butilo
butyl 9,10-epoxyocta-decanoate
9,10-epoxiocta-decanoato de butilo
butyl ether
éter butílico
n-butyl ethyl ether
éter n-butiletílico

43

butyl ethyl ketone
cetona butiletílica,
butiletilcetona
butyl formate
formiato de butilo
n-butyl furfuryl
ether
éter de n-butil-
furfurilo
butyl furoate
furoato de butilo
n-butyl glycidyl
ether
éter de n-butilglicidilo
butyl glycol acetate
acetato de glicol
butílico, acetato de
butilglicol
n-butyl glycol
phthalate
ftalato de n-butilglicol
butyl hydride
hidruro de butilo
tert-butyl
hydroperoxide
hidroperóxido de terc-
butilo
tert-butyl hypochlorite
hipoclorito terc-
butílico
n-butyl iodide
yoduro de n-butilo
sec-butyl iodide
yoduro de sec-butilo
n-butyl isocyanate
isocianato de n-butilo
butyl isodecyl
phthalate
ftalato de butilisodecilo
n-butyl lactate
lactato de n-butilo
N-n-butyl lauramide
lauramida N-n-
butílica, N-n-butil
lauramida
butyl laurate
laurato de butilo
butyl mercaptan
mercaptano butílico,
butilmercaptano
butyl mesityl oxide
óxido butil mesitílico
n-butyl methacrylate
metacrilato n-butílico,
n-butilmetacrilato
tert-butyl methacrylate
metacrilato terc-
butílico, terc-
butilmetacrilato

butyl methoxy-
dibenzoylmethane
butilmetoxidi-
benzoilmetano
n-butyl myristate
miristato n-butílico
n-butyl nitrate
nitrato n-butílico
n-butyl nitrite
nitrito n-butílico
tert-butyl nitrite
nitrito terc-butílico
butyl nonanoate
nonanoato de butilo
butyl octadecanoate
octadecanoato de
butilo
butyl octyl
phthalate
octilftalato de butilo
butyl oleate
oleato de butilo
n-butyl pelargonate
pelargonato de n-butilo
sec-butyl
pelargonate
pelargonato de sec-
butilo
tert-butyl peracetate
peracetato de terc-
butilo
tert-butylperbenzoate
perbenzoato de terc-
butilo
tert-butyl periso-
butyrate
perisobutirato de terc-
butilo
tert-butyl permaleic
acid
ácido permaleico terc-
butílico
tert-butyl peroctoate
peroctoato de terc-
butilo
tert-butyl peroxide
peróxido terc-butílico
tert-butyl peroxy-
acetate
peroxiacetato de terc-
butilo
tert-butyl peroxy-
benzoate
peroxibenzoato de terc-
butilo
tert-butyl peroxy-2-
ethylhexanoate
peroxi-2-etilhexanoato
de terc-butilo

tert-butyl peroxyiso-
butyrate
peroxiisobutirato de
terc-butilo
tert-butyl peroxy-
maleic acid
ácido peroximaleico
terc-butílico
tert-butyl peroxy-
phthalic acid
ácido peroxiftálico
terc-butílico
tert-butyl peroxy-
pivalate
peroxipivalato terc-
butílico
tert-butyl perphthalic
acid
ácido perftálico terc-
butílico
n-butyl phthalate
ftalato de n-butilo
butyl phthalylbutyl
glycolate
ftalilbutilglicolato de
butilo
n-butyl propionate
propionato de n-butilo
butyl ricinoleate
ricinoleato de butilo
butyl rubber
caucho butílico
butyl sebacate
sebacato de butilo
butyl sorbate
sorbato de butilo
butyl stearamide
estearamida butílica
butyl stearate
estearato de butilo
butyl sulfide
sulfuro de butilo
butyl titanate
titanato de butilo
n-butyl vinyl ether
éter n-butil vinílico, n-
butil vinil éter
butyl xanthate
xantato de butilo
butyl xanthic acid
ácido butilxántico
tert-butylacetic acid
ácido terc-butilacético
N-tert-butyl-
acrylamide
N-terc-butilacrilamida
butylaldehyde
aldehído butílico,
butilaldehído

n-butylamine
n-butilamina
sec-butylamine
sec-butilamina
tert-butylamine
terc-butilamina
butyl-o-aminobenzoate
o-aminobenzoato de
butilo
n-butyl-p-amino-
benzoate
p-aminobenzoato de n-
butilo
N-n-butylamino-
ethanol
N-n-butilaminoetanol
tert-butylaminoethyl
methacrylate
metacrilato de terc-
butilaminoetilo
N'-n-butylaniline
N'-n-butilanilina
2-tert-butylanthra-
quinone
2-terc-butil-
antraquinona
butylate
butilato
butylated hydroxy-
anisole
hidroxianisol butilado
butylated hydroxy-
toluene, BHT
hidroxitolueno
butilado, HTB
n-butylbenzene
n-butilbenceno
sec-butylbenzene
sec-butilbenceno
tert-butylbenzene
terc-butilbenceno
butylbenzene
sulfonamide
sulfonamida
butilbencénica
N-tert-butyl-2-
benzothiazol
sulfenamide
sulfenamida
N-terc-butil-2-benzo-
tiazólica
butylcarbamoyl-
sulfanilamide
sulfanilamida
butilcarbamoílica,
butilcarbamoil-
sulfanilamida
p-tert-butylcatechol
p-terc-butilcatecol

44

6-tert-butyl-m-cresol
6-terc-butil-m-cresol
n-butyldiamylamine
n-butildiamilamina
n-butyldichlorarsine
n-butildiclorarsina
1-n-butyl-3-(3,4-dichlorophenyl)-1-methylurea
1-n-butil-3-(3,4-diclorofenil)-1-metilurea
n-butyldiethanol-amine
n-butildietanolamina
tert-butyldiethanol-amine
terc-butildietanolamina
4-tert-butyl-1,2-dihydroxybenzene
4-terc-butil-1,2-dihidroxibenceno
4-butyl-1,2-diphenyl-3,5-pyrazolidine-dione
4-butil-1,2-difenil-3,5-pirazolidindiona
butyldithiocarbonic acid
ácido butilditio-carbónico
butylene
butileno
α-butylene dibromide
dibromuro α-butilénico
butylene dimethacrylate
dimetacrilato butilénico
1,3-butylene glycol
glicol 1,3-butilénico, 1,3-butilenglicol
butylene glycol
glicol butilénico, butilenglicol
1,2-butylene oxide
óxido de 1,2-butileno
butylepoxystearate
epoxiestearato de butilo
n-butylethanolamine
n-butiletanolamina
butylethyl-acetaldehyde
acetoaldehído butiletílico, butiletilacetaldehído

5-butyl-5-ethyl-barbituric acid
ácido 5-butil-5-etilbarbitúrico
2-butyl-2-ethyl-propanediol-1,3
2-butil-2-etil-propanodiol-1,3
tert-butylformamide
terc-butilformamida
tert-butylhydro-quinone
terc-butilhidroquinona
4,4'-butylidene bis(6-tert-butyl-m-cresol)
4,4'-butilideno bis(6-terc-butil-m-cresol)
butylidene chloride
cloruro de butilideno
tert-butylisopropyl-benzene hydro-peroxide
hidroperóxido de terc-butilisopropilbenceno
butyllithium
butil litio
n-butylmagnesium chloride
cloruro de magnesio n-butílico
n-butylmalonic acid
ácido n-butilmalónico
butylmercuric chloride
cloruro de butilmercurio
1-butyl-3-metanilyl-urea
1-butil-3-metanililurea
tert-butyl-4-methoxyphenol
terc-butil-4-metoxifenol
sec-butyl-6-methyl-3-cyclohexane-1-carboxylate
1-carboxilato de sec-butil-6-metil-3-ciclohexano
p-tert-butyl-α-methylhydro cinnamaldehyde
hidrocinamaldehído p-terc-butil-α-metílico
tert-butylmethyl-methane
metano terc-butilmetílico, terc-butilmetilmetano

2-tert-butyl-4-methylphenol
4-metilfenol 2-terc-butílico
3-butyl-1-ol
3-butil-1-ol
butylparaben
butilparabeno
tert-butylperoxy isopropyl carbonate
carbonato terc-butil peroxi isopropílico, carbonato de terc-butil peroxiso-propilo
o-sec-butylphenol
fenol o-sec-butílico, o-sec-butilfenol
o-tert-butylphenol
fenol o-terc-butílico, o-terc-butilfenol
p-tert-butylphenol
fenol p-terc-butílico, p-terc-butilfenol
2-(p-tert-butyl-phenoxy)isopropyl -2-chloroethyl sulfite
sulfito de 2-(p-terc-butilfenoxi)isopropil-2-cloroetilo
n-butylphenyl acetate
fenilacetato de n-butilo
n-butylphenyl ether
éter n-fenilbutílico
4-tert-butylphenyl salicylate
salicilato de 4-terc-butilfenilo
n-butylphosphoric acid
ácido fosfórico n-butílico
butylscopol-ammonium bromide
bromuro butílico de escopolamonio, bromuro de butilescopolamonio
n-butylstannic acid
ácido estánnico n-butílico, ácido n-butilestánnico
n-butylstannoic acid
ácido estannoico n-butílico, ácido n-butilestannoico

4-tert-butyl-o-thiocresol
o-tiocresol 4-terc-butílico, 4-terc-butil-o-vtiocresol
4-tert-butylthiophenol
tiofenol 4-terc-butílico, 4-terc-butiltiofenol
n-butyltin trichloride
tricloruro de n-butilestaño
p-tert-butyltoluene
tolueno p-terc-butílico, p-terc-butiltolueno
n-butyltin trichloride
tricloruro de estaño n-butílico, tricloruro de n-butilestaño
n-butyltrichlorosilane
triclorosilano n-butílico, n-butiltriclorosilano
tert-butyltrimethyl-methane
terc-butiltrimetil-metano
N-n-butylurea
N-n-butilurea
butylxanthic acid
ácido butilxántico
butynamine
butinamina
1-butyne
1-butino
butynediol
butinodiol
butyraldehyde
aldehído butírico, butiraldehído
butyramide
butiramida
butyrate
butirato
butyric acid
ácido butírico
butyric alcohol
alcohol butírico
butyric aldehyde
aldehído butírico
butyric anhydride
anhídrido butírico
butyrin
butirina
butyroin
butiroína
butyroyl chloride
cloruro de butiroílo
butyrolactam
butirolactano

butyrolactone
butirolactona
butyrone
butirona
butyronitrile
butironitrilo

**N-butyryl p-amino-
phenol**
N-butiril-p-aminofenol
butyroil chloride
cloruro de butiroílo
butyryl chloride
cloruro de butirilo

buzepide
bucépido
buzepide metiodide
metioduro de
bucépido
by hand
manual, a mano

bypass, by-pass
derivación, desvío
bypass valve
válvula de derivación
by-product
producto secundario,
subproducto, derivado

C

ca.
aproximadamente
cabenegrins
cabenegrinas
cabergoline
cabergolina
cabinet
gabinete, botiquín
cacao butter
manteca de cacao
cacao shell
cáscara de cacao
cachet
oblea, sello
C acid
ácido C (ácido 2-
naftilamino-4,8-
disulfónico)
cacodyl
cacodilo
cacodylic acid
ácido cacodílico
cacotheline
cacotelina
cactinomycin
cactinomicina
cadalene
cadaleno, cadalina
cadaverine
cadaverina
cade oil
aceite de cada, aceite
de enebro
cadiene
cadieno
cadinene
cadineno
cadmium
cadmio
cadmium acetate
acetato de cadmio
**cadmium ammonium
bromide**
bromuro de cadmio y
amonio
cadmium antimonide
antimoniuro de
cadmio
**cadmium
borotungstate**
borotungstato de
cadmio
cadmium bromate
bromato de cadmio

cadmium bromide
bromuro de cadmio
cadmium carbonate
carbonato de cadmio
cadmium chlorate
clorato de cadmio
cadmium chloride
cloruro de cadmio
cadmium cyanide
cianuro de cadmio
**cadmium diethyl-
dithiocarbamate**
dietilditiocarbamato de
cadmio
cadmium fluoride
fluoruro de cadmio
cadmium hydroxide
hidróxido de cadmio
cadmium iodate
yodato de cadmio
cadmium iodide
yoduro de cadmio
**cadmium mercury
lithopone**
litopona con cadmio y
mercurio
cadmium molybdate
molibdato de cadmio
cadmium nitrate
nitrato de cadmio
cadmium oxalate
oxalato de cadmio
cadmium oxide
óxido de cadmio
cadmium pigment
pigmento de cadmio
cadmium plating
cadmiado
**cadmium potassium
cyanide**
cianuro de cadmio y
potasio
**cadmium potassium
iodide**
yoduro de cadmio y
potasio
cadmium propionate
propionato de cadmio
cadmium ricinoleate
ricinoleato de cadmio
cadmium salicylate
salicilato de cadmio
cadmium selenate
seleniato de cadmio

cadmium selenide
seleniuro de cadmio
**cadmium selenide
lithopone**
litopona con seleniuro
de cadmio
cadmium stearate
estearato de cadmio
cadmium succinate
succinato de
cadmio
cadmium sulfate
sulfato de cadmio
cadmium sulfide
sulfuro de cadmio
cadmium telluride
telururo de cadmio
cadmium tungstate
tungstato de cadmio
cadmiun yellow
amarillo de cadmio
cadmium-base Babbitt
Babbitt con base de
cadmio
cadralazine
cadralacina,
cadralazina
cafaminol
cafaminol
cafedrine
cafedrina
cafestol
cafestol
caffeic acid
ácido cafeico
caffeine
cafeína, trimetilxantina
caffeine bromide
bromuro de cafeína
**caffeine
hydrobromide**
bromhidrato de cafeína
**caffeine sodium
benzoate**
benzoato de cafeína y
sodio
caframinol
caframinol
cage mill
molino de tambor
metálico
cajeput
cayeputi, árbol de la
India

cajeput oil
esencia (aceite) de
cayeputi
cajeputene
cayeputeno, cineno
cajeputol
cayeputol, cineol,
eucaliptol
cajuput oil
esencia (aceite) de
cayeputi
cajuputene
cayeputeno, cineno
cajuputol
cayeputol, cineol,
eucaliptol
cake
bizcocho
cake, to
agrumar, aglutinar,
aglomerar
cake alum
sulfato de alúmina,
alumbre en bloque
caking
apelmazado,
apelmazamiento,
endurecimiento
calabarine
calabarina
calamine
calamina
calamintha oil
aceite de
calaminta
calamus oil
esencia (aceite) de
cálamo
calandria
calandria (azúcar)
calaverite
calaverita
calcareous
calcáreo
calcifediol
calcifediol, calcidiol
calciferol
calciferol,
ergocalciferol,
vitamina D$_2$
calcimine
lechada de cal con cola
calcimycin
calcimicina

calcinate, to
calcinar
calcinated magnesia
magnesia calcinada
calcination
calcinación
calcine
calcinar
calcining furnace
horno de calcinación
calcipotriene
calcipotrieno
calcite
calcita, espato calizo, piedra caliza
calcitonin(e)
calcitonina
calcitriol
calcitriol
calcium
calcio
calcium abietate
abietato de calcio
calcium acetate
acetato de calcio
calcium acetylsalicylate
acetilsalicilato de calcio
calcium acid sulfite
sulfito ácido de calcio
calcium acrylate
acrilato de calcio
calcium alginate
alginato de calcio
calcium aluminate
aluminato de calcio
calcium aluminium hydride
hidruro de calcio y aluminio
calcium aluminosilicate
aluminosilicato de calcio
calcium ammoniun nitrate
nitrato de calcio y amonio
calcium arsenate
arseniato de calcio
calcium arsenite
arsenito de calcio
calcium ascorbate
ascorbato de calcio
calcium 3-aurothio-2-propanol-1-sulfonate
3-aurotío-2-propanol-1-sulfonato de calcio

calcium benzamido-salicylate
benzamidosalicilato de calcio
calcium biphosphate
bifosfato de calcio
calcium bisulfide
bisulfuro de calcio
calcium bisulfite
bisulfito de calcio
calcium borate
borato de calcio
calcium borogluconate
borogluconato de calcio
calcium bromate
bromato de calcio
calcium bromide
bromuro de calcio
calcium bromolacto-bionate
bromolactobionato de calcio
calcium carbide
carburo de calcio
calcium carbimide
carbimida de calcio
calcium N-carbamoyl-aspartate
N-carbamoil-aspartato de calcio, aspartato N-carbamoílico de calcio
calcium carbonate
carbonato de calcio
calcium caseinate
caseinato de calcio
calcium chlorate
clorato de calcio
calcium chloride
cloruro de calcio
calcium chloride solution
solución de cloruro de calcio
calcium chlorite
clorito de calcio
calcium chromate
cromato de calcio
calcium citrate
citrato de calcio
calcium clofibrate
clofibrato de calcio
calcium cyanamide
cianamida cálcica
calcium cyanamide citrated
cianamida cálcica citratada

calcium cyanide
cianuro de calcio
calcium cyclamate
ciclamato de calcio
calcium cyclobarbital
ciclobarbital cálcico
calcium cyclohexane-sulfamate
ciclohexansulfamato de calcio
calcium dehydro-acetate
dihidroacetato de calcio
calcium diacetate
diacetato de calcio
calcium dibromo-benehate
dibromobenehato de calcio
calcium dichromate
dicromato de calcio
calcium dihydrogen sulfite
sulfito biácido de calcio
calcium dioxide
dióxido de calcio
calcium disodium edetate
edetato de calcio disódico
calcium disodium ethylenediamine-tetraacetate
etilendiamintetracetato de calcio disódico
calcium dobesilate
dobesilato de calcio
calcium ethylhexoate
etilhexoato de calcio
calcium 2-ethyl-butanoate
2-etilbutanoato de calcio
calcium ferrocyanide
ferrocianuro de calcio
calcium ferrous citrate
citrato de calcio ferroso
calcium fluoride
fluoruro de calcio
calcium fluoro-phosphate
fluorfosfato de calcio
calcium fluosilicate
fluosilicato de calcio
calcium folinate
folinato de calcio

calcium formate
formiato de calcio
calcium glubionate
glubionato de calcio
calcium gluco-heptonate
glucoheptonato de calcio
calcium gluconate
gluconato de calcio
calcium glutamate
glutamato de calcio
calcium glycero-phosphate
glicerofosfato de calcio
calcium glycolate
glicolato de calcio
calcium hexafluoro-silicate
hexafluorosilicato de calcio
calcium hexasilico-fluorate
hexasilicofluorato de calcio
calcium hydrate
hidrato de calcio
calcium hydride
hidruro de calcio
calcium hydrogen sulfite
sulfito ácido de calcio
calcium hydro-phosphite
hidrofosfito de calcio
calcium hydrosulfide
sulfhidrato de calcio
calcium hydrosulfite
hidrosulfito de calcio
calcium hydroxide
hidróxido de calcio
calcium hypochlorite
hipoclorito de calcio
calcium hypo-phosphite
hipofosfito de calcio
calcium hyposulfite
hiposulfito de calcio
calcium iodate
yodato de calcio
calcium iodide
yoduro de calcio
calcium iodobehenate
yodobehenato de calcio
calcium iodostearate
yodoestearato de calcio
calcium ipodate
ipodato de calcio

calcium lactate
lactato de calcio
calcium laurate
laurato de calcio
calcium leucovorin
leucovorina cálcica,
folinato de calcio
calcium levulinate
levulinato de calcio
calcium lignosulfonate
lignosulfonato de
calcio
calcium linoleate
linoleato de calcio
calcium magnesium
aconitate
aconitato de calcio y
magnesio
calcium magnesium
carbonate
carbonato de calcio y
magnesio
calcium magnesium
chloride
cloruro de calcio y
magnesio
calcium malonate
malonato de calcio
calcium mandelate
mandelato de calcio
calcium metasilicate
metasilicato de calcio
calcium mesoxalate
mesoxalato de calcio
calcium methionate
metionato de calcio
calcium molybdate
molibdato de calcio
calcium naphthenate
naftenato de calcio
calcium nitrate
nitrato de calcio
calcium nitride
nitruro de calcio
calcium nitrite
nitrito de calcio
calcium novobiocin
novobiocina cálcica
calcium octoate
octoato de calcio
calcium oleate
oleato de calcio
calcium ortho-
phosphate
ortofosfato de calcio,
o-fosfato de calcio
calcium ortho-tungstate
ortotungstato de calcio,
o-tungstato de calcio

calcium oxalate
oxalato de calcio
calcium oxide
óxido de calcio
calcium oxychloride
cloruro básico de
calcio
calcium palmitate
palmitato de calcio
calcium panthotenate
pantotenato de calcio
calcium pectate
pectato de calcio
calcium perborate
perborato de calcio
calcium perchlorate
perclorato de calcio
calcium permanganate
permanganato de
calcio
calcium peroxide
peróxido de calcio
calcium phenosulfonate
fenosulfonato de calcio
calcium phenoxide
fenóxido de calcio
calcium phenylate
fenilato de calcio
calcium persulfate
persulfato de calcio
calcium phosphate
fosfato de calcio
calcium phosphate,
dibasic
fosfato dibásico de
calcio
calcium phosphate,
monobasic
fosfato monobásico de
calcio
calcium phosphate,
precipitated
fosfato de calcio
precipitado
calcium phosphide
fosfuro de calcio
calcium phosphite
fosfito de calcio
calcium phytate
fitato de calcio
calcium plumbate
plumbato de calcio
calcium poly-
carbophil
policarbofil cálcico
calcium polysilicate
polisilicato de calcio
calcium propionate
propionato de calcio

calcium propyl
arsenate
propilarseniato de
calcio, arseniato
propílico de calcio
calcium pyrophosphate
pirofosfato de calcio
calcium resinate
resinato de calcio
calcium ricinoleate
ricinoleato de calcio
calcium saccharate
sacarato de calcio
calcium d-saccharate
d-sacarato de calcio
calcium saccharin
sacarina cálcica
calcium salicylate
salicilato de calcio
calcium selenate
seleniato de calcio
calcium selenide
seleniuro de calcio
calcium silicate
silicato de calcio
calcium silicide
siliciuro de calcio
calcium silicofluoride
silicofluoruro de
calcio
calcium-silicon alloy
aleación de calcio y
silicio
calcium sodium
ferriclate
ferriclato de calcio y
sodio
calcium sorbate
sorbato de calcio
calcium stannate
estannato de calcio
calcium stearate
estearato de calcio
calcium stearyl
lactylate
lactilato esteárílico de
calcio
calcium strontium
sulfide
sulfuro de calcio y
estroncio
calcium succinate
succinato de calcio
calcium sulfamate
sulfamato de calcio
calcium sulfate
sulfato de calcio
calcium sulfhydrate
sulfhidrato de calcio

calcium sulfide
sulfuro de calcio
calcium sulfite
sulfito de calcio
calcium sulfocarbolate
sulfocarbolato de calcio
calcium sulfocyanide
sulfocianuro de calcio
calcium sulfocyanate
sulfocianato de calcio
calcium superoxide
superóxido de calcio
calcium tallate
talato (resinato) de
calcio
calcium tannate
tanato de calcio
calcium tartrate
tartrato de calcio
calcium thiocyanate
tiocianato de calcio
calcium thioglycolate
tioglicolato de calcio
calcium thiosulfate
tiosulfato de calcio
calcium titanate
titanato de calcio
calcium trisodium
pentetate
pentetato de calcio
trisódico
calcium tungstate
tungstato de calcio
calcium undecylenate
undecilenato de calcio
calcium zirconate
circonato de calcio
calcium zirconium
silicate
silicato de calcio y
circonio
caldariomycin
caldariomicina
C-calebassine
C-calebasina
calendula
caléndula
caliche
caliche (nitrato sódico)
caliper
calibrador
calmagite
calmagita
calmodulin
calmodulina
calomel
calomel, monocloruro
de mercurio, cloruro
mercurioso

calomelol
calomel coloidal
calorie
caloría
calorific
calorífico
calorimetric
calorimétrico
calotropin(e)
calotropina
calumba
colombo
calusterone
calusterona
calutron
calutrón
calycanthine
calicantina
camazepam
camacepán,
camazepam
cambendazole
cambendazol
camiverine
camiverina
camomile
manzanilla,
camomila
camomile oil
esencia (aceite) de
manzanilla
camostat
camostat
campesterol
campesterol
2-camphanol
2-canfanol
2-camphanone
2-canfanona
camphene
canfeno
camphenol
canfenol
d-camphocarboxylic
acid
ácido d-canfo-
carboxílico
camphor
alcanfor
camphor bromate
bromato de alcanfor
camphor,
Malayan
alcanfor de
Malaya,
alcanfor malayo
camphor oil
esencia (aceite) de
alcanfor

di-camphoroquinine
di-canforoquinina
camphoric acid
ácido canfórico
d-camphorsulfonic
acid
ácido d-canfor-
sulfónico
camphotamide
canfotamida
camptothecin
camptotecina
Camps quinoline
synthesis
síntesis de quinolinas
de Camps
camsilate
cansilato
camylofin(e)
camilofina
Canada balsam
bálsamo del Canadá
canadine
canadina
cananga oil
esencia (aceite) de
cananga, esencia
(aceite) de ilang ilang
canavanine
canavanina
canbisol
cambisol
candelilla wax
cera de candelilla
candicidin
candicidina
candidin
candidina
cane sugar
azúcar de caña,
sacarosa
cane wax
cera de caña
canella
canela
cannabidiol
cannabidiol
cannabinol
cannabinol
cannabis
cannabis, marijuana,
marihuana
Cannizzaro reaction
reacción de
Cannizzaro
canrenoic acid
ácido canrenoico
canrenone
canrenona

cantharidis
cantáridas
cantharidin
cantaridina
canthaxanthin
cantaxantina
cap torque
torsión de la tapa
capillarity
capilaridad
capillary action
acción capilar
capillary tension
tensión capilar
capillary tube
tubo capilar
capobenic acid
ácido capobénico
capping
tendencia a formar
sobrecapas (tabletas)
capraldehyde
capraldehído
capreomycin
capreomicina
capreomycin sulfate
sulfato de
capreomicina
capric acid
ácido cáprico
caproic acid
ácido caproico
caproic aldehyde
aldehído caproico
caprolactam
caprolactama,
caprolactámico
caprolactone
caprolactona
caproxamine
caproxamina
caproyl chloride
cloruro de caproílo
capryl alcohol
alcohol caprílico
capryl compounds
compuestos caprílicos
caprylene
caprileno
caprylic acid
ácido caprílico
caprylic alcohol
alcohol caprílico
caprylic aldehyde
aldehído caprílico
capsaicin
capsaicina
capsanthin
capsantina

capsicum
cápsico, pimienta roja
capsule
cápsula
capsule (botton & top)
cartucho y casco
captafol
captafol
captamine
captamina
captan
captán
captodiame
captodiamo
captodiamine
captodiamina
captopril
captopril
capture a neutron, to
capturar un neutrón
capuride
capurida
caramel
caramelo
caramiphen
caramifeno
caramiphen
ethanedisulfonate
etandisulfonato de
caramifeno
caramiphen
hydrochloride
clorhidrato de
caramifeno
caraway
alcaravea
caraway oil
esencia (aceite) de
alcaravea
carazolol
carazolol
carbachol
carbacol
carbacrylic resins
resinas carbacrílicas
carbadox
carbadox
carbamate
carbamato
carbamazepine
carbamacepina
carbamic acid
ácido carbámico
carbamide
carbamida
carbamide peroxide
peróxido de carbamida
carbamidine
carbamidina

carbamite
carbamita
cardamom oil
esencia (aceite) de
cardamomo
carbamylarsanilic acid
ácido carbamil-
arsanílico
carbamylcholine
chloride
cloruro de
carbamilcolina
carbamylguanidine
sulfate
sulfato de carbamil-
guanidina
carbamylhydrazine
hydrochloride
clorhidrato de
carbamilhidrazina
carbamylmethyl-
choline chloride
cloruro de carbamil-
metilcolina
carbamylurea
carbamilurea
carbanil
carbanilo
carbanilic acid
ácido carbanílico
carbanilide
carbanilida
carbanion
carbanión
carbantel
carbantel
carbarsone
carbarsona, ácido p-
ureidobencenarsónico
carbaryl
carbarilo
carbasalate calcium
carbasalato cálcico
carbazeran
carbacerán
carbazide
carbazida
carbazochrome
salicylate
salicilato de
carbazocromo
carbazochrome sodium
sulfonate
sulfonato de
carbazocromo sódico
carbazocine
carbazocina
carbazole
carbazol

carbazoleacetic acid
ácido carbazolacético
carbazolic acid
ácido carbazólico
carbendazim
carbendacima
carbene
carbeno
carbenicillin
carbenicilina
carbenoxolone
carbenoxolona
carbenzide
carbencida
carbesilate
carbesilato
carbetapentane
carbetapentano
carbetapentane tannate
tanato de
carbetapentano
2-carbethoxycyclo-
hexanone
2-carbetoxiciclo-
hexanona
ß-carbethoxyethyl-
triethoxy silane
ß-carbetoxietiltrietoxi
silano
N-carbethoxypiperazine
N-carbetoxipiperazina
ß-carbethoxy-
propylmethyl-
diethoxysilane
ß-carbetoxipropil-
metildietoxisilano
carbetidine
carbetidina
carbetocin(e)
carbetocina
carbic anhydride
anhídrido cárbico
carbide
carburo
carbidopa
carbidopa
carbifene
carbifeno
carbimazole
carbimazol
carbinol
carbinol
carbinoxamine
carbinoxamina
carbinoxamine maleate
maleato de
carbinoxamina
carbiphene
carbifeno

carbobenzoxy
chloride
cloruro de
benciloxicarbonilo
carbobenzyloxy-l-
alanine
benciloxicarbonilo-l-
alanina,
carbobenciloxi-l-
alanina
carbocaine
carbocaína
carbocisteine
carbocisteína
carbocloral
carbocloral
carbocromen
carbocromeno
carbocyclic
carbocíclico
carbocyclic
compound
compuesto
carbocíclico
carbocysteine
carbocisteína
carbodihydrazide
carbodihidrazida
carbodiimide
carbodiimida
carbofenotion
carbofenotión
carbofuran
carbofurano
carbohydrase
carbohidrasa
carbohydrate
hidrato de carbono,
carbohidrato
carbohydrazide
carbohidrazida
carboline
carbolina
carbolineum
carbolíneo
carbolfuchsin
carbolfucsina
carbolic acid
ácido fénico
carbolic oil
aceite fénico
carbomer
carbómero
3-carbomethoxy-1-
methyl-4-piperidone
hydrochloride
clorhidrato de 3-
carbometoxi-1-metil-4-
piperidona

2-carbomethoxy-1-
methylvinyl dimethyl-
phosphate
dimetilfosfato de 2-
carbometoxi-1-
metilvinilo
carbomycin
carbomicina
carbon
carbono
carbon, amorphous
carbono amorfo
carbon bisulfide
bisulfuro de carbono
carbon black
negro de humo
carbon black oil
aceite de negro de
humo
carbon combined
carbono combinado
carbon content
contenido de carbono
carbon cycle
ciclo del carbono
carbon dichloride
dicloruro de carbono
carbon dioxide
anhídrido carbónico,
bióxido de carbono,
dióxido de carbono
carbon dioxide ice
hielo seco
carbon diselenide
diseleniuro de carbono
carbon disulfide
disulfuro de carbono
carbon, divalent
carbono divalente
carbon fiber
fibra de carbón
carbon filament lamp
lámpara con filamento
de carbón
carbon fluoride
fluoruro de carbono
carbon hexachloride
hexacloruro de carbono
carbon monoxide
monóxido de carbono
carbon oxybromide
bromuro básico de
carbono
carbon oxychloride
cloruro básico de
carbono
carbon oxycianide
cianuro básico de
carbono

51

carbon oxyfluoride
fluoruro básico de
carbono
carbon oxysulfide
sulfuro básico de
carbono
carbon paper
papel carbón, papel
carbónico
carbon residue
residuo de carbón
carbon suboxide
subóxido de carbono
carbon tetrabromide
tetrabromuro de
carbono
carbon tetrachloride
tetracloruro de
carbono,
tetraclorometano
carbon tetrafluoride
tetrafluoruro de
carbono
carbon tetraiodide
tetrayoduro de
carbono
carbon trichloride
tricloruro de carbono
carbonate
carbonato
carbonate mineral
mineral de carbonato
carbonic acid
ácido carbónico
carbonic acid gas
gas carbónico
carbonic anhydrase
anhidrasa carbónica
carbonic anhydride
anhídrido carbónico
carbonic ester
éster carbónico
carbonium ion
ion carbonio
carbonization
carbonización
carbonization
index
índice de
carbonización
carbonize, to
carbonizar
carbonizing
carbonización
carbonyl
carbonilo
carbonyl chloride
cloruro de
carbonilo

N,N'-carbonyl bis(4-
methoxy metanilic
acid) disodium salt
sal disódica de N,N'-
carbonil bis(ácido 4-
metoximetanílico)
carbonyl bromide
bromuro de carbonilo
carbonyl chloride
cloruro de carbonilo
carbonyl cyanide
cianuro de carbonilo
carbonyl fluoride
fluoruro de carbonilo
carbonyl group
grupo carbonilo
carbonyl sulfide
sulfuro de carbonilo
1,1'-carbonyldi-
imidazole
1,1'-carbonildi-
imidazol
carbophenothion
carbofenotiona
carboplatin
carboplatino
carboprost
carboprost
carboquone
carbocuona
carborane
carborano
carborundum
carborundo, carburo
de silicio
carbosand
carboarena
carbostyryl
carboestirilo
carboxin
carboxina
ß-carboxyaspartic acid
ácido ß-carboxi-
aspártico
carboxybenzene
carboxibenceno
carboxyglutamic acid
ácido carboxi-
glutámico
2-carboxy-2'-hydroxy-
5'-sulfoformazyl-
benzene
2-carboxi-2'-hidroxi-
5'-sulfoformacil-
benceno
carboxyl
carboxilo
carboxyl group
grupo carboxilo

carboxylase
carboxilasa
carboxylic acid
ácido carboxílico
carboxylic group
grupo carboxílico
carboxymethoxyl-
amine hemyhydro-
chloride
hemiclorhidrato de
carboximetoxilamina
carboxymethyl-
cellulose
celulosa carboxi-
metílica, carboxi-
metilcelulosa
carboxymethyl-
mercaptosuccinic acid
ácido mercapto-
succínico carboxi-
metílico, ácido
carboximetil-
mercaptosuccínico
carboxymethyl-
pyridinium chloride
hydrazide
hidrazida de cloruro de
piridinio carboxi-
metílico, hidrazida de
cloruro de
carboximetilpiridinio
carboxymethyltri-
methylammonium
chloride hydrazide
hidrazida de cloruro
de amonio carboxi-
metiltrimetílico,
hidrazida de cloruro de
carboximetiltri-
metilamonio
carboxypeptidase
carboxipeptidasa
carboxypoly-
methylene
carboxipolimetileno
4-carboxyresorcinol
4-carboxirresorcinol,
4-carboxirresorcina
6-carboxyuracil
6-carboxiuracilo
carbromal
carbromal
carbubarb
carbubarbo
carburazepam
carburacepán,
carburazepam
carburet, to
carburar

carburet of sulfur
carburo de azufre
carburetted hydrogen
hidrógeno carburado
carbutamide
carbutamida
carbuterol
carbuterol
carcainium chloride
cloruro de carcainio
card cabinet
fichero
cardamom oil
esencia (aceite) de
cardamomo
cardamom seed
semilla de cardamomo
cardiotoxin
cardiotoxina
σ-3-carene
σ-3-careno
carfecillin
carfecilina
carfecillin sodium
carfecilina sódica
carfenazine
carfenacina,
carfenazina
carfentanil citrate
citrato de carfentanilo
carfimate
carfimato
cargutocin
cargutocina
carindacillin
carindacilina
carisoprodol
carisoprodol
Carlsbad salt artificial
sal artificial de
Carlsbad
carmantadine
carmantadina
carmellose
carmellosa
carmetizide
carmetizida
carmine
carmín
carminic acid
ácido carmínico
carmofur
carmofur
carmustine
carmustina
carnallite
carnalita
carnauba wax
cera carnaúba

carnegine
carnegina
carnidazole
carnidazol
carnitine
carnitina
capsaicin
capsaicina
carocainide
carocainida
caroverine
caroverina
caroxazone
caroxazona
carnosine
carnosina
carnotite
carnotita
Carnot's cycle
ciclo de Carnot
Carnot's reagent
reactivo de Carnot
carob-seed gum
goma de semilla de
algarrobo
Caro's acid
ácido de Caro
carotene
caroteno
carotenoid
carotenoide
carotol
carotol
caroverine
caroverina
caroxazone
caroxazona
carpaine
carpaína
carperidine
carperidina
carperone
carperona
carphenazine
carfenacina,
carfenazina
carpindolol
carpindolol
carpipramine
carpipramina
carprazidil
carpracidilo
carprofen
carprofeno
carpronium chloride
cloruro de
carpronio
carrier
portador

carrier compound
compuesto portador
carrier gas
gas portador
Carroll reaction
reacción de Carroll
carrot oil
aceite de zanahorias
carry on, to
mantener, continuar
carry through, to
llevar a cabo, llevar a
buen término
carsalam
carsalamo
cartap
ácido carbamótioco
cartazolate
cartazolato
carteolol
carteolol
carteolol hydrochloride
clorhidrato de
carteolol
carthamic acid
ácido cartámico
carthamin
cartamina
carthamus
alazor, cártamo,
azafrán falso
cartridge
cartucho
carubicin
carubicina
carvacrol
carvacrol
carvedilol
carvedilol
carvone
carvona
caryophyllene
cariofileno
caryophyllic acid
ácido cariofílico
carzenide
carcenida
carzinophillin
carcinofilina
casanthranol
casantranol
cascara amara
corteza amarga, corteza
de Honduras
cascara sagrada bark
corteza de cáscara
sagrada
cascarilla
cascarilla

cascarilla oil
esencia (aceite) de
cascarilla
cascarillin
cascarillina
casein
caseína
casein formaldehyde
resins
resinas formaldehídicas
de caseína
casein glue
cola de caseína
casein-sodium
caseína sódica
cashew gum
goma de anacardo
cashew nutshell oil
esencia (aceite) de
cáscara de nuez de
anacardo
casimiroedine
casimiroedina
casimiroin
casimiroína
cassaidine
casaidina
cassaine
casaína
cassamine
casamina
cassava
mandioca, yuca
Cassel brown
marrón de Cassel
Cassel green
verde de Cassel
Cassella's acid
ácido de Cassella
cassia bark
canela, casia
cassia fistula
cañafístula
cassia oil
esencia (aceite) de
casia, aceite de canela
cassiterite
casiterita
castanea
castaña
Castle's intrinsic
factor
factor intrínseco de
Castle
castor oil
aceite de ricino
castor seed oil meal
harina de aceite de
semilla de ricino

catalase
catalasa
catalposide
catalpósido
catalyse, to
catalizar
catalyser
catalizador
catalysis
catálisis
catalyst
catalizador
catalyst activity
actividad del
catalizador
catalyst, negative
catalizador negativo
catalyst, organic
catalizador orgánico
catalyst, shape
selective
catalizador selectivo de
forma
catalyst, stereospecific
catalizador
estereoespecífico
catalyst, thermo-
nuclear
catalizador
termonuclear
catalytic
catalítico
catalytic action
acción catalítica
catechin
catequina
catechol
catecol
catecholborane
catecolborano
catechu black
negro catecú
catenane
catenano
catharanthine
catarantina
cathepsins
catepsinas
cathine
catina
cathinone
catinona
cathode
cátodo
cathode sputtering
desintegración
catódica,
pulverización
catódica

cation
catión
cation exchange
intercambio de
cationes
cationic reagent
reactivo catiónico
catlinite
catlinita
catnep
nébeda
caulophylline
caulofilina
caulophyllum
caulófilo
caustic potash
potasa cáustica
caustic soda
soda cáustica, sosa
cáustica
caution
precaución
cavitation
cavitación
ceanothic acid
ácido ceanótico
cedar leaf oil
esencia (aceite) de
hojas de cedro
cedar wood oil
esencia (aceite) de
madera de cedro
cedrin
cedrina
cedrol
cedrol
cedryl acetate
acetato de
cedrilo
cefacetrile
cefacetrilo
cefaclor
cefaclor
cefadroxil
cefadroxilo
cefalexin
cefalexina
cefaloglycin
cefaloglicina
cefalonium
cefalonio
cefaloram
cefaloramo
cefaloridine
cefaloridina
cefalotin
cefalotina
cefamandole
cefamandol

cefamandole nafate
nafato de
cefamandol
cefaparole
cefaparol
cefapirin
cefapirina
cefatrizine
cefatricina
cefazaflur
cefazaflur
cefazedone
cefacedona
cefazolin
cefazolina
cefbuperazone
cefbuperazona
cefepime
hydrochloride
clorhidrato de
cefepima
cefetrizole
cefetrizol
cefixime
cefixima
cefmenoxime
cefmenoxima
cefmetazole
cefmetazol
cefodizime
cefodicima
cefonicid
cefonicida
cefonizide
cefonicida
cefoperazone
cefoperazona
ceforanide
ceforanida
cefotaxime
cefotaxima
cefotetan
cefotetán
cefotiam
cefotián
cefoxazole
cefoxazol
cefoxitin
cefoxitina
cefpimizole
cefpimizol
cefpiramide
cefpiramida
cefpodoxime
proxetil
cefpodoxima
proxetílica
cefprozil
cefprocil

cefradine
cefradina
cefrotil
cefrotilo
cefroxadine
cefroxadina
cefsulodin
cefsulodina
cefsumide
cefsumida
ceftazidime
ceftacidima
ceftezole
ceftezol
ceftibuten
ceftibuteno
ceftioxide
ceftióxido
ceftizoxime
ceftizoxima
ceftriaxone
ceftriaxona
cefuracetime
cefuracetima
cefuroxime
cefuroxima
celery oil
aceite de apio
celesticetin
celesticetina
celestin blue
azul celestino
celestine, celestite
celestina
celiprolol
celiprolol
cell
célula, celdilla, celda
cell kill
destrucción de células
cell lines
líneas celulares, linajes
celulares
cell flock filter aid
ayuda de filtración
para floculación
cellular
cellaburate
celaburato
cellacefate
celacefato
cellobiose
celobiosa
cellocidin
celocidina
celloidin
celoidina
cellophane
celofán

cellulase
celulasa
celluloid
celuloide
cellulose
celulosa
cellulose acetate
acetato de celulosa
cellulose acetate
butyrate
butirato acetato de
celulosa
cellulose acetate
phthalate
ftalato acetato de
celulosa
cellulose acetate
propionate
propionato acetato de
celulosa
cellulose acetate rayon
rayón de acetato de
celulosa
cellulose aceto-
butyrate
acetobutirato de
celulosa
cellulose ester
éster de celulosa
cellulose ether
éter de celulosa
cellulose ethyl
hydroxyethyl ether
éter etilhidroxietílico
de celulosa
cellulose gum
goma de celulosa
cellulose, hydrated
celulosa hidratada
cellulose methyl ether
éter metílico de
celulosa
cellulose, modified
celulosa modificada
cellulose nitrate
nitrato de celulosa
cellulose, oxidized
celulosa oxidada
cellulose propionate
propionato de
celulosa
cellulose regenerated
celulosa regenerada
cellulose sponge
esponja de celulosa
cellulose triacetate
triacetato de celulosa
cellulose xanthate
xantato de celulosa

cellulosic plastic
plástico celulósico
cellulosic
thiocarbonate
tiocarbonato celulósico
celucloral
celucloral
celylic alcohol
alcohol celílico
cement, aluminous
cemento alumínico
cement, Portland
cemento Portland
cement, rubber
adhesivo
centaurein
centaureína
center of gravity
centro de gravedad
center of gyration
centro de giro
centigrade heat unit
unidad centígrada de
calor
centigrade degree
grado Celsius, grado
centígrado
centipoise
centipoise (submúltiplo
de unidad de
viscosidad dinámica)
centistoke
centistoke (submúltiplo
de unidad de
viscosidad cinemática)
centrifugation
centrifugación
centrifuge
centrífuga
centripetal force
fuerza centrípeta
cephacetrile sodium
cefacetrilo sódico
cephaeline
cefaelina
cephalin(e)
cefalina
cephalosporin
cefalosporina
cephamycin
cefamicina
cephalexin
cefalexina
cephalexin
hydrochloride
clorhidrato de
cefalexina
cephalins
cefalinas

cephaloglycin
cefaloglicina
cephalonic acid
ácido cefalónico
cephaloridine
cefaloridina
cephalosporins
cefalosporinas
cephalothin
cefalotina
cephamycins
cefamicinas
cephapirin
sodium
cefapirina sódica
cepharanthine
cefarantina
cephradine
cefradina
ceramic
cerámica
ceramic, glass
vidrio de cerámica
cerberoside
cerberósido
cerebrosides
cerebrósidos
cereous
ceroso
ceresin
ceresina, cerina
ceresin wax
cera de ceresina
ceria
ceria, óxido de cerio
ceric ammonium
nitrate
nitrato cérico de
amonio
ceric fluoride
fluoruro cérico
ceric hydroxide
hidróxido cérico
ceric oxide
óxido cérico
ceric sulfate
sulfato cérico
ceric sulfide
sulfuro cérico
cerin
cerina
ceritamic acid
ácido ceritámico
cerite
cerita
cerium
cerio
cerium carbonate
carbonato de cerio

cerium chloride
cloruro de cerio
cerium dioxide
dióxido de cerio
cerium hydrate
hidrato de cerio
cerium
naphthenate
naftenato de cerio
cerium nitrate
nitrato de cerio
cerium oxalate
oxalato de cerio
cerium oxide
óxido de cerio
cerium sulfate
sulfato de cerio
cerium sulfide
sulfuro de cerio
cerium-ammonium
nitrate
nitrato de cerio y
amonio
cerivastatin sodium
cerivastatina sódica
cerosiline
cerosilina
cerosin
cerosina
cerotic acid
ácido cerótico
cerous
ceroso
cerous bromide
bromuro ceroso
cerous carbonate
carbonato ceroso
cerous chloride
cloruro ceroso
cerous fluoride
fluoruro ceroso
cerous hydroxide
hidróxido ceroso
cerous iodide
yoduro ceroso
cerous nitrate
nitrato ceroso
cerous oxalate
oxalato ceroso
cerous sulfate
sulfato ceroso
certified color
color certificado
cerulean blue
azul cerúleo
cerulenin
cerulenina
ceruletide
cerulétido

ceruloplasmin
ceruloplasmina
cerussite
cerusita
cervicarcin
cervicarcina
ceryl alcohol
alcohol cerílico
ceryl cerotate
cerotato cerílico
cesium, caesium
cesio
cesium acid sulfate
sulfato ácido de
cesio
cesium aluminum
sulfate
sulfato de cesio y
aluminio
cesium antimonide
antimoniuro de cesio
cesium arsenide
arseniuro de cesio
cesium bromide
bromuro de cesio
cesium carbonate
carbonato de cesio
cesium chloride
cloruro de cesio
cesium dioxide
dióxido de cesio
cesium flouride
fluoruro de cesio
cesium hexafluoro-
germanate
hexafluorogermanato
de cesio
cesium hydrate
hidrato de cesio
cesium hydroxide
hidróxido de cesio
cesium iodide
yoduro de cesio
cesium nitrate
nitrato de cesio
cesium oxide
óxido de cesio
cesium pentachloro-
carbonylosmium (III)
pentaclorocarbonil-
osmio de cesio (III)
cesium perchlorate
perclorato de cesio
cesium peroxide
peróxido de cesio
cesium phosphide
fosfuro de cesio
cesium sulfate
sulfato de cesio

cesium tetróxido
tetróxido de cesio
cesium trioxide
trióxido de cesio
cetaben
cetabeno
cetalkonium chloride
cloruro de cetalconio
cetamolol
cetamolol
cetane
cetano, n-hexadecano
cetane index
índice de cetano
cetane number
número de cetano
cethexonium bromide
bromuro de cetexonio
cethexonium chloride
cloruro de cetexonio
cetiedil
cetiedilo
cetin
cetina
cetirizine
hydrochloride
clorhidrato de
cetiricina
cetocycline
cetociclina
cetofenicol
cetofenicol
cetohexazine
cetohexacina,
cetohexazina
cetomacrogol 1000
cetomacrogol 1000
cetotiamine
cetotiamina
cetoxime
cetoxima
cetraria
cetraria
cetraric acid
ácido cetrárico
cetraxate
cetraxato
cetrimide
cetrimida
cetrimonium bromide
bromuro de cetrimonio
cetrimonium
pentachlorophenoxide
pentaclorofenóxido de
cetrimonio
cetrimonium stearate
estearato de cetrimonio
cetyl
cetilo

cetyl alcohol
alcohol cetílico
cetyl bromide
bromuro de cetilo
cetyl ether
éter cetílico
cetyl lactate
lactato cetílico
cetyl mercaptan
mercaptano cetílico,
cetilmercaptano
cetyl palmitate
palmitato de cetilo
cetyl vinyl ether
éter cetilvinílico
cetyldimethylbenzyl-
ammonium chloride
cloruro de cetildimetil-
bencilamonio
cetyldimethylethyl-
ammonium bromide
bromuro de
cetildimetiletil-
amonio
cetyldimethylethyl-
ammonium chloride
cloruro de
cetildimetiletil-
amonio
cetylic acid
ácido cetílico
cetylic alcohol
alcohol cetílico
cetylpyridinium
bromide
bromuro de
cetilpiridinio
cetylpyridinium
chloride
cloruro de
cetilpiridinio
cetyltrimethyl-
ammonium
bromide
bromuro de
cetiltrimetilamonio
cetyltrimethyl-
ammonium
chloride
cloruro de
cetiltrimetilamonio
cetyltrimethyl-
ammonium tosylate
tosilato de
cetiltrimetilamonio
cevadine
cevadina
cevine
cevina

CFU
unidades formadoras
de colonias, UFC
chain branching
ramificación
chain compound
compuesto en cadena
chain decay
descomposición
en cadena,
desintegración
en cadena
chain iniciation
iniciación de la cadena
chalcocite
chalcocita
chalcomycin
chalcomicina
chalcone
chalcona
chalcopyrite
calcopirita
D-chalcose
D-chalcosa
chalk, drop
pastillas de creta
chalk, French
creta francesa
chalk, precipitated
creta precipitada
challenge
agresión
chalybeate
chalibita
chamazulene
camazuleno
chamber
cámara
chamomile
manzanilla
chamomile oil-German
esencia (aceite)
de manzanilla alemana
chamomile oil-Roman
esencia (aceite) de
manzanilla romana
champaca oil
esencia (aceite) de
champacán
change, to
cambiar
change of state
cambio de estado
Chapman
rearrangement
transformación de
Chapman
char, to
carbonizar

characteristic frecuency
frecuencia característica
charcoal, activated
carbón activado
charcoal, animal
carbón animal
charcoal, bone
carbón de huesos
charcoal, vegetable
carbón vegetal
charcoal, wood
carbón de madera
charge
carga
Charles' Law
ley de Charles
Charpy impact test
prueba de elasticidad
de Charpy
charring
carbonización
chart
gráfico
chartreusin
chartreusina,
lambdamicina
chaulmoogra oil
aceite de
chaulmugra
chaulmoogric acid
ácido chaulmúgrico
chaulmoogric oil
aceite chaulmúgrico
chaulmosulfone
chaulmosulfona
chavicine
chavicina
chavicol
chavicol
check
verificar, comprobar
checking
verificación
cheirolin
queirolina, quirolina
chelant
quelante
chelate
quelato
chelate ring
anillo quelatado
chelate, to
quelar
chelating agent
agente quelante
chelation
quelación
chelator
quelador

chelen
queleno, cloruro de
etilo
chelerytrine
queleritrina
chelidonate
quelidonato
chelidonic acid
ácido quelidónico
chelidonine
quelidonina
chemical
agente químico,
producto químico
chemical adsorption
adsorción química
chemical activity
actividad química
chemical affinity
afinidad química
chemical air- pollutant
contaminante químico
del aire
chemical analysis
análisis químico
chemical analyzer
analizador químico
chemical anti-detonant
antidetonante químico
chemical balance
equilibrio químico;
balanza química,
balanza de laboratorio
chemical bench
banco de laboratorio
chemical bending
curvatura con
productos químicos
chemical bleaching
blanqueo químico
chemical bond
enlace químico
chemical change
cambio químico
chemical combustion
combustión química
chemical data storage
almacenamiento de
datos químicos
chemical desiccator
desecador químico
chemical data
datos químicos
chemical energy
energía química
chemical equivalent
equivalente químico
chemical fibers
fibras químicas

chemical glass
vidrio apropiado para
aparatos de laboratorio
chemical grade
grado químico
chemical grinding
rectificado químico
chemical ignition
ignición química
chemical industry
industria química
chemical laws
leyes químicas
chemical leaching
lixiviación química
chemical literature
publicaciones
químicas, literatura
química
chemical microscopy
microscopía química
chemical milling
abrasión química,
molienda química
chemical nomenclature
nomenclatura química
chemical oxygen demand (COD)
demanda química de
oxígeno
chemical performance
rendimiento químico,
comportamiento
químico
chemical reaction
reacción química
chemical reagent
reactivo químico
chemical research
investigación química
chemical sediment
sedimento químico
chemical separation
separación química
chemical shift
desplazamiento
químico
chemical smoke
humo químico,
emanación química
chemical technology
tecnología química
chemical treatment
tratamiento químico
chemical waste
desechos químicos
chemically pure
químicamente puro

chemicals
agentes químicos,
productos químicos
chemiluminescence
quimioluminiscencia
chemisorption
adsorción química
chemist
químico
chemistry
química
chemistry history
historia química
chemistry in space
química en el espacio,
química espacial
chemodynamics
quimiodinámica
chemonite
cemonita, arsenito de
cobre amoniacal
chemonuclear production
producción
quimionuclear
chemosterilant
quimioesterilizante
chemotaxis
quimiotaxis
chemotherapy
quimioterapia
chenodeoxycholic acid
ácido
quenodeoxicólico
chenodiol
quenodiol
chenopodium oil
esencia (aceite) de
quenopodio
cherry bark oil, wild
aceite de corteza de
cerezo silvestre
cherry laurel oil
esencia (aceite) de
lauroceraso o laurel
real
chert
pedernal, horsteno,
sílex
chi acid
ácido antraquinona-
1,8-disulfónico
Chichibabin pyridine synthesis
síntesis de piridinas de
Chichibabin
Chichibabin reaction
reacción de Chichibabin

chicle
chicle
child proof
a prueba de niños
child resistant
resistente a la
manipulación por parte
de menores
Chilean nitrate
nitrato de Chile
Chilean saltpeter
salitre de Chile
chill, to
enfriar
chimaphila
quimafila
chimaphilin
quimafilina
chimonanthine
quimonantina
chimyl alcohol
alcohol quimílico
China bark
corteza china
China clay
arcilla de China
china ink
tinta china
chinaldine
quinaldina
chinaphthol
quinaftol
China-wood oil
aceite de madera de
China
Chinese bean oil
aceite de soja
Chinese blue
azul de Prusia,
ferricianuro férrico,
azul de China
Chinese gelatin
gelatina china
Chinese rhubarb
ruibarbo chino
Chinese wax
cera china
Chinese white
blanco de cinc,
blanco
de China
chinic acid
ácido quínico
chinidine
quinidina
chiniofon
quiniofón
chinone
quinona

57

chip	chloraminophenamide	chlordiazepoxide	chlorinated paraffin
fragmento	cloraminfenamida	hydrochloride	parafina clorada
chiral	**chloramphenicol**	clorhidrato de	**chlorinated polyether**
quiral	cloranfenicol	clordiacepóxido	poliéter clorado
chirality	**chloramphenicol**	**chlordimeform**	**chlorinated polyolefin**
quiralidad	**palmitate**	clordimeformo	poliolefina clorada
chirata	palmitato de	**chlordimorine**	**chlorinated rubber**
chirata	cloranfenicol	clordimorina	caucho clorado
chitin	**chloramphenicol**	**chlorendic anhydride**	**chlorinated trisodium**
quitina	**panthothenate**	anhídrido cloréndico	**phosphate**
chitinase	pantotenato de	**chlorethane**	fosfato trisódico
quitinasa	cloranfenicol	cloretano	clorado
chitosamine	**chloramphenicol**	**chlorethanol**	**chlorination**
glucosamina,	**sodium succinate**	cloretanol	cloración
quitosamina	succinato sódico de	**chlorfenac**	**chlorindanol**
chitosan	cloranfenicol	clorfenaco	clorindanol
quitosán	**chloranil**	**chlorfenvinphos**	**chlorine**
chlophedianol	cloranilo,	clorofenvinfós	cloro
clofedianol	tetracloroquinona,	**chlorguanide**	**chlorine addition**
chlophedianol	**chloranilic acid**	clorguanida	adición de cloro
hydrochloride	ácido cloranílico	**chlorhexadol**	**chlorine bromide**
clorhidrato de	**chloranthrene**	clorhexadol	bromuro de cloro
clofedianol	**yellow**	**chlorhexidine**	**chlorine dioxide**
chloracetyl chloride	amarillo de	clorhexidina	dióxido de cloro
cloruro de cloracetilo	clorantreno	**chlorhexidine gluconate**	**chlorine heptoxide**
chloracyzine	**chlorapatite**	gluconato de	heptóxido de cloro
cloracicina,	clorapatita	clorhexidina	**chlorine**
cloracizina	**chlorate**	**chlorhydrin**	**monofluoride**
chloral	clorato	clorhidrina	monofluoruro de cloro
cloral, aldehído	**chlorauric acid**	**chlorhydroquinone**	**chlorine monoxide**
tricloracético	ácido cloráurico	clorhidroquinona	monóxido de cloro
chloral alcoholate	**chlorazanil**	**chloric acid**	**chlorine number**
alcoholato de cloral	clorazanilo	ácido clórico	índice de cloro
chloral betaine	**chlorazine**	**chloride**	**chlorine substitution**
cloral betaína	cloracina, clorazina	cloruro	substitución de cloro
chloral formamide	**chlorazodin(e)**	**chloride of lime**	**chlorine trifluoride**
cloral formamida	clorazodina	hipoclorito de calcio	trifluoruro de cloro
chloral hydrate	**chlorbenside**	**chloridizing**	**chlorine water**
hidrato de cloral	clorobénsido	clorado	agua de cloro
chloral hydrate	**chlorbenzoxamine**	**chlorinate, to**	**chloriodized oil**
antipyrine	clorobenzoxamina	clorar	aceite cloroyodado
hidrato de cloral	**chlorbetamide**	**chlorinated acetone**	**chlorisondamine**
antipirina	clorobetamida	acetona clorada	**chloride**
chloralamide	**chlorbyciclen**	**chlorinated camphene**	cloruro de
cloralamida	clorobicicleno	canfeno clorado	clorisondamina
chloralantipyrine	**chlorcyclizine**	**chlorinated diphenyl**	**chlormadinone**
cloralantipirina	clorciclicina	difenilo clorado	clormadinona
chloralodol	**chlorcyclizine**	**chlorinated**	**chlormadinone acetate**
cloralodol	**hydrochloride**	**hydrocarbon**	acetato de
chloralose	clorhidrato de	hidrocarburo clorado	clormadinona
cloralosa	clorciclicina	**chlorinated isocyanuric**	**chlormerodrin**
chloramben	**chlordan(e)**	**acid**	clormerodrina
clorambeno	clordano	ácido isocianúrico	**chlormequat**
chlorambucil	**chlordantoin**	clorado	clorocolina
clorambucilo	clordantoína	**chlorinated lime**	**chlormequat chloride**
chloramination	**chlordecone**	cal clorada	cloruro de clorocolina,
cloraminación	clordecona	**chlorinated**	dicloruro de colina
chloramine	**chlordiazepoxide**	**naphthalene**	**chlormerodrin**
cloramina	clordiacepóxido	naftaleno clorado	clormerodrina

chlormethine
clormetina
chlormezanone
clormezanona
chlormidazole
clormidazol
chlornaphazine
clornafacina
chloroacetaldehyde
cloracetaldehído
chloroacetaldehyde
dimethyl acetal
acetal de
cloracetaldehído
dimetílico,
cloracetaldehído
dimetil acetal
chloroacetamide
cloracetamida
chloroacetanilide
cloracetanilida
chloroacetic acid
ácido cloracético
chloroacetic anhydride
anhídrido cloracético
o-chloroaceto-
acetanilide
o-cloracetoacetanilida
chloroacetocatechol
cloracetocatecol
α-chloroaceto-3,4-
dihydroxybenzene
α-cloraceto-3,4-
dihidroxibenceno
chloroacetone
cloracetona
chloroacetonitrile
cloracetonitrilo
α-chloroaceto-
phenone
α-cloracetofenona
chloroacetopyro-
catechol
cloracetopirocatecol
chloroacetyl chloride
cloruro de cloracetilo
chloroacetyl isocyanate
isocianato de
cloracetilo
chloroacetylurethane
cloracetiluretano
chloroacrolein
cloracroleína
α-chloroacrylonitrile
α-cloracrilonitrilo
2-chloroallyl diethyl-
dithiocarbamate
dietilditiocarbamato de
2-cloralilo

N-(3-chloroallyl)-
hexaminium chloride
cloruro de N-(3-
cloralil)hexaminio
chloroaluminium
diisopropoxide
diisopropóxido de
cloraluminio
chloroamine
cloramina
2-chloro-5-amino-
benzoic acid
ácido 2-cloro-5-
aminobenzoico
p-chloro-o-
aminophenol
p-cloro-o-
aminofenol
2-chloro-4-tert-
amylphenol
2-cloro-4-terc-
amilfenol
m-chloroaniline
m-cloranilina
o-chloroaniline
o-cloranilina
4-chloroaniline-3-
sulfonic acid
ácido 4-cloranilina-3-
sulfónico
2-chloroanthra-
quinone
2-clorantraquinona
chloroarsenol
clorarsenol
chloroauric acid
ácido cloroáurico
chloroazodin
clorazodina
chloroazotic acid
ácido clorazótico
chlorobenzal
clorobenzal
chlorobenzaldehyde
clorobenzaldehído
o-chlorobenzal-
malononitrile
o-clorobenzal-
malononitrilo
3-chloro-4-
benzamido-6-
methylaniline
3-cloro-4-
benzamido-6-
metilanilina
chlorobenzanthrone
clorobenzantrona
chlorobenzene
clorobenceno

p-chlorobenzene-
sulfonamide
sulfonamida p-
clorobencénica, p-
clorobenceno
sulfonamida
p-chlorobenzene-
sulfonic acid
ácido p-cloro-
bencensulfónico
1-(p-chlorobenzene-
sulfonyl)-3-propylurea
1-(p-clorobenceno-
sulfonilo)-3-propilurea
o-chlorobenzenethiol
o-clorobencentiol
chlorobenzilate
clorobencilato
chlorobenzil chloride
cloruro de clorobencilo
p-chlorobenzohydrol
p-clorobenzohidrol
chlorobenzoic acid
ácido clorobenzoico
p-chlorobenzo-
phenone
p-clorobenzofenona
chlorobenzotriazole
clorobenzotriazol
o-chlorobenzo-
trichloride
tricloruro o-cloro-
benzoico, o-cloro-
benzotricloruro
p-chlorobenzo-
trifluoride
trifluoruro p-cloro-
benzoico, p-cloro-
benzotrifluoruro
chlorobenzoyl chloride
cloruro de
clorobenzoílo
p-chlorobenzoyl
peroxide
peróxido de p-cloro-
benzoílo
p-chlorobenzyl
cyanide
cianuro de p-
clorobencilo
p-chlorobenzyl-p-
chlorophenyl sulfide
sulfuro de p-cloro-
bencil-p-clorofenilo
p-chlorobenzyl-p-
fluorophenyl
sulfide
sulfuro de p-cloro-
bencil-p-fluorofenilo

o-chlorobenzylidene
malononitrile
o-clorobencilideno
malononitrilo
chlorobenzylpseudo-
thiuronium
clorobencilpseudo-
tiuronio
2-(p-chlorobenzyl)
pyridine
2-(p-clorobencil)
piridina
chlorobromo
clorobromo
2-chlorobutadiene-1,3
2-clorobutadieno-1,3
1-chlorobutane
1-clorobutano
chlorobutanol
clorobutanol,
1,1,1-tricloro-2-
metil-2-propanol
1-chloro-2-butene
1-cloro-2-buteno
3-chloro-1-butene
3-cloro-1-buteno
4-chloro-2-
butynyl-m-
chlorocarbanilate
m-clorcarbanilato
de 4-cloro-2-
butinilo
3-chloro-d-camphor
3-cloro-d-alcanfor
chlorocarbon
clorocarbono
chlorocarbonyl
ferrocene
ferroceno
clorocarbonílico
chlorochromic
anhydride
anhídrido clorocrómico
chlorocosane
clorocosano
3-chlorocoumarin
3-clorocumarina
chlorocresol
clorocresol
p-chloro-m-cresol
p-cloro-m-cresol
chlorocyanohydrin
clorcianohidrina
chlorodecone
clordecona
α-chloro-N,N-diallyl-
acetamide
α-cloro-N,N-
dialilacetamida

59

1-chloro-2-dichloro-
arsinoethene
1-cloro-2-dicloro-
arsinoeteno
2-chloro-1-(2,4-
dichlorophenyl) vinyl
diethyl phosphate
dietilfosfato de 2-
cloro-1-(2,4-
diclorofenil)vinilo
chlorodifluoroacetic
acid
ácido clorodi-
fluoroacético
1,1,1-chlorodifluoro-
ethane
1,1,1-clorodifluoro-
etano
chlorodifluoro-
methane
clorodifluorometano
1-chloro-2,4-dini-
trobenzene
1-cloro-2,4-
dinitrobenceno
chlorodiphenyl
clorodifenilo
4-chlorodiphenyl
sulfone
sulfona clorodi-
fenílica, 4-clorodi-
fenilsulfona
1-chloro-2,3-epoxy-
propane
1-cloro-2,3-epoxi-
propano
2-chloroethanamide
2-cloretanamida
chloroethane
cloretano
chloroethane nitrile
cloretanonitrilo
chloroethanoic
anhydride
anhídrido cloretanoico
2-chloroethanol
2-cloretanol
chloroethene
cloreteno
chloroethyl acetate
acetato de cloretilo
chloroethyl alcohol
alcohol cloretílico
2-chloro-4-ethyl-
amino-s-triazine
2-cloro-4-etil-amino-
s-triacina, 2-cloro-
4-etil-amino-s-
triazina

ß-chloroethyl
chloroformate
cloroformiato de ß-
cloretilo
ß-chloroethyl
chlorosulfonate
clorosulfonato de ß-
cloretilo
2-chloroethyl methyl
sulfide
metilsulfuro de 2-
cloretilo
2-chloroethyl vinyl
ether
éter 2-cloretil vinílico,
2-cloretil vinil éter
N-(chloroethyl)
dibenzylamine
hydrochloride
clorhidrato de N-
(cloretil)dibencilamina
chloroethylene
cloretileno
2-chloroethyl-
phosphonic acid
ácido 2-cloretil-
fosfónico
2-chloroethyltri-
methylammonium
chloride
cloruro de 2-
cloretiltrimetilamonio
chlorofenethol
clorfenetol
chlorofenvinphos
clorfenvinfós
chloroform
cloroformo,
triclorometano
chloroformoxime
cloroformoxima
chloroformyl chloride
cloruro de clorformilo
chlorofluorocarbon
clorofluorcarbono
chlorogenic acid
ácido clorogénico
chlorogenin
clorogenina
chloroguanidine
hydrochloride
clorhidrato de
cloroguanidina
chlorohexane
clorohexano
chlorohydrin
clorhidrina
chlorohydrin rubber
caucho clorhidrínico

chlorohydroquinone
clorhidroquinona
chlorohydroxybenzene
clorhidroxibenceno
5-chloro-2-hydroxy-
benzophenone
5-cloro-2-hidroxi-
benzofenona
2-chloro-4-(hydroxy-
mercuri)phenol
2-cloro-4-(hidroxi-
mercuri)fenol
4-chloro-1-hydroxy- 3-
methylbenzene
4-cloro-1-hidroxi-3-
metilbenceno
6-chloro-3-hydroxy-
toluene
6-cloro-3-
hidroxitolueno
2-chloro-N-iso-
propylacetanilide
2-cloro-N-isopropil-
acetanilida
chloroisopropyl alcohol
alcohol
clorisopropílico
6-chloro-4-isopropyl-1-
methyl-3-phenol
6-cloro-4-isopropil-1-
metil-3-fenol
chloromadinone
acetate
acetato de
cloromadinona
chloromaleic
anhydride
anhídrido
cloromaleico
chloromercuri-
ferrocene
cloromercuriferroceno
1[3-(chloromercuri)-2-
methoxypropyl] urea
1[3-(cloromercuri)-2-
metoxipropil]urea
o-chloromercuri-
phenol
o-cloromercurifenol
chloromethane
clorometano
chloromethapyrilene
citrate
citrato de
clorometapirileno
chloromethyl
cyanide
cianuro de
clorometilo

chloromethyl methyl
ether
éter clorometil metílico
3-chloro-2-
methylaniline
3-cloro-2-metilanilina
chloromethylated
diphenyl oxide
óxido clorometilado de
difenilo
chloromethylbenzene
clorometilbenceno
1-chloro-3-methyl-
butane
1-cloro-3-metilbutano
chloromethyl-
chloroformate
cloroformiato de
clorometilo
chloromethyl-
chlorosulfonate
clorosulfonato de
clorometilo
1-chloromethylethyl-
benzene
1-clorometiletil-
benceno
1-chloromethyl-
naphthalene
1-clorometilnaftaleno
4-chloro-3-
methylphenol
4-cloro-3-
metilfenol
4-chloro-2-methyl-
phenoxyacetic acid
ácido 4-cloro-2-
metilfenoxiacético
chloromethyl-
phosphonic acid
ácido clorometil-
fosfónico
chloromethyl-
phosphonic dichloride
dicloruro
clorometilfosfónico
1-chloro-2-methyl-
propene
1-cloro-2-metilpropeno
3-chloro-2-methyl-1-
propene
3-cloro-2-metil-1-
propeno
chloronaphthalene
cloronaftaleno
α-chloro-m-nitro-
acetophenone
α-cloro-m-
nitroacetofenona

2-chloro-4-nitro-
aniline
2-cloro-4-
nitroanilina
m-chloronitrobenzene
m-cloronitrobenceno
2-chloro-5-nitro-
benzenesulfonamide
sulfonamida 2-cloro-5-
nitrobencénica, 2-
cloro-5-nitrobencen-
sulfonamida
6-chloro-3-nitro-
benzenesulfonic acid,
sodium salt
sal sódica del ácido
6-cloro-3-nitro-
bencensulfónico
4-chloro-3-
nitrobenzoic acid
ácido 4-cloro-3-
nitrobenzoico
4-chloro-3-nitro-
benzotrifluoride
trifluoruro de 4-cloro-
3-nitrobenzoico, 4-
cloro-3-nitrobenzotri-
fluoruro
p-chloro-m-nitro-
fluorotoluene
p-cloro-m-
nitrofluorotolueno
4-chloro-2-nitro-
phenol, sodium salt
sal sódica de 4-cloro-2-
nitrofenol
1-chloro-1-nitro-
propane
1-cloro-1-
nitropropano
2-chloro-6-nitro-
toluene
2-cloro-6-nitrotolueno
chloronitrous acid
ácido cloronitroso
chloropentafluoro-
acetone
acetona cloropenta-
fluorada, cloropenta-
fluoroacetona
chloropentafluoro-
ethane
etano cloropenta-
fluorado, cloro-
pentafluoretano
1-chloropentane
1-cloropentano
chlorophacinone
clorofacinona

p-chlorophenacyl
bromide
bromuro de p-
clorofenacilo
chlorophene
clorofeno
chlorophenol
clorofenol
m-chlorophenol
m-clorofenol
p-chlorophenyl
benzenesulfonate
bencensulfonato de
p-clorofenilo
m-chlorophenyl
isocyanate
isocianato de m-
clorofenilo
p-chlorophenyl
phenylsulfone
p-clorofenilfenil-
sulfona
p-chlorophenyl-p-
chlorobenzene-
sulfonate
p-clorobencen-
sulfonato de p-
clorofenilo
4-chloro-α-phenyl-o-
cresol
4-cloro-α-fenil-o-cresol
3-p-chlorophenyl-1,1-
dimethylurea
3-p-clorofenil-1,1-
dimetilurea
3-(p-chlorophenyl)-5-
methylrhodamine
3-(p-clorofenil)-5-
metilrodamina
chloro-o-phenyl-
phenol
cloro-o-fenilfenol
chlorophenyltri-
chlorosilane
clorofeniltricloro-
silano
chlorophosphine
clorofosfina
4-chlorophthalic acid
ácido 4-cloroftálico
chlorophyll
clorofila
chlorophyllin
clorofilina
chloropicrin
cloropicrina,
tricloronitrometano
chloroplatinic acid
ácido cloroplatínico

chloroprednisone
cloroprednisona
ß-chloroprene
ß-cloropreno
chloroprocaine
cloroprocaína
chloroprocaine
hydrochloride
clorhidrato de
cloroprocaína
1-chloropropane
1-cloropropano
3-chloropropane-1,2-
diol
3-cloropropano-1,2-
diol
1-chloro-2-propanol
1-cloro-2-propanol
1-chloro-2-propanone
1-cloro-2-propanona
1- or 3-chloropropene
1- ó 3-cloropropeno
2-chloropropionic acid
ácido 2-cloro-
propiónico
3-chloropropionitrile
3-cloropropionitrilo
chloropropylene oxide
óxido de
cloropropileno
3-chloropropyl
mercaptan
mercaptano 3-
cloropropílico, 3-
cloropropilmercaptano
3-chloro-1-propyne
3-cloro-1-propino
6-chloropurine
6-cloropurina
chloropyramine
cloropiramina
2-chloropyridine
2-cloropiridina
chloropyrilene
cloropirileno
6-chloroquinaldine
6-cloroquinaldina
chloroquine
cloroquina
chloroquine hydro-
chloride
clorhidrato de
cloroquina
chloroquine phosphate
fosfato de cloroquina
5-chlorosalicylanilide
5-clorsalicilanilida
5-chlorosalicylic acid
ácido 5-clorosalicílico

chloroselenic acid
ácido cloroselénico
chloroserpidine
cloroserpidina
chlorosilan
clorosilano
o-chlorostyrene
o-clorestireno
N-chlorosuccinimide
N-clorosuccinimida
chlorosulfonic acid
ácido clorosulfónico
4-chlorosulfonyl-
benzoic acid
ácido 4-cloro-
sulfonilbenzoico
chlorosulfuric acid
ácido clorosulfúrico
chloroten
cloroteno
chlorotetracyclina
clortetraciclina
chlorotetrafluoro-
ethane
clortetrafluoretano
chlorothalonil
clortalonilo
chlorothen
cloroteno
chlorothen citrate
citrato de cloroteno
chlorothiazide
clorotiazida
chlorothricin
clorotricina
p-chlorothiophenol
p-clorotiofenol
chlorothymol
clorotimol
α-chlorotoluene
α-clorotolueno
2-chlorotoluene-4-
sulfonic acid
ácido 2-clorotolueno-
4-sulfónico
4-chloro-o-toluidine
hydrochloride
clorhidrato de 4-cloro-
o-toluidina
2-chloro-p-toluidine
2-cloro-p-toluidina
2-chloro-5-toluidine-4-
sulfonic acid
ácido 2-cloro-5-
toluidina-4-
sulfónico
chlorotrianisene
clortrianiseno, tri-p-
anisilcloroetileno

chlorotriazinyl dye
colorante
clortriacinílico
chlorotrifluoro-
ethylene
clortrifluoretileno
chlorotrifluoro-
ethylene polymer
polímero de
clortrifluoretileno
chlorotrifluoro-
methane
clortrifluorometano
2-chloro-5-trifluoro-
methylaniline
2-cloro-5-trifluoro-
metilanilina
chlorotrifluoro-
methylbenzene
clortrifluorometil-
benceno
chloro-α,α,α-
trifluorotoluene
cloro-α,α,α-
trifluorotolueno
chlorotris(p-
methoxyphenyl)-
ethylene
clorotris(p-metoxi-
fenil)etileno
chlorotris(triphenyl-
phosphine) rhodium
clorotris (trifenil-
fosfina) rodio
ß-chlorovinyl
ethyl ethynyl
carbinol
ß-clorovinil etil etinil
carbinol
ß-chlorovinyldi-
chloroarsine
ß-clorovinildi-
clorarsina
ß-chlorovinylmethyl-
chloroarsine
ß-clorovinilmetil-
clorarsina
chloroxine
cloroxina
chloroxuron
cloroxurón
chloroxylenol
cloroxilenol
p-chloro-m-xylenol
p-cloro-m-xilenol
6-chloro-3,4,-xylyl-
methylcarbamate
metilcarbamato de 6-
cloro-3,4-xililo

chlorozotozin
clorozotocina
chlorphenamine
clorfenamina
chlorphenesin
clorfenesina
chlorphenesin
carbamate
carbamato de
clorfenesina
chlorpheniramine
clorfeniramina
chlorpheniramine
maleate
maleato de
clorfeniramina
chlorpheniramine
tannate
tanato de
clorfeniramina
chlorphenoctium
amsonate
ansonato de
clorfenoctio
chlorphenol red
rojo de clorofenol
chlorphenoxamide
clorfenoxamida
chlorphenoxamine
clorfenoxamina
chlorphentermine
clorfentermina
chlorphentermine
hydrochloride
clorhidrato de
clorfentermina
chlorphenvisphos
clorfenvisfós
chlorproethazine
clorproetacina,
clorproetazina
chlorproguanil
clorproguanilo
chlorpromazine
clorpromacina,
clorpromazina
chlorpromazine
hydrochloride
clorhidrato de
clorpromazina
chlorpropamide
clorpropamida
chlorprophan
cloroprofano
chlorprophen-
pyridamine
maleate
maleato de clor-
profenpiridamina

chlorprothixene
clorprotixeno
chlorpyrifos
clorpirifós
chlorquinaldol
clorquinaldol
chlortetracycline
clortetraciclina
chlorthalidone
clortalidona
chlorthenoxazin(e)
clortenoxacina,
clortenoxazina
chlorthion
clorotión
chlorzoxazone
clorzoxazona
choice
selección
cholaic acid
ácido colaico
cholane
colano
cholanic acid
ácido colánico
cholanthrene
colantreno
cholecalciferol
colecalciferol,
vitamina D_3
cholecystokinin
colecistoquinina,
pancreocimina
choleic acid
ácido coleico
cholestane
colestano
cholestanol
colestanol
cholesteric
colestérico
cholesterol
colesterol
cholestyramine
colestiramina
cholestyramine
resin
resina de
colestiramina
cholic acid
ácido cólico
choline
colina
choline bicarbonate
bicarbonato de colina
choline bitartrate
bitartrato de colina
choline chloride
cloruro de colina

choline dehydro-
cholate
dehidrocolato de colina
choline dihydrogen
citrate
citrato biácido de
colina
choline esterase
colinesterasa
choline esterase
inhibitor
inhibidor de la
colinesterasa
choline gluconate
gluconato de colina
choline salicylate
salicilato de colina
choline theophyllinate
teofilinato de colina
cholytaurine
colitaurina
chondrillasterol
condrilasterol
chondrocurine
condrocurina
chondrofiline
condrofilina
chondroitin sulfate
sulfato de condroitina
chondrosine
condrosina
chonemorphine
conemorfina
chorionic gonadotropin
gonadotropina
coriónica
chorismic acid
ácido corísmico
chromate
cromato
chromated zinc
chloride
cloruro de cinc
cromado
chromatic
cromático
chromatin
cromatina
chromatogram
cromatograma
chromatographic
cromatográfico
chromatografic
analysis
análisis cromatográfico
chromatography
cromatografía
chrome
cromo

chrome alum
alumbre crómico
chrome ammonium
alum
alumbre de cromo y
amonio
chrome dye
colorante de cromo,
colorante cromado
chrome green
verde de cromo, verde
cromado
chrome molybdenum
steel
acero al cromo
molibdeno
chrome nickel steel
acero al cromo níquel
chrome orange
anaranjado de cromo
chrome oxide green
óxido verde de cromo
chrome pigment
pigmento de cromo
chrome potash alum
alumbre de cromo y
potasa
chrome red
rojo de cromo
chrome steel
acero al cromo
chrome tanning
curtido al cromo
chrome vanadium
steels
aceros al cromo
vanadio
chrome yellow
amarillo de cromo
chromia
cromia, óxido de
cromo, cinabrio verde
chromia-alumina gel
gel de óxido de cromo
y aluminio
chromic acetate
acetato crómico
chromic acid
ácido crómico
chromic anhydride
anhídrido crómico
chromic bromide
bromuro crómico
chromic chloride
cloruro crómico
chromic fluoride
fluoruro crómico
chromic formate
formiato crómico

chromic hydroxide
hidróxido crómico
chromic nitrate
nitrato crómico
chromic oxide
óxido crómico
chromic phospate
fosfato crómico
chromic potassiun
oxalate
oxalato crómico de
potasio
chromic potassium
sulfate
sulfato crómico de
potasio
chromic sulfate
sulfato crómico
chromite
cromita
chromium
cromo
chromium acetate
acetato de cromo
chromium
acetylacetonate
acetilacetonato de
cromo
chromium ammonium
sulfate
sulfato de cromio y
amonio
chromium boride
boruro de cromo
chromium bromide
bromuro de cromo
chromium carbide
carburo de cromo
chromium carbonate
carbonato de cromo
chromium carbonyl
carbonilcromo
chromium chlorate
clorato de cromo
chromium chloride
cloruro de cromo
chromium copper
cromo cobre
chromium dioxide
dióxido de cromo
chromium fluoride
fluoruro de cromo
chromium
hexacarbonyl
hexacarbonilcromo
chromium hydrate
hidrato de cromo
chromium hydroxide
hidróxido de cromo

chromium oxide
óxido de cromo
chromium manganese
antimonide
antimoniuro de cromo
y manganeso
chromium naphthenate
naftenato de cromo
chromium nitrate
nitrato de cromo
chromium oxide
óxido de cromo
chromium oxychloride
cloruro básico de
cromo
chromium oxyfluoride
fluoruro básico de
cromo
chromium phosphate
fosfato de cromo
chromium potassium
sulfate
sulfato de cromo y
potasio
chromium
sesquichloride
sesquicloruro de cromo
chromium sesquioxide
sesquióxido de cromo
chromium steel
acero al cromo
chromium sulfate
sulfato de cromo
chromium trichlorate
triclorato de cromo
chromium trifluoride
trifluoruro de
cromo
chromium
tetrafluoride
tetrafluoruro de cromo
chromium trioxide
trióxido de cromo
chromocarb
cromocarbo
chromogen
cromógeno
chromomycins
cromomicinas
chromonar
cromonar,
carbocromeno
chromophore
cromóforo,
cromatóforo
chromotrope 2B
cromótropo 2B
chromotropic acid
ácido cromotrópico

chromosome
cromosoma
chromous acetate
acetato cromoso
chromous bromide
bromuro cromoso
chromous
carbonate
carbonato cromoso
chromous chloride
cloruro cromoso
chromous fluoride
fluoruro cromoso
chromous formate
formiato cromoso
chromous oxalate
oxalato cromoso
chromous sulfate
sulfato cromoso
chromyl chloride
cloruro de cromilo
chromyl fluoride
fluoruro de
cromilo
chronometer
cronómetro
chrysamine G
crisamina G
chrysamminic acid
ácido crisamínico
chrysanthemaxanthin
crisantemaxantina
chrysantemic acid
ácido crisantémico
chrysanthemummono-
carboxylic acid, ethyl
ester
éster etílico del ácido
crisantemo-
monocarboxílico
chrysanthenone
crisantenona
chrysarobin
crisarrobina
chrysazin
crisacina
6-chrysenamine
6-crisenamina
chrysene
criseno
chrysergonic acid
ácido
crisergónico
chrysin
crisina
chrysocolla
crisocola
chrysoidine
crisoidina

chrysoidine
hydrochloride
clorhidrato de
crisoidina
chrysolite
crisolita
chrysophanic acid
ácido crisofánico
chrysotile
crisótilo
Chugaev reaction
reacción de
Chugaev
churn, to
batir
chymopapain
quimopapaína
chymosin
quimosina
chymotrypsin
quimotripsina
chymotrypsinogen
quimotripsinógeno
ciadox
ciadox
ciafos
ciafós
Ciamician-Dennstedt
rearrangement
transposición de
Ciamician y Dennstedt
cianergoline
cianergolina
cianidanol
cianidanol
cianogen
cianógeno
cianopramine
cianopramina
ciaphos
ciafós
ciapilome
ciapiloma
cibenzoline
cibenzolina
cicarperone
cicarperona
cichoriin
cicoriína
ciclacillin
ciclacilina
ciclactate
ciclactato
ciclafrine
ciclafrina
ciclafrine
hydrochloride
clorhidrato de
ciclafrina

ciclazindol
ciclacindol
cicletanine
cicletanina
ciclindole
ciclindol
cicliomenol
cicliomenol
ciclobendazole
ciclobendazol
ciclofenazine
ciclofenacina,
ciclofenazina
ciclofoxacin
hydrochloride
clorhidrato de
ciclofoxacina
cicloheximide
cicloheximida
ciclonicate
ciclonicato
ciclonium bromide
bromuro de ciclonio
ciclopirox
ciclopirox
ciclopramine
ciclopramina
cicloprofen
cicloprofeno
ciclosidomine
ciclosidomina
ciclosporin
ciclosporina
ciclotate
ciclotato
ciclotizolam
ciclotizolán,
ciclotizolam
cicloxilic acid
ácido cicloxílico
cicloxolone
cicloxolona
cicortonide
cicortónido
cicrotoic acid
ácido cicrotoico
cicutoxin
cicutoxina
cideferron
cideferrón
cidofovir
cidofovir
cidoxepin
cidoxepina
cifenline
cifenlina
cigarette tar
alquitrán de
cigarrillos

ciguatoxin
ciguatoxina
ciheptolane
ciheptolano
cilastatin
cilastatina
cilobamine
cilobamina
cilostamide
cilostamida
cilostazol
cilostazol
ciltoprazine
ciltopracina,
ciltoprazina
cimaterol
cimaterol
cimemoxin
cimemoxina
cimepanol
cimepanol
cimetidine
cimetidina
cimetropium bromide
bromuro de cimetropio
cimicifuga
cimicífuga
cimigenol
cimigenol
cimoxatone
cimoxatona
cinametic acid
ácido cinamético
cinamiodyl
cinamiodilo
cinamolol
cinamolol
cinanserin
cinanserina
cinchocaine
cincocaína
cincholepidine
cincolepidina
cinchomeronic acid
ácido cincomerónico
cinchona
quina, quinquina,
cincona, cascarillo
cinchona bark
quina, quinquina,
cincona
cinchonamine
cinconamina
cinchonidine
cinconidina
cinchonin(e)
cinconina
cinchophen
cincofeno

cinchotoxine
cincotoxina
cinders
carboncillos, cenizas
cinecromen
cinecrómeno
cinene
cineno, cayeputeno
cineol
cineol, eucaliptol
cinepazet
cinepaceto
cinepazet maleate
maleato de cinepaceto
cinepazic acid
ácido cinepácico
cinepazide
cinepazida
cinerins
cinerinas
cinfenine
cinfenina
cinfenoac
cinfenoaco
cingestol
cingestol
cinitapride
cinitaprida
cinmetacin
cinmetacina
cinnabar
cinabrio
cinnabarine
cinabarina
cinnamaldehyde
cinamaldehído
cinnamate
cinamato
cinnamaverine
cinamaverina
cinnamedrine
cinamedrina
cinnamein
cinameína
cinnamene
cinameno
cinnamic
cinámico, de
canela
cinnamic acid
ácido cinámico
cinnamic alcohol
alcohol cinámico
cinnamic aldehyde
aldehído cinámico
cinnamic ether
éter cinámico
cinnamon
canela

cinnamon, Ceylon
canela de Ceilán
cinnamon, Saigon
canela de Saigón
cinnamon oil
esencia (aceite) de
canela
cinnamon oil, Ceylon
esencia (aceite) de
canela de Ceilán
cinnamoyl chloride
cloruro de cinamoílo
cinnamoylcocaine
cinamoilcocaína
cinnamyl acetate
acetato de cinamilo
cinnamyl alcohol
alcohol cinamílico
cinnamyl aldehyde
aldehído cinamílico,
cinamaldehído
cinnamyl
anthranilate
antranilato de cinamilo
cinnamyl
cinnamate
cinamato de cinamilo
cinnamylic acid
ácido cinamílico
cinnarizine
cinaricina, cinarizina,
cinipirina
cinnofuradione
cinofuradiona
cinnoline
cinolina
cinnopentazone
cinopentazona
cinobufotalin
cinobufotalina
cinoctramide
cinoctramida
cinolazepam
cinolacepán,
cinolazepam
cinoquidox
cinoquidox
cinoxacin
cinoxacina
cinoxate
cinoxato
cinoxolone
cinoxolona
cinperene
cimpereno
cinprazole
cimprazol
cinpropazide
cimpropazida

cinromide
cinromida
cintramide
cintramida
cipionate
cipionato
ciprafamide
ciprafamida
ciprefadol
ciprefadol
ciprocinonide
ciprocinonida
ciprofibrate
ciprofibrato
ciprofloxacin
ciprofloxacina
ciprofloxacin
hydrochloride
clorhidrato de
ciprofloxacina
cipropride
ciproprida
ciproquazone
ciprocuazona
ciproquinate
ciproquinato
ciproximide
ciproximida
ciramadol
ciramadol
cirazoline
cirazolina
circle
círculo
circuit
circuito
circulating reflux
reflujo circulante
circulation of air
circulación de aire
circulins
circulinas
circumference
circunferencia
circumscribe
circunscribir
cirolemycin
cirolemicina
cis
cis
cis isomer
isómero cis
cisapride
cisaprida
cisatracurium besylate
besilato de cisatracurio
cis-13-docosenoic acid
ácido cis-13-
docosenoico

cis-9-hexadecenoic acid
ácido cis-9-
hexadecenoico
cis-12-hydroxy-
octadec-9-enoic acid
ácido cis-12-
hidroxioctadec-9-
enoico
cismadinone
cismadinona
cisplatin
cisplatino
cis-platinum II
cis-platino II,
cisplatino
cis-N-[(1,1,2,2-tetra-
chloroethyl)thio]-4-
cyclohexene-1,2-
dicarboximide
cis-N-[(1,1,2,2-tetra-
cloroetil)tío]-4-
ciclohexeno-1,2-
dicarboximida
cis-tetradec-9-enoic
acid
ácido cis-tetradec-9-
enoico
citalopram
citaloprán, citalopram
citenamide
citenamida
citenazone
citenazona
citicoline
citicolina
citiolone
citiolona
citraconic acid
ácido citracónico
citraconic anhydride
anhídrido citracónico
citral
citral
citramalic acid
ácido citramálico
citrate
citrato
ß-citraurin
ß-citraurina
citrazinic acid
ácido citracínico
citric acid
ácido cítrico
citric acid cycle
ciclo del ácido cítrico
citrinin
citrinina
citromycetin
citromicetina

citron yellow
amarillo limón
citronella
citronela
citronella oil
esencia (aceite) de
citronela
citronellal
citronelal
citronellal hydrate
hidrato de citronelal
citronellol
citronelol
ß-citronellol
ß-citronelol, citrolenol
citronellyl acetate
acetato de citronelilo
citronellyl butyrate
butirato de citronelilo
citronellyl formate
formiato de citronelilo
citronine
citronina
citrovorum factor
factor citrovorum,
ácido folínico
citrulline
citrulina
citrullol
citrulol
citrus red 2
rojo 2 cítrico
civet
civeto
civetone
civetona
civettal
civetal
cladribine
cladribina
claim
afirmación, declaración,
reivindicación
Claisen condensation
condensación de
Claisen
Claisen flask
matraz de Claisen
Claisen rearrangement
transposición de
Claisen
Claise-Schmidt
condensation
condensación de
Claisen Schmidt
Clapeyron equation
ecuación de Clapeyron
clamidoxic acid
ácido clamidóxico

clamoxyquine
clamoxiquina
clamp
pinza, abrazadera,
tornillo de banco
clamp, to
sujetar, pinzar
clanobutin
clanobutina
clantifen
clantifeno
clarification
aclaración,
clarificación
clarification bed
lecho de clarificación
clarify, to
aclarar, clarificar
clarithromycin
claritromicina
Clark-Lubs indicators
indicadores de Clark
Lubs
clary sage oil
esencia (aceite) de
salvia de amara
class
clase
classification
clasificación
clathrates
clatráticos
Claude system
sistema de Claude
clavulanate potassium
clavulanato potásico
clavulanic acid
ácido clavulánico
clay
arcilla
clay coated paper
papel estucado con
arcilla
clay filter
filtro de arcilla
clazolam
clazolán, clazolam
clazolimine
clazolimina
clean, to
limpiar, purificar
clear
transparente
clearance
depuración
cleared
depurado
cleavage
escición, segmentación,

ruptura, separación,
hendidura
cleave
segmentar, escindir,
partir
clebopride
clebóprido
clefamide
clefamida
cleft
hendidura, muesca,
fisura
Cleland's reagent
reactivo de Cleland
clemastine
clemastina
clemeprol
clemeprol
clemizole
clemizol
clemizole penicillin
penicilina clemizólica,
clemisol penicilina
Clemmensen reaction
reacción de
Clemmensen
clenbuterol
clembuterol
clenpirin
clempirina
cletoquine
cletoquina
Cleveland open cup
copa abierta de
Cleveland
Cleve's acid
ácido de Cleve
clibucaine
clibucaína
clidanac
clidanaco
clidinium bromide
bromuro de clidinio
climbazole
climbazol
climiqualine
climicualina
clindamycin
clindamicina
**clindamycin
hydrochloride**
clorhidrato de
clindamicina
clindamycin phosphate
fosfato de clindamicina
cling, to
adherirse
clinical chemistry
química clínica

clinofibrate
clinofibrato
clinolamide
clinolamida
clioquinol
clioquinol
clioxanide
clioxanida
clip, to
cortar, sujetar
clobazam
clobazán, clobazam
clobenfurol
clobenfurol
clobenoside
clobenósido
clobenzepam
clobencepán,
clobenzepam
clobenzorex
clobenzorex
clobenztropine
clobenzotropina
**clobenztropine
hydrocloride**
clorhidrato de
clobenzotropina
**clobenztropine
hydrobromide**
bromhidrato de
clobenzotropina
**clobenztropine
methobromide**
metobromuro de
clobenzotropina
clobetasol
clobetasol
clobetasol propionate
propionato de
clobetasol
clobetasone
clobetasona
clobutinol
clobutinol
clobuzarit
clobuzarit
clocanfamide
clocanfamida
clocapramine
clocapramina
clociguanil
clociguanil
clocinizine
clocinicina, clocinizina
clock wise
en sentido horario,
hacia la derecha, en
sentido de las
manecillas del reloj

cloconazole
cloconazol
clocortolone
clocortolona
clocortolone pivalate
pivalato de
clocortolona
clodacaine
clodacaína
clodanolene
clodanoleno
clodantoin
clodantoína
clodazon
clodazona
clodoxopone
clodoxopona
clodronic acid
ácido clodrónico
clofazimine
clofacimina
clofedanol
clofedanol
clofenamic acid
ácido clofenámico
clofenamide
clofenamida
clofenciclan
clofenciclano
clofenetamine
clofenetamina
clofenotane
clofenotano
clofenoxyde
clofenoxida
clofentezine
clofentecina
clofenvinfos
clofenvinfós
clofeverine
clofeverina
clofexamide
clofexamida
clofezone
clofezona
clofibrate
clofibrato
clofibric acid
ácido clofíbrico
clofibride
clofibrida
clofilium phosphate
fosfato de clofilio
clofluperol
clofluperol
clofoctol
clofoctol
cloforex
cloforex

clofucarban
clofucarbano
clofurac
clofuraco
clog, to
obturar, tapar
clogestone
clogestona
cloguanamil
cloguanamil
clomacran
clomacrano
clomegestone
clomegestona
clomestrone
clomestrona
clometacin
clometacina
clometerone
clometerona
clomethiazole
clometiazol
clometocillin
clometocilina
clomifene, clomiphene
clomifeno
clominorex
clominorex
clomiphene citrate
citrato de clomifeno
clomipramine
clomipramina
clomocycline
clomociclina
clonazepam
clonacepán,
clonazepam
clonazoline
clonazolina
clonidine
clonidina
clonidine
hydrochloride
clorhidrato de
clonidina
clonitazene
clonitaceno
clonitrate
clonitrato
clonixeril
clonixeril
clopamide
clopamida
clopenthixol
clopentixol
cloperastine
cloperastina
cloperidone
cloperidona

clopidogrel
bisulfate
bisulfato de
clopidrogrel
clopidol
clopidol
clopimozide
clopimozida
clopipazan
clopipazán
clopirac
clopiraco
cloponone
cloponona
cloprednol
cloprednol
cloprostenol
cloprostenol
cloprothiazole
cloprotiazol
clopyralid
clopirálido
cloquinate
cloquinato
cloquinozine
cloquinocina,
cloquinozina
cloracetadol
cloracetadol
cloral betaine
cloral betaína
cloranolol
cloranolol
clorazepate
cloracepato
cloretate
cloretato
clorexolone
clorexolona
cloridanol
cloridanol
clorindanic acid
ácido clorindánico
clorindanol
clorindanol
clorindione
clorindiona
clormecaine
clormecaína
clorofene, clorophene
clorofeno
cloroperone
cloroperona
cloroqualone
clorocualona
clorotepine
clorotepina
clorprenaline
clorprenalina

clorsulon
clorsulón
clortermine
clortermina
closantel
closantel
close, to
cerrar, concluir
closed chain
hydrocarbon
hidrocarburo de
cadena cerrada
closed circuit
circuito cerrado
closilate
closilato
closiramine
closiramina
clospirazine
clospiracina,
clospirazina
closure
cierre, tapa, tapón, fin
clostebol
clostebol
clot
coágulo, grumo
clothiapine
clotiapina
clotiapine
clotiapina
clotiazepam
clotiacepán, clotiazepam
clotioxone
clotioxona
clotrimazole
clotrimazol
cloud chamber
cámara de ionización,
cámara de niebla
cloud point
temperatura de
enturbiamiento,
temperatura de
opacidad
cloud seeding
siembra artificial de
nubes
cloud test
prueba de opacidad
cloudy
turbio, opaco, nebuloso
clove
clavo de olor
clove oil
esencia (aceite) de
clavo de olor, esencia
(aceite) de clavo
aromático

clovoxamine
clovoxamina
cloxacepride
cloxaceprida
cloxacillin
cloxacilina
cloxazolam
cloxazolán, cloxazolam
cloxestradiol
cloxestradiol
cloximate
cloximato
cloxotestosterone
cloxotestosterona
cloxypendyl
cloxipendilo
cloxyquin(e)
cloxiquina
clozapine
clozapina
clupanodonic acid
ácido
clupanodónico
clupeine
clupeína
cluster
agrupación, racimo
CM-cellulose
CM-celulosa (celulosa
carboximetílica)
coacervation
coacervación
coagel
precipitado
gelatinoso
coagulant
coagulante
coagulate, to
coagular
coagulation
coagulación
Coahran process
proceso Coahran
coal
carbón, hulla
coal char
escorias de hulla
coal gas
gas de hulla
coal gasification
gasificación del carbón
coal hydrogenation
hidrogenación del
carbón
coalites
coalitas
coal oil
petróleo, aceite de
hulla

coal tar
alquitrán de hulla,
alquitrán mineral
coal tar creosote
creosota de alquitrán
de hulla
coal tar distillate
destilado de alquitrán
de hulla
coal tar dye
colorante de alquitrán
coal tar ligth oil
aceite ligero de
alquitrán de hulla .
coal tar naphtha
benzol, nafta de
alquitrán de hulla
coal tar oil
aceite de alquitrán de
hulla
coal tar pitch
brea de alquitrán de
hulla, pez de alquitrán
de hulla
coal tar resin
resina de alquitrán de
hulla
coalesce, to
unirse, fundirse
coalescense
coalescencia
coarse
grueso
coat, to
revestir
coating
revestido,
revestimiento
coaxial
coaxial
cobalamin
cobalamina
cobalt
cobalto
cobalt acetate
acetato de cobalto
cobalt ammonium
sulfate
sulfato de cobalto y
amonio
cobalt arsenate
arseniato de cobalto
cobalt black
óxido de cobalto, negro
de cobalto
cobalt bloom
eritrita, flores de
cobalto, arseniato de
cobalto hidratado

cobalt blue
azul de cobalto
cobalt bromide
bromuro de cobalto
cobalt bromide test
prueba de bromuro de
cobalto
cobalt carbonate
carbonato de cobalto
cobalt carbonyl
cobalto carbonílico
cobalt chloride
cloruro de cobalto
cobalt chromate
cromato de cobalto
cobalt chromate,
basic
cromato básico de
cobalto
cobalt difluoride
difluoruro de cobalto
cobalt hydrate
hidrato de cobalto
cobalt hydroxide
hidróxido de cobalto
cobalt iodide
yoduro de cobalto
cobalt linoleate
linoleato de cobalto
cobalt molybdate
molibdato de cobalto
cobalt monoxide
monóxido de
cobalto
cobalt naphthenate
naftenato de cobalto
cobalt neodecanoate
neodecanoato de
cobalto
cobalt nitrate
nitrato de cobalto
cobalt octoate
octoato de cobalto
cobalt oleate
oleato de cobalto
cobalt oxide
óxido de cobalto
cobalt peroxide
peróxido de cobalto
cobalt phosphate
fosfato de cobalto
cobalt potassium
cyanide
cianuro de cobalto y
potasio
cobalt potassium
nitrate
nitrato de cobalto y
potasio

cobalt potassium nitrite
nitrito de cobalto y
potasio
cobalt powder
polvo de cobalto,
cobalto en polvo
cobalt resinate
resinato de cobalto
cobalt selenite
selenito de cobalto
cobalt silicide
siliciuro de cobalto
cobalt soap
jabón de cobalto
cobalt sodium nitrite
nitruro de cobalto y
sodio
cobalt stearate
estearato de cobalto
cobalt sulfate
sulfato de cobalto
cobalt tallate
talato (resinato) de
cobalto
cobalt tetracarbonyl
cobalto
tetracarbonílico
cobalt titanate
titanato de cobalto
cobalt trifluoride
trifluoruro de
cobalto
cobalt tungstate
tungstato de cobalto
cobalt ultramarine
azul de cobalto
cobalt yellow
amarillo de cobalto, sal
de Fischer
cobalt violet
violeta de cobalto
cobalt wolframate
wolframato de cobalto
cobaltammine
cobaltamina
cobalt-2-ethylhexoate
2-etilhexoato de
cobalto
cobalt-gold alloy
aleación de cobalto y
oro
cobaltic acetate
acetato cobáltico
cobaltic
acetylacetonate
acetilacetonato
cobáltico
cobaltic boride
boruro cobáltico

cobaltic fluoride
fluoruro cobáltico
cobaltic hydroxide
hidróxido cobáltico
cobaltic oxide
óxido cobáltico
cobaltic oxide
monohydrate
óxido cobáltico
monohidratado
cobaltic potassium
nitrite
nitrito cobáltico de
potasio
cobaltic-cobaltous
oxide
óxido cobáltico
cobaltoso
cobaltine
cobaltina
cobaltocene
cobaltoceno
cobalto-cobaltic oxide
óxido cobáltico de
cobalto
cobaltous acetate
acetato cobaltoso
cobaltous aluminate
aluminato cobaltoso
cobaltous ammonium
phosphate
fosfato cobaltoso de
amonio
cobaltous ammonium
sulfate
sulfato cobaltoso de
amonio
cobaltous arsenate
arseniato cobaltoso
cobaltous bromide
bromuro cobaltoso
cobaltous carbonate
carbonato cobaltoso
cobaltous carbonate,
basic
carbonato cobaltoso
básico
cobaltous chloride
cloruro cobaltoso
cobaltous chromate
cromato cobaltoso
cobaltous citrate
citrato cobaltoso
cobaltous cyanide
cianuro cobaltoso
cobaltous ferrite
ferrita cobaltosa
cobaltous fluoride
fluoruro cobaltoso

cobaltous formate
formiato cobaltoso
cobaltous hydroxide
hidróxido cobaltoso
cobaltous iodide
yoduro cobaltoso
cobaltous linoleate
linoleato cobaltoso
cobaltous naphthenate
naftenato cobaltoso
cobaltous nitrate
nitrato cobaltoso
cobaltous nitrite
nitrito cobaltoso
cobaltous oleate
oleato cobaltoso
cobaltous oxalate
oxalato cobaltoso
cobaltous oxide
óxido cobaltoso
cobaltous perchlorate
perclorato cobaltoso
cobaltous phosphate
fosfato cobaltoso
cobaltous potassium
sulfate
sulfato cobaltoso de
potasio
cobaltous resinate
resinato cobaltoso
cobaltous silicofluoride
silicofluoruro
cobaltoso
cobaltous succinate
succinato cobaltoso
cobaltous sulfate
sulfato cobaltoso
cobaltous sulfide
sulfuro cobaltoso
cobaltous tungstate
tungstato cobaltoso
cobaltous thiocyanate
tiocianato cobaltoso
cobamamide
cobamamida
cobrotoxin
cobrotoxina
coca
coca
cocaethylene
cocaetileno
cocaine
cocaína
cocaine hydrochloride
clorhidrato de cocaína
cocarboxylase
cocarboxilasa
coccus
coco

cocculin
coculina
cocculus
cóculo, coca de
Levante
cocculus, solid
cóculo sólido, coca de
Levante sólida
cochineal
cochinilla, carmín
cocillana
cocillana
cock
grifo, llave de paso
coclaurine
coclaurina
cocoa
cacao
cocoa butter
manteca de cacao
cocoa oil
aceite de cacao
coconut acid
ácido de coco
coconut cake
bizcocho de coco
coconut carbon
carbón de coco
coconut oil
aceite de coco
coconut oil meal
harina de aceite de
coco
cocoyl sarcosine
cocoilsarcosina
codactide
codactida
codamine
codamina
codehydrogenase I
codehidrogenasa I
codeine
codeína
codeine phosphate
fosfato de codeina
codeine
hydrochloride
clorhidrato de
codeína
codeine methyl
bromide
metilbromuro de
codeína
codeine N-oxide
N-óxido de codeína
codeine phosphate
fosfato de codeína
codeine sulfate
sulfato de codeína

cod liver oil
aceite de hígado de
bacalao
codoxime
codoxima
coefficient
coeficiente
coelute
coeluir junto con,
coeluido
coenzyme
coenzima
coercitive
coercitivo, por la
fuerza
coffee oil
aceite de granos de
café
coffearine
cafearina, trigonelina
cofisatin
cofisatina
cogazocine
cogazocina
cogeneration
cogeneración
cognac oil, green
esencia verde de
coñac
coherent ligth
luz coherente
coherin
coherina
cohesion
cohesión
cohesive failure
resistencia a la pérdida
de cohesión
cohesive power
fuerza de cohesión
cohune oil
aceite de nuez de
cohuna
coil
espiral, muelle,
serpentín, retorcido
coil (DNA)
hélice (del ADN)
coiler
enrollador,
enroscador
coil spring
resorte
coke
coque
cola
cola
colamine
colamina

colchiceine
colchiceína,
colquiceína
colchicine
colchicina
cold flow
flujo en frío
cold rubber
caucho sintético
producido al frío
colecalciferol
colecalciferol
colemanite
colemanita
colestipol
colestipol
colestyramine
colestiramina
colfenamate
colfenamato
colfosceril palmitate
palmitato de
colfoscerilo
colicins
colicinas
colimecycline
colimeciclina
colistin
colistina
collagen
colágeno
collagenase
colagenasa
collect
obtener, reunir
collide, to
chocar
2,4,6-collidine
2,4,6-colidina
collinomycin
colinomicina
collinsonia
colinsonia
collodion, collodium
colodión
collodium, cantharidal
colodión cantarídeo,
colodión vesicante,
colodión ampollante
colloid
coloide
colloid, association
asociación coloide
colloid chemistry
química coloidal
colloid mill
molino coloidal
colloid, protective
protector coloidal

colloidal
coloidal
colloidal clay
arcilla coloidal
colloidal dispersion
dispersión coloidal
colloidal gold
oro coloidal
colloidal silicates
silicatos coloidales
colloidal silver
plata coloidal
colloidal solution
solución coloidal
colloidal sulfur
azufre coloidal
colocynthin
colocintina,
coloquíntida
Cologne spirits
alcohol de Colonia
colophony
colofonía
color (USA)
colour (UK)
color
color hold test
prueba de retención del
color
color stability
estabilidad del color
colorant
colorante
coloration
coloración
colorimeter
colorímetro
colorimetric
colorimétrico
colorimetry
colorimetría
coloring gels
geles colorantes
colorless
incoloro
colorless dye
colorante incoloro
colostrokinin
calostrocinina
colpormon
colpormona
colterol
colterol
coltsfoot
fárfara, tusílago
columbamine
columbamina
columbin
columbina, calumbina

columbite
columbita
columbium
niobio, columbio
column
columna
column, distillation
columna de destilación
column efficiency
eficiencia de la
columna
Combes quinoline
synthesis
síntesis de quinolinas
de Combes
combination
combinación
combining number
número de
combinación
combining weight
peso de combinación
combustible material
material combustible
combustion
combustión
combustion chamber
cámara de combustión
combustion method
método de
combustión
combustion residue
residuo de la
combustión
combustion
temperature
temperatura de
combustión
comirin
comirina
commercial scale
escala comercial
commercial yield
rendimiento comercial,
producción comercial
comminution
desmenuzado
compact
compacto
compact, to
comprimir
compaction
compresión
comparable
similar
comparison
comparación
compartment
compartimiento

compatibility
compatibilidad
compatible
compatible
compensate, to
compensar
complaint
queja, reclamación
complement
complemento
complete analysis
análisis completo
complex
complejo
complex compound
compuesto complejo
complex ion
ion complejo
complex salt
sal compleja
complexing agent
agente formador de
complejos
component
componente
composite
compuesto, mixto
composition
composición
compound
compuesto, mezcla
compounding
mezclar
compressed gas
gas comprimido
computational
chemistry
química de cálculo
concanavalin A
concanavalina A,
conA, con A
concave
cóncavo
concentrated
concentrado
concentration
concentración
concentric
concéntrico
conchiolin
conquiolina
conchoidal
concoidal
conclusion
conclusión
condensate
condensado
condensation
condensación

condensation
column
columna de
condensación
condense, to
condensar
conductance
conductancia
conduction
conducción
conductivity
conductividad
condurangin
condurangina
cone
cono
conessine
conesina
confectioners glaze
barniz farmacéutico
confectioners sugar
azúcar impalpable
configuration
configuración
confine, to
aislar
conformation
conformación
congeal point
punto de congelación
conglomerate
conglomerado
Congo red
rojo Congo
Congo resin
resina del Congo
congressane
congresano
conhydrine
conhidrina
conic
cónico
conical flask
frasco erlenmeyer,
erlenmeyer
ß-coniceine
ß-coniceína
coniferin
coniferina
coniferyl alcohol
alcohol coniferílico
coniine
coniína, conicina,
cicutina
coniine hydrobromide
bromhidrato de coniína,
bromhidrato de
conicina, bromhidrato
de cicutina

70

coniine hydrochloride
clorhidrato de
coniína, clorhidrato
de conicina, clor-
hidrato de cicutina
conium fruit
conio, cicuta
conjugated
conjugado
conjugated double
bonds
enlaces dobles
conjugados
conjugated estrogenic
hormones
hormonas estrógenas
conjugadas
conjugated layers
capas conjugadas
conjugation
conjugación
connected
conectado
connection
conexión
conorfone
conorfona
conquinamine
conquinamina
Conrad-Limpach
reaction
reacción de Conrad
Limpach
conservation of energy,
law
ley de conservación de
la energía
consistency
consistencia,
regularidad,
uniformidad,
coherencia
consistent with
correspondiente a,
guarda
correspondencia con,
concordante con
consolidate, to
consolidar
consolute
miscible
constant
constante
constant boiling
ebullición constante
constant boiling
mixture
mezcla de ebullición
constante

constant pressure
presión constante
constant volume
volumen constante
constituent
componente, elemento
constituyente
constitutional formula
fórmula estructural,
fórmula constitucional
constraints
limitaciones
consume, to
consumir
consumed oxygen
oxígeno consumido
contact acid
ácido de contacto
contact process
método de contacto
contact resin
resina de contacto
contact surface
superficie de contacto
contain, to
contener
container
envase, recipiente,
contenedor
contaminant
contaminante
contaminated
contaminado
content
contenido
continuing testing
prueba continua
continuos distillation
destilación continua
continuos phase
fase contínua
contrast
prueba de control
controlled release
liberación
controlada
convallamarogenin
convalamarogenina
convallaria
convalaria
convallatoxin
convalatoxina
convection
convección
conventional
tradicional, clásico,
convencional
convergence
convergencia

conversion
conversión
converting
conversión
convex
convexo
conveyor
cinta transportadora,
correa transportadora
convicine
convicina
cooking
cocción
cool, to
enfriar
cooling rack
rejilla de enfriamiento
coordinates
coordenadas
coordinate axis
eje de coordenadas
coordination
compound
compuesto de
coordinación
coordination number
número de
coordinación
copaene
copaeno
copaiba
copaiba
copaiba oil
esencia (aceite) de
copaiba
copaiba resin
resina de copaiba
copaibic acid
ácido copáibico
copal
copal
copal resine
resina de copal, goma
de copal
coparaffinate
coparafinato
Cope elimination
reaction
reacción de
eliminación de Cope
Cope rearrangement
transposición de
Cope
Cope's rule
regla de Cope
copolymer
copolímero
copolymerization
copolimerización

copper
cobre
copper abietate
abietato de cobre
copper acetate
acetato de cobre
copper acetate, basic
acetato básico de cobre
copper acetoarsenite
acetoarsenito de cobre
copper acetylacetonate
acetilacetonato de
cobre
copper amalgam
amalgama de cobre
copper aminoacetate
aminoacetato de cobre
copper aminosulfate
aminosulfato de cobre
copper ammonium
acetate
acetato de cobre y
amonio
copper ammonium
sulfate
sulfato de cobre y
amonio
copper arsenate
arseniato de cobre
copper arsenite
arsenito de cobre
copper arsenite,
ammoniacal
arsenito de cobre
amoniacal
copper benzoate
benzoato de cobre
copper, blister
cobre negro, cobre
bruto, cobre sin
refinar
copper blue
azul de cobre
copper borate
borato de cobre
copper bromide
bromuro de cobre
copper carbonate
carbonato de cobre
copper chloride
cloruro de cobre
copper chromate
cromato de cobre
copper cyanide
cianuro de cobre
copper deoxidized
cobre desoxidado
copper dichromate
dicromato de cobre

copper dihydrazinium
sulfate
  sulfato dihidracínico de
cobre
copper dimethyldi-
thiocarbamate
  ditiocarbamato
dimetílico de cobre,
dimetilditiocarbamato
de cobre
copper, electrolytic
  cobre electrolítico
copper ethylaceto-
acetate
  etilacetoacetato de
cobre
copper ferrocyanide
  ferrocianuro de cobre
copper fluoride
  fluoruro de cobre
copper fluosilicate
  fluosilicato de cobre
copper glance
  calcosita, cobre
sulfurado vidrioso
copper gluconate
  gluconato de cobre
copper glycinate
  glicinato de cobre
copper hemioxide
  semióxido de cobre
copper hydrate
  hidrato de cobre
copper hydroxide
  hidróxido de cobre
copper iodide
  yoduro de cobre
copper lactate
  lactato de cobre
copper mercury
iodide
  yoduro de cobre y
mercurio
copper metaborate
  metaborato de cobre
copper methane
arsenate
  metanoarseniato de
cobre
copper molybdate
  molibdato de cobre
copper monoxide
  monóxido de cobre
copper naphthenate
  naftenato de cobre
copper nitrate
  nitrato de cobre
copper nitrite
  nitrito de cobre

copper nitrite, basic
  nitrito básico de cobre
copper nucleinate
  nucleinato de cobre
copper octoate
  octoato de cobre
copper oleate
  oleato de cobre
copper oxalate
  oxalato de cobre
copper oxide, black
  óxido negro de cobre
copper oxide,
hydrated
  óxido de cobre
hidratado
copper oxide, red
  óxido rojo de cobre
copper oxinate
  oxinato de cobre
copper oxychloride
  cloruro básico de cobre
copper phthalo-
cyanine
  ftalocianina cúprica
copper phenol-
sulfonate
  fenolsulfonato de
cobre
copper phosphate
  fosfato de cobre
copper phosphide
  fosfuro de cobre
copper phthalate
  ftalato de cobre
copper phthalo-
cyanine blue
  azul de ftalocianina
cúprica
copper phthalo-
cyanine green
  verde de ftalocianina
cúprica
copper potassium
ferrocyanide
  ferrocianuro de cobre y
potasio
copper protoxide
  protóxido de cobre
copper pyrites
  piritas de cobre
copper resinate
  resinato de cobre
copper ricinoleate
  ricinoleato de cobre
copper scale
  película de cobre
copper selenate
  seleniato de cobre

copper silicate
  silicato de cobre
copper silicide
  siliciuro de cobre
copper silicofluoride
  silicofluoruro de cobre
copper sodium chloride
  cloruro de cobre y
sodio
copper sodium cyanide
  cianuro de cobre y
sodio
copper stearate
  estearato de cobre
copper subacetate
  subacetato de cobre
copper suboxide
  subóxido de cobre
copper sulfate
  sulfato de cobre
copper sulfate
ammoniated
  sulfato de cobre
amoniacal
copper sulfate, tribasic
  sulfato tribásico de
cobre
copper sulfide
  sulfuro de cobre
copper sulfocarbolate
  sulfocarbolato de
cobre
copper sulfocyanide
  sulfocianuro de cobre
copper tallate
  talato (resinato) de
cobre
copper trifluoro-
acetylacetonate
  trifluoroacetil-
acetonato de cobre
copper tungstate
  tungstato de cobre
copper undecylenate
  undecilenato de cobre
copper wire
  alambre de cobre
copper yellow
  amarillo de cobre
copper zinc chromate
  cromato de cobre y
cinc
copper-8-hydroxy-
quinoline
  8-hidroxiquinolina de
cobre
copper-2,4-pentane-
dione
  cobre-2,4-pentandiona

copper-8-
quinolinolate
  8-quinolinolato de
cobre
copperas
  caparrosa
copperas, blue
  caparrosa azul
copperas, green
  caparrosa verde
copperas, white
  caparrosa blanca
copra
  copra
copra oil
  aceite de copra
coprecipitation
  coprecipitación
coproergostane
  coproergostano,
pseudoergostano
coprogen
  coprogén
coprostane
  coprostano
coprosterol
  coprosterol
coptine
  coptina
coptis
  coptis
coptisine
  coptisina
coral
  coral
corbadrine
  corbadrina
cordite
  cordita
cordycepin
  cordicepina
core
  núcleo, centro
core of the earth
  centro de la tierra
Corey-Winter olefin
synthesis
  síntesis de olefinas de
Corey Winter
coriamyrtin
  coriamirtina
coriander
  coriandro, cilantro,
culantro
coriander oil
  esencia (aceite) de
coriandro
coriandrol
  coriandrol

Cori ester
éster de Cori
cork
corcho, tapón
corkboard
tabla de corcho
cork oak
alcornoque
cork stopper
tapón de corcho
cormetasone
cormetasona
corn oil
aceite de maíz
corn steep liquor
licor de maíz macerado
corn sugar
glucosa
corn syrup
jarabe de maíz
cornstarch
almidón de maíz
cornus
corno, cornejo
coroxon ·
coroxón
correcting factor
factor de corrección
correlation
correlación
corresponding states
estados
correspondientes
corrosion
corrosión
corrosion test
prueba de corrosión
corrosive material
material corrosivo
corrosive mercury
chloride
cloruro de mercurio
corrosivo
corrosive sublimate
sublimado corrosivo
corrugated
corrugado, ondulado
corticoid hormone
hormona corticoide
corticosterone
corticosterona
corticotropin
corticotropina
cortisol
cortisol, hidrocortisona
cortisone
cortisona
cortisone acetate
acetato de cortisona

cortisone, 21ß-
cyclopentane
propionate
cortisona, propionato
de 21ß-ciclopentano
cortisone phosphate
fosfato de cortisona
cortisuzol
cortisuzol
cortivazol
cortivazol
cortol
cortol
cortolone
cortolona
cortodoxone
cortodoxona
corundum
corindón, óxido de
aluminio
corybulbine
coribulbina
corycavamine
coricavamina
corycavidine
coricavidina
corydaldine
coridaldina
corydaline
coridalina
corydine
coridina
corynantheine
corinanteína
corynanthine
corinantina
corynine
corinina
corypalmine
coripalmina
corytuberine
corituberina
cosin
cosina
cosmetic
cosmético
cosmochemistry
cosmoquímica
cosyntropin
cosintropina
cotarnine
cotarnina
cotarnine chloride
cloruro de
cotarnina
cotinine
cotinina
cotoin
cotoína

cotriptyline
cotriptilina
cotton, acetylated
algodón acetilado
cotton, aminized
algodón aminado
cotton, cyanoethylated
algodón cianoetilado
cotton, mercerized
algodón mercerizado
cotton oil
aceite de algodón
cottonseed
semilla de algodón
cottonseed meal
harina de semilla de
algodón
cottonseed oil
aceite de semilla de
algodón
coulomb
culombio
coumachlor
cumacloro
coumafos
cumafós
coumafuryl
cumafurilo
coumalic acid
ácido cumálico
coumamycin
cumamicina
coumaphos
cumafós
coumaran
cumarán,
dihidrocumarona
p-coumaric acid
ácido p-cumárico
coumarilic acid
ácido cumarílico
coumarin(e)
cumarina
coumarine 3-
carboxylic acid
ácido cumarin-3-
carboxílico
coumarone
cumarona
coumarone-indene
resin
resina de cumarona
indeno
coumazoline
cumazolina
coumestrol
cumestrol
coumetarol
cumetarol

coumingine
cumingina
coumithoate
cumitoato
counter clockwise
contra horario, hacia la
izquierda, en sentido
contrario a las
manecillas del reloj
countercurrent
contracorriente,
corriente contraria
countercurrent
extraction
extracción en
contracorriente
countercurrent flow
flujo a contracorriente
couple
par, conectar, asociar
coupling constant
constante de
acoplamiento
course
dirección, camino
covalence
covalencia
covalency
covalencia
covalent bond
enlace covalente
covalent compound
compuesto covalente
cover
cubierta, recubrimiento
covering
recubrimiento
covering power
cobertura
coverglass
cubreobjeto
Cox chart
diagrama de Cox
crack the tablet
partir, quebrar la
tableta
Craig method
método de Craig
Cram's rule of
asymmetric induction
ley de la inducción
asimétrica de Cram
crataegus
cratáego, espino
crazing
agrietamiento
cream of tartar
bitartrato de potasio,
crémor tártaro

73

creatine
creatina
creatinine
creatinina
creatinolfosfate
creatinolfosfato,
fosfato creatinólico
Creighton process
proceso de Creighton
creoline
creolina
creosol
creosol
creosote
creosota
creosote carbonate
carbonato de
creosota
creosote, coal tar
creosota de alquitrán
de hulla
creosote, wood
creosota vegetal
creosote, wood tar
creosota de alquitrán
vegetal
creosotic acid
ácido creosótico
p-cresidine
p-cresidina
cresol
cresol, tricresol,
hidroxitolueno,
metilfenol
cresol purple
violeta de cresol,
púrpura de cresol
cresol red
rojo de cresol
cresolphthalein
cresolftaleína
cresotamide
cresotamida
m-cresotic acid
ácido m-cresótico
p-cresotic acid
ácido p-cresótico
m-cresyl acetate
acetato de m-cresilo
cresyl diglycol
carbonate
diglicolcarbonato de
cresilo
cresyl diphenyl
phosphate
difenilfosfato de
cresilo
p-cresyl isobutyrate
isobutirato de p-cresilo

cresyl methyl ether
éter cresilmetílico
cresyl phenyl
phosphate
fosfato fenilcresílico
cresyl silicate
silicato de cresilo
o-cresyl-α-glyceril
ether
éter o-cresil-α-
glicerílico
cresylic acids
ácidos cresílicos
cresyl-p-toluene
sulfonate
sulfonato de cresil-p-
tolueno
crevise
grieta, fisura
CRF (corticotropin
releasing factor)
FLC (factor de
liberación de
corticotropina)
Criegge reaction
reacción de Criegge
crimidine
crimidina
crimp seal
cierre o sello
corrugado
crimson
carmesí
criptoxanthin
criptoxantina
critical assembly
conjunto crítico
critical constant
constante crítica
critical humidity
humedad crítica
critical mass
masa crítica
critical point
punto crítico
critical temperature
temperatura crítica
criticality
estado crítico
croceic acid
ácido croceico
crocein acid
ácido croceínico
crocetin
crocetina
crocidolite
crocidolita
crocin
crocina

crocking
desteñido
cromacate
cromacato
cromesilate
cromesilato
cromitrile
cromitrilo
cromoglycic acid
ácido
cromoglícico
cromolyn
cromolín
cropropamide
cropropamida
cross lines
retículo
cross reference
remisión, referencia
de una parte a otra
cross section
sección transversal
cross-link
eslabón,
conjugación cruzada
crosslinking
entrecruzamiento,
conjugación cruzada
crotamine
crotamina
crotamiton
crotamitón
crotethamide
crotetamida
crotoniazide
crotoniazida
crotonaldehyde
crotonaldehído,
aldehído crotónico
crotonic acid
ácido crotónico
crotonic aldehyde
aldehido crotónico
croton oil
aceite de crotón
crotonyl alcohol
alcohol crotonílico,
alcohol crotílico
crotonylene
crotonileno
crotoxin
crotoxina
crotoxyphos
crotoxifós
crotyl alcohol
alcohol crotílico,
alcohol crotonílico
crown ethers
éteres de corona

crown glass
vidrio de potasio y boro
CRP
PCR (proteína c-
reactiva)
crucial
decisivo, crítico
crucible
crisol
crucible furnace
mufla, horno de crisol
crude
crudo
crude acid
ácido crudo
crude wax
cera cruda, parafina
cruda
crufomate
crufomato
crusher
triturador
crusher, gyratory
trituradora giratoria
crushing
trituración
crust
costra
cryochemistry
crioquímica
cryofluorane
criofluorano
cryogenics
criogenia,
criogénicos
cryohydrate
criohidrato
cryolite
criolita
cryoscopic
crioscópico
cryptenamine
tannates
tanatos de
criptenamina
cryptocyanine
criptocianina
cryptopine
criptopina
cryptoxanthin
criptoxantina
crypts cells
células de las
criptas
crystal
cristal
crystal growth
crecimiento
cristalino

crystal lattice
red cristalina,
retículo cristalino,
estructura reticular
del cristal
crystal structure
estructura cristalina
crystal violet stain
tinción de violeta
cristalina
crystalline
cristalina
crystalline rocks
rocas cristalinas
crystallite
cristalita
crystallization
cristalización
crystallizing dish
cristalizador, placa de
cristalización
crystallography
cristalografía
C-stage resin
resina termofija en
fase final
cubeb
cubeba
cubeb oil
esencia (aceite) de
cubeba
cubebin
cubebina
cucurbitacins
cucurbitacinas
cudbear
orcina u orcinol
cullet
vidrio de desecho
culm
polvo de antracita
cultivate, to
cultivar
culture medium
medio de cultivo
cumaldehyde
cumaldehído
cumaric acid
ácido cumárico
cumarinic acid
ácido cumarínico
cumene
cumeno, cumol
cumerone
cumerona
cumic acid
ácido cúmico
cumic alcohol
alcohol cúmico

cumic aldehyde
aldehído cúmico
cumidin(e)
cumidina
cuminaldehyde
cumaldehído, aldehído
cumínico
cuminaldehyde
thiosemicarbazole
tiosemicarbazol
cumaldehídico,
cumaldehído
tiosemicarbazol
cumin, cummin
comino
cumin oil
esencia (aceite) de
comino
cuminic alcohol
alcohol cumínico
cuminic aldehyde
aldehído cumínico
cumulene
cumuleno
cumyl phenol
cumilfenol, fenol
cumílico
cupellation process
proceso de copelación
cupferron
cupferrona
cuprammonium
process
método cuproamoniacal
cupreine
cupreína
cupressin
cupresina
cupriaseptol
cupriaseptol
cupric
cúprico
cupric acetate
acetato cúprico
cupric acetoarsenite
acetoarsenito cúprico
cupric arsenite
arsenito cúprico
cupric acetate
acetato cúprico
cupric borate
borato cúprico
cupric bromide
bromuro cúprico
cupric butyrate
butirato cúprico
cupric carbonate, basic
carbonato cúprico
básico

cupric chlorate
clorato cúprico
cupric chloride
cloruro cúprico
cupric chromate acid
cromato cúprico ácido
cupric chromate basic
cromato cúprico
básico
cupric chromate
cromato cúprico
cupric chromite
cromito cúprico
cupric citrate
citrato cúprico
cupric cyanide
cianuro cúprico
cupric ferrocyanide
ferrocianuro cúprico
cupric fluoride
fluoruro cúprico
cupric formate
formiato cúprico
cupric gluconate
gluconato cúprico
cupric glycinate
glicinato cúprico
cupric hexafluoro-
silicate
hexafluorosilicato
cúprico
cupric hydroxide
hidróxido cúprico
cupric nitrate
nitrato cúprico
cupric oleate
oleato cúprico
cupric oxalate
oxalato cúprico
cupric oxide
óxido cúprico
cupric perchlorate
perclorato cúprico
cupric p-phenol-
sulfonate
p-fenosulfonato
cúprico
cupric phosphate
fosfato cúprico
cupric salicylate
salicilato cúprico
cupric selenate
seleniato cúprico
cupric selenide
seleniuro cúprico
cupric selenite
selenito cúprico
cupric stearate
estearato cúprico

cupric sulfate
sulfato cúprico
cupric sulfate, basic
sulfato cúprico básico
cupric sulfide
sulfuro cúprico
cupric tartrate
tartrato cúprico
cupric tungstate
tungstato cúprico
cupriethylene diamine
diamina cuprietilénica,
cuprietilendiamina
cuprimyxin
cuprimixina
cuprinol
cuprinol
cuprite
cuprita
cuprobam
cuprobán
cupronickel
cuproníquel
cuprotungsten
cuprotungsteno
cuprous
cuproso
cuprous acetate
acetato cuproso
cuprous acetate
ammoniacal
acetato cuproso
amoniacal
cuprous acetylide
acetilida cuprosa
cuprous bromide
bromuro cuproso
cuprous chloride
cloruro cuproso
cuprous cyanide
cianuro cuproso
cuprous iodide
yoduro cuproso
cuprous mercuric
iodide
yoduro cuproso
mercúrico
cuprous oxide
óxido cuproso
cuprous phosphate
fosfato cuproso
cuprous potassium
cyanide
cianuro cuproso de
potasio
cuprous selenide
seleniuro cuproso
cuprous sulfide
sulfuro cuproso

cuprous sulfite
sulfito cuproso
cuprous thiocyanate
tiocianato cuproso
cuproxoline
cuproxolina
curangin
curangina
curare
curare
curarine
curarina
C-curarine I
C-curarina I
curcumin
curcumina
curdle, to
cuajar
curie
curie
curine
curina
curium
curio
current
corriente, vigente
current assay
ensayo vigente
curvularin
curvularina
cuscohygrine
cuscohigrina
cusconidine
cusconidina
cuspareine
cuspareína
cusparine
cusparina
Curtius rearrangement
transposición de
Curtius
cyacetacide
ciacetacida, hidrazida
malononitrílica
cyamelide
ciamelida
cyamemazine
ciamemacina,
ciamemazina
cyanalcohol
cianalcohol
cyanamide
cianamida
cyanate
cianato
cyanazine
cianacina, cianazina
cyanic acid
ácido ciánico

cyanide
cianuro
cyanide pulp
pasta de cianuro
cyanidin chloride
cloruro de cianidina
cyanine dye
colorante de cianina
cyanoacetamide
cianacetamida
cyanoacetic acid
ácido cianacético
cyanocarbon
carbocianuro
cyanocobalamin
cianocobalamina
2-cyanoethyl acrylate
acrilato de 2-cianetilo
cyanoethyl sucrose
sacarosa cianetílica,
cianetilsacarosa
cyanofenphos
cianofenfós
cyanoformic chloride
cloruro cianofórmico
cyanogen
cianógeno
cyanogen azide
azida cianógena
cyanogen bromide
bromuro de cianógeno
cyanogen chloride
cloruro de cianógeno
cyanogen fluoride
fluoruro de cianógeno
cyanogen iodide
yoduro de cianógeno
cyanogenamide
cianogenamida
cyanoguanidine
cianoguanidina
cyano(methyl-
mercuri)guanidine
ciano(metilmercuri)
guanidina
cyanophenfos
cianofenfós
cyanophos
cianofós
cyanopsin
cianopsin
3-cyanopyridine
3-cianopiridina
cyanuramide
cianuramida
cyanurdiamide
cianurdiamida
cyanuric acid
ácido cianúrico

cycasin
cicasina
cyclacillin
ciclacilina
cyclamate
ciclamato
cyclamic acid
ácido ciclámico
cyclamin
ciclamina
cyclandelate
ciclandelato
cyclarbamate
ciclarbamato
cyclazocine
ciclazocina
ciclazodone
ciclazodona
cycle
ciclo
cyclethrin
cicletrina
cyclexanone
ciclexanona
cyclexedrine
ciclexedrina
cyclic AMP
monofosfato
adenosínico cíclico
cyclic compound
compuesto cíclico
cyclic GMP
monofosfato
guanosínico cíclico
cycliramine
cicliramina
cyclizine
ciclicina, ciclizina
cyclizine
hydrochloride
clorhidrato de ciclicina,
clorhidrato de ciclizina
cycloaliphatic epoxy
resin
resina epóxido
cicloalifática
cyclobarbital
ciclobarbital
cyclobendazole
ciclobendazol
cyclobenzaprine
ciclobenzaprina
cyclobenzaprine
hydrochloride
clorhidrato de
ciclobenzaprine
cyclobutane
ciclobutano,
tetrametileno

cyclobutene
ciclobuteno
cyclobutilene
ciclobutileno
cyclobutoic acid
ácido ciclobutoico
cyclobutyrol
ciclobutirol
cyclobuxine
ciclobuxina
cyclocitrylidenacetone
acetona
ciclocitrilidénica,
ciclocitrilidenacetona
cyclocumarol
ciclocumarol
cyclodextrins
ciclodextrinas
cyclodrine
ciclodrina
cyclofenil
ciclofenilo
cycloguanil
cicloguanilo
cycloguanil embonate
embonato de
cicloguanil
cycloheptane
cicloheptano
cycloheptanone
cicloheptanona
cyclohexadiene
ciclohexadieno
cyclohexane
ciclohexano
cyclohexanecarboxylic
acid
ácido ciclohexan-
carboxílico
1,4-cyclohexane-
dimethanol
1,4-ciclohexan-
dimetanol
cyclohexanesulfamic
acid
ácido ciclohexan-
sulfámico
cyclohexanol
ciclohexanol
cyclohexanone
ciclohexanona
cyclohexanyl acetate
acetato de
ciclohexanilo
cyclohexene
ciclohexeno
cyclohexenylethyl-
barbituric acid
ácido barbitúrico

ciclohexeniletílico,
ácido ciclohexenil-
etilbarbitúrico
cyclohexenylethylene
etileno ciclohexenílico,
ciclohexeniletileno
cyclohexenyltri-
chlorosilane
triclorosilano
ciclohexenílico,
ciclohexeniltri-
clorosilano
cycloheximide
cicloheximida
cyclohexyl
ciclohexilo
cyclohexyl bromide
bromuro de
ciclohexilo
cyclohexyl chloride
cloruro de
ciclohexilo
cyclohexylisocyanate
isocianato de
ciclohexilo
cyclohexyl
methacrylate
metacrilato de
ciclohexilo
cyclohexyl stearate
estearato de
ciclohexilo
cyclohexyl
trichlorosilane
triclorosilano
ciclohexílico
cyclohexylamine
ciclohexilamina
cyclohexylbenzene
ciclohexilbenceno
cyclohexylcarbinol
carbinol ciclo-
hexílico, ciclohexil-
carbinol
2-cyclohexylcyclo-
hexanol
ciclohexanol 2-
ciclohexílico, 2-
ciclohexilciclo-
hexanol
2-cyclohexyl-4,6-
dinitrophenol
2-ciclohexil-4,6-
dinitrofenol
1-cyclohexyl-2-
methylamino-
propane
1-ciclohexil-2-
metilaminopropano

p-cyclohexylphenol
fenol
p-ciclohexílico, p-
ciclohexilfenol
cyclohexylphenyl-1-
piperidinepropanol
hydrochloride
clorhidrato de
ciclohexilfenil-1-
piperidinpropanol
N-cyclohexyl-
piperidine
piperidina N-
ciclohexílica, N-
ciclohexilpiperidina
cyclohexylsulfamic
acid
ácido sulfámico
ciclohexílico, ácido
ciclohexilsulfámico
N-cyclohexyl-p-
toluenesulfonamide
sulfonamida N-
ciclohexil-p-toluénica,
N-ciclohexil-p-toluen-
sulfonamida
cycloleucine
cicloleucina
cyclomenol
ciclomenol
cyclomethycaine
ciclometicaína
cyclonite
ciclonita
cyclonium iodide
yoduro de ciclonio
3-cyclooctadiene
3-cicloctadieno
cyclooctane
cicloctano
1,3,5,7-cycloocta-
tetraene
1,3,5,7-ciclocta-
tetraeno
cycloolefin
ciclolefina
cycloparaffin
cicloparafina
cyclopentadiene
ciclopentadieno
cyclopentamine
ciclopentamina
cyclopentane
ciclopentano
1,2,3,-cyclopentane-
tetracarboxylic acid
ácido 1,2,3-
ciclopentano
tetracarboxílico

cyclopentanol
ciclopentanol
cyclopentanone
ciclopentanona
cyclopentanone
oxime
oxima ciclo-
pentanónica
cyclopentene
ciclopenteno
1,2-cyclopentene-
phenanthrene
1,2-ciclopenten-
fenantreno
cyclopenthiazide
ciclopentiazida
cyclopentobarbital
ciclopentobarbital
cyclopentolate
ciclopentolato
cyclopentyl alcohol
alcohol ciclopentílico
cyclopentyl bromide
bromuro de
ciclopentilo
cyclopentyl phenyl
ketone
cetona ciclopentil
fenílica, ciclopentil
fenil cetona
cyclopentylacetone
acetona ciclopentílica,
ciclopentilacetona
1-cyclopentyl-2-
methylaminopropane
hydrochloride
clorhidrato de 1-
ciclopentil-2-
metilaminopropano
1-cyclopentyl-2-
propanone
1-ciclopentil-2-
propanona
cyclopentylpropionic
acid
ácido ciclopentil-
propiónico
cyclopentylpropionyl
chloride
cloruro de ciclo-
pentilpropionilo
cyclophosphamide
ciclofosfamida
cyclophane
ciclofano
cyclophosphamide
ciclofosfamida
cyclopregnol
ciclopregnol

cyclopropane
ciclopropano,
trimetileno
cyclopropanespiro-
cyclopropane
ciclopropanespiro-
ciclopropano
cyclopropyl methyl
ether
éter ciclopropil-
metílico
cyclopyrronium
bromide
bromuro de
ciclopirronio
cyclorphan
ciclorfán
cycloserine
cicloserina
cyclosilane
ciclosilano
cyclosporine
ciclosporina
cyclothiazide
ciclotiazida
cyclotrimethylene-
trinitramine
trinitramina
ciclotrimetilénica,
ciclotrimetilén
trinitramina
cyclotron
ciclotrón
cyclovalone
ciclovalona
cycothiamin(e)
cicotiamina
cycrimine
cicrimina
cycrimine
hydrochloride
clorhidrato de
cicrimina
cyhalothrin
cialotrina
cyheptamide
ciheptamida
cyheptropine
ciheptropina
cyhexatin
cihexatina
cylinder
cilindro
cylinder, graduate
probeta
cymarin
cimarina
cymarose
cimarosa

cymene	**cyprenorphine**	**cystathionine**	**cytochalasins**
cimeno	ciprenorfina	cistationina	citocalasinas
cymiazole	**cypress oil**	**cysteamine**	**cytochemistry**
cimiazol	esencia (aceite) de	cisteamina	citoquímica
cymol	ciprés	**cysteic acid**	**cytochrome**
cimol	**cypridol**	ácido cisteico	citocromo
cynanchogenin	cipridol	**cysteine**	**cytochrome oxidase**
cinancogenina	**cypripedium**	cisteína	citocromo
cynapine	cipripedio	**cystine**	oxidasa
cinapina	**cyprodenate**	cistina	**cytohemin**
cynarase	ciprodenato	**cystopurin**	citohemina
cinarasa	**cyproheptadine**	cistopurina	**cytokinins**
cynarin(e)	ciproheptadina	**cytarabine**	citoquininas
cinarina	**cyproquinate**	citarabina, ß-citosina	**cytolipin H**
cynotoxin	ciproquinato	arabinósida,	citolipina H
cinotoxina	**cyprolidol**	aracitidina	**cytosine**
cypermethrin	ciprolidol	**cythioate**	citosina
cipermetrina	**cyproterone**	citioato	**cytosine**
cypenamine	ciproterona	**cytidine**	**monophosphate**
cipenamina	**cyromazine**	citidina	monofosfato de
cyphenotrin	ciromacina,	**3'-cytidylic acid**	citosina
cifenotrina	ciromazina	ácido 3'-citidílico	**cytosylic acid**
cyprazepam	**cystamine**	**cytisine**	ácido
cipracepán, ciprazepam	cistamina	citisina	citosílico

D

dacarbazine
dacarbacina,
dacarbazina
daclizumab
daclizumabo
dactinomycin
dactinomicina
dacuronium bromide
bromuro de
dacuronio
daily
diario, diariamente
daily output
producción diaria
daidzein
daidceína
dairy
lácteo
Dakin reaction
reacción de Dakin
Dakin's solution
solución de Dakin
Dakin-West reaction
reacción de Dakin
West
dalapon
dalapón
daledalin
daledalina
dalhin
dalina, inulina
dalton
dalton
Dalton's law
ley de Dalton
damage
daño, lesión
damar
damara
damascenine
damascenina, nigelina
daminozide
daminocida
dammar
damara
damotepine
damotepina
damp
húmedo
damp-proof
resistente a la
humedad
damped oscillation
oscilación moderada

damper
moderador,
amortiguador
damping
amortiguador
dampness
humedad
danaparoid
sodium
danaparoide sódico
danazol
danazol
dandy roll
cilindro de afiligranar,
cilindro escurridor
danger
peligro
danitracen
danitraceno,
danitracino
dansyl chloride
cloruro de dansilo
danthron
dantrón, dantrona,
crisacina
dantrolene
dantroleno
dantrolene sodium
dantroleno sódico
dantron
dantrón, dantrona,
crisacina
daphnandrine
dafnandrina
daphnetin
dafnetina
daphnin
dafnina
daphnoline
dafnolina
dapiprazole
dapiprazol
dapsone
dapsona
dark room
cuarto oscuro
darken, to
oscurecer
darkness
oscuridad
Darzens
condensation
condensación de
Darzens

Darzens-Nenitzescu
synthesis of ketones
síntesis de cetonas de
Darzens Nenitzescu
Darzens synthesis of
tetralin derivatives
síntesis de derivados
de tetralina de
Darzens
dash
raya, guion
data
datos
date
fecha
datiscetin
datiscetina
datum
dato
datura
datura
daturic acid
ácido datúrico
daucol
daucol
daughter element
elemento hijo
daunomycin
daunomicina
daunorubicin
daunorrubicina
daunorubicin
hydrochloride
clorhidrato de
daunorrubicina
dauricine
dauricina
day light
luz natural,
luz del día
dazadrol
dazadrol
dazidamine
dazidamina
dazolicine
dazolicina
dazomet
dazomet
dazoxiben
dazoxibeno
dazzling
deslumbrante,
resplandeciente,
encandilante

Deacon process
proceso de Deacon
deactivate, to
desactivar
dead point
punto muerto
DEAE-cellulose
celulosa dietil-
aminoetílica, celulosa
DEAE, dietilamino-
etilcelulosa
DEAE-dextran
dextrano
dietilaminoetílico,
dextrano DEAE,
dietilamino-
etildextrano
deaminooxytocin
desaminoxitocina
deanil
deanilo
deanol
deanol
deanol aceglumate
aceglumato de deanol
deblooming agents
agentes
antifluorescentes
deboxamet
deboxameto
debris
desechos, restos,
despojos
debrisoquin(e)
debrisoquina
debrominate, to
desbromar
Debye-Huckel theory
teoría de Debye
Huckel
decaborane
decaborano
decachloro-1,1'-bi-
2,4-cyclopentadienyl
decacloro-1,1'-bi-2,4-
ciclopentadienilo
decachlorooctahydro-
1,2,4-metheno-2H-
cyclobuta(cd)-
pentalen-2-one
decacloroctahidro-
1,2,4-meten-2H-
ciclobuta(cd)-pentalen-
2-ona

decaglycerol
decaglicerol,
decaglicerina
decahydronaphthalene
decahidronaftaleno
decalactone
decalactona
decalin
decalina
decamethonium
bromide
bromuro de
decametonio
decamethrin
decametrina
decamethylcyclo-
pentasiloxane
pentasiloxano
decametilcíclico,
decametilciclo-
pentasiloxano
decamethylene-bis(4-
aminoquinaldinium)
acetate
acetato de deca-
metilenbis(4-amino-
quinaldinio)
decamethylene-bis(tri-
methylammonium)
bromide
bromuro de
decametilen-bis-
(trimetilamonio)
decamethyl-
tetrasiloxane
tetrasiloxano
decametílico,
decametiltetrasiloxano
n-decanal
n-decanal
n-decane
n-decano
decanedioic acid
ácido decandioico
decanoic acid
ácido decanoico
1-decanol
1-decanol
decanoyl chloride
cloruro de decanoílo
decanoyl peroxide
peróxido de
decanoílo
decant, to
decantar
decantation
decantación
decantation glass
vaso de decantación

decanter
decantador, licorera
decanting vessel
vasija de
decantación
decarbonization
descarbonización
decarbonize, to
descarbonizar
decarboxylase
decarboxilasa
decay
descomposición,
desintegración
decay, radioactive
desintegración
radiactiva
1-decene
1-deceno
decigram
decigramo
decil
decilo
decimemide
decimemida
decimeter
decímetro
decinormal
décimo normal
decitropine
decitropina
deck
platina, plataforma
declenperone
declenperona
declination
declinación
decline curve
curva de declinación
decloxizine
decloxicina
decoction
decocción
decoic acid
ácido decoico
decolorization
descoloramiento,
descoloración
decolorizing agent
agente descolorante
decolorizing carbon
carbón descolorante
decominol
decominol
decomposition
descomposición
decomposition product
producto de
descomposición

decomposition
temperature
temperatura de
descomposición
decontaminating agent
agente de
descontaminación
decontamination
descontaminación
decoquinate
decoquinato
decoquinate, to
descarbonizar,
descoquinar
decrease
disminución, reducción
decrease, to
disminuir, reducir,
aminorar
dectaflur
dectafluoro
decyl
decilo
decyl acetate
acetato decílico
n-decyl alcohol
alcohol n-decílico
n-decyl aldehyde
aldehído n-decílico
C-decyl betaine
betaína C-decílica, C-
decilbetaína
decyl carbinol
carbinol decílico,
decilcarbinol
decyl hydride
hidruro decílico
decyl mercaptan
mercaptano decílico,
decilmercaptano
n-decylamine
n-decilamina
decylene
decileno
decylic acid
ácido decílico
decyl-octyl
methacrylate
metacrilato de
deciloctilo
deditonium bromide
bromuro de deditonio
deep
profundo
deet
N,N-dietil-3-
metilbenzamida
default
valor por omisión

defect
defecto
defensins
defensinas
deferoxamine
deferoxamina
deferoxamine mesylate
mesilato de
deferoxamina
defibrotide
defibrótido
definition
definición
deflagration
deflagración
deflazacort
deflazacort
deflocculate, to
desfloculación
defoaming agent
agente antiespumante
defoliant
defoliante
deformation
deformation
defosfamide
defosfamida
degass, to
desgasificar
degassed
desgasificado
degeneration
degeneración
degradation
degradación
degree
grado
degree of accuracy
grado de precisión
degree of acidity
grado de acidez
degree of dispersion
grado de dispersión
degree of dissociation
grado de disociación
degree of hardness
grado de dureza
degree of
polymerization
grado de
polimerización
degree of purity
grado de pureza
degree of saturation
grado de saturación
degree of stability
grado de estabilidad
dehumidification
deshumidificación

dehydrate, to
deshidratar
dehydratation
deshidratación
dehydroabietic acid
ácido
dehidroabiético
dehydroabietylamine
dehidroabietilamina
dehydroacetic acid
ácido dehidroacético
dehydroascorbic acid
ácido dehidroascórbico
7-dehydrocholesterol
7-dehidrocolesterol
dehydrocholic acid
ácido dehidrocólico
dehydrocorticosterone
dehidrocorticosterona
dehydrocyclo-
dimerization
dehidrociclo-
dimerización
dehydroemetine
dehidroemetina
dehydro-
epiandrosterone
dehidroepi-
androsterona
dehydroergosterol
dehidroergosterol
dehydrogenase
deshidrogenasa
dehydrogenation
deshidrogenación
11-dehydro-17-
hydroxy-
corticosterone
11-dehidro-17-hidroxi-
corticosterona
dehydroiso-
androsterone
dehidroiso-
androsterona
3-dehydroretinol
3-dehidrorretinol
dehydrositosterol
dehidrositosterol
dehydrothio-p-
toluidine
dehidrotio-p-toluidina
deicing
deshelar,
descongelación
deicing compound
compuesto
descongelante
deionized
desionizada

delanterone
delanterona
delavirdine mesylate
mesilato de delavirdina
delay
demora
delay, to
retardar, demorar
delayed
demorado, tardío,
diferido
delergotrile
delergotrilo
Delepine reaction
reacción de Delepine
deleterious
deletéreo, dañino,
lesivo
delergotrile
delergotrilo
delfantrine
delfantrina
deliquescent
delicuescente
delivery
liberación, rescate,
descarga, entrega
delmadinone
delmadinona
delmadinone
acetate
acetato de
delmadinona
delmetacin
delmetacina
delorazepam
deloracepán,
delorazepam
delphinidin
delfinidina
delphinine
delfinina
delphinoidine
delfinoidina
delprostenate
delprostenato
delsoline
delsolina
deltamethrin
deltametrina
delta acid
ácido delta
delustrant
deslustrante
demanyl phosphate
fosfato de demanilo
De Mayo reaction
reacción de De
Mayo

demecarium bromide
bromuro de
demecario
demeclocycline
demeclociclina
demecolcine
demecolcina
demecycline
demeciclina
demegestone
demegestona
demelverine
demelverina
11-demethoxy-
reserpine
11-demetoxireserpina
demethylchlor-
tetracycline
hydrochloride
clorhidrato de
demetilclortetraciclina
demeton
demetona
demeton methyl
demetona metílica,
metildemetona
demexiptiline
demexiptilina
demineralization
desmineralización
Demjanov
rearrangement
transposición de
Demjanov
democonazole
democonazol
demoxepam
demoxepán,
demoxepam
demoxytocin
demoxitocina
demulsification
desmulsificación
denatonium benzoate
benzoato de
denatonio
denaturant
desnaturalizante
denaturatium
desnaturalización
denatured alcohol
alcohol
desnaturalizado
denaverine
denaverina
denitrate
desnitrificar, desnitrar
denopamine
denopamina

denopterin
denopterina
denpinazone
dempinazona
dense
denso
densimeter
densímetro,
densitómetro,
densitométrico
density
densidad
deodorant
desodorante
deoxidation
desoxidación
deoxy-
desoxi-
deoxyanisoin
desoxianisoína
6-deoxy-L-ascorbic acid
ácido 6-desoxi-L-
ascórbico
deoxybenzoin
desoxibenzoína
deoxycholic acid
ácido desoxicólico
deoxycorticosterone
desoxicorticosterona
deoxycorticosterone
acetate
acetato de
desoxicorticosterona
deoxydizer
desoxidante
deoxydihydro-
streptomycin
desoxidihidro-
estreptomicina
deoxyephedrine
hydrochloride
clorhidrato de
desoxiefedrina
deoxyepinephrine
desoxiepinefrina
2-deoxy-D-glucose
2-desoxi-D-glucosa
1-deoxynojirimycin
1-desoxinojirimicina
deoxyribonucleases
desoxirribonucleasas
deoxyribonucleic
acid
ácido
desoxirribonucleico
D-deoxyribose
D-desoxirribosa
deoxystreptamine
desoxiestreptamina

deoxyuridine
desoxiuridina

department
departamento

deperdition
pérdida

depict, to
representar,
describir

depilatory
depilatorio

depleted
agotado

depletion
agotamiento,
empobrecimiento

depolarizer
despolarizador

depolymerization
despolimerización

deposit
depósito

depramine
depramina

deprenyl
deprenilo

deprodone
deprodona

deprostil
deprostilo

deptropine
deptropina

dequalinium
decualinio

dequalinium acetate
acetato de decualinio

dequalinium chloride
cloruro de decualinio

derivatized
derivado

dermostatin
dermostatina

derris root
raíz de tuba

desalination
desalinación

desaspidin
desaspidina

desatrine
desatrina

descending paper
chromatography
cromatografía
descendente sobre
papel

descent
descenso

descinolone
descinolona

description
descripción

deserpidine
deserpidina

desflurane
desflurano

desglugastrin
desglugastrina

deshydrating agent
agente deshidratante

desiccant
desecante

desiccator
desecador

design
diseño

designate, to
designar

desiodothyroxine
desyodotiroxina

desipramine
desipramina

deslanoside
deslanósido

desmethylmoramide
moramida desmetílica,
desmetilmoramida

desmopressin
desmopresina

desmopressin
acetate
acetato de desmopresina

desocriptine
desocriptina

desogestrel
desogestrel

desomorphine
desomorfina

desonide
desónido

desorption
desabsorción

desosamine
desosamina

desoximetasone
desoximetasona

desoxy-
desoxi-

desoxychloric acid
ácido desoxiclórico

6-desoxy-D-glucosamine
6-desoxi-D-
glucosamina

desoxycortone
desoxicortona

11-desoxy-17-hydroxy-
corticosterone
11-desoxi-17-hidroxi-
corticosterona

desoxypyridoxine
hydrochloride
clorhidrato de
desoxipiridoxina

desoxyribose nucleic
acid
ácido
desoxirribonucleico

desthiobiotin
destiobiotina

destomycin A
destomicina A

destructive
distillation
destilación destructiva

detajmium bitartrate
bitartrato de detajmio

detanosal
detanosal

detaxtran
detaxtrán

detect, to
descubrir, averiguar,
detectar

detection limit
límite de detección

deterenol
deterenol

detergent
detergente

detergent index
índice de detergencia

determine
determinar, calcular

detomidine
detomidina

detonation
detonación

detorubicin
detorrubicina

detoxicate, to
desintoxicar

detoxin complex
complejo de detoxina

detralfate
detralfato

detrothyronine
detrotironina

deuteride
deutérido, hidruro
pesado

deuterium
deuterio

deuterium oxide
óxido de deuterio

deutero-
deutero-

deuteron
deuterón

Devarda's metal
aleación de Devarda,
metal de Devarda

developed (in
photograph)
revelado

developer
revelador

development
revelado, desarrollo

development of heat
producción de calor

Development
Pharmaceutics
Desarrollo
Farmacéutico

development solvent
solvente de revelado

deviation
desviación

device
aparato, dispositivo,
artefacto

devitrification
desvitrificación

De Vrys reagent
reactivo de De Vrys

dewatering
extracción de agua

dew point
punto de rocío,
temperatura de
rocío

dexamethasone
dexametasona

dexamethasone
acetate
acetato de
dexametasona

dexamethasone
sodium phosphate
fosfato de sodio y
dexametasona

dexamisole
dexamisol

dexamphetamine
dexanfetamina

dexbrompheniramine
dexbromfeniramina

dexchlorpheniramine
dexclorfeniramina

dexclamol
dexclamol

dexetimide
dexetimida

dexetozoline
dexetozolina

deximafen
deximafeno

dexivacaine
dexivacaína
dexoxadrol
dexoxadrol
dexpanthenol
dexpantenol
dexpropanolol
dexpropanolol
dexproxibutene
dexproxibuteno
dexrazoxane
dexrazoxano
dextilidine
dextilidina
dextran
dextrán, dextrano
dextranase
dextranasa
dextranomer
dextranómero
dextran sulfate
sulfato de dextrán,
sulfato de dextrano
dextriferron
dextriferrona
dextrin
dextrina
dextroamphetamine
sulfate
sulfato de
dextroanfetamina
dextrofemine
dextrofemina
dextrogyre
dextrógiro
dextromethorphan
dextrometorfán,
dextrometorfano
dextromethorphan
hydrobromide
bromhidrato de
dextrometorfán
dextromoramide
dextromoramida
dextropropoxyphene
dextropropoxifeno
dextrorotation
dextrorrotación
dextrorotator
dextrorrotatorio
dextrorotatory
dextrógiro,
dextrorrotatorio
dextrorphan
dextrorfano
dextrose
dextrosa, glucosa
dextrose equivalent
equivalente de dextrosa

dextrothyroxine
sodium
dextrotirosina sódica
dezocine
dezocina
dhurrin
durrina
1,4-diabicyclo-
(2,2,2)octane
1,4-diabiciclo-
(2,2,2)octano
diaboline
diabolina
diacetamate
diacetamato
diacetazotol
diacetazotol
diacetic acid
ácido diacético
diacetic ether
éter diacético
diacetin
diacetina
diacetolol
diacetolol
diacetonamine
diacetonamina
diacetone acrylamide
acrilamida diacetónica
diacetone alcohol
alcohol diacetónico
diacetoneglucose
glucosa diacetónica,
diacetonglucosa
diacetonyl alcohol
alcohol diacetonílico
diacetonyl sulfide
sulfuro de diacetonilo
diacetyl
diacetilo
1,1'-diacetyl ferrocene
1,1'-diacetilferroceno
diacetyl peroxide
péroxido de diacetilo
diacetyl resorcine
resorcina diacetílica,
diacetilresorcina
diacetylamino-
azotoluene
azotolueno
diacetilamínico,
diacetilamino-
azotolueno
diacetyldihydro-
morphine
dihidromorfina
diacetílica,
diacetildihidro-
morfina

diacetylene
diacetileno
1,2-diacetylethane
1,2-diacetiletano
diacetylmethane
metano diacetílico,
diacetilmetano
diacetylmorphine
morfina diacetílica,
diacetilmorfina
diacid
diácido
diacynadiamidine
sulfate
sulfato de
diacinadiamidina
diagenesis
diagénesis
diagonal
diagonal
diagram
diagrama
dial
dial, rueda, ruedecilla,
esfera, disco
dialdehyde starch
almidón
dialdehídico
dialifor
dialifor
dialkylchloroalkyl-
amine hydro-
chlorides
chloridratos de
dialquilcloro-
alquilamina
diallate
dialato
diallyl adipate
adipato dialílico
diallyl
chlorendate
clorendato dialílico,
clorendato de dialilo
diallyl cyanamide
cianamida dialílica,
dialilcianamida
diallyl diglycollate
diglicolato dialílico,
diglicolato de dialilo
diallyl isophthalate
isoftalato dialílico,
isoftalato de dialilo
diallyl maleate
maleato dialílico,
maleato de dialilo
diallyl phosphite
fosfito dialílico,
fosfito de dialilo

diallyl phtalate
ftalato dialílico,
ftalato de dialilo
diallyl sulfide
sulfuro dialílico,
sulfuro de dialilo
diallylamine
amina dialílica,
dialilamina
diallylbarbituric
acid
ácido
dialilbarbitúrico
diallylmelamine
melamina dialílica,
dialilmelamina
diamantane
diamantano
diameter
diámetro
diamfenetide
dianfenetida
diamide hydrate
hidrato de
diamida
diamil phthalate
ftalato diamílico,
ftalato de diamilo
diamine
diamina
diamine black
negro de diamina
diamine fast red F
rojo F estable de
diamina
diamine gold yellow
amarillo oro de
diamina
diamine violet N
violeta N de diamina
diamine hydrate
hidrato de diamina
3,6-diaminoacridine
3,6-diaminoacridina
3,6-diamino-
acridinium hydrogen
sulfate
sulfato ácido de 3,6-
diaminoacridinio
p-diaminoazobenzene
p-diaminoazobenceno
m-diaminoazobenzene
hydrochloride
clorhidrato de m-
diaminoazobenceno
diaminoazoxytoluene
diaminoazoxitolueno
diaminobenzene
diaminobenceno

3,3'-diaminobenzidine
3,3'-diaminobencidina
**3,5-diaminobenzoic
acid**
ácido 3,5-diamino-
benzoico
1,3-diaminobutane
1,3-diaminobutano
**2,6-diamino-2'-butoxy-
3,5'-azopyridine**
2,6-diamino-2'-butoxi-
3,5'-azopiridina
diaminocaproic acid
ácido diamino-
caproico
diaminocarbanilide
diaminocarbanilida
diaminochrysazin
diaminocrisazina
**trans-1,2-diamino-
cyclohexanetetraacetic
acid**
ácido trans-1,2-
diaminociclohexano
tetraacético
**diaminodiethyl
sulfide**
sulfuro de
diaminodietilo
**1,8-diamino-4,5-
dihydroxy-
antraquinone**
1,8-diamino-4,5-
dihidroxiantraquinona
**diaminodihydroxy-
arsenobenzene
dihydrochloride**
diclorhidrato de
diamindihidroxi-
arsenobenceno
**di-p-aminodi-
methoxydiphenyl**
di-p-aminodi-
metoxidifenilo
diaminodiphenic acid
ácido diaminodifénico
p-diaminodiphenyl
p-diaminodifenilo
**diaminodiphenyl-
amine**
diaminodifenilamina
**diaminodiphenyl-
ethylene**
etileno diamino-
difenílico,
diaminodifeniletileno
**p,p'-diaminodiphenyl
methane**
metano p,p'-di-

aminodifenílico, p,p'-
diaminodifenilmetano
**diaminodiphenyl-
thiourea**
diamino difeniltiourea
**diaminodiphenylurea
disulfonic acid**
ácido disulfónico
diaminodifenilureico,
ácido diaminodifenil-
ureadisulfónico
**3,3'-diaminodipropyl-
amine**
3,3'-diaminodi-
propilamina
diaminoditolyl
diaminoditolilo
**p,p'-diaminoditolyl-
methane**
metano p,p'-
diaminoditolílico,
p,p'-diaminoditolil-
metano
1,2-diaminoethane
1,2-diaminoetano
**6,9-diamino-2-
ethoxyacridine lactate
monohydrate**
lactato monohidratado
de 6,9-diamino-2-
etoxiacridina
**di-p-aminoethoxy-
diphenyl**
di-p-aminoetoxi-
difenilo
**diaminoethyl ether
tetraacetic acid**
ácido de éter tetra-
acético diamino-
etílico, ácido
diaminoetil éter
tetraacético
1,6-diaminohexane
1,6-diaminohexano
**2,4-diamino-6-
hydroxypyrimidine**
2,4-diamino-6-
hidroxipirimidina
diaminomesitylene
diaminomesitileno
**3,6-diamino-10-
methylacrydinium
chloride**
cloruro de 3,6-diamino-
10-metilacridinio
diaminonaphthalene
diaminonaftaleno
1,5-diaminopentane
1,5-diaminopentano

2,3-diaminophenazine
2,3-diaminofenazina
2,4-diaminophenol
2,4-diaminofenol
o-diaminophenol
o-diaminofenol
**2,4-diaminophenol
hydrochloride**
clorhidrato de 2,4-
diaminofenol
**2,4-diamino-6-phenyl-
S-triazine**
2,4-diamino-6-fenil-S-
triazina
1,2-diaminopropane
1,2-diamino-
propano
**2,3-diaminopropionic
acid**
ácido 2,3-
diaminopropiónico
2,3-diaminopurine
2,3-diaminopurina
2,6-diaminopyridine
2,6-diaminopiridina
p-diaminostilbene
p-diaminoestilbeno
**4,4'-diamino-2,2'-
stilbene disulfonic
acid**
ácido 4,4'-diamino-
2,2'-estilbeno
disulfónico
**diaminothio-
carbanilide**
diaminotio-
carbanilida
**di-α-amino-ß-thiol-
propionic acid**
ácido di-α-amino-ß-
tiolpropiónico
diaminotoluene
diaminotolueno
**4,6-diamino-m-
toluenesulfonic acid**
ácido 4,6-diamino-m-
toluensulfónico
**4,6-diamino-S-triazine-
2-ol**
4,6-diamino-S-triazina-
2-ol
2,5-diaminovaleric acid
ácido 2,5-
diaminovalérico
**diammonium
ethylenebis-
dithiocarbamate**
etilenbisditio-
carbamato diamónico

**diammonium
hydrogen phosphate**
fosfato ácido diamónico
diammonium phosphate
fosfato diamónico
diamocaine
diamocaína
diamond
diamante, rombo
diamond black F
negro de humo F
diamond, industrial
diamante industrial
diamond ink
tinta grabadora
diamond shape
romboidal
diampromide
diampromida
**diamthazole
dihydrochloride**
diclorhidrato de
diantazol
**di-tert-amyl
disulfide**
disulfuro de di-terc-
amilo
diamyl maleate
maleato diamílico,
maleato de diamilo
diamyl phenol
fenol diamílico,
diamilfenol
diamyl phtalate
ftalato diamílico,
ftalato de diamilo
**diamyl sodium
sulfosuccinate**
sulfosuccinato de
diamil sodio
diamyl sulfide
sulfuro diamílico,
sulfuro de diamilo
di-n-amylamine
di-n-amilamina
N,N-diamylaniline
N,N-diamilanilina
diamylene
diamileno
**2,5-di(tert-amyl)-
hydroquinone**
2,5-di(terc-amil)-
hidroquinona
dianhydrosorbitol
dianhidrosorbitol
**1,4,3,6-dianhydro-
sorbitol**
1,4,3,6-dianhidro-
sorbitol

1,2-dianilinoethane
1,2-dianilinetano
dianisidine
dianisidina
dianisidine
diisocyanate
diisocianato de
dianisidina
di-p-anisyl-p-
phenetylguanidine
hydrochloride
clorhidrato de
di-p-anisil-p-
fenetilguanidina
diaphoretic
diaforético,
sudorífico
diaphragm cell
cuba diafragmática,
célula diafragmática
diarbarone
diarbarona
diaspore
diásporo
diassemble, to
desmontar, desarmar
diastase
diastasa
diastase of malt
diastasa de malta
diastatic
diastático
diastereoisomer
diastereoisómero
diathymosulfone
diatimosulfona
diatomaceous earth
tierra diatomácea,
tierra de infusorios
diatomic
diatómico
diatomite
diatomita
diatretyne
diatretina
diatrizoate sodium
diatrizoato de sodio
diaveridine
diaveridina
1,4-diazabicyclo-
(2,2,2)octane
1,4-diazabiciclo-
(2,2,2)octano
diazepam
diacepán, diazepam
1,3-diazine
1,3-diazina
diazinon
diacinona

diaziquone
diacicuona
diazoacetic ester
éster diazoacético
diazo
diazo
diazo compound
compuesto diazo
diazoaminobenzene
diazoaminobenceno
4,4'-diazoamino-
dibenzamidine
4,4'-diazoamino-
dibenzamidina
diazobenzeneaniline
anilina diazo-
bencénica, diazo-
bencenanilina
p-diazobenzene-
sulfonic acid
ácido sulfónico p-
diazobencénico, ácido
p-diazo-
bencensulfónico
diazomethane
p-diazodimethyl-
aniline zinc
chloride double
salt
sal doble de
diazometano p-
diazodimetilanilina y
cloruro de cinc
2-diazo-4,6-dinitro-
benzene-1-oxide
1-óxido de 2-diazo-
4,6-dinitrobenceno
diazodinitrophenol
diazodinitrofenol
p-diazodiphenylamine
sulfate
sulfato de p-diazo-
difenilamina
diazol green B
verde B diazol
1,2-diazole
1,2-diazol
diazomethane
diazometano
1-diazo-2-naphtol-4-
sulfonic acid
ácido 1-diazo-2-naftol-
4-sulfónico
diazonium
diazonio
6-diazo-5-oxo-L-
norleucine
6-diazo-5-oxo-L-
norleucina

diazotization
diazoación
diazotizing salt
sales diazoantes
diazouracil
diazouracilo
diazoxide
diazóxido
dibasic
dibásico
dibekacin
dibekacina, dibecacina
dibemethine
dibemetina
dibenzalacetone
dibenzalacetona
1,2:5,6-dibenz-
anthracene
1,2:5,6-dibenzo-
antraceno
dibenzanthrone
dibenzantrona
3,3'-dibenzanthronyl
3,3'-dibenzantronilo
dibenzepin
dibencepina
2,3,6,7-dibenzo-
anthracene
2,3,6,7-dibenzo-
antraceno
dibenzocyclo-
heptadienone
dibenzociclo-
heptadienona
dibenzofuran
dibenzofurano
dibenzopyran
dibenzopirano
dibenzopyrone
dibenzopirona
dibenzopyrrole
dibenzopirrol
dibenzothiophene
dibenzotiofeno
dibenzoyl
dibenzoílo
trans-1,2-dibenzoyl-
ethylene
trans-1,2-dibenzoil-
etileno
dibenzoylmethane
metano dibenzoílico,
dibenzoilmetano
dibenzoyl peroxide
peróxido de dibenzoílo
dibenzoyl-p-
quinonedioxime
dibenzoíl-p-
quinonadioxima

2,4-dibenzoyl-
resorcinol
2,4-dibenzoíl resor-
cinol, resorcinol 2,4-
dibenzoílico
2,3:6,7-dibenz-
phenanthrene
2,3:6,7-dibenzo-
fenantreno
dibenzyl chloro-
phosphonate
clorofosfonato
dibencílico,
clorofosfonato de
dibencilo
dibenzyl disulfide
disulfuro di-bencílico,
disulfuro de dibencilo
dibenzyl ether
éter dibencílico
dibenzyl phosphide
fosfuro dibencílico,
fosfuro de dibencilo
dibenzyl sebacate
sebacato dibencílico,
sebacato de dibencilo
dibenzyl succinate
succinato dibencílico,
succinato de dibencilo
dibenzylamine
dibencilamina
N,N-dibenzyl-p-
aminophenol
N,N-dibencil-p-
aminofenol
N,N-dibenzylaniline
N,N-dibencilanilina
dibenzylidene acetone
acetona
dibencilidénica,
dibencilidenacetona
N,N-dibenzyl-
methylamine
N,N-dibencilmetilamina
2,5-dibiphenyloxazole
2,5-dibifeniloxazol
diborane
diborano
diboron tetrachloride
tetracloruro de diboro
diboron tetrahydroxide
tetrahidróxido de
diboro
dibromoacetylene
dibromoacetileno
9,10-dibromo-
anthracene
9,10-dibromo-
antraceno

o-dibromobenzene
o-dibromobenceno
N,N-dibromobenzene-sulfonamide
sulfonamida N,N-dibromobencénica,
N,N-dibromo-bencensulfonamida
α,α'-dibromo-d-camphor
α,α'-dibromo-d-alcanfor
dibromochloromethane
dibromoclorometano
1,2-dibromo-3-chloropropane
1,2-dibromo-3-cloropropano
dibromochloro-propane
dibromocloropropano
1,2-dibromo-2,4-dicyanobutane
1,2-dibromo-2,4-dicianobutano
dibromodiethyl sulfide
sulfuro dibromo-dietílico, sulfuro de dibromodietilo
dibromodiethyl sulfone
sulfona dibromo-dietílica, dibromo-dietilsulfona
dibromodiethyl sulfoxide
sulfóxido dibromo-dietílico, sulfóxido de dibromodietilo
dibromodifluoro-methane
dibromodifluoro-metano
1,3-dibromo-5,5-di-methylhydantoin
1,3-dibromo-5,5-dimetilhidantoína
1,2-dibromoethane
1,2-dibromoetano
4,5-dibromofluorescein
4,5-dibromo-fluoresceína
2,4-dibromofluoro-benzene
2,4-dibromofluoro-benceno
dibromodifluoro-methane
dibromodifluoro-metano

ar-dibromoethyl-benzene
ar-dibromoetilbenceno
dibromoformoxime
dibromoformoxima
dibromogallic acid
ácido dibromogálico
3,5-dibromo-4-hydroxibenzene sulfonic acid
ácido 3,5-dibromo-4-hidroxibencen-sulfónico
dibromoiodoethylene
dibromoyodoetileno
dibromomalonic acid
ácido dibromomalónico
dibromomalonyl chloride
cloruro dibromo-malonílico, cloruro de dibromomalonilo
dibromomethane
dibromometano
dibromomethyl ether
éter dibromometílico
9,10-dibromoocta-decanoic acid
ácido 9,10-dibromo-octadecanoico
1,5-dibromopentane
1,5-dibromopentano
dibromopropamidine
dibromopropamidina
1,3-dibromopropane
1,3-dibromopropano
dibromopropanol
dibromopropanol
2,3-dibromopropene
2,3-dibromopropeno
2,6-dibromoquinone-4-chlorimide
2,6-dibromoquinona-4-clorimida
3,5-dibromosalicyl-aldehyde
aldehído 3,5-dibromosalicílico, 3,5-dibromosalicil-aldehído
4,5-dibromosalicyl-anilide
anilida 4,5-dibromo-salicílica, 4,5-di-bromosalicilanilida
3,5-dibromosalicylic acid
ácido 3,5-bromosalicílico

9,10-dibromostearic acid
ácido 9,10-dibromo-esteárico
2,3-dibromosuccinic acid
ácido 2,3-dibromo-succínico
2,5-dibromo-terephthalic acid
ácido 2,5-dibromotereftálico
sym-dibromotetra-fluoroethane
sim-dibromotetra-fluoroetano
3,5-dibromo-L-tyrosine
3,5-dibromo-L-tirosina
dibrompropamidine
dibrompropamidina
dibromsalan
dibromsalán
dibromsalicil
dibromsalicilo
dibucaine
dibucaína
dibucaine hydrochloride
clorhidrato de dibucaína
dibudinate
dibudinato
dibunate sodium
dibunato de sodio
dibuprol
dibuprol
dibupyrone
dibupirona
dibusadol
dibusadol
dibutoline sulfate
sulfato de dibutolina
2,5-dibutoxyaniline
2,5-dibutoxianilina
1,4-dibutoxybenzene
1,4-dibutoxibenceno
dibutoxyethyl adipate
adipato de dibutoxietilo
dibutoxyethyl phthalate
ftalato de dibutoxietilo
dibutoxymethane
dibutoximetano
dibutoxytetraglycol
dibuxitetraglicol

N,N-di-n-butyl acetamide
acetamida N,N-di-n-butílica, N,N-di-n-butilacetamida
2,5-di-tert-butyl benzoquinone
benzoquinona 2,5-di-terc-butílica, 2,5-di-terc-butil-benzoquinona
2,5-di-tert-butyl hydroquinone
hidroquinona 2,5-di-terc-butílica, 2,5-di-terc-butil hidroquinona
dibutyl butyl phosphonate
fosfonato dibutil butílico
dibutyl chloro-phosphate
clorofosfato dibutílico
dibutyl diphenyl tin
dibutildifenilestaño
di-tert-butyl disulfide
disulfuro di-terc-butílico
n-dibutyl ether
éter n-dibutílico
dibutyl fumarate
fumarato dibutílico, fumarato de dibutilo
dibutyl hexahydro-phthalate
hexahidroftalato dibutílico, hexahidroftalato de dibutilo
di-n-butyl itaconate
itaconato di-n-butílico, itaconato de di-n-butilo
N,N-di-n-butyl lauramide
lauramida N,N-di-n-butílica, N,N-di-n-butil lauramida
dibutyl maleate
maleato dibutílico, maleato de dibutilo
di-tert-butyl malonate
malonato di-terc-butílico, malonato de di-terc-butilo
dibutyl oxalate
oxalato dibutílico, oxalato de dibutilo

di-tert-butyl
peroxide
  peróxido di-terc-
  butílico, peróxido de
  di-terc-butilo
dibutyl phosphate
  fosfato dibutílico,
  fosfato de dibutilo
dibutyl phosphite
  fosfito dibutílico,
  fosfito de dibutilo
dibutyl phthalate
  ftalato dibutílico,
  ftalato de dibutilo
di-tert-butylpyridine
  di-terc-butilpiridina
dibutyl sebacate
  sebacato dibutílico,
  sebacato de dibutilo
dibutyl succinate
  succinato dibutílico,
  succinato de dibutilo
di-tert-butyl succinate
  succinato di-terc-
  butílico, succinato de
  di-terc-butilo
di-tert-butyl sulfide
  sulfuro di-terc-butílico,
  sulfuro de di-terc-
  butilo
dibutyl tartrate
  tartrato dibutílico,
  tartrato de dibutilo
dibutyl xanthogen
disulfide
  disulfuro de
  dibutilxantógeno
di-n-butylamine
  di-n-butilamina
di-sec-butylamine
  di-sec-butilamina
dibutylamine
pyrophosphate
  pirofosfato de
  dibutilamina
N,N-di-n-butyl-
aminoethanol
  N,N-di-n-butil-
  aminoetanol
3-dibutylaminopropyl-
p-aminobenzoate
sulfate
  sulfato de 3-dibutil-
  aminopropil-p-
  aminobenzoato
dibutylammonium
oleate
  oleato de dibutil-
  amonio

di-n-butylammonium
tetrafluoroborate
  tetrafluoroborato de
  di-n-butilamonio
N,N-di-n-butylanilide
  N,N-di-n-butilanilida
4,6-di-tert-butyl-m-
cresol
  4,6-di-terc-butil-m-
  cresol
2,6-di-tert-butyl-α-
dimethylamino-p-
cresol
  2,6-di-terc-butil-α-
  dimetilamino-p-cresol
di-tert-butyl-
diperphthalate
  diperftalato de di-terc-
  butilo
dibutyldithiozinc-
carbamate
  carbamato de dibutil
  ditiocinc
2,6-di-tert-butyl-4-
methylphenol
  4-metilfenol 2,6-di-
  terc-butílico, 2,6-di-
  terc-butil-4-metilfenol
2,4-di-tert-butyl-
phenol
  fenol 2,4-di-terc-
  butílico, 2,4-di-terc-
  butilfenol
N,N-di-sec-butyl-p-
phenylenediamine
  p-fenilendiamina
  N,N-di-sec-butílica,
  N,N-di-sec-butil-p-
  fenilendiamina
2,6-di-tert-
butylpyridine
  piridina 2,6-di-terc-
  butílica, 2,6-di-terc-
  butilpiridina
2,5-di-tert-butyl-
quinone
  quinona 2,5-di-terc-
  butílica, 2,5-di-terc-
  butilquinona
N,N-dibutyl-
stearamide
  N,N-dibutil-
  estearamida
dibutylthiourea
  dibutiltiourea
dibutyltin bis(lauryl-
mercaptide)
  bis(laurilmercáptido)
  de dibutilestaño

dibutyltin
diacetate
  diacetato de
  dibutilestaño
dibutyltin
dichloride
  dicloruro de
  dibutilestaño
dibutyltin di-2-
ethylhexoate
  di-2-etilhexoato de
  dibutilestaño
dibutyltin dilaurate
  dilaurato de
  dibutilestaño
dibutyltin maleate
  maleato de
  dibutilestaño
dibutyltin oxide
  óxido de
  dibutilestaño
dibutyltin sulfide
  sulfuro de
  dibutilestaño
2,6-di-tert-butyl-p-
tolyl-N-methyl-
carbamate
  N-metilcarbamato de
  2,6-di-terc-butil-p-
  tolilo
1,1-dibutylurea
  1,1-dibutilurea
dicalcium magnesium
diaconitate
  diaconitato de dicalcio
  y magnesio
dicalcium orthophos-
phate
  ortofosfato de dicalcio
dicalcium
orthophosphite
  ortofosfito de dicalcio
dicalcium phosphate
dihydrate
  fosfato de dicalcio
  dihidratado
dicalcium silicate
  silicato de dicalcio
dicamba
  dicamba, dianat
dicapryl adipate
  adipato dicaprílico,
  adipato de dicaprilo
dicapryl phthalate
  ftalato dicaprílico,
  ftalato de dicaprilo
dicapryl sebacate
  sebacato dicaprílico,
  sebacato de dicaprilo

dicapthon
  dicaptona
dicarbine
  dicarbina
dicarboxylic acid
  ácido dicarboxílico
dicarfen
  dicarfeno
dicentrine
  dicentrina
dicetyl
  dicetilo
dicetyl ether
  éter dicetílico
dicetyl sulfide
  sulfuro dicetílico
dichlobenil
  diclobenilo
dichlofenthion
  diclofentión
dichlone
  diclona
dichlor-
  diclor-
dichloramine T
  dicloramina T
dichloracetaldehyde
  dicloroacetaldehído
dichlofuanid
  diclofuanida
dichloralphenazone
  dicloralfenazona
dichlorisone
  diclorisona
dichlorisone acetate
  acetato de
  diclorisona
dichlorisoproterenol
  diclorisoproterenol
dichlormezanone
  diclormezanona
dichloroacetic acid
  ácido dicloracético
sym-dichloroacetic
anhydride
  anhídrido sim-
  dicloracético
2,5-dichloroaceto-
acetanilide
  acetanilida 2,5-
  dicloracética, 2,5-
  dicloraceto-
  acetanilida
1,1-dichloroacetone
  1,1-dicloracetonaa
α,α-dichloroaceto-
phenone
  α,α-dicloraceto-
  fenona

dichloroacetyl
chloride
  cloruro de
  dicloracetilo
dichloroacetylene
  dicloracetileno
2,3-dichloroallyl
diisopropylthiol-
carbamate
  diisopropil-
  tiolcarbamato
  2,3-dicloroalílico
2,4-dichloro-6-
aminophenol
  2,4-dicloro-6-
  aminofenol
2,5-dichloroaniline
  2,5-dicloranilina
3,6-dichloro-o-anisic
acid
  ácido 3,6-dicloro-o-
  anísico
dichlorobenzaldehyde
  diclorobenzaldehído
dichlorobenzalkonium
chloride
  cloruro de
  diclorobenzalconio
m-dichlorobenzene
  m-diclorobenceno
1,3.dichlorobenzene
  1,3-diclorobenceno, m-
  diclorobenceno
N,N-dichlorobenzene-
sulfonamide
  sulfonamida N,N-
  diclorobencénica, N,N-
  diclorobenceno-
  sulfonamida
2,2'-dichlorobenzidine
  2,2'-diclorobencidina
2,4-dichlorobenzoic
acid
  ácido 2,4-
  diclorobenzoico
2,6-dichlorobenzo-
nitrile
  2,6-dicloro-
  benzonitrilo
3,4-dichlorobenzo-
trichloride
  tricloruro 3,4-
  diclorobenzoico, 3,4-
  diclorobenzo-
  tricloruro
dichlorobenzoyl
chloride
  cloruro de
  diclorobenzoílo

dichlorobenzyl alcohol
  alcohol
  diclorobencílico
1,1-dichloro-2,2-bis(p-
chloro-phenyl)ethane
  1,1-dicloro-2,2-bis(p-
  clorofenil) etano
1,1-dichloro-2,2-bis(p-
ethylphenyl) ethane
  1,1-dicloro-2,2-bis(p-
  etilfenil) etano
1,4-dichlorobutane
  1,4-diclorobutano
1,3-dichlorobutene-2
  1,3-diclorobuteno-2
dichlorocarbene
  diclorocarbeno
1,1'-dichlorocarbonyl
ferrocene
  ferroceno 1,1-
  diclorocarbonílico, 1,1-
  diclorocarbonil
  ferroceno
2,4-dichloro-6-o-
chloroanilino-S-
triazine
  2,4-dicloro-6-o-
  cloroanilino-S-
  triazina
dichloro(2-chloro-
vinyl)arsine
  dicloro(2-
  clorovinil)arsina
3,3'-dichloro-4,4'-
diaminodiphenyl-
methane
  3,3'-dicloro-4,4'-
  diaminodifenil-
  metano
2,3-dichloro-5,6-
dicyanobenzoquinone
  2,,3-dicloro-5,6-
  dicianobenzoquinona
2,2'-dichlorodiethyl
ether
  éter 2,2'-dicloro
  dietílico
dichlorodiethyl formal
  formal dicloro-
  dietílico, dicloro-
  dietilformal
dichlorodiethyl sulfide
  sulfuro dicloro-
  dietílico, sulfuro de
  diclorodietilo
dichlorodiethyl sulfone
  sulfona dicloro-
  dietílica, dicloro-
  dietilsulfona

2,2-dichloro-1,1-
difluoroethyl methyl
ether
  éter 2,2-dicloro-1,1-
  difluoretilmetílico
dichlorodifluoro-
methane
  diclorodifluorometano
1,3-dichloro-5,5-
dimethylhydantoin
  1,3-dicloro-5,5-
  dimetilhidantoína
dichlorodimethyl-
silane
  silano dicloro-
  dimetílico, dicloro-
  dimetilsilano
dichlorodiphenyl-
dichloroethane
  dicloretano
  diclorodifenílico,
  diclorodifenil-
  dicloretano
dichlorodiphenyl-
dichloroethylene
  dicloretileno
  diclorodifenílico,
  diclorodifenil-
  dicloretileno
dichlorodiphenyl-
trichloroethane
  tricloretano
  diclorodifenílico,
  diclorodifenil-
  tricloretano
dichloroethane
  dicloretano
dichloroether
  dicloroéter
dichloroethoxymethane
  dicloretoximetano
1,2-dichloroethyl
acetate
  acetato 1,2-
  dicloretílico, acetato de
  1,2-dicloretilo
dichloroethyl
carbonate
  carbonato dicloretílico,
  carbonato de dicloretilo
sym-dichloroethyl
ether
  éter sim-dicloretílico
dichloroethyl formal
  formal dicloretílico,
  dicloretilformal
dichloroethyl oxide
  óxido dicloretílico,
  óxido de dicloretilo

dichloroethyl sulfide
  sulfuro dicloretílico,
  sulfuro de dicloretilo
p-di-(2-chloroethyl)-
aminophenylalanine
  p-di-(2-cloretil)
  aminofenilalanina
dichloroethylarsine
  dicloretilarsina
sym-dichloroethylene
  sim-dicloretileno
dichloroethylene
  dicloretileno
dichlorofluorescein
  diclorofluoresceína
dichlorofluoro-
methane
  diclorofluorometano
dichloroformoxime
  dicloroformoxima
α-dichlorohydrin
  α-diclorohidrina
5,7-dichloro-8-
hydroxyquinaldine
  5,7-dicloro-8-
  hidroxiquinaldina
2,6-dichloroindo-
phenol sodium
  2,6-diclorindofenol
  sódico
dichloroisocyanuric
acid
  ácido diclorisoci-
  anúrico
sym-dichloroisopropyl
alcohol
  alcohol sim-diclor-
  isopropílico
dichloroisopropyl
ether
  éter diclor-
  isopropílico
dichloromethane
  diclorometano
3,4-dichloro-2-methyl-
acrylanilide
  3,4-dicloro-2-
  metilacrilanilida
sym-dichloromethyl
ether
  éter sim-dicloro-
  metílico
dichloromethyl sulfate
  sulfato diclorometílico,
  sulfato de diclorometilo
5,7-dichloro-2-methyl-
8-quinolinol
  5,7-dicloro-2-metil-8-
  quinolinol

dichloromethylsilane
silano diclorometílico,
dicloro-metilsilano
dichloromono-
fluoromethane
dicloromonofluoro-
metano
dichloronaphthalene
dicloronaftaleno
2,3-dichloro-1,4-
naphthoquinone
2,3-dicloro-1,4-
naftoquinona
2,6-dichloro-4-
nitroaniline
2,6-dicloro-4-
nitroanilina
1,2-dichloro-4-
nitrobenzene
1,2-dicloro-4-
nitrobenceno
2,5-dichloronitro-
benzene
2,5-dicloronitro-benceno
1,2-dichloro-1-
nitroethane
1,2-dicloro-1-nitroetano
dichloropentane
dicloropentano
dichlorophenarsine
diclorofenarsina
dichlorophenarsine
hydrochloride
clorhidrato de
diclorofenarsina
dichlorophen(e)
diclorofeno
2,4-dichlorophenol
2,4-diclorofenol
2,4-dichlorophenoxy-
acetic acid
ácido 2,4-dicloro-
fenoxiacético
2,4-dichlorophenoxy-
butiric acid
ácido 2,4-dicloro-
fenoxibutírico
di-(4-chlorophenoxy)
methane
di-(4-clorofenoxi)
metano
2-(2,4-chlorophenoxy)
propionic acid
ácido 2-(2,4-
clorofenoxi) propiónico
2,4-dichlorophenyl-
benzene sulfonate
sulfonato de 2,4-
diclorofenilbenceno

3,4-dichlorophenyl
isocyanate
isocianato de 3,4-
diclorofenilo
O-(2,4-dichloro-
phenyl)-O,O-diethyl
phosphorothioate
fosfotioato de O-(2,4-
diclorofenil)-O,O-
dietilo
3-(3,4-dichloro-
phenyl)-1,1-
dimethylurea
3-(3,4-diclorofenil)-
1,1-dimetilurea
di-(p-chlorophenyl)
ethanol
di-(p-clorofenil) etanol
3-(3,4-dichloro-
phenyl)-1-methoxy-1-
methylurea
3-(3,4-diclorofenil)-1-
metoxi-1-metilurea
di(p-chlorophenyl)
methyl carbinol
di(p-clorofenil)
metilcarbinol
o-(2,4-dichloro-
phenyl)o-methyl-
isopropylphosphoro-
amidothioate
fosfamidotioato
de o-(2,4-diclorofenil)
o-metilisopropilo
2,4-dichlorophenyl-4-
nitrophenyl ether
éter 2,4-diclorofenil-
4-nitrofenílico
dichlorophenyl-
trichloro silane
triclorosilano
diclorofenílico,
diclorofenil-
triclorosilano
3,6-dichlorophthalic
acid
ácido 3,6-dicloroftálico
dichloroprop
ácido 2-(2,4-
diclorofenoxi)
propanoico
1,2-dichloropropane
1,2-dicloropropano
1,3-dichloro-2-
propanol
1,3-dicloro-2-
propanol
1,3-dichloropropene
1,3-dicloropropeno

dichloropropene-
dichloropropane
mixture
mezcla de
dicloropropeno y
dicloropropano
3,4-dichloropropion-
anilide
anilida 3,4-dicloro-
propiónica, 3,4-
dicloropropion-
anilida
2,2-dichloropropionic
acid
ácido 2,2-dicloro-
propiónico
2,6-dichloroquinone-
chlorimide
clorimida 2,6-
dicloroquinónica, 2,6-
dicloro quinona
clorimida
4,6-dichlororesorcine
4,6-diclororesorcina
dichlororiboflavin
diclororriboflavina
dichlorosilan
diclorosilano
2,6-dichlorostyrene
2,6-dicloroestireno
p-N,N-dichloro-
sulfamylbenzoic acid
ácido p-N,N-
diclorosulfamil-
benzoico
dichorosulfonphthalein
diclorosulfoftaleína
dichlorotetra-
fluoroacetone
diclorotetra-
fluoracetona
sym-dichlorotetra-
fluorethane
sim-diclorotetra-
fluoretano
2,5-dichlorothiopene
2,5-diclorotiopeno
dichlorotoluene
diclorotolueno
dichloro-sym-trazine-
2,4,6-trione
dicloro-sim-tracino-
2,4,6-triona
2,2-dichlorovinyl
dimethyl phosphate
dimetilfosfato 2,2-
diclorovinílico,
dimetilfosfato de 2,2-
diclorovinilo

ß,ß'-dichlorovinyl-
chloroarsine
clorarsina ß,ß'-
diclorovinílica, ß,ß'-
diclorovinil-
clorarsina
ß,ß'-dichlorovinyl-
methylarsine
arsina ß,ß'-dicloro-
vinilmetílica, ß,ß'-
diclorovinilmetil-
arsina
dichloroxylenol
dicloroxilenol
dichlorphenamide
diclorfenamida
dichlorprop
ácido dicloro-
propanoico
dichlorvos
diclorvós
dichroic
dicroico
dichromatic
dicromático
diciferron
diciferrón
diclobutrazol
diclobutrazol
diclofenac
diclofenaco
diclofenac sodium
diclofenaco sódico
diclofenac potassium
diclofenaco potásico
diclofenamide
diclofenamida
diclofensine
diclofensina
diclofurime
diclofurima
diclometide
diclometida
diclonixin
diclonixina
dicloralurea
dicloralurea
dicloxacillin
dicloxacilina
dicobalt edetate
edetato dicobáltico
dicobalt
octacarbonyl
octacarbonilo
dicobáltico
dicofol
dicofol
dicolinium iodide
yoduro de dicolinio

89

dicophane
dicofano, DDT,
diclorodifenil
tricloroetano
dicoumarol
dicumarol
dicresulene
dicresuleno
dicresyl glyceril
ether
éter dicresilglicerílico
dicresyl glyceril ether
acetate
acetato de éter
dicresilglicerílico
dicrotophos
dicrotofós
dicryl
dicrilo
dictamnine
dictamnina
dicumarol
dicumarol
dicumyl peroxide
peróxido de
dicumilo
dicyan
diciano, cianógeno,
etandinitrilo
dicyandamide
diciandamida
dicyanine
dicianina
o-dicyanobenzene
o-dicianobenceno
1,4-dicyanobutane
1,4-dicianobutano
2,4-dicyanobutene-1
2,4-dicianobuteno-1
dicyanodiamide
dicianodiamida
dicyanodiamidine
sulfate
sulfato de diciano-
diamidina
9-dicyanomethylene-
2,4,7-trinitrofluorene
9-dicianometileno-
2,4,7-trinitrofluoreno
dicyclodiepoxy-
carboxilate
carboxilato de
diciclodiepóxido
dicyclohexyl
diciclohexilo
dicyclohexyl adipate
adipato diciclo-
hexílico, adipato de
diciclohexilo

dicyclohexylamine
hexilamina dicíclica,
diciclohexilamina
dicyclohexyl-
carbodiimide
carbodiimida
diciclohexílica,
diciclohexil-
carbodiimida
dicyclohexyl-
phthalate
ftalato diciclohexílico,
ftalato de diciclohexilo
dicyclomine
hydrochloride
chlorhidrato de
diciclomina
dicyclopentadiene
pentadieno dicíclico,
diciclopentadieno
dicyclopentadiene
dioxide
dióxido de pentadieno
dicíclico, dióxido de
diciclopentadieno
dicyclopenta-
dienylcobalt
cobalto diciclo-
pentadienílico,
diciclopenta-
dienilcobalto
dicyclopenta-
dienyliron
hierro diciclopenta-
dienílico, diciclo-
pentadienilhierro
dicyclopenta-
dienylnickel
níquel diciclo-
pentadienílico,
diciclopenta-
dienilníquel
dicyclopenta-
dienylosmium
osmio diciclopenta-
dienílico, diciclo-
pentadienilosmio
dicyclopenta-
dienyltitanium
dichloride
dicloruro de titanio
diciclopentadienílico,
dicloruro de
diciclopenta-
dieniltitanio
dicyclopenta-
dienylzirconium
dichloride
dicloruro de circonio

diciclopentadienílico,
dicloruro de
diciclopenta-
dienilcirconio
dicycloverine
verina dicíclica,
dicicloverina
didanosine
didanosina
didecyl adipate
adipato didecílico,
adipato de didecilo
didecyl ether
éter didecílico
didecyl phthalate
ftalato didecílico,
ftalato de didecilo
didecyl sulfide
sulfuro didecílico,
sulfuro de didecilo
didecyl thioether
tioéter didecílico
didecylamine
amina didecílica,
didecilamina
didecyldimethyl-
ammonium chloride
cloruro de amonio
didecildimetílico,
cloruro de didecil-
dimetilamonio
dideoxyadenosine
dideoxiadenosina
dideoxycytidine
dideoxicitidina
di(diphenylmercury)
dodecenyl succinate
succinato de
di(difenilmercuri)
dodecenilo
didodecyl ether
éter didodecílico
didodecyl
thioether
tioéter didodecílico
didodecyl 3,3-thio-
dipropionate
3,3-tiodipropionato
didodecílico, 3,3-
tiodipropionato de
didodecilo
didodecylamine
didodecilamina
didrovaltrate
didrovaltrato
didymium
didimio
didymiun oxide
óxido de didimio

die
troquel, molde,
matriz
Dieckmann reaction
reacción de Dieckmann
dieldrin
dieldrina
dielectric
dieléctrico
dielectric constant
constante dieléctrica
dielectric strengh
resistencia dieléctrica,
potencia dieléctrica
Diels-Alder reaction
reacción de Diels
Alder
diene
dieno
dienestrol
dienestrol
dienochlor
dienoclor
diethadione
dietadiona
N,N-diethanoglycine
N,N-dietanoglicina
diethanolamine
dietanolamina
N,N-diethanolglycine
N,N-dietanolglicina
diethazine
dietazina
2,5-diethoxyaniline
2,5-dietoxianilina
1,4-diethoxybenzene
1,4-dietoxibenceno
diethoxyethyl
phthalate
ftalato dietoxietílico,
ftalato de dietoxietilo
diethyl acetal
acetal dietílico,
dietilacetal
diethyl acetaldehyde
acetaldehído dietílico,
dietilacetaldehído
diethyl adipate
adipato dietílico,
adipato de dietilo
diethyl cadmium
cadmio dietílico,
dietilcadmio
diethyl carbinol
carbinol dietílico,
dietilcarbinol
diethyl carbonate
carbonato dietílico,
carbonato de dietilo

90

diethyl chlorophosphate
clorofosfato dietílico,
clorofosfato de dietilo
diethyl diethylmalonate
dietilmalonato dietílico,
dietilmalonato de
dietilo
diethyl ether
éter dietílico
diethyl ethoxymethylene malonate
malonato dietílico de
etoximetileno,
etoximetilenmalonato
dietílico
diethyl ethylmalonate
etilmalonato dietílico,
etilmalonato de dietilo
diethyl ethylphosphonate
etilfosfonato dietílico,
etilfosfonato de dietilo
1,1'-diethyl ferrocenoate
ferrocenoato de 1,1'-
dietilo
diethyl isoamylethylmalonate
malonato isoamiletil
dietílico, isoamiletil-
malonato de dietilo
diethyl ketone
cetona dietílica,
dietilcetona
diethyl maleate
maleato dietílico,
maleato de dietilo
diethyl malonate
malonato dietílico,
malonato de dietilo
diethyl (1-methyl-butyl) malonate
(1-metilbutil) malonato
dietílico, (1-metilbutil)
malonato de dietilo
diethyl oxalate
oxalato dietílico,
oxalato de dietilo
diethyl oxide
óxido dietílico, óxido
de dietilo
diethyl phosphite
fosfito dietílico, fosfito
de dietilo
diethyl phthalate
ftalato dietílico, ftalato
de dietilo

diethyl succinate
succinato dietílico,
succinato de dietilo
diethyl sulfate
sulfato dietílico,
sulfato de dietilo
diethyl sulfide
sulfuro dietílico,
sulfuro de dietilo
diethyl tartrate
tartrato dietílico,
tartrato de dietilo
N,N-diethylacetamide
acetamida N,N-
dietílica, N,N-
dietilacetamida
diethylacetic acid
ácido dietilacético
N,N-diethylacetoacetamide
acetoacetamida N,N-
dietílica, N,N-
dietilacetoacetamida
diethylaluminium chloride
cloruro de dietilaluminio
diethylaluminium hydride
hidruro de
dietilaluminio
diethylamine
amina dietílica,
dietilamina
1-diethylamino-4-aminopentane
1-dietilamino-4-
aminopentano
diethylaminoaniline
anilina dietilamínica,
dietilaminoanilina
diethylaminocelullose
celulosa dietilamínica,
dietilaminocelulosa
2-diethylamino-ethanethiol hydrochloride
clorhidrato de 2-
dietilaminetantiol
diethylaminoethanol
dietilaminetanol
diethylaminoethoxy ethanol
dietilaminetoxietanol
N,N-diethyl-3-amino-4-methoxybenzene-sulfonamide
sulfonamida N,N-

dietil-3-amino-4-
metoxibencénica
1-diethylamino-2-methylbenzene
1-dietilamino-2-
metilbenceno
7-diethylamino-1-methylcoumarin
7-dietilamino-1-
metilcumarina
5-diethylamino-2-pentanone
5-dietilamino-2-
pentanona
m-diethylaminophenol
m-dietilaminofenol
3-diethylamino-propylamine
propilamina 3-
dietilamínica, 3-
dietilaminopropilamina
diethylaniline
dietilanilina
diethylbarbituric acid
ácido
dietilbarbitúrico
diethylbenzhydryl-amine
bencidrilamina
dietílica, dietil-
bencidrilamina
diethylberyllium
berilio dietílico,
dietilberilio
diethylbromo-acetamide
bromacetamida
dietílica, dietilbrom-
acetamida
di(2-ethylbutyl) azelate
acelato de di-(2-
etilbutilo)
di(2-ethylbutyl) phthalate
ftalato de di-(2-
etilbutilo)
diethylcarbamazine
dietilcarbamazina,
carbamazina dietílica
diethylcarbamazine citrate
citrato de
dietilcarbamazina
N,N-diethyl-carbanilide
N,N-dietil-
carbanilida

1,1'-diethyl-4,4'-carbocyanine iodide
yoduro de 1,1'-dietil-
4,4'-carbocianina
diethylcyclohexane
ciclohexano dietílico,
dietilciclohexano
N,N-diethylcyclo-hexylamine
ciclohexilamina N,N-
dietílica,
N,N-dietilciclo-
hexilamina
diethyl-1-(2,4-dichlorophenyl)-2-chlorovinyl phosphate
fosfato de dietil-1-
(2,4-diclorofenil)-2-
clorovinilo
diethyldichlorosilane
diclorosilano dietílico,
dietildiclorosilano
O,O-diethyl-S-2-diethylaminoethyl phosphorothioate hydrogen oxalate
oxalato ácido de S-2-
dietilaminoetil-
fosfotioato de O,O-
dietilo
diethyldiphenyl-dichloroethane
dicloroetano
dietildifenílico,
dietildifenildi-
cloroetano
sym-diethyldiphenyl-urea
sim-dietildifenilurea
diethyldithio zinc carbamate
dietilditiocarbamato
de cinc
diethylendiamine
dietilendiamina
diethylene disulfide
disulfuro de dietileno
diethylene ether
éter dietilénico
diethylene glycol
glicol dietilénico,
dietilenglicol
diethylene glycol acetate
acetato de glicol
dietilénico, acetato de
dietilenglicol

91

diethylene glycol bis(allyl carbonate)
bis(alilcarbonato) de glicol dietilénico

diethylene glycol bis(n-butylcarbonate)
bis(n-butilcarbonato) de glicol dietilénico

diethylene glycol bis(chloroformate)
bis(cloroformiato) de glicol dietilénico

diethylene glycol bis(cresyl carbonate)
bis(cresilcarbonato) de glicol dietilénico

diethylene glycol bis(2,2-dichloro propionate)
bis(2,2-dicloropropionato) de glicol dietilénico

diethylene glycol diacetate
diacetato de glicol dietilénico

diethylene glycol dibenzoate
dibenzoato de glicol dietilénico

diethylene glycol dibutyl ether
éter dibutílico de glicol dietilénico

diethylene glycol dicarbamate
dicarbamato de glicol dietilénico

diethylene glycol diethyl ether
éter dietílico de glicol dietilénico

diethylene glycol dimethyl ether
éter dimetílico de glicol dietilénico

diethylene glycol dinitrate
dinitrato de glicol dietilénico

diethylene glycol dipelargonate
dipelargonato de glicol dietilénico

diethylene glycol distearate
diestearato de glicol dietilénico

diethylene glycol monoacetate
monoacetato de glicol dietilénico

diethylene glycol monobutyl ether acetate
acetato de éter monobutílico de glicol dietilénico

diethylene glycol monoethyl ether
éter monoetílico de glicol dietilénico

diethylene glycol monoethyl ether acetate
acetato de éter monoetílico de glicol dietilénico

diethylene glycol monohexyl ether
éter monohexílico de glicol dietilénico

diethylene glycol monolaurate
monolaurato de glicol dietilénico

diethylene glycol monomethyl ether
éter monometílico de glicol dietilénico

diethylene glycol monomethyl ether acetate
acetato de éter monometílico de glicol dietilénico

diethylene glycol monooleate
monoleato de glicol dietilénico

diethylene glycol monoricinoleate
monorricinoleato de glicol dietilénico

diethylene glycol monostearate
monoestearato de glicol dietilénico

diethylene glycol phthalate
ftalato de glicol dietilénico

diethylene glycol stearate
estearato de glicol dietilénico

diethylene oxide
óxido dietilénico, óxido de dietileno

1,4-diethylene oxide
óxido de 1,4-dietileno

diethylene triamine
triamina dietilénica, dietilentriamina

diethylene triamine pentaacetic acid
ácido dietilentriamina pentaacético

N,N-diethylethanolamine
N,N-dietiletanolamina

uns-diethylethylene
asim-dietiletileno

N,N-diethylethylenediamine
diamina N,N-dietiletilénica, N,N-dietiletilendiamina

p,p'-(1,2-diethylethylene) diphenol
p,p'-(1,2-dietiletilén) difenol

diethylgermanium dichloride
dicloruro de dietilgermanio

diethylglycol phthalate
ftalato de dietilglicol

di(2-ethylhexyl) adipate
adipato de di(2-etilhexilo)

di(2-ethylhexyl) amine
di(2-etilhexil)amina

di(2-ethylhexyl) aminoethanol
di(2-etilhexil) aminoetanol

di(2-ethylhexyl) azelate
acelato de di(2-etilhexilo)

di(2-ethylhexyl) ethanolamine
di(2-etilhexil) etanolamina

di(2-ethylhexyl) ether
éter de di(2-etilhexilo)

di(2-ethylhexyl)2-ethylhexyl-phosphonate
2-etilhexilfosfonato de di(2-etilhexilo)

di(2-ethylhexyl) fumarate
fumarato de di(2-etilhexilo)

di(2-ethylhexyl) hexahydrophthalate
hexahidroftalato de di(2-etilhexilo)

di(2-ethylhexyl) hydrogen phosphate
fosfato ácido de di(2-etilhexilo)

di(2-ethylhexyl) isophthalate
isoftalato de di(2-etilhexilo)

di(2-ethylhexyl) maleate
maleate de di(2-etilhexilo)

di(2-ethylhexyl) phosphite
fosfito de di(2-etilhexilo)

di(2-ethylhexyl) phosphoric acid
ácido di(2-etilhexil) fosfórico

di(2-ethylhexyl) phthalate
ftalato de di(2-etilhexilo)

di(2-ethylhexyl) sebacate
sebacato de di(2-etilhexilo)

di(2-ethylhexyl) sodium sulfosuccinate
sulfosuccinato sódico de di(2-etilhexilo)

di(2-ethylhexyl) succinate
succinato de di(2-etilhexilo)

diethylhydroxylamine
hidroxilamina dietílica, dietilhidroxilamina

diethylmagnesium
magnesio dietílico, dietilmagnesio

diethylmalonic acid
ácido dietilmalónico

diethylmalonylurea
malonilurea dietílica, dietilmaloniurea

diethylmethyl-
methane
  metano dietilmetílico,
  dietilmetilmetano
O,O-diethyl-O-p-
nitrophenyl
phosphorothioate
  O-p-nitrofenil-
  fosfotioato de O,O-
  dietilo
O,O-diethyl-O-p-
nitrophenyl
thiophosphate
  O-p-nitrofeniltiofosfato
  de O,O-dietilo
di-p(ethylphenyl)di-
chloroethane
  di-p(etilfenil)
  dicloroetano
N,N-diethyl-p-
phenylenediamine
  N,N-dietil-p-
  fenilendiamina
2,2-diethyl-1,3-
propanediol
  2,2-dietil-1,3-
  propandiol
diethylpropion
  dietilpropión
O,O-diethyl-O-2-
pyrazinyl
phosphorothioate
  O-2-pirazinil-
  fosfotioato de O,O-
  dietilo
diethylpyrocarbonate
  pirocarbonato dietílico,
  pirocarbonato de
  dietilo
diethylsilane
  dietilsilano
diethylstilbestrol
  diestilestilbestrol
diethylstilbestrol
dipropionate
  dipropionato de
  dietilestilbestrol
diethylthiambutene
  tiambuteno dietílico,
  dietiltiambuteno
1,3-diethylthiourea
  1,3-dietiltiourea
N,N-diethyl-m-
toluamide
  N,N-dietil-m-toluamida
N,N-diethyl-m-toluidine
  N,N-dietil-m-toluidina
N,N-diethyl-o-toluidine
  N,N-dietil-o-toluidina

O,O-diethyl-O-3,5,6-
trichloro-2-pyridil
phosphorothioate
  O-3,5,6-tricloro-2-
  piridilfosfotioato de
  O,O-dietilo
3,9-diethyl-6-
tridecanol
  3,9-dietil-6-tridecanol
1,1-diethylurea
  1,1-dietilurea
diethylzinc
  cinc dietílico, dietilcinc
dietifen
  dietifeno
difebarbamate
  difebarbamato
difedipine
  difedipina
difemerine
  difemerina
difemetorex
  difemetorex
difenamizole
  difenamizol
difencloxazine
  difencloxazina
difenidol
  difenidol
difenoximide
  difenoximida
difenoxin
  difenoxina
difenoxin hydro-
chloride
  clorhidrato de
  difenoxina
difenpiramide
  difempiramida
difetarsone
  difetarsona
difeterol
  difeterol
differential gravimetric
analysis
  análisis gravimétrico
  diferencial
differential thermal
analysis
  análisis térmico
  diferencial
diffraction, neutron
  difracción de neutrones
difraction, X ray
  difracción de rayos X
diffusion
  difusión
diffusion, gaseous
  difusión gaseosa

diffusion pump
  bomba de difusión
diffussion velocity
  velocidad de difusión
diffusivity
  difusividad,
  coeficiente de
  difusión
diffusor
  difusor
diflorasone
  diflorasona
diflorasone diacetate
  diacetato de
  diflorasona
difluanazine
  difluanacina,
  difluanazina
diflubenzuron
  diflubenzurón
diflucortolone
  diflucortolona
diflucortolone
21-valerate
  21-valerato de
  diflucortolona
diflumidone
  diflumidona
diflunisal
  diflunisal
2,4-difluoroaniline
  2,4-difluoranilina
p-difluorobenzene
  p-difluorobenceno
1,1,1-difluorochloro-
ethane
  1,1,1-difluoro-
  cloretano
difluorochloro-
methane
  difluoroclorometano
difluorodiazine
  difluorodiazina
difluorodibromo-
methane
  difluorodibromo-
  metano
difluorodichloro-
methane
  difluorodicloro-
  metano
4,4'-difluorodiphenyl
  4,4'-difluorodifenilo
difluorodiphenyl-
trichloroethane
  tricloroetano
  difluorodifenílico,
  difluorodifenil-
  tricloroetano

1,1-difluoroethane
  1,1-difluoretano
1,1-difluoroethylene
  1,1-difluoretileno
difluoromethane
  difluorometano
difluoromono-
chloroethane
  difluoromono-
  cloroetano
difluoromono-
chloromethane
  difluoromono-
  clorometano
difluorophosphoric
acid
  ácido difluoro-
  fosfórico
difluprednate
  difluprednato
difluron
  diflurón
difolaton
  difolatón
diftalone
  diftalona
digallic acid
  ácido digálico
digalogenin
  digalogenina
digest
  digestión
digest, to
  digerir
digester
  equipo de digestión
digestion
  digestión
digestor
  equipo de
  digestión
diginatigenin
  diginatigenina
diginatin
  diginatina
diginin
  diginina
digital integrator
  integrador digital
digitalin
  digitalina
digitalis
  digital
digitalose
  digitalosa
digitogenin
  digitogenina
digitonin
  digitonina

digitoxigenin
digitoxigenina
digitoxin
digitoxina
digitoxose
digitoxosa
diglycerol
diglicerina, diglicerol
diglycidyl ether
éter diglicidílico
**1,3-diglycidyloxy-
benzene**
oxibenceno 1,3-
diglicidílico, 1,3-
diglicidiloxibenceno
diglycol
diglicol
diglycol acetate
acetato diglicólico,
acetato de diglicol
diglycol carbamate
carbamato diglicólico,
carbamato de diglicol
**diglycol
chloroformate**
cloroformiato
diglicólico,
cloroformiato de
diglicol
diglycol chlorohydrin
clorhidrina diglicólica,
clorhidrina de diglicol
diglycolic acid
ácido diglicólico
diglycol laurate
laurato diglicólico,
laurato de diglicol
diglycol methyl ether
éter metil diglicólico
diglycol monostearate
monoestearato
diglicólico,
monoestearato de
diglicol
diglycol nitrate
nitrato diglicólico,
nitrato de diglicol
diglycol oleate
oleato diglicólico,
oleato de diglicol
diglycol phthalate
ftalato diglicólico,
ftalato de diglicol
diglycol ricinoleate
ricinoleato diglicólico,
ricinoleato de diglicol
diglycol stearate
estearato diglicólico,
estearato de diglicol

diglyme
diglima
digoxigenin
digoxigenina
digoxin
digoxina
**diheptyl-p-phenylene-
diamine**
diheptil-p-
fenilendiamina
dihexadecyl ether
éter dihexadecílico
dihexadecyl sulfide
sulfuro dihexa-
decílico, sulfuro de
dihexadecilo
dihexadecyl thioether
tioéter dihexadecílico
dihexadecylamine
dihexadecilamina
dihexyl
dihexilo
di-n-hexyl adipate
adipato de di-n-hexilo
di-n-hexyl maleate
maleato de di-n-hexilo
dihexyl phthalate
ftalato diexílico, ftalato
de diexilo
dihexyl sebacate
sebacato dihexílico,
sebacato de dihexilo
di-n-hexylamine
di-n-hexilamina
dihexyverine
dihexiverina
dihydralazine
dihidralazina
dihydrate
dihidrato
dihydrazine sulfate
sulfato de dihidrazina
dihydric
dihídrico
dihydric alcohol
alcohol dihídrico
dihydric phenol
fenol dihídrico
dihydroabietyl alcohol
alcohol
dihidroabietílico
**1,8-dihydro-
acenaphthylene**
1,8-dihidro-
acenaftileno
dihydrochalcone
dihidrocalcona
dihydrocholesterol
dihidrocolesterol

dihydrocodeine
dihidrocodeína
**dihydrocodeine
tartrate**
tartrato de
dihidrocodeína
**dihydrocodeinone
bitartrate**
bitartrato de
dihidrocodeinona
**dihydrocodeinone
enol acetate**
acetato enólico de
dihidrocodeinona
dihydrocortisone
dihidrocortisona
dihydrocoumarin
dihidrocumarina
**6,7-dihydrodipyrol
(1,2-a:2',1'-c)
pyrazidinium salt**
sal de 6,7-
dihidrodipirol
(1,2-a: 2',1'-c)-
piracidinio
dihydroequillin
dihidroequilina
dihydroergotamine
dihidroergotamina
**dihydroergotamine
mesylate**
mesilato de
dihidroergotamina
dihydro-ß-erytroidine
dihidro-ß-eritroidina
dihydrofolic reductase
reductasa
dihidrofólica
**dihydrogen ferrous
EDTA**
AEDT dihidroferroso
**dihydro-2,(3)-
imidazolone**
dihidro-2,(3)-
imidazolona
2,3-dihydroindene
2,3-dihidroindeno
dihydroisocodeine
dihidroisocodeína
dihydromorphine
dihidromorfina
**9,20-dihydro-9-
oxoanthracene**
9,20-dihidro-9-
oxoantraceno
dihydroperoxide
dihidroperóxido
2,3-dihydropyran
2,3-dihidropirano

**1,2-dihydro-3,6-
pyridazinedione**
1,2-dihidro-3,6-
piridacindiona
dihydrostreptomycin
dihidro-
estreptomicina
**dihydrostreptomycin
sulfate**
sulfato de dihidro-
estreptomicina
dihydrotachysterol
dihidrotaquisterol
dihydrothebaine
dihidrotebaína
**2,5-dihydrothiophene
1,1-dioxide**
1,1-dióxido de 2,5-
dihidrotiofeno
**1,2-dihydro-
2,2,4-trimethyl-
quinoline**
1,2-dihidro-2,2,4-
trimetilquinolina, 1,2-
dihidro-2,2,4-
trimetilquinoleína
dihydrovitamin K
dihidrovitamina K
dihydroxyacetone
dihidroxiacetona
**2,4-dihydroxy-
acetophenone**
2,4-dihidroxi-
acetofenona
**dihydroxyaluminum
acetylsalicylate**
acetilsalicilato de
dihidroxialuminio
**dihydroxyaluminium
amino acetate**
aminoacetato de
dihidroxialuminio
**dihydroxyaluminum
sodium carbonate**
carbonato de
dihidroxialuminio y
sodio
**1,3-dihydroxy-2-
amino-4-octadecene**
1,3-dihidroxi-2-amino-
4-octadeceno
**1,8-dihydroxy-
anthranol**
1,8-dihidroxi-
antranol
**1,2-dihydroxy-
anthraquinone**
1,2-dihidroxi-
antraquinona

m-dihydroxybenzene
m-dihidroxibenceno
2,4-dihydroxybenzene carboxylic acid
ácido 2,4-dihidroxibencencarboxílico
2,4-dihydroxybenzoic acid
ácido 2,4-dihidroxibenzoico
2,4-dihydroxybenzophenone
2,4-dihidroxibenzofenona
2,5-dihydroxybenzoquinone
2,5-dihidroxibenzoquinona
2,3-dihydroxybutane
2,3-dihidroxibutano
2,5-dihydroxychlorobenzene
2,5-dihidroxiclorobenceno
3-(3,4-dihydroxycinnamoyl)quinic acid
ácido 3-(3,4-dihidroxicinamoíl) quínico
dihydroxydiaminomercurobenzene
dihidroxidiaminomercurobenceno
2,2'-dihydroxy-5,5'-dichlorophenylmethane
2,2'-dihidroxi-5,5'-diclorofenilmetano
dihydroxydiethyl ether
éter dihidroxidietílico
2,2'-dihydroxy-5,5'-difluorodiphenyl sulfide
sulfuro de 2,2'-dihidroxi-5,5'-difluorodifenilo
2,4'-dihydroxy-3,3-dimethylbutyric acid gamma lactone
gamma lactona de ácido 2,4'-dihidroxi-3,3-dimetil butírico
n-(2,4-dihydroxy-3,3-di-methylbutyryl)-ß-alanine
n-(2,4-dihidroxi-3,3-dimetilbutiril)-ß-alanina

5,7-dihydroxydimethylcoumarin
5,7-dihidroxidimetilcumarina
dihydroxydiphenyl sulfone
sulfona dihidroxidifenílica, dihidroxidifenil sulfona
5,5'-dihydroxy-7,7'-disulfonic-2,2'-dinaphthylurea
2,2'-dinaftilurea 5,5'-dihidroxi-7,7'-disulfónica
p-di(2-hydroxyethoxy)benzene
p-di(2-hidroxietoxi) benceno
N,N-dihydroxyethyl ethylenediamine
etilendiamina N,N-dihidroxietílica, N,N-dihidroxietiletilendiamina
dihydroxyethyl sulfide
sulfuro dihidroxietílico, sulfuro de dihidroxietilo
di(2-hydroxyethyl) amine
di(2-hidroxietil) amina
N,N-dihydroxy ethyl-m-toluidine
N,N-dihidroxietil-m-toluidina
2.2'-dihydroxy-3,5,6,3',5',6'-hexachlorodiphenyl methane
metano 2.2'-dihidroxi-3,5,6,3',5',6'-hexacloro difenílico, 2.2'-dihidroxi-3,5,6,3',5',6'-hexaclorodifenil metano
1,3-dihydroxy-4-hexylbenzene
benceno 1,3-dihidroxi-4-hexílico, 1,3-dihidroxi-4-hexilbenceno
3',4'-dihydroxy-2-isopropylamine acetophenone hydrochloride
clorhidrato de 3',4'-dihidroxi-2-

isopropilaminoacetofenona
dihydroxymaleic acid
ácido dihidroximaleico
3,4-dihydroxy-α-(methylaminomethyl)benzyl alcohol
alcohol 3,4-dihidro-α-(metilaminometil) bencílico
1,8-dihydroxy-3-methyl-anthraquinone
1,8-dihidroxi-3-metilantraquinona
5,7-dihydroxy-4-methylcoumarin
5,7-dihidroxi-4-metilcumarina
1,1'-dihydroxy-methylferrocene
1,1-dihidroximetil-ferroceno
1,3-dihydroxy-naphthalene
1,3-dihidroxinaftaleno
4,5-dihydroxy-2,7-naphthalene disulfonic acid
ácido 4,5-dihidroxi-2,7-naftalen-disulfónico
2,3-dihydroxy-naphthalene-6-sulfonic acid, sodium salt
sal sódica del ácido 2,3-dihidroxinaftalén-6-sulfónico
2,8-dihydroxy-3-naphthoic acid
ácido 2,8-dihidroxi-3-naftoico
L-dihydroxyphenyl-alanine
L-dihidroxifenil-alanina
1,2-dihydroxypropane
1,2-dihidroxipropano
dihydroxypropanone
dihidroxipropanona
dihydroxystearic acid
ácido dihidroxiesteárico
dihydroxysuccinic acid
ácido dihidroxisuccínico
dihydroxytartaric acid
ácido dihidroxitartárico

3,5-dihydroxytoluene
3,5-dihidroxitolueno
dihyprilone
dihiprilona
diiodoacetylene
diyodoacetileno
diiodoaniline
diyodoanilina
diiodobrassidinic acid ethyl ester
éster etílico de ácido diyodobrasidínico
sym-diiododibromo-ethylene
sim-diyododibrom-etileno
diiododiethyl sulfide
sulfuro dietílico de diyodo, sulfuro de diyododietilo
4',5'-diiodofluorescein
4',5'-diyodofluoresceína
diiodoformoxime
diyodoformoxima
diiodohydroxyquinoleine
diyodohidroxiquinoleína
diiodomethane
diyodometano
3,5-diiodosalicylic acid
ácido 3,5-diyodosalicílico
diiodothyronine
diyodotironina
diisoamylamine
diisoamilamina
diisobutyl
diisobutilo
diisobutyl adipate
adipato de diisobutilo
diisobutyl aluminum chloride
cloruro de diisobutil aluminio
diisobutyl aluminum hydride
hidruro de diisobutil aluminio
diisobutylcarbinyl acetate
acetato de diisobutil carbinilo
diisobutyl ketone
cetona diisobutílica, diisobutilcetona

diisobutyl phenol
fenol diisobutílico,
diisobutil fenol
diisobutyl phthalate
ftalato diisobutílico,
ftalato de diisobutilo
diisobutyl sodium
sulfosuccinate
sulfosuccinato
diisobutílico de sodio
diisobutylamine
diisobutilamina
diisobutylcarbinol
diisobutilcarbinol
diisobutylene
diisobutileno
diisocyanate
diisocianato
diisodecyl adipate
adipato diisodecílico,
adipato de diisodecilo
diisodecyl phthalate
ftalato diisodecílico,
ftalato de diisodecilo
diisodecyl-4,5-epoxy-
tetrahydrophthalate
4,5-epoxitetra-
hidroftalato de
diisodecilo
diisononyl adipate
adipato diisononílico,
adipato de
diisononilo
diisooctyl acid
phosphate
fosfato ácido de
diisoctilo
diisooctyl adipate
adipato diisoctílico,
adipato de diisoctilo
diisooctyl azelate
acelato diisoctílico,
acelato de diisoctilo
diisooctyl phthalate
ftalato diisoctílico,
ftalato de diisoctilo
diisooctyl sebacate
sebacato diisoctílico,
sebacato de diisoctilo
diisopromine
diisopromina
diisopropanolamine
diisopropanolamina
diisopropyl
diisopropilo
diisopropyl carbinol
carbinol diiso-
propílico, diisopropil
carbinol

diisopropyl cresol
cresol diisopropílico,
diisopropil cresol
diisopropyl
dixanthogen
dixantógeno
diisopropílico,
diisopropil
dixantógeno
diisopropyl ether
éter diisopropílico
diisopropyl
fluorophosphate
fluorofosfato
diisopropílico,
fluorofosfato de
diisopropilo
diisopropyl ketone
cetona diisopropílica,
diisopropilcetona
diisopropyl oxide
óxido diisopropílico,
óxido de diisopropilo
diisopropylparaoxon
paraoxón diiso-
propílico, diiso-
propilparaoxón
diisopropyl
peroxydicarbonate
peroxidicarbonato
diisopropílico,
peroxidicarbonato de
diisopropilo
diisopropylamine
diisopropilamina
diisopropylamine
dichloroacetate
dicloroacetato de
diisopropilamina
diisopropylamino-
ethanol
diisopropilamino-
etanol
ß-diisopropylamino-
ethyl chloride
hydrochloride
clorhidrato del
cloruro de ß-
diisopropilamino-
etilo
m-diisopropyl-
benzene
m-diisopropilbenceno
diisopropylbenzene
diisopropilbenceno
diisopropylbenzene
hydroperoxide
hidroperóxido de
diisopropilbenceno

N,N'-diisopropyl-
diaminophosphoryl
fluoride
fluoruro de N,N'-
diisopropildi-
aminofosforilo
N,N-diisopropyl-
ethanolamine
N,N-diisopropil-
etanolamina
2,6-diisopropyl-
naphthalene
2,6-diisopropil-
naftaleno
2,6-diisopropylphenol
fenol 2,6-diisopropílico,
2,6-diisopropilfenol
diisopropyl-p-
phenylenediamine
diisopropil-p-
fenilendiamina
N,N'-diisopropyl-
thiourea
N,N'-diisopropil-
tiourea
dikegulac
dicegulac
diketene
diceteno
diketobutane
dicetobutano
2,5-diketohexane
2,5-dicetohexano
diketone
dicetona
diketopiperazina
dicetopiperazina
2,5-diketopyrrolidone
2,5-dicetopirrolidona
2,5-diketotetrahydro-
furane
2,5-dicetotetrahidro-
furano
dilatability
expansibilidad,
dilatabilidad
dilatation
dilatación
dilatometer
dilatómetro
dilaudid
dilaudid
dilaurylamine
dilaurilamina
dilauryl ether
éter dilaurílico
dilauryl phosphite
fosfito dilaurílico,
fosfito de dilaurilo

dilauryl sulfide
sulfuro dilaurílico,
sulfuro de dilaurilo
dilauryl thio-
dipropionate
tiodipropionato
dilaurílico,
tiodipropionato
de dilaurilo
dilazep
dilacepán, dilazepam
dilevalol
dilevalol
dilinoleic acid
ácido dilinoleico
dilithium sodium
phosphate
fosfato de dilitio
y sodio
dilituric acid
ácido dilitúrico
dill oil
esencia (aceite) de
eneldo
dillweed oil, American
aceite de arbusto de
eneldo americano
dilmefone
dilmefona
diloxanide
diloxanida
diltiazem
diltiacén, diltiazem
diltiazem hydro-
chloride
clorhidrato de diltiacén
diluent
diluyente, diluente
dilute, to
diluir
dilute solution
solución diluida
diluted
diluido
dilution ratio
proporción de
dilución
dim
opaco, oscuro, débil,
borroso
dimabefylline
dimabefilina
dimagnesium
phosphate
fosfato de dimagnesio
dimantine
dimantina
dimazol(e)
dimazol

dimazol
dihydrochloride
diclorhidrato de dimazol
dimecamine
dimecamina
dimecolonium iodide
yoduro de dimecolonio
dimecrotic acid
ácido dimecrótico
dimedone
dimedona
dimefadane
dimefadano
dimefline
dimeflina
dimefox
dimefox
dimelazine
dimelazina
dimemorfan
dimemorfano
dimenhydrinate
dimenhidrinato
di-p-mentha-1,8-diene
di-p-menta-1,8-dieno
dimenoxadol
dimenoxadol
dimension
dimensión
dimensionless
adimensional
dimepheptanol
2-dimetilamino-4,4-
difenil-5-heptanol, di-
metadol
dimepranol
dimepranol
dimepregnen
dimepregneno
dimeprozan
dimeprozano
dimer
dímero
«dimer» impurity
impureza «dímera»
dimercaprol
dimercaprol
2,3-dimercapto-1-
propanesulfonic acid
ácido 2,3-di-mercapto-
1-propansulfónico
2,3-dimercapto-
propanol
2,3-dimercapto-
propanol
dimeric
dimérico
dimerization
dimerización

dimesna
dimesna
dimesone
dimesona
dimestrol
dimestrol
dimetacrine
dimetacrina
dimetamfetamine
dimetanfetamina
dimetan
dimetán
dimethadione
dimetadiona
dimethallyl
dimetalilo
1,4-dimethano-
sulfonoxybutane
1,4-dimetansulfon-
oxibutano
dimethazan
dimetazano
dimethicone
dimeticona
dimethindene
dimetindeno
dimethiodal
sodium
dimetiodal sódico
dimethirimol
dimetirimol
dimethisoquin
dimetisoquina
dimethisoquin
hydrochloride
clorhidrato de
dimetisoquina
dimethisterone
dimetisterona
dimethoate
dimetoato
dimethocaine
dimetocaína
dimetholizine
dimetolicina
dimethoxanate
dimetoxanato
dimethoxane
dimetoxano
1,2-dimethoxy-4-
allylbenzene
1,2-dimetoxi-4-
alilbenceno
2,5-dimethoxyaniline
2,5-dimetoxianilina
2,5-dimethoxy-
benzaldehyde
2,5-dimetoxi-
benzaldehído

1,2-dimethoxy-
benzene
1,2-dimetoxi-
benceno
dimethoxybenzidine
dimetoxibencidina
3,3'-dimethoxy-
benzidine-4,4'-
diisocyanate
4,4'-diisocianato de
3,3'-dimetoxi-
bencidina
3,4-dimethoxybenzyl
alcohol
alcohol 3,4-
dimetoxibencílico
2,4-dimethoxy-5-
chloroaniline
2,4-dimetoxi-5-
cloranilina
p,p-dimethoxy-
diphenylamine
p,p-dimetoxidifenil-
amina
1,2-dimethoxyethane
1,2-dimetoxietano
(2-dimethoxyethyl)
adipate
adipato de (2-
dimetoxietilo)
di-(2-methoxyethyl)
phthalate
ftalato de di-(2-
metoxietilo)
dimethoxymethane
dimetoximetano
2,5-dimethoxy-4-
methylamphetamine
2,5-dimetoxi-4-
metilanfetamina
3,4-dimethoxy-
phenetylamine
3,4-dimetoxi-
fenetilamina
3,4-dimethoxy-
phenylacetic
acid
ácido 3,4-dimetoxi-
fenilacético
2,6-dimethoxy-
phenyllithium
2,6-dimetoxifenil litio
1-(3,4-dimethoxy-
phenyl)-2-nitro-1-
propene
1-(3,4-dimetoxifenil)-
2-nitro-1-propeno
3-(dimethoxy-
phosphinyloxy)-N,N-

dimethyl-cis-
crotonamide
3-(dimetoxi-
fosfiniloxi)-N,N-
dimetil-cis-
crotonamida
dimethoxystrychnine
dimetoxiestricnina
dimethoxytetra-
glycol
dimetoxitetraglicol
dimethrin
dimetrina
dimethyl
dimetilo
dimethyl
anthranilate
antranilato dimetílico,
antranilato de
dimetilo
dimethyl brassylate
brasilato dimetílico,
brasilato de dimetilo
dimethyl benzyl-
phosphonate
bencilfosfonato
dimetílico,
bencilfosfonato de
dimetilo
dimethyl cadmium
cadmio dimetílico,
dimetilcadmio
dimethyl carbate
carbato dimetílico,
carbato de dimetilo
dimethyl carbinol
carbinol dimetílico,
dimetilcarbinol
dimethyl carbonate
carbonato dimetílico,
carbonato de dimetilo
dimethyl cyanamide
cianamida dimetílica,
dimetilcianamida
dimethyl dioxane
dioxano dimetílico,
dimetildioxano
dimethyl ether
éter dimetílico
dimethyl ethyl
carbinol
carbinol dimetiletílico,
dimetiletilcarbinol
dimethyl
ferrocenoate
ferrocenoato
dimetílico,
ferrocenoato de
dimetilo

dimethyl glycol
phthalate
ftalato dimetil
glicólico, ftalato de
dimetilglicol
dimethyl hexynol
hexinol dimetílico,
dimetilhexinol
dimethyl itaconate
itaconato dimetílico,
itaconato de dimetilo
dimethyl maleate
maleato dimetílico,
maleato de dimetilo
dimethyl malonate
malonato dimetílico,
malonato de dimetilo
dimethyl nitrosamine
nitrosamina dimetílica,
dimetilnitrosamina
dimethyl phosphite
fosfito dimetílico,
fosfito de dimetilo
dimethyl phthalate
ftalato dimetílico,
ftalato de dimetilo
dimethyl resorcinol
resorcinol dimetílico,
dimetilresorcinol,
dimetilresorcina
dimethyl sebacate
sebacato dimetílico,
sebacato de dimetilo
dimethyl silicone
silicona dimetílica,
dimetilsilicona
dimethyl sulfate
sulfato dimetílico,
sulfato de dimetilo
dimethyl sulfide
sulfuro dimetílico,
sulfuro de dimetilo
dimethyl sulfoxide
dimetilsulfóxido,
sulfóxido dimetílico,
sulfóxido de dimetilo
dimethyl terephthalate
tereftalato dimetílico,
tereftalato de dimetilo
dimethyl 2,3,5,6-
tetrachloro-
terephthalate
2,3,5,6-tetracloro-
tereftalato dimetílico,
2,3,5,6-tetracloro-
tereftalato de dimetilo
dimethylacetal
acetal dimetílico,
dimetilacetal

N,N-dimethyl-
acetamide
acetamida N,N-
dimetílica, N,N-
dimetilacetamida
N,N-dimethyl
acetoacetamide
acetoacetamida N,N-
dimetílica, N,N-
dimetilaceto-
acetamida
2,4-dimethyl
acetophenone
acetofenona 2,4-di-
metílica, 2,4-di-
metilacetofenona
dimethylacetylene
acetileno dimetílico,
dimetilacetileno
dimethylamine
amina dimetílica,
dimetilamina
dimethylaminoaniline
aminoanilina
dimetílica,
dimetilaminoanilina
dimethylamino-
antipyrine
aminoantipirina
dimetílica,
dimetilaminoantipirina
dimethylamino-
azobenzene
aminoazobenceno
dimetílico,
dimetilamino-
azobenceno
p-dimethylamino-
benzaldehyde
aminobenzaldehído p-
dimetílico, p-
dimetilamino-
benzaldehído
p-dimethylamino-
benzalrhodanine
aminobenzal-
rodanina p-dimetílica,
p-dimetilamino-
benzalrodanina
dimethylamino-
benzene
aminobenceno
dimetílico,
dimetilaminobenceno
p-dimethylamino-
benzene diazonium
chloride, zinc chloride
double salt
sal doble de cloruro de

p-dimetilamino-
bencendiazonio y
cloruro de cinc
p-dimethylamino-
benzenediazo sodium
sulfonate
sulfonato de p-
dimetilamino-
bencendiazo sódico
3-dimethylamino-
benzoic acid
ácido 3-dimetil-
aminobenzoico
p-dimethylamino-
benzophenone
p-dimetilamino-
benzofenona
dl-dimethylamino-
4,4-diphenyl-3-
heptanone hydro-
chloride
clorhidrato de dl-
dimetilamino-
4,4-difenil-3-
heptanona
2-dimethylamino-
ethanol
2-dimetilaminoetanol
ß-dimethylamino
ethyl chloride
hydrochloride
clorhidrato de cloruro
de ß-dimetilaminoetilo
3-(ß-dimethylamino-
ethyl)-5-hydroxyindole
3-(ß-dimetilamino-
etil)-5-hidroxiindol
dimethylaminoethyl
methacrylate
metacrilato
dimetilaminoetílico,
metacrilato de
dimetilaminoetilo
dimethylaminomethyl
phenol
fenol dimetil-
aminometílico,
dimetilamino-
metilfenol
4-dimethylamino-3-
methylphenolmethyl
carbamate (ester)
(éster) carbamato
de 4-dimetilamino-3-
metilfenolmetilo
1-dimethylamino-2-
propanol
1-dimetilamino-2-
propanol

3-dimethylamino-
propylamine
3-dimetilamino-
propilamina
1-dimethylamino-2-
propyl chloride
cloruro de 1-
dimetilamino-2-
propilo
1-dimethylamino-
3-propyl
chloride
cloruro de 1-
dimetilamino-3-
propilo
1-dimethylamino-
3-propyl chloride
hydrochloride
clorhidrato de cloruro
de 1-dimetilamino-3-
propilo
dimethylaminopropyl
methacrylamide
metacrilamida
dimetilaminopropílica,
dimetilamino-
propilmetacrilamida
4-dimethylamino-m-
tolyl N-methyl-
carbamate
N-metilcarbamato de
4-dimetilamino-m-
tolilo
4-dimethylamino-
3,6-xylyl-N-
methylcarbamate
N-metilcarbamato de
4-dimetilamino-3,6-
xililo
N,N-dimethylaniline
N,N-dimetilanilina
dimethylarsinic acid
ácido dimetilarsínico
9,10-dimethyl-1,2-
benzanthracene
9,10-dimetil-1,2-
benzantraceno
1,2-dimethylbenzene
1,2-dimetilbenceno
3,3-dimethylbenzidine
3,3-dimetilbencidina
5,6-dimethylbenz-
imidazole
5,6-dimetil-
bencimidazol
p,α-dimethylbenzyl
alcohol
alcohol p, α-
dimetilbencílico

2,5-dimethylbenzyl chloride
cloruro 2,5-dimetilbencílico, cloruro de 2,5-dimetilbencilo

2,4-dimethylbenzyl chrysanthemumate
crisantemumato de 2,4-dimetilbencilo

α,α-dimethylbenzyl hydroperoxide
hidroxiperóxido de α,α-dimetilbencilo

dimethylbenzylcarbinyl acetate
acetato dimetilbencilcarbinílico, acetato de dimetilbencilcarbinilo

dimethylberyllium
berilio dimetílico, dimetilberilio

3,3'-dimethyl-4,4'-biphenylene diisocyanate
diisocianato de 3,3'-dimetil-4,4'-bifenileno

1,1'-dimethyl-4,4-bipyridinium salt
sal de 1,1'-dimetil-4,4'-bipiridinio

2,2-dimethylbutane
2,2-dimetilbutano

2,3-dimethyl-1,3-butadiene
2,3-dimetil-1,3-butadieno

2,2-dimethyl-1,3-butanediol
2,2-dimetil-1,3-butandiol

2,3-dimethylbutene-1
2,3-dimetilbuteno-1

2,4-dimethyl-6-tert-butylphenol
2,4-dimetil-6-terc-butilfenol

dimethylcarbamoyl chloride
cloruro de dimetilcabamoílo

dimethylchloroacetal
cloroacetal dimetílico, dimetilcloroacetal

2,5-dimethyl-α-chlorotoluene
2,5-dimetil-α-clorotolueno

dimethylcyclohexane
ciclohexano dimetílico, dimetilciclohexano

dimethyl-1,4-cyclohexane dicarboxylate
dicarboxilato dimetílico de 1,4-ciclohexano, 1,4-ciclohexandicarboxilato de dimetilo

5-5-dimethyl-1,3-cyclohexanedione
5,5-dimetil-1,3-ciclohexanodiona

N,N-dimethylcyclohexane ethylamine
ciclohexanetilamina N,N-dimetílica, N,N-dimetilciclohexano etilamina

N,N-dimethylcyclohexylamine
ciclohexilamina N,N-dimetílica, N,N-dimetilciclohexilamina

1,2-dimethylcyclopentane
ciclopentano 1,2-dimetílico, 1,2-dimetilciclopentano

2,2'-dimethyl-1,1'-dianthraquinone
1,1'-diantraquinona 2,2'-dimetílica, 2,2'-dimetil-1,1' diantraquinona

2,5-dimethyl-2,5-di(tert-butylperoxy)hexane
2,5-dimetil-2,5-di(terc-butilperoxi) hexano

dimethyldichlorosilane
diclorosilano dimetílico, dimetil-diclorosilano

dimethyl dichlorovinyl phosphate
fosfato dimetílico de diclorovinilo, fosfato de dimetildicloro-vinilo

5,5-dimethyldihydro-resorcinol dimethylcarbamate
dimetilcarbamato de

5,5-dimetildihidro-resorcinol

1,1-dimethyl-3,5-diketocyclohexane
3,5-dicetociclohexano 1,1-dimetílico, 1,1-dimetil-3,5-dicetociclohexano

dimethyldiketone
dicetona dimetílica, dimetildicetona

N,N'-dimethyl-N,N-di-(1-methylpropyl)-p-phenylenediamine
N,N'-dimetil-N,N-di-(1-metilpropil)-p-fenilendiamina

2,2-dimethyl-1,3-dioxolane-4-methanol
2,2-dimetil-1,3-dioxolano-4-metanol

N,N-dimethyl-N,N-dinitrosterephthalamide
N,N-dimetil-N,N-dinitroestereftalamida

N,N-dimethyl-2,2-diphenylacetamide
N,N-dimetil-2,2-difenilacetamida

dimethyldiphenylurea
urea dimetil difenílica, dimetildifenilurea

dimethyldithio zinc carbamate
carbamato de dimetilditio cinc

dimethylenemethane
metano dimetilénico, dimetilenmetano

dimethylethanolamine
etanolamina dimetílica, dimetiletanolamina

dimethylethylene
etileno dimetílico, dimetiletileno

sym-dimethylethylene glycol
etilenglicol sim-dimetílico, sim-dimetiletilenglicol

O,O-dimethyl-S-(ethylsulfinyl) ethyl phosphoro-thioate
S-(etilsulfinil)etil-fosfotioato de O,O-dimetilo

5,5-dimetildihidro-resorcinol

1,1-dimethyl-3,5-diketocyclohexane

N,N-dimethylformamide
formamida N,N-dimetílica, N,N-dimetilformamida

dimethylfuran
furano dimetílico, dimetilfurano

N,N-dimethylglycine
N,N-dimetilglicina

N,N-dimethylglycine hydrazide hydrochloride
clorhidrato de hidrazida N,N-dimetilglicínica

dimethylglyoxal
glioxal dimetílico, dimetilglioxal

dimethylglyoxime
glioxima dimetílica, dimetilglioxima

2,6-dimethyl-4-heptane
4-heptano 2,6-dimetílico, 2,6-dimetil-4-heptano

2,6-dimethyl-4-heptanone
4-heptanona 2,6-dimetílica, 2,6-dimetil-4-heptanona

2,6-dimethyl-5-hepten-1-al
2,6-dimetil-5-hepten-1-al

2,6-dimethyl-heptene-3
2,6-dimetil- hepteno-3

2,5-dimethyl-hexadiene-1,5
2,5-dimetilhexadieno-1,5

2,5-dimethylhexane-2,5-dihydroperoxide
2,5-dihidro-peróxido de 2,5-dimetilhexano

dimethylhexanediol
hexandiol dimetílico, dimetilhexandiol

2,5-dimethylhexane-2,5-diperoxybenzoate
2,5-diperoxibenzoato de 2,5-dimetilhexano

dimethylhexynediol
hexindiol dimetílico, dimetilhexindiol

99

5,5-dimethylhydantoin
hidantoína 5,5-
dimetílica, 5,5-
dimetilhidantoína
dimethylhydantoin-
formaldehyde
polymer
polímero de
dimetilhidantoína y
formaldehído
1,1-dimethylhydrazine
1,1-dimetilhidracina
dimethylhydro-
quinone
hidroquinona
dimetílica,
dimetilhidroquinona
dimethylhydroxy-
benzene
hidroxibenceno
dimetílico,
dimetilhidroxibenceno
dimethyl-3-hydroxy-
glutaconate dimethyl
phosphate
dimetilfosfato de 3-
hidroxiglutaconato de
dimetilo
3,7-dimethyl-7-
hydroxyoctenal
3,7-dimetil-7-
hidroxioctenal
dimethylisopropanol-
amine
isopropanolamina
dimetílica,
dimetilisopropanol-
amina
dimethylketol
cetol dimetílico,
dimetilcetol
dimethylketone
cetona dimetílica,
dimetilcetona
dimethylmethane
metano
dimetílico,
dimetilmetano
2,6-dimethyl-
morpholine
morfolina 2,6-
dimetílica, 2,6-
dimetilmorfolina
2-(2,6-dimethyl-4-
morpholinothio)
benzothiazole
2-(2,6-dimetil-4-
morfolintio)
benzotiazol

dimethyl-α-naphthyl-
amine
α-naftilamina
dimetílica, dimetil-α-
naftilamina
dimethyl-β-naphthyl-
amine
β-naftilamina
dimetílica, dimetil-β-
naftilamina
dimethylnitrobenzene
nitrobenceno
dimetílico,
dimetilnitrobenceno
O,O-dimethyl-O-p-
nitrophenyl
phosphorothioate
fosforotioato O-p-
nitrofenil O,O-
dimetílico, O-p-
nitrofenil fosforotioato
de O,O-dimetilo
N,N-dimethyl-p-
nitrosoaniline
N,N-dimetil-p-
nitrosoanilina
3,6-dimethyl-3,6-
octanediol
3,6-octandiol 3,6-
dimetílico, 3,6-dimetil-
3,6-octandiol
dimethyloctanoic
acid
ácido dimetiloctanoico
3,6-dimethyl-3-octanol
3-octanol 3,6-
dimetílico, 3,6-dimetil-
3-octanol
2,6-dimethyl-1,5,7-
octatriene
1,5,7-octatrieno 2,6-
dimetílico, 2,6-dimetil-
1,5,7-octatrieno
3,7-dimethyl-6-octenal
6-octenal 3,7-
dimetílico, 3,7-dimetil-
6-octenal
3,7-dimethyl-6(or 7)-
octen-1-ol
3,7-dimetil-6(ó 7)-
octen-1-ol
dimethyloctynediol
octindiol dimetílico,
dimetiloctindiol
dimethylol ethylene
urea
urea dimetilol
etilénica, dimetilol
etilenurea

dimethylolethyl-
triazone
triazona dimetilol
etílica, dimetilol-
tiltriazona
dimethylolpropionic
acid
ácido dimetilol-
propiónico
dimethylolurea
urea dimetilólica,
dimetilolurea
2,3-dimethyl-
pentaldehyde
pentaldehído 2,3-
dimetílico, 2,3-
dimetilpentaldehído
2,4-dimethylpentane
pentano 2,4-dimetílico,
2,4-dimetilpentano
2,4-dimethylpentanol-3
2,4-dimetilpentanol-3
2,4-dimethyl-
pentanone-3
2,4-dimetilpentanona-3
α,α-dimethyl-
phenethyl acetate
acetato de α,α-
dimetilfenetilo
dimethylphenol
fenol dimetílico,
dimetilfenol
dimethyl-p-phenylene-
diamine
p-fenilendiamina
dimetílica, dimetil-p-
fenilendiamina
N,ß-dimethyl-
phenylethylamine
amina N,ß-dimetilfenil
etílica, N,ß-
dimetilfeniletilamina
2,3-dimethyl-1-phenyl-
3-pyrazolin-5-one
2,3-dimetil-1-fenil-3-
pirazolín-5-ona
O,O-dimethyl-
phosphoro-
chloridothioate
fosfocloridotioato de
O,O-dimetilo
N,N'-dimethyl-
piperazine
piperazina N,N'-
dimetílica, N,N'-
dimetilpiperazina
2,6-dimethyl-
piperidine
piperidina 2,6-

dimetílica, 2,6-
dimctilpiperidina
dimethylpolysiloxane
polisiloxano
dimetílico,
dimetilpolisiloxano
2,2-dimethylpropane
propano 2,2-dimetílico,
2,2-dimetilpropano
2,2-dimethyl-1,3-
propanediol
1,3-propandiol 2,2-
dimetílico, 2,2-dimetil-
1,3-propandiol
dimethylpyridine
piridina dimetílica,
dimetilpiridina
2,7-dimethyl-
quinoline
quinolina 2,7-
dimetílica, 2,7-
dimetilquinolina
2,4-dimethyl-
sulfolane
sulfolano 2,4-
dimetílico, 2,4-
dimetilsulfolano
dimethylsulfone
sulfona dimetílica,
dimetilsulfona
dimethylsulfonyl-
oxybutane
oxibutano dimetil
sulfonílico,
dimetilsulfonil-
oxibutano
3,5-dimethyltetra-
hydro-1,3,5-(2H)-
thiadiazine-2-thione
3,5-dimetiltetrahidro-
1,3,5-(2H)-tiadiazina-
2-tiona
dimethylthiambutene
tiambuteno dimetílico,
dimetiltiambuteno
dimethylthiazole
tiazol dimetílico,
dimetiltiazol
N,N-dimethylthiourea
tiourea N,N-dimetílica,
N,N-dimetiltiourea
dimethyltin dichloride
dicloruro de
dimetilestaño
dimethyltin oxide
óxido de dimetilestaño
N,N-dimethyl-
tryptamine
triptamina N,N-

dimetílica, N,N-
dimetiltriptamina
dimethyltubocurarine
chloride
cloruro de dimetiltubo-
curarina
N,N'-dimethylurea
urea
N,N-dimetílica, N,N-
dimetilurea
1,3-dimethyl-
xanthine
xantina 1,3-dimetílica,
1,3-dimetilxantina
dimethylzinc
cinc dimetílico,
dimetilcinc
dimeticone
dimeticona
dimetilan
dimetilán
dimetindene
dimetindeno
dimetipirium bromide
bromuro de dimetipirio
dimetofrine
dimetofrina
dimetothiazine
dimetotiazina
dimetracine
dimetracina
dimetridazole
dimetridazol
dimevamide
dimevamida
diminazene
diminaceno
diminazene aceturate
aceturato de
diminaceno
diminish, to
disminuir, reducir
dimolecular
bimolecular
dimolybdenum trioxide
trióxido de
dimolibdeno
dimorphic
dimorfo
dimorphism
dimorfismo
dimorpholamine
dimorfolamina
dimorphous
dimorfo
dimoxyline
dimoxilina, dimoxilinio
dimpylate
dimpilato

Dimroth rearrangement
transposición de
Dimroth
dimyristyl amine
amina dimiristílica,
dimiristilamina
dimyristyl ether
éter dimiristílico
dimyristyl sulfide
sulfuro dimiristílico,
sulfuro de dimiristilo
ß,ß-dinaphtylamine
ß,ß-dinaftilamina
N,N'-di-ß-2-naphtyl-
p-phenylenediamine
N,N'-di-ß-2-naftil-p-
fenilendiamina
dinazafone
dinazafona
diniconazole
diniconazol
diniprofylline
diniprofilina
dinitolmide
dinitolmida
dinitraniline orange
anaranjado de
dinitranilina
dinitroaminophenol
dinitroaminofenol
2,4-dinitroaniline
2,4-dinitroanilina
2,4-dinitroanisole
2,4-dinitroanisol
2,4-dinitrobenz-
aldehyde
2,4-dinitrobenz-
aldehído
dinitrobenzene
dinitrobenceno
2,4-dinitrobenzene-
sulfenyl chloride
cloruro sulfenílico de
2,4-dinitrobenceno
3,5-dinitrobenzoic acid
ácido 3,5-dinitro-
benzoico
5,7-dinitro-1,2,3-
benzoxadiazole
5,7-dinitro-1,2,3-
benzoxadiazol
3,5-dinitrobenzoyl
chloride
cloruro de 3,5-
dinitrobenzoílo
2-(2,4-dinitrobenzyl)
pyridine
2-(2,4-dinitrobencil)
piridina
2,4-dinitrophenol
2,4-dinitrofenol

2,4-dinitro-6-sec-
butylphenol
2,4-dinitro-6-sec-
butilfenol
4,4'-dinitro-
carbanilide
4,4'-dinitro-
carbanilida
dinitrochlorbenzol
dinitroclorbenzol
dinitrochlorbenzene
dinitroclorbenceno
dinitrocresol
dinitrocresol
4,6-dinitro-o-cresol
4,6-dinitro-o-cresol
2,6-dinitro-p-cresol
2,6-dinitro-p-cresol
dinitrocyclohexyl-
phenol
dinitrociclohexil-
fenol
2,4-dinitrofluoro-
benzene
2,4-dinitrofluoro-
benceno
dinitrogen tetroxide
tetróxido de
dinitrógeno
dinitrogen trioxide
trióxido de dinitrógeno
dinitroglycol
dinitroglicol
2,4-dinitro-4-
hydroxydiphenyl-
amine
2,4-dinitro-4-
hidroxidifenilamina
dinitro(1-methyl-
heptyl) phenyl
crotonate
crotonato de dinitro(1-
metilheptil) fenilo
4,6-dinitro-2-
methylphenol
4,6-dinitro-2-
metilfenol
dinitronaphthalene
dinitronaftaleno
2,4-dinitro-1-naphtol-
7-sulfonic acid
ácido 2,4-dinitro-1-
naftol-7-sulfónico
3,7-dinitro-5-oxo-
phenothiazine
3,7-dinitro-5-oxo-
fenotiazina

dinitrophenyl-
hydrazine
hidracina dinitro-
fenílica, dinitrofenil-
hidracina
2,4-dinitrophenyl
methyl ether
éter metil 2,4-
dinitrofenílico
2,4-dinitroresorcinol
2,4-dinitrorresorcinol,
2,4-dinitrorresorcina
5,5'-dinitrosalicil
5,5'-dinitrosalicilo
3,5-dinitrosalicylic acid
ácido 3,5-dinitro-
salicílico
dinitrosopenta-
methylenetetramine
tetramina dinitroso
pentametilénica,
dinitrosopenta-
metilentetramina
2,4-dinitrosoresorcinol
2,4-dinitroso-
resorcinol, 2,4-
dinitrosorresorcina
3,5-dinitro-o-
toluamide
3,5-dinitro-o-toluamida
dinitrotoluene
dinitrotolueno
dinobuton
dinobutón
dinocap
dinocap
dinonyl adipate
adipato dinonílico,
adipato de dinonilo
dinonyl carbonate
carbonato dinonílico,
carbonato de dinonilo
dinonyl ether
éter dinonílico
dinonyl maleate
maleato dinonílico,
maleato de dinonilo
dinonyl phenol
fenol dinonílico,
dinonilfenol
dinonyl phthalate
ftalato dinonílico,
ftalato de dinonilo
dinoprostone
dinoprostona
dinoprost
dinoprosta
dinoseb
dinoseb

dinosterol
dinosterol
dinsed
dinsedo
dinuclear
dinuclear, dinucleado
dioctadecylamine
dioctadecilamina
2,6-dioctadecyl-p-cresol
2,6-dioctadecil-p-cresol
dioctadecyl ether
éter dioctadecílico
dioctadecyl sulfide
sulfuro dioctadecílico, sulfuro de dioctadecilo
3,3'-dioctadecyl thiodipropionate
tiodipropionato de 3,3'-dioctadecilo
dioctyl adipate
adipato dioctílico, adipato de dioctilo
dioctylaminoethanol
aminoetanol dioctílico, dioctilaminoetanol
dioctyl azelate
acelato dioctílico, acelato de dioctilo
dioctyl chlorophosphate
clorofosfato dioctílico, clorofosfato de dioctilo
di-n-octyl diphenylamine
difenilamina di-n-octílica, di-n-octildifenilamina
dioctyl ether
éter dioctílico
dioctyl fumarate
fumarato dioctílico, fumarato de dioctilo
dioctyl hexahydrophthalate
hexahidroftalato dioctílico, hexahidroftalato de dioctilo
dioctyl maleate
maleato de dioctilo
dioctyl phosphite
fosfito dioctílico, fosfito de dioctilo
dioctyl phosphoric acid
ácido dioctil fosfórico

dioctyl phosphorochloridate
fosfoclorhidrato dioctílico, fosfoclorhidato de dioctilo
dioctyl phthalate
ftalato dioctílico, ftalato de dioctilo
dioctyl sebacate
sebacato dioctílico, sebacato de dioctilo
dioctyl sodium sulfosuccinate
sulfosuccinato dioctil sódico, sulfosuccinato de dioctil sodio
dioctyl succinate
succinato dioctílico, succinato de dioctilo
dioctyl sulfide
sulfuro dioctílico, sulfuro de dioctilo
dioctyl thioether
tioéter dioctílico, dioctil tioéter
dioctyl thiopropionate
tiopropionato dioctílico, tiopropionato de dioctilo
di(n-octyl-n-decyl) adipate
adipato de di(n-octil-n-decilo)
di(n-octyl-n-decyl) phthalate
ftalato de di(n-octil-n-decilo)
N,N'-di-n-octyl-p-phenylenediamine
p-fenilendiamina N,N'-di-n-octílica, N,N'-di-n-octil-p-fenilendiamina
di(2-octyl)phthalate
ftalato (2-octílico), ftalato de (2-octilo)
di-(n-octyl)tin -S,S'-bis-(isooctyl-mercaptoacetate)
S,S'-bis-(isoctil-mercaptoacetato) de di-(n-octil) estaño
diode
diodo
diodone
diodona
diol
diol

diolamine
diolamina
diolefin
diolefina
dioptase
dioptasa
diopter
dioptría
diopterin
diopterina
dioscin
dioscina
dioscorea
dioscorea
dioscorine
dioscorina
diosgenin
diosgenina
diosmetin
diosmetina
diosmin
diosmina
dioxadrol
dioxadrol
dioxamate
dioxamato
1,4-dioxane
1,4-dioxano
dioxaphetyl butyrate
butirato dioxafetílico, butirato de dioxafetilo
dioxathion
dioxatión
dioxethedrin(e)
dioxetedrina
dioxide
dióxido, bióxido
dioxifedrine
dioxifedrina
dioxin
dioxina
3,5-dioxo-1,2-diphenyl-4-n-butylpyrazolidine
3,5-dioxo-1,2-difenil-4-n-butil-pirazolidina
1,3-dioxolane
1,3-dioxolano
dioxolone-2
dioxolona-2
dioxopurine
dioxopurina
dioxyacetone
dioxiacetona
dioxyanthraquinone
dioxiantraquinona
dioxybenzene
dioxibenceno

dioxybenzone
dioxibenzona
dioxyethylene ether
éter dioxietilénico, éter de dioxietileno
dioxyline phosphate
fosfato de dioxilina
dioxynaphthalenes
dioxinaftalenos
dioxypyramidon
dioxipiramidón
dip, to
sumergir
dip dyeing
teñido por inmersión
dipalmitylamine
amina dipalmitílica, dipalmitilamina
dipentaerythritol
dipentaeritritol
dipentamethylene-thiouram tetrasulfide
tetrasulfuro de dipentametilén tiourano
dipentene
dipenteno
dipentene dioxide
dióxido de dipenteno
dipentene glycol
glicol dipenténico, dipentenglicol
dipentene monoxide
monóxido de dipenteno
di-n-pentylamine
di-n-pentilamina
2,5-di-tert-pentyl-hydroquinone
2,5-di-terc-pentil-hidroquinona
diperodon
diperodón
diperodon hydrochloride
clorhidrato de diperodón
diphacinone
difacinona
diphemanil methylsulfate
sulfato difemanil metílico, metilsulfato de difemanilo
diphemethoxidine
difemetoxidina
diphenadione
difenadiona
diphenamid
difenamida

102

diphenan(e)
difenano
diphenatrile
difenatrilo
diphenazoline
difenazolina
diphencyprone
difenciprona
diphenhydramine
difenhidramina
diphenhydramine citrate
citrato de difenhidramina
diphenhydramine hydrochloride
clorhidrato de difenhidramina
diphenic acid
ácido difénico
diphenidol
difenidol
diphenolic acid
ácido difenólico
diphenoxylate
difenoxilato
diphenyl
difenilo
diphenyl carbonate
carbonato difenílico, carbonato de difenilo
diphenyl chlorinated
difenil clorado
diphenyl ether
éter difenílico
diphenyl isophthalate
isoftalato difenílico, isoftalato de difenilo
diphenyl oxide
óxido difenílico, óxido de difenilo
diphenyl phosphite
fosfito difenílico, fosfito de difenilo
diphenyl phthalate
ftalato difenílico, ftalato de difenilo
diphenyl sulfone
sulfona difenílica, difenilsulfona
diphenylacetamide
acetamida difenílica, difenilacetamida
diphenylacetic acid
ácido difenilacético
diphenylacetonitrile
acetonitrilo difenílico, difenilacetonitrilo

diphenylacetylene
acetileno difenílico, difenilacetileno
2-diphenylacetyl-1,3-indanedione
2-difenilacetil-1,3-indandiona
diphenylamine
difenilamina
diphenylamine chloroarsine
cloroarsina difenilamínica, difenilamina-cloroarsina
diphenylamine-2,2'-dicarboxilic acid
ácido difenilamina-2,2'-dicarboxílico
9,10-diphenyl-anthracene
9,10-difenil-antraceno
1,4-diphenylbenzene
1,4-difenilbenceno
diphenylbenzidine
bencidina difenílica, difenilbencidina
2,5-diphenyl-p-benzo-quinone
p-benzoquinona 2,5-difenílica, 2,5-difenil-p-benzo-quinona
diphenylbromoarsine
bromarsina difenílica, difenilbromarsina
1,4-diphenyl-1,3-butadiene
1,4-difenil-1,3-butadieno
1,3-diphenyl-2-buten-1-one
1,3-difenil-2-buten-1-ona
diphenylcarbazide
carbazida difenílica, difenilcarbazida
diphenylcarbazone
carbazona difenílica, difenilcarbazona
diphenylcarbinol
carbinol difenílico, difenilcarbinol
diphenylchloroarsine
clorarsina difenílica, difenilclorarsina

diphenyldecyl phosphite
fosfito difenil decílico, fosfito de difenildecilo
2,4'-diphenyldiamine
2,4'-difenildiamina
diphenyldichloro-silane
diclorosilano difenílico, difenildiclorosilano
diphenyldi-n-dodecylsilane
difenildi-n-dodecilsilano
diphenyldiimide
diimida difenílica, difenildiimida
diphenyldimethoxy-silane
dimetoxisilano dimetílico, dimetildimetoxi-silano
n-diphenylene-methane
metano n-difenilénico, n-difenilenmetano
diphenylene oxide
óxido difenilénico, óxido de difenileno
uns-diphenylethane
asim-difeniletano
sym-diphenylethane
sim-difeniletano
diphenylethene
eteno difenílico, difenileteno
diphenylethylene
etileno difenílico, difeniletileno
N,N'-diphenyl-ethylenediamine
diamina N,N'-difeniletilénica, N,N'-difeniletilen-diamina
N-(1,2-diphenylethyl) nicotinamide
N-(1,2-difeniletil) nicotinamida
diphenylglycolic acid
ácido difenilglicólico
N,N'-diphenyl-guanidine
N,N'-difenilguanidina
1,6-diphenyl-hexatriene
1,6-difenilhexatrieno

1,1-diphenylhydrazine
1,1-difenilhidracina
diphenylketene
ceteno difenílico, difenilceteno
diphenylketone
cetona difenílica, difenilcetona
diphenylmagnesium
magnesio difenílico, difenilmagnesio
diphenylmethane
metano difenílico, difenilmetano
diphenylmethane-4,4'-diisocyanate
4,4'-diisocianato de difenilmetano
diphenylmethane-4,4'-disulfonamide
difenilmetano-4,4'-disulfonamida
diphenylmethanol
etanol difenílico, difenilmetanol
diphenylmethyl bromide
bromuro difenil metílico, bromuro de difenilmetilo
diphenylmethyl-chlorosilane
clorosilano difenil metílico, difenil-metilclorosilano
diphenylnaphthylene-diamine
diamina difenil naftilénica, difenilnaftilen-diamina
diphenylnitrosamine
nitrosamina difenílica, difenilnitrosamina
2,5-diphenyloxazole
2,5-difeniloxazol
diphenylpenta-erythritol diphosphite
difosfito de difenilpentaeritritol
N,N'-diphenyl-m-phenylenediamine
N,N'-difenil-m-fenilendiamina
1,1-diphenyl-2-picryl-hydrazyl (free radical)
1,1-difenil-2-picril-hidracilo (radical libre)

103

diphenyl-4-
piperidine methanol
hydrochloride
  chlorhidrato de difenil-
  4-piperidinmetanol
α,α-diphenyl-2-
piperidine propanol
  α,α-difenil-2-
  piperidinpropanol
diphenyl-4-piperidyl-
methane
  difenil-4-piperidil-
  metano
diphenylpyraline
  piralina difenílica,
  difenilpiralina
diphenylpyro-
phosphorodiaminic
acid
  ácido difenil
  pirofosfodiamínico
diphenylsilanediol
  silanodiol difenílico,
  difenilsilanodiol
p,p-diphenylstilbene
  p,p-difenilestilbeno
N,N'-diphenylthiourea
  N,N'-difeniltiourea,
  tiocarbanilida,
  sulfocarbanilida
1,3-diphenyltriazene
  1,3-difeniltriaceno
diphenylurea
  urea difenílica,
  difenilurea
diphenyl-o-xenyl
phosphate
  fosfato de difenil-o-
  xenilo
diphetarsone
  difetarsona
diphosgene
  difosgeno
diphosphopyridine
nucleotide
  nucleótido de
  difosfopiridina
diphosphoric acid
  ácido difosfórico
diphoxazide
  difoxazida
dipicrylamine
  dipicrilamina
dipicryl sulfide
  sulfuro dipicrílico,
  sulfuro de dipicrilo
1,3-di-4-piperydil
propane
  propano 1,3-di-4-

piperidílico, 1,3-di-4-
piperidil propano
dipin
  dipina
dipipanone
  dipipanona
dipiproverine
  dipiproverina
dipivefrine
  dipivefrina
diplet
  doblete
diploicin
  diploicina
dipole
  dipolo
dipole moment
  momento dipolar
diponium bromide
  bromuro de diponio
dippel's oil
  aceite de huesos, aceite
  animal, aceite de
  dippel
dipping microscope
  microscopio de
  inmersión
dipping
refractometer
  refractómetro de
  inmersión
dipotassium
clorazepate
  cloracepato
  dipotásico
dipotassium
orthophosphate
  ortofosfato dipotásico,
  ortofosfato de
  dipotasio
diprenorphine
  diprenorfina
diprobutine
  diprobutina
diprofene
  diprofeno
diprogulic acid
  ácido diprogúlico
diproleandomycin
  diproleandomicina
dipropargyl
  dipropargilo
dipropenyl
  dipropenilo
di-2-propenyl amine
  di-2-propenilamina
di-n-propenyl
amine
  di-n-propenil amina

dipropetryn
  dipropetrina
diprophylline
  diprofilina
dipropyl ketone
  cetona dipropílica,
  dipropilcetona
dipropyl phthalate
  ftalato dipropílico,
  ftalato de dipropilo
dipropylamine
  dipropilamina
dipropylene
  dipropileno
dipropylene glycol
  glicol dipropilénico,
  dipropilenglicol
dipropylene glycol
dibenzoate
  dibenzoato de glicol
  dipropilénico,
  dibenzoato de
  dipropilenglicol
dipropylene glycol
dipelargonate
  dipelargonato de glicol
  dipropilénico,
  dipelargonato de
  dipropilenglicol
dipropylene glycol
monomethyl ether
  éter monometílico de
  glicol dipropilénico,
  éter monometílico de
  dipropilenglicol
dipropylene glycol
monosalicylate
  monosalicilato de
  glicol dipropilénico,
  monosalicilato de
  dipropilenglicol
dipropylene triamine
  triamina
  dipropilénica,
  dipropilentriamina
dipropylmethane
  metano dipropílico,
  dipropilmetano
5,5-dipropyl-2,4-
oxazolidinedione
  5,5-dipropil-2,4-
  oxazolidindiona
diproqualone
  diprocualona
diprotrizoate sodium
  diprotrizoato sódico,
  diprotrizoato de sodio
diproxadol
  diproxadol

dipyridamole
  dipiridamol
α,α'-dipyridyl
  α,α'-dipiridilo
2,2-dipyridylamine
  2,2-dipiridilamina
dipyridylethyl sulfide
  sulfuro dipiridil
  etílico, sulfuro de
  dipiridiletilo
dipyrithione
  dipiritiona
dipyrocetyl
  dipirocetilo
dipyrone
  dipirona
diquat
  diquat
diquat dibromide
  dibromuro de diquat
1,3-di-6-
quinolylurea
  1,3-di-6-quinolilurea
diradical
  birradical
direct current
  corriente continua
direct dye
  colorante directo
directions (for use)
  instrucciones
directive
  directiva
diresorsinol
  dirresorcina,
  dirresorcinol
diresorcinolphthalein
  ftaleína
  dirresorcinólica,
  dirresorcinolftaleína
dirithromycin
  diritromicina
N,N'-disalicylidene-
1,2-diaminopropane
  N,N'-disalicildén-1,2-
  diaminopropano
disassemble, to
  desmontar, desarmar
disc, disk
  disco
discharge
  descarga
discharging agent
  agente de descarga
Dische reaction
  reacción de Dische
discolor
  descolorar, decolorar,
  desteñir

discoloration
descoloración,
decoloración
disconnect, to
desconectar
disconnection
desconexión
discontinue, to
suspender, finalizar
discrete
discreto
discussion
comentarios, debate,
presentación,
exposición
disengage, to
liberar, desconectar
dish
placa
disilicoethane
disilicoetano, disilano
disilane
disilano, disilicoetano
disilanyl
disilanilo
disiloxane
disiloxano
disinfectant
desinfectante
disintegration
desintegración
disintegrator
desintegrador
disjoint, to
desmontar,
desconectar
dislocation
dislocación
dismount, to
desmontar
disobutamide
disobutamida
disodium
acetarsenate
acetarseniato
disódico
2,7-disodium dibromo-
4-hydroxymercuri-
fluorescein
dibromo-4-
hidroximercurio-
fluoresceína 2,7-
disódica disodium
phosphate
disodium dibutyl-o-
phenylphenol-
disulfonate
dibutil-o-fenilfenoldi-
sulfonato disódico

disodium dihydrogen
pyrophosphate
pirofosfato diácido
disódico
disodium dihydrogen
hypophosphate
hipofosfato diácido
disódico
disodium 1,2-
dihydroxybenzene-3,5-
disulfonate
1,2-dihidrobenceno-
3,5-disulfonato
disódico
disodium
diphosphate
difosfato disódico
disodium EDTA
EDTA disódico
disodium endothal
endotal disódico
disodium
ethylenebisdi-
thiocarbamate
etilenbisditio-
carbamato disódico
disodium guanylate
guanilato disódico
disodium hydrogen
phospate
fosfato ácido disódico
disodium inosinate
inosinato disódico
disodium
methanearsonate
metanarsoniato
disódico
disodium
methylarsenate
metilarseniato disódico
disodium
orthophosphate
ortofosfato disódico
disodium phenyl
phosphate
fenilfosfato disódico
disodium phosphate
fosfato disódico
disodium
pyrophosphate
pirofosfato disódico
disodium tartrate
tartrato disódico
disofenin
disofenina
disogluside
disoglúsido
disolution ratio
proporción de

disolución, índice
de disolución
disophenol
disofenol
disopyramide
disopiramida
disopyramide
phosphate
fosfato de
disopiramida
disordered state
estado desordenado,
estado desorganizado
disparity
discrepancia,
diferencia
dispensability
facilidad de suministro
dispense
dispensar, repartir,
distribuir
dispenser
dispensador,
distribuidor, repartidor
dispersal
dispersión
disperse, to
dispersar
disperse phase
fase dispersa
dispersing agent
agente de dispersión
dispersion
dispersión
dispersion medium
medio dispersante
displace, to
desplazar
displaced phase
fase desplazada
displacement force
fuerza de
desplazamiento
displacement series
serie de
desplazamiento
disposal, waste
eliminación de
desperdicios
disproportionation
desproporción
disruption
ruptura
dissemble, to
ocultar, disimular
disseminate, to
diseminar
dissimilar
diferente

dissociation
disociación
dissociation energies
energías de
disociación
dissociative ionization
ionización disociativa
dissolution
disolución
dissolved
disuelto
dissolved oxygen
oxígeno disuelto
dissolvent
disolvente
dissolving
intermediary
intermediario
disolvente
distance
distancia
distearylamine
distearilamina
2,6-distearyl-p-cresol
2,6-distearil-p-cresol
distearyl ether
éter distearílico
distearyl sulfide
sulfuro distearílico,
sulfuro de distearilo
distearyl thiodi-
propionate
tiodipropionato
distearílico,
tiodipropionato de
distearilo
distearyl thioether
tioéter distearílico
distigmine bromide
bromuro de distigmina
distillate
destilado
distillation
destilación
distillation column
columna de destilación
distillation loss
pérdida por
destilación
distilled water
agua destilada
distillery
destilería
distorted
deformado,
distorsionado,
tergiversado
distribution
distribución

disulergine
disulergina
disulfamide
disulfamida
disulfide
disulfuro, bisulfuro
disulfiram
disulfiram,
disulfiramo
3,5-disulfobenzoic acid
ácido 3,5-disulfo-
benzoico
disulfoton
disulfotón
disulfuryl chloride
cloruro disulfurílico,
cloruro de disulfurilo
disulsodium
disul sódico, disulsodio
dita bark
corteza de alstonia,
corteza de dita
ditamine
ditamina
ditaine
ditaína
ditazol(e)
ditazol
ditetradecylamine
ditetradecilamina
ditetradecyl ether
éter ditetradecílico
ditetradecyl sulfide
sulfuro ditetradecílico,
sulfuro de ditetradecilo
1,4-dithiane
1,4-ditiano
dithiane methyliodide
metilyoduro de ditiano
dithianone
ditianona
dithiazanine iodide
yoduro de ditiazanina
ß,ß'-dithiobisalanine
ß,ß'-ditiobisalanina
**2,2'-dithiobis(benzo-
thiazole)**
2,2'-ditiobis(benzo-
tiazol)
2,4-dithiobiuret
2,4-ditiobiuret
dithiocarbamato
ditiocarbamato
dithiocarbamic acid
ácido ditiocarbámico
**2,2'-dithiodibenzoic
acid**
ácido 2,2-ditio-
dibenzoico

**4,4'dithiodi-
morpholine**
4,4'-ditiodimorfolina
**3,3-dithiodipyridine
dihydrochloride**
diclorhidrato de 3,3-
ditiodipiridina
1,2-dithioglycerol
1,2-ditioglicerol, 1,2-
ditioglicerina
**6,8-dithiooctanoic
acid**
ácido 6,8-ditioctanoico
dithiooxamide
ditioxamida
dithiosalicylic acid
ácido ditiosalicílico
dithiothreitol
ditiotreitol
dithizone
ditizona
dithranol
ditranol
dithymol diiodide
diyoduro de ditimol
ditiocarb sodium
ditiocarb sódico
ditolamide
ditolamida
**1,4-di-p-toluidino-
anthraquinone**
antraquinona 1,4-di-p-
toluidínica, 1,4-di-p-
toluidino antraquinona
1,2-di-p-tolylethane
1,2-di-p-toliletano
ditophal
ditofal
**di-o-tolyl
carbodiimide**
carbodiimida di-o-
tolílica, di-o-tolil
carbodiimida
**N,N'-di-o-tolyl-
ethylenediamine**
etilendiamina N,N'-di-
o-tolílica, N,N'-di-o-
toliletilendiamina
di-o-tolylguanidine
guanidina di-o-
tolílica, di-o-
tolilguanidina
p-ditolylmercury
mercurio p-ditolílico,
p-ditolilmercurio
**2,7-di-p-tolyl-
naphthylenediamine**
2,7-di-p-tolil-
naftilendiamina

**1,3-di-p-tolyl-
phenylenediamine**
1,3-di-p-tolil-
fenilendiamina
di-o-tolylthiourea
di-o-toliltiourea
ditridecyl phthalate
ftalato ditridecílico,
ftalato de ditridecilo
**ditridecyl thio-
dipropionate**
tiodipropionato
ditridecílico,
tiodipropionato de
ditridecilo
diurazin
diuracina
diuretic
diurético
diuretin
diuretina
diuron
diurón
divalent
bivalente, divalente
divalent carbon
carbono bivalente,
carbono divalente
divalproex sodium
divalproex sódico
divanadyl tetrachloride
tetracloruro
divanadílico,
tetracloruro de
divanadilo
divergence
divergencia, separación
divicine
divicina
divide, to
dividir
divinyl
divinilo
divinyl acetylene
acetileno
divinílico,
divinilacetileno
divinylbenzene
benceno divinílico,
divinilbenceno
divinyl ether
éter divinílico
divinyl oxide
óxido divinílico, óxido
de divinilo
**3,9-divinylspirobi-m-
dioxane**
3,9-divinilespirobi-m-
dioxano

divinyl sulfide
sulfuro divinílico,
sulfuro de divinilo
divinyl sulfone
sulfona divinílica,
divinilsulfona
division
división,
separación
dixanthogen
dixantógeno
**di-o-xenyl phenyl
phosphate**
fosfato di-o-xenil
fenílico, fenilfosfato
de di-o-xenilo
di-p-xylylene
di-p-xilileno
dixylil ethane
etano dixilílico,
dixililetano
dixyrazine
dixirazina
djenkolic acid
ácido djencólico
DNA technology
tecnología del ADN
dobesilate calcium
dobesilato cálcico
dobutamine
dobutamina
docetaxcel
docetaxcelo
n-docosane
n-docosano
doconazole
doconazol
docosanoic acid
ácido docosanoico
1-docosanol
1-docosanol
cis-1,3-docosenoic acid
ácido cis-1,3-
docosenoico
document
documento, documentar
docusate calcium
docusato cálcico
docusate sodium
docusato sódico
dodecahedron
dodecahedro
dodecahydrosqualane
dodecahidro-
escualano
**dodecamethyl-
cyclohexasiloxane**
dodecametilciclo-
hexasiloxano

dodecamethyl-
pentasiloxane
dodecametil-
pentasiloxano
dodecanal
dodecanal
n-dodecane
n-dodecano
1,12-dodecanedioic
acid
ácido 1,12-
dodecanodioico
dodecanoic acid
ácido dodecanoico
n-dodecanol
n-dodecanol
dodecanoyl peroxide
peróxido de
dodecanoílo
3-(1,3,5,7,9-
dodecapentaenyloxy)
1,2-propanediol
3-(1,3,5,7,9-
dodecapentaeniloxi)-
1,2-propandiol
dodecarbonium
chloride
cloruro de
dodecarbonio
dodecene
dodeceno
dodecenylsuccinic acid
ácido dodecenil-
succínico
dodecenylsuccinic
anhydride
anhídrido dodecenil-
succínico
dodeclonium bromide
bromuro de dodeclonio
dodecyl
dodecilo
dodecyl acetate
acetato dodecílico
n-dodecyl alcohol
alcohol n-dodecílico
dodecyl aldehyde
aldehído dodecílico
dodecylaniline
dodecilanilina
dodecylbenzene
dodecilbenceno
dodecylbenzene-
sulfonic acid
ácido dodecil-
bencensulfónico
dodecylbenzyl
mercaptan
mercaptano

dodecilbencílico,
dodecilbencil-
mercaptano
n-dodecyl bromide
bromuro n-dodecílico,
bromuro de n-dodecilo
6-dodecyl-1,2-dihydro-
2,2,4-trimethyl-
quinoline
6-dodecil-1,2-dihidro-
2,2,4-trimetilquinolina
dodecyldimethyl(2-
phenoxyethyl)
ammonium bromide
bromuro de
dodecildimetil(2-
fenoxietil)amonio
dodecyl gallate
galato dodecílico,
galato de dodecilo
n-dodecylguanidine
acetate
acetato de n-
dodecilguanidina
n-dodecyl mercaptan
mercaptano n-
dodecílico, n-
dodecilmercaptano
tert-dodecyl mercaptan
mercaptano terc-
dodecílico, terc-
dodecilmercaptano
4-dodexyloxy-2-
hydroxybenzophenone
4-dodexiloxi-2-
hidroxibenzofenona
dodecylphenol
fenol dodecílico,
dodecilfenol
dodecyltrichloro-silane
triclorosilano
dodecílico,
dodeciltriclorosilano
dodecyltrimethyl-
ammonium chloride
cloruro de dodecil
trimetilamonio
dodemorph
dodemorfo
dodine
dodina
Doebner-Miller
reaction
reacción de Doebner
Miller
Doebner reaction
reacción de Doebner
dofamium chloride
cloruro de dofamio

doisynoestrol
doisinestrol
doisynolic acid
ácido doisinólico
dolasetron mesylate
mesilato de
dolasetrona
Dollo's law
ley de Dollo
dolomite
dolomita
domazoline
domazolina
domesticine
domesticina
domiodol
domiodol
domiphen bromide
bromuro de
domifeno
domopregnate
domopregnato
domoxin
domoxina
domperidone
domperidona
donepezil
hydrochloride
clorhidrato de
donepecilo
Donovan's solution
solución de
Donovan
dopa
dopa
dopamantine
dopamantina
dopamine
dopamina
dopamine
hydrochloride
clorhidrato de
dopamina
dopan
dopán
dopastin
dopastina
dope
droga, narcótico
dopexamine
dopexamina
Doppler effect
efecto Doppler
dorastine
dorastina
dorzolamide hydro-
chloride
clorhidrato de
dorzolamida

dosage form
forma posológica
dose (radiation)
dosis (de radiación)
dosimeter
dosímetro
dosing
dispensación,
administración,
dosificación
dossier
legajo, expediente
dosulepin
dosulepina
dotefonium bromide
bromuro de dotefonio
dothiepin
dotiepina
dotriacontane
dotriacontano
double bond
enlace doble
double salt
sal doble
doublet
doblete, doble
dowicide 9
dowicida 9
downcomer
tubo de descenso,
bajante
doxacurium chloride
cloruro de doxacurio
doxaminol
doxaminol
doxapram
doxapram, doxapramo
doxaprost
doxaprost
doxazosin
doxazosina
doxazosin mesylate
mesilato de doxazosina
doxefazepam
doxefacepán,
doxefazepam
doxenitoin
doxenitoína
doxepin
doxepina
doxepin hydrochloride
clorhidrato de
doxepina
doxibetasol
doxibetasol
doxifluridine
doxifluridina
doxofylline
doxofilina

doxorubicin
doxorrubicina
doxorubicin
hydrochlorate
clorhidrato de
doxorrubicina
doxpicomine
doxpicomina
doxycycline
doxiciclina
doxycycline hyclate
hiclato de doxyciclina
doxylamine
doxilamina
dragee
gragea
dragonic acid
ácido dragónico
dragon's blood
sangre de dragón
dram
dracma
draw, to
extraer, estirar
drazidox
drazidox
drazoxolon
drazoxolón
dried cake
bizcocho drier
drier
equipo secador, secante
drimenin
drimenina
drinidene
drinideno
drobuline
drobulina
drocarbil
drocarbilo
drocinonide
drocinonida
droclidinium bromide
bromuro de
droclidinio
drofenine
drofenina
drometrizole
drometrizol
dromostanolone
propionate
propionato de
dromostanolona
dronabinol
dronabinol
drop
gota, caída
dropempine
dropempina

droperidol
droperidol
droprenilamine
droprenilamina
dropropizine
dropropicina
dropwise
gota a gota
drosera
drosera
drosophilin A
drosofilina A
drostanolone
drostanolona
drotaverine
drotaverina
drotebanol
drotebanol
droxacin
droxazina
droxicainide
droxicainida
droxicam
droxican
droxypropine
droxipropina
drug
fármaco, medicamento,
droga
Drug Master Files
Archivos Maestros
de Fármacos
drug product
producto farmacológico
drug substance
sustancia
farmacológica
dry cell
pila seca
dry chemical
compuesto químico
seco, compuesto
químico en polvo
dry deposition
deposición seca
dryer
desecador
dry gas
gas seco
dry ice
hielo seco
drying
desecado
drying oil
aceite desecante
drying oven
horno desecante
duazomycin
duazomicina

Duff reaction
reacción de Duff
Duhring's rule
regla de
Duhring
dulcamara
dulcamara
dulcin
dulcina
dulcitol
dulcitol
dulofibrate
dulofibrato
Dulong and Petit's law
ley de Dulong y Petit
Dumas method
método de Dumas
dumortierite
dumortierita
duometacin
duometacina
Duo-Sol process
proceso de Duo Sol
dupracetam
dupracetán
duralumin
duraluminio
durapatite
durapatita
durene
dureno
durometer hardness
dureza durométrica
duroquinone
duroquinona
dusting agent
agente espolvoreante
Dutch method
método holandés
Dutt-Wormall reaction
reacción de Dutt
Wormall
dwarf pine needles
oil
esencia (aceite) de
agujas de pino enano
dyclonine
diclonina
dyclonine
hydrochloride
clorhidrato de
diclonina
dydrogesterone
didrogesterona
dye
colorante, color, tinte
dye, azo
colorante azoico,
azocolorante

dye, certified
colorante certificado
dye, direct
colorante directo
dye, disperse
colorante de
dispersión
dye, fiber reactive
colorante reactivo a
fibras
dyeing assistant
auxiliar de teñido
dyeing, solvent
teñido al disolvente
dye intermediate
intermediario
colorante
dye, metal
colorante metálico
dye, natural
colorante natural
dye retarding
agents
agentes retardantes
del teñido
dye, solvent
colorante
disolvente
dye, synthetic
colorante
sintético
dyfonate
difonato
dymanthine
dimantina
dynamite
dinamita
dynorphin
dinorfina
dyphilline
difilina
dypnone
dipnona
dysprosia
disprosia
dysprosium
disprosio
dysprosium nitrate
nitrato de
disprosio
dysprosium oxide
óxido de
disprosio
dysprosium salt
sal de disprosio
dysprosium sulfate
sulfato de disprosio
dystrophin
distrofina

E

each
cada
early
inicial, precoz
earth
tierra
earth wax
cera térrea,
ceresina
easily
fácilmente
easy
fácil
ebonite
ebonita
ebullioscope
ebulloscopio
ebullioscopy
ebulloscopía
ebullition
ebullición, hervor
eburnamonine
eburnamonina
ecdysones
ecdisonas
ecgonidine
ecgonidina
ecgonine
ecgonina
echinacea
equinácea
echinenone
equinenona
echinochrome A
equinocromo A
echinomycin
equinomicina
echinopsine
equinopsina
echinuline
equinulina
echitamine
equitamina
echothiophate iodide
yoduro de ecotiofato
ecipramidil
ecipramidilo
ECM
Mercado Común
Europeo
ecology
ecología
econazole
econazol

econazole nitrate
nitrato de econazol
economics, chemical
economía de los
productos químicos
economizer
economizador,
recuperador
ecosystem
sistema ecológico,
ecosistema, biocenosis
ectylurea
urea ectílica, ectilurea
Edeleanu process
proceso de Edeleanu
edestin
edestina
edetate
edetato
edetate calcium
disodium
edetato disódico de
calcio
edetate disodium
edetato disódico
edetate sodium
edetato de sodio,
edetato sódico
edetate trisodium
edetato trisódico
edetic acid
ácido edético
edge
borde, filo
edible
comestible
edible fat
grasa comestible
edible oil
aceite comestible
edifenphos
edifenfós
edisilate
edisilato
Edman degradation
degradación de Edman
edogestrone
edogestrona
edoxudine
edoxudina
edrophonium chloride
cloruro de edrofonio
edulcorate, to
endulzar

EEC
Comunidad Económica
Europea
efface, to
borrar
effect
efecto
effect, to
afectar
effective
eficaz, efectivo
efficacy
eficacia
efficiency
eficiencia
efflorescence
eflorescencia, floración
effluence
efluencia, emanación,
descarga
effluent
agua residual, efluente
effluvium
efluvio
efflux
emanación, descarga,
salida
eflornithine
eflornitina
efloxate
efloxato
efrotomycin
efrotomicina
egg oil
aceite de yema de
huevo
egg yolk
yema de huevo
Ehrlich-Sachs reaction
reacción de Ehrlich
Sachs
eicosamethyl
nonasiloxane
nonasiloxano
eicosametílico
eicosapentanenoic acid
ácido eicosa-
pentaenoico
eicosane
eicosano
eicosanoic acid
ácido eicosanoico
eicosanoid
eicosanoide

1-eicosanol
1-eicosanol
5,8,11,14-eicosa-
pentaenoic acid
ácido 5,8,11,14-
eicosapentanoico
5,8,11,14-eicosa-
tetraenoic acid
ácido 5,8,11,14-
eicosatetranoico
Einhorn-Brunner
reaction
reacción de
Einhorn Brunner
einstenium
einstenio
ekahafnium
ecahafnio
elaboration
elaboración,
fabricación
elaidic acid
ácido elaídico
elaidinization
elaidinización
elaiomycin
elaiomicina
elantrine
elantrina
elanzepine
elancepina
elastase
elastasa
elastic modulus
módulo elástico
elasticity
elasticidad
elastin
elastina
elastomer
elastómero
Elbs persulfate
oxidation
oxidación de
persulfato de Elbs
Elbs reaction
reacción de Elbs
elcatonin
elcatonina
electric double layer
capa doble
eléctrica
electric furnace
horno eléctrico

electric steel
acero de electro-
horno, acero
eléctrico, acero
al silicio
electride
electruro
electrochemical
equivalent
equivalente
electroquímico
electrochemistry
electroquímica
electrocoating
capa galvánica
electrocortin
electrocortina
electrocratic
electrocrático
electrode
electrodo
electrode, glass
electrodo de vidrio
electrode, hydrogen
electrodo de hidrógeno
electrodeposition
deposición
galvanoplástica,
deposición
electrolítica,
electrodeposición
electrodialysis
electrodiálisis
electroforming
electroplastia,
electromoldeo
electroless coating
revestimiento por vía
química, revestimiento
no electrolítico
electroluminescence
electroluminiscencia
electrolysis
electrólisis
electrolyte
electrólito
electrolytic acid
ácido electrolítico
electrolytic cell
cuba electrolítica
electrolytic zinc
cinc electrolítico
electromagnet
electroimán
electromagnetic
electromagnético
electromagnetic field
campo
electromagnético

electromagnetic
radiation
radiación
electromagnética
electromagnetic
separation
separación
electromagnética
electromagnetic
spectrum
espectro
electromagnético
electrometallurgy
electrometalurgia
electrometer
electrómetro
electrometric
electrométrico
electrometric tritration
titulación
electrométrica
electromotive force
fuerza electromotriz
electromotive series
serie electromotriz
electron
electrón
electron beam
haz de electrones
electron microscope
microscopio
electrónico
electron paramagnetic
resonance
resonancia electrónica
paramagnética
electronegativity
electronegatividad
electron-volt
electrón voltio, eV
electrophile
electrófilo
electrophoresis
electroforesis
electropositive
electropositivo
electrostatic
electrostático
electrostatic bond
enlace electrostático
electrostatic coating
revestimiento
electrostático
electrostatic field
campo electrostático
electrostatic
precipitator
precipitador
electrostático

electrovalency
electrovalencia
electrovalent bond
enlace electrovalente
electrovalent
compound
compuesto
electrovalente
electrowinning
electroextracción,
extracción
electrolítica
electrum
plata alemana
eledoisin
eledoisina
element
elemento
elementary
elemental
elementary analysis
análisis elemental
elementary particle
partícula elemental
elemi
elemí
elenolide
elenólido
elevation
elevación
elfazepam
elfacepán, elfazepam
eliminate, to
eliminar
elimination
eliminación
elixir
elixir
ellagic acid
ácido elágico
elliptic
elíptico
ellipticine
elipticina
elliptinium acetate
acetato de eliptinio
elliptone
eliptona, eliptón
elongate, to
alargar
elongation
alargamiento
Eltekoff reaction
reacción de Eltekoff
eluate, to
eluir, separar, lavar,
filtrar
eluate
eluido, eluato

elucaine
elucaína
elute, to
eluir, separar, lavar
elution
elución
elutriation
elución, separación,
levigación
elymoclavine
elimoclavina
emanate, to
emanar
emanation
emanación
embelin
embelina
embody, to
incorporar, incluir
embonate
embonato
embosser
estampador
embramine
embramina
embrittle, to
fragilizar
embutramide
embutramida
Emde degradation
degradación de Emde
emendation
emendation
corrección, enmienda
emepronium bromide
bromuro de emepronio
emerald
esmeralda
emerald green
verde esmeralda
emeralds, synthetic
esmeraldas sintéticas
emerge, to
surgir, aparecer
emery, emeryl
esmeril, lija
emery cloth
tela de esmeril
emery papel
papel de lija, papel de
esmeril
emetamine
emetamina
emetic
emético
emetin(e)
emetina
emilium tosilate
tosilato de emilio

110

emission spectra
espectros de emisión
emission
spectrometer
espectrómetro de
emisión
emission
spectroscopy
espectroscopía de
emisión
emit
emitir
emmenagogue
emenagogo, hemagogo
(menstrual)
Emmert reaction
reacción de Emmert
emodin
emodina
emollient
emoliente
emorfazone
emorfazona
emphasize, to
destacar, recalcar,
puntualizar
empirical
empírico
empirical formula
fórmula empírica
empirical rule
regla empírica
emplacement
emplazamiento
empty
vacío
empty, to
vaciar
emulgator
emulgador
emulsifiable
emulsionable
emulsification
emulsificación
emulsifier
emulsionante
emulsifier oil
aceite emulsionante
emulsify, to
emulsionar
emulsifying agent
agente emulsionante
emulsin
emulsina
emulsion
emulsión
emulsion breaker
cortador de emulsión,
rompedor de emulsión

emulsion
polymerization
polimerización en
emulsión
emulsionize, to
emulsionar
emulsive power
potencia emulsiva,
poder emulsivo
emulsoid
emulsoide
emylcamate
emilcamato
enalapril
enalapril
enalapril maleate
maleato de enalapril
enalaprilat
enalaprilato
enallylpropymal
enalilpropimal
enamel
esmalte
enamine
enamina
enantate
enantato
enanthaldehyde
enantaldehído
enanthic acid
ácido enántico
enanthotoxin
enantotoxina
enanthyl alcohol
alcohol enantílico
enantiomer
enantiómero
enantiomorph
enantiomorfo
enantiomorphism
enantiomorfismo
enantiomorphous
enantiomórfico
enantiotropy
enantiotropía
enbucrilate
embucrilato
encainide
encainida
encapsulation
encapsulación
enciprazine
encipracina,
enciprazina
enclomifene
enclomifeno
encoded
codificado, introducido
en el código

encyprate
enciprato
end
fin
endiandric acids
ácidos endiándricos
end point
punto final
end product
producto final,
producto terminado
endo-
endo-
endobenzyline bromide
bromuro de
endobencilina
endo-cis-
biclyclo(2,2,1)-5-
heptene-2,3-dicarboxy-
lic anhydride
anhídrido endo-cis-
biciclo(2,2,1)-5-
hepteno-2,3-
dicarboxílico
endomide
endomida
endomycin
endomicina
endophenolphthalein
endofenolftaleína
endorphins
endorfinas
endosmosis
endósmosis
endosulfan
endosulfán
endothall
endotal
endothermal
endotérmico
endothermic
endotérmico
endothion
endotiona
endotoxins
endotoxinas
endoxan
ciclofosfamida
endralazine
endralacina,
endralazina
endrin
endrín
endrisone
endrisona
enduracidin
enduracidina
enercology
enercología

Ene reaction
reacción eno
energize, to
activar
energy
energía
energy converter
conversor de energía,
convertidor de energía
energy sources
fuentes de energía
energy storage
almacenamiento de
energía
enestebol
enestebol
enfenamic acid
ácido enfenámico
enfleurage
enfloración
enflurane
enflurano
engage, to
captar, atraer, ocuparse,
engranar
engine
máquina
engineered
manipulado, alterado
artificialmente
engineering material
materiales industriales
engrain, to
teñir
enhance, to
destacar, realzar,
fomentar, aumentar
enhancer
intensificador
eniclobrate
eniclobrato
enilconazole
enilconazol
enlarge, to
agrandar, aumentar,
expandir
electric coil heater
calentador eléctrico a
serpentina
enniatins
enniatinas
enocitabine
enocitabina
enol
enol
enolicam
enolicán, enolicam
enolisation
enolización

enolase
enolasa
enology
enología
enoxacin
enoxacina
enoxaparin
enoxaparina
enoximone
enoximona
enoxolone
enoxolona
enpiprazole
empiprazol
enprazepine
empracepina
enprofylline
emprofilina
enpromate
empromato
enprostil
emprostilo
enramycin
enramicina
enrich, to
enriquecer
enriching
enriquecimiento
enrichment
enriquecimiento
enrofloxacin
enrofloxacina
ensilage
ensilado,
ensilaje
enter, to
entrar, introducir
entering
entrada
enterobactin
enterobactina
enterogastrone
enterogastrona
enterolactone
enterolactona
enteromycin
enteromicina
entprol
entprol, cuadrol
enterprise
empresa
enterokinase
enterocinasa
entity
entidad
entrain, to
arrastrar
entrainer
arrastrante

entrainment
arrastre
entrapped air
burbuja de aire, aire
atrapado
entropy
entropía
entprol
entprol
entsufon
entsufona
envelope
envoltura
enviomycin
enviomicina
environment
medio ambiente
environmental
chemistry
química del ambiente,
química ambiental
Environmental
Protection Agency
Agencia de Protección
del Medio Ambiente
enviroxime
enviroxima
enzyme
enzima
eosin(e)
eosina
eosine I bluish
eosina I azulada
eosine yellowish
eosina amarillenta
epalrestat
epalrestato
epanolol
epanolol
eperisone
eperisona
ephedrine
efedrina
ephedrine sulfate
sulfato de efedrina
ephedrine tannate
tanato de efedrina
epiandrosterone
epiandrosterona
epicainide
epicainida
epichlorohydrin
epiclorhidrina
epoxide
epichlorohydrin tri-
ethanolamine
cellulose
celulosa epiclorhidrín
trietanolamínica,

epiclorhidrina
trietanolamincelulosa
epicholestanol
epicolestanol
epicholesterol
epicolesterol
epicillin
epicilina
epiestriol
epiestriol
epimer
epímero
epimestrol
epimestrol
epinastine
epinastina
epinephrine
epinefrina, adrenalina
epinephrine bitartrate
bitartrato de
epinefrina
epipropidine
epipropidina
epiquinidine
epiquinidina
epiquinine
epiquinina
epirizole
epirizol
epiroprim
epiroprima
epirubicin
epirrubicina
epistaxis
epistaxis
epitaxis
epitaxia
epithiazide
epitiazida
epitiostanol
epitiostanol
epitizide
epitizida
epoprostenol
epoprostenol
epoxide
epóxido, epoxídico
epoxy
epoxi
epoxy novolak
epoxi novolaca
epoxy resin
resina epoxídica
1,2-epoxybutane
1,2-epoxibutano
3,4-epoxycyclohexane
carbonitrile
carbonitrilo 3,4-
epoxiciclohexánico

epoxyethane
epoxietano
2,3-epoxy-2-ethyl-
hexanol
2,3-epoxi-2-etil-
hexanol
2,3-epoxy-1-propanol
2,3-epoxi-1-propanol
eprazinone
epracinona
eprozinol
eprocinol
epsilon acid
ácido epsilón
Epsom salt
sal de Epson, sulfato
de magnesio
eptazocine
eptazocina
eptifibatide
eptifibatida
equal
igual
equal, to
igualar
equality
igualdad
equalize, to
igualar
equation
ecuación
equation of
a reaction
ecuación de una
reacción
equidistant
equidistante
equilenin
equilenina
equilibrate, to
equilibrar
equilibrium
equilibrio
equilibrium
constant
constante de equilibrio
equilibrium
position
posición de equilibrio
equilin
equilina
equimolar
equimolar
equipment
equipo
equivalence
equivalencia
equivalent
equivalente

equivalent
concentración
concentración
equivalente
equivalent solution
solución equivalente
equivalent weight
peso equivalente
equol
ecuol
erabutoxins
erabutoxinas
eradicate, to
erradicar
erase, to
borrar
eraser
borrador
erbia
erbia, óxido de erbio
erbium
erbio
erbium nitrate
nitrato de erbio
erbium oxalate
oxalato de erbio
erbium oxide
óxido de erbio
erbium sulfate
sulfato de erbio
erbon
erbón
erdin
erdina
Erdmann's salt
sal de Erdmann
erect, to
erigir
erepsin
erepsina
erg
ergio
ergamine
ergamina
ergin
ergina
ergobasine
ergobasina, ergonovina
ergocalciferol
ergocalciferol,
vitamina D_2
ergochrysins
ergocrisinas
ergocornine
ergocornina
ergocorninine
ergocorninina
ergocristine
ergocristina

ergocriptinine
ergocriptinina
ergocryptine
ergocriptina
ergocryptinine
ergocriptinina
ergoflavin
ergoflavina
ergoloid mesylates
mesilatos ergoloides
ergometrine
ergometrina,
ergonovina
ergometrinine
ergometrinina
ergonovine
ergonovina,
ergometrina,
ergobasina, ergotocina,
ergostetrina
ergosine
ergosina
ergostane
ergostano
ergostanol
ergostanol
α-ergostenol
α-ergostenol
ergosterine
ergosterina, ergosterol
ergosterol
ergosterol, ergosterina
ergot
cornezuelo de centeno
ergotamine
ergotamina
ergotamine tartrate
tartrato de ergotamina
ergotaminine
ergotaminina
ergothioneine
ergotioneína, tioneína,
tiohistidilbetaína
ergotine
ergotina
ergotinine
ergotinina
ergotoxine
ergotoxina
erigeron
erigerona
eriodictyol
eriodictiol
eriodictyon
eriodictión, bálsamo
montañez, yerba santa
eritadenine
eritadenina,
lentinacina, lentisina

eritrityl tetranitrate
tetranitrato de eritritilo
Erlenmeyer flask
erlenmeyer, frasco
erlenmeyer, matraz
erlenmeyer
Erlenmeyer-Plochl
azlactone and amino
acids synthesis
síntesis de azlactona y
aminoácidos de
Erlenmeyer Plochl
erode, to
corroer, socavar,
menoscabar
erratic
errático, irregular,
desigual
error
error
error calculation
cálculo de error
erucamide
erucamida
erucic acid
ácido erúcico
erucyl alcohol
alcohol erucílico
erythrin
eritrina
erythrite
eritrita, eritrina, flor de
cobalto, cobalto
arseniado, arseniato de
cobalto
erythritol
eritritol, eritrita,
eritroglucina,
tetrahidroxibutano
erythritol anhydride
anhídrido de eritritol
erythrityl tetranitrate
tetranitrato de eritritilo
erythroascorbic acid
ácido eritro ascórbico
erythrocentaurin
eritrocentaurina
erythrocyte
eritrocito
erytrogenic acid
ácido eritrogénico
α-erythroidine
α-eritroidina
ß-erythroidine
ß-eritroidina
erythrol
eritrol
erythrol tetranitrate
tetranitrato de eritrol

erythromycin
eritromicina
erythromycin acistrate
acistrato de
eritromicina
erythromycin estolate
estolato de eritromicina
erythromycin
ethylsuccinate
etilsuccinato de
eritromicina
erythromycin
glucoheptonate
glucoheptonato de
eritromicina
erythromycin
lactobionate
lactobionato de
eritromicina
erythromycin
propionate
propionato de
eritromicina
erythromycin stearate
estearato de
eritromicina
erythrophlamine
eritroflamina
erythrophleine
eritrofleína
erythropoietin
eritropoyetina
erythropterin
eritropterina
d-erythrose
d-eritrosa
l-erythrose
l-eritrosa
d-erythrose-4-
phosphate
4-fosfato de d-eritrosa,
d-eritrosa-4-fosfato
erythrosine
eritrosina
l-erythrulose
l-eritrulosa
esaprazole
esaprazol,
esaprazola
escape
fuga
Eschweiler-Clark
reaction
reacción de Eschweiler
Clark
escigenin
escigenina
escin
escina

esculamine
esculamina
esculetin
esculetina
esculin
esculina, esculósido,
bicolorina, policromo
eseridine
eseridina
eserine
eserina, fisostigmina
esilate
esilato
esmonol
esmonol
esmolol hydrochloride
clorhidrato de esmolol
esorubicin
esorrubicina
esparto
esparto
esparto wax
cera de esparto
esproquine
esproquina
essential
esencial, indispensable,
volátil (aceite)
essential fatty acids
ácidos grasos
esenciales
essential oil
aceite esencial, aceite
volátil
establish, to
establecer
establishment
establecimiento
estazolam
estazolán, estazolam
ester
éster
ester condensation
condensación estérea
ester gum
goma éster, goma
esterificada
ester of an acid
éster de un ácido
ester value
índice de éster
esterification
esterificación
esterify, to
esterificar
estimate, to
calcular
estimation
cálculo

estolate
estolato
estradiol
estradiol
α-estradiol
α-estradiol
estradiol benzoate
benzoato de estradiol
estradiol 17ß-cypionate
17ß-cipionato de
estradiol
estradiol undecylate
undecilato de estradiol
estradiol valerate
valerato de estradiol
estragole
estragol
estramustine
estramustina
estrapronicate
estrapronicato
estrazinol
estracinol
estriol
estriol
estriol succinate
succinato de estriol
estrofurate
estrofurato
estrogen
estrógeno
estrone
estrona
estropipate
estropipato
Etard reaction
reacción de Etard
etabenzarone
etabenzarona
etafedrine
etafedrina
etafenone
etafenona
etamestrol
etamestrol
etaminile
etaminilo
etamiphyllin
etamifilina
etamivan
etamiván
etamocycline
etamociclina
etamycin
etamicina
etaqualone
etacualona
etasuline
etasulina

etazolate
etazolato
etebenecid
etebenecida
eterobarb
eterobarbo
etersalate
etersalato
ethacridine
etacridina
ethacrynic acid
ácido etacrínico
ethadione
etadiona
ethalfluralin
etalfluralina
ethambutol
etambutol
ethamivan
etamiván
ethamoxytriphetol
etamoxitrifetol
ethamsylate
etansilato
ethanal
etanal
ethanamide
etanamida
ethane
etano
ethane hydrate
hidrato de etano
ethanearsonic acid
ácido etanarsónico
ethanedioyl chloride
cloruro de
etanodioílo
1,2-ethanedisulfonic
acid
ácido 1,2-etan-
disulfónico
1,2-ethanedithiol
1,2-etanditiol
ethanethiol
etantiol
ethanethiolic acid
ácido etantiólico
ethanoic acid
ácido etanoico
ethanol
etanol
ethanol formamide
formamida etanólica,
etanol formamida
ethanol hydrazine
hidracina etanólica,
etanolhidracina,
hidrazina etanólica,
etanolhidrazina

ethanolamine
etanolamina
ethanolamine oleate
oleato de etanolamina
ethanolurea
urea etanólica,
etanolurea
ethaverine
etaverina
ethchlorvynol
etclorvinol
ethebenecid
etebenécido
ethene
eteno
ethenoid linking
enlace etenoide
ethenoid resin
resina etenoide
ethenol
etenol, alcohol vinílico
ethenyl
vinilo
ethenylbenzene
estireno, etenilbenceno
ethenylen
vinilideno
ethenzamine
etenzamina
ethephon
etefón
ether
éter
ethereal
etéreo
etherification
eterificación
etherify, to
eterificar
ethiazide
etiazida
ethical drug
fármaco ético
ethidene
etilideno, etideno
ethinamate
etinamato
ethinyl estradiol
etinilestradiol
ethiodized oil
aceite etiyodado
ethion
etión
ethionamide
etionamida
ethionine
etionina
ethiozin
etiocina, etiozina

ethirimol
etirimol
ethisterone
etisterona
ethodin
etodina
ethofumesate
etofumesato
ethoheptazine
etoheptacina,
etoheptazina
ethohexadiol
etohexadiol
ethomoxane
etomoxano
ethopabate
etopabato
ethoprop
etoprop
ethopropazine
etopropacina,
etopropazina
ethosuximide
etosuximida
ethotion
etotiona
ethoxazene
etoxaceno
ethoxazorutoside
etoxazorutósido
ethoxy group
grupo etoxi
p-ethoxyacetanilide
p-etoxiacetanilida
ethoxybenzidine
etoxibencidina
ethoxycarbonyl
isothiocyanate
isotiocianato de
etoxicarbonilo
2-ethoxy-3,4-dihydro-
2H-pyran
2-etoxi-3,4-dihidro-
2H-pirano
6-ethoxy-1,2-dihydro-
2,2,4-trimethyl-
quinoline
6-etoxi-1,2-dihidro-
2,2,4-trimetil-
quinolina
2-ethoxyethanol
2-etoxietanol
2-ethoxyethyl acetate
acetato de 2-
etoxietilo
2-ethoxyethyl-p-
methoxycinnamate
p-metoxicinamato de
2-etoxietilo

3-ethoxy-4-hydroxy-
benzaldehyde
3-etoxi-4-hidroxi-
benzaldehído
1-ethoxy-2-hydroxy-4-
propenylbenzene
1-etoxi-2-hidroxi-4-
propenilbenceno
4-ethoxy-3-methoxy-
benzaldehyde
4-etoxi-3-metoxi-
benzaldehído
4-ethoxy-3-
methoxyphenylacetic
acid
ácido 4-etoxi-3-
metoxifenilacético
1-ethoxy-2-methoxy-4-
propenylbenzene
1-etoxi-2-metoxi-4-
propenilbenceno
ethoxymethylene-
malononitrile
etoximetilen-
malononitrilo
2-ethoxynaphthalene
2-etoxinaftaleno
4-ethoxyphenol
4-etoxifenol
ethoxyquin
etoxiquina
ethoxytriglycol
etoxitriglicol
ethoxzolamide
etoxzolamida
ethyl
etilo
ethyl abietate
abietato etílico,
abietato de etilo
ethyl acetate
acetato etílico, acetato
de etilo
ethyl acetate,
anhydrous
acetato de etilo
anhidro
ethyl acetic acid
ácido etilacético
ethyl acetoacetate
acetoacetato etílico,
acetoacetato de etilo
ethyl acetone
acetona etílica,
etilacetona
ethyl acetylsalicylate
acetilsalicilato
etílico, acetil-
salicilato de etilo

ethyl acrylate
acrilato etílico, acrilato
de etilo
ethyl alcohol
alcohol etílico
ethyl alcohol dena-
tured
alcohol etílico
desnaturalizado
ethyl aldehyde
aldehído etílico
ethyl aluminum
dichloride
dicloruro etílico de
aluminio, dicloruro de
etilaluminio
ethyl amyl ketone
cetona etilamílica,
etilamilcetona
ethyl antranilate
antranilato etílico,
antranilato de etilo
ethyl benzoate
benzoato etílico,
benzoato de etilo
ethyl benzoylacetate
benzoilacetato etílico,
benzoilacetato de etilo
ethyl biscoumacetate
biscumacetato etílico,
biscumacetato de etilo
ethyl borate
borato etílico, borato
de etilo
ethyl bromide
bromuro etílico,
bromuro de etilo
ethyl bromoacetate
bromacetato etílico,
bromacetato de etilo
ethyl α-bromo-
propionate
α-bromopropionato
etílico, α-bromo-
propionato de etilo
ethyl butanoate
butanoato etílico,
butanoato de etilo
ethyl tert-butyl ether
éter terc-butil etílico
ethyl butyl ketone
cetona etilbutílica,
etilbutilcetona
ethyl butyrate
butirato etílico, butirato
de etilo
ethyl caffeate
cafeato etílico, cafeato
de etilo

ethyl caprate
caprato etílico, caprato
de etilo
ethyl caproate
caproato etílico,
caproato de etilo
ethyl caprylate
caprilato etílico,
caprilato de etilo
ethyl carbamate
carbamato etílico,
carbamato de etilo
ethyl carbazate
carbazato etílico,
carbazato de etilo
ethyl ß-carboline-3-
carboxylate
3-carboxilato de etil ß-
carbolina
ethyl carbonate
carbonato etílico,
carbonato de etilo
ethyl carfluzepate
carflucepato etílico,
carflucepato de etilo
ethyl cartrizoate
cartrizoato etílico,
cartrizoato de etilo
ethyl cellulose
etilcelulosa, celulosa
etílica
ethyl chloride
cloruro etílico, cloruro
de etilo
ethyl chloroacetal
etilcloracetal
ethyl chloroacetate
cloracetato etílico,
cloracetato de etilo
ethyl chloro-
carbonate
clorocarbonato etílico,
clorocarbonato de
etilo
ethyl chloroformate
cloroformiato etílico,
cloroformiato de etilo
ethyl α-chloro-
propionate
α-cloropropionato
etílico, α-cloro-
propionato de etilo
ethyl chlorosulfonate
clorosulfonato
etílico, cloro-
sulfonato de etilo
ethyl cinnamate
cinamato etílico,
cinamato de etilo

115

ethyl citrate
citrato etílico, citrato
de etilo
ethyl crotonate
crotonato etílico,
crotonato de etilo
ethyl cyanide
cianuro etílico, cianuro
de etilo
ethyl cyanoacetate
cianoacetato etílico,
cianoacetato de etilo
ethyl dichloro-
phenoxyacetate
diclorofenoxiacetato
de etilo
ethyl dimethyl-9-
octadecenyl
ammonium bromide
bromuro de etildimetil-
9-octadecenilamonio
S-ethyl di-N,N-
propylthiocarbamate
di-N,N-propiltio-
carbamato de S-etilo
ethyl dirazepate
diracepato etílico,
diracepato de etilo
ethyl enanthate
enantato etílico,
enantato de etilo
ethyl ether
éter etílico
ethyl 3-ethoxy-
propionate
3-etoxipropionato de
etilo
ethyl ferrocenoate
ferrocenoato etílico,
ferrocenoato de etilo
ethyl fluid
líquido etílico, fluido
etílico
ethyl fluoroformate
fluoroformiato etílico,
fluoroformiato de etilo
ethyl fluorosulfonate
fluorosulfonato etílico,
fluorosulfonato de
etilo
ethyl formate
formiato etílico,
formiato de etilo
ethyl o-formate
o-formiato etílico, o-
formiato de etilo
ethyl furoate
furoato etílico, furoato
de etilo

ethyl glyme
glima etílica
ethyl heptazine
heptacina etílica,
heptazina etílica
ethyl hexanoate
hexanoato etílico,
hexanoato de etilo
ethyl hexoate
hexoato etílico,
hexoato de etilo
ethyl hydroxyethyl
cellulose
celulosa etilhidroxi-
etílica, etilhidroxi-
etilcelulosa
ethyl iodide
yoduro etílico, yoduro
de etilo
ethyl iodoacetate
yodacetato etílico,
yodacetato de etilo
ethyl iodophenyl-
undecylate
yodofenilundecilato
etílico, yodofenil-
undecilato de etilo
ethyl isothiocyanate
isotiocianato etílico,
isotiocianato de etilo
ethyl isovalerate
isovalerato etílico,
isovalerianato
etílico, isova-
lerianato de etilo
ethyl lactate
lactato etílico, lactato
de etilo
ethyl laurate
laurato etílico, laurato
de etilo
ethyl levulinate
levulinato etílico,
levulinato de etilo
ethyl linoleate
linoleato etílico,
linoleato de etilo
ethyl loflazepate
loflacepato etílico,
loflacepato de etilo
ethyl malonate
malonato etílico,
malonato de etilo
ethyl mercaptan
mercaptano etílico,
etilmercaptano
ethyl mesoxalate
mesoxalato etílico,
mesoxalato de etilo

ethyl methane-
sulfonate
metansulfonato etílico,
metansulfonato de
etilo
ethyl methylcellulose
celulosa etilmetílica,
etilmetilcelulosa
ethyl methyl ether
éter etilmetílico
ethyl methyl ketone
cetona etilmetílica,
etilmetilcetona
ethyl methylphenyl-
glycidate
metilfenilglicidato
etílico, metilfenil-
glicidato de etilo
ethyl mustard oil
aceite etílico de
mostaza, aceite de
etilmostaza
ethyl myristate
miristato etílico,
miristato de etilo
ethyl nitrate
nitrato etílico, nitrato
de etilo
ethyl nitrile
nitrito etílico, nitrito de
etilo
ethyl nitrobenzoate
nitrobenzoato
etílico, nitro-
benzoato de etilo
ethyl nonanoate
nonanoato etílico,
nonanoato de etilo
ethyl nonoate
nonoato etílico,
nonoato de etilo
ethyl octanoate
octanoato etílico,
octanoato de etilo
ethyl octoate
octoato etílico, octoato
de etilo
ethyl oenanthate
oenantato etílico,
oenantato de etilo
ethyl oleate
oleato etílico, oleato de
etilo
ethyl orthoacetate
ortoacetato etílico,
ortoacetato de etilo
ethyl orthoformate
ortoformiato etílico,
ortoformiato de etilo

ethyl orthopropionate
ortopropionato etílico,
ortopropionato de
etilo
ethyl oxalacetate
oxalacetato etílico,
oxalacetato de etilo
ethyl oxalate
oxalato etílico, oxalato
de etilo
ethyl parathion
paratión etílico,
etilparatión
ethyl PCT
etil PCT (fosfo-
cloridotionato de O,O-
dietilo)
ethyl pelargonate
pelargonato etílico,
pelargonato de etilo
ethyl phenyl acetate
acetato feniletílico,
fenilacetato de etilo
ethyl phenyl
acrylate
acrilato feniletílico,
fenilacrilato de etilo
ethyl phenyl-
carbamate
carbamato feniletílico,
fenilcarbamato etílico,
fenilcarbamato de
etilo
ethyl phenyl
dichlorosilane
diclorosilano
feniletílico,
etilfenildiclorosilano
ethyl phenyl ketone
cetona feniletílica,
etilfenilcetona
ethyl phosphoro-
chloridite
fosforocloridita etílica
ethyl phthalate
ftalato etílico, ftalato
de etilo
ethyl phthalyl ethyl
glyconate
etilgliconato
ftaliletílico,
ftaliletilgliconato de
etilo
ethyl propiolate
propiolato etílico,
propiolato de etilo
ethyl propionate
propionato etílico,
propionato de etilo

ethyl propyl ketone
cetona propiletílica,
etilpropilcetona
ethyl
pyrophosphate
pirofosfato etílico,
pirofosfato de etilo
ethyl salicylate
salicilato etílico,
salicilato de etilo
ethyl sebacate
sebacato etílico,
sebacato de etilo
ethyl silicate
silicato etílico, silicato
de etilo
ethyl silicate,
condensed
silicato etílico
condensado, silicato de
etilo condensado
ethyl sodium
oxalacetate
oxalacetato de sodio
etílico, oxalacetato
sódico de etilo
ethyl sulfate
sulfato etílico, sulfato
de etilo
ethyl sulfhydrate
sulfhidrato etílico,
sulfhidrato de etilo
ethyl sulfide
sulfuro etílico, sulfuro
de etilo
ethyl tartrate
tartrato etílico, tartrato
de etilo
ethyl tartrate, acid
tartrato etílico
ácido, tartrato
ácido de etilo
ethyl triacetylgallate
triacetilgalato etílico,
triacetilgalato de etilo
ethyl uretane
etiluretano, uretano
etílico
ethyl valerate
valerato etílico,
valerato de etilo
ethyl vanillate
vainillato etílico,
vainillato de etilo
ethyl vanillin
etilvainillina, vainillina
etílica
ethyl vinyl ether
éter vinil etílico

ethyl xanthic acid
ácido etilxántico
ethyl zinc
etilcinc, cinc
etílico
n-ethylacetamide
acetamida n-etílica, n-
etilacetamida
ethylacetamido-
cyanoacetate
acetamidociano acetato
de etilo
n-ethylacetanilide
n-etilacetanilida
ethylacetylene
acetileno etílico,
etilacetileno
ethyl-n-acetyl-α-
cyanoglycine
α-cianoglicina etil-
n-acetílica, etil-
n-acetil-α-ciano-
glicina
ethyl-α-allylaceto-
acetate
α-alilacetoacetato
etílico, α-alilaceto-
acetato de etilo
ethylaluminum
sesquichloride
sesquicloruro etílico
de aluminio,
sesquicloruro
de etilaluminio
ethylamine
etilamina
ethylamine
hydrobromide
bromhidrato de
etilamina
ethyl-o-amino-
benzoate
o-aminobenzoato
etílico, o-amino-
benzoato de etilo
ethyl-p-amino-
benzoate
p-aminobenzoato
etílico, p-amino-
benzoato de etilo
ethyl-p-amino-
benzoate
hydrochloride
clorhidrato de p-
aminobenzoato de
etilo
ethylaminoethanol
etanol etilamínico,
etilaminoetanol

2-ethylamino-4-
isopropylamino-6-
methylthio-s-triazine
2-etilamino-4-
isopropilamino-6-
metiltio-s-triacina, 2-
etilamino-4-
isopropilamino-6-
metiltio-s-triazina
ethyl-1-(p-amino-
phenyl)-4-phenyl-
isonipecotate
4-fenilisonipecotato de
etil-1-(p-aminofenilo)
ethylamphetamine
anfetamina etílica,
etilanfetamina
n-ethylaniline
n-etilanilina
o-ethylaniline
o-etilanilina
2-ethylanthraquinone
antraquinona 2-etílica,
2-etilantraquinona
ethylarsenious oxide
óxido etilarsenioso
ethylate, to
etilar
ethylation
etilación
2-ethylaziridine
2-etilaciridina
ethylbenzene
benceno etílico,
etilbenceno
4-ethylbenzene-
sulfonic acid
ácido 4-etilbencen-
sulfónico
ethylbenzhydramine
etilbenzhidramina
ethyl-o-benzoyl-
benzoate
o-benzoilbenzoato
etílico, o-benzoil-
benzoato de etilo
ethylbenztropine
etilbenztropina
1-ethylbenzyl alcohol
alcohol 1-etil-bencílico
ethylbenzyl chloride
cloruro etilbencílico,
cloruro de etilbencilo
ethylbenzylaniline
etilbencilanilina
ethyl-bis(4-hydroxy-
coumarinyl) acetate
acetato de bis(4-
hidroxicumarinil) etilo

ethylbromopyruvate
bromopiruvato etílico,
etilbromopiruvato
2-ethylbutanol
butanol 2-etílico,
2-etilbutanol
2-ethyl-1-butene
2-etil-1-buteno
3-(2-ethylbutoxy)-
propionic acid
ácido 3-(2-
etilbutoxi)propiónico
2-ethylbutyl acetate
acetato 2-etilbutílico,
acetato de 2-etilbutilo
2-ethylbutyl alcohol
alcohol 2-etilbutílico
ethylbutyl carbonate
carbonato etilbutílico,
carbonato de etilbutilo
ethyl-n-butyl ether
éter etil-n-butílico
2-ethylbutyl silicate
silicato 2-etilbutílico,
silicato de 2-etilbutilo
2-ethylbutyl aldehyde
aldehído 2-etilbutílico
ethylene
n-ethylbutylamine
amina n-etilbutílica, n-
etilbutilamina
2-ethyl-2-butyl-
propanediol-1,3
2-etil-2-butil-
propanodiol-1,3
2-ethylbutyric acid
ácido 2-etilbutírico
N-ethylcarbazole
N-etilcarbazol
5-ethyl-5-cyclo-
heptenylbarbituric
acid
ácido 5-etil-5-
cicloheptenil
barbitúrico
ethylcyclohexane
etilciclohexano,
ciclohexano etílico
N-ethylcyclohexyl-
amine
N-etilciclohexilamina,
ciclohexilamina N-
etílica
ethylcyclopentane
etilciclopentano,
ciclopentano etílico
ethyldichloroarsine
diclorarsina etílica,
etildiclorarsina

ethyl-4,4'-dichloro-
benzilate
4,4-diclorobencilato de
etilo
ethyldichlorosilane
etildiclorosilano,
diclorosilano etílico
ethyldiethanolamine
etildietanolamina,
dietanolamina etílica
ethyldimethylmethane
dimetilmetano etílico,
etildimetilmetano
ethyldipropylmethane
dipropilmetano etílico,
etildipropilmetano
ethylene
etileno
ethylene bis(imino-
diacetic acid)
ácido etilenbis
(iminodiacético)
ethylene bis(oxy-
ethylenenitrile)
tetraacetic acid
ácido etilenbis
(oxietilen nitrilo)
tetracético
ethylene bond
enlace etilénico
ethylene bromide
bromuro de etileno
ethylene bromohydrin
etilenbromohidrina,
bromohidrina etilénica
ethylene carbonate
carbonato etilénico,
carbonato de etileno
ethylene chloride
cloruro etilénico,
cloruro de etileno
ethylene chloro-
bromide
clorobromuro etilénico,
clorobromuro de
etileno
ethylene chloro-
hydrin(e)
clorhidrina etilénica,
clorhidrina de etileno
ethylene cyanide
cianuro etilénico,
cianuro de etileno
ethylene
cyanohydrin
cianhidrina etilénica
ethylene dibromide
dibromuro etilénico,
dibromuro de etileno

ethylene dichloride
dicloruro etilénico,
dicloruro de etileno
ethylene dicyanide
dicianuro etilénico,
dicianuro de etileno
ethylene diphenyl
diamine
etilendifenildiamina,
difenildiamina
etilénica
ethylene glycol
glicol etilénico,
etilenglicol
ethylene glycol
bis(ß-aminoethyl
ether)-N,N-
tetraacetic acid
ácido etilenglicol-
bis(ß-aminoetil éter)-
N,N-tetracético
ethylene glycol
bis(mercapto-
propionate)
bis(mercapto-
propionato) de glicol
etilénico
ethylene glycol
bisthioglycolate
bistioglicolato de glicol
etilénico
ethylene glycol
diacetate
diacetato de glicol
etilénico
ethylene glycol dibutyl
ether
éter dibutílico de glicol
etilénico
ethylene glycol
dibutyrate
dibutirato de glicol
etilénico
ethylene glycol diethyl
ether
éter dietílico de glicol
etilénico
ethylene glycol
diformate
diformiato de glicol
etilénico
ethylene glycol
dimethyl ether
éter dimetílico de
glicol etilénico
ethylene glycol
dinitrate
dinitrato de glicol
etilénico

ethylene glycol
dipropionate
dipropionato de glicol
etilénico
ethylene glycol
monoacetate
monoacetato de glicol
etilénico
ethylene glycol
monobenzyl ether
éter monobencílico de
glicol etilénico
ethylene glycol
monobutyl ether
éter monobutílico de
glicol etilénico
ethylene glycol
monobutyl ether
laurate
laurato de éter
monobutílico de glicol
etilénico
ethylene glycol mono-
butyl ether oleate
oleato de éter
monobutílico de glicol
etilénico
ethylene glycol
monobutyl ether
stearate
estearato de éter
monobutílico de glicol
etilénico
ethylene glycol
monoethyl ether
éter monoetílico de
glicol etilénico
ethylene glycol
monoethyl ether
acetate
acetato de éter
monoetílico de glicol
etilénico
ethylene glycol
monoethyl ether
laurate
laurato de éter
monoetílico de glicol
etilénico
ethylene glycol
monoethyl ether
ricinoleate
ricinoleato de éter
monoetílico de glicol
etilénico
ethylene glycol
monohexyl ether
éter monohexílico de
glicol etilénico

ethylene glycol
monomethyl ether
éter monometílico
de glicol etilénico
ethylene thiourea
ethylene glycol
monomethyl ether
acetate
acetato de éter
monometílico
de glicol
etilénico
ethylene glycol
monomethyl ether
acetyl ricinoleate
acetilrricinoleato de
éter monometílico de
glicol etilénico
ethylene glycol
monomethyl ether
ricinoleate
ricinoleato de éter
monometílico de glicol
etilénico
ethylene glycol
monomethyl ether
stearate
estearato de éter
monometílico de glicol
etilénico
ethylene glycol
monooctyl ether
éter monoctílico de
glicol etilénico
ethylene glycol
monophenyl ether
éter monofenílico de
glicol etilénico
ethylene glycol
monoricinoleate
monorricinoleato de
glicol etilénico
ethylene glycol
monostearate
monoestearato de
glicol etilénico
ethylene glycol
silicate
silicato de glicol
etilénico
ethylene hexene-1-
copolymer
copolímero de hexeno-
1 y etileno
ethylene hydrate
hidrato de etileno
ethylene oxide
óxido etilénico, óxido
de etileno

ethylene thiourea
tiourea etilénica
ethylene urea
ethylene urea
urea etilénica
ethylenediamine
etilendiamina, diamina
etilénica
ethylenediamine
carbamate
carbamato de
etilendiamina
ethylenediamine
dihydroiodide
dihidroyoduro de
etilendiamina
ethylenediamine
tartrate
tartrato de
etilendiamina
ethylenediamine
tetraacetic acid
ácido etilendiamino
tetracético
ethylenediamine
tetraacetonitrile
etilendiamino
tetracetonitrilo
ethylenediamine-di-o-
hydroxyphenylacetic
acid
ácido etilendiamino-
di-o-hidroxifenil-
acético
ethylenedinitrile
tetraacetic acid
ácido etilendinitrilo
tetracético
ethylenedinitrile tetra-
2-propanol
etilendinitrilotetra-2-
propanol
1,1'-ethylene-2,2'-
dipyridinium
dibromide
dibromuro de 1,1-
etilén-2,2'-
dipiridinio
ethyleneimine
etilenimina, imina
etilénica
ethylene-maleic
anhydride
copolymer
copolímero de
anhídrido maleico y
etileno
ethylenenaphthalene
naftaleno etilénico

ethylene-propylene-
diene monomer
monómero de
propilendienetileno
ethylene-propylene
rubber
caucho de
propilenetileno
ethylene-vinyl acetate
copolymer
copolímero de acetato
de vinilo y etileno
ethylenic hydrocarbons
hidrocarburos
etilénicos
ethylestrenol
etilestrenol, estrenol
etílico
n-ethylethanolamine
n-etiletanolamina,
etanolamina n-etílica
ethylethylene
etileno etílico,
etiletileno
ethylethyleneimine
etiletilenimina, imina
etiletilénica
ethyl-3-formyl-
propionate
3-formilpropionato
etílico, 3-formil-
propionato de etilo
2-ethylfurane
2-etilfurano, furano 2-
etílico
ethylglycol acetate
acetato de glicol
etílico
4-ethylheptane
4-etilheptano, heptano
4-etílico
ethylheptanoate
heptanoato etílico,
heptanoato de etilo
2-ethylhexaldehyde
hexaldehído 2-etílico
2,2'-(2-ethylhexamido)
diethyl di(2-ethyl-
hexoate)
di(2-etilhexoato) de
2,2'-(2-etilhexamido)
dietilo
2-ethylhexanal
2-etilhexanal
2-ethylhexanediol-1,3
2-etilhexandiol-1,3
2-ethylhexanol
2-etilhexanol, hexanol
2-etílico

2-ethylhexenal
2-etilhexenal, hexenal
2-etílico
2-ethyl-1-hexene
2-etil-1-hexeno
2-ethylhexoic acid
ácido 2-etilhexoico
2-ethylhexyl
2-etilhexilo
2-ethylhexyl acetate
acetato 2-etilhexílico,
acetato de 2-etilhexilo
2-ethylhexyl acrylate
acrilato 2-etilhexílico,
acrilato de 2-etilhexilo
2-ethylhexyl alcohol
alcohol 2-etilhexílico
2-ethylhexyl bromide
bromuro 2-etilhexílico,
bromuro de 2-
etilhexilo
2-ethylhexyl chloride
cloruro 2-etilhexílico,
cloruro de 2-etilhexilo
2-ethylhexylcyano-
acetate
cianoacetato 2-
etilhexílico,
cianoacetato de 2-
etilhexilo
2-ethylhexyl isodecyl
phthalate
isodecilftalato 2-
etilhexílico,
isodecilftalato de 2-
etilhexilo
2-ethylhexyl
octylphenyl phosphite
fosfito 2-etilhexil-
octilfenílico, fosfito
de 2-etilhexil-
octilfenilo
2-ethylhexylamine
2-etilhexilamina, amina
2-etilhexílica
n-2-ethylhexylaniline
n-2-etilhexilanilina,
anilina n-2-
etilhexílica
2-ethylhexyl-
magnesium chloride
cloruro de 2-
etilhexilmagnesio
3,3'-(2-ethylhexyl)
thiodipropionate
tiodipropionato de 3,3'-
(2-etilhexilo)
ethylhydrocupreine
etilhidrocupreína

ethyl-2-hydroxy-2,2-
bis(4-chlorophenyl)
acetate
acetato de etil-2-
hidroxi-2,2-bis(4-
clorofenilo)
ethyl-3-hydroxy-
butyrate
3-hidroxibutirato
etílico, 3-hidroxi-
butirato de etilo
ethyl-α-hydroxyiso-
butyrate
α-hidroxiisobutirato
etílico, α-hidroxi-
isobutirato de etilo
ethylic
etílico
ethylidene chloride
cloruro etilidénico,
cloruro de etilideno
ethylidene diacetate
diacetato etilidénico,
diacetato de etilideno
ethylidene dicoumarol
etilidendicumarol,
dicumarol etilidénico
ethylidene fluoride
fluoruro etilidénico,
fluoruro de etilideno
ethylidenediethyl
ether
éter etilidendietílico
ethylidenedimethyl
ether
éter etiliden-
dimetílico
5-ethylidene-2-
norbornene
5-etilideno-2-
norborneno
5-ethyl-5-isoamyl-
barbituric acid
ácido 5-etil-5-
isoamilbarbitúrico
ethylisobutylmethane
metano etilisobutílico,
etilisobutilmetano
ethylisobutyrate
isobutirato etílico,
isobutirato de etilo
ethylisocyanate
isocianato etílico,
isocianato de etilo
2-ethylisohexanol
isohexanol 2-etílico, 2-
etilisohexanol
ethyllithium
etil litio

ethylmagnesium
bromide
bromuro de
etilmagnesio
ethylmagnesium
chloride
cloruro de etilmagnesio
N-ethylmaleimide
N-etilmaleimida,
maleimida N-etílica
ethylmercuric acetate
acetato etilmercúrico
ethylmercuric chloride
cloruro etilmercúrico
ethylmercuric
phosphate
fosfato etilmercúrico
ethylmercurithio-
salicylic acid,
sodium salt
sal sódica del
ácido etilmercuri-
tiosalicílico
ethylmercury-2,3-
dihydroxypropyl
mercaptide
2,3-dihidroxipropil-
mercaptida
etilmercúrica
ethylmercury-p-
toluenesulfonanilide
p-toluensulfonanilida
etilmercúrica
n-ethylmercury-p-
toluenesulfonanilide
p-toluensulfonanilida
n-etilmercúrica
ethylmethacrylate
etilmetacrilato,
metacrilato etílico,
metacrilato de etilo
N-ethyl-3-methyl-
aniline
3-metilanilina N-
etílica, N-etil-3-
metilanilina
5-ethyl-5-(1-methyl-1-
butenil) barbituric
acid
ácido 5-etil-5-(1-metil-
1-butenil) barbitúrico
ethyl-2-methyl-
butyrate
2-metilbutirato etílico,
2-metilbutirato de
etilo
ethylmethyl-
thiambutene
tiambuteno

etilmetílico,
etilmetiltiambuteno
2-ethyl-4-methyl-
imidazole
imidazol 2-etil-4-
metílico, 2-etil-4-
metilimidazol
1-ethyl-1-methyl-
propyl carbamate
carbamato de 1-etil-1-
metilpropilo
5-ethyl-2-methyl-
pyridine
2-metilpiridina 5-
etílica, 5-etil-2-
metilpiridina
α-ethyl-α-methyl-
succinimide
α-metilsuccinimida α-
etílica, α-etil-α-
metilsuccinimida
7-ethyl-2-methyl-4-
undecanol
4-undecanol 7-etil-2-
metílico, 7-etil-2-metil-
4-undecanol
ethylmorphine
etilmorfina
ethylmorphine
hydrochloride
clorhidrato de
etilmorfina
N-ethylmorpholine
N-etilmorfolina
n-ethyl-α-naphthyl-
amine
α-naftilamina n-etílica,
n-etil-α-naftilamina
ethylparaben
etilparabeno
n-ethyl-n-nitrosourea
n-nitrosurea n-etílica,
n-etil-n-nitrosurea
ethylnorepinephrine
noradrenalina etílica,
norepinefrina etílica,
etilnorepinefrina
ethyl 2-oxocyclo-
pentanecarboxylate
pentancarboxilato 2-
oxociclo etílico, 2-
oxociclopentano-
carboxilato de etilo
3-ethylpentane
pentano 3-etílico, 3-
etilpentano
m-ethylphenol
fenol m-etílico, m-
etilfenol

p-ethylphenol
fenol p-etílico, p-
etilfenol
ethylphenylacetamide
acetamina feniletílica,
etilfenilacetamida
5-ethyl-5-phenyl-
barbituric acid
ácido 5-etil-5-
fenilbarbitúrico
N,N-ethylphenyl-
ethanolamine
etanolamina N,N-
etilfenílica, N,N-
etilfeniletanolamina
2-ethyl-2-phenyl-
glutarimide
glutarimida 2-etil-2-
fenílica, 2-etil-2-
fenilglutarimida
ethylphenylurethane
uretano feniletílico,
etilfeniluretano
ethylphosphoric acid
ácido etilfosfórico
4-ethyl-2-picoline
2-picolina 4-etílica, 4-
etil-2-picolina
2-ethylpiperidine
piperidina 2-etílica, 2-
etilpiperidina
5-ethyl-5-(1-piperidyl)-
barbituric acid
ácido 5-etil-5-(1-
piperidil) barbitúrico
1-ethyl-3-
piperidinol
3-piperidinol 1-etílico,
1-etil-3-piperidinol
1-ethyl-1-propanol
1-propanol 1-etílico,
1-etil-1-propanol
ethylpropionyl
propionilo etílico,
etilpropionilo
2-ethyl-3-propyl-
acrolein
3-propilacroleína 2-
etílica, 2-etil-3-
propilacroleína
α-ethyl-ß-propyl-
acrylanilide
ß-propilacrilanilida
α-etílica, α-etil-ß-
propilacrilanilida
2-ethyl-3-propyl-
acrylic acid
ácido 2-etil-3-
propilacrílico

2-ethyl-3-propyl-
glycinamide
3-propilglicinamida 2-
etílica, 2-etil-3-
propilglicinamida
3-ethyl-3-propyl-1,3-
propanediol
1,3-propanediol 3-etil-3-
propílico, 3-etil-3-
propil-1,3-propanediol
4-ethylpyridine
4-etilpiridina, piridina
4-etílica
2-(5-ethyl-2-
pyridyl)ethyl acrylate
acrilato 2-(5-etil-2-
piridil)etílico, acrilato
de 2-(5-etil-2-
piridil)etilo
ethylstibamine
etilestibamina,
estibamina etílica
ethylsulfonylethyl
alcohol
alcohol
etilsulfoniletílico
2-(ethylsulfonyl)
ethanol
etanol 2-
(etilsulfonílico), 2-
(etilsulfonil)etanol
ethylsulfuric acid
ácido etilsulfúrico
4-ethyl-1,4-thiazane
1,4-tiazano 4-etílico, 4-
etil-1,4-tiazano
ethylthiocarbimide
tiocarbimida etílica,
etiltiocarbimida
ethylthioethanol
tioetanol etílico,
etiltioetanol
ethylthiopyro-
phosphate
tiopirofosfato etílico,
tiopirofosfato de etilo
n-ethyl-p-toluene-
sulfonamide
p-toluensulfonamida n-
etílica, n-etil-p-
toluensulfonamida
ethyl-p-toluene-
sulfonate
p-toluensulfonato
etílico, p-toluen-
sulfonato de etilo
N-ethyl-m-toluidine
m-toluidina N-etílica,
N-etil-m-toluidina

ethyltrichlorosilane
triclorosilano etílico,
etiltriclorosilano
ethyne
etino
ethynerone
etinerona
ethynilation
etinilación
ethynodiol
etindiol
ethynodiol diacetate
diacetato de etindiol
ethynylbenzene
etinilbenceno, benceno
etinílico
1-ethynylcyclohexanol
1-etinilciclohexanol,
ciclohexanol
1-etinílico
1-ethynylcyclohexyl
carbamate
carbamato 1-
etinilciclohexílico,
carbamato de 1-
etinilciclohexilo
ethynylestradiol
etinilestradiol
ethypicone
etipicona
ethythrin
etitrina
eticyclidine
eticiclidina
etidocaine
etidocaína
etidocaine
hydrochloride
clorhidrato de
etidocaína
etidronic acid
ácido etidrónico
etidronate disodium
etidronato disódico
etifelmin(e)
etifelmina
etifenin
etifenina
etifoxine
etifoxina
etilamfetamine
etilanfetamina,
anfetamina etílica
etilefrin(e)
etilefrina
etintidine
etintidina
etiocholane
etiocolano

etiocholanic acid
ácido etiocolánico
etiocobalamin
etiocobalamina
etioporphyrin
etioporfirina
etipirium iodide
yoduro de etipirio
etiproston
etiprostón
etiracetam
etiracetán
etiroxate
etiroxato
etisazol(e)
etisazol
etisomicin
etisomicina
etisulergine
etisulergina
etizolam
etizolán, etizolam
etocarlide
etocarlida
etocrilene
etocrileno
etodolac
etodolac, etodolaco
etodroxizine
etodroxicina,
etodrixizina
etofamide
etofamida
etofenamate
etofenamato
etofibrate
etofibrato
etoformin
etoformina
etofuradine
etofuradina
etofylline
etofilina
etofylline clofibrate
clofibrato de etofilina
etofylline nicotinate
nicotinato de etofilina
etoglucid
etoglúcido
etolorex
etolorex
etoloxamine
etoloxamina
etomidate
etomidato
etomidoline
etomidolina
etonam
etonamo

etonitazene
etonitaceno
etoperidone
etoperidona
etoposide
etopósido
etoposide phosphate
fosfato de etopósido
etoprindole
etoprindol
etorphine
etorfina
etosalamide
etosalamida
etoxadrol
etoxadrol
etoxazene
etoxaceno
etoxeridine
etoxeridina
etozolin
etozolina
etretinate
etretinato
etrimfos
etrinfós
etryptamine
etriptamina
etybenzatropine
etibenzatropina
etymemazine
etimemacina,
etimemazina
etynodiol
etinodiol
ß-eucaine
ß-eucaína
eucalyptol(e)
eucaliptol, cineol
eucalyptus
eucalipto
eucalyptus gum
goma de eucalipto
eucalyptus oil
esencia (aceite) de
eucalipto
eucalyptus tar
brea de eucalipto
eucatropine
eucatropina
eucatropine
hydrochloride
clorhidrato de
eucatropina
eucryptite
eucriptita, silicato de
aluminio y litio
eugenic acid
ácido eugénico

eugenol
eugenol
eugenyl methyl ether
éter metileugenílico
euonymus
raiz de evónimo
euparin
euparina
eupatorin
eupatorina
eupatorium
eupatorio
euphorbia
euforbia
euprocin
euprocina
europia
europia, óxido de
europio
europium
europio
europium chloride
cloruro de europio
europium fluoride
fluoruro de europio
europium nitrate
nitrato de europio
europium oxalate
oxalato de europio
europium oxide
óxido de europio
europium sulfate
sulfato de europio
eutectic
eutéctico
eutectic point
punto eutéctico
eutrophication
eutroficación
evacuate, to
evacuar, vaciar
evacuated
vacío, evacuado
evaluate, to
evaluar, valorar
Evan's blue
azul de Evan
evaporate, to
evaporar
evaporate down, to
concentrar
evaporate to dryness,
to
evaporar a sequedad
evaporation
evaporación
evaporation cooling
refrigeración por
evaporación

121

evaporation losses
pérdidas por
evaporación

evaporation residue
residuo de evaporación

evaporating dish
placa de evaporación,
evaporadora

evaporator
evaporador

evaporite
evaporita

even
plano, uniforme,
parejo, liso, par

even bubble patern
burbujeo parejo,
burbujeo uniforme

even number
número par

evidence
evidencia

evodiamine
evodiamina

evolution
evolución

evolve, to
evolucionar,
desarrollar

exactness
exactitud

exalamide
exalamida

examination
examen

exaprolol
exaprolol

exceeding
en exceso,
sobrepasando

excessive
excesivo

exchange
intercambio

exchange, to
cambiar, intercambiar

exchange reaction
reacción de
intercambio

exepanol
exepanol

excipient
excipiente

excited atom
átomo excitado

excited state
estado de excitación

exclude, to
excluir

exercise
ejercicio

exhaust
escape, agotar

exhaust emission
control
control de emisión de
gases de escape

exhibit, to
exhibir, demostrar,
exponer

exifone
exifona

exiproben
exiprobeno

exothermic
exotérmico

exotic
exótico

exotoxins
exotoxinas

expand, to
expandir, extender,
dilatar

expander
alargador, expansor

expected values
valores previstos

expedient
expediente,
conveniente, oportuno

experiment, to
experimentar, probar

experimental
experimental

experimental
chemistry
química experimental

experimental
conditions
condiciones
experimentales

experimental error
error experimental

experimental method
método experimental

expert
experto

explosion-proof
a prueba de
explosiones

explosive, initiation
explosivo de iniciación

exposure testing
pruebas de exposición

expression
expresión

extender
diluyente, expansor

extinguishing agent
agente extinguidor

extract of malt
extracto de malta

extractible
extractable

extraction
extracción

extraction apparatus
equipo extractor,
extractor

extraction column
columna de extracción

extraction method
método de extracción

extractive distillation
destilación extractiva

extractive
metallurgy
metalurgia extractiva

extractor
extractor

extrapolate, to
extrapolar

extrapolation
extrapolación

extreme pressure
additives
aditivos para presiones
extremas

extruder
extruidor

extrusion
extrusión

exudate, to
exudar

n-exyl bromide
bromuro n-exílico,
bromuro de n-exilo

eyepiece
ocular (sistema de
lentes)

F

fabric
tejido
F, acid
ácido F (ácido 2-naftol-7-sulfónico)
facilities
instalaciones
factice
aceite vegetal vulcanizado
factor
factor
factor I
factor I, fibrinógeno
factor II
factor II, protrombina
factor III
factor III, factor hístico, tromboplastina hística
factor IV
factor IV
factor V
factor V, proacelerina
factor VI
factor VI, acelerina
factor VII
factor VII, proconvertina
factor VIII
factor VIII, globulina antihemofílica
factor IX
factor IX, autoprotrombina II
factor X
factor X, factor de Stuart Prower, autoprotrombina III
factor XI
factor XI, factor antihemofílico C
factor XII
factor XII, factor de activación
factor XIII
factor XIII, factor de Laki Lorand
fagarine
fagarina
Fahrenheit
Fahrenheit
failed
no pasó la prueba

falipamil
falipamilo, falipamil
fallout
lluvia radioactiva
famciclovir
fanciclovir
famotidine
famotidina
famotine
famotina
famphur
fanfur
famprofazone
famprofazona
fantridone
fantridona
faraday
faraday
α-farnesene
α-farneseno
ß-farnesene
ß-farneseno
farnesol
farnesol
fast
rápido, fijo
fast atom bombardment
bombardeo atómico rápido
fast electron
electrón rápido
fast reaction
reacción rápida
fat
grasa
fat acids
ácidos grasos
fat alcohol
alcohol graso
fat dyes
colorantes grasos
fat like
lipoide, adipoide
fat liquoring agents
agentes engrasantes emulsionados
fat soluble
liposoluble
fat solvent
disolvente de grasas
fat splitting
división de grasas

fat test
prueba de grasa
fatty
grasoso, graso (ácido), alifático
fatty acid
ácido graso
fatty acid enol ester
ester enólico de ácido graso
fatty acid pitch
pez de ácido graso
fatty alcohol
alcohol graso
fatty amines
aminas grasas
fatty ester
éster graso
fatty matter
materia grasa
fatty nitrile
nitrilo graso
fatty series
serie alifática
fazadinium bromide
bromuro de fazadinio
FDA
Administración de Alimentos y Medicamentos
FD&C dyes
colorantes FD&C, colorantes clasificados bajo la Ley de Alimentos, Medicamentos y Cosméticos de EE.UU.
feasibility
viabilidad, posibilidad de
febantel
febantel
febarbamate
febarbamato
febrifugine
febrifugina
febuprol
febuprol
febuverine
febuverina
feclemine
feclemina
feclobuzone
feclobuzona

fecula
fécula
fedrilate
fedrilato
feedback
retroaccion, retrorreacción, retroinformación
feeder
alimentador
feedstock
material básico, materia prima de alimentación
Fehling's solution
solución de Fehling
Feist-Benary synthesis
síntesis de Feist Benary
feldspar, felspar
feldespato
felbinac
felbinaco
felinine
felinina
felipyrine
felipirina
felodipine
felodipina
felsit rock
felsita
felt
fieltro
felypressin
felipresina
femoxetine
femoxetina
femto-
femto-
fenabutene
fenabuteno
fenac
fenaco, fenac
fenacetinol
fenacetinol
fenaclon
fenaclona
fenadiazole
fenadiazol
fenalamide
fenalamida
fenalcomine
fenalcomina

fenamifuril	**fendizoate**	**fenoxazoline**	(etilenpropileno
fenamifurilo	fendizoato	fenoxazolina	fluorado)
fenamiphos	**fendosal**	**fenoxedil**	**fepromide**
fenamifós	fendosal	fenoxedilo	fepromida
fenamisal	**feneritrol**	**fenozolone**	**feprosidnine**
fenamisal	feneritrol	fenozolona	feprosidnina
fenamole	**fenestrel**	**fenpentadiol**	**ferbam**
fenamol	fenestrel,	fempentadiol	ferbán
fenapanil	fenestrelo	**fenpiclonil**	**fermentation**
fenapanilo	**fenethazine**	fempiclonil	fermentación
fenaperone	fenetacina, fenetazina	**fenpiprane**	**fermentation alcohol**
fenaperona	**fenethylline**	fempiprano	alcohol de
fenarimol	fenetilina	**fenpiverinium bromide**	fermentación
fenarimol	**fenetradil**	bromuro de	**fermium**
fenbendazole	fenetradil, fenetradilo	fempiverinio	fermio
fembendazol	**fenetylline**	**fenpropathrin**	**ferrate**
fenbenicillin	fenetilina	fempropatrino	ferrato
fembenicilina	**fenflumizol**	**fenproporex**	**ferredoxin**
fenbufen	fenflumizol	femproporex	ferredoxina
fembufeno, fembufén	**fenfluramine**	**fenprostalene**	**ferreous**
fenbutatin oxide	fenfluramina	femprostaleno	ferroso, férreo
óxido de fembutatina	**fenharmane**	**fenquizone**	**ferric**
fenbutrazate	fenharmano	fenquizona	férrico
fembutrazato	**fenimide**	**fenson**	**ferric acetate**
fencamfamin	fenimida	fensona	acetato férrico
fencanfamina	**feniodium chloride**	**fenspiride**	**ferric acetate basic**
fencamine	cloruro de fenodio	fenspirida,	acetato férrico básico
fencamina	**fenipentol**	decaspirida	**ferric acetylacetonate**
fencarbamide	fenipentol	**fensulfothion**	acetilacetonato férrico
fencarbamida	**fenisorex**	fensulfotión	**ferric albuminate**
2-fenchanol	fenisorex	**fentanyl**	albuminato férrico
2-fencanol	**fenitrothion**	fentanilo, fentanila	**ferric ammonium alum**
fenchol	fenitrotión	**fentanyl citrate**	alumbre férrico
fencol	**fenmetozole**	citrato de fentanilo	amónico
fenchone	fenmetozol	**fenthion**	**ferric ammonium**
fencona	**fennel oil**	fentión, fentiona	**citrate**
fenchyl alcohol	esencia (aceite) de	**fentiazac**	citrato férrico amónico
alcohol fenquílico	hinojo	fentiazaco	**ferric ammonium**
fencibutirol	**fenocitol**	**fenticlor**	**oxalate**
fencibutirol	fenocitol	fenticloro	oxalato férrico
fenclexonium	**fenoctimine**	**fenticonazole**	amónico
methylsulfate	fenoctimina	fenticonazol	**ferric ammonium**
metilsulfato de	**fenofibrate**	**fentonium bromide**	**sulfate**
fenclexonio	fenofibrato	bromuro de	sulfato férrico
fenclofenac	**fenoldopam**	fentonio	amónico
fenclofenaco,	fenoldopán	**fenuron**	**ferric ammonium**
fenclofenac	**fenoldopam mesylate**	fenurón	**tartrate**
fenclofos	mesilato de	**fenvalerate**	tartrato férrico
fenclofós	fenoldopán	fenvalerato	amónico
fenclonine	**fenoprofen**	**fenyramidol**	**ferric arsenate**
fenclonina	fenoprofeno	feniramidol	arseniato férrico
fenclorac	**fenoprofen calcium**	**fenyripol**	**ferric arsenite**
fencloraco, fenclorac	fenoprofeno cálcico	feniripol	arsenito férrico
fenclozic acid	**fenoprop**	**fepitrizol**	**ferric benzoate**
ácido fenclócico	fenoprop	fepitrizol	benzoato férrico
fendiline	**fenoterol**	**feprazone**	**ferric bromide**
fendilina	fenoterol	feprazona	bromuro férrico
fendiline hydrochloride	**fenoverine**	**FEP resin**	**ferric cacodylate**
clorhidrato de fendilina	fenoverina	resina EPF	cacodilato férrico

ferric chloride,
anhydrous
cloruro férrico anhidro
ferric chloride, hydrate
cloruro férrico
hidratado
ferric chromate
cromato férrico
ferricyanic
ferriciánico
ferricyanide
ferricianuro
ferric citrate
citrato férrico
ferric dichromate
dicromato férrico
ferric dimethyl-
dithiocarbamate
dimetilditiocarbamato
férrico
ferric ferrocyanide
ferrocianuro
férrico
ferric fluoride
fluoruro férrico
ferric formate
formiato férrico
ferric fructose
fructosa férrica
ferric glycero-
phosphate
glicerofosfato férrico
ferrichrome
ferricromo
ferric hydrate
hidrato férrico
ferric hydroxide
hidróxido férrico
ferric hypophosphite
hipofosfito férrico
ferric malate
malato férrico
ferric naphthenate
naftenato férrico
ferric nitrate
nitrato férrico
ferric octoate
octoato férrico
ferric oleate
oleato férrico
ferric oxalate
oxalato férrico
ferric oxide
óxido férrico
ferric oxide, yellow
óxido férrico
amarillo
ferric perchloride
percloruro férrico

ferric phosphate
fosfato férrico
ferric potassium citrate
citrato férrico potásico
ferric pyrophosphate,
pirofosfato férrico
ferric pyrophosphate,
soluble
pirofosfato férrico
soluble
ferric resinate
resinato férrico
ferric sodium oxalate
oxalato férrico
sódico
ferric sodium edetate
edetato férrico sódico
ferric sodium
pyrophosphate
pirofosfato férrico
sódico
ferric stearate
estearato férrico
ferric subsulfate
solution
solución de subsulfato
férrico
ferric succinate
succinato férrico
ferric sulfate
sulfato férrico
ferric phthalate
ftalato férrico
ferric tannate
tanato férrico
ferric thiocyanate
tiocianato férrico
ferric tribromide
tribromuro férrico
ferric trichloride
tricloruro férrico
ferric trioxide
trióxido férrico
ferric trisulfate
trisulfato férrico
ferric vanadate
vanadato férrico
ferricyanic
ferriciánico
ferricyanide
ferricianuro
ferrite
ferrita
ferritin
ferritina
ferro⁻
ferro⁻
ferroboron
ferroboro

ferrocene
ferroceno
ferrocenecarboxylic
acid ethyl ester
éster etílico del ácido
ferrocencarboxílico
1,1'-ferrocene-
dicarboxylic acid
diethyl ester
éster dietílico del ácido
1,1'-ferrocen-
dicarboxílico
1,1'-ferrocene-
dicarboxylic acid
dimethyl ester
éster dimetílico del
ácido 1,1'-ferrocen-
dicarboxílico
1,1'-ferrocenediyl di-
chlorosilane
1,1'-ferrocenediílo
diclorosilano
ferrocenoyl chloride
cloruro de ferrocenoílo
ferrocenoyl dichloride
dicloruro de
ferrocenoílo
ferrocenyl borane
polymer
polímero de
ferrocenilborano
ferrocenyl methyl
ketone
ferrocenil metil cetona,
cetona ferrocenil
metílica
ferrocerium
ferrocerio
ferrocholinate
ferrocolinato
ferrochromium
ferrocromo
ferrocyanic
ferrociánico
ferrocyanide
ferrocianuro
ferroglycine sulfate
sulfato de
ferroglicina
ferromagnesite
ferromagnesita
ferromagnetic oxide
óxido ferromagnético
ferromanganese
ferromanganeso
ferromolybdenum
ferromolibdeno
ferron
ferrón, ácido 7-yodo-8-

hidroxiquinoleín-5-
sulfónico
ferronickel
ferroníquel
ferroniobium
ferroniobio
ferrophosphorus
ferrofósforo
ferropolimaler
ferropolimalero
ferrosilicon
ferrosilicio
ferrosoferric oxide
óxido ferroso férrico
ferrotitanium
ferrotitanio
ferrotrenine
ferrotrenina
ferrotungsten
ferrotungsteno
ferrous
ferroso
ferrous acetate
acetato ferroso
ferrous ammonium
sulfate
sulfato ferroso
amónico
ferrous arsenate
arseniato ferroso
ferrous bromide
bromuro ferroso
ferrous carbonate
carbonato ferroso
ferrous chloride
cloruro ferroso
ferrous citrate
citrato ferroso
ferrous 2-ethylhexoate
2-etilhexoato ferroso
ferrous ferricyanide
ferricianuro ferroso
ferrous ferric oxide
óxido ferroso férrico
ferrous fluoride
fluoruro ferroso
ferrous fumarate
fumarato ferroso
ferrous gluconate
gluconato ferroso
ferrous hydroxide
hidróxido ferroso
ferrous iodide
yoduro ferroso
ferrous lactate
lactato ferroso
ferrous
naphthenate
naftenato ferroso

ferrous octoate
octoato ferroso
ferrous oxalate
oxalato ferroso
ferrous oxide
óxido ferroso
ferrous phosphate
fosfato ferroso
ferrous phosphide
fosfuro ferroso
ferrous selenide
seleniuro ferroso
ferrous succinate
succinato ferroso
ferrous sulfate
sulfato ferroso
ferrous sulfide
sulfuro ferroso
ferrous
thiocyanate
tiocianato ferroso
ferrovanadium
ferrovanadio
ferrozirconium
ferrocirconio
ferruginous
ferruginoso
ferrum
hierro
fertile material
material fértil
fertilizer
fertilizante
fertilysin
fertilisina
fertirelin
fertirelina
ferulic acid
ácido ferúlico
fervenulin
fervenulina
fetoxilate
fetoxilato
fexicaine
fexicaína
fexinidazole
fexinidazol
fexofenadine
hydrochloride
clorhidrato de
fexofenadina
fezatione
fezationa
fiber
fibra
fiber glass
fibra de vidrio
fiber, graphite
fibra de grafito

fiber optical
fibra óptica
fiber-reactive dye
colorante reactivo a
fibra
fibracillin
fibracilina
fibrid
fíbrido
fibrin
fibrina
fibrinogen
fibrinógeno
fibrinolysin
fibrinolisina
fibroin
fibroína
fibrolite
fibrolita
fibronectin
fibronectina
ficin
ficina
fictile
fictilo
fiducial limits
límites fiduciarios
field
campo, área
field intensity
intensidad del campo
field-ion microscope
microscopio de campo
iónico
figure
cifra, número, valor
filament
filamento
filenadol
filenadol
filicin
filicina
filicinic acid
ácido filicínico
filipin
filipina
filixic acid
ácido filíxico
fill
cargar, promedio de
llenado, carga
film
película,
revestimiento
filter
filtro
filter aid
auxiliar de filtro, ayuda
de filtración

filter alum
sulfato de aluminio
filter bed
lecho filtrante
filter cake
torta (de filtro),
bizcocho de filtro
filter funnel
embudo filtrante
filter media
medios de
filtración
filter paper
papel de filtro
filter residue
residuo de filtración
filter sand
arena filtrante
filter support
portafiltro
filtrate
filtrado, material
filtrado
filtration
filtración
final pressure
presión final
final product
producto final,
producto terminado
final temperature
temperatura final
finasteride
finastérida
fine chemical
sustancias químicas
finas, sustancias
químicas de alta
calidad
fines
finos
finished product
producto terminado,
producto final
finishing
compounds
compuestos de
acabado, compuestos
de terminación
Finkelstein reaction
reacción de Finkelstein
fire clay
arcilla refractaria
fire extinguisher
extinguidor de
incendios,
extintor
fire point
punto de llama

fire sand
arena refractaria
fireproof
resistente al fuego
fir oil
esencia (aceite)
de abeto
fir oil-Siberian
esencia (aceite)
de abeto siberiano
Fischer indole
synthesis
síntesis de indol
de Fischer
Fischer oxazole
synthesis
síntesis de oxazol
de Fischer
Fischer peptide
synthesis
síntesis de péptidos de
Fischer
Fischer phenyl-
hydrazine synthesis
síntesis de
fenilhidracina de
Fischer, síntesis de
fenilhidrazina de
Fischer
Fischer's reagent
reactivo de
Fischer
Fischer's salt
sal de Fischer
Fischer's solution
solución de Fischer
Fischer-Speier
esterification
method
método de
esterificación de
Fischer Speier
Fischer-Tropsch
process
proceso de Fischer
Tropsch
Fischer-Tropsch
synthesis
síntesis de Fischer
Tropsch
fisetin
fisetina
Fisher's solution
solución de Fisher
fish glue
cola de pescado
fish-liver oil
aceite de hígado de
pescado

fish meal
harina de pescado
fish oil
aceite de pescado
fish protein
concentrate
proteína concentrada
de pescado
fissile
fisil
fissiochemistry
fisioquímica,
fisicoquímica
fission
fisión, escisión nuclear
Fittig's synthesis
síntesis de Fittig
fitting
montaje, ajuste
five membered ring
anillo de cinco
carbonos
fix
fijar
fixation
fijación
fixatives, perfume
fijadores de perfumes
fixed nitrogen
nitrógeno fijo
fixed oil
aceite fijo
fixing agent,
chemical
agente químico de
fijación
fixing agent,
mechanical
agente mecánico de
fijación
fixing agent, perfume
agente de fijación de
perfume
flamenol
flamenol
flake
escama
flameproofing agent
agente
incombustibilizante
flammability
combustibilidad
flammable material
material inflamable,
material combustible
flash
destello, llamarada,
fogonazo,
fulguración

flash destillation
destilación instantánea
flash point
punto de inflamación,
temperatura de
inflamación
flask
matraz, frasco, balón
flecainide
flask neck
cuello del matraz
flask, volumetric
matraz aforado
flatting agent
agente opacificante
flavamine
flavamina
flavanol
flavanol
flavanone
flavanona
flavanthrene
flavantreno
flavaspidic acid
ácido flavaspídico
flavianic acid
ácido flaviánico
flavin(e)
flavina
flavin enzyme
enzima flavínica
flavin mononucleotide
mononucleótido
flavínico
flavipucine
flavipucina
flavone
flavona
flavonoid
flavonoide
flavonol
flavonol
flavopereine
flavopereína
flavoprotein
flavoproteína
flavopurpurine
flavopurpurina
flavor
sabor
flavoxanthin
flavoxantina
flavoxate
flavoxato
flax
lino
flaxseed oil
aceite de semilla de
lino

flazalone
flazalona
flecainide
flecainida
flecainide acetate
acetato de
flecainida
fleroxacin
fleroxacina
fletazepam
fletacepán, fetazepam
flindersine
flindersina
flint
pedernal
flint glass
vidrio flint
flip-off seal
sello de arrancar, sello
fácil de levantar
flocculant
floculante
flocculation
floculación
floctafenine
floctafenina
Flood reaction
reacción de Flood
flopropione
flopropiona
florantyrone
florantirona
floredil
floredil, floredilo
florfenicol
florfenicol
flotation
flotación
floverine
floverina
flow
flujo, corriente
flow control
control de flujo
flow diagram
organigrama, diagrama
de flujo
flow rate
velocidad de flujo, tasa
de flujo
floxacillin
floxacilina
floxacrine
floxacrina
floxuridine
floxuridina
fluacizine
fluacicina,
fluacizina

fluconazole
fluconazol
flualamide
flualamida
fluanisone
fluanisona
fluazacort
fluazacort
flubanilate
flubanilato
flubendazole
flubendazol
flubenzimine
flubencimina
flubepride
flubeprida
flucarbril
flurcarbrilo
flucetorex
flucetorex
fluchloralin
flucloralina
flucindole
flucindol
fluciprazine
flucipracina,
fluciprazina
fluclorolone acetonide
acetónido de
flucorolona
flucloronide
fluclorónido
flucoxacillin
flucoxacilina
flucrilate
flucrilato
flucytosine
flucitosina
fludalanine
fludalanina
fludarabine phosphate
fosfato de fludarabina
fludazonium chloride
cloruro de fludazonio
fludiazepam
fludiacepán,
fludiazepam
fludorex
fludorex
fludoxopone
fludoxopona
fludrocortisone
fludrocortisona
fludrocortisone
acetate
acetato de
fludrocortisona
fludroxycortide
fludroxicortida

flufenisal
flufenisal
flufenamic acid
ácido flufenámico
fluffy
liviano, suave,
esponjoso, sedoso
flufosal
flufosal
flugestone
flugestona
fluid
líquido, fluido
fluid bed process
proceso del lecho
fluido
fluid bed granulator
dryer
secador de lecho fluido
granulador
fluidization
licuación,
fluidificación
fluidize
licuar, fluidificar
fluid ounce
onza líquida
fluindarol
fluindarol
fluindione
fluindiona
flumazenil
flumacenil
flumecinol
flumecinol
flumedroxone
flumedroxona
flumequine
flumequina
flumeridone
flumeridona
flumethasone
flumetasona
flumethiazide
flumetiazida
flumetramide
flumetramida
flumexadol
flumexadol
flumezapine
flumezapina
fluminorex
fluminorex
flumizole
flumizol
flumoxonide
flumoxonida
flunamine
flunamina

flunarizine
flunaricina
flunidazole
flunidazol
flunisolide
flunisolida
flunitrazepam
flunitracepán,
flunitrazepam
flunixin
flunixina
flunoxaprofene
flunoxaprofeno
fluoboric acid
ácido fluobórico
fluocinolone acetonide
acetónido de
fluocinolona
fluocinonide
fluocinonida
fluocortin
fluocortina
fluocortolone
fluocortolona
fluometuron
fluometurona
fluophosphate alkyl
ester
alquiléster de
fluofosfato
fluor
fluoro, flúor
p-fluoraniline
p-fluoranilina
fluoranthene
fluoranteno
fluorapatite
fluorapatita
fluorbenside
fluobensida
fluorene
fluoreno
N-2-fluorenyl-
acetamide
N-2-fluorenil-
acetamida
9-fluorenone
9-fluorenona
fluorescamine
fluorescamina
fluorescein
fluoresceína
fluorescein paper
papel de
fluoresceína
fluorescence
fluorescencia
fluorescin
flurescina

fluoresone
fluoresona
fluoric
fluórico
fluoridamid
fluoridamida
fluoridate
fluorar, tratar con
flúor
fluoridated ethylene-
propylene resin
resina de
etilenpropileno
fluorado
fluoridated water
agua fluorada
fluoridation
fluoración
fluoride
fluoruro
fluorinate
tratar o combinar con
fluoro, fluorar
fluorine
flúor
fluorine cyanide
cianuro de flúor
fluorine dioxide
dióxido de flúor
fluorine monoxide
monóxido de flúor
fluorine nitrate
nitrato de flúor
fluorine percolate
percolato de flúor
fluorite
fluorita
fluoro-
fluoro-
fluoroacetamide
fluoracetamida
fluoroacetic acid
ácido fluoracético
fluoroacetone
fluoracetona
fluoroacetophenone
fluoracetofenona
fluoroaniline
fluoranilina
fluoroapatite
fluorapatita
fluorobenzene
fluorobenceno
fluoroboric acid
ácido fluorobórico
fluorocarbon
fluorocarburo,
hidrocarburo
fluorado

fluorocarbon polymer
polímero de
fluorocarburo
fluorochemical
fluoroquímico, agente
fluoroquímico
5-fluorocytosine
5-fluorocitosina
fluorodichloro-
methane
fluorodiclorometano
1-fluoro-2,4-dinitro-
benzene
1-fluoro-2,4-
dinitrobenceno
fluoroelastomer
fluoroelastómero,
elastómero fluorado
fluoroethylene
fluoretileno
fluoroform
fluoroformo
fluoroformyl fluoride
fluoruro de
fluoroformilo
fluorol
fluorol
fluorometer
fluorómetro
fluoromethane
fluorometano
fluorometholone
fluorometolona
p-fluorophenol
p-fluorofenol
p-fluorophenyl-
acetic acid
ácido p-fluoro-
fenilacético
fluorophosphate
alkyl ester
alquiléster de
fluorofosfato,
alquiléster de
fluofosfato
fluorophosphoric
acid
ácido fluorofosfórico,
ácido fluofosfórico
fluoroquinolone
fluoroquinolona
fluorosalan
fluorosalano
fluorosilicic acid
ácido fluoro-
silícico, ácido
fluosilícico
fluorosulfonic acid
ácido fluorosulfónico

fluorosulfuric acid
ácido fluorosulfúrico,
ácido fluosulfúrico
fluorothane
fluorotano, fluotano
fluorothene
fluoroteno, fluoteno
fluorotoluene
fluorotolueno
fluorotrichloro-
methane
fluorotriclorometano,
fluotriclorometano
fluorouracil
fluoruracilo
5-fluorouracil
5-fluoruracilo
fluorspar
espato flúor, flúor
espato
fluosilicate
fluorosilicato,
fluosilicato
fluosilicic acid
ácido fluorosilícico,
ácido fluosilícico
fluosulfonic acid
ácido fluoro-
sulfónico, ácido
fluosulfónico
fluotracen
fluotraceno
fluoxetine
fluoxetina
fluoxetine
hydrochloride
clorhidrato de
fluoxetina
fluoxymesterone
fluoximesterona
flupentixol
flupentixol
fluperamide
fluperamida
fluperlapine
fluperlapina
fluperolone
fluperolona
fluperolone acetate
acetato de
fluperolona
fluphenazine
flufenacina,
flupenazina
fluphenazine
hydrochloride
clorhidrato de
flufenacina, clorhidrato
de flufenazina

flupimazine
flupimacina,
flupimazina
flupirtine
flupirtina, flupirtino
flupranone
flupranona
fluprazine
flupracina, fluprazina
fluprednidene
fluprednideno
fluprednidene acetate
acetato de
fluprednideno
fluprednisolone
fluprednisolona
fluprofen
fluprofeno
fluproquazone
fluprocuazona
fluprostenol
fluprostenol
fluquazone
flucuazona
flurandrenolide
flurandrenólido
flurantel
flurantel
flurazepam
flurazepán, fluracepam
flurazepam
hydrochloride
clorhidrato de
flurazepán
flurazolidine
flurazolidina
flurbiprofen
flurbiprofeno
fluretofen
fluretofeno
flurocitabine
flurocitabina
flurofamide
flurofamida
flurogestone acetate
acetato de
flurogestona
flurothyl
flurotilo
fluroxene
fluroxeno
fluroxypyr
fluroxipiro
flurprimidol
flurprimidol
flusalan
flusalán
flush
lavar, enjuagar, enrasar

fluspiperone
fluspiperona
fluspirilene
fluspirileno
flutamide
flutamida
flutazolam
flutazolán, flutazolam
flutiazin
flutiazina
fluticasone propionate
propionato de
fluticasona
flutizenol
fluticenol
flutonidine
flutonidina
flutoprazepam
flutopracepán,
flutoprazepam
flutriafol
flutriafol
flutroline
flutrolina
flutropium bromide
bromuro de flutropio
fluvalinate
fluvalinato
fluvastatin sodium
fluvastatina sódica
fluvoxamine
fluvoxamina
fluvoxamine maleate
maleato de fluvoxamina
flux
fundente, fluidificante,
flujo
fluzoperine
fluzoperina
foam
espuma
foam breaker
antiespumante
foam inhibitor
inhibidor de espuma
foam, plastic
espuma de material
plástico
foaming
espumante
foaming agent
agente espumante
focal point
foco
fog
niebla
foil
lámina metálica,
película metálica

folacin
folacina, ácido fólico
fold
[número de] veces
(doble, triple, etc.),
doblez
folded
plegado
folded filter
filtro plegado
folescutol
folescutol
folic acid
ácido fólico
folinic acid
ácido folínico
follitropin alfa
alfa folitropina
follow-up
seguimiento,
vigilancia
folpet
folpet
fomecin
fomecina
fominoben
fominobeno
fomocaine
fomocaína
fonazine
fonacina, fonazina
fonofos
fonofós
fonophos
fonofós
food additive
aditivo para
alimentos
food color
colorante de
alimentos, color de
alimentos
foot candle
bujía por pie
fopirtoline
fopirtolina
foreign matters
materias extrañas,
impurezas
foreign
substances
materias extrañas,
impurezas
forensic chemistry
química forense
formal
formal
formaldehyde
formaldehído

formaldehyde aniline
anilina formaldehídica,
formanilina
formaldehyde
cyanohydrin
cianhidrina
formaldehídica
formaldehyde-p-
toluidine
formaldehído-p-
toluidina, p-toluidina
formaldehídica
formalin
formalina
formamide
formamida
formanilide
formanilida
formaniline
formanilina
formate
formiato
formation
formación
formebolone
formebolona
formetanate
formetanato
formetorex
formetorex,
formetamida
formic acid
ácido fórmico
formic aldehyde
aldehído fórmico
formic ether
éter fórmico
formicin
formicina
forminitrazole
forminitrazol
formocortal
formocortal
formol
formol
formonitrile
formonitrilo
formononetin
formononetina
formosulfathiazole
formosulfatiazol
formoterol
formoterol
formothion
formotión
formula, chemical
fórmula química
formula, product
fórmula del producto

formulary
formulario
formulation
fórmula
formula weight
peso de la fórmula
formyl
formilo
formyl fluoride
fluoruro de formilo
formyldienolone
formildienolona
2-formyl-3,4-dihydro-
2H-pyran
2-formil-3,4-dihidro-
2H-pirano
1-formylpiperidine
1-formilpiperidina
4'-formylsuccinanilic
acid thiosemi-
carbazone
tiosemicarbazona de
ácido 4'-formil-
succinanílico
N²-formyl-
sulfisomidine
N²-formil-
sulfisomidina
Forster reaction
reacción de Forster
fortification
fortificación
fortimicin
fortimicina
fosazepam
fosazepam,
fosacepán
foscarnet sodium
foscarnet sódico
fosenazide
fosenazida
fosfamide
fosfamida
fosfestrol
fosfestrol
fosfomycin
fosfomicina
fosfonet sodium
fosfoneto sódico
fosfosal
fosfosal
fosinopril
fosinopril
fosinopril sodium
fosinopril sódico
fosmidomycin
fosmidomicina
fosphenitoin sodium
fosfenitoína sódica

fospirate
fospirato
fosthietan
fostietano
fraction
fracción
fractional destillation
destilación fraccionada
fractionation
fraccionamiento
fragance
fragancia
fragment
fragmento
fraissite
fraisita
framicetyn
framicetina
Franchimont reaction
reacción de
Franchimont
francium
francio
frangula
frángula
frankincense
incienso
Frankland-Duppa
reaction
reacción de Frankland
Duppa
Frankland synthesis
síntesis de Frankland
franklinite
franklinita
Frary metal
metal de Frary
Frasch process
proceso de Frasch
Fraunhofer lines
líneas de
Fraunhofer
fraxetin
fraxetina
fraxin
fraxina
fredericamycin A
fredericamicina A
free
libre
free electron
electrón libre
free energy
energía libre
free radical
radical libre
free radical mechanism
mecanismo de radical
libre

free sulfur
azufre libre
freely
libremente
freely soluble
fácilmente soluble,
libremente soluble
freeze-dry
secado por
congelación,
criodesecado
freeze-thaw cycle
ciclo de congelación y
descongelación
freezing point
punto de congelación
frenolicin
frenolicina
frentizole
frentizol
freon
freón, dicloro-
difluorometano
frequentin
frecuentina
Freund synthesis
síntesis de Freund
friability
friabilidad
friction
fricción
friedelin
friedelina
fritted (glass)
vidrio poroso, vidrio
sinterizado
front
frente
frosted glass
vidrio esmerilado
froth flotation
flotación por espuma
frozen
congelado
fructose
fructosa
fructose-1,6-
diphosphate
1,6-difosfato de
fructosa, fructosa 1,6-
difostato
fruit sugar
azúcar de frutas
FT black
negro TF (térmico fino)
ftalofyne
ftalofino
ftaxilide
ftaxilida

ftivazide
ftivazida
ftormetazine
ftormetacina,
ftormetazina
fubrogonium iodide
yoduro de fubrogonio
fuchsin
fucsina
fucosamine
fucosamina
fucosterol
fucosterol
fucoxanthin
fucoxantina
full-scale
escala completa
fulminates
fulminatos
fulminate of mercury
fulminato de mercurio
fulvoplumierin
fulvoplumierina
fumagillin
fumagilina
fumaric acid
ácido fumárico
fumarine
fumarina
fumaryl
fumarilo
fumaryl chloride
cloruro de fumarilo,
cloruro fumarílico
fume
emanación, humo,
vapores, gases
fumigant
producto fumigante
fumigation
fumigación
function
función
fundamental particle
partícula fundamental,
partícula básica
fundametal research
investigación básica,
investigación
fundamental
fungal protease
enzyme
enzima proteas
micótica
fungicide
fungicida
fungicidin
fungicidina

fungichromin
fungicromina
fungistatic
fungistático
fungisterol
fungisterol
fungus
hongo
funnel
embudo
funnel holder
portaembudo
funnel, separatory
embudo de separación
funtumine
funtumina
fuprazole
fuprazol
furacrylic acid
ácido furacrílico
furalazine
furalacina, fluralazina
furaltadone
furaltadona
furamide
furamida
furan(e)
furano
furan carboxylic acid
ácido furancarboxílico
furan polymer
polímero de furano
furanacrylic acid
ácido furanacrílico
furanacrylonitrile
furanacrinonitrilo
2,5-furandione
2,5-furandiona
2-furanmethanethiol
2-furanmetantiol
furaprofen
furaprofeno
furazabol
furazabol
furazolidone
furazolidona
furazolium chloride
cloruro de furazolio
furbucillin
furbucilina
furcellaran
furcelarán
furcloprofen
furcloprofeno
furethidine
furetidina
furethrin
furetrina

furfenorex
furfenorex
furfural
furfural, aldehído
piromúcico
furfural acetic acid
ácido furfural acético
furfuraldehyde
aldehído furfurílico
furfuramide
furfuramida
furfuran
furfurano
furfurol
furfurol
furfuryl acetate
acetato de furfurilo,
acetato furfurílico
furfuryl alcohol
alcohol furfurílico
α-furfuryl amine
α-furfurilamina
furfuryl mercaptan
mercaptano
furfurílico, furfuril
mercaptano
6-furfurylamino-
purine
6-furfurilaminopurina
5-furfuryl-5-iso-
propylbarbituric acid
ácido 5-furfuril-5-
isopropilbarbitúrico
furfurylmethyl-
amphetamine
metilanfetamina
furfurílica,
furfurilmetil-
anfetamina
furidarone
furidarona
α-furildioxime
α-furildioxima
furmethoxadone
furmetoxadona
furnace
horno
furoamide
furoamida,
furamida
furobufen
furobufeno
furosimide
furosimida
furodazole
furodazol
furofenac
furofenaco

2-furoic acid
ácido 2-furoico
furoic acid
ácido furoico, ácio
piromúcico
furomazine
furomacina,
furomazina
furonazide
furonazida
furosemide
furosemida
furostilbestrol
furoestilbestrol
furoxicillin
furoxicilina
furoyl chloride
cloruro de furoílo
fursalan
fursalán
fursultiamine
fursultiamina
furterene
furtereno
furtrethonium iodide
yoduro de
furtretonio
further dilute
seguir diluyendo,
diluir aún más
furyl carbinol
furilcarbinol
furylacrylic acid
ácido furilacrílico
fusafungine
fusafungina
fusarubin
fusarrubina
fuscin
fuscina
fused alumina
alúmina fundida
fused ring
anillo condensado
fused salt
sal fundida
fused silica
silicio fundido
fusel oil
aceite de fusel
fusidic acid
ácido fusídico
fusion
fusión, unión
fustin
fustina
fuzlocillin
fuzlocilina

G

g
abreviatura de gramo
gabapentin
gabapentina
gabexate
gabexato
G acid
ácido G (ácido 2-naftol-6,8-disulfónico)
gadolinium
gadolinio
gadolinium chloride
cloruro de gadolinio
gadolinium fluoride
fluoruro de gadolinio
gadolinium nitrate
nitrato de gadolinio
gadolinium oxalate
oxalato de gadolinio
gadolinium oxide
óxido de gadolinio
gadolinium sulfate
sulfato de gadolinio
gage
calibre, medidor, indicador de presión, nivel, manómetro
gage pressure
presión barométrica
galactaric acid
ácido galactárico
galactitol
galactitol
galactoflavin
galactoflavina
D-galactosamine
D-galactosamina
D-galactosamine hydrochloride
clorhidrato de D-galactosamina
D-galactose
D-galactosa, cerebrosa
D(+)-galacturonic acid
ácido D(+)-galacturónico
galanga
galanga, galangal, gengibre de la China
galangin
galangina
galanthamine, galantamine
galantamina

galegine
galegina, isoamilenguanidina
galena
galena, sulfuro de plomo
galenical
farmacológica, galénica
galipine
galipina
gallacetophenone
galacetofenona
gallamine triethiodide
trietilyoduro de galamina
gallate
galato
gallein
galeína
gallic
gálico
gallic acid
ácido gálico, ácido 3,4,5-trihidroxi-benzoico
gallimycin
galimicina
gallium
galio
gallium antimonide
antimoniuro de galio
gallium arsenide
arseniuro de galio
gallium (67 GA) citrate
citrato de galio (67 GA)
gallium oxide
óxido de galio
gallium phosphide
fosfuro de galio
gallium sesquioxide
sesquióxido de galio
gallium trifluoride
trifluoruro de galio
gallocyanine
galocianina
gallon
galón
gallopamil
galopamilo
gallotannic acid
ácido galotánico

galonidite
galonidita
galosemide
galosemida
gamabufotalin
gamabufotalina, gamabufogenina, gamabufagina
gambir
gambir, catecú
gamboge
cambogia
gambogic acid
ácido cambógico
gametocide
gametocida
gamfexine
ganfexina
gamma
gamma
gamma acid
ácido gamma (ácido 2-amino-8-naftol-6-sulfónico)
gamma ray
rayo gamma
gamma ray spectroscopy
espectroscopía con rayos gamma
gamma-globulina
gammaglobulina, globulina gamma
ganciclovir
ganciclovir
ganglefene
ganglefeno
gangliosides
gangliósidos
gapicomine
gapicomina
gardenins
gardeninas
gardinol type detergens
detergentes tipo gardinol
garlic
ajo
garlic oil
esencia (aceite) de ajo
garnet, natural
granate sintético

garnierite
garnierita
garryine
garriína
gas
gas
gas absorption
absorción de gases
gas análisis
análisis de gases
gas black
negro de humo de gas natural
gas chromatography
cromatografía de gases
gas, compressed
gas comprimido
gas hydrate
gas hidratado
gas, inert
gas inerte
gas laws
leyes de los gases
gas liquid
gas líquido
gas, noble
gas noble
gaseous
gaseoso
gaseous diffusion
difusión gaseosa, difusión de gases
gasification
gasificación
gasket
guarnición, junta, empaquetadura
gasoline
gasolina
gassing
saturación por gas, gaseamiento
gastric fluid
jugo gástrico
gastrins
gastrinas
gauge
calibre, medidor, indicador de presión, nivel, manómetro
gaultheria
gaulteria
gaultherin
gaulterina

Gay-Lussac's law
ley de Gay Lussac
gear plate
placa de engranajes,
plato de engranajes
gefarnate
gefarnato
geissoschizoline
geissosquizolina,
pereirina
geissospermine
geissospermina
gel
gel, jalea coloidal
gel filtration
filtración por gel
gelatin
gelatina
gelation
gelación, gelificación,
transformación de un
sol a un gel
gelled hydrogen
hidrógeno
gelificado
gelsemine
gelsemina
gelsemium
gelsemio, jazmín
amarillo
gemazocine
gemazocina
gemcadiol
gencadiol
gemcitabine
hydrochloride
clorhidrato de
gencitabina
gemeprost
gemeprost
gemfibrozil
genfibrozil
gene
gen
gene splicing
empalme de genes
generic formula
fórmula genérica
genetic code
código genético
Geneva System
Sistema de
Ginebra
genin
genina
genistein
genisteína
gentamicin
gentamicina

gentamicin
hydrochloride
clorhidrato de
gentamicina
gentian
genciana
gentian violet
violeta de genciana
gentianine
gencianina
gentiobiose
gentiobiosa
gentiopicrin
gentiopicrina
gentisic acid
ácido gentísico
gentisin
gentisina
gentisyl alcohol
alcohol gentisílico
gentrogenin
gentrogenina
geochemistry
geoquímica
geometric isomer
isómero geométrico
geosmin
geosmina
gepefrine
gepefrina
gephyrotoxin
gefirotoxina
geranial
geranial
geranialdehyde
geranialdehído
geraniol
geraniol
geranium
geranio
geranium oil
esencia (aceite) de
geranio
geranyl acetate
acetato de geranilo
geranyl butyrate
butirato de geranilo
geranyl formiate
formiato de geranilo
geranyl propionate
propionato de geranilo
geranylhydroquinone
hidroquinona
geranílica
germane
germano, hidruro de
germanio
germanium
germanio

germanium dichloride
dicloruro de germanio
germanium dioxide
dióxido de germanio
germanium monoxide
monóxido de germanio
germanium potassium
fluoride
fluoruro de germanio y
potasio
germanium telluride
telururo de germanio
germanium tetra-
chloride
tetracloruro de
germanio
germanium tetra-
fluoride
tetrafluoruro de
germanio
germanium
tetrahydride
tetrahidruro de
germanio
germicide
germicida
germine
germina
geroquinol
geroquinol
gestaclone
gestaclona
gestadienol
gestadienol
gestodene
gestodeno
gestonorone
caproate
caproato de
gestonorona
gestrinone
gestrinona
gethermal energy
energía geotérmica
getter
desgasificador,
eliminador de residuos
gaseosos
ghatti gum
goma ghatti, goma de
la India
ghee, ghi
manteca clarificada
gibberellic acid
ácido giberélico
gibberellin
giberelina
Gibbs reagent
reactivo de Gibbs

gigantine
gigantina
gin
ginebra, desmotadora,
licor de enebro
ginger
jengibre
ginger oil
esencia de jengibre
[6]-gingerol
[6]-gingerol
ginkgo
ginkgo
ginkgo biloba extract
extracto de ginkgo
biloba
ginseng
ginseng, ginsén
giparmen
giparmena
giractide
giractida
Girard's reagent
reactivo de Girard
gitalin
gitalina
gitalin amorphous
gitalina amorfa
gitaloxin
gitaloxina
gitoformate
gitoformiato
gitogenin
gitogenina
F-gitonin
F-gitonina
gitoxigenin
gitoxigenina
gitoxin
gitoxina
glacial
glacial
glacial acetic acid
ácido acético glacial
gladiolic acid
ácido gladiólico
glafenine
glafenina
glass
vidrio
glass, borosilicate
vidrio de
borosilicato
glass enamel
esmalte de vidrio
glass fiber
fibra de vidrio
glass, metalic
vidrio metálico

glass, optical
vidrio óptico
glass, photochromic
vidrio fotocrómico
glass, photosensitive
vidrio fotosensible
glass, resistant
vidrio resistente al
calor
glass, safety
vidrio inastillable,
vidrio de seguridad
glass wool
lana de vidrio
glass-ceramic
vidrio cerámico
glassine
papel cristal
glassware
utensilios de vidrio,
objetos de vidrio
glaucarubin
glaucarubina
glaucine
glaucina
glauconite
glauconita
glaze
vidriado
glaze stain
color para vidriado
glaziovine
glaciovina, glaziovina
GLC
CGL (cromatografía de
gases y líquidos)
gleptoferron
gleptoferrón, heptonato
de hierro
gliadin
gliadina
gliamilide
gliamilida
glibenclamide
glibenclamida
glibornuride
glibornurida
glibutimine
glibutimina
glicaramide
glicaramida
glicetanile
glicetanila
gliclazide
gliclazida
glicondamide
glicondamida
glidant
deslizante

glidazamide
glidazamida
gliflumide
gliflumida
glimepiride
glimepirida
gliotoxin
gliotoxina
glipentide
glipentida
glipizide
glipicida
gliquidone
gliquidona
glisamuride
glisamurida
glisindamide
glisindamida
glisolamide
glisolamida
glisoxepid(e)
glisoxepida
globin
globina
globulin
globulina
gloxazone
gloxazona
glucagon
glucagón
glucalox
glucalox
glucametacin
glucametacina
glucamine
glucamina
D-glucaric acid
ácido D-glucárico
glucase
glucasa
gluceptate
gluceptato
glucinum, glucinium
glucinio
glucinium oxide
óxido de glucinio
D-glucoascorbic
acid
ácido D-gluco-
ascórbico
glucofrangulin
glucofrangulina
ß-glucogallin
ß-glucogalina
glucoheptonic acid
ácido gluco-
heptónico
gluconic acid
ácido glucónico

glucono-delta-lactose
glucón delta-lactosa,
delta-lactosa glucónica
gluconolactone
glucón lactona, lactona
glucónica
glucosamine
glucosamina
glucose
glucosa
glucose (liquid)
glucosa (líquida)
glucose oxidase
glucosa oxidasa
glucose syrup
jarabe de maíz, jarabe
de glucosa
α-glucose-1-phosphate
1-fosfato de α-glucosa
glucose-6-phosphate
6-fosfato de glucosa
glucose-1-phosphoric
acid
ácido glucosa 1-
fosfórico
α-glucosidase
α-glucosidasa
ß-glucosidase
ß-glucosidasa
glucoside
glucósido
glucosulfamide
glucosulfamida
glucosulfone
glucosulfona
glucosulfone
sodium
glucosulfona sódica
glucurolactone
glucurolactona
glucuronamide
glucuronamida
D(+)glucuronic acid
ácido D(+)-
glucurónico
N⁴ß-D-glucosyl-
sulfanilamide
N⁴ß-D-glucosil-
sulfanilamida
glucovanillin
glucovainillina
ß-glucuronidase
ß-glucuronidasa
gluside
glusida
glusoferron
glusoferrón
glutamic acid
ácido glutámico

L-glutamic acid 5-ethyl
ester
éster etílico del ácido
L-glutámico
glutamic acid
hydrochloride
chlorhidrato de ácido
glutámico
glutamine
glutamina
gamma-glutamyl-
cysteinglycine
gamma-glutamil-
cisteinglicina
glutaral
glutaral
glutaraldehyde
glutaraldehído
glutaric acid
ácido glutárico
glutaric
anhydride
anhídrido glutárico
glutaronitrile
glutaronitrilo
glutathione
glutatión
glutaurine
glutaurina
gluten
gluten
glutenin
glutenina
glutethimide
glutetimida
glyburide
gliburida
glybuthiazol(e)
glibutiazol
glybuzole
glibuzol
glycarbylamide
glicarbilamida
glycarsamide
glicarsamida
glyceraldehyde
gliceraldehído
glyceraldehyde 3-
phosphate
3-fosfato de
gliceraldehído
glycerate
glicerato
glyceric acid
ácido glicérico
glyceride
glicérido
glycerin(e)
glicerina

134

glycerin carbonate
carbonato de glicerina
glycerine oleate
oleato de glicerina
glycerol
glicerol, glicerina
glycerol boriborate
boriborato de glicerol,
boriborato de glicerina
glycerol dichlorhydrin
diclorhidrin glicerólica,
diclorhidrina de
glicerina
glycerol 1,3-distearate
1,3-diestearato de
glicerol, 1,3-diestearato
de glicerina
glycerol formal
formalglicerol glycerol
monolaurate
monolaurato de
glicerol, monolaurato
de glicerina
glycerol monooleate
monoleato de glicerol,
monoleato de glicerina
glycerol mono-
ricinoleate
monorricinoleato
de glicerol,
monorricinoleato
de glicerina
glycerol monostearate
monoestearato de
glicerol, monoestearato
de glicerina
glycerol phthalate
ftalato de glicerol,
ftalato de glicerina
glycerol tributyrate
tributirato de glicerol,
tributirato de glicerina
glycerol tripropionate
tripropionato de
glicerol, tripropionato
de glicerina
glycerol tristearate
triestearato de glicerol,
triestearato de
glicerina
glycerophosphates
glicerofosfatos
glycerophosphoric acid
ácido glicerofosfórico
glyceryl abietate
abietato glicerílico,
abietato de glicerilo
glyceryl p-amino-
benzoate

p-aminobenzoato de
glicerilo, p-
aminobenzoato
glicerílico
glyceryl α-
chlorohydrin
gliceril α-clorhidrina,
α-clorhidrina
glicerílica
glyceryl diacetate
diacetato de glicerilo,
diacetato glicerílico
glyceryl 1,3-
distearate
1,3-diestearato de
glicerilo, 1,3-
diestearato glicerílico
glyceryl ditolylether
éter gliceril ditolílico,
glicerilditoliléter
glyceryl guaiacolate
guayacolato de
glicerilo
glyceryl iodide
yoduro de glicerilo,
yoduro glicerílico
glyceryl monoacetate
monoacetato de
glicerilo, monoacetato
glicerílico
glyceryl monolaurate
monolaurato de
glicerilo, monolaurato
glicerílico
glyceryl monooleate
monoleato de glicerilo,
monoleato glicerílico
glyceryl
monoricinoleate
monorricinoleato
de glicerilo,
monorricinoleato
glicerílico
glyceryl
monostearate
monoestearato de
glicerilo, monoestearato
glicerílico
glyceryl phthalate
ftalato de glicerilo,
ftalato glicerílico
glyceryl ricinoleate
ricinoleato de glicerilo,
ricinoleato glicerílico
glyceryl triacetate
triacetato de glicerilo,
triacetato glicerílico
glyceryl tri-(12-
acetoxystearate)

tri-(12-acetoxi-
estearato) de glicerilo,
tri-(12-acetoxiestearato)
glicerílico
glyceryl tri-(12-
acetylricinoleate)
tri-(12-acetil-
rricinoleato) de
glicerilo, tri-(12-
acetilrricinoleato)
glicerílico
glyceryl tributyrate
tributirato de glicerilo,
tributirato glicerílico
glyceryl tri-(hydroxy-
estearate)
tri-(hidroxiestearato)
de glicerilo, tri-
(hidroxiestearato)
glicerílico
glyceryl trinitrate
trinitrato de glicerilo,
trinitrato glicerílico
glyceryl trioleate
trioleato de glicerilo,
trioleato glicerílico
glyceryl tripalmitate
tripalmitato de
glicerilo, tripalmitato
glicerílico
glyceryl tripropionate
tripropionato de
glicerilo, tripropionato
glicerílico
glyceryl triricinoleate
trirricinoleato de
glicerilo, trirricinoleato
glicerílico
glyceryl tristearate
triestearato de glicerilo,
triestearato glicerílico
glycidol
glicidol
Υ-glycidoxypropyl-
trimethoxysilane
Υ-glicidoxi-
propiltrimetoxisilano
glycidyl acrylate
acrilato de glicidilo,
acrilato glicidílico
glycidyl ether
éter de glicidilo, éter
glicidílico
glycine
glicina
glycine sulfate
sulfato de glicina
glycinin
glicinina

glyclopyramide
gliclopiramida
glycobiarsol
glicobiarsol
glycocholic acid
ácido glicocólico
glycocoll
glicocola, ácido
aminoacético
glycocoll-p-
phenetidine
hydrochloride
clorhidrato de
glicocola-p-fenetidina
glycocyamine
glicociamina
glycogen
glucógeno
glycogenesis
glucogénesis,
glucogenia
glycogenetic
glucogenético
glycogenic
glucogénico
glycogenic acid
ácido glucogénico
glycol
glicol
glycol boriborate
boriborato de glicol,
boriborato glicólico
glycol bromohydrin
bromhidrina de glicol,
bromhidrina glicólica
glycol carbonate
carbonato de glicol,
carbonato glicólico
glycol chlorohydrin
clorhidrina de glicol,
clorhidrina glicólica
glycol diacetate
diacetato de glicol,
diacetato glicólico
glycol dibutyrate
dibutirato de glicol,
dibutirato glicólico
glycol diformate
diformiato de glicol,
diformiato glicólico
glycol dilaurate
dilaurato de glicol,
dilaurato glicólico
glycol dimercapto-
acetate
dimercaptoacetato de
glicol,
dimercaptoacetato
glicólico

glycol dimercapto-
propionate
dimercaptopropionato
de glicol, dimercapto-
propionato glicólico
glycol dimethyl ether
éter dimetil glicólico,
glicoldimetiléter
glycol dipropionate
dipropionato de glicol,
dipropionato glicólico
glycol monoacetate
monoacetato de
glicol, monoacetato
glicólico
glycol propionate
propionato de glicol,
propionato glicólico
glycol salicilate
salicilato de glicol
glycol stearate
estearato de glicol,
estearato glicólico
glycolic
glicólico
glycolic acid
ácido glicólico
glycolilurea
glucolilurea, urea
glucolílica
glycolonitrile
glicolonitrilo
glycolthiourea
glucoltiourea, tiourea
glicólica
glycolysis
glucólisis
glyconiazide
gluconiazida
glyconic acid
ácido glucónico
glyconitrile
gluconitrilo
glycopyrrolate
glicopirrolato
glycopyrronium
bromide
bromuro de
glucopirronio
glycoprotein
glucoproteína
glycoside
glucósido
glycosine
glucosina
glycyclamide
gliciclamida
glycyl alcohol
alcohol glucílico,

alcohol glicílico
N-glycylglycine
N-glicilglicina
glycyrrhiza
glucirriza
glycyrrhizic acid
ácido glucirrícico
glycyrrhizin
glicirricina
glyhexamide
glihexamida
glymidine
glimidina ·
glymidine sodium
glimidina sódica
glyoctamide
glioctamida
glyodin
gliodina
glyoxal
glioxal
glyoxaline
glioxalina
glyoxal-sodium
bisulfite
bisulfito
glioxalsódico
glyoxyldiureide
glioxildiureído
glyoxylic acid
ácido glioxílico
glyphosate
glifosato
glyphosine
glifosina
glypinamide
glipinamida
glyprothiazol
gliprotiazol
glyptal
gliptal
glysobuzole
glisobuzol
goitrin
goitrina
gold
oro
gold, artificial
oro artificial
gold bromide
bromuro de oro
gold bronze
bronce dorado
gold bronze
powder
polvo de bronce
dorado
gold chloride
cloruro de oro

gold cobalt alloys
aleaciones de oro y
cobalto
gold cyanide
cianuro de oro
gold explosive
oro fulminante
gold filled
chapado en oro, relleno
de oro
gold hydroxide
hidróxido de oro
gold, liquid bright
oro líquido brillante
gold monochloride
monocloruro de oro
gold monocyanide
monocianuro de oro
gold monoiodide
monoyoduro de oro
gold monosulfide
monosulfuro de oro
gold monoxide
monóxido de oro
gold oxide
óxido de oro
gold potassium
chloride
cloruro de oro y
potasio
gold potassium cyanide
cianuro de oro y ·
potasio
gold, radioctive,
colloidal
oro radioactivo
coloidal
gold salts
sales de oro
gold selenate
seleniato de oro
gold selenide
seleniuro de oro
gold silicon alloy
aleación de oro y
silicio
gold sodium chloride
cloruro de oro y sodio
gold sodium cyanide
cianuro de oro y sodio
gold sodium
thiomalate
tiomalato de oro y
sodio
gold sodium thiosulfate
tiosulfato de oro y
sodio
gold solder
soldadura de oro

gold stannate
estannato de sodio
gold thioglucose
tioglucosa de oro
gold tin precipitate
precipitado de oro
y estaño
gold tin purple
violeta de oro y estaño,
púrpura de oro y estaño
gold tribromide
tribromuro de oro
gold tribromide, acid
tribromuro ácido de
oro
gold trichloride
tricloruro de oro
gold trichloride, acid
tricloruro ácido de oro
gold tricyanide
tricianuro de oro
gold trihydroxide
trihidróxido de oro
gold trioxide
trióxido de oro
gold trisulfide
trisulfuro de oro
gold, white
oro blanco
GMP (Good Manufac-
turing Practices)
BPM (Buenas Prácticas
de Manufactura)
gonadorelin
gonadorelina
gonadorelin
hydrochloride
clorhidrato de
gonadorelina
goserelin
goserelina
goserelin acetate
acetato de goserelina
gossyplure
gosiplura
gossypol
gosipol
gougerotin
gougerotina
G-proteins
proteínas G
grade
calidad
graduate
probeta, frasco
graduado, vaso
graduado
graduated cylinder
probeta

graduated pipette
pipeta graduada
Graham's salt
sal de Graham
grain alcohol
alcohol de cereales
grain oil
aceite de cereales
grained
granulado
gram
gramo
gram atomic weight
peso molecular gramo,
peso molecular
expresado en gramos
gramicidin
gramicidina
gramicidin S
gramicidina S
gramine
gramina
Gram-positive,
negative
Grampositivo o
gramnegativo
Gram stain
tinción de Gram
granaticin
granaticina
grandisol
grandisol
granisetron
granisetrona
granisetron hydro-
chloride
clorhidrato de
granisetrona
granule
gránulo
grapefruit oil
esencia (aceite) de
toronja, esencia
(aceite) de pomelo
grape sugar
azúcar de uva
griseoviridin
graph
gráfica, gráfico
graph paper
papel cuadriculado,
papel de gráficos
graphic formula
fórmula de
constitución
graphite
grafito
graphitic oxide
óxido grafítico

graphitic acid
ácido grafítico, óxido
grafítico, óxido de
grafito
gratiogenin
gratiogenina
gratioside
gratiosida
gravimetric analysis
análisis gravimétrico
gravitol(e)
gravitol
gravity
gravedad, peso
específico
gray acetate
acetato gris
gray antimony
antimonio gris
grayanotoxins
grayanotoxinas
green cinnabar
cinabrio verde
green liquor
licor verde
grepafloxacin
hydrochloride
clorhidrato de
grepafloxacina
Grignard reagent
reactivo de Grignard
grind
moler
grindelia
grindelia
grindelic acid
ácido grindélico
grisein
griseína
griseofulvin
griseofulvina
griseoviridin
griseoviridina
grog
ron, bebida alcohólica
gross weight
peso bruto
ground glass
vidrio esmerilado
ground-nut oil
aceite de maní
grown culture
cultivo
growth
proliferación
G salt
sal G (sal sódica o
potásica del ácido 2-
naftol-6,8-disulfónico)

guabenxan
guabenxano
guacetisal
guacetisal
guafecainol
guafecainol
guaiac, guaiacum
guayaco, guayacán,
resina de guayaco
guaiac-copper sulfate
paper
papel con sulfato
de cobre y resina de
guayaco
guaiacol
guayacol
guaiacol benzoate
benzoato de guayacol
guaiacol carbonate
carbonato de guayacol
guaiacol phosphate
fosfato de guayacol
guaiacol valerate
valerato de guayacol
guaiactamine
guayactamina
guaiac-wood oil
aceite de madera de
guayacol
guaiol
guayol
guaiapate
guayapato
guaietolin
guayetolino,
guayetolina
guaifenesin
guayafenesina
(guayacolato de
glicerol)
guaifylline
guayafilina
guaithylline
guaitilina
guamecycline
guameciclina
guanabenz
guanabenzo
guanabenz acetate
acetato de
guanabenzo
guanacline
gluanaclina
guanadrel
guanadrel
guanadrel sulfate
sulfato de guanadrel
guanazodine
guanazodina

guancidine
guancidina
guanclofine
guanclofina
guanethidine
guanetidina
guanethidine sulfate
sulfato de guanetidina
guanfacine
guanfacina
guanicaine
guanicaína
guanidine
guanidina
guanidine amino-
valeric acid
ácido guanidín
aminovalérico
guanidine carbonate
carbonato de
guanidina, carbonato
guanidínico
guanidine
hydrochloride
clorhidrato de gua-
nidina, clorhidrato
guanidínico
guanidine nitrate
nitrato de guanidina,
nitrato guanidínico
guanidine thiocyanate
tiocianato de
guanidina, tiocianato
guanidínico
guanidinium
aluminum sulfate
hexahydrate
sulfato de aluminio y
guanidinio
hexahidratado
guanine
guanina
guanisoquine
guanisoquina
guano
guano
guanoclor
gluanocloro
guanoctine
guanoctina
guanosine
guanosina
guanosine
monophosphate
monofosfato de
guanosina, monofosfato
guanosínico
guanosine phosphates
fosfatos de guanosina,

137

fosfatos guanosínicos
guanosine phosphoric
acid
ácido guanosín
fosfórico
guanoxabenz
guanoxabenzo
guanoxan
guanoxano
guanoxyfen
guanoxifeno
guanylic acid
ácido guanílico
guanyl nitrosamino
guanylidene
hydrazine
guanilnitrosamino-
guanilidenhidracina,
guanilnitrosamino-
guaniliden hidrazina
guanyl nitrosamino-
guanyl tetrazene

guanilnitrosamino-
guanil tetraceno
guanylurea sulfate
sulfato de guanilurea
guar gum
goma guar
guaran
guarana
guayule
guayule
guidelines
principios
generales,
directivas
Guignet's green
verde de Guignet
guinea green B
verde guinea B
D-gulonic acid
ácido D-gulónico
D,L-gulose
D,L-gulosa

gum arabic
goma arábiga
gum benzoin
resina de benzoína,
resina de benjuí
gum camphor
goma de alcanfor
gum natural
goma natural
gum rosin
gomorresina
gum sugar
goma de azúcar
gum, synthetic
goma sintética
gum tragacanth
goma
tragacanto
gum thus
goma de incienso
gum turpentine
goma de

trementina
gun metal
bronce de cañón
gutta percha
gutapercha
guvacine
guvacina
gymnemic acid
ácido gimnémico
gynocardia oil
aceite de
ginocardia
gyplure
giplura
gypsogenin
gipsogenina
gypsum
yeso
gypsum cement
escayola, yeso

H

H-acid
ácido H (ácido 1-
amino-8-naftol-3,6-
disulfónico)
hachimycin
hachimicina
hadacidin
hadacidina
hafnia
hafnia
hafnium
hafnio
hafnium boride
boruro de hafnio
hafnium carbide
carburo de hafnio
hafnium disulfide
disulfuro de hafnio
hafnium nitride
nitruro de hafnio
hafnium oxide
óxido de hafnio
hair-like
capilar
halazepam
halazepán, halazepam
halazone
halazona
halcinonide
halcinonida
halethazole
haletazol
half-life
vida media
halibut liver oil
aceite de
hígado de
hipogloso
halides
haluros
halite
halita
hallucinogen
alucinógeno
halobetasol
propionate
propionato de
halobetasol
halocarban
halocarbano
halocarbon
hidrocarburo
halogenado,
halocarbón

halocortolone
halocortolona
halofantrine
halofantrina
halofenate
halofenato
halofuginone
halofuginona
halogen
halógeno
halogen derivatives
derivados halogenados
halogenate
halogenar
halogenation
halogenación
haloid
haloideo
halometasone
halometasona
halonamine
halonamina
halopemide
halopemida
halopenium chloride
cloruro de halopenio
haloperidol
haloperidol
haloperidol decanoate
decanoato de
haloperidol
halopredone
halopredona
halopredone acetate
acetato de halopredona
haloprogesterone
haloprogesterona
haloprogin
haloprogina
halopropane
halopropano
halostachine
halostacina
halothane
halotano
haloxazolam
haloxazolán,
haloxazolam
haloxon
haloxona
halquinol
halquinol
hamamelis
hamamelis

hamamelitannin
hamamelitanina
hamamelose
hamamelosa
hammer mill
molino triturador,
trituradora de martillos
hamycin
hamicina
hand over scale
escala de transferencia
haplophytine
haplofitina
haptens
haptenos
haptoglobins
haptoglobinas
hard
duro
hard water
agua dura
hardness
dureza
harmaline
harmalina
harmalol
harmalol
harman
harman
harmine
harmina
hartshorn oil
aceite de cuerno de
ciervo, aceite de dippel
hashish
hachís
hasubanonine
hasubanonina
hazardous material
material peligroso
hazardous waste
residuos peligrosos,
desperdicios peligrosos
hazy
nebuloso, turbio
head space
cabezal, espacio libre
entre el cierre y el
material, espacio
de cabeza
heat
calor
heat exchanger
termopermutador,

intercambiador de
calor
heat seal coat
cubierta termosellable
heat transfer
transferencia de calor
heating block
plancha de
calentamiento
heavy
pesado
heavy chemical
producto químico
pesado
heavy hydrogen
hidrógeno pesado
heavy metal
metal pesado
heavy oil
aceite pesado
heavy oxygen
oxígeno pesado
heavy spar
espato pesado
heavy water
agua pesada
hecogenin
hecogenina
hectorite
hectorita
hedaquinium chloride
cloruro de
hedaquinio
hedeoma oil
esencia (aceite) de
hedeoma, esencia
(aceite) de poleo
hederagenin
hederagenina
α-hederin
α-hederina
hedonal
hedonal
helenalin
helenalina
helenine
helenina
helenynolic acid
ácido heleninólico
helianthine B
heliantina B
helicin
helicina
heliomycin
heliomicina
heliosupine
heliosupina

heliotropin
heliotropina
heliotropyl acetate
acetato de
heliotropilo,
acetato heliotropílico
helium
helio
hellebrin
helebrina
helminthosporal
helmintosporal
helminthosporol
helmintosporol
helonias
helonias
helveticoside
helveticósido
helvolic acid
ácido helvólico
hematein
hemateína
hematin
hematina
hematite, brown
hematita parda
hematite, red
hematita roja
hematoporphyrin
hematoporfirina
hematoxylin
hematoxilina
hematoxylon
hematoxilona
heme
hem, hematina
reducida
hem-, hema-, hemo-
hemático, prefijos que
significan sangre
hemel
hemel
hemellitic acid
ácido hemelítico
hementin
hementina
hemerythrin
hemeritrina
hemiacetal
hemiacetal
hemic
hémico, hemático
hemicellulose
hemicelulosa,
celulosano
hemicholinium
hemicolinio
hemihydrate
hemihidrato

hemiketal
hemicetal
hemimellitene
hemimeliteno
hemin
hemina
hemipyocianine
hemipiocianina
hemisulfur mustard
mostaza hemiazufrada,
gas semimostaza
hemocyanins
hemocianinas
hemoglobin
hemoglobina
hemlock oil
esencia (aceite) de
cicuta
hempa
hempa, triamida
hexametil-
fosfórica, hexa-
metilfosforamida,
hexametapol
hempseed oil
aceite de semilla de
cáñamo
n-heneicosanoic acid
ácido
n-henicosanoico
henna
alheña
Henry reaction
reacción de Henry
Henry's law
ley de Henry
heparamine
heparamina
heparin
heparina
hepaxanthin
hepaxantina
hepronicate
hepronicato
heptabarb
heptabarbo,
heptabarbital
heptabarbital
heptabarbital
heptachlor
heptacloro
heptachlorepoxide
heptaclorepóxido
**heptachlorotetra-
hydrometanoindene**
heptaclortetra-
hidrometanindeno
n-heptacosane
n-heptacosano

n-heptadecane
n-heptadecano
n-heptadecanoic acid
ácido n-
heptadecanoico
heptadecane
heptadecano
heptadecanol
heptadecanol
n-heptadecanol
n-heptadecanol
**2-(8-heptadecenyl)-2-
imidazoline-1-ethanol**
2-(8-heptadecenil)-2-
imidazolín-1-etanol
**2-heptadecyl-
glyoxalidine**
2-heptadecil-
glioxalidina
**2-heptadecyl-
glyoxalidine acetate**
acetato de 2-
heptadecilglioxalidina
**2-heptadecyl-
imidazoline**
2-heptadecil-
imidazolina
**2-heptadecil-2-
imidazolidine acetate**
acetato de 2-
heptadecil-2-
imidazolidina
**heptafluorobutyric
acid**
ácido heptafluoro-
butírico
heptaldehyde
heptaldehído, heptanal,
enantal
heptalin acetate
acetato de heptalina
heptalin formate
formiato de heptalina
heptamethylene
heptametileno
heptamethylnonane
heptametilnonano
heptaminol
heptaminol
heptanal
heptanal, enantal,
heptaldehído
**heptanal sodium
bisulfite**
bisulfito sódico de
heptanal, bisulfito
sódico de enantal
n-heptane
n-heptano

**1,7-heptane-
dicarboxylic acid**
ácido 1,7-heptan-
dicarboxílico
1,7-heptanedioc acid
ácido 1,7-heptandioico
n-heptanoic acid
ácido n-heptanoico
heptanol
heptanol
heptanone
heptanona
heptanoyl chloride
cloruro de heptanoílo,
cloruro heptanoílico
heptavalent
heptavalente
heptaverine
heptaverina
heptene
hepteno
heptenophos
heptenofós
heptine carbonic acid
ácido heptincarbónico
heptoic acid
ácido heptoico
heptoic aldehyde
aldehído heptoico
heptolamide
heptolamida
heptose
heptosa
heptoxime
heptoxima
heptyl
heptilo
1-heptyl acetate
acetato de 1-heptilo,
acetato de 1-heptílico
heptyl alcohol
alcohol heptílico
heptyl formate
formiato de heptilo,
formiato heptílico
heptyl heptoate
heptoato de heptilo,
heptoato heptílico
heptyl pelargonate
pelargonato de heptilo,
pelargonato heptílico
heptylamine
heptilamina
n-heptylic acid
ácido n-heptílico
hepzidine
hepcidina
hercynine
hercinina

heroin
heroína
herqueinone
herqueinona
herring oil
aceite de arenque
Herz compounds
compuestos herzianos
Herz reaction
reacción herziana
Herzig-Meyer
determination
of N-alkyl groups
determinación de
Herzig Meyer
de grupos N-alquílicos
hesperetin
hesperetina
hesperidin
hesperidina
hetacillin
hetacilina
hetaflur
hetaflur
hetastarch
almidón hidroxietílico
heteroaromic
heteroaromático
heteroatom
heteroátomo
heteroatomic
heteroatómico
heterocycles
heterociclos
heterocyclic
heterocíclico
heterocyclic compound
compuesto
heterocíclico
heterogeneous
heterogéneo
heterogeneous
catalysis
catálisis heterogénea
heteromolybdates
heteromolibdatos
heteronium
heteronio
heteronium bromide
bromuro de
heteronio
heteropolar
heteropolar
heteropolarity
heteropolaridad
heuristic
heurístico
hexaaminocobalt
trichloride

tricloruro de
hexaminocobalto
hexabasic
hexabásico
hexaborane(10)
decahidruro de
hexaborón, borohexano
hexabromohethane
hexabromoetano
hexacalcium phytate
fitato hexacálcico
hexacarbacholine
bromide
bromuro de
hexacarbacolina
hexachloroacetone
hexacloracetona
hexachlorobenzene
hexaclorobenceno
hexachlorobutadiene
hexaclorobutadieno
1,2,3,4,5,6-hexachloro-
cyclohexane
1,2,3,4,5,6-
hexaclorociclohexano
hexachlorocyclo-
pentadiene
hexaclorociclo-
pentadieno
hexachlorodiphenyl
oxide
óxido de hexa-
clorodifenilo,
óxido hexacloro-
difenílico
hexachloroendo-
metylene tetra-
hydrophtalic-
anhydride
anhídrido hexa-
cloroendometilén-
tetrahidroftálico
hexachloroethane
hexacloroetano
hexachlorohexane
hexaclorohexano
hexachloromethyl
carbonate
carbonato de
hexaclorometilo,
carbonato hexacloro
metílico
hexachloromethyl
ether
éter hexacloro-
metílico, hexa-
clorometiléter
hexachloro-
naphthalene

hexacloronaftaleno
hexachlorophene
hexaclorofeno
hexachloro-2-propane
hexacloro-2-propano
hexachloropropylene
hexacloropropileno
hexacontane
hexacontano
hexacosanoic acid
ácido hexacosanoico
hexacyclic
hexacíclico
hexacyclonate sodium
hexaciclonato de
sodio
hexacyprone
hexaciprono
hexad
átomo de seis valencias
n-hexadecane
n-hexadecano
hexadecanoic acid
ácido hexadecanoico
1-hexadecanol
1-hexadecanol
hexadecanoyl chloride
cloruro de
hexadecanoílo, cloruro
hexadecanoílico
1-hexadecene
1-hexadeceno
cis-9-hexadecenoic
acid
ácido cis-9-
hexadecenoico
6-hexadecenolide
6-hexadecenólido
hexadecylmercaptan
hexadecyl mercaptan
hexadecilmercaptano,
mercaptano
hexadecílico
tert-hexadecyl
mercaptan
terc-hexadecil-
mercaptano,
mercaptano terc-
hexadecílico
1-hexadecyl-
pyridinium chloride
cloruro de 1-
hexadecilpiridinio
hexadecyltrichloro-
silane
hexadeciltri-
clorosilano
hexadecyltrimethyl-
ammonium bromide

bromuro de hexadecil
trimetilamonio
1,4-hexadiene
1,4-hexadieno
2,4-hexadienoic acid
ácido 2,4-hexadienoico
hexadiline
hexadilina
hexadimethrine
bromide
bromuro de
hexadimetrina
1,5-hexadiyne
1,5-hexadiíno
hexaethyl
tetraphosphate
tetrafosfato de
hexaetilo, tetrafosfato
hexaetílico
hexa-2-ethylbutoxy-
disiloxane
hexa-2-etilbutoxi-
disiloxano
hexafluorenium
bromide
bromuro de
hexafluorenio
hexafluoroacetone
hexafluoracetona
hexafluorobenzene
hexafluorobenceno
hexafluoroethane
hexafluoretano
hexafluorophosphoric
acid
ácido hexafluoro-
fosfórico
hexafluoropropylene
hexafluoropropileno
hexafluoropropylene
epoxide
epóxido de hexafluoro-
propileno
hexafluorosilicic
acid
ácido
hexafluorosilícico
hexafluronium
bromide
bromuro de
hexafluronio
hexaglycerol
hexaglicerol
hexahydrate
hexahidrato
hexahydric
hexahídrico
hexahydric alcohol
alcohol hexahídrico

hexahydroaniline
hexahidroanilina
hexahydrobenzene
hexahidrobenceno
hexahydrobenzoic acid
ácido hexahidro-
benzoico
hexahydrocresol
hexahidrocresol
hexahydroequilenin
hexahidroequilenina
hexahydromethyl
phenol
hexahidrometilfenol
hexahydrophenol
hexahidrofenol
hexahydrophthalic
anhydride
anhídrido
hexahidroftálico
hexahydropyridine
hexahidropiridina
hexahydrotoluene
hexahidrotolueno
hexahydro-1,3,5-
trinitro-sym-
triazine
hexahidro-1,3,5-
trinitro-sim-triacina,
hexahidro-1,3,5-
trinitro-sim-triazina
hexahydroxy-
cyclohexane
hexahidroxiciclo-
hexano
hexahydroxylene
hexahidroxileno
hexakis(methoxy-
methyl) melamine
hexaquis (metoxi-
metil) melamina
n-hexaldehyde
n-hexaldehído
hexalin
hexalina
hexalin formate
formiato de hexalina
hexalure
hexaluro
hexametapol
hexametapol
hexamethonium
hexametonio
hexamethonium
chloride
cloruro de
hexametonio
hexamethylbenzene
hexametilbenceno

hexamethyldiamino-
isopropanol diiodide
diyoduro de
hexametildiamino
isopropanol
hexamethyldisilazane
hexametildisilazano
hexamethylene
hexametileno
hexamethylene
diisocyanate
diisocianato de
hexametileno,
diisocianato
hexametilénico
hexamethylene
glycol
hexametilenglicol,
glicol hexametilénico
hexamethylene-
diamine
hexametilendiamina,
diamina
hexametilénica
hexamethylene-
diamine carbamate
carbamato de
hexametilendiamina
hexamethyleneimine
hexametilenimina,
imina hexametilénica
hexamethylene-
tetramine
hexametilentetramina,
tetramina
hexametilénica
hexamethylene-
tetramine mandelate
mandelato de
hexametilentetramina,
mandelato de tetramina
hexametilénica
hexamethylene-
tetramine salicylate
salicilato de
hexametilentetramina,
salicilato de tetramina
hexametilénica
1,1,2,3,3,5-
hexamethylindan
methyl ketone
1,1,2,3,3,5-
hexametilindano-
metilcetona, cetona
1,1,2,3,3,5-
hexametilindano-
metílica
hexamethylmelamine
hexametilmelamina,

melamina hexametílica
hexamethylolmelamine
hexametilolmelamina,
melamina
hexametilólica
hexamethylpara-
rosaniline chloride
cloruro de hexa-
metilpararrosanilina,
cloruro de
pararrosanilina
hexametílica
hexamethyl-
phosphoramide
hexametilfosforamida,
fosforamida
hexametílica
hexamethylphosphoric
triamide
triamida
hexametilfosfórica
hexamethyltetra-
cosahexaene
hexametiltetracosa-
hexaeno, escualeno
hexamethyltetra-
cosane
hexametiltetracosano
hexamidine
hexamidina
hexamine
hexamina
hexanaphthene
hexanafteno
n-hexane
n-hexano
1,6-hexanediamine
1,6-hexandiamina
hexanedioic acid
ácido hexandioico
1,6-hexanediol
1,6-hexandiol
hexanedione-2,5
hexandiona-2,5
1,2,6-hexanetriol
1,2,6-hexantriol
hexanitrodiphenyl-
amine
hexanitrodifenilamina
hexanitrodiphenyl-
sulfide
sulfuro de
hexanitrodifenilo,
sulfuro
hexanitrodifenílico
hexanitromannite
hexanitromanita
hexanoic acid
ácido hexanoico

1-hexanol
1-hexanol
2-hexanone
2-hexanona
hexanoyl chloride
cloruro de hexanoílo,
cloruro hexanoílico
hexaphenyldisilane
hexafenildisilano
hexapradol
hexapradol
hexaprofen
hexaprofeno
hexapropymate
hexapropimato
hexasonium iodide
yoduro de hexasonio
hexatriacontane
hexatriacontano
hexavalent
hexavalente
hexazinone
hexacinona
hexazole
hexazol
hexcarbacholine
bromide
bromuro de
hexacarbacolina
hexedine
hexedina
1-hexene
1-hexeno
5-hexene-2-one
5-hexeno-2-ona
hexenol
hexenol
hexestrol
hexestrol
hexetidine
hexetidina
hexethal sodium
hexetal sódico
hexite
hexita
hexetidine
hexetidina
hexobarbital
hexobarbital
hexobendine
hexobendina
hexocyclium methyl
sulfate
sulfato hexociclo
metílico
hexoic acid
ácido hexoico
hexokinase
hexocinasa

hexone
hexona
hexoprenaline
hexoprenalina,
hexoprenalino
hexopyrronium
bromide
bromuro de
hexopirronio
hexose
hexosa
hexyl
hexilo, hexil
hexyl acetate
acetato de hexilo,
acetato hexílico
sec-hexyl acetate
acetato de sec-hexilo,
acetato sec-hexílico
hexyl alcohol
alcohol hexílico
n-hexyl ether
éter n-hexílico
hexyl mercaptan
hexilmercaptano,
mercaptano hexílico
hexyl methacrylate
metacrilato de hexilo,
metacrilato hexílico
hexyl methyl ketone
hexilmetil cetona,
cetona hexilmetílica
n-hexylamine
n-hexilamina
n-hexylbromide
bromuro de n-hexilo,
bromuro n-hexílico
hexylcaine
hexilcaína
hexylcaine
hydrochloride
clorhidrato de
hexilcaína
hexylcinnamaldehyde
hexilcinamaldehído,
cinamaldehído
hexílico
2-hexyldecanoic acid
ácido 2-hexil-
decanoico
hexylene
hexileno
hexylene glycol
glicol hexilénico,
hexilenglicol
hexylic acid
ácido hexílico
p-tert-hexylphenol
p-terc-hexilfenol

hexylresorcinol
hexilresorcinol,
hexilresorcina
hexyltrichlorosilane
hexiltriclorosilano,
triclorosilano hexílico
1-hexyne
1-hexino
hexynol
hexinol
hibenzate
hibenzato
high
alto, elevado
high-boiling
temperatura de
ebullición elevada
high-frequency
alta frecuencia,
hiperfrecuencia,
frecuencia elevada
high grade
de alto grado
high melting point
punto de fusión alto,
temperatura alta de
fusión
high polymer
alto polímero, polímero
elevado
high-pressure
alta presión
high speed
alta velocidad
high temperature
temperatura elevada
high vacuum
distillation
destilación a alto
vacío
hightly active
muy activo
hightly volatile
muy volátil
hinderin
hinderina
hindrance
impedimento,
obstáculo
Hinsberg sulfone
synthesis
síntesis de sulfonas de
Hinsberg
hippuric acid
ácido hipúrico
hirsutic acid C
ácido hirsútico C
hirudin
hirudina

histaminase
histaminasa
histamine
histamina
histapyrrodine
histapirrodina
histidine
histidina
histochemistry
histoquímica
histone
histona
history, chemical
historia química
Hofmann degradation
degradación de
Hofmann
Hofmann isonitrile
synthesis
síntesis de isonitrilo de
Hofmann
Hofmann-Martius
rearrangement
transposición de
Hofmann Martius
Hofmann's reaction
reacción de Hofmann
Hofmann rule
regla de Hofmann
Hofmann's violet
violeta de Hofmann
holarrhenine
holarrenina
hold-back agent
agente de retención
holder
soporte, asidero,
asa, mango,
empuñadura
holding tank
tanque, depósito
holmic
hólmico
holmium
holmio
holmiun chloride
cloruro de holmio
holmium fluoride
fluoruro de holmio
holmium oxide
óxido de holmio
holocellulose
holocelulosa
holomycin
holomicina
holothurin
holoturina
homarine
homarina

homarylamine
homarilamina
homatropine
homatropina
homatropine
methylbromide
metilbromuro de
homatropina
home light
luz normal del hogar
homidium
homidio
homidium bromide
bromuro de homidio
homocamfin
homocanfina
homochelidonine
homoquelidonina
homochlorcyclizine
homoclorciclicina,
homoclorciclizina
homocyclic
homocíclico
homocyclic compound
compuesto
homocíclico
homocysteine
homocisteína
homocystine
homocistina
homoeriodictyol
homoeriodictiol
homofenazine
homofenacina,
homofenazina
homogeneous
homogéneo
homogeneous catalysis
catálisis homogénea
homogeneous mixture
mezcla homogénea
homogeneous reaction
reacción homogénea
homogeneity
homogeneidad
homogenization
homogenización
homogenized
homogenizado
homogenizer
homogenizador
homogenizing
homogenización
homogentisic acid
ácido homogentísico
homologous series
serie homóloga
homolytic reaction
reacción homolítica

homomenthyl
salicylate
salicilato de
homomentilo
homomorphs
homomorfos
homonicotinic acid
ácido homonicotínico
homophthalic acid
ácido homoftálico
homopipramol
homopipramol
homopolymer
homopolímero
homosalate
homosalato
o-homosalicylic
acid
ácido o-homosalicílico
homoserine
homoserina
4-homosulfanilamide
hydrochloride
chlorhidrato de 4-
homosulfanilamida
homoveratric acid
ácido homoverátrico
homoveratrylamine
homoveratrilamina
homprenorphine
homprenorfina
hood
campana
Hooke's law
ley de Hooke
Hooker reaction
reacción de Hooker
hopantenic acid
ácido hopanténico
hopcalite
hopcalita
hops oil
esencia (aceite) de
lúpulo
hoquizil
hoquicilo
hordenine
hordenina
hormone, animal
hormona animal
hormone, plant
hormona vegetal
hot air
aire caliente
hot air drying
secado con aire
caliente
hot hand
guante térmico

hot plate
hornilla eléctrica,
calentador eléctrico
Houben-Fischer
shyntesis
síntesis de Houben
Fischer
Houben-Hoesch
reaction
reacción de Houben
Hoesch
Huber's reagent
reactivo de Huber
Hubl's reagent
reactivo de Hubl
Hudson isorotation
rules
reglas de isorrotación
de Hudson
Hudson lactone rule
regla de la lactona de
Hudson
humectant
humectante
humic
húmico
humic acid
ácido húmico
humidity, absolute
humedad absoluta
humidity indicator
indicador de humedad
humidity, relative
humedad relativa
humulene
humuleno
humulon
humulón
humus
humus
hyalobiuronic acid
ácido hialobiurónico
hyaluronic acid
ácido hialurónico
hyaluronidase
hialuronidasa
hycanthone
hicantona
hydantoin
hidantoína
hydnocarpic acid
ácido hidnocárpico
hydrabamine
penicillin V
penicilina V
hidrabamínica
hydracarbazine
hidracarbacina,
hidracarbazina

hydracid
hidrácido
hydracrylic acid
ácido hidracrílico
hydralazine
hidralacina,
hidralazina
hydralazine
hydrochloride
clorhidrato de
hidralacina, clorhidrato
de hidralazina
hydrallostane
hidralostano
hydramethylnon
hidrametilnona
hydramitrazine
hidramitracina,
hidramitrazina
hydrangea
Hydrangea
hydrargaphen
hidrargafeno
hydrargyrum
hidrargiro, hidrargirio,
mercurio
hydrase
hidrasa
hydrastine
hidrastina
hydrastine
hydrochloride
clorhidrato de
hidrastina
hydrastinine
hidrastinina
hydrastis
hidrastis, cúrcuma
hindú
hydrate
hidrato
hydrate, to
hidratar
hydrated
hidratado
hydrated aluminum
oxide
óxido de aluminio
hidratado
hydrated silica
sílice hidratado
hydration
hidratación
hydrazine
hidracina, hidrazina
hydrazine acid tartrate
tartrato ácido de
hidracina, tartrato
ácido de hidrazina

hydrazine
dihydrochloride
diclorhidrato de
hidracina, diclorhidrato
de hidrazina
hydrazine hydrate
hidrato de hidracina,
hidrato de hidrazina,
hidracina hidratada,
hidrazina hidratada
hydrazine
monobromide
monobromuro de
hidracina,
monobromuro de
hidrazina
hydrazine
monochloride
monocloruro de
hidracina, monocloruro
de hidrazina
hydrazine nitrate
nitrato de hidracina,
nitrato de hidrazina
hydrazine perchlorate
perclorato de hidracina,
perclorato de hidrazina
hydrazine sulfate
sulfato de hidracina,
sulfato de hidrazina
hydrazine tartrate
tartrato de hidracina,
tartrato de hidrazina
hydrazinebenzene-
sulfonic acid
ácido hidracin-
bencensulfónico, ácido
hidrazinbencen-
sulfónico
2-hydrazinoethanol
2-hidracinetanol, 2-
hidrazinetanol
hydrazinophthalazine
hydrochloride
chlorhidrato de
hidracinoftalacina,
chlorhidrato de
hidrazinoftalazina
hydrazobenzene
hidrazobenceno
hydrazoic
hidrazoico
hydrazoic acid
ácido hidrazoico
hydrazone
hidrazona
hydrazonium sulfate
sulfato de hidracina,
sulfato de hidrazina

hydric
hídrico
hydride
hidruro
hydrindene
hidrindeno
hydrindantin
hidrindantina
hydriodic
yodhídrico
hydriodic acid
ácido yodhídrico
hydroabietyl alcohol
alcohol hidro-
abietílico
hydrobentizide
hidrobenticida,
hidrobentizida
hydrobenzoin
hidrobenzoína
hydrobiotite
hidrobiotita
hydroboration
hidroboración
hydrobromic acid
ácido bromhídrico
hydrobromide
bromhidrato
hydrocarbon
hidrocarburo
hydrocarbon halogenated
hidrocarburo
halogenado
hydrocarbostyril
hidrocarbostirilo
hydrocellulose
hidrocelulosa
hydrochloric acid
ácido clorhídrico
hydrochloride
clorhidrato
hydrochlorothiazide
hidroclorotiazida
hydrocinchonidine
hidrocinconidina
hydrocinchonine
hidrocinconina
hydrocinnamic acid
ácido hidrocinámico
hydrocinnamic alcohol
alcohol hidro-
cinámico
hydrocinnamic aldehyde
aldehído hidrocinámico
hydrocinnamyl acetate
acetato de
hidrocinamilo

hydrocodone
hidrocodona
hydrocodone bitartrate
bitartrato de
hidrocodona
hydrocolloid
hidrocoloide
hydrocortamate
hidrocortamato
hydrocortisone
hidrocortisona
hydrocortisone acetate
acetato de
hidrocortisona
hydrocortisone phosphate
fosfato de hidro-
cortisona
hydrocortisone sodium phosphate
fosfato de hidro-
cortisona sódica
hydrocortisone 21-sodium succinate
succinato de hidro-
cortisona 21-sódica,
succinato de 21-sodio
hidrocortisona
hydrocortisone tebutate
tebutato de
hidrocortisona
hydrocotarnine
hidrocotarnina
hydrocyanic acid
ácido cianhídrico,
ácido prúsico
hydrodealkylation
hidrodealquilación
hydrodistillation
hidrodestilación
hydroflumethiazide
hidroflumetiazida
hydrofluoric acid
ácido fluorhídrico,
ácido hidrofluórico
hydrofluorosilicic acid
ácido hidro-
fluorosilícico
hydroforming
hidroformación
hydrofuramide
hidrofuramida
hydrogasification
hidrogasificación
hydrogel
hidrogel
hydrogen
hidrógeno

o-hydrogen
o-hidrógeno
p-hydrogen
p-hidrógeno
hydrogenation
hidrogenación
hydrogen azide
azida hidrogenada
hydrogen bond
enlace de hidrógeno
hydrogen bromide
ácido bromhídrico
hydrogen bromide, anhydrous
ácido bromhídrico
anhidro
hydrogen chloride
ácido clorhídrico
hydrogen cyanide
ácido cianhídrico
hydrogen dioxide
dióxido de hidrógeno
hydrogen electrode
electrodo de
hidrógeno
hydrogen fluoride
ácido fluorhídrico
hydrogen fluoride, anhydrous
ácido fluorhídrico
anhidro
hydrogenhexa-fluorosilicate
hexafluorosilicato
hidrogenado
hydrogen iodide
ácido yodhídrico
hydrogen iodode, anhydrous
ácido yodhídrico anhidro
hydrogen ion
ion hidrógeno,
hidrogenión
hydrogen ion concentration
concentración de iones
hidrógeno
hydrogen oxide
óxido de hidrógeno
hydrogen peroxide
peróxido de hidrógeno,
agua oxigenada
hydrogen peroxide solution 3%
solución de peróxido
de hidrógeno al 3%
hydrogen phosphide
fosfuro de hidrógeno,
ácido fosfhídrico

hydrogen phosphoretted
hidrógeno fosforado
hydrogen selenide
seleniuro de
hidrógeno, ácido
selenhídrico
hydrogen sulfide
ácido sulfhídrico,
sulfuro de hidrógeno
hydrogen tellurate
telurato hidrogenado
hydrogen telluride
ácido telurhídrico,
telururo de hidrógeno
hydrogenolysis
hidrogenólisis
hydrohydrastinine
hidrohidrastinina
hydrol
hidrol
hydrolase
hidrolasa
hydroliquefaction
hidrolicuacíon
hydrolysis
hidrólisis
hydrolytic
hidrolítico
hydrolyzable
hidrolizable
hydrolyze
hidrolizar
hydromadinone
hidromadinona
hydrometer
hidrómetro
hydromorphinol
hidromorfinol
hydromorphone
hidromorfona
hydromorphone hydrochloride
clorhidrato de
hidromorfona
hydronium ion
ion hidronio
hydroorotic acid
ácido hidrorótico
hydroperoxide
peróxido de
hidrógeno,
hidroperóxido
hydrophobic
hidrófobo
hydrophylic
hidrófilo
hydroquinidine
hidroquinidina

hydroquinol
hidroquinol
hydroquinine
hidroquinina
hydroquinone
hidroquinona
hydroquinone benzyl ether
éter bencil hidroquinónico, éter bencílico de hidroquinona
hydroquinone dibenzyl ether
éter dibencil hidroquinónico, éter dibencílico de hidroquinona
hydroquinone di-n-butyl ether
di-n-butiléter de hidroquinona, éter di-n-butil hidroquinónico
hydroquinone di(ß-hydroxyethyl) ether
di(ß-hidroxietil) éter de hidroquinona, éter di(ß-hidroxietil) hidroquinónico
hydroquinone dimethyl ether
éter dimetil hidroquinónico, éter dimetílico de hidroquinona
hydroquinone mono-n-butyl ether
éter mono-n-butil hidroquinónico, éter mono-n-butílico de hidroquinona
hydroquinone monomethyl ether
éter monometil hidroquinónico, éter monometílico de hidroquinona
hydrosilicate
hidrosilicato
hydrosilicofluoric acid
ácido hidrosilico-fluórico
hydrosol
hidrosol
hydrosolvation
hidrosolvatación
hydrosulfide
sulfhidrato, hidrosulfuro

hydrosulfite
hidrosulfito
hydrosulfite-formaldehyde
hidrosulfito formaldehído
hydrosulfurous
hidrosulfuroso
hydrotalcite
hidrotalcita
hydrothermal energy
energía hidrotérmica
hydrotrope
hidrótropo
hydrous
hidratado
hydrous oxide
óxido hidratado
hydroxamic acid
ácido hidroxámico
hydroxidation
hidroxidación
hydroxide
hidróxido
hydroxide ion
ion hidroxilo, ion oxhidrilo
hydroxindasate
hidroxindasato
hydroxindasol
hidroxindasol
hydroxocobalamin(e)
hidroxocobalamina
hydroxyacetal
hidroxiacetal
p-hydroxyacetanilide
p-hidroxiacetanilida
hydroxyacetic acid
ácido hidroxiacético
hydroxyacetone
hidroxiacetona
o-hydroxy-acetophenone
o-hidroxi-acetofenona
hydroxyacid
ácido hidroxilado, hidroxiácido, oxiácido
2-hydroxyadipaldehyde
2-hidroxiadipaldehído
ß-hydroxyalanine
ß-hidroxialanina
hydroxyaldehide
hidroxialdehído
5-hydroxy-3-(ß-aminoethyl)indole
5-hidroxi-3-(ß-aminoetil)indol

hydroxyamphetamine
hidroxianfetamina
hydroxyaniline
hidroxianilina
o-hydroxyanisole
o-hidroxianisol
9-hydroxyanthracene
9-hidroxiantraceno
hydroxyapatite
hidroxiapatita
p-hydroxyazobenzene-p-sulfonic acid
ácido p-hidroxi-azobenceno-p-sulfónico
m-hydroxybenz-aldehyde
m-hidroxi-benzaldehído
o-hydroxybenzamide
o-hidroxibenzamida
hydroxybenzene
hidroxibenceno
2-hydroxy-1',2'-benzocarbazole-3-carboxylic acid
ácido 2-hidroxi-1',2'-benzocarbazol-3-carboxílico
m-hydroxybenzoic acid
ácido m-hidroxi-benzoico
o-hydroxybenzoic acid
ácido o-hidroxi-benzoico
2-hydroxybenzo-phenone
2-hidroxibenzo-fenona
o-hydroxybenzyl-alcohol
alcohol o-hidroxi-bencílico
p-hydroxybenzyl-penicillin sodium
p-hidroxibencil-penicilina sódica
p-hydroxybenzyl-phosphinic acid
ácido p-hidroxi-bencilfosfínico
ß-hydroxybutyr-aldehyde
aldehído ß-hidroxibutírico
p-hydroxybutyranilide
anilida p-hidroxi-butírica

ß-hydroxybutyric acid
ácido ß-hidroxibutírico
2-hydroxycamphane
2-hidroxicanfano
3-hydroxycamphor
3-hidroxicanfor
hydroxycarbamide
hidroxicarbamida
hydroxy-ß-carotene
hidroxi-ß-caroteno
hydroxychloroquine
hidroxicloroquina
hydroxychloroquine sulfate
sulfato de hidroxicloroquina
1α-hydroxychole-calciferol
1α-hidroxicole-calciferol
3-ß-hydroxy-cholestane
3-ß-hidroxicolestano
24-hydroxy-cholesterol
24-hidroxicolesterol
25-hydroxy-cholesterol
25-hidroxicolesterol
hydroxycitronellal
hidroxicitronelal
hydroxycitronellal dimethyl acetal
dimetilacetal de hidroxicitronelal
hydroxycodeinone
hidroxicodeinona
hydroxycortisone butyrate
butirato de hidroxicortisona
17-hydroxy-costicosterone
17-hidroxi-costicosterona
3-hydroxy-p-cymene
3-hidroxi-p-cimeno
1-hydroxy-2,4-diamylbenzene
1-hidroxi-2,4-diamilbenceno
hydroxydione sodium
hidroxidiona sódica
hydroxydione sodium succinate
succinato de hidroxidiona sódica

hydroxydiphenyl
hidroxidifenilo
p-hydroxydiphenyl-
amine
p-hidroxidifenil-
amina, amina p-
hidroxidifenílica
p-hydroxyephedrine
p-hidroxiefedrina
2-hydroxyethane-
sulfonic acid
ácido 2-hidroxi-
etansulfónico
2-hydroxyethyl
acrylate
2-hidroxietilacrilato,
acrilato 2-
hidroxietílico
2-hydroxyethyl
carbamate
carbamato 2-
hidroxietílico
2-hydroxyethyl
methacrylate
metacrilato 2-
hidroxietílico,
metacrilato de 2-
hidroxietilo
N-hydroxyethyl
piperazine
N-hidroxietil-
piperazina, piperazina
N-hidroxietílica
hydroxyethyl-
acetamide
hidroxietilacetamida,
acetamida
hidroxietílica
2-hydroxyethylamine
2-hidroxietilamina,
amina 2-hidroxietílica
hydroxyethylcellulose
hidroxietilcelulosa,
celulosa hidroxietílica
hydroxyethyl-
ethylenediamine
hidroxietiletilen-
diamina, diamina
hidroxietil etilénica
hydroxyethyl-
ethylenediamine-
triacetic acid
ácido triacético
hidroxietiletilen-
diamínico
n-(2-hydroxyethyl)-
ethyleneimine
n-(2-hidroxietil)
etilenimina,

imina n-(2-hidroxietil)
etilénica
1-(2-hydroxyethyl)-2-
n-heptadecenyl-2-
imidazole
1-(2-hidroxietil)-2-n-
heptadecen-2-imidazol
ß-hydroxyethyl-
hydrazine
ß-hidroxietilhidracina,
hidracina ß-
hidroxietílica, ß-
hidroxietilhidrazina,
hidrazina ß-
hidroxietílica
N-hydroxyethyl-
morpholine
N-hidroxietil-
morfolina, morfolina
N-hidroxietílica
N-2-hydroxyethyl-
piperidine
N-2-hidroxietil-
piperidina, piperidina
N-2-hidroxietílica
N-hydroxyethyl-
promethazine chloride
cloruro de N-
hidroxietil-
prometazina,
cloruro de prometazina
N-hidroxietílica
hydroxyethyl-
trimethylammonium
bicarbonate
bicarbonato de
hidroxietil
trimetilamonio,
bicarbonato
de amonio hidroxietil
trimetílico
ß-hydroxyethyl-
trimethylammonium
hydroxide
hidróxido de ß-
hidroxietil
trimetilamonio,
hidróxido de amonio ß-
hidroxietil trimetílico
1-hydroxyfenchane
1-hidroxifencano
hydroxyglutamic
acid
ácido hidroxiglutámico
8-hydroxy-7-iodo-5-
quinolinesulfonic acid
ácido 8-hidroxi-7-
yodo-5-quinolin-
sulfónico

4-hydroxyisophthalic
acid
ácido 4-hidroxiisoftálico
4-hydroxy-2-keto-4-
methylpentane
4-hidroxi-2-ceto-4-
metilpentano
hydroxyl
hidroxilo, oxhidrilo
hydroxyl group
grupo hidroxilo
hydroxyl ion
ion hidroxilo
hydroxyl value
valor hidroxilo
hydroxylamine
hidroxilamina
hydroxylamine acid
sulfate
sulfato ácido de
hidroxilamina
hydroxylamine
hydrochloride
clorhidrato de
hidroxilamina
hydroxylamine sulfate
sulfato de hidroxilamina
hydroxylammonium
acid sulfate
sulfato ácido
de hidroxilamonio
hydroxylammonium
chloride
cloruro de
hidroxilamonio
hydroxylammonium
sulfate
sulfato de
hidroxilamonio
hydroxylate, to
hidroxilar
hydroxylation
hidroxilación
hydroxylupanine
hidroxilupanina
hydroxymercury-
chlorophenol
hidroximercuri-
clorofenol
hydroxymercurycresol
hidroximercuricresol
hydroxymercury-
nitrophenol
hidroximercuri-
nitrofenol
2-hydroxy-3-methyl-
benzoic acid
ácido 2-hidroxi-3-
metilbenzoico

3-hydroxy-3-methyl-
butanone-2
3-hidroxi-3-metil-
butanona-2
7-hydroxy-4-methyl-
coumarin
7-hidroxi-4-metil-
cumarina
1-(hydroxymethyl)-5,5-
dimethylhydantoin
1-(hidroximetil)-5,5-
dimetilhidantoína
4-hydroxymethyl-
2,6-di-tert-butyl-
phenol
4-hidroximetil-2,6-di-
terc-butilfenol
hydroxymethyl-
ethylene carbonate
carbonato de
hidroximetiletileno,
carbonato hidroximetil
etilénico
5-hydroxymethyl-2-
furaldehyde
5-hidroximetil-2-
furaldehído
Dl-α-hydroxy-δ-
methylmercapto-
butyric acid,
calcium salt
sal cálcica del
ácido Dl-α-hidroxi-δ-
metilmercapto-
butírico
N-(hydroxymethyl-
nicotinamide
N-(hidroximetil)
nicotinamida
2-hydroxymethyl-5-
norbornene
2-hidroximetil-5-
norborneno
4-hydroxy-4-
methylpentanone-2
4-hidroxi-4-
metilpentanona-2
2-(2'-hydroxy-5'-
methylphenyl)
benzotriazole
2-(2'-hidroxi-5'-
metilfenil)
benzotriazol
3-hydroxy-2-methyl-
1,4-pyrone
3-hidroxi-2-metil-1,4-
pirona
hydroxynaphthalene
hidroxinaftaleno

3-hydroxy-2-naphthoic acid
ácido 3-hidroxi-2-naftoico
ß-hydroxynaphthol anilide
anilida ß-hidroxinaftólica
2-hydroxy-1,4-naphtho quinone
2-hidroxi-1,4-naftoquinona
5-hydroxy-1,4-naphthoquinone
5-hidroxi-1,4-naftoquinona
N-(7-hydroxy-1-naphthyl)acetamide
N-(7-hidroxi-1-naftil)acetamida
4-hydroxy-3-nitrobenzene arsonic acid
ácido 4-hidroxi-3-nitrobencenarsónico
4-hydroxynonanoic acid, δ-lactone
δ-lactona del ácido 4-hidroxi-nonanoico
4-hydroxy-19-nortestosterone
4-hidroxi-19-nortestosterona
cis-12-hydroxy-octadec-9-enoic acid
ácido cis-12-hidroxioctadec-9-enoico
12-hydroxyoleic acid
ácido 12-hidroxioleico
15-hydroxypenta-decanoic acid lactone
lactona del ácido 15-hidroxipentadecanoico
hydroxypethidine
hidroxipetidina
hydroxyphenamate
hidroxifenamato
3-hydroxyphenol
3-hidroxifenol
2-hydroxy-2-phenylacetophenone
2-hidroxi-2-fenilacetofenona
ß-p-hydroxyphenyl-alanine
ß-p-hidroxifenil-alanina

2-(2'-hydroxyphenyl)-benzotriazole
2-(2'-hidroxifenil) benzotriazol
p-hydroxyphenyl-benzyl ether
p-hidroxifenil bencil éter, éter p-hidroxifenil bencílico
4-(p-hydroxyphenyl)-2-butanone acetate
acetato de 4-(p-hidroxifenil)-2-butanona
N-(p-hydroxyphenyl)-glycine
N-(p-hidroxifenil) glicina
2-hydroxyphenyl-mercuric chloride
cloruro 2-hidroxifenil mercúrico
1-(p-hydroxyphenyl)-2-methylaminoethanol tartrate
tartrato de 1-(p-hidroxifenil)-2-metilaminoetanol
hydroxyphenylstearic acid
ácido hidroxifenil esteárico
1-hydroxypiperidine
1-hidroxipiperidina
hydroxyprocaine
hidroxiprocaína
11-α-hydroxy-progesterone
11-α-hidroxi-progesterona
hydroxyprogesterone
hidroxiprogesterona
hydroxyprogesterone caproate
caproato de hidroxi-progesterona
4-hydroxyproline
4-hidroxiprolina
2-hydroxy-1,2,3-propanetricarboxylic acid
ácido 2-hidroxi-1,2,3-propán tricarboxílico
α-hydroxypropionic acid
ácido α-hidroxi-propiónico

α-hydroxypropionitrile
α-hidroxipropionitrilo
ß-hydroxypropio-nitrile
ß-hidroxipropionitrilo
2-hydroxypropyl acrylate
acrilato de 2-hidroxipropilo
hydroxypropyl cellulose
hidroxipropil-celulosa, celulosa hidroxipropílica
hydroxypropyl methacrylate
metacrilato de hidroxipropilo, metacrilato hidroxipropílico
hydroxypropyl methylcellulose
hidroxipropilmetil-celulosa, celulosa hidroxipropil metílica
2-hydroxypropyl-amine
2-hidroxipropilamina
hydroxypropyl-glicerine
hidroxipropilglicerina, glicerina hidroxipropílica
N-ß-hydroxy-propyl-o-toluidine
N-ß-hidroxipropil-o-toluidina, o-toluidina N-ß-hidroxipropílica
4-hydroxy-2H-pyran-3,3,5,5-(4H,6H) tetramethanol
4-hidroxi-2H-pirán-3,3,5,5-(4H,6H) tetrametanol
hydroxypyridine tartrate
tartrato de hidroxipiridina
2-hydroxypyridine-N-oxide
N-óxido de 2-hidroxipiridina
1-hydroxy-2-pyridine thione
1-hidroxi-2-piridintiona
4-hydroxy-2-pyrrolidine-carboxylic acid
ácido 4-hidroxi-2-pirrolidín carboxílico

8-hydroxyquinoline
8-hidroxiquinolina
8-hydroxyquinoline benzoate
benzoato de 8-hidroxiquinolina
8-hydroxyquinoline sulfate
sulfato de 8-hidroxiquinolina
8-hydroxy-5-quinoline sulfonic acid
ácido 8-hidroxi-5-quinolín sulfónico
4-hydroxysalicylic acid
ácido 4-hidroxi-salicílico
12-hydroxystearic acid
ácido 12-hidro-esteárico
1,12-hydroxystearyl alcohol
alcohol 1,12-hidroxiestearílico
hydroxystenozole
hidroxistenozol
hydroxystilbamidine
hidroxiestilbamidina
hydroxystreptomycin
hidroxiestreptomicina
hydroxysuccinic acid
ácido hidroxisuccínico
hydroxytetracaine
hidroxitetracaína
hydroxytoluene
hidroxitolueno
hydroxytoluic acid
ácido hidroxitolúico
1-hydroxytriacontane
1-hidroxitriacontano
5-hydroxytriptamine
5-hidroxitriptamina
5-hydroxytryptophan
5-hidroxitriptofano
4-hydroxyundecanoic acid, δ-lactone
δ-lactona del ácido 4-hidroxiundecanoico
hydroxyurea
hidroxiurea
hydrozincite
hidrocincita
hydroxyzine
hidroxicina, hidroxizina
hydroxyzine hydrochloride
chlorhidrato de hidroxicina,

chlorhidrato de
hidroxizina
**hydroxyzine
pamoate**
pamoato de
hidroxicina, pamoato
de hidroxizina
hydyne
hidina
hyenanchin
hienanquina
hygrine
higrina
hygromycin
higromicina
hygroscopic
higroscópico
hymecromone
himecromona
hymecromone
**O,O-diethyl
phosphorothionate**
O,O-dietil
fosforotionato de
himecromona
hyodeoxycholic acid
ácido hiodeoxicólico
hyoscine
hioscina
hyoscyamine
hiosciamina
hyoscynamous

hioscinamo
hypaphorine
hipaforina
**hyperglycemic glyco-
genolytic factor**
factor hiperglicémico
glicogenolítico
hypericin
hipericina
hypersorption
hiperabsorción
hypertensin
hipertensina
hypnocarpic acid
ácido hipnocárpico
hypnone
hipnona
hypoallergenic
hipoalergénico
hypobromous acid
ácido hipobromoso
hypochlorite
hipoclorito
hypochlorite solution
solución de hipoclorito
hypoclorous
hipocloroso
hypoclorous acid
ácido hipocloroso
hypoglycine A
hipoglicina A
hypoglicine B

hipoglicina B
hyponitrite
hiponitrito
hyponitrous
hiponitroso
hyponitrous acid
ácido hiponitroso
α-hypophamine
α-hipofamina
ß-hypophamine
ß-hipofamina
hypophosphate
hipofosfato
hypophosphite
hipofosfito
hypophosphoric acid
ácido hipofosfórico
hypophosphorous
hipofosforoso
hypophosphorous acid
ácido hipofosforoso
hyposulfite
hiposulfito
hyposulfurous
hiposulfuroso
hyposulfurous acid
ácido hiposulfuroso
hypoxanthine
hipoxantina
hypoxanthine riboside
hipoxantin ribósido,
ribósido hipoxantínico

**hypoxanthine riboside
5-phosphoric acid**
ácido hipoxantin-
ribósido-5-fosfórico
hypromellose
hipromelosa
hypsocromic
hipsocrómico
hyssop oil
aceite (esencia) de
hisopo
hyzone
hizona

I

ibazocine
ibazocina
ibogaine
ibogaina
ibopamine
ibopamina
ibotenic acid
ácido iboténico
ibrotamide
ibrotamida
ibudilast
ibudilast
ibufenac
ibufenac, ibufenaco
ibuprofen
ibuprofén, ibuprofeno
ibuproxam
ibuproxán, ibuproxam
ibuterol
ibuterol
ibutilide fumarate
fumarato de ibutilido
ibuverine
ibuverina
ice
hielo
ice, to
helar
ice dye
colorante glacial
ice-cold
helado
ice water
agua helada
Iceland moss
liquen de Islandia
Iceland spar
espato de Islandia
ichthammol
ictamol
icthyopterin
ictiopterina
iclazepam
iclacepán, iclazepam
icthyol
ictiol
idarubicin
idarrubicina
idarubicin hydro-
chloride
clorhidrato de
idarrubicina
ideal conditions
condiciones ideales

ideal gas
gas ideal
ideal solution
solución ideal
idebenone
idebenona
identical
idéntico
identification
identificación
identification reaction
reacción de
identificación
identity period
período de identidad
identify, to
identificar
idose
idosa
idoxuridine
idoxuridina
idrocilamide
idrocilamida
idropranolol
idropranolol
ifenprodil
ifenprodil, ifenprodilo
ifosfamide
ifosfamida
igneous
ígneo
ignitability
combustibilidad,
inflamabilidad
ignite
quemar, encender,
inflamar
igniter
encendedor
igniting
encendido
ignition
ignición
ignition temperature
temperatura de
ignición
ignition tube
tubo de ignición
ignotine
ignotina
ilmenite
ilmenita
iloprost
iloprost

iludins
iludinos
imandrite
imandrita
imbibition
imbibición
imcarbofos
incarbofós
imexon
imexón
imiclopazine
imiclopacina,
imiclopazina
imidazole
imidazol
4-imidazole ethylamine
etilamina 4-
imidazólica, 4-imidazol
etilamina
imidazole salicilate
salicilato de imidazol
4,5-imidazoledi-
carboxamide
dicarboxamida 4,5-
imidazólica, 4,5-
imidazoldi-
carboxamida
2-imidazolidinethione
idinotiona 2-
imidazólica, 2-
imidazolidinotiona
2-imidazolidinone
idinona 2-imidazólica,
2-imidazolidinona
2-imidazolidone
2-imidazolidona
imidazolyl
imidazolil
imidazo(4,5-d)
pyrimidine
imidazo(4,5-d)
pirimidina
imide
imida
imido-
imido-
imidocarb
imidocarbo
imido group
grupo imido
imidole
imidol, pirrol
imidoline
imidolina

imine
imina
imino acids
iminoácidos
3,3'-iminobis-
propylamine
3,3'-iminobis
propilamina
iminocarbonyl
iminocarbonilo
iminodiacetic acid
ácido iminodiacético
iminodiacetic acid
disodium salt hydrate
hidrato de sal sódica
del ácido imino-
diacético
iminodiacetonitrile
iminodiacetonitrilo
4,4-iminodicyclo-
hexanecarboxylic acid
ácido 4,4-imino-
diciclohexán-
carboxílico
iminophenimide
iminofenimida
iminourea
iminourea
imipenem
imipenem
imipramine
imipramine
imipramine
hydrochloride
clorhidrato de
imipramina
imipramine N-oxide
N-óxido de imipramina
imipramine pamoate
pamoato de
imipramina
imipraminoxide
óxido de imipramina,
imipraminóxido
imiquimod
imiquimod
immerse, to
sumergir
immiscibility
inmiscibilidad
immiscible
inmiscible
immiscible fluid phase
fase fluida inmiscible

immune serum globulin
globulina sérica
inmune, inmunoseroglobulina
immunochemistry
inmunoquímica
immunoglobulin
inmunoglobulina
imolamine
imolamina
impacarzine
impacarcina, impacarzina
impact strenght
resistencia al impacto
impalpable
impalpable
impeller
impulsor
imperatorin
imperatorina
imperial green
verde imperial
imperialine
imperialina
impromidine
impromidina
improsulfan
improsulfán
impure
impuro
impurities
impurezas
impurity
impureza
impurity profile
contenido de impurezas
imuracetam
imuracetán, imuracetam
inaccuracy
imprecisión, inexactitud
inactive
inactivo
inactivity
inactividad
in bulk
a granel
incendiary gel
geles incendarios
incineration
incineración
inclusion complex
complejo de inclusión
indaconitine
indaconitina

indalpine
indalpino
indan
indano
indanazoline
indanazolina
indanorex
indanorex
indanthrene
indantreno
indanthrene yellow
amarillo indantreno
indanthrone
indantrona
indapamide
indapamida
1H-indazole
1H-indazol
indecainide
indecainida
indeloxazine
indeloxacina, indeloxazina
indeloxazine hydrochloride
clorhidrato de indeloxacina, clorhidrato de indeloxazina
indene
indeno
indenolol
indenolol
indian red
rojo de la India, óxido férrico
indian yellow
amarillo de la India, nitrito de cobalto y potasio
indican
indicano, indicán
indicator
indicador
indigo
índigo, añil
indinavir sulfate
sulfato de indinavir
indirect dye
colorante indirecto
indium
indio
indium acetylacetonate
acetilacetonato de indio
indium antimonide
antimoniuro de indio
indium arsenide
arseniuro de indio

indium chloride
cloruro de indio
indium oxide
óxido de indio
indium phosphide
fosfuro de indio
indium selenide
selenuro de indio
indium sesquioxide
sesquióxido de indio
indium telluride
teluriuro de indio
indium trichloride
tricloruro de indio
indium trifluoride
trifluoruro de indio
indium trioxide
trióxido de indio
indobufen
indobufén, indobufeno
indocate
indocato
indocianine green
verde de indocianina
indole
indol
indoleacetic acid
ácido indolacético
ß-indoleacetic acid
ácido ß-indolacético
indole-α-aminopropionic acid
ácido indol-α-aminopropiónico
indolebutyric acid
ácido indolbutírico
indole-2,3-dione
indol-2,3-diona
ß-indolylacetic acid
ácido ß-indolilacético
indolmycin
indolmicina
3-indolylacetone
3-indolilacetona
indomethacin
indometacina
indopine
indopina
indoprofen
indoprofeno
indoramin
indoramina
indoretane
indoretano
indospicine
indospicina
indoxole
indoxol

indoxyl
indoxilo
indriline
indrilina
induline
indulina
indurite
indurita
industrial alcohol
alcohol industrial
industrial carbon
carbón industrial
industrial, chemistry
química industrial
inert
inerte
inert gas
gas inerte
influx
entrada, flujo de entrada
infrared
infrarrojo
infrared radiation
radiación infrarroja
infrared rays
rayos infrarrojos
infrared spectroscopy
espectroscopía infrarroja
infrared spectrum
espectro infrarrojo
infusion
infusión
infusorial earth
tierra de infusorios
ingot iron
hierro de lingotes
ingrain dye
colorante en rama
ingredient
ingrediente
inhibin
inhibina
inhibitor
inhibidor
inicarone
inicarona
initial
inicial
initial boiling point
punto de ebullición inicial
initial pressure
presión inicial
initial temperature
temperatura inicial
initial velocity
velocidad inicial

initiator
iniciador

inject, to
inyectar

injection
inyección

injector
inyector

inlet
entrada

inlet temperature
temperatura del puerto
de entrada

inodorous
inodoro

inorganic
inorgánico

inorganic chemistry
química inorgánica

inorganic
constituents
componentes
inorgánicos

inosine
inosina

inosinic acid
ácido inosínico

inosite
inosita

inositol
inositol

inositol hexa-
phosphoric acid
ácido hexafosfórico de
inositol

inositol hexa-
phosphoric acid ester,
sodium salt
sal sodica de ácido
hexafosfórico de
inositol

inositol mono-
phophate
monofosfato de
inositol

inositol niacinate
niacinato de inositol

inositol nicotinate
nicotinato de inositol

in-process tests
pruebas durante la
manufactura del
producto

inproquone
improcuona

insecticide
insecticida

insect wax
cera de insectos

inside diameter
diámetro interior

in situ
in situ

insolubility
insolubilidad

insoluble
insoluble

inspect, to
inspeccionar, examinar

instability
inestabilidad

instable
inestable

instantaneous value
valor instantáneo

instruction manual
manual de
instrucciones

instrument
instrumento

instrumental analysis
análisis instrumental

instrumentation
instrumental,
instrumentación

insufficient
insuficiente

insulate, to
aislar

insulator
aislante

insularine
insularina

insulin
insulina

insulin zinc suspension
suspensión de insulina
con cinc

insulinase
insulinasa

intensity of light
intensidad de la luz

interaction
interacción

interatomic
interatómico

intercalation
compound
compuesto de
intercalación

intercept, to
interceptar

interchange
intercambio iodate

interface
interfaz

interferon
interferón

intermediate
compuesto o producto
intermedio

intermetallic
compound
compuesto
intermetálico

internal
interno

interpolation
interpolación

interstitial cell-
stimulating hormone
hormona estimulante
de células intersticiales

intramolecular
reaction
reaction intramolecular

intrazole
intrazol

intriptyline
intriptilina

introns
intrones

inulin
inulina

in vacuo
al vacío

invention
invento

invertase
invertasa

invert sugar
azucar invertida

in vitro
in vitro

iobenzamic acid
ácido yodo-
benzámico

iocarmic acid
ácido yodocármico

iocetamic acid
ácido yodocetámico

iodamine
yodamina

iodate
yodato

iodation
tratamiento con yodo

iodeosin
yodoeosina, eosina
yodada

iodic
yódico

iodic acid
ácido yódico

iodic acid anhydride
anhídrido del ácido
yódico

iodide
yoduro

iodinated glycerol
glicerol yodado

iodination
yodación, tratamiento o
impregnación con yodo

iodine
yodo

iodine 131
yodo 131

iodine bisulfide
bisulfuro de yodo

iodine bromide
bromuro de yodo

iodine chloride
cloruro de yodo

iodine colloidal
yodo coloidal

iodine cyanide
cianuro de yodo

iodine disulfide
disulfuro de yodo

iodine heptafluoride
heptafluoruro de yodo

iodine monobromide
monobromuro de yodo

iodine monochloride
monocloruro de yodo

iodine number
índice de yodo

iodine pentafluoride
pentafluoruro de yodo

iodine pentoxide
pentóxido de yodo

iodine trichloride
tricloruro de yodo

iodine value
valor de yodo

iodinin
yodinina

iodipamide
yodipamida

iodisan
yodisán

iodism
yodismo,
envenenamiento
causado por el yodo

iodival
yodival

iodize
yodurar

iodized oil
aceite yodado

iodoacetic acid
sodium salt
sal sódica de ácido
yodoacético

α-iodoacetophenone
α-yodoacetofenona
iodoalphionic acid
ácido yodoalfiónico
iodobenzene
yodobenceno
iodobenzoic acid
ácido yodobenzoico
iodochlorohydroxy-
quinoleine
yodoclorohidroxi-
quinoleína
iodochlorhydroxyquin
yodoclorhidroxiquina
iodochloroxyquinoline
yodocloroxiquinoleína
5-iodo-2'-deoxy-
uridine
5-yodo-2'-deoxi-
uridina
iodoethane
yodoetano
iodoethylene
yodoetileno
iodofenphos
yodofenfós
iodoform
yodoformo,
triyodometano
o-iodohippurate
sodium
o-yodohipurato de
sodio
7-iodo-8-hydroxy-
quinoline 5-sulfonic
acid
ácido 7-yodo-8-
hidroxiquinolín-5-
sulfónico
iodol
yodol
iodomethane
yodometano
iodometric
yodométrico
iodometry
yodometría
1-iodooctadecane
1-yodoctadecano
iodopanoic acid
ácido yodopanoico
o-iodophenol
o-yodofenol
p-iodophenol
p-yodofenol
iodophor
yodóforo
iodophosphonium
yodofosfonio

iodophthalein sodium
yodoftaleína sódica
2-iodopropane
2-yodopropano
iodoprotein
yodoproteína,
proteína
yodada
iodopsin
yodopsina
iodopyracet
yodopiracet
iodoquinol
yodoquinol
N-iodosuccinimide
N-yodosuccinimida
iodous
yodoso
iofendylate
yodofendilato,
yofendilato
ioglucol
yodoglucol
ioglucomide
yodoglucomida
ioglunide
yodoglunida
iohexol
yodohexol
iometer
iómetro, iómero
iometin
yodometina
ion
ion
ion exchange
intercambio de iones
ion exchange
chromatography
cromatografía de
intercambio de iones
ion-exchange resin
resinas de intercambio
iónico
ion exclusion
exclusión de iones
ion pair
par iónico
ionic
iónico, relativo a los
iones
ionic bond
enlace iónico
ionic compound
compuesto iónico
ionic detergent
detergente iónico
ionic reaction
reacción iónica

ionium
ionio, isótopo
radioactivo del torio
ionization
ionización, disociación
ionization constant
coeficiente de
ionización
ionize
ionizar, separar en iones
ionizer
ionizador
ionomer resine
resina ionómera
ionone
ionona
ion retardation
retardo iónico
iopamidol
yodopamidol
iopanoic acid
ácido yodopanoico
iopentol
yodopentol, iopentol
iophendilate
yodofendilato,
iofendilato
iophenoxic acid
ácido yodofenóxico
iopromide
yodopromida,
iopromida
iopronic acid
ácido yodoprónico,
ácido ioprónico
iopydol
yodopidol, iopidol
iopydone
yodopidona, iopidona
iosulamide
yodosulamida,
iosulamida
iothalamic acid
ácido yodotalámico,
ácido iotalámico
iotasul
yodotasul, iotasul
iothion
yodotiona, iotiona
iothiuracil
yodotiuracilo,
iotiuracilo
iotrol
yodotrol, iotrol
iotrolan
yodotrolán, iotrolán
ioxaglic acid
ácido yodoxáglico,
ácido ioxáglico

ipecac
ipecacuana
ipecacuanha
ipecacuana
ipexidine
ipexidina
ipomea
ipomea
ipragratine
ipragratina
ipratropium bromide
bromuro de ipratropio
iprazochrome
iprazocromo
ipriflavone
ipriflavona
iprindole
iprindol
iproclozide
iproclozida
iprocrolol
iprocrolol
iprodione
iprodiona
iproheptine
iproheptina
iproniazid(e)
iproniazida
ipronidazole
ipronidazol
iproxamine
iproxamina
iproxilamine
iproxilamina
ipsapirone
ipsapirona
iquindamine
iquindamina
irbesartan
irbesartano
iridic
del iridio
iridic chloride
cloruro irídico
iridium
iridio
iridium 192
iridio 192
iridium bromide
bromuro de iridio
iridium chloride
cloruro de iridio
iridium
hexafluoride
hexafluoruro de iridio
iridium potassium
chloride
cloruro de iridio y
potasio

iridium sesquioxide
sesquióxido de iridio
iridium tetrachloride
tetracloruro de iridio
iridium tribromide
tribromuro de iridio
iridium trichloride
tricloruro de iridio
iridomyrmecin
iridomirmecina
iridosmine
iridosmina
irigenin
irigenina
Irish moss
musgo irlandés
irisolone
irisolona
iron
hierro
iron 55
hierro 55
iron acetate liquor
licor de acetato de
hierro
iron alum
alumbre de hierro,
sulfato de amonio
férrico
iron ammonium sulfate
sulfato de amonio y
hierro
iron bisulfite
bisulfito de hierro
iron black
negro de hierro
iron blue
ferrocianuro férrico,
azul Prusia, azul
Berlín, azul París
iron carbonate,
precipitated
carbonato de hierro
precipitado
iron carbonyl
carbonilo de hierro
iron chromate
cromato de hierro
iron compounds
compuestos de hierro
iron formation
formación de hierro
iron mass
masa de hierro
iron octoate
octoato de hierro
iron ore, chrome
mineral cromado de
hierro

iron oxide
óxido de hierro
iron oxide black
óxido de hierro negro
iron oxide brown
óxido de hierro marrón
iron oxide, hydrated
óxido de hierro
hidratado
iron oxide, metallic
brown
óxido de hierro
metálico marrón
iron oxide, process
proceso del óxido de
hierro
iron oxide red
óxido de hierro rojo
iron oxide, synthetic
óxido de hierro
sintético
iron oxide, wet
óxido de hierro
húmedo
iron oxide yellow
óxido de hierro
amarillo
iron pentacarbonyl
pentacarbonilo de
hierro
iron powder
polvo de hierro
iron potassium sulfate
sulfato de hierro y
potasio
iron protochloride
protocloruro de hierro
iron protoiodide
protoyoduro de hierro
iron protosulfide
protosulfuro de hierro
iron pyrite
pirita de hierro
iron pyrolignite
pirolignito de hierro
iron pyrophosphate
pirofosfato de hierro
iron red
hierro rojo
iron reduced
hierro reducido
iron resinate
resinato de hierro
iron saccharate
sacarato de hierro
irone
irona, 6-metilionona
α-irone
α-irona

irons, stainless
hierros inoxidables
irradiation
irradiación
irreversible
irreversible
irreversible process
proceso irreversible
irreversible reaction
reacción irreversible
irsogladine
irsogladina
isamfazone
isanfazona
isamoxole
isamoxol
isanic acid
ácido isánico
isanolic acid
ácido isanólico
isatide
isatida
isatin
isatina
isatoic anhydride
anhídrido isatoico
isaxonine
isaxonina
isazofos
isazofós
isethionic acid
ácido isetiónico
isetionate
isetionato
iso
iso
isoalloxazine
isoaloxazina
isoaminile
isoaminilo
isoamyl acetate
acetato de isoamilo,
acetato isoamílico
isoamyl alcohol,
primary
alcohol isoamílico
primario
isoamyl alcohol,
secundary
alcohol isoamílico
secundario
isoamyl benzoate
benzoato de isoamilo,
benzoato isoamílico
isoamyl benzyl
ether
éter isoamil
bencílico, isoamil
bencil éter

isoamyl bromide
bromuro de isoamilo,
bromuro isoamílico
isoamyl butyrate
butirato de isoamilo,
butirato isoamílico
isoamyl caprate
caprato de isoamilo,
caprato isoamílico
isoamyl chloride
cloruro de isoamilo,
cloruro isoamílico
isoamyl dichloroarsine
isoamildicloroarsina,
dicloroarsina
isoamílica
isoamyl ether
éter isoamílico
isoamyl formate
formiato isoamílico,
formiato de isoamilo
isoamyl furoate
furoato de isoamilo,
furoato isoamílico
isoamyl iodide
yoduro de isoamilo,
yoduro isoamílico
isoamyl isovalerate
isovalerato isoamílico,
isovalerianato de
isoamilo
sec-isoamyl mercaptan
mercaptano sec-
isoamílico, sec-
isoamilmercaptano
isoamyl nitrate
nitrato de isoamilo,
nitrato isoamílico
isoamyl nitrite
nitrito de isoamilo,
nitrito isoamílico
isoamyl pelargonate
pelargonato de
isoamilo, pelargonato
isoamílico
isoamyl phthalate
ftalato de isoamilo,
ftalato isoamílico
isoamyl propionate
propionato de isoamilo,
propionato isoamílico
isoamyl salicylate
salicilato de isoamilo,
salicilato isoamílico
isoamyl valerate
valerato isoamílico,
valerianato de isoamilo
isoamylamine
isoamilamina

α-isoamylene
α-isoamileno
ß-isoamylene
ß-isoamileno
isoapo-ß-erythroidine
isoapo-ß-eritroidina
isoascorbic acid
ácido isoascórbico
isobar
isobara, isóbaro
isobaric
isobárico
isobenzan
isobenzano
isoborneol
isoborneol
isobornyl acetate
acetato de isobornilo,
acetato isobornílico
isobornyl salicylate
salicilato de isobornilo,
salicilato isobornílico
isobornyl
thiocyanoacetate
tiocianoacetato de
isobornilo,
tiocianacetato
isobornílico
isobornyl valerate
valerato de isobornilo,
valerato isobornílico,
valerianato de
isobornilo, valerianato
isobornílico
isobornyl hydrate
hidrato de isobornilo,
isobornilo hidratado
isobutamben
isobutambeno
isobutane
isobutano
isobutane hydrate
isobutano hidratado
isobutanol
isobutanol
isobutanolamine
isobutanolamina
isobutene
isobuteno
isobutyl acetate
acetato de isobutilo,
acetato isobutílico
isobutyl acrylate
acrilato de isobutilo,
acrilato isobutílico
isobutyl alcohol
alcohol isobutílico
isobutyl aldehyde
aldehído isobutílico

isobutyl benzoate
benzoato isobutílico
isobutyl bromide
bromuro de isobutilo,
bromuro isobutílico
isobutyl n-butyrate
n-butirato de isobutilo,
n-butirato isobutílico
isobutyl carbamate
carbamato de isobutilo,
carbamato isobutílico
isobutyl carbinol
isobutilcarbinol,
carbinol isobutílico
isobutyl chloride
cloruro de isobutilo,
cloruro isobutílico
isobutyl
chlorocarbonate
clorocarbonato de
isobutilo,
clorocarbonato
isobutílico
isobutyl chloroformate
cloroformiato de
isobutilo,
cloroformiato
isobutílico
isobutyl cinnamate
cinamato de isobutilo,
cinamato isobutílico
isobutyl cyano
acrylate
cianoacrilato de
isobutilo, cianocrilato
isobutílico
isobutyl formate
formiato de isobutilo,
formiato isobutílico
isobutyl furoate
furoato de isobutilo,
furoato isobutílico
isobutyl heptyl
ketone
isobutil heptil cetona,
cetona isobutil
heptílica
isobutyl iodide
yoduro de isobutilo,
yoduro isobutílico
isobutyl isobutyrate
isobutirato de isobutilo,
isobutirato isobutílico
isobutyl isovalerate
isovalerato de
isobutilo, isovalerato
isobutílico,
isovalerianato
isobutílico

isobutyl mercaptan
isobutil mercaptano,
mercaptano isobutílico
isobutyl
methacrylate
metacrilato de
isobutilo, metacrilato
isobutílico
isobutyl nitrate
nitrato de isobutilo,
nitrato isobutílico
isobutyl nitrite
nitrito de isobutilo,
nitrito isobutílico
isobutyl
phenylacetate
fenilacetato de
isobutilo, fenilacetato
isobutílico
isobutyl propionate
propionato de
isobutilo, propionato
isobutílico
isobutyl salicylate
salicilato de isobutilo,
salicilato isobutílico
isobutyl stearate
estearato de isobutilo,
estearato isobutílico
isobutyl sulfide
sulfuro de isobutilo,
sulfuro isobutílico
isobutyl thiocyanate
tiocianato de isobutilo,
tiocianato isobutílico
isobutyl urethane
isobutil uretano,
uretano isobutílico
isobutyl valerate
valerato de isobutilo,
valerato isobutílico,
valerianato
isobutílico
isobutyl vinyl ether
éter isobutil vinílico,
isobutil vinil éter
isobutylamine
isobutilamina
isobutyl-p-
aminobenzoate
p-aminobenzoato de
isobutilo, p-
aminobenzoato
isobutílico
isobutylbenzene
isobutilbenceno,
benceno isobutílico
isobutylene
isobutileno

isobutylene-isoprene
rubber
caucho de isobutileno e
isopreno
N-isobutyl-
hendecenamide
N-isobutilhendecen-
amida, hendecenamida
N-isobutílica
isobutylic alcohol
alcohol isobutílico
N-isobutylundecylen-
amide
N-isobutilundecilen-
amida, undecilen-
amida N-isobutílica
isobutyraldehyde
isobutiraldehído,
aldehído isobutírico
isobutyric acid
ácido isobutírico
isobutyric anhydride
anhídrido isobutírico
isobutyronitrile
isobutironitrilo, nitrilo
isobutírico
isobutyroyl chloride
cloruro de isobutiroilo,
cloruro isobutiroílico
isobutyryl chloride
cloruro de isobutirilo,
cloruro isobutirílico
isocarboxazid
isocarboxazida
isocetyl laurate
laurato de isocetilo,
laurato isocetílico
isocetyl myristate
miristato de isocetilo,
miristato isocetílico
isocetyl oleate
oleato de isocetilo,
oleato isocetílico
isocetyl stearate
estearato de isocetilo,
estearato isocetílico
isochinoline
isoquinolina
isochondrodendrine
isocondrodendrina
isocil
isocilo
isocinchomeronic acid
ácido
isocincomerónico
isochromatic
isocromático
isoconazole
isoconazol

isocorybulbine
isocoribulbina
isocorydine
isocoridina
isocorypalmine
isocoripalmina
isocromil
isocromilo
isocrotonic acid
ácido isocrotónico
isocyanate
isocianato
isocyanate resin
resina de isocianato
isocyanic acid
ácido isociánico
isocyanine
isocianina
isocyanurate
isocianurato
isocyanuric acid
ácido isocianúrico
isodapamide
isodapamida
isodecaldehyde
isodecaldehído
isodecane
isodecano
isodecanoic acid
ácido isodecanoico
isodecanol
isodecanol
isodecyl chloride
cloruro de isodecilo,
cloruro isodecílico
isodecyl octyl adipate
adipato isodecil
octílico
isodecyl pelargonate
pelargonato de
isodecilo, pelargonato
isodecílico
isodrin
isodrina
isodurene
isodureno
isoelectric point
punto isoeléctrico
isoestradiol
isoestradiol
8-isoestrone
8-isoestrona
isoetharine
isoetarina
isoeugenol
isoeugenol
isoeugenol acetate
acetato de
isoeugenol

isoeugenol ethyl ether
éter etílico de
isoeugenol
isofenphos
isofenfós
isofezolac
isofezolaco
isoflavone
isoflavona
isoflupredone
isoflupredona
isoflurane
isoflurano
isoflurophate
isofluorfato
L-isoglutamine
L-isoglutamina
isoheptane
isoheptano
isohexane
isohexano
isoladol
isoladol
isolan
isolán
isolation
aislamiento
isoleucine
isoleucina
isologous
isólogo
isolysergic acid
ácido isolisérgico
isomaltol
isomaltol
isomer
isómero
isomerase
isomerasa
isomeric
isomérico, isómero
isomerism
isomerismo
isomerization
isomerización
**isometamidium
chloride**
cloruro de
isometamidio
isomethadol
isometadol
isomethadone
isometadona
isomethéptene
isomethepteno
**isometheptene
mucate**
mucato de
isomethepteno

α-**isomethylionone**
α-isometilionona
isometric
isométrico
isomorph
isomorfo, isomórfico
isomorphic
isomorfo, isomórfico
isomorphism
isomorfismo
isomorphous
isomorfo, isomórfico
isoniazid
isoniazida
**isoniazid
methanesulfonate**
metansulfonato de
isoniazida
isonicotinic acid
ácido
isonicotínico
**isonicotinic acid
diethylamine**
dietilamina de ácido
isonicotínico
**isonipecaine
hydrochloride**
clorhidrato de
isonipecaína
isonipecotic acid
ácido
isonipecótico
isonitrile
isonitrilo
isonitrosoacetone
isonitrosacetona
**isonitroso-
acetophenone**
isonitrosacetofenona
isonixin
isonixina
isononyl alcohol
alcohol isononílico
isoocetene
isoceteno
isooctane
isoctano, 2,2,4
trimetilpentano
isooctene
isocteno
isooctyl adipate
adipato de isoctilo,
adipato isoctílico
isooctyl alcohol
alcohol isoctílico
**isooctyl isodecyl
phthalate**
ftalato isoctil
isodecílico

**isooctyl
mercaptoacetate**
mercaptoacetato de
isoctilo,
mercaptoacetato
isoctílico
isooctyl palmitate
palmitato de isoctilo,
palmitato isoctílico
**isooctylphenoxy-
polyoxyethylene
ethanol**
etanol isoctil
fenoxipolioxietilénico,
isoctilfenoxi-
polioxietilenetanol
isooctyl thioglycolate
tioglicolato de isoctilo,
tioglicolato isoctílico
**isooctylphenyl-
polyethylene glycol
ether**
éter de glicol isoctil
fenil polietilénico,
isoctilfenil-
polietilenglicol éter
isopentaldehyde
isopentaldehído
isopentane
isopentano
isopentanoic acid
ácido isopentanoico
isopentyl alcohol
alcohol isopentílico
isophane insulin
insulina isofánica
**isophane insulin
suspension**
suspensión de insulina
isofánica
isophorone
isoforona
**isophorone
diisocyanate**
diisocianato de
isoforona
isophthalic acid
ácido isoftálico
isophthaloyl chloride
cloruro de isoftaloilo,
cloruro isoftaloílico
isophytol
isofitol
isopilosine
isopilosina
isopimaric acid
ácido isopimárico
isopolyester
isopoliéster

isopral
isopral
isoprazone
isoprazona
isopregnidene
isopregnideno
isoprenaline
isoprenalina
isoprene
isopreno
isoprenoid
isoprenoide
isoprofen
isoprofeno
isopromethazine
isoprometacina,
isoprometazina
isopropalin
isopropalina
isopropamide
isopropamida
isopropamide iodide
yoduro de
isopropamida
isopropanol
isopropanol
isopropanolamine
isopropanolamina
isopropenyl acetate
acetato de
isopropenilo, acetato
isopropenílico
isopropenyl
chloride
cloruro de
isopropenilo, cloruro
isopropenílico
isopropenylacetylene
isopropenilacetileno,
acetileno
isopropenílico
isopropenylchloro-
formate
cloroformiato de
isopropenilo,
cloroformiato
isopropenílico
4-(5-isopropenyl-2-
methyl-1-cyclopenten-
1-yl)-2-butanone
4-(5-isopropenil-2-
metil-1-ciclopenten-1-
il)-2-butanona
isopropicillin
isopropicilina
p-isopropoxy-
diphenylamine
p-isopropoxi-
difenilamina

2-isopropoxyethanol
2-isopropoxietanol
o-isopropoxyphenyl-N-
methylcarbamate
N-metilcarbamato de
o-isopropoxifenilo, N-
metilcarbamato o-iso-
propoxifenílico
ß-isopropoxy-
propionitrile
ß-isopropoxi-
propionitrilo
isopropyl acetate
acetato de isopropilo,
acetato isopropílico
isopropyl alcohol
alcohol isopropílico
isopropyl acetoacetate
acetoacetato de
isopropilo,
acetoacetato
isopropílico
isopropyl bromide
bromuro de isopropilo,
bromuro isopropílico
isopropyl butyrate
butirato de isopropilo,
butirato isopropílico
isopropyl chloride
cloruro de isopropilo,
cloruro isopropílico
isopropyl
chloroformate
cloroformiato de
isopropilo,
cloroformiato
isopropílico
isopropyl cyanide
cianuro de isopropilo,
cianuro isopropílico
isopropyl dichloro-
phenoxyacetate
diclorofenoxiacetato de
isopropilo,
diclorofenoxiacetato
isopropílico
isopropyl ether
éter isopropílico
isopropyl glycidyl
ether
isopropilglicidil éter,
éter isopropil
glicidílico
isopropyl iodide
yoduro de isopropilo,
yoduro isopropílico
isopropyl
meprobamate
meprobamato de

isopropilo,
meprobamato
isopropílico
isopropyl mercaptan
isopropilmercaptano,
mercaptano
isopropílico
isopropyl myristate
miristato de isopropilo,
miristato isopropílico
isopropyl nitrate
nitrato de isopropilo,
nitrato isopropílico
isopropyl nitrite
nitrito de isopropilo,
nitrito isopropílico
isopropyl palmitate
palmitato de
isopropilo, palmitato
isopropílico
isopropyl
percarbonate
percarbonato de
isopropilo,
percarbonato
isopropílico
isopropyl
peroxydicarbonate
peroxidicarbonato de
isopropilo,
peroxidicarbonato
isopropílico
isopropyl titanate
titanato de isopropilo,
titanato isopropílico
isopropylacetone
isopropilacetona,
acetona isopropílica
N-isopropyl-
acrylamide
N-isopropilacrilamida,
acrilamida N-
isopropílica
isopropylamine
isopropilamina
p-isopropylamino-
diphenylamine
p-isopropilamino-
difenilamina,
aminodifenilamina p-
isopropílica
isopropylamino-
ethanol
isopropilaminoetanol,
etanol
isopropilamínico
N-isopropylaniline
N-isopropilanilina,
anilina N-iso-propílica

p-isopropylaniline
p-isopropilanilina,
anilina p-isopropílica
isopropylantimonite
isopropilantimonita,
antimonita
isopropílica
p-isopropyl-
benzaldehyde
p-isopropil-
benzaldehído,
benzaldehído p-
isopropílico
isopropylbenzene
isopropilbenceno,
benceno
isopropílico
p-isopropylbenzyl
alcohol
alcohol p-isopropil
bencílico
isopropylcarbinol
isopropilcarbinol,
carbinol isopropílico
N-isopropyl-α-chloro-
acetanilide
N-isopropil-α-
cloroacetanilida, α-
cloroacetanilida N-
isopropílica
isopropyl-3-chloro-
carbanilate
3-clorocarbanilato de
isopropilo, 3-
clorocarbanilato
isopropílico
isopropyl-N-(3-
chlorophenyl)-
carbamate
N-(3-clorofenil)
carbamato de
isopropilo, N-(3-
clorofenil) carbamato
isopropílico
isopropyl-m-cresol
isopropil-m-cresol, m-
cresol isopropílico
isopropyl-o-cresol
isopropil-o-cresol,
o-cresol
isopropílico
isopropylcresol
isopropilcresol, cresol
isopropílico
isopropyldiethanol-
amine
isopropildietanol-
amina, dietanolamina
isopropílica

2-isopropyl-4-di-
methylamino-5-
methylphenyl-1-
piperidine carboxylate
methyl chloride
metilcloruro de 2-
isopropil-4-dimetil-
amino-5-metilfenil-1-
piperidin carboxilato
isopropylethanol-
amine
isopropiletanolamina,
etanolamina
isopropílica
isopropylethylene
isopropiletileno,
etileno isopropílico
isopropylfuroate
furoato de isopropilo,
furoato isopropílico
isopropylidene acetone
isopropilidenacetona,
acetona
isopropilidénica
p,p-isopropylidene
diphenol
p,p-isopropiliden-
difenol, difenol p,p-
isopropilidénico
isopropylidene glycerol
glicerol
isopropilidénico
2-isopropyl-5-methyl-
benzoquinone
2-isopropil-5-
metilbenzoquinona, 5-
metilbenzoquinona 2-
isopropílica
5-isopropyl-2-methyl-
1,3-cyclohexadiene
5-isopropil-2-metil-
1,3-ciclohexadieno
3-isopropyl-6-
methylene-1-
cyclohexene
3-isopropil-6-metilén-
1-ciclohexeno
1-isopropyl-2-methyl-
ethylene
1-isopropil-2-
metiletileno, 2-
metiletileno 1-
isopropílico
N-isopropyl-2-methyl-
2-propyl-1,3-
propanediol
dicarbamate
dicarbamato de N-
isopropil-2-metil-2-

propil-1,3-propandiol
1-isopropyl-3-methyl-
5-pyrazolyl dimethyl
carbamate
dimetilcarbamato de 1-
isopropil-3-metil-5-
pirazolilo
2-isopropyl-
naphthalene
2-isopropilnaftaleno,
naftaleno 2-isopropílico
m,p-isopropylphenol
m,p-isopropilfenol,
fenol m,p-isopropílico
o-isopropylphenol
o-isopropilfenol, fenol
o-isopropílico
isopropyl-N-phenyl-
carbamate
N-fenilcarbamato de
isopropilo, N-
fenilcarbamato
isopropílico
N-isopropyl-N'-phenyl-
p-phenylenediamine
N'-fenil-p-
fenilendiamina N-
isopropílica
4-isopropylpyridine
4-isopropilpiridina,
piridina 4-iso-propílica
isopropyltoluene
isopropiltolueno,
tolueno isopropílico
isopropyl-2,4,5-
trichlorophenoxy-
acetate
2,4,5-triclorofenoxi-
acetato de isopropilo,
2,4,5-
triclorofenoxiacetato
isopropílico
isopropyltrimethyl-
methane
isopropiltrimetil-
metano,
trimetilmetano
isopropílico
isoproterenol
isoproterenol
isoproterenol
hydrochloride
clorhidrato de
isoproterenol
isoproturon
isoproturón
isopulegol
isopulegol
isopurpurin

isopurpurina
isopyrocalciferol
isopirocalciferol
isoquassin
isocuasina
isoquercitrin
isoquercitrina
isoquinoline
isoquinolina
1,3-isoquinolinediol
1,3-isoquinolindiol
isorubijervine
isorrubijervina
isosafrole
isosafrol
isosorbide
isosórbido, isosorbida
isosorbide
mononitrate
mononitrato de
isosorbida,
mononitrato de
isosórbido
isosorbide dinitrate
dinitrato de isosorbida,
dinitrato de isosórbido
ß-isosparteine
ß-isosparteína
isostearic acid
ácido isoesteárico
isosterism
isosterismo
isostilbene
isostilbeno
isosulpride
isosulprida
isotactic polymer
polímero isotáctico
isothebaine
isotebaína
isotherm
isoterma
isothermal
isotérmico
isothermal process
proceso isotérmico
isothiocyanic acid
ácido isotiociánico
isothipendyl
isotipendilo
isotone
isótono
isotonic
isotónico
isotonicity
isotonicidad
isotope
isótopo
isotopic

isotópico
isotopy
isotopía
isotretinoin
isotretinoína
isotropy
isotropía
isovaleraldehyde
isovaleraldehído
isovaleramide
isovaleramida
isovaleric aldehyde
aldehído
isovaleriánico,
aldehído isovalérico
isovaleric acid
ácido isovalérico, ácido
isovaleriánico
isovalerianic acid
ácido isovaleriánico,
ácido isovalérico
isovaleroyl chloride
cloruro de isovaleroílo,
cloruro isovaleroílico
isovaleryl chloride
cloruro de isovalerilo,
cloruro isovalerílico
isovaleryl diethylamide
isovaleril dietilamida,
dietilamida
isovalerílica
2-isovalerylindane-1,3-
dione
2-isovalerilindano-1,3-
diona
isovaleryl-p-
phenetidine
isovaleril-p-fenetidina
isovaline
isovalina
isoxaben
isoxabeno
isoxaprolol
isoxaprolol
isoxepac
isoxepac
isoxicam
isoxicán, isoxicamo
isoxsuprine
isoxsuprina
isradipine
isradipina
issue
emisión,
publicación
itaconic acid
ácido itacónico
itanoxone
itanoxona

itraconazole
itraconazol

itramin tosylate
tosilato de itramina

Ivanov
reagent
reactivo de
Ivanov

ivermectin
ivermectina

ivory black
negro de marfil

ixbut
ixbut

ixodin
ixodina

J

J acid
ácido J (ácido 2-amino-5-naftol-7-sulfónico)
J acid urea
urea del ácido J
jacketed
encamisado
Jacobsen rearrangement
transposición de Jacobsen
jalap
jalapa
jambul
jambul
jamolin
jamolina
Janovsky reaction
reacción de Janovsky
Jantsen column for acid and bases
columna de Jantzen de separación de ácidos y bases

japan
barniz del Japón, laca de China, barniz opaco
Japan wax
cera del Japón
japanese agar
agar agar
japanned
esmaltado
japonic acid
ácido japónico
Japp-Klingemann reaction
reacción de Japp Klingemann
jar
bote, vasija, frasco
jasmine aldehyde
aldehído jazmínico, aldehído de jazmín
jasmine oil
esencia (aceite) de jazmín
jasmone
jazmona

jatrophone
jatropona
jatrorrhizine
jatrorricina
javanicin
javanicina
Javel (Javelle) water
agua de Javel
jaws
mandíbula, mordazas
jell, to
gelatinizar
jellied
gelatinizado
jellification
gelatinización
jelly
jalea, gelatina
jelly-like
gelatinoso
jellying ability
capacidad para gelificar
Jeppel's oil
aceite de huesos

jervine
jervina
jesaconitine
jesaconitina
jojoba oil
aceite de jojoba
Jones oxidation
oxidación de Jones
josamycin
josamicina
juglone
juglona
julocrotine
julocrotina
juniper berries
enebrina
juniper oil
esencia (aceite) de enebro, enebrina
juniper tar oil
esencia (aceite) de brea de enebro
justicidins
justicidinas
jute
yute
juvenile hormone
hormona juvenil

K

K acid
ácido K (ácido 1-
amino-8-naftol-4,6-
disulfónico)
kaempferol
kaempferol
kainic acid
ácido caínico
kaitine
caitina
kalafungin
kalafungina
kallidinogenase
kalidinogenasa
kallidin
calidín
kallikrein
calicreína
kalomel
calomel
kamala
kamala
kanamycin
kanamicina
kanamycin sulfate
sulfato de kanamicina
kaolin
caolín
kaolinite
caolinita
kapok
capoc, miraguano, lana
de ceibo
karanjin
caranjina
karaya gum
goma karaya
Karl Fischer reagent
reactivo de Karl
Fischer
karsil
karsil
kauri
kauri
kauri-butanol value
valor de kauri en
butanol
kava
kava
kawain
kawaina, kavaína
kcal
kcal (abreviatura de
kilogramo caloría)

K-capture
captura K
kebuzone
quebuzona
Kekulé theory
teoría de Kekulé
kelp
alga marina
Kelvin scale
escala de Kelvin
Kendall-Mattox
reaction
reacción de Kendall y
Mattox
kerabitumen
cerabitumen
keracyanin
keracianina
keratin
queratina
keratinase
queratinasa
kermesic acid
ácido quermésico
kernite
kernita
kerosene, kerosine
queroseno
ketal
cetal
ketamine
cetamina
ketanserin
ketanserina
ketazocine
ketazocina
ketazolam
ketazolán, ketazolam
ketene
cetena
kethoxal
quetoxal
ketimine
cetimina
ketimipramine
ketimipramina
ketipic acid
ácido quetípico
keto
ceto
ketoacids
ácidos cetónicos
ketobemidone
cetobemidona

4-ketobenzotriazine
4-cetobenzotriacina,
4-cetobenzotriazina
ketocaine
cetocaína
ketocainol
ketocainol
ketoconazole
ketoconazol
keto-enol
ceto enólico
ketogenesis
cetogénesis
α-ketoglutaric acid
ácido α-cetoglutárico
ß-ketoglutaric acid
ácido ß-cetoglutárico
2-keto-L-gulonic acid
ácido 2-ceto-L-
gulónico
ketohexamethylene
cetohexametileno
ketol(e)
cetol
ketone
cetona
ketone body
cuerpo cetónico
ketonimide dye
colorante de
cetonimida
ketoprofen
cetoprofeno
ketoprogesterone
cetoprogesterona
α-ketopropionic acid
ácido α-cetopropiónico
ketorolac
tromethamine
cetorolac trometamina
ketose
quetosa
ketotetrahydro-
naphthalene
cetotetrahidro-
naftaleno
ketotifen
ketotifeno
Υ-ketovaleric acid
ácido Υ-cetovalérico
ketoxime
cetoxima
kettle
caldera

key
tecla
Keyes process
proceso de Keyes
khat
cat
khellin
quelina
khellol glucoside
quelol glucósido
khelloside
quelosido
khurchatovium
khurchatorio
kieselguhr
tierra diatomácea
kieserite
kieserita
kiku oil
aceite de kiku
kilogram
kilogramo
kiloliter
kilolitro
kinematic viscosity
viscosidad cinemática
kinetics, chemical
química cinética
kinetic theory
teoría cinética
kinetin
kinetina
king's green
verde real
kinin
quinina
kino
resina de quino
kinoprene
kinopreno
Kishner
cyclopropane
synthesis
síntesis de
ciclopropano de
Kishner
kit
juego
kitasamycin
quitasamicina
kitol
kitol
Kjeldahl flask
matraz de Kjeldahl

Kjeldahl test
prueba de
Kjeldahl
kneading
amasado
Knorr pyrazole
synthesis
síntesis de pirazoles de
Knorr
Knorr pyrrole
synthesis
síntesis de pirroles de
Knorr
Knorr quinoline
synthesis
síntesis de quinoleína
de Knorr
Koch acid
ácido de Koch (ácido
1-naftil-amino-3,6,8-
tri-sulfónico)

Kochi reaction
reacción de
Kochi
Koerings-Knorr
synthesis
síntesis de Koering
y Knorr
kojic acid
ácido cójico
kola
cola
kola nut
nuez de cola
Kolbe elctrolytic
synthesis
síntesis electroltica de
Kolbe
Komarowsky
reaction
reacción de
Komarowsky

kopsine
kopsina
korax
korax
kosin
kosina
Kostanecki acylation
acilación de
Kostanecki
kraft paper
papel de estraza
krantzite
crancita
Kroll process
proceso de Kroll
ìrypton
criptón
krypton 85
criptón 85
krypton 86
criptón 86

kryptonates
criptonatos
Kucherov reaction
reacción de Kucherov
Kuhn-Roth method for
C-methyl
determination
método para la
determinación de
C-metilo de Kuhn y
Roth
kurchessine
kurchesina
kyanmethin
kianmetina
kyanite
cianita
kynurenic acid
ácido quinurénico
kynurenine
quinurenina

L

L acid
ácido L (ácido 1-naftol
5-sulfónico)
label
etiqueta, marca
label strength (L.S.)
potencia declarada en
el rótulo
labeled
marcado
labeled compound
compuesto marcado
labeled molecule
molécula marcada
labeling machine
rotuladora
labetalol
labetalol
**labetalol hydro-
chloride**
clorhidrato de labetalol
labil(e)
lábil, inestable
laboratory
laboratorio
laboratory assistant
auxiliar de laboratorio
laboratory conditions
condiciones de
laboratorio
**laboratory
machinery**
maquinaria de
laboratorio
laboratory test
prueba de laboratorio
lac
laca
lac dye
laca colorante,
colorante de laca
lac wax
cera de laca
laccaic acid
ácido lacaico
laccase
lacasa
lachesine
laquesina
lachrymatory
lacrimógeno
lacmoid
lacmoide, azul de
resorcina

lacquer
laca
lacrimatory
lacrimógeno
lactalbumin
lactoalbúmina
lactam
lactama
lactaroviolin
lactaroviolina
lactase
lactasa
lactate
lactato
lactate dehydrogenase
lactato deshidrogenasa
lactic
láctico
lactic acid
ácido láctico
D-lactic acid
D-ácido láctico
DL-lactic acid
DL-ácido láctico
L-lactic acid
L-ácido láctico
**lactic acid dehydro-
genase**
ácido láctico
deshidrogenasa
lactic acid lactate
lactato del ácido láctico
lactitol
lactitol, lactositol
lactobacillic acid
ácido lactobacílico
lactobionic acid
ácido lactobiónico
lactoflavin
lactoflavina
lactogenic hormone
hormona lactogénica
lactoglobulin
lactoglobulina
lactometer
lactómetro
lactone
lactona
lactonitrile
lactonitrilo
lactonisation
lactonización
lactonitrile
lactonitrilo

p-lactophenetide
p-lactofenetida
lactophenine
lactofenina
lactoprotein
lactoproteína
lactose
lactosa
lactucin
lactucina
lactulose
lactulosa
ladder polymer
polímero escalonado
**Ladenburg
rearrangement**
transposición de
Ladenburg
ladle
caldero de colada
lake
laca (de pintor)
lake Red C
rojo de laca C
lake Red C amine
amina de laca roja C
lake Red carbon
rojo de laca y carbono
lakes
lacas
lamepon
lamepón
laminate
laminado
laminaran
laminarina, laminarán
laminin
laminina
lamivudine
lamivudina
lamotrigine
lamotrigina
lampblack
negro de humo
lanatoside C
lanatósido C
lane (electrophoresis)
hilera, pista
langbeinite
langbeinita
lanital
lanital
lankamycin
lankamicina

lanoconazole
lanoconazol
lanolin
lanolina
lanolin, anhydrous
lanolina anhidra
lanosterol
lanosterol
lansoprazole
lansoprazol
lanthana
lantana
lanthanide series
series de los lantánidos
lanthanoid series
serie de los lantanoides
lanthanum
lantano
lanthanum acetate
acetato de lantano
**lanthanum ammonium
nitrate**
nitrato de lantano y
amonio
lanthanum antimonide
antimoniuro de lantano
lanthanum arsenide
arseniuro de lantano
lanthanum carbonate
carbonato de lantano
lanthanum chloranilate
cloranilato de lantano
lanthanum chloride
cloruro de lantano
lanthanum fluoride
fluoruro de lantano
lanthanum nitrate
nitrato de lantano
lanthanum oxalate
oxalato de lantano
lanthanum oxide
óxido de lantano
lanthanum phosphide
fosfuro de lantano
lanthanum sesquioxide
sesquióxido de lantano
lanthanum sulfate
sulfato de lantano
lanthanum trioxide
trióxido de lantano
lanthionine
lantionina
lapachol
lapacol

lapirium chloride
cloruro de lapirio
lappa
bardana, lampazo, lapa
lappaconitine
lapaconitina
lapyrium chloride
cloruro de lapirio
larch turpentine
trementina de alerce
lard, benzoinated
manteca benzoinada
lard oil
aceite de manteca de
cerdo
larkspur
consuelda, espuela de
caballero
larvicide
larvicida
lasalocid
lasalócido
lasalocid A
lasalócido A
laser
láser
laserpitin
laserpitina
lasiocarpine
lasiocarpina
latamoxef
latamoxef
latent heat
calor latente
latent solvent
solvente latente
latex
látex
latex paint
pintura de látex
lattice
red cristalina
latrunculins
latrunculinas
laudanidine
laudanidina,
tritopina
laudanine
laudanina
laudanosine
laudanosina
laudanum
láudano
laudexium methyl
sulfate
metilsulfato de
laudexio
laughing gas
gas hilarante

laundry sour
neutralizador de
lavandería
lauraldehyde
aldehido láurico
laurate
laurato
lauralkonium chloride
cloruro de lauralconio
laurel oil
aceite de laurel
laurel oil volatile
aceite volátil de laurel
laureline
laurelina
Laurent's acid
ácido de Laurent
laurepukine
laurepuquino
lauric acid
ácido láurico
lauroguadine
lauroguadina
laurolinium acetate
acetato de laurolinio
lauromacrogol 400
lauromacrogol 400
laurone
laurona
laurotetanine
laurotetanina
lauroyl chloride
cloruro de lauroilo
lauroyl peroxide
peróxido de lauroilo
N-lauroyl-p-
aminophenol
N-lauroil-p-
aminofenol
3-O-lauroylpyridoxol
diacetate
diacetato de 3-O-
lauroilpiridoxol
N-lauroylsarcosine
N-lauroilsarcosina
lauryl acetate
acetato de laurilo
lauryl alcohol
alcohol laurílico
lauryl aldehyde
aldehido laurílico
lauryl bromide
bromuro de laurilo
lauryl chloride
cloruro de laurilo
lauryl lactate
lactato de laurilo
lauryl mercaptan
laurilmercaptano

lauryl methacrylate
metacrilato de laurilo
lauryl pyridium
chloride
cloruro de lauril piridio
lauryl pyridium-5-
chloro-2-benzothiazyl
sulfide
5-cloro-2-
benzotiazilsulfuro de
laurilpiridinio
lauryldimethylamine
laurildimetilamina
lauryldimethylamine
oxide
óxido de
laurildimetilamina
lavandin oil, abrial
aceite de lavanda
abrial
lavander
lavanda
lavander oil
esencia (aceite) de
lavanda, esencia
(aceite) de espliego
lavender oil,
terpeneless
esencia (aceite) de
lavanda sin terpeno
lawrencium
lawrencio
lawsone
lawsona
layer
capa
lazaroids
lazaroides
lazurite
lazurita, lapislázuli
L-dopa
L-dopa
leaching
lixiviación
lead
plomo
lead acetate
acetato de plomo
lead acetate water
agua blanca, solución
de acetato de plomo
lead alloy
aleación de plomo
lead, antimonial
plomo antimonial
lead antimonate
antimoniato de plomo
lead antimonite
antimonito de plomo

lead arsenate
arseniato de plomo
lead arsenite
arsenito de plomo
lead azide
azida de plomo
lead-base Babbitt
metal Babbitt con base
de plomo
lead bath
baño de plomo
lead biorthophosphate
biortofosfato de plomo
lead blue
plomo azul
lead borate
borato de plomo
lead borosilicate
borosilicato de plomo
lead bromate
bromato de plomo
lead bromide
bromuro de plomo
lead butyrate
butirato de plomo
lead carbolate
carbolato de plomo
lead carbonate
carbonato de plomo
lead carbonate, basic
carbonato básico de
plomo
lead chloride
cloruro de plomo
lead chlorosilicate
complex
complejo de
clorosilicato de plomo
lead chromate
cromato de plomo
lead chromate, basic
cromato básico de
plomo
lead cyanide
cianuro de plomo
lead dimethyldithio-
carbamate
dimetilditiocarbamato
de plomo
lead dioxide
dióxido de plomo
lead electrolytic
plomo electrolítico
lead ethylhexoate
etilhexoato de plomo
lead flakes
plomo de escamas
lead fluoborate
fluoborato de plomo

lead fluoride
fluoruro de plomo
lead fluosilicate
fluosilicato de plomo
lead formate
formiato de plomo
lead fumarate,
tetrabasic
fumarato tetrabásico de
plomo
lead glass
vidrio de plomo
lead hexafluoro-
silicate
hexafluorosilicato de
plomo
lead hydroxide
hidróxido de plomo
lead hypophosphite
hipofosfito de plomo
lead hyposulfite
hiposulfito de plomo
lead iodide
yoduro de plomo
lead lactate
lactato de plomo
lead linoleate
linoleato de plomo
lead maleate
maleato de plomo
lead maleate tribasic
maleato tribásico de
plomo
lead metavanadate
metavanadato de
plomo
lead molybdate
molibdato de plomo
lead monohydrogen
phosphate
fosfato monohidrógeno
de plomo, fosfato
dibásico de plomo
lead mononitro-
resorcinate
mononitrorresorcinato
de plomo
lead monoxide
monóxido de plomo
lead ß-naphthalene-
sulfonate
ß-naftalensulfonato de
plomo
lead naphthenate
naftenato de plomo
lead nitrate
nitrato de plomo
lead nitrite
nitrito de plomo

lead nitrite, basic
nitrito básico de plomo
lead ocher
ocre de plomo
lead octoate
octoato de plomo
lead oleate
oleato de plomo
lead ore
mineral de plomo
lead orthoarsenate
ortoarseniato de plomo
lead orthophosphate,
normal
ortofosfato de plomo
normal
lead orthosilicate
ortosilicato de plomo
lead oxalate
oxalato de plomo
lead oxide, black
óxido negro de plomo,
subóxido de plomo,
litargirio negro
lead oxide, brown
óxido pardo de plomo
lead oxide hydrated
óxido hidratado de
plomo
lead oxide, red
óxido rojo de plomo
lead oxide, yellow
óxido amarillo de
plomo, litargirio
lead perchlorate
perclorato de plomo
lead peroxide
peróxido de plomo
lead phenate
fenato de plomo
lead phenolsulfonate
fenolsulfonato de
plomo
lead phosphate
fosfato de plomo
lead phosphate,
dibasic
fosfato dibásico de
plomo
lead phosphite, dibasic
fosfito dibásico de
plomo
lead phthalate, dibasic
ftalato dibásico de
plomo
lead protoxide
protóxido de plomo
lead, read
plomo rojo

lead resinate
resinato de plomo
lead salicylate
salicilato de plomo
lead selenate
seleniato de plomo
lead selenide
seleniuro de plomo
lead selenite
selenita de plomo
lead sesquioxide
sesquióxido de plomo
lead silicate
silicato de plomo
lead silicate, basic
silicato básico de
plomo
lead silicochromate
silicocromato de plomo
lead silicofluoride
silicofluoruro de plomo
lead soap lubricants
lubricantes de jabón de
plomo
lead sodium
hyposulfite
hiposulfito de plomo y
sodio
lead sodium
thiosulfate
tiosulfato de plomo y
sodio
lead stannate
estannato de plomo
lead stearate
estearato de plomo
lead styphnate
estifnato de plomo
lead subacetate
subacetato de plomo
lead subcarbonate
subcarbonato de plomo
lead subnitrite
subnitrito de plomo
lead suboxide
subóxido de plomo
lead, sugar of
azúcar de plomo
lead sulfate
sulfato de plomo
lead sulfate, basic
sulfato básico de
plomo
lead sulfate, blue basic
sulfato azul básico de
plomo
lead sulfate, tribasic
sulfato tribásico de
plomo

lead sulfide
sulfuro de plomo
lead sulfite
sulfito de plomo
lead sulfocarbolate
sulfocarbolato de
plomo
lead sulfocyanide
sulfocianuro de plomo
lead superoxide
superóxido de plomo
lead tallate
talato de plomo
lead telluride
teluluro de plomo
lead tetraacetate
tetracetato de
plomo
lead tetraethyl
tetraetilo de plomo
lead tetrafluoride
tetrafluoruro de plomo
lead tetroxide
tetróxido de plomo
lead thiocyanate
tiocianato de plomo
lead thiosulfate
tiosulfato de plomo
lead titanate
titanato de plomo
lead trinitro-
resorcinate
trinitrorresorcinato de
plomo
lead tungstate
tungstato de plomo
lead vanadate
vanadato de plomo
lead water
agua de plomo
lead white
plomo blanco
lead wolframate
wolframato de plomo
lead wool
lana de plomo
lead yellow
amarillo de plomo
lead zirconate titanate
circonato titanato de
plomo, zirconato
titanato de plomo
lead-coated
revestido de plomo
lead-silver Babbitt
Babbitt de plata y
plomo
leaf, filter
filtro de hojas

leak
escape, fuga, pérdida
leak detector
detector de fugas
leak test
prueba de pérdida
lecithin
lecitina
lectin
lectina
ledol
ledol
lefetamine
lefetamina
leflunomide
leflunomida
legal chemistry
química legal
leghemoglobin
legemoglobina
legumin
legúmina
leiopyrrole
leiopirrol
lemon chrome
cromo limón
lemon, essential
salt of
sal esencial de limón
lemon grass oil
esencia (aceite) de
hierba luisa
lemon oil
esencia (aceite) de
limón
lemon peel
cáscara de limón
lenacil
lenacil
lenampicillin
lenampicilina
lencine
lencina
lencite
lencita
leniquinsin
leniquinsina
lenperone
lemperona
lentinan
lentinan
lenthionine
lentionina
leonurine
leonurina
lepidine
lepidina
lepidolite
lepidolita

leptacline
leptaclina
leptandra
leptandra
leptin
leptina
leptodactyline
leptodactilina
leptophos
leptofós
lergotrile
lergotrilo
letimide
letimida
letosteine
letosteína
Letts nitrile synthesis
síntesis de nitrilos de
Letts
leucine
leucina
leucinocaine
leucinocaína
leucinocaine
mesylate
mesilato de
leucinocaína
leuco alizarin
leucoalizarina
leucocianidol
leucocianidol
leucocyanidin
leucocianidina
leucocyte
leucocito
leucodrin
leucodrina
leucoglycodrin
leucoglicodrina
leucomycin
leucomicina
leucopterin
leucopterina
leucovorin
leucovorina
leukotriene
leucotrieno
leupeptins
leupeptinas
leuprolide
leuprolida
leuprolide acetate
acetato de leuprolida
leuprorelin
leuprorrelina
levacetylmethadol
levacetilmetadol
levallorphan
levalorfano

levallorphan tartrate
tartrato de levalorfano
levamfetamine
levanfetamina
levamisole
levamisol
level
concentración, valores,
nivel (plano inclinado)
leveling
igualador
levisoprenaline
levisoprenalina
levobunolol
levobunolol
levocarnitine
levocarnitina
levodopa
levodopa
levofacetoperane
levofacetoperano
levofloxacin
levofloxacina
levofuraltadone
levofuraltadona
levoglutamide
levoglutamida
levomenol
levomenol
levomepate
levomepato
levomepromazine
levomepromacina,
levomepromazina
levomethadone
levometadona
levomethadyl acetate
acetato de
levometadilo, acetato
levometadílico
levomethorphan
levometorfano
levometiomeprazine
levometiomepracina,
levometiomeprazina
levomoramide
levomoramida
levonantradol
levonantradol
levonordefrin
levonordefrina
levonorgestrel
levonorgestrel
levophacetoperane
levofacetoperano
levophenacylmorphan
levofenacilmorfano
levopimaric acid
ácido levopimárico

levopropicillin
levopropicilina
levopropoxyphene
levopropoxifeno
levopropylhexedrine
levopropilhexedrina
levorin
levorina
levorotatory
levorrotatorio, levógiro
levorphanol
levorfanol
levorphanol tartrate
tartrato de levorfanol
levothyroxine sodium
levotiroxina sódica
levoxadrol
levoxadrol
levulinic acid
ácido levulínico
levulose
levulosa
Lewis acid
ácido de Lewis
Lewis base
base de Lewis
Lewis electron theory
teoría de los electrones
de Lewis
lewisite
lewisita
Lewis metal
metal de Lewis
lexofenac
lexofenaco
liatris
liatris
libecillide
libecilida
liberate
liberar, separar
licanic acid
ácido licánico
lichenic acid
ácido liquénico
licheniformins
liqueniforminas
lichenin
liquenina
licorice
regaliz
lidamidine
lidamidina
lidding
cubierta
lidimycin
lidimicina
lidocaine
lidocaína

lidocaine
hydrochloride
clorhidrato de
lidocaína
lidofenin
lidofenino
lidoflazine
lidoflazina
Lieben iodoform
reaction
reacción del
yodoformo de Lieben
lifibrate
lifibrato
ligand
ligando
ligase
ligasa
light green SF
yellowish
verde claro SF
amarillento
light hydrocarbon
hidrocarburo ligero
light metal
metal ligero
light microscope
microscopio de luz
light oil
aceite ligero
light water
agua ligera
lignans
lignanas
lignin
lignina
lignin sulfonate,
lignosulfonate
sulfonato de lignina,
ligninsulfonato
lignite
lignita
lignoceric acid
ácido lignocérico,
ácido tetracosanoico
ligroin(e)
ligroína
limaprost
limaprost
lime
cal
lime acetate
acetato de cal
lime, agricultural
cal agrícola
lime, air-slaked
cal apagada al aire
lime chlorinated
cal clorada

lime citrate
citrato de cal
lime compounds
compuestos de cal
lime, fat
cal grasa
lime, hydrated
cal hidratada
lime, hydraulic
cal hidráulica
lime hypophosphite
hipofosfito de cal
lime, lean
cal magra
lime oil destilled
aceite de
lima destilado
lime oil, expressed
aceite exprimido de
lima
lime saltpeter
salitre cálcico
lime, slaked
cal apagada
lime sulfurated
solution
solución de cal
sulfurada
lime unslaked
cal viva
lime water
agua de cal
lime-ammonium
nitrogen
cal nitrógeno amónico
lime-nitrogen
cal nitrogenada
limestone
caliza
limestone, hydraulic
caliza hidráulica
limettin
limetina, citropteno
limit
límite
limit concentration
concentración límite
limit of measurement
límite de medida
limit value
valor límite
limonene
limoneno
limonene dioxide
dióxido de limoneno
limonene, inactive
limoneno inactivo
limonene monoxide
monóxido de limoneno

limonin
limonina
limonite
limonita
linaloe
lináloe
linaloe oil
acite de lináloe
linalool, linalol
linalol
linalool oxide
óxido de linalol
linalyl acetate
acetato de linalilo
linalyl formate
formiato de linalilo
linalyl isobutyrate
isobutirato de linalilo
linalyl propionate
propionato de linalilo
linamarin
linamarina
linarin
linarina
linatine
linatina
lincomycin
lincomicina
lindane
lindano
Lindlar catalyst
catalizador Lindlar
linear alkyl
sulfonate
alquilsulfonato lineal
linear molecule
molécula lineal
lineatin
lineatina
liner
revestimiento interior
lingot iron
hierro de lingote
linin
linina
lining
revestimiento interior
link
enlace
link, to
unir, ligar, enlazar
linkage
enlace, acoplo
linoleates
linoleatos
linoleic
linoleico
linoleic acid
ácido linoleico

linolein
linoleína
linolenic acid
ácido linolénico
linolenin
linolenina
linolenyl alcohol
alcohol linolenílico
linoleyl alcohol
alcohol linoleílico
linoleyltrimethyl-
ammonium bromide
bromuro de
linoleiltrimetilamonio
linolic acid
ácido linólico
linseed cake
torta de linaza
linseed oil
aceite de linaza
linseed oil, blown
aceite de linaza
polimerizado
linseed oil, boiled
aceite de linaza
hervido
linseed oil, heat-bodied
aceite de linaza
espesado por calor
linseed oil, meal
harina de aceite de
linaza
linseed oil, raw
aceite crudo de linaza
linseed oil, refined
aceite refinado de
linaza
lint
pelusas
linters, cotton
pelusas de algodón
linuron
linurón
liophilic
liofílico
liothyronine
liotironina
liothyronine sodium
liotironina sódica
lipase
lipasa
lipid
lípido
lipide-soluble
liposoluble
di-α-lipoic acid
ácido di-α-lipoico
lipolysis
lipólisis

lipoprotein lipase
lipasa lipoproteína
liposomes
liposomas
lipotropic agent
agente lipotrópico
lipotropic hormone
hormona lipotrópica
Lipowitz' alloy
aleación de Lipowitz
Lipowitz' metal
metal de Lipowitz
lipoxidase
lipoxidasa
liquate, to
licuar
liquation
licuación
liquefaction
licuación de gases
liquefiable
licuable
liquefied
licuado
liquefied hydrocarbon
gas
gas de hidrocarburo
licuado
liquefied natural gas
gas natural licuado
liquefied petroleum
gas
gas de petróleo licuado
liquefy
licuarse, licuar
liquid
líquido
liquid air
aire líquido
liquid ammonia
amoniaco líquido
liquid chromatography
cromatografía de
líquido
liquid crystal
cristal líquido
liquid dioxide
dióxido líquido
liquid film
película líquida
liquid level
concentración del
líquido
liquid Newtonian
líquido newtoniano
liquid oxygen
oxígeno líquido
liquid phase
fase líquida

liquid pitch oil
aceite de pez líquida
liquid rosin
colofonia líquida
liquid-liquid
extraction
extracción líquido
líquido
liquor, waste
licores residuales
lisinopril
lisinopril
lisuride
lisurida
liter
litro
litharge
litargirio
litharge leaded
litargirio plomado,
óxido de plomo negro
lithia
litia
lithic
lítico
lithic acid
ácido lítico
lithium
litio
lithium acetate
acetato de litio
lithium acetate,
dihydrate
acetato de litio
dihidratado
lithium acetylsalycilate
acetilsalicilato de litio
lithium aluminate
aluminato de litio
lithium aluminum
deuteride
deuteruro de litio y
aluminio
lithium aluminum
hydride
hidruro de litio y
aluminio
lithium aluminum
hydride, ethereal
hidruro etéreo de litio y
aluminio
lithium aluminum tri-
tert-butoxyhydride
tri-terc-butoxihidruro
de litio y aluminio
lithium amide
litioamida
lithium arsenate
arseniato de litio

lithium benzoate
benzoato de litio
lithium
bicarbonate
bicarbonato de litio
lithium bitartrate
bitartrato de litio
lithium borate
borato de litio
lithium
borohydride
borohidruro de litio
lithium bromate
bromato de litio
lithium bromide
bromuro de litio
lithium carbide
carburo de litio
lithium carbonate
carbonato de litio
lithium chlorate
clorato de litio
lithium chloride
cloruro de litio
lithium chromate
cromato de litio
lithium citrate
citrato de litio
lithium cobaltine
cobaltina de litio
lithium deuteride
deuteruro de litio
lithium dichromate
dicromato de litio
lithium ferrosilicon
ferrosilicio de litio
lithium fluoride
fluoruro de litio
lithium
fluorophosphate
fluorfosfato de litio
lithium formate
formiato de litio
lithium gallate
galato de litio
lithium grease
grasa de litio
lithium hydride
hidruro de litio
lithim hydroxide
hidróxido de litio
lithium
hydroxystearate
hidroxiestearato de
litio
lithium hypochlorite
hipoclorito de litio
lithium iodate
yodato de litio

lithium iodide
trihydrate
yoduro de litio
trihidratado
lithium lactate
lactato de litio
lithium manganite
manganito de litio
lithium metaborate
dihydrate
metaborato de litio
dihidratado
lithium metasilicate
metasilicato de litio
lithium metavanadate
metavanadato de litio
lithium methoxide
metóxido de litio
lithium methylate
metilato de litio
lithium molybdate
molibdato de litio
lithium niobate
litio niobato
lithium nitrate
nitrato de litio
lithium nitride
nitruro de litio
lithium
orthophosphate
ortofosfato de litio
lithium oxalate
oxalato de litio
lithium oxide
óxido de litio
lithium perchlorate
perclorato de litio
lithium peroxide
peróxido de litio
lithium phosphate
fosfato de litio
lithium ricinoleate
ricinoleato de litio
lithium salicylate
salicilato de litio
lithium selenate
seleniato de litio
lithium selenite
selenita de litio
lithium silicate
silicato de litio
lithium silicon
silicona de litio
lithium stearate
estearato de litio
lithium sulfate
sulfato de litio
lithium tetraborate
tetraborato de litio

lithium tetracyano-
platinate
tetracianoplatinato de
litio
lithium titanate
titanato de litio
lithium tri-tert-
butoxyalumino-
hydride
tri-terc-butoxi-
aluminohidruro de
litio
lithium tungstate
tungstato de litio
lithiumn vanadate
vanadato de litio
lithium zirconate
circonato de litio,
zirconato de litio
lithium-zirconium
silicate
silicato de litio y
circonio, silicato de
litio y zirconio
lithocholic acid
ácido litocólico
lithol rubine
rubina de litol
lithopone
litopón
litmus
tornasol
litmus paper
papel de tornasol
litracen
litraceno
liver extract
extracto de
hígado
livetins
livetinas
lividomycin
lividomicina
lixiviation
lixiviación
load
carga
loam
limo
lobelanidine
lobelanidina
lobelanine
lobelanina
lobelia
lobelia
lobeline
lobelina
lobendazole
lobendazol

lobenzarit
lobenzarit
Lobry de Bruyn-van
Ekenstein
transformation
transformación de
Lobry de Bruyn y van
Ekenstein
lochnericine
locnericina
lochneridine
locneridina
locust bean gum
goma de algarrobilla
lodiperone
lodiperona
lodoxamide
lodoxamida
lofemizole
lofemizol
lofendazam
lofendazán,
lofendazam
lofentanil
lofentanila
lofepramine
lofepramina
lofexidine
lofexidina
loflucarban
loflucarbano
loganin
loganina
log book
anotador
logwood
palo campeche
loline
lolina
lombazole
lombazol
lomefloxacin
lomefloxacina
lometraline
lometralina
lomifylline
lomifilina
lomustine
lomustina
lonaprofen
lonaprofeno
lonazolac
lonazolaco
London purple
púrpura de Londres
long chain
cadena larga
longifolene
longifoleno

lonidamine
lonidamina
lonomycins
lonomicinas
loop
asa, ansa
loperamide
loperamida
loperamide
hydrochloride
clorhidrato de
loperamida
lophophorine
lofoforina
lophotoxin
lofotoxina
lopirazepam
lopiracepán,
lopirazepam
loprazolam
loprazolán,
loprazolam
loprodiol
loprodiol
lorajmine
lorajmina
lorapride
loraprida
loratadine
loratadina
lorazepam
loracepán, lorazepam
lorbamate
lorbamato
lorcainide
lorcainida
loretin
loretina
lormetazepam
lormetacepán,
lormetazepam
lortalamine
lortalamina
losartan potassium
losartan potásico
losindole
losindola
Lossen
rearrangement
transposición de
Lossen
loss on drying
pérdida por desecación
lotifazole
lotifazol
lotrifen
lotrifeno
lotucaine
lotucaína

lovage oil
aceite de ligústico
lovastatin
lovastatina
low boiling
de bajo punto de
ebullición
low-alloy steel
acero de aleación baja
low-melting alloy
aleaciones de bajo
punto de fusión
low-pressure resin
resina de baja presión
low-soda aluminas
alúminas de poca sosa
low-temperature
carbonization
carbonización a
temperatura baja
loxanast
loxanast
loxapine
loxapina
loxoprofen
loxoprofeno
lozilurea
lozilurea
lubricant, solid
lubricante sólido
lubricant, synthetic
lubricante sintético
lubricating grease
grasa lubricante
lubricating oil
aceite lubricante
lubrication
lubricación
lucanthone
lucantona
lucanthone
hydrochloride
clorhidrato de
lucantona
lucensomycin
lucensomicina
lutein
luteína
luciferase
luciferasa
luciferin
luciferina
lucimycin
lucimicina
luer tip
punta «luer»
Lugol's solution
solución Lugol
lumazine
lumacina, lumazina

lumichrome
lumicromo
lumiflavine
lumiflavina
luminescence
luminiscencia
luminol
luminol
lumisterol
lumisterol
lunacridine
lunacridina
lunacrine
lunacrina
lunasine
lunasina
lunine
lunina
lunularic acid
ácido lunulárico
lupanine
lupanina
lupeol
lupeol
2,6-lupetidine
2,6-lupetidina
lupinine
lupinina
luprostiol
luprostiol
lupulin
lupulina
lupulon
lupulona
Lurgi process
método de Lurgi
luster
brillo

lutecia
lutecia
lutecium
lutecio
lutein
luteína
luteolin
luteolina
luteotropin
luteotropina
lutetia
lutecia
lutetium
lutecio
lutetium chloride
cloruro de lutecio
lutetium fluoride
fluoruro de lutecio
lutetium nitrate
nitrato de lutecio
lutetium oxide
óxido de lutecio
lutetium sulfate
sulfato de lutecio
lutidine
lutidina
2,6-lutidine
2,6-lutidina
lututrin
lututrina
lyapolate
sodium
liapolato de
sodio
lyase
liasa
lycoctonine
licoctonina

lycopodium
licopodio
lycodine
licodina
lycopene
licopeno
lycophyll
licofil
lycopodine
licopodina
lycopidium
licopodio
lycopus
licopos
lycoramine
licoramina
lycorine
licorina
lycoxanthin
licoxantina
lye
lejía
lymecycline
limeciclina
lynestrenol
linestrenol
lyocratic
liocrático
lyosol
liosol
lyophilic
liofílico
lyophilization
liofilización
lyophilize
liofilizar
lyophobic
liófobo

lypressin
lipresina
lysalbinic acid
ácido lisalbínico
lysergamide
lisergamida
lysergic acid
ácido lisérgico
D-lysergic acid
diethylamine
dietilamina del ácido
D-lisérgico
lysergide
lisergido
lysidine
lisidina
lysine
lisina
lysine acetyl
salicylate
acetilsalicilato
de lisina
L-lysine L-
glutamate
L-glutamato de
L-lisina
lysol
lisol
lysosomes
lisosomas
lysostaphin
lisostafina
lysozyme
lisozima
lyxoflavine
lixoflavina
D-lyxose
D-lixosa

M

M acid
ácido M (ácido 1-
amino-5-naftol-7-
sulfónico)
mabuterol
mabuterol
macassar oil
aceite de macasar
mace oil
aceite de macis, aceite
de macia
macerate
macerar
maceration
maceración
maclurin
maclurina
macrogol
macrogol
macrogol ester
éster de macrogol
macromerine
macromerina
macromolecular
macromolecular
macromolecule
macromolécula
macroscopic
macroscópico
macrosalb
macrosalbo
macrose
macrosa, dextrano
macusines
macusinas
madder
rubia (planta), raíz de
rubia
Maddrell's salt
sal de Maddrell
Madelung synthesis
síntesis de Madelung
maduramicin
maduramicina
mafenide
mafenida
mafenide acetate
acetato de mafenida
**mafenide
hydrochloride**
clorhidrato de
mafenida
magainins
magaininas

magaldrate
magaldrato
magenta
rojo violáceo (color),
magenta (agente
colorante) (coloración)
magma
magma
magnalium
magnalio
magnesia
magnesia, óxido de
magnesio
magnesia alba
magnesia blanca,
carbonato de magnesio
hidratado
magnesia, burnt
magnesia quemada,
calcinada
magnesia, calcined
magnesia calcinada
**magnesia caustic
calcined**
magnesia cáustica
calcinada
magnesia, dead burned
magnesia anhidra
magnesia, fused
magnesia fundida
magnesia-alumina
magnesia y alúmina
magnesia-chromia
magnesia y óxido de
cromo
magnesian
magnesiano
magnesite
magnesita
magnesite burnt
magnesita quemada,
calcinada
**magnesite, caustic
calcined**
magnesita cáustica
calcinada
magnesite dead burned
magnesita anhidra
magnesite, synthetic
magnesita sintética
magnesium
magnesio
magnesium acetate
acetato de magnesio

**magnesium
acetylacetonate**
acetilacetonato de
magnesio
**magnesium acetyl-
salicylate**
acetilsalicilato de
magnesio
magnesium amide
amida magnésica
**magnesium ammonium
phosphate**
fosfato de magnesio y
amonio
magnesium arsenate
arseniato de magnesio
magnesium benzoate
benzoato de magnesio
**magnesium
biphosphate**
bifosfato de magnesio
magnesium bisulfate
bisulfato de magnesio
magnesium borate
borato de magnesio
**magnesium
borocitrate**
borocitrato de
magnesio
**magnesium boron
fluoride**
fluoruro de magnesio y
boro
magnesium bromate
bromato de magnesio
magnesium bromide
bromuro de magnesio
**magnesium calcium
chloride**
cloruro de magnesio
cálcico, cloruro de
calcio y magnesio
magnesium carbonate
carbonato de magnesio
**magnesium carbonate,
basic**
carbonato básico de
magnesio
magnesium chlorate
clorato de magnesio
magnesium chloride
cloruro de magnesio
magnesium chromate
cromato de magnesio

magnesium citrate
citrato de magnesio
**magnesium citrate,
dibasic**
citrato de magnesio
dibásico, citrato
dibásico de magnesio
magnesium clofibrate
clofibrato de magnesio
magnesiun dichromate
dicromato de magnesio
magnesium dioxide
dióxido de magnesio
magnesium fluoride
fluoruro de magnesio
magnesium fluosilicate
fluosilicato de
magnesio
magnesium flux
fundente de magnesio
magnesium formate
formiato de magnesio
magnesium germanide
germanuro de
magnesio
magnesium gluconate
gluconato de magnesio
**magnesium
glycerinophosphate**
glicerinfosfato de
magnesio
**magnesium glycero-
phosphate**
glicerofosfato de
magnesio
**magnesium
hexafluorosilicate**
hexafluorosilicato de
magnesio
magnesium hydrate
hidrato de magnesio
magnesium hydride
hidruro de magnesio
magnesium hyposulfite
hiposulfito de
magnesio
**magnesium hydrogen
phosphate**
fosfato ácido de
magnesio
magnesium hydroxide
hidróxido de magnesio
magnesium iodide
yoduro de magnesio

magnesium lactate
lactato de magnesio
magnesium lauryl
sulfate
sulfato laurílico de
magnesio, sulfato de
lauril magnesio
magnesium lime
cal de magnesio
magnesium limestone
caliza de magnesio
magnesium methoxide
metóxido de magnesio
magnesium methylate
metilato de magnesio
magnesium
molybdate
molibdato de magnesio
magnesium nitrate
nitrato de magnesio
magnesium oleate
oleato de magnesio
magnesium oxide
óxido de magnesio
magnesium
oxichloride
oxicloruro de
magnesio
magnesium palmitate
palmitato de magnesio
magnesium pemoline
pemolina magnésica
magnesium
perborate
perborato de magnesio
magnesium
perchlorate
perclorato de magnesio
magnesium
permanganate
permanganato de
magnesio
magnesium peroxide
peróxido de magnesio
magnesium
phosphate
fosfato de magnesio
magnesium phosphate,
dibasic
fosfato dibásico de
magnesio
magnesium phosphate,
neutral
fosfato neutro de
magnesio
magnesium phosphate,
secundary
fosfato de magnesio
secundario

magnesium phosphate,
tribasic
fosfato tribásico de
magnesio
magnesium potassium
selenate
seleniato de potasio y
magnesio
magnesium
pyrophosphate
pirofosfato de
magnesio
magnesium resinate
resinato de magnesio
magnesium ricinoleate
ricinoleato de
magnesio
magnesium salicylate
salicilato de magnesio
magnesium selenate
seleniato de magnesio
magnesium selenide
seleniuro de magnesio
magnesium silicate
silicato de magnesio
magnesium silicide
siliciuro de magnesio
magnesium
silicofluoride
silicofluoruro de
magnesio
magnesium stannate
estannato de magnesio
magnesium stannide
estanniuro de magnesio
magnesium stearate
estearato de magnesio
magnesium sulfate
sulfato de magnesio
magnesium sulfide
sulfuro de magnesio
magnesium sulfite
sulfito de magnesio
magnesium superoxide
superóxido de
magnesio
magnesium
tetrahydrogen
phosphate
fosfato de magnesio
tetrahidrogenado
magnesium
thiocyanate
tiocianato de magnesio
magnesium
thiosulfate
tiosulfato de magnesio
magnesium titanate
titanato de magnesio

magnesium trisilicate
trisilicato de magnesio
magnesium tungstate
tungstato de magnesio
magnesium zirconate
circonato de magnesio
magnesium zirconium
silicate
silicato de circonio y
magnesio
magneson
magnesona
magnetic pyrite
pirita magnética
magnetic separation
separación magnética
magnetite
magnetita
magnetochemistry
magnetoquímica
magnetohydro-
dynamics
magnetohidro-
dinámica
magnoflorine
magnoflorina
magnoline
magnolina
Maillard reaction
reacción de Maillard
maitansine
maitansina
maize oil
aceite de maíz
maizenate
maicenato (sal del
ácido maicénico)
maizenic acid
ácido maicénico
malachite green
verde malaquita, verde
Victoria B, verde de
benzaldehído
malachite green G
verde malaquita G
malachite green toner
colorante de verde
malaquita
malakin
malaquina
Malaprade reaction
reacción de
Malaprade
malate
malato
malathion
malatión
maleamic acid
ácido maleámico

maleanilic acid
ácido maleanílico
maleic acid
ácido maleico
maleic anhydride
anhídrido maleico
maleic hydrazide
hidrazida maleica
maleic resins
resinas maleicas
maleinic acid
ácido maleínico
maletamer
maletámero
maleuric acid
ácido maléurico
maleylsulfathiazole
maleilsulfatiazol
malic acid
ácido málico
malleability
maleabilidad
malleable
maleable
malonamide nitrile
nitrilmalonamida,
malonamida nitrílica
malonic acid
ácido malónico
malonic acid
diethylester
éster dietílico de ácido
malónico
malonic dinitrile acid
ácido dinitril malónico
malonic ester
éster malónico
malonic ester synthesis
síntesis de éster
malónico
malonic ethyl ester
nitrile
éster nitril etil
malónico
malonic methyl ester
nitrile
éster nitril metil
malónico
malonic mononitrile
mononitrilo malónico
malononitrile
malononitrilo
malonylurea
malonilurea
malotilate
malotilato
malt
malta, cebada
fermentada

malt extract
extracto de malta
maltase
maltasa
maltha
malta, brea mineral,
pez mineral
maltol
maltol
maltose
maltosa
malvidin chloride
cloruro de malvidina
manaca
manaca, manaco
mancozeb
mancozeb
mandarin oil
esencia (aceite) de
mandarina
mandelic acid
ácido mandélico
mandelic acid isoamyl
ester
éster isoamílico de
ácido mandélico
mandelonitrile
mandelnitrilo
mandelonitrile
glucoside
glucósido
mandelnitrílico,
glucósido nitril
mandélico
maneb
maneb
manganate
manganato
manganese
manganeso
manganese abietate
abietato de manganeso
manganese acetate
acetato de manganeso
manganese ammonium
sulfate
sulfato de manganeso y
amonio
manganese arsenate
arseniato de
manganeso
manganese bioxide
bióxido de manganeso
manganese black
negro de manganeso
manganese borate
borato de manganeso
manganese bromide
bromuro de manganeso

manganese bronze
bronce manganoso
manganese carbonate
carbonato de
manganeso
manganese carbonyl
carbonilo manganésico
manganese chloride
cloruro de manganeso
manganese chromate
cromato de manganeso
manganese citrate
citrato de manganeso
manganese
cyclopentadienyl
tricarbonyl
manganeso tricarbonil
ciclopentadienílico,
tricarbonil
ciclopentadienil
manganeso
manganese difluoride
difluoruro de
manganeso
manganese dioxide
dióxido de manganeso
manganese dithionate
ditionato de
manganeso
manganese
ethylenebisdithio-
carbamate
etilenbisditio-
carbamato de
manganeso
manganese
ethylhexoate
etilhexoato de
manganeso
manganese fluoride
fluoruro de manganeso
manganese gluconate
gluconato de
manganeso
manganese glycero-
phosphate
glicerofosfato de
manganeso
manganese green
verde de manganeso
manganese hydrate
hidrato de manganeso
manganese hydrogen
phosphate
fosfato ácido de
manganeso
mangenese hydroxide
hidróxido de
manganeso

manganese
hypophosphite
hipofosfito de
manganeso
manganese iodide
yoduro de manganeso
manganese linoleate
linoleato de manganeso
manganese monoxide
monóxido de
manganeso
manganese
naphthenate
naftenato de
manganeso
manganese nitrate
nitrato de manganeso
manganese octoate
octoato de manganeso
manganese oleate
oleato de manganeso
manganese oxalate
oxalato de manganeso
manganese oxide
óxido de manganeso
manganese peroxide
peróxido de
manganeso
manganese phosphate
fosfato de manganeso
manganese phosphate,
dibasic
fosfato dibásico de
manganeso
manganese protoxide
protóxido de
manganeso
manganese
pyrophosphate
pirofosfato de
manganeso
manganese resinate
resinato de manganeso
manganese selenide
seleniuro de
manganeso
manganese
sesquioxide
sesquióxido de
manganeso
manganese silicate
silicato de manganeso
manganese stearate
estearato de
manganeso
manganese sulfate
sulfato de manganeso
manganese sulfide
sulfuro de manganeso

manganese sulfite
sulfito de manganeso
manganese tallate
talato de manganeso
manganese tetraoxide
tetraóxido de
manganeso
manganese trifluoride
trifluoruro de
manganeso
manganese-boron
manganeso y boro
manganese-titanium
manganeso y titanio
manganic
acetylacetonate
acetilacetonato
mangánico
manganic fluoride
fluoruro mangánico
manganic hydroxide
hidróxido mangánico
manganic oxide
óxido mangánico
manganic oxide,
hydrated
óxido mangánico
hidratado
manganite
manganita
manganous ammonium
sulfate
sulfato manganoso de
amonio
manganous arsenate
arseniato manganoso
manganous bromide
bromuro manganoso
manganous carbonate
carbonato manganoso
manganous chloride
cloruro manganoso
manganous chromate
cromato manganoso
manganous citrate
citrato manganoso
manganous fluoride
fluoruro manganoso
manganous hydroxide
hidróxido manganoso
manganous iodide
yoduro manganoso
manganous nitrate
nitrato manganoso
manganous
orthophosphate
ortofosfato manganoso
manganous oxide
óxido manganoso

manganous phosphate
fosfato manganoso
manganous phosphate acid
fosfato manganoso ácido
manganous pyrophosphate
pirofosfato manganoso
manganous silicate
silicato manganoso
manganous sulfate
sulfato manganoso
manganous sulfide
sulfuro manganoso
manganous sulfite
sulfito manganoso
mangostin
mangostina
Manila fiber
cáñamo de Manila, fibra de abacá
Manila resin
resina de Manila
manna
maná
Mannheim furnace
horno Mannheim
Mannich reaction
reacción de Mannich
mannite
manita, manitol
mannitol
manitol, manita
mannitol hexanitrate
hexanitrato de manitol
mannomustine
manomustina
mannose
manosa, manitosa
mannosulfan
manosulfano
manozodil
manozodil
manufacture
producción, fabricación, manufactura
manufacturer
fabricante
manufacturing process
proceso de producción, proceso de fabricación, proceso de manufactura
manufacturing source
sitio de producción, fabricación, manufactura; lugar de

producción, fabricación, manufactura
maprotiline
maprotilina
maprotiline hydrochloride
clorhidrato de maprotilina
Marathon-Howard process
método de Marathon y Howard
marble
mármol
marbofloxacin
marbofloxacina
marfanil
marfanilo
margaric acid
ácido margárico, ácido heptadecanoico
maridomycin
maridomicina
marihuana
marihuana
marijuana
marihuana
mariptiline
mariptilina
marjoram oil
esencia (aceite) de mejorana
Markownikoff rule
regla de Markownikoff
maroon
rojo oscuro
marrubiin
marrubiína
marsh gas
gas de los pantanos
Mars red
rojo Marte
martensite
martensita
Martinet dioxindol synthesis
síntesis de dioxindol de Martinet
martonite
martonita
masonry cement
cemento de mampostería
mass
masa
mass action law
ley de acción de masas

mass conservation law
ley de conservación de la masa
mass defect
defecto de masa
mass number
número de masa
mass production
producción en serie
mass spectrometry
espectrometría de masa
mass spectrum
espectro de masa
massicot
masicote, monóxido de plomo
master batch
lote matriz, mezcla madre
mastic
masilla, lentisco, mástico, almáciga, alfóncigo, alfónsigo
maté
yerba mate
material
material
material balance
equilibrio de materiales
materials handling
manejo de materiales
matico
mático, matico
matrass
matraz
matricaria
matricaria
matricarin
matricarina
matrine
matrina
matrix
matriz
matter
materia, sustancia
mauve
lila
mauveine
malveína, violeta de anilina
maximum output
capacidad máxima
maximum speed
velocidad máxima, rendimiento máximo
Mayer's reagent
reactivo de Mayer
maytansine
maitansina

mazaticol
mazaticol
mazindol
macindol
mazipredone
macipredona
McFadyen-Stevens reaction
reacción de McFadyen y Stevens
McLafferty rearrangement
transposición de McLafferty
mean
media
mean value
valor medio
mean free path
recorrido libre medio
measurable
mensurable, que puede medirse
measure
medida
measuring glass
probeta
mebamazine
mebamacina, mebamazina
mebendazole
mebendazol
mebenoside
mebenósido
mebeverine
mebeverina
mebezonium iodide
yoduro de mebezonio
mebehydrolin
mebehidrolina
mebhydroline
mebhidrolina
mebiquine
mebiquina
mebolazine
mebolacina, mebolazina
mebrofenin
mebrofenina
mebutamate
mebutamato
mebutizide
mebutizida
mecamylamine
mecamilamina
mecamylamine hydrochloride
clorhidrato de mecamilamina

mecarbam
mecarbán, mecarbam
mecarbinate
mecarbinato
mechanochemistry
mecanoquímica,
química mecánica
mechlorethamine
mecloretamina
mechlorethamine
hydrochloride
clorhidrato de
mecloretamina
mechlorethamine oxide
hydrochloride
clorhidrato de
oximecloretamina
mecinarone
mecinarona
meclizine
meclicina, meclizina
meclizine
hydrochloride
clorhidrato de
meclicina, clorhidrato
de meclizina
meclocycline
meclociclina
meclofenamate sodium
meclofenamato sódico
meclofenamic acid
ácido meclofenámico
meclofenoxate
meclofenoxato
meclofenoxate
hydrochloride
clorhidrato de
meclofenoxato
meclonazepam
meclonacepán,
meclonazepam
mecloqualone
meclocualona
mecloralurea
mecloralurea
meclorisone
meclorisona
mecloxamine
mecloxamina
meclozine
meclocina, meclozina
mecobalamin
mecobalamina
meconic acid
ácido mecónico
meconin
meconina
mecoprop
mecoprop

mecrylate
mecrilato
mecysteine
mecisteína
mecysteine
hydrochloride
clorhidrato de
mecisteína
medazepam
medacepán,
medazepam
medazepam
hydrochloride
clorhidrato de
medacepán, clorhidrato
de medazepam
medazomide
medazomida
medetomidine
medetomidina
medibazine
medibacina,
medibazina
medicagol
medicagol
medicinal chemistry
química medicinal
medixofamine
medixofamina
medmain
medmaína
medorubicin
medorrubicina
medrogestone
medrogestona
medronic acid
ácido medrónico
medroxalol
medroxalol
medroxyprogesterone
medroxiprogesterona
medroxyprogesterone
acetate
acetato de medroxi-
progesterona
medrylamine
medrilamina
medrysone
medrisona
Meerwein-Ponndorf-
Verley reduction
reducción de
Meerwein, Ponndorf y
Verley
meet, to
satisfacer, cumplir con
mefeclorazine
mefecloracina,
mefeclonazina

mefenamic acid
ácido mefenámico
mefenorex
mefenorex
mefeserpine
mefeserpina
mefexamide
mefexamida
mefloquine
mefloquina
mefloquine
hydrochloride
clorhidrato de
mefloquina
mefluidide
mefluidida
mefruside
mefrusida
megallate
megalato
megacins
megacinas
megalomicin
megalomicina
megatomoic acid
ácido megatomoico
megaton
megatonelada,
megatón, un millón de
toneladas
megestrol
megestrol
megestrol acetate
acetato de megestrol
meglitinide
meglitinido
meglucycline
megluciclina
meglumine
meglumina
meglumine acetrizoate
acetrizoato de
meglumina
meglumine diatrizoate
diatrizoato de
meglumina
meglutol
meglutol
Meisenheimer
complexes
complejos de
Meisenheimer
Meisenheimer
rearrangement
transposición de
Meisenheimer
meladrazine
meladracina,
meladrazina

melamine
melamina, 2,4,6-
triamino-s-triazina
melamine resin
resina de melamina
melaniline
melanilina
melanin
melanina
melanostatin
melanostatina
melarsonyl potassium
potasio melarsonílico,
melarsonil potásico
melarsoprol
melarsoprol
melatonin
melatonina
Meldrum's acid
ácido de Meldrum
melengestrol
melengestrol
meletimide
meletimida
melezitose
melecitosa
melibiose
melibiosa
melilot
meliloto, trébol dulce
melilotoside
melilotósido
melinamide
melinamida
melinonine A
melinonina A
melissic acid
ácido melísico
melissyl alcohol
alcohol melisílico
melitracen
melitraceno
melittin
melitina
melizame
melizamo
mellitic acid
ácido melítico
melperone
melperona
melphalan
melfalano, melfalán
melt index
índice de fusión
melting point
punto de fusión,
temperatura de fusión
melting range
zona de fusión

memantine
memantina
membrane cell
célula de membrana
membrane,
semipermeable
membrana
semipermeable
memtetrahydro-
phthalic anhydride
anhídrido mentetra-
hidroftálico
menadiol diacetate
diacetato de menadiol
menadiol dibutyrate
dibutirato de
menadiol
menadiol diphosphate
(tetrasodium salt)
difosfato de menadiol
(sal tetrasódica)
menadiol disulfate
disulfato de menadiol
menadiol sodium
sulfate
sulfato sódico de
menadiol
menadione
menadiona
menadione
dimethylpyrimidol
bisulfite
bisulfito de
dimetilpirimidol
menadiona
menadione sodium
bisulfite
bisulfito sódico de
menadiona
menadoxime
menadoxima
menatetrenone
menatetrenona
menazon
menazona
menbutone
membutona
mendelevium
mendelevio, Md
menfegol
menfegol
menglytate
menglitato
menhaden oil
aceite de sábalo
menichlopholan
meniclofolano
meniscus
menisco

menitrazepam
menitracepán,
menitrazepam
menoctone
menoctona
menotropins
menotropinas
Menschutkin reaction
reacción de
Menschutkin
menthanediamine
mentandiamina
p-menthane-8-
hydroperoxide
8-hidroperóxido de p-
mentano
p-menthan-3-one
p-mentan-3-ona
menthol
mentol
menthol acetic ester
éster mentolacético
menthol valerate
valerato de mentol,
valerianato de mentol
menthone
mentona
menthyl acetate
acetato de mentilo
menthyl borate
borato de mentilo
menthyl isovalerate
isovalerato de mentilo
menthyl salicylate
salicilato de mentilo
menthyl valerate
valerato de mentilo,
valerianato de mentilo
meobentine
meobentina
mepacrine
mepacrina
meparfynol
meparfinol
meparfynol carbamate
carbamato de
meparfinol
mepartricin
mepartricina
mepazine
mepacina, mepazina
mepazine
hydrochoride
clorhidrato de
mepacina, clorhidrato
de mepazina
mepenzolate bromide
bromuro de
mepenzolato

meperidine
hydrochloride
clorhidrato de
meperidina
mephenesin
mefenesina
mephenhydramine
mefenhidramina
mephenoxalone
mefenoxalona
mephentermine
mefentermina,
N-α,α-trimetil-
fenetilamina
mephenytoin
mefenitoína
mephobarbital
mefobarbital
mephosfolan
mefosfolano,
mefosfalán
mepindonol
mepindonol
mepiprazole
mepiprazol
mepiquat chloride
cloruro de mepiquat
mepiroxol
mepiroxol
mepitiostane
mepitiostano
mepivacaine
mepivacaína
mepixanox
mepixanox
mepramidil
mepramidil
meprednisone
meprednisona
meprobamate
meprobamato
meproscillarin
meproscilarina
meprotixol
meprotixol
meprylcaine
meprilcaína
meprylcaine
hydrochloride
clorhidrato de
meprilcaína
meptazinol
meptacinol
mepyramine
mepiramina
mequidox
mequidox
mequinol
mequinol

mequitazine
mequitacina,
mequitazina
meralein sodium
meraleína sódica
meralluride
meralurida
merbromin
merbromina
mercamphamide
mercanfamida
mercaptamine
mercaptamina
mercaptan
mercaptán
mercaptoacetic acid
ácido mercapto-
acético
2-mercaptobenzoic
acid
ácido 2-mercapto-
benzoico
mercaptobenzo-
thiazole
mercaptobenzotiazol
2-mercaptobenzo-
thiazole acid
ácido 2-mercapto-
benzotiazólico
2-mercaptobenzo-
thiazyl disulfide
disulfuro de 2-
mercaptobenzotiacilo
mercaptobutanedioic
acid
ácido mercapto-
butandioico
2-mercaptoethanol
2-mercaptoetanol
ß-mercaptoethylamine
hydrochloride
clorhidrato de ß-
mercaptoetilamina
N-(2-mercaptoethyl)-
benzenesulfonamide
bencenosulfonamida
N-(2-mercaptoetílica)
N-(2-mercaptoethyl)
benzenesulfonamide
S-(O,O-diisopropyl-
phosphorodithionate)
S-(O,O-diisopropil-
fosforoditionato) de N-
(2-mercaptoetil)
bencenosulfonamida
2-mercapto-
imidazoline
2-mercapto-
imidazolina

176

mercaptomerin
mercaptomerina
mercaptomerin sodium
mercaptomerina sódica
ß-mercaptopropionic
acid
ácido ß-mercapto-
propiónico
6-mercaptopurine
6-mercaptopurina
mercaptosuccinic acid
ácido mercapto-
succínico
2-mercaptothiazoline
2-mercaptotiazolina
D-3-mercaptovaline
D-3-mercaptovalina
mercerized cotton
algodón mercerizado
mercerizing assistant
auxiliar de la
mercerización
mercuderamine
mercuderamina
mercufenol chloride
cloruro de mercufenol
mercumallylic acid
ácido mercumalílico
mercumatilin sodium
mercumatilina sódica
mercuric
mercúrico
mercuric acetate
acetato mercúrico
mercuric ammonium
chloride
cloruro mercúrico de
amonio, cloruro de
amonio mercúrico
mercuric arsanilate
arsanilato mercúrico
mercuric arsenate
arseniato mercúrico
mercuric barium
bromide
bromuro mercúrico de
bario, bromuro de
bario mercúrico
mercuric barium
iodide
yoduro mercúrico de
bario, yoduro de bario
mercúrico
mercuric benzoate
benzoato mercúrico
mercuric bromide
bromuro mercúrico
mercuric chloride
cloruro mercúrico

mercuric chloride,
ammoniated
cloruro mercúrico
amoniacal
mercuric cuprous
iodide
yoduro cuproso
mercúrico
mercuric cyanate
cianato mercúrico
mercuric cyanide
cianuro mercúrico
mercuric dichromate
dicromato mercúrico
mercuric dimethyl-
dithiocarbamate
dimetilditiocarbamato
mercúrico
mercuric dioxylsulfate
dioxilsulfato mercúrico
mercuric fluoride
fluoruro mercúrico
mercuric iodate
yodato mercúrico
mercuric iodide
yoduro mercúrico
mercuric lactate
lactato mercúrico
mercuric naphthenate
naftenato mercúrico
mercuric nitrate
nitrato mercúrico
mercuric oleate
oleato mercúrico
mercuric oxide
óxido mercúrico
mercuric oxide, red
óxido mercúrico rojo
mercuric oxide, yellow
óxido mercúrico
amarillo
mercuric oxycyanide
oxicianuro mercúrico
mercuric phosphate
fosfato mercúrico
mercuric potassium
cyanide
cianuro mercúrico de
potasio, cianuro de
potasio mercúrico
mercuric potassium
iodide
yoduro mercúrico de
potasio, yoduro de
potasio mercúrico
mercuric salicylate
salicilato mercúrico
mercuric silver iodide
yoduro mercúrico de

plata, yoduro de plata
mercúrico
mercuric sodium p-
phenosulfonate
p-fenosulfonato
mercúrico de sodio, p-
fenosulfonato de sodio
mercúrico
mercuric stearate
estearato mercúrico
mercuric subsulfate
subsulfato mercúrico
mercuric succinimide
succinimida mercúrica
mercuric sulfate
sulfato mercúrico
mercuric sulfate, basic
sulfato mercúrico
básico
mercuric sulfide,
black
sulfuro mercúrico
negro
mercuric sulfide, red
sulfuro mercúrico rojo
mercuric thiocyanate
tiocianato mercúrico
mercurobutol
mercurobutol
mercurol
mercurol
mercurophen
mercurofeno
mercurophylline
mercurofilina
mercurous
mercurioso
mercurous acetate
acetato mercurioso
mercurous acetylide
acetiluro mercurioso
mercurous bromide
bromuro mercurioso
mercurous chlorate
clorato mercurioso
mercurous chloride
cloruro mercurioso
mercurous chromate
cromato mercurioso
mercurous fluoride
fluoruro mercurioso
mercurous iodide
yoduro mercurioso
mercurous nitrate
hydrated
nitrato mercurioso
hidratado
mercurous oxide
óxido mercurioso

mercurous sulfate
sulfato mercurioso
mercury
mercurio
mercury ammoniated
mercurio amoniacal
mercury atoxylate
atoxilato de mercurio
mercury bichloride
bicloruro de mercurio
mercury cell
pila de mercurio
mercury chloride
cloruro de mercurio
(sublimado corrosivo)
mercury compounds
compuestos de
mercurio
mercury dichromate
dicromato de mercurio
mercury fulminate
fulminato de mercurio
mercury mass
masa de mercurio,
masa azul
mercury selenide
seleniuro de mercurio
mercury telluride
telururo de mercurio
mercury thiocyanate
tiocianato de mercurio
merethoxylline
procaine
procaína
meretoxilínica
merisoprol
merisoprol
merisoprol Hg 197
merisoprol Hg 197
merocyanine
merocianina
meropenem
meropenem,
meropenem
merphyrin
merfirina
Merrifield solid-phase
peptide synthesis
síntesis de péptidos en
fase sólida de
Merrifield
mersalyl
mersalilo
mesabolone
mesabolona
mesaconic acid
ácido mesacónico
mesalamine
mesalamina

mescaline
mescalina, 3,4,5-
trimetoxifenetilamina
meseclazone
meseclazona
mesembrine
mesembrina
mesh
malla (de red, de
tamiz), reticulado
mesilate
mesilato
mesityl oxide
óxido de mesitilo,
óxido mesitílico
mesitylene
mesitileno
2-mesitylenesulfonyl
chloride
cloruro de 2-
mesitilensulfonilo
mesna
mesna
meso-
meso-
mesocarb
mesocarbo
mesomerism
mesomerismo
mesomorphic
mesomórfico
mesoridazine
mesorridacina,
mesorridazina
mesoridazine
besylate
besilato de
mesorridacina, besilato
de mesoridazina
mesothorium
mesotorio
mesoxalic acid
ácido mesoxálico
mesquite gum
resina de mezquita
messenger RNA
ARN (ácido
ribonucleico)
mensajero
mestanolone
mestanolona
mesterolone
mesterolona
mestilbol
mestilbol
mestranol
mestranol
mesudipine
mesudipino

mesulergine
mesulergina
mesulfamide
mesulfamida
mesulphen
mesulfeno
mesuprine
mesuprina
mesuximide
mesuximida
mesyl chloride
cloruro de mesilo,
cloruro mesílico
meta-
meta-
metabisulfite
metabisulfito
metabolism
metabolismo
metabolite
metabolito
metaboric acid
ácido metabórico
metabromsalan
metabromosalán
metabutoxycaine
hydrochloride
clorhidrato de
metabutoxicaína
metacetamol
metacetamol
metacetone
metacetona
metachrome yellow
amarillo
metacrómico
metaclazepam
metaclacepán,
metaclazepam
metacrylates
metacrilatos
metacycline
metaciclina
metacyclophane
metaciclofano
metaformaldehyde
metaformaldehído
metaglycodol
metaglicodol
metahexamide
metahexamida
metal
metal
metal deactivator
desactivador de metal
metal dye
colorante metálico
metal fiber
fibra metálica

metal glass
vidrio metálico
metal, powdered
metal pulverizado,
metal en polvo
metalaxyl
metalaxil, metalaxilo
metaldehyde
metaldehído
metallibure
metalibura
metallic soap
jabón metálico
metallized dyes
colorantes metalizados
metallizing
metalización
metallocene
metaloceno
metalloid
metaloide
metallurgical coke
coque metalúrgico
metamelfalan
metamelfalán
metameric
metamérico
metamfazone
metanfazona
metamfepramone
metanfepramona
metamitron
metamitrón
metampicillin
metampicilina
metandienone
metandienona
metanephrine
metanefrina
metanilic acid
ácido metanílico
metanil yellow
amarillo metanilo
metanixin
metanixina
metaphanine
metafanina
metapon
metapona
metapramine
metapramina
metaproterenol
metaproterenol
metaproterenol
sulfate
sulfato de
metaproterenol
metaraminol
metaraminol

metaraminol bitartrate
bitartrato de
metaraminol
metaterol
metaterol
metaxalone
metaxalona
metazamide
metazamida
metazide
metazida
metazocine
metazocina
metbufen
metbufeno
metcaraphen
metcarafeno
metembonate
metembonato
meteneprost
meteneprost
metenolone
metenolona
meteloidine
meteloidina
metepa
metepa
meter
metro
metergoline
metergolina
metergotamine
metergotamina
metescufylline
metescufilina
metesculetol
metesculetol
metethoheptazine
metetoheptacina,
metetoheptazina,
metetoin
metetoína
metformin
metformina
metformin
hydrochloride
clorhidrato de
metformina
methabenzthiazuron
metabenzotiazurona
methacetin
metacetina
methacholine bromide
bromuro de
metacolina
methacholine chloride
cloruro de metacolina
methacrifos
metacrifós

methacrolein
metacroleína
methachrome yellow
amarillo metacrómico
methacrylaldehyde
aldehído metacrílico,
metacrilaldehído
methacrylamide
amida metacrílica,
metacrilamina
methacrylamido-
propyltrimethyl-
ammonium chloride
cloruro de
metacrilamido
propiltrimetil amonio
methacrylate ester
éster de metacrilato
methacrylate resin
resina de metacrilato
methacrylatochromic
chloride
cloruro de metacrilato
crómico
methacrylic acid
ácido metacrílico
ß-methacrylic acid
ácido ß-metacrílico
methacrylonitrile
metacrilonitrilo
Υ-methacryloxy-
propyltrimethoxy-
silane
Υ-metacriloxipropil-
trimetoxisilano
methacryloyl chloride
cloruro de metacriloílo
methacycline
metaciclina
methadone
metadona
methadone
hydrochloride
clorhidrato de
metadona
methadyl acetate
acetato de metadilo
methafurylene
metafurileno
methallenestril
metalenestrilo
methallibure
metaliburo
methallyl acetate
acetato de metalilo
methallyl alcohol
alcohol metalílico
ß-methallyl chloride
cloruro de ß-metalilo

methallylidene
diacetate
diacetato de
metalilideno
methamidophos
metamidofós
methamphetamine
metanfetamina
methamphetamine
hydrochloride
clorhidrato de
metanfetamina
methampyrone
metampirona
metham sodium
metam sódico,
metilditiocarbamato de
sodio
methanal
metanal
methanamide
metanamida
methandriol
metandriol
methandrostenolone
metandrostenolona
methandrosterone
metandrosterona
methane
metano
methanearsonic acid
ácido metanarsónico
methanearsonic acid,
disilver salt
sal diargéntica del
ácido metanarsónico
methanearsonic acid,
disodium salt
sal disódica del ácido
metanarsónico
methanecarboxylic
acid
ácido metan-
carboxílico
methanedicarbonic
acid
ácido metan-
dicarbónico
methanedicarboxylic
acid
ácido metandi-
carboxílico
methanesulfonic
acid
ácido metansulfónico
methanesulfonyl
chloride
cloruro de
metansulfonilo

methanethiol
metanotiol
methane
thiomethane
metantiometano
methaniazide
metaniazida
methanilic acid
ácido metanílico
methanoic acid
ácido metanoico
methanol
metanol
methantheline
bromide
bromuro de
metantelina
methanthelinium
bromide
bromuro de
metantelinio
methaphenilene
metafenileno
methapyrilene
metapirileno
methaqualone
metacualona
metharbital
metarbital
methargen
metargeno
methastyridone
metastiridona
methazolamide
metazolamida
methazole
metazol
methcathinone
metcatinona
methdilazine
metdilacina,
metdilazina
methemoglobin
metahemoglobina
methenamine
metenamina
methenamine allyl
iodide
yoduro de
metenaminalilo
methenamine
anhydromethylenecitrate
anhidrometilen-
citrato de
metenamina
methenamine
hippurate
hipurato de
metenamina

methenamine
mandelate
mandelato de
metenamina
methenamine salycilate
salicilato de
metenamina
methenamine
sulfosalycilate
sulfosalicilato de
metenamina
methenamine
tetraiodine
tetrayodo
metenamínico
methene
meteno
methenolone
metenolona
methenyl tribromide
tribromuro de metenilo
metheptazine
meteptacina,
meteptazina
methestrol
metestrol
methetoin
metetoína
methicillin
meticilina
methicillin sodium
meticilina sódica
methidathion
metidatión
methimazole
metimazol
methiocarb
metiocarbo
methiodal sodium
metiodal sódico
methiomeprazine
metiomepracina,
metiomeprazina
methionic acid
ácido metiónico
methionine
metionina
methionine hydroxy
analog
análogo de
hidroximetionina
methioprim
metioprima
methiotepa
metiotepa
methisazone
metisazona
methitural
metitural

methixene
metixeno
methixene
hydrochloride
clorhidrato de
metixeno
methocarbamol
metocarbamol
methocidin
metocidina
method of analysis
método de análisis
methohexital
metohexital
methohexital sodium
metohexital sódico
methomyl
metomilo
methoprene
metopreno
methopromazine
metopromacina,
metopromazina
methopterin
metopterina
methoserpidine
metoserpidina
methotrexate
metotrexato
methotrexate sodium
metotrexato sódico
methotrimeprazine
metotrimeprazina,
metotrimepazina
methoxamine
metoxamina
methoxamine
hydrochloride
clorhidrato de
metoxamina
methoxsalen
metoxsaleno
methoxyacetaldehyde
metoxiacetaldehído
methoxyacetic acid
ácido metoxiacético
p-methoxyaceto-
phenone
p-metoxiacetofenona
methoxyacetyl-p-
phenetidine
p-fenetidina
metoxiacetílica
methoxyamine
metoxiamina
methoxybenzaldehyde
metoxibenzaldehído
methoxybenzene
metoxibenceno

p-methoxybenzoic
acid
ácido p-metoxi-
benzoico
p-methoxybenzyl
acetate
acetato de p-metoxi-
bencilo, acetato p-
metoxibencílico
p-methoxybenzyl
alcohol
alcohol p-metoxi-
bencílico
p-methoxybenzyl
formate
formiato de p-
metoxibencilo,
formiato p-
metoxibencílico
2-methoxy-4,6-bis-
(isopropylamino)-
s-triazine
2-metoxi-4,6-bis-
(isopropilamino)-s-
triacina, 2-metoxi-4,6-
bis-(iso-propilamino)-
s-triazina
3-methoxybutanol
3-metoxibutanol
1-methoxycarbonyl-1-
propen-1-yl
dimethylphosphate
dimetilfosfato de 1-
metoxicarbonil-1-
propen-1-ilo
methoxychlor
metoxicloro, 1,1,1-
tricloro-2,2-bis(p-
metoxifenil)etano
2-methoxy-3,6-di-
chlorobenzoic acid
ácido 2-metoxi-3,6-
diclorobenzoico
2-methoxy-3,6-
dichlorobenzoic acid,
dimethylamine salt
sal dimetilamínica del
ácido 2-metoxi-3,6-
diclorobenzoico
2-(ß-methoxyethoxy)
ethanol
2-(ß-metoxietoxi)
etanol
methoxyethylene
metoxietileno
2-methoxyethyl-
mercury acetate
acetato de 2-metoxi-
etilmercurio

methoxyethyl oleate
oleato de metoxietilo,
oleato metoxietílico
methoxyethyl stearate
estearato de
metoxietilo, estearato
metoxietílico
methoxyflurane
metoxiflurano
methoxyharmalan
metoxiharmalano
3-methoxy-4-hydroxy-
benzaldehyde
3-metoxi-4-hidroxi-
benzaldehído
methoxyhydroxy-
mercuripropylsuccinyl
urea
metoxihidroxi-
mercuripropil-
succinilurea
3-methoxy-4-
hydroxyphenylglycol
3-metoxi-4-hidroxi-
fenilglicol
4'-methoxy-2-(p-
methoxyphenyl)
acetophenone
4'-metoxi-2-(p-
metoxifenil)
acetofenona
2-methoxy-5-
methylaniline
2-metoxi-5-
metilanilina
2-(methoxymethyl)-5-
nitrofuran
2-(metoximetil)-5-
nitrofurano
4-methoxy-4-
methylpentanol-2
4-metoxi-4-metil-
pentanol-2
4-methoxy-4-methyl-
pentanone-2,4
4-metoxi-4-metil-
pentanona-2,4
2-methoxy-4-
methylphenol
2-metoxi-4-metilfenol
2-methoxy-
naphthalene
2-metoxinaftaleno
1-methoxy-4-
nitrobenzene
1-metoxi-4-
nitrobenceno
methoxyphedrine
metoxifedrina

methoxyphenamine
metoxifenamina
4-methoxyphenol
4-metoxifenol
3-(o-methoxy-
phenoxy)-1,2-
propanediol-1-
carbamate
1-carbamato de 3-(o-
metoxifenoxi)-1,2-
propandiol
p-methoxyphenyl-
acetic acid
ácido p-metoxi-
fenilacético
p-methoxyphenyl-
butanone
p-metoxifenilbutanona
4-methoxy-m-
phenylene diamine
4-metoxi-m-
fenilendiamina
methoxypolyethylene
glycol
glicol metoxi-
polietilénico
3-(o-methoxyphenyl)-
2-phenylacrylic acid
ácido 3-(o-metoxi-
fenil)-2-fenilacrílico
N-(p-methoxyphenyl)-
phenylenediamine
N-(p-metoxifenil)-
fenilendiamina
methoxypromazine
metoxipromacina,
metoxipromazina
methoxypropanol
metoxipropanol
p-methoxypropenyl-
benzene
p-metoxipropenil-
benceno
p-methoxypropio-
phenone
p-metoxipropiofenona
3-methoxypropyl-
amine
3-metoxipropilamina
8-methoxypsoralen
8-metoxipsoraleno
6-methoxy-α-tetralone
6-metoxi-α-tetralona
p-methoxytoluene
p-metoxitolueno
p-methoxy-α-toluic
acid
ácido p-metoxi-α-
toluídico

methoxytriethylene
glycol acetate
acetato de glicol
metoxitrietilénico
methoxytriglycol
metoxitriglicol
methoxytriglycol
acetate
acetato de
metoxitriglicol
1-methoxy-3-
(trimethylsilyloxy)-1,3-
butadiene
1-metoxi-3-
(trimetilsililoxi)-1,3-
butadieno
5-methoxytryptamine
5-metoxitriptamina
methscopolamine
bromide
bromuro de
metescopolamina
methscopolamine
nitrate
nitrato de
metescopolamina
methsuximide
metsuximida, N-2-
dimetil-2-fenil-
succinimida
methyclothiazide
meticlotiazida
methyl
metilo
methyl abietate
abietato de metilo,
abietato metílico
methyl acetate
acetato de metilo,
acetato metílico
methyl acetic acid
ácido metilacético
methyl acetoacetate
acetoacetato de metilo,
acetoacetato metílico
methyl acetone
acetona metílica
methyl acetylene
acetileno metílico
methyl acetylene-
propadiene, stabilized
acetileno metílico-
propadieno,
estabilizado
methyl acetyl-
ricinoleate
acetilricinoleato de
metilo, acetilricinoleato
metílico

methyl acetylsalicylate
acetilsalicilato de
metilo, acetilsalicilato
metílico
methyl acid phosphate
fosfato ácido de metilo
methyl acrylate
acrilato de metilo,
acrilato metílico
methyl alcohol
alcohol metílico
ß-methyl allyl chloride
cloruro de ß-metilalilo,
cloruro ß-metilalílico
methyl allyl trisulfide
trisulfuro de metilalilo,
trisulfuro metilalílico
methyl anthranilate
antranilato de metilo,
antranilato metílico
methyl apholate
afolato de metilo,
afolato metílico
methyl arachidate
araquidato de metilo,
araquidato metílico
methyl arecaidinate
arecaidinato de metilo,
arecaidinato metílico
methyl azinphos
azinfós metílico
methyl behenate
behenato de metilo,
behenato metílico
methyl blue
azul de metilo
methyl borate
borato de metilo,
borato metílico
methyl bromide
bromuro de metilo,
bromuro metílico
methyl bromoacetate
bromoacetato de
metilo, bromoacetato
metílico
methyl benzoate
benzoato de metilo,
benzoato metílico
methyl benzoyl-
salicylate
benzoilsalicilato de
metilo, benzoil-
salicilato metílico
methyl butyl ketone
cetona
metilbutílica
methyl butynol
butinol metílico

methyl butyrate
butirato de metilo,
butirato metílico
methyl caprate
caprato de metilo,
caprato metílico
methyl caproate
caproato de metilo,
caproato metílico
methyl caprylate
caprilato de metilo,
caprilato metílico
methyl carbamate
carbamato de metilo,
carbamato metílico
methyl carbonate
carbonato de metilo,
carbonato metílico
methyl ceroate
ceroato de metilo,
ceroato metílico
methyl chloride
cloruro de metilo,
cloruro metílico
methyl chloroacetate
cloracetato de metilo,
cloracetato metílico
methyl chloro-
carbonate
clorocarbonato de
metilo, clorocarbonato
metílico
methyl chloroform
cloroformo metílico
methyl chloroformate
cloroformiato de
metilo, cloroformiato
metílico
methyl chlorosilane
metilclorosilano,
clorosilano metílico
methyl chloro-
sulfonate
clorosulfonato de
metilo, clorosulfonato
metílico
methyl cinnamate
cinamato de metilo,
cinamato metílico
methyl cyanide
cianuro de metilo,
cianuro metílico
methyl
cyanoacetate
cianoacetato de metilo,
cianoacetato metílico
methyl cyano-
ethanoate
cianoetanoato de

metilo, cianoetanoato
metílico
methyl cyanoformate
cianoformiato de
metilo
methyl decanoate
decanoato de metilo,
decanoato metílico
methyl demeton
demetona metílica
methyl dichloracetate
dicloracetato de metilo,
dicloracetato metílico
methyl dichloroarsine
diclorarsina metílica
methyl dichloro-
stearate
diclorestearato de
metilo, diclorestearato
metílico
methyl diphenyl
phosphate
fosfato de
metildifenilo, fosfato
metildifenílico
methyl docosanoate
docosanoato de metilo,
docosanoato metílico
methyl dodecanoate
dodecanoato de metilo,
dodecanoato metílico
methyl eicosanoate
eicosanoato de metilo,
eicosanoato metílico
methyl elaidate
elaidato de metilo,
elaidato metílico
methyl ester
éster metílico
methyl ether
éter metílico
methyl ethyl diketone
dicetona metiletílica
methyl ethyl ketone
cetona metiletílica
methyl ethyl ketone
peroxide
peróxido de cetona
metiletílica
methyl eugenol
metileugenol, eugenol
metílico
methyl fluoride
fluoruro de metilo,
fluoruro metílico
methyl fluorosulfonate
fluorosulfonato de
metilo, fluoro-
sulfonato metílico

methyl formate
formiato de metilo,
formiato metílico
methyl fuel
combustible de metilo,
combustible metílico
methyl gallate
galato de metilo, galato
metílico
α-methyl glucoside
α-metilglucósido,
glucósido α-metílico
methyl glycocoll
glicocola metílica
methyl glycol
glicol metílico
methyl green
verde de metilo
methyl group
grupo metilo
**methyl heptyne
carbonate**
carbonato de
heptinmetilo,
carbonato
heptinmetílico
methyl hexacosanoate
hexacosanoato de
metilo, hexacosanoato
metílico
methyl hexadecanoate
hexadecanoato de
metilo, hexadecanoato
metílico
methyl heneicosanoate
heneicosanoato de
metilo, heneicosanoato
metílico
**methyl hepta-
decanaoate**
heptadecanoato de
metilo, hepta-
decanoato metílico
methyl hexanoate
hexanoato de metilo,
hexanoato metílico
methyl hexyl ketone
cetona metilhexílica
methyl hydride
hidruro de metilo
methyl iodide
yoduro de metilo,
yóduro metílico
methyl isoamyl ketone
cetona metilisoamílica
**methyl isobutenyl
ketone**
cetona metil-
isobutenílica

methyl isobutyl ketone
cetona metilisobutílica
methyl isobutyrate
isobutirato de metilo,
isobutirato metílico
methyl isocyanate
isocianato de metilo,
isocianato metílico
methyl isonicotinate
isonicotinato de metilo,
isonicotinato metílico
methyl isothiocyanate
isotiocianato de
metilo, isotiocianato
metílico
methyl isovalerate
isovalerato de metilo,
isovalerianato de
metilo
methyl lactate
lactato de metilo,
lactato metílico
methyl actonitrile
metilactonitrilo,
actonitrilo metílico
methyl laurate
laurato de metilo,
laurato metílico
methyl lauroleate
lauroleato de metilo,
lauroleato metílico
methyl lignocerate
lignocerato de metilo,
lignocerato metílico
methyl linoleate
linoleato de metilo,
linoleato metílico
methyl linolenate
linolenato de metilo,
linolenato metílico
methyl malonate
malonato de metilo,
malonato metílico
methyl margarate
margarato de metilo,
margarato metílico
methyl methacrylate
metacrilato de metilo,
metacrilato metílico
**methyl methane-
sulfonate**
metansulfonato de
metilo, metan-
sulfonato metílico
**N-methyl methyl
anthranilate**
antranilato de N-
metilmetilo, antranilato
N-metilmetílico

methyl myristate
miristato de metilo,
miristato metílico
methyl myristoleate
miristoleato de metilo,
miristoleato metílico
methyl naphthyl ether
éter metilnaftílico
methyl nicotinate
nicotinato de metilo,
nicotinato metílico
methyl nitrate
nitrato de metilo,
nitrato metílico
methyl nitrite
nitrito de metilo, nitrito
metílico
methyl nonyl ketone
cetona metilnonílica
**methyl norbornene
dicarboxylic anhydride**
anhídrido
metilnorborneno
dicarboxílico
methyl octadecanoate
octadecanoato de
metilo, octadecanoato
metílico
methyl oleate
oleato de metilo, oleato
metílico
methyl orange
naranja de metilo,
anaranjado de metilo
methyl oxalate
oxalato de metilo,
oxalato metílico
methyl oxide
óxido de metilo, óxido
metílico
methyl palmitate
palmitato de metilo,
palmitato metílico
methyl parathion
metilparatión
methyl PCT
FCT (fosfoclor-
idotionato de O,O-
dimetilo) metílico
methyl pelargonate
pelargonato de metilo,
pelargonato metílico
**methyl penta-
decanoate**
pentadecanoato de
metilo, penta-
decanoato metílico
methyl phenyl ether
éter metilfenílico

**methyl phenyl
phosphate**
fosfato de metilfenilo,
fosfato metilfenílico
**methyl o-phosphoric
acid**
ácido metil o-fosfórico
methyl nonanoate
nonanoato de metilo,
nonanoato metílico
**methyl phthalyl ethyl
glycollate**
glicolato de
metilftaliletilo,
glicolato
metilftaliletílico
methyl picrate
picrato de metilo,
picrato metílico
methyl propionate
propionato de metilo,
propionato metílico
methyl propyl ether
éter metilpropílico
methyl propyl ketone
cetona metilpropílica
**methyl pyridyl
ketone**
cetona metilpiridílica
methyl pyromucate
piromucato de metilo,
piromucato metílico
methyl red
rojo de metilo
methyl resorcinol
resorcinol metílico,
metilresorcinol
methyl ricinoleate
ricinoleato de metilo,
ricinoleato metílico
methyl salicylate
salicilato de metilo,
salicilato metílico
methyl silicone
silicona metílica
methyl silicone resins
resinas de
metilsilicona, resinas
de silicona metílica
methyl stearate
estearato de metilo,
estearato metílico
methyl styryl ketone
cetona metilestirílica
methyl succinic acid
ácido metilsuccínico
methyl sulfate
sulfato de metilo,
sulfato metílico

methyl sulfide
sulfuro de metilo,
sulfuro metílico
methyl tetracosanoate
tetracosanoato de
metilo, tetracosanoato
metílico
methyl tetradecanoate
tetradecanoato de
metilo, tetradecanoato
metílico
**methyl trimethylol-
methane**
metiltrimetilolmetano,
trimetilolmetano
metílico
methyl undecanoate
undecanoato de metilo,
undecanoato metílico
methyl violet
violeta de metilo
methyl yellow
amarillo de metilo
ß-methylacrylic acid
ácido ß-metilacrílico
N-methylacetanilide
acetanilida N-metílica
methylacetophenone
acetofenona metílica
methylacetopyranone
acetopiranona
metílica
ß-methylacrolein
ß-metilacroleína
methylacrylamine
metilacrilamina
methylal
metilal
2-methylalamine
2-metilalamina
2-methylalanine
2-metilalanina
methylallyl acetate
acetato de metilalilo,
acetato metilalílico
methylallyl alcohol
alcohol metilalílico
**methylaluminium
sesquibromide**
sesquibromuro de
metilaluminio,
sesquibromuro de
aluminio metílico
**methylaluminium
sesquichloride**
sesquicloruro de
metilaluminio,
sesquicloruro de
aluminio metílico

methylamine
metilamina
**methylaminoacetic
acid**
ácido metilamino-
acético
**methyl-o-amino-
benzoate**
o-aminobenzoato de
metilo
**methylamino-
dimethylacetal**
metilamino-
dimetilacetal
**1-methylamino-
ethanolcatechol**
catecol 1-metil-
aminoetanólico, 1-
metilaminoetanol-
catecol
**p-methylamino-
ethanolphenol
tartrate**
tartrato de p-metil-
aminoetanolfenol
**2-(methylamino)
glucose**
2-(metilamino) glucosa
**2-methylamino-
heptane**
2-metilaminoheptano
**methyl-m-amino-p-
hydroxy benzoate**
m-amino-p-
hidroxibenzoato de
metilo
**3-methylamino-
isocamphane
hydrochloride**
clorhidrato de 3-
metilaminoisocanfano
**2-methylamino-6-
methyl-5-heptene**
2-metilamino-6-metil-
5-hepteno
**N-methyl-p-
aminophenol**
N-metil-p-aminofenol,
p-aminofenol N-
metílico
**p-methylaminophenol
sulfate**
sulfato de p-
metilaminofenol
methylamylacetate
acetato de metilamilo,
acetato metilamílico
methylamyl alcohol
alcohol metilamílico

**methyl-n-amyl
carbinol**
metil-n-amilcarbinol,
n-amilcarbinol metílico
methyl-n-amylketone
n-amilcetona metílica
N-methylaniline
N-metilanilina
α-methylanisalacetone
anisalacetona α-
metílica
5-methyl-o-anisidine
5-metil-o-anisidina, o-
anisidina 5-metílica
p-methylanisole
p-metilanisol
α-methylanthracene
α-metilantraceno
methylanthraquinone
metilantraquinona
methylarbutin
metilarbutina
methylate
metilato
methylated spirit
alcohol metílico,
alcohol desnaturalizado
**methylbenactyzium
bromide**
bromuro de
metilbenacticio
methylbenzaldehydes
benzaldehídos
metílicos,
metilbenzaldehídos
methylbenzene
metilbenceno
**methylbenzethonium
chloride**
cloruro de
metilbencetonio
methylbenzoic acid
ácido metilbenzoico
methylbenzophenone
metilbenzofenona
**methyl-o-benzoyl-
benzoate**
o-benzoilbenzoato de
metilo, o-
benzoilbenzoato
metílico
α-methylbenzyl acetate
acetato de α-
metilbencilo, acetato
α-metilbencílico
**α-methylbenzyl
alcohol**
alcohol α-metil-
bencílico

α-methylbenzylamine
α-metilbencilamina
**α-methylbenzyl-
diethanolamine**
α-metilbencil-
dietanolamina
**α-methylbenzyl-
dimethylamine**
α-metilbencil-
dimetilamina
**α-methylbenzyl
ether**
éter α-metilbencílico
**methyl-bis(2-chloro-
ethyl)amine-hydrochlo-
ride**
clorhidrato de metil-
bis(2-cloroetil)amina
2-methyl-1,3-butadiene
2-metil-1,3-butadieno
2-methyl-2-butanethiol
2-metil-2-butantiol
2-methyl-1-butanal
2-metil-1-butanal
2-methylbutane
2-metilbutano
2-methyl-1-butanol
2-metil-1-butanol
3-methyl-2-butanone
3-metil-2-butanona
**methylbutanoyl
chloride**
cloruro de
metilbutanoílo
2-methyl-1-butene
2-metil-1-buteno
**cis-2-methyl-2-
butenoic acid**
ácido cis-2-metil-2-
butenoico
**trans-2-methyl-2-
butenoic acid**
ácido trans-2-metil-2-
butenoico
**2-methyl-1-buten-3-
yne**
2-metil-1-buten-3-ino
1-methylbutyl alcohol
alcohol 1-metilbutílico
methyl-tert-butyl ether
éter metil-terc-butílico
N-methylbutylamine
N-metilbutilamina
**2-methyl-6-tert-
butylphenol**
2-metil-6-terc-
butilfenol
2-methylbutyl-3-thiol
2-metilbutil-3-tiol

2-methyl-4-tert-butylthiophenol
2-metil-4-terc-butiltiofenol
2-methylbutyraldehyde
2-metilbutiraldehído
3-methylbutyric acid
ácido 3-metilbutírico
methylcellulose
metilcelulosa
methylcellulose propylene glycol ether
éter propilenglicólico de metilcelulosa
methylchloromethyl ether
éter metilclorometílico
2-methyl-4-chlorophenoxyacetic acid
ácido 2-metil-4-clorofenoxiacético
4-(2-methyl-4-chlorophenoxy)-butyric acid
ácido 4-(2-metil-4-clorofenoxi)butírico
4-(2-methyl-4-chlorophenoxy)-propionic acid
ácido 4-(2-metil-4-clorofenoxi)-propiónico
methylcholanthrene
metilcolantreno
methylclothiazide
metilclotiazida
methylconiine
metilconiína
methylcoumarin
metilcumarina
methyl-p-cresol
metil-p-cresol
methylchromone
metilcromona
cis-α-methylcrotonic acid
ácido cis-α-metilcrotónico
trans-α-methylcrotonic acid
ácido trans-α-metilcrotónico
methyl-2-cyano-acrylate
2-cianoacrilato de metilo

methylcyclohexane
metilciclohexano
methylcyclohexanol
metilciclohexanol
methylcyclohexanol acetate
acetato de metil-ciclohexanol
methylcyclohexanone
metilciclohexanona
methylcyclohexanone glyceryl acetal
metilciclohexanona glicerilacetal
methylcyclohexanyl oxalate
oxalato de metil-ciclohexanilo, oxalato metilciclo-hexanílico
4-methylcyclo-hexene-1
4-metilciclohexeno-1
6-methyl-3-cyclo-hexenecarbox-aldehyde
carboxaldehído 6-metil-3-ciclohexeno
N-methyl-5-cyclo-hexenyl-5-methyl-barbituric acid
ácido N-metil-5-ciclohexenil-5-metilbarbitúrico
N-methylcyclohexyl-amine
N-metilciclohexil-amina, ciclohexil-amina N-metílica
methylcyclo-pentadiene dimer
dímero de metil-ciclopentadieno
methylcyclopenta-dienyl manganese tricarbonyl
tricarbonil metil-ciclopentadienil manganeso
methylcyclopentane
metilciclopentano, ciclopentano metílico
methylcyclo-pentenolone
metilciclo-pentenolona, ciclopentenolona metílica

3'-methyl-1,2-cyclopenteno-phenanthrene
3'-metil-1,2-ciclopentenfenantreno
5-methylcytosine
5-metilcitosina
methyldesorphine
metildesorfina
methyl-3,4-dichloro-carbanilate
3,4-diclorocarbanilato de metilo, 3,4-diclorocarbanilato metílico
methyl-N-3,4-dichlorophenyl-carbamate
N-3,4-diclorofenil-carbamato de metilo, N-3,4-diclorofenil-carbamato metílico
methyldichlorosilane
metildiclorosilano, diclorosilano metílico
methyldiethanol-amine
metildietanolamina, dietanolamina metílica
methyldiethylamine
metildietilamina, dietilamina metílica
4-methyl-7-(diethyl-amino)coumarin
4-metil-7-(dietil-amino)cumarina
methyldihydro-morphine
metildihidromorfina, dihidromorfina metílica
6-methyldihydro-morphine hydrochloride
clorhidrato de 6-metildihidromorfina, clorhidrato de dihidromorfina 6-metílica
3-methyl-2,5-dihydro-thiophene-1,1-dioxide
1,1-dióxido de 3-metil-2,5-dihidrotiofeno
methyl-3-(dimethoxy-phosphinyloxy) crotonate
3-(dimetoxi-fosfiniloxi) crotonato de metilo

methyl-N-3,7-di-methyl-7-hydroxy octyliden-anthranilate
N-3,7-dimetil-7-hidroxioctiliden-antranilato de metilo
methyldioxolane
metildioxolano
p-methyldiphen-hydramine
p-metildifen-hidramina, difenhidramina p-metílica
methyldiphenylamine
metildifenilamina, difenilamina metílica
methyldipropyl-methane
metildipropilmetano, metano metildipropílico
2-methyl-1,2-di-3-pyridyl-1-propanone
2-metil-1,2-di-3-piridil-1-propanona
methyldopa
metildopa
methyldopate hyrochloride
clorhidrato de metildopato
methylene
metileno
methylene azure
azul celeste de metileno
methylene blue
azul de metileno
methylene bromide
bromuro de metileno
methylene chloride
cloruro de metileno
methylene chlorobromide
clorobromuro de metileno
methylene dichloride
dicloruro de metileno
methylene glutaronitrile
metilenglutaronitrilo, glutaronitrilo metilénico
methylene iodide
yoduro de metileno

methylene succinic acid
ácido metilensuccínico

N,N'-methylenebisacrylamine
N,N'-metilenbisacrilamina

4,4'-methylenebis(2-chloroaniline)
4,4'-metilenbis(2-cloroanilina)

p,p'-methylenebis(o-chloroaniline)
p,p'-metilenbis(o-cloroanilina)

2,2'-methylenebis(4-chlorophenol)
2,2'-metilenbis(4-clorofenol)

4,4'-methylenebis-(2,6-tert-butylphenol)
4,4'-metilenbis-(2,6-terc-butil-fenol)

3,3'-methylenebis(4-hydroxycoumarin)
3,3'-metilenebis(4-hidroxicumarina)

methylenebis (phenylisocyanate)
bis(fenilisocianato) de metileno

2,2'-methylenebis (3,4,6-trichlorophenol)
2,2'-metilenbis (3,4,6-triclorofenol)

4,4-methylenedianiline
4,4'-metilendianilina

methylenedigallic acid
ácido metilendigálico

3,4-methylenedioxy benzaldehyde
3,4-metilendioxi-benzaldehído

1,2-(methylenedioxy-4-[2-(octylsulfinyl) propyl]benzene)
1,2-(metilendioxi-4-[2(octilsulfinil)-propil]benceno)

3,4-methylenedioxy-propylbenzene
3,4-metilendioxi-propilbenceno

methylene-di-p-phenylene isocyanate
isocianato de metilen-di-p-fenileno

5,5'-methylene-disalicylic acid
ácido 5,5'-metilen-disalicílico

5-methylene-2-norbornene
5-metileno-2-norborneno

methylene-p-toluidine
metilen-p-toluidina, p-toluidina metilénica

methylenomycins
metilenomicinas

methylephedrine
metilefedrina, efedrina metílica

N-methyl-ephinephrine
N-metilepinefrina

methylergometrine
metilergometrina, ergometrina metílica

methylergonovine maleate
maleato de metilergonovina

N-methylethanol-amine
N-metiletanolamina, etanolamina N-metílica

4-methyl-7-ethoxy-coumarin
4-metil-7-etoxicumarina, 7-etoxicumarina 4-metílica

2-(1-methylethoxy) phenol methyl-carbamate
metilcarbamato de 2-(1-metiletoxi)fenol

methylethylcarbinol
metiletilcarbinol, carbinol metiletílico

methylethylcellulose
metiletilcelulosa, celulosa metiletílica

2-methyl-2-ethyl-1,3-dioxolane
2-metil-2-etil-1,3-dioxolano

sym-methylethyl-ethylene
sim-metiletiletileno

methylethylglyoxal
metiletilglioxal, glioxal metiletílico

methylethylhydantoin formaldehyde resin
resina formaldehídica de metiletilhidantoína, resina formaldehídica de hidantoína metiletílica

2-methyl-5-ethylpyridine
2-metil-5-etilpiridina, 5-etilpiridina 2-metílica

α-methylfentanyl
α-metilfentanilo, fentanilo α-metílico

methylfluorosulfate
fluorosulfato de metilo, fluorosulfato metílico

N-methylformanilide
N-metilformanilida, formanilida N-metílica

2-methylfuran
2-metilfurano, furano 2-metílico

N-methylfurfuryl-amine
N-metilfurfurilamina, furfurilamina N-metílica

methyl-2-furoate
2-furoato de metilo, 2-furoato metílico

N-methylglucamine
N-metilglucamina, glucamina N-metílica

methyl-α-d-glucopyranoside
metil-α-d-glucopiranósido

N-methyl-L-glucosamide
N-metil-L-glucosamida, L-glucosamida N-metílica

methylglyoxanilide
metilglioxanilida, glioxanilida metílica

4-methylguaiacol
4-metilguayacol, guayacol 4-metílico

methylguanidine
metilguanidina, guanidina metílica

N-methyl-N-guanylglycine
N-metil-N-guanilglicina, N-

guanilglicina N-metílica

2-methylheptane
2-metilheptano, heptano 2-metílico

3-methyl-1,4,6-heptatriene
3-metil-1,4,6-heptatrieno, 1,4,6-heptatrieno 3-metílico

methylheptenone
metilheptenona, heptenona metílica

2-(1-methylheptyl)-4,6-dinitrophenyl-crotonate
4,6-dinitrofenil-crotonato de 2-(1-metilheptilo)

methylhexamine
metilhexamina, hexamina metílica

2-methylhexane
2-metilhexano, hexano 2-metílico

methylhexaneamine
metilhexanoamina, hexanoamina metílica

5-methyl-2-hexanone
5-metil-2-hexanona, 2-hexanona 5-metílica

methylhydantoin formaldehyde resin
resina formaldehídica de metilhidantoina

methylhydrazine
metilhidracina, hidracina metílica, metilhidrazina, hidrazina metílica

methylhydrogen sulfate
sulfato ácido de metilo

methyl-p-hydroxy-benzoate
p-hidroxibenzoato de metilo

methylhydroxy-butanone
metilhidroxibutanona, hidroxibutanona metílica

4-methyl-7-hydroxy-coumarine diethoxyphosphate
dietoxifosfato de 4-metil-7-hidroxi-cumarina

methyl-3-hydroxy-α-crotonate dimethyl phosphate
dimetilfosfato de metil-3-hidroxi-α-crotonato, fosfato dimetílico de metil-3-hidroxi-α-crotonato
methylhydroxyisopropylcyclohexane
metilhidroxiisopropilciclohexano, hexano metilhidroxiisopropílico
methyl-N-3,7-hydroxyoctyliden anthranilate
N-3,7-hidroxioctilidenantranilato de metilo
methyl-12-hydroxystearate
12-hidroxiestearato de metilo
2-methylimidazole
2-metilimidazol
3-methylindole
3-metilindol
methylionone
metilionona
methylisobutyl carbinol
metilisobutilcarbinol, carbinol metilisobutílico
methylisobutyl carbinol acetate
acetato de metilisobutilcarbinol, acetato de carbinol metilisobutílico
methylisoeugenol
metilisoeugenol, isoeugenol metílico
methylisopropenyl ketone
cetona metilisopropenílica
1-methyl-4-isopropenylcyclohexan-3-ol
1-metil-4-isopropenilciclo hexano-3-ol
methylisopropyl ketone
cetona metilisopropílica

2-methyl-5-isopropylphenol
2-metil-5-isopropilfenol, 5-isopropilfenol-2-metílico
methyl-p-isopropylphenyl propyl aldehyde
aldehído metil-p-isopropilfenil propílico
methylisothiazolinone
metilisotiazolinona
methyllithium
metillitio, litio metílico
methylmagnesium bromide
bromuro de metilmagnesio, bromuro de magnesio metílico
methylmagnesium chloride
cloruro de metilmagnesio, cloruro de magnesio metílico
methylmagnesium iodide
yoduro de metilmagnesio, yoduro de magnesio metílico
methylmaleic anhydride
anhídrido metilmaleico
metilmercaptan
metilmercaptano, mercaptano metílico
methylmercury acetate
acetato de metilmercurio, acetato de mercurio metílico
methylmercury cyanide
cianuro de metilmercurio, cianuro de mercurio metílico
methylmercury dicyandiamide
metilmercurio diciandiamida, diciandiamida de metilmercurio, diciandiamida de mercurio metílico
methylmercury-2,3-dihydroxypropylmercaptide
2,3-dihidroxipropil-mercaptida de

metilmercurio, 2,3-dihidroxipropil-mercaptida de mercurio metílico
methylmercury-8-hydroxyquinoleate
8-hidroxiquinoleato de metilmercurio, 8-hidroxiquinoleato de mercurio metílico
methylmercury quinolinoleate
quinolinoleato de metilmercurio, quinolinoleato de mercurio metílico
7-methyl-3-methylene-1,6-octadiene
7-metil-3-metileno-1,6-octadieno
methylmethane
metilmetano, metano metílico
3-methyl-6,7-methylenedioxy-1-piperonylisoquinoline
3-metil-6,7-metilendioxi-1-piperonilisoquinolina
methyl N-methyl-nipecotate
N-metilnipecotato de metilo
methylmorphine
metilmorfina, morfina metílica
N-methylmorpholine
N-metilmorfolina
N-methylmyosmine
N-metilmiosmina
α-methylnaphthalene
α-metilnaftaleno, naftaleno α-metílico
ß-methylnaphthalene
ß-metilnaftaleno, naftaleno ß-metílico
2-methyl-1,4-naphthoquinone
2-metil-1,4-naftaquinona, 1,4-naftaquinona 2-metílica
methyl naphthyl dodecyl dimethyl-ammonium chloride
cloruro de metilnaftil-dodecildimetilamonio
methylnitrobenzene
nitrobenceno metílico

methyl-p-nitrobenzene sulfonate
p-nitrobencensulfonato de metilo, p-nitro-bencensulfonato metílico
N-methyl-N'-nitro-N-guanidine
N-metil-N'-nitro-N-guanidina
4-methyl-2-nitrophenol
4-metil-2-nitrofenol, 2-nitrofenol 4-metílico
methyl-4-nitrosoperfluorobutyrate
4-nitrosoperfluoro-butirato de metilo, 4-nitrosoperfluoro-butirato metílico
N-methyl-N-nitroso-p-toluenesulfonamide
N-metil-N-nitroso-p-toluensulfonamida, p-toluensulfonamida N-metil-N-nitrosa
2-methylnonane
2-metilnonano, nonano 2-metílico
methyl-2-nonenoate
2-nonenoato de metilo, 2-nonenoato metílico
methylnonylacetaldehyde
acetaldehído metilnonílico
methyl-2-octynoate
2-octinoato de metilo, 2-octinoato metílico
methylol imidazolidone
imidazolidona metilólica, metilol-imidazolidona
methylol riboflavine
riboflavina metilólica
methylol urea
urea metilólica
methylol dimethyl-hydantoin
dimetilhidantoína metilólica, metiloldimetil-hidantoína
methylolacrylamide
acrilamida metilólica
methylparaben
metilparabeno
methylparafynol
metilparafinol

methylpentadiene
metilpentadieno
2-methylpentaldehyde
pentaldehído 2-
metílico
2-methylpentane
2-metilpentano
2-methyl-1,3-
pentanediol
2-metil-1,3-
pentanodiol, 1,3-
pentanodiol 2-metílico
2-methyl-2,4-
pentanediol
2-metil-2,4-
pentanodiol, 2,4-
pentanodiol 2-metílico
2-methylpentanoic acid
ácido 2-metil-
pentanoico
2-methyl-1-pentanol
2-metil-1-pentanol, 1-
pentanol 2-metílico
4-methyl-2-pentanol
acetate
acetato de 4-metil-2-
pentanol, acetato de 2-
pentanol 4-metílico
3-methyl-3-pentanol
carbamate
carbamato de 3-metil-
3-pentanol, carbamato
de 3-pentanol 3-
metílico
4-methyl-2-pentanone
4-metil-2-pentanona,
2-pentanona 4-metílica
2-methyl-1-pentene
2-metil-1-pentene, 1-
penteno 2-metílico
4-methyl-3-penten-2-
one
4-metil-3-penten-2-
ona, 3-penten-2-ona 4-
metílica
methylpentynol
metilpentinol
3-methyl-1-pentyn-
3-ol
3-metil-1-pentin-3-ol,
1-pentin-3-ol 3-
metílico
5-methyl-5-(3-
phenanthryl)-
hydantoin
5-metil-5-(3-
fenantril)hidantoína,
5-(3-fenantil)-
hidantoína 5-metílica

N-methyl-
phenazonium
methosulfate
metosulfato de N-
metilfenazonio
methylphenetylamine
metilfenetilamina,
fenetilamina metílica
methylphenidate
metilfenidato, fenidato
metílico
methylphenobarbital
metilfenobarbital,
fenobarbital metílico
methylphenylacetate
fenilacetato de metilo,
fenilacetato metílico
methylphenylcarbinol
metilfenilcarbinol,
fenilcarbinol metílico
methylphenylcarbinyl
acetate
acetato de
metilfenilcarbinilo
methylphenyldichloro-
silane
metilfenildicloro-
silano, diclorosilano
metilfenílico
3-methyl-5-phenyl-
hydantoin
3-metil-5-fenil-
hidantoína, 5-fenil-
hidantoína 3-metílica
4-methyl-1-phenyl-2-
pentanone
4-metil-1-fenil-2-
pentanona, 2-
pentanona 4-metil-1-
fenílica
2-methyl-2-phenyl-
propane
2-metil-2-fenil-
propano, propano 2-
metil-2-fenílico
3-methyl-1-phenyl-2-
pyrazolin-5-one
3-metil-1-fenil-2-
pirazolin-5-ona, 2-
pirazolin-5-ona 3-
metil-1-fenílica
methylphosphonic acid
ácido metilfosfónico
methylphosphoric acid
ácido metilfosfórico
3'-methylphthalanilic
acid
ácido 3'-metil-
ftalanílico

methyl nona-
decanoate
nonadecanoato de
metilo, nonadecanoato
metílico
N-methylpiperazine
N-metilpiperazina,
piperazina N-metílica
2-methylpiperidine
2-metilpiperidina,
piperidina 2-metílica
1-methyl-4-piperidinol
1-metil-4-piperidinol,
4-piperidinol 1-
metílico
3-(2-methyl-
piperidino) propyl-3,4-
dichlorobenzoate
3,4-diclorobenzoato de
3-(2-metilpiperidin)
propílico
methylprednisolone
metilprednisolona,
prednisolona metílica
2-methylpropane
2-metilpropano,
propano 2-metílico
p-(2-methylpropenyl)
phenol acetate
acetato de p-(2-
metilpropenil)fenol
2-methylpropane-
nitrile
2-metilpropanonitrilo,
propanonitrilo 2-
metílico
2-methyl-1-
propanethiol
2-metil-1-propanotiol,
1-propanotiol 2-
metílico
2-methylpropanoic
acid
ácido 2-metil-
propanoico
2-methyl-1-propanol
2-metil-1-propanol, 1-
propanol 2-metílico
2-methylpropanoyl
chloride
cloruro de 2-
metilpropanoílo
2-methylpropene
2-metilpropeno,
propeno 2-metílico
2-methyl-2-propen-1-ol
2-metil-2-propen-1-ol,
2-propen-1-ol 2-
metílico

2-methylpropionic acid
ácido 2-metil-
propiónico
methylpropyl-
benzene
metilpropilbenceno,
benceno metil-
propílico
methylpropylcarbinol
metilpropilcarbinol,
carbinol metilpropílico
methylpropylcarbinol
urethane
uretano de
metilpropilcarbinol,
metilpropilcarbinol
uretano
2-methyl-2-n-propyl-
1,3-propanediol
dicarbamate
dicarbamato de 2-
metil-2-n-propil-1,3-
propandiol
5-methylpyrazole-3-
carboxylic acid
ácido 5-metilpirazol-
3-carboxílico
methylpyridine
metilpiridina, piridina
metílica
methyl-4-pyridyl
ketone thiosemi-
carbazone
tiosemicarbazona de
metil-4-piridilcetona
N-methylpyrrole
N-metilpirrol, pirrol N-
metílico
N-methylpyrrolidine
N-metilpirrolidina,
pirrolidina N-metílica
N-methyl-2-
pyrrolidone
N-metil-2-pirrolidona,
2-pirrolidona N-
metílica
N-methylpyrroline
N-metilpirrolina,
pirrolina N-metílica
α-methylquinoline
α-metilquinolina,
quinolina α-metílica
2-methylquinoline
2-metilquinolina,
quinolina 2-metílica
6-methyl-2,3-
quinoxaline dithiol
cyclic carbonate
carbonato cíclico de

2,3,-quinoxalinditiol
6-metílico
methylrosaniline
chloride
cloruro de
metilrosanilina, cloruro
de rosanilina metílica
α-methylstyrene
α-metilestireno,
estireno α-metílico
4'-(methylsulfamoyl)
sulfanilanilide
4'-(metilsulfamoíl)
sulfanilanilida, anilida
4'-(metilsulfamoíl)-
sulfanílica
3-methylsulfolane
3-metilsulfolano,
sulfolano 3-metílico
3-methylsulfolene
3-metilsulfoleno,
sulfoleno 3-metílico
methylsulfonic acid
ácido metilsulfónico
methylsulfuric acid
ácido metilsulfúrico
N-methyltaurine
N-metiltaurina, taurina
N-metílica
17-methyltestosterone
17-metiltestosterona,
testosterona 17-
metílica
2-methyltetrahydro-
furan
2-metiltetrahidro-
furano, tetrahidro-
furano 2-metílico
3-methyltetrahydro-
thiophene-1,1-
dioxide
1,1-dióxido de 3-
metiltetrahidro-
tiofeno
N-methylteurine
N-metilteurina, teurina
N-metílica
4-methyl-5-thiazol-
ethanol
4-metil-5-tiazoletanol,
etanol 4-metil-5-
tiazólico
methyl-2-thienyl
ketone
cetona metil-2-tienílica
m-(methylthio)aniline
m-(metiltío)anilina
methylthiocyanate
metiltiocianato

4-(methylthio)-3,5-
dimethylphenyl-n-
methylcarbamate
n-metilcarbamato de 4-
(metiltío)-3,5-
dimetilfenilo
methylthionine
chloride
cloruro de metiltionina
methylthioninium
chloride
cloruro de metiltioninio
methylthiouracil
metiltiouracilo,
tiouracilo metílico
methyltin
metilestaño, estaño
metílico
methyl-p-toluate
p-toluato de metilo, p-
toluato metílico
methyl-p-toluene-
sulfonate
p-toluensulfonato de
metilo, p-toluen-
sulfonato metílico
methyl-p-tolyl ketone
cetona metil-p-tolílica
methyltrichlorosilane
metiltriclorosilano,
triclorosilano metílico
methyl tricosanoate
tricosanoato de metilo,
tricosanoato metílico
methyltridecanoate
tridecanoato de metilo,
tridecanoato metílico
methyltrienolone
metiltrienolona,
trienolona metílica
α-methyl-m-tyrosine
α-metil-m-tirosina, m-
tirosina α-metílica
ß-methyl-
umbelliferone
ß-metilumbeliferona,
umbeliferona ß-
metílica
2-methylundecanal
2-metilundecanal,
undecanal 2-metílico
5-methyluracil
5-metiluracilo, uracilo
5-metílico
methylvinyldichloro-
silane
metilvinildicloro-
silano, diclorosilano
metilvinílico

2-methyl-5-vinyl-
pyridine
2-metil-5-vinilpiridina,
5-vinilpiridina 2-
metílica
methymycin
metimicina
methysergid(e)
metisérgido
methysticin
metisticina
metiamide
metiamida
metiapine
metiapina
metiazinic acid
ácido metiacínico
meticillin
meticilina
meticrane
meticrano
metildigoxin
metildigoxina,
digoxina metílica
metilsulfate
metilsulfato, sulfato
metílico
metindizate
metindizato
metipranolol
metipranolol
metioprim
metioprima
metioxate
metioxato
metipirox
metipirox
metipranolol
metipranolol
metiprenaline
metiprenalina
metirosine
metirosina
metisazone
metisazona
metitepine
metitepina
metixene
metixeno
metizoline
metizolina
metkefamide
metkefamida
metobromuron
metobromurón
metochalcone
metocalcona
metocinium iodide
yoduro de metocinio

metoclopramide
metoclopramida
metocurine iodide
yoduro de metocurina
metofenazate
metofenazato
metofoline
metofolina
metogest
metogesto
metol
metol
metolachlor
metolaclor
metolazone
metolazona
metomidate
metomidato
metopimazine
metopimacina,
metopimazina
metopon
metopón
metopon
hydrochloride
clorhidrato de metopón
metoprolol
metoprolol
metoprolol succinate
succinato de
metoprolol
metoprolol tartrate
tartrato de metoprolol
metoquinone
metoquinona
metoquizine
metoquicina,
metoquizina
metoserpate
metoserpato
metoxepin
metoxepina
metrafazoline
metrafazolina
metralindole
metralindol
metrazifone
metracifona
metribolone
metribolona
metribuzin
metribucina,
metribuzina
metrifonate
metrifonato
metrifudil
metrifudil
metrizamide
metrizamida

metrizoic acid
ácido metrizoico
metronidazole
metronidazol
metron S
metrón S (N-isopropil-
1,5-dimetilhexilamina)
meturedepa
meturedepa
metynodiol
metinodiol
metyrapone
metirapona
metyridine
metiridina
metyrosine
metirosina
mevaldic acid
ácido meváldico
mevalonic acid
ácido mevalónico
mevastatin
mevastatina
mevinphos
mevinfós
mexacarbate
mexacarbato
mexazolam
mexazolán, mexazolam
mexenone
mexenona
mexicain
mexicaína
mexiletine
mexiletina
mexiletine
hydrochloride
clorhidrato de
mexiletina
mexoprofen
mexoprofeno
mexrenoate potassium
mexrenoato de potasio
mezepine
mecepina
mezereum
mecereón
mezilamina
mecilamina
mezlocillin
mezlocilina
mezlocillin sodium
mezlocilina sódica
Meyer reaction
reacción de Meyer
Meyer-Schuster
rearrangement
transposición de Meyer
y Schuster

Meyer synthesis
síntesis de Meyer
Meyer aldehyde
synthesis
síntesis de aldehídos de
Meyer
mianserin
mianserina
miazine
miazina
mibolerone
mibolerona
micinicate
micinicato
mica
mica
micellar flooding
inundación micelar
micelle
micela
Michael reaction
reacción de
Michael
Michaelis-Arbuzov
reaction
reacción de Michaelis
y Arbuzov
Michler's base
base de Michler
Michler's hydrol
hidrol de Michler
Michler's ketone
cetona de Michler
miconazole
miconazol
miconazole nitrate
nitrato de
miconazol
micranthine
micrantina
micro-activity
microactividad
microanalysis
microanálisis
microbial limit test
prueba de límites
microbianos
microburette
microbureta
microchemistry
microquímica
micrococcin P
micrococcina P
microcosmic salt
sal microcósmica
microcrystalline
microcristalino
microcurie
microcurio

microencapsulation
microencapsulación,
microencapsulado
microgram
microgramo
micrometer
micrómetro
micron
micrón, micra,
micrómetro,
millonésima
parte del metro
micronomicin
micronomicina
micronutrient
micronutriente
microorganism
microorganismo
microscope
microscopio
microscopy chemistry
química microscópica
microsphere
microesfera
microwave
spectroscopy
espectroscopía de
microondas
midaflur
midaflur
midamaline
midamalina
midazolam
midazolán,
midazolam
middle oil
aceite medio
midecamycin
midecamicina
midodrine
midodrina
midodrine
hydrochloride
clorhidrato de
midodrina
Miescher degradation
degradación de
Miescher
Mignonac reaction
reacción de
Mignonac
migration
migración
migration area
área de migración
mikamycin
micamicina
mil
milésima

Milas hydroxylation of
olefins
hidroxilación de
olefinas de Milas
milbemycins
milbemicinas
mildew preventive
preventivos contra
mohos
mildiomycin
mildiomicina
milenperone
milemperona
milestones
hitos, puntos
importantes
milipertine
milipertina
milk acid
ácido de la leche
milk glass
vidrio de criolita
milk of lime
lechada de cal
milk of magnesia
leche de magnesia
milk sugar
azúcar de leche
mill
molino
milli-
mili-
millicurie
milicurio
milligram
miligramo
milliequivalent
miliequivalente
milliliter
mililitro
millimeter
milímetro
millimicron
milimicrón
millimol
milimol
millirem
milirremio
Millon's reagent
reactivo de Millon
Mills-Nixon effect
efecto de Mills y
Nixon
Milori blue
azul de Milori
miloxacin
miloxacina
mimbane
mimbano

189

mimosine
mimosina
minaprine
minaprina
minaxolone
minaxolona
mindoperone
mindoperona
minepentate
minepentato
mineral
mineral
mineral acid
ácido mineral
mineral black
negro mineral
mineral blue
azul mineral
mineral cotton
algodón mineral
mineral dust
polvo mineral
mineral graphite
grafito mineral
mineral green
verde mineral
mineral jelly
jalea mineral
mineral oil
aceite mineral
mineral oil white
aceite mineral blanco
mineral pitch
brea mineral
mineral rouge
rojo mineral
mineral rubber
caucho mineral
mineral spirits
alcoholes
minerales
mineral thinner
diluyente mineral
mineral water
agua mineral
mineral wax
cera mineral
mineral wool
lana mineral
minium
minio
minocycline
minociclina
minocycline
hydrochloride
clorhidrato de
minociclina
minoxidil
minoxidil

miokamycin
miocamicina,
miokamicina
mipafox
mipafox
miracle fruit
fruta milagrosa
mirbane oil
aceite de mirbana
mirex
mirex
mirincamycin
mirincamicina
miristalkonium
chloride
cloruro de
miristalconio
miroprofen
miroprofeno
mirtazapine
mirtazapina
mirtle wax
cera de mirto
mischmetal
mischmetal,
mezcla de tierras
raras, cerio,
lantano y
didimio
miscibility
miscibilidad
miscible
miscible
misonidazole
misonidazol
misoprostol
misoprostol
mithramycin
mitramicina
miticide
acaricida
mitobronitol
mitobronitol
mitocarcin
mitocarcina
mitochondria
mitocondria
mitoclomine
mitoclomina
mitogillin
mitogilina
mitoguazone
mitoguazona
mitolactol
mitolactol
mitomalcin
mitomalcina
mitomycin
mitomicina

mitomycin C
mitomicina C
mitonafide
mitonafida
mitopodozide
mitopodócido
mitosis
mitosis
mitosper
mitospero
mitotane
mitotano
mitotenamine
mitotenamina
mitoxantrone
mitoxantrona
mitoxantrone
hydrochloride
clorhidrato de
mitoxantrona
mitragynine
mitraginina
Mitsunobu reaction
reacción de
Mitsunobu
mivacurium chloride
cloruro de mivacurio
mixed acid
ácido mixto, ácido
mezclado
mixed lead alkyl
alquilo de plomo mixto
mixidine
mixidina
mixing
mezclar
mixture
mezcla
mizoribine
mizoribina
mobecarb
mobecarbo
mobenzoxamine
mobenzoxamina
mobility
movilidad
mocimycin
mocimicina
mociprazine
mocipracina,
mociprazina
moclobemide
moclobemida
moctamide
moctamida
modacrylic fiber
fibra modacrílica
modaline
modalina

model
modelo
moderator
moderador
modification
modificación
modulus of elasticity
módulo de elasticidad
moexipril
hydrochloride
clorhidrato de
moexiprilo
mofebutazone
mofebutazona
mofloverine
mofloverina
mofoxime
mofoxima
mohair
pelo de cabra de
angora, mohair (tejido)
Mohr's salt
sal de Mohr,
sulfato ferroso-
amónico,
Mohs' scale
escala de Mohs
moiety
porción, mitad
moisture content
contenido de
humedad
molal
molal
molal concentration
concentración molal
molality
molalidad
molar
molar
molarity
molaridad
molassess
melaza
mold
moho, verdín, molde,
estampa
mold preventive
preventivo del moho
molding
moldeo
molding powder
polvo de moldeo
molding sand
arena para moldeo
mole
mol
mole fraction
fracción molar

molecular biology
biología molecular
molecular bond
enlace molecular
molecular diffusion
difusión molecular
molecular
distillation
destilación molecular
molecular
entanglement
agrupación molecular
molecular formula
fórmula molecular
molecular heat
calor molecular
molecular mass
masa molecular
molecular model
modelo molecular
molecular
rearrangement
transposición molecular
molecular sandwich
sándwich molecular,
emparedado molecular
molecular sieve
criba molecular
molecular structure
estructura molecular
molecular weight
peso molecular
molecularity
molecularidad
molecule
molécula
molinazone
molinazona
molindone
molindona
molindone
hydrochloride
clorhidrato de
molindona
molsidomine
molsidomina
molten mass
masa fundida
molten salt
sal fundida
molybdate
molibdato
molybdate chrome
orange
anaranjado de
molibdato y cromo
molybdate orange
anaranjado de
molibdato

molybdenic
molibdénico
molybdenite
molibdenita
molybdenite
concentrate
concentrado de
molibdenita
molybdenum
molibdeno
molybdenum acetyl
acetonate
acetilacetonato de
molibdeno
molybdenum
anhydride
anhídrido de
molibdeno
molybdenum boride
boruro de molibdeno
molybdenum carbonyl
carbonil molibdeno,
molibdeno carbonílico
molybdenum dioxide
dióxido de molibdeno
molybdenum
diselenide
diseleniuro de
molibdeno
molybdenum
disilicide
disiliciuro de
molibdeno
molybdenum
disulfide
disulfuro de molibdeno
molybdenum
ditelluride
ditelururo de
molibdeno
molybdenum glance
lustre de molibdeno,
molibdenita
molybdenum
hexacarbonyl
hexacarbonil
molibdeno,
molibdeno
hexacarbonílico
molybdenum
hexafluoride
hexafluoruro de
molibdeno
molybdenum lake
laca de molibdeno
molybdenum
methaphosphate
metafosfato de
molibdeno

molybdenum
naphthalene
naftaleno molibdénico
molybdenum orange
anaranjado de
molibdeno
molybdenum III oxide
óxido de molibdeno III
molybdenum oxides
óxidos de molibdeno
molybdenum
pentachloride
pentacloruro de
molibdeno
molybdenum
sesquioxide
sesquióxido de
molibdeno
molybdenum silicide
siliciuro de molibdeno
molybdenum sulfide
sulfuro de molibdeno
molybdenum trioxide
trióxido de molibdeno
molybdic
molíbdico
molybdic acid
ácido molíbdico
molybdic acid,
anhydride
ácido molíbdico
anhidro
molybdic oxide
óxido molíbdico
molybdic sulfide
sulfuro molíbdico
molybdophosphates
molibdofosfatos
12-molybdo-
phosphoric acid
ácido 12-molibdo-
fosfórico
molybdosilicates
molibdosilicatos
12-molybdosilicic acid
ácido 12-molibdo-
silícico
molibdous
molibdoso
monacetin
monacetina
monalazone disodium
monalazona disódica
monarda
monarda
monardein chloride
cloruro de monardeína
monatomic
monatómico

monazite
monacita
Mond process
proceso de Mond
monellins
monelinas
monensin
monensina
monitor
monitor, observar,
monitorear
mono acid
monoácido
mono acid F
monoácido F
(ácido 2-
naftol-7-sulfónico)
monoamine oxidase
monoamino oxidasa
monoazo dye
colorante monoazoico
monobasic
monobásico
monobenzone
monobenzona
monocalcic
monocálcico
monocalcium
phosphate
fosfato monocálcico
monochloroacetic
acid
ácido monocloracético
monochloroacetone
monocloracetona
monochlorobenzene
monoclorobenceno
monochlorodifluoro-
methane
monoclorodifluoro-
metano
monochloroethane
monocloretano
monochloromethane
monoclormetane
monochloropenta-
fluoroethane
monoclorpenta-
fluoretano
monochlorophenol
monoclorofenol
monochlorotetra-
fluoroethane
monoclorotetra-
fluoretano
monochlorotriazinyl
dye
colorante de
monoclortriacinilo

191

monochlorotrifluoro-methane
monoclorotrifluoro-metano
monocrotaline
monocrotalina
monocrotophos
monocrotofós
monoethanolamine
monoetanolamina
monoethanolamine oleate
oleato de monoetanolamina
monoethylamine
monoetilamina
monofilament
monofilamento
monoglyceride
monoglicérido
monoglyme
monoglima
monohydrate
monohidrato
monohydric
monohídrico
monohydric alcohol
alcohol monohídrico
mononer
monómero
monometacrine
monometacrina
monomethylamine
monometilamina
monomolecular film
película monomolecular
monomolecular reaction
reacción monomolecular
monooctanoin
monooctanoíno
monophospho-thiamine
monofosfotiamina
monopropellant
monopropulsor
monorden
monordeno
monosaccharide
monosacárido
monosodium glutamate
glutamato monosódico
monostearin
monoestearina
monotropein
monotropeína

monoxerutin
monoxerutina
monoxychlor
monoxicloro
montan wax
cera montana
montmorillonite
montmorilonita
monuron
monurón
moperone
moperona
mopidamol
mopidamol
moprolol
moprolol
moquizone
moquizona
morantel
morantel
morazone
morazona
morclofone
morclofona
mordant
mordiente
mordant rouge
mordiente rojo
morforex
morforex
moricizine
moricicina, moricizina
moricizine hydrochloride
clorhidrato de moricicina, clorhidrato de moricizina
morin
morina
morinamide
morinamida
morindin
morindina
morniflumate
morniflumato
morocromen
morocromeno
moroxydine
moroxidina
morphazinamide
morfazinamida
morphenol
morfenol
morpheridine
morferidina
morpherinan
morferinán
morphine
morfina

p-morphine
p-morfina
morphine benzyl ether hydrochloride
clorhidrato de éter de bencil morfina, clorhidrato de éter de morfina bencílica, clohridrato de benciléter morfina
morphine hydrobromide
bromhidrato de morfina
morphine meconate
meconato de morfina
morphime methylbromide
metilbromuro de morfina
morphine mucate
mucato de morfina
morphine oleate
oleato de morfina
morphine N-oxide
N-óxido de morfina
morpholine
morfolina
morpholine borane
morfolinborano
morpholine salicylate
salicilato de morfolina
2-(morpholinothio) benzothiazole
2-(morfolintío) benzotiazol
6-(N-morpholino)-4,4-diphenyl-3-heptanone hydrochloride
clorhidrato de 6-(N-morfolino)-4,4-difenil-3-heptanona
7-morpholinomethyl-theophylline teofilina
7-morfolinmetílica, 7-morfolinmetilteofilina
morphology
morfología
morphothebaine
morfotebaína
morphothion
morfototiona
morsuximide
morsuximida
mortar
argamasa, mortero
mortar, metallic
argamasa metálica, mortero metálico

Mossbauer effect
efecto de Mossbauer
mossy zinc
cinc musgoso
mother
madre
motilin
motilina
motrazepam
motracepán, motrazepam
motretinide
motretinida
mottled tablet
tableta moteada, tableta jaspeada
mountain blue
azul de montaña
moveltipril
moveltiprilo
moxadolen
moxadolena
moxalactam
moxalactama, moxalactán
moxaprindine
moxaprindina
moxastine
moxastina
moxaverine
moxaverina
moxazocine
moxazocina
moxestrol
moxestrol
moxicoumone
moxicumona
moxipraquine
moxipraquina
moxisylite
moxisilita
moxnidazole
moxnidazol
mucic
múcico
mucic acid
ácido múcico
mucilage
mucílago
mucins
mucinas
mucochloric anhydride
anhídrido mucoclórico
muconic acid
ácido mucónico
mucopolysaccharide
mucopolisacárido

muffle furnace
horno de copela, horno
de mufla
muffle oven
horno de copela, horno
de mufla
muguet
muguet (infección por
Candida albicans),
muguete (planta de
España)
muguet, synthetic
muguete sintético
mull
dispersión
muller
moleta
mullite combustion
tube
tubo de
combustión de mulita
multinuclear
multinuclear
multipolar
multipolar
Muntz metal
metal de Muntz
mupirocin
mupirocina
muramic acid
ácido murámico
muramyl dipeptide
dipéptido muramílico
murexide
murexida
murexine
murexina
muriate
muriato
muriatic
muriático
muriatic acid
ácido muriático
murocainide
murocainida
muroctasin
muroctasina
murvesco
murvesco
muscalure
muscalura

muscarine
muscarina
muscarine chloride
cloruro de muscarina
muscazone
muscazona
muscimol
muscimol
muscone
muscona
muscovite
mica, moscovita
musk
almizcle
musk ketone
cetona de almizcle
musk xylene
xileno de almizcle
mustard black
negro de mostaza
mustard gas
gas de mostaza, sulfuro
de dicloroetilo
mustard oil
aceite de mostaza
mustard oil, artificial
aceite artificial de
mostaza
mutagenic agent
agente mutagénico
muzolimine
muzolimina
mycaminose
micaminosa
mycarose
micarosa
mycelianamide
micelianamida
mycetins
micetinas
myclobutanil
miclobutanil
mycobactins
micobactinas
mycobacidin
micobacidina
mycobacillin
micobacilina
mycofenolate mofetil
micofenolato
mofetílico

mycolic acids
ácidos micólicos
mycomycin
micomicina
mycophenolic acid
ácido micofenólico
mycosamine
micosamina
mycotoxin
micotoxina
myelin
mielina
myfadol
mifadol
mylabris
cantárida China
myoglobin
mioglobina
myo-inositol
mio-inositol
myokinase
miocinasa
myosin
miosina
myralact
miralacto
myrcene
mirceno
myrcia oil
aceite de mircia
myrica
mirica
myrica oil
aceite de mirica
myricetin
miricetina
myricyl alcohol
alcohol miricílico
myricyl palmitate
palmitato de miricilo,
palmitato miricílico
myristic acid
ácido mirístico, ácido
tetradecanoico
myristica oil
esencia (aceite) de
nuez moscada
myristicin
miristicina
myristin
miristina

myristoleic acid
ácido miristoleico
myristoyl peroxide
peróxido de miristoílo,
peróxido miristoílico
myristyl alcohol
alcohol miristílico,
alcohol
tetradecílico,
1-tetradecanol
myristyl chloride
cloruro de miristilo,
cloruro miristílico
myristyl
dimethylamine
dimetilamina
miristílica,
miristildimetilamina
myristyl dimethyl-
benzylammonium
chloride
cloruro de amonio
miristil dimetil-
bencílico
myristyl lactate
lactato de miristilo,
lactato miristílico
myristyl mercaptan
mercaptano
miristílico,
miristilmercaptano
myristyltrimethyl-
ammonium bromide
bromuro de miristil-
trimetilamonio,
bromuro de trimetil-
amonio miristílico
myrophine
mirofina
myrrh
mirra
myrtecaine
mirtecaína
myrtle oil
esencia de mirto
myrtle wax
cera de mirto
myrtol
mirtol
myxin
mixina

N

nabam
nabán
nabilone
nabilón
nabitan
nabitán
nabitan hydrochloride
clorhidrato de nabitán
naboctate
naboctato
nabumetone
nabumetona
nacre
nácar
nacreous pigment
pigmento nacarado
nadide
nadida
nadolol
nadolol
nadoxolol
nadoxolol
nadroparin
nadroparina
nafarelin
nafarelina
nafarelin acetate
acetato de nafarelina
nafazatrom
nafazatrón, nafazatrom
nafcillin
nafcilina
nafcillin sodium
nafcilina sódica
nafenopin
nafenopino
nafetolol
nafetolol
nafiverine
nafiverina
nafomine
nafomina
nafoxidine
nafoxidina
nafronyl
nafronilo
naftalofos
naftalofós
naftazone
naftazona
naftidrofuryl
naftidrofurilo
naftifine
naftifina

naftifine hydrochoride
clorhidrato de naftifina
naftoxate
naftoxato
naftypramide
naftipramida
nalbuphine
nalbufina
nalbuphine
hydrochloride
cloruro de nalbufina
naled
naled, bromoclorfós
nalidixic acid
ácido nalidíxico
nalmefene
nalmefeno
nalmefene
hydrochloride
clorhirato de
nalmefeno
nalmetrene
nalmetreno
nalmexone
nalmexona
nalorphine
nalorfina
nalorphine dinicotinate
dinicotinato de
nalorfina
naloxone
naloxona
naloxone
hydrochloride
clorhirato de naloxona
naltrexone
naltrexona
naltrexone
hyrochloride
cloruro de naltrexona
namoxyrate
namoxirato
nandinine
nandinina
nandrolone
nandrolona
nandrolone
decanoate
decanoato de
nandrolona
nandrolone p-
hexyloxyphenyl
propionate
p-hexiloxifenil-

propionato de
nandrolona
nandrolone
phenpropionate
fenpropionato de
nandrolona
nandrolone propionate
propionato de
nandrolona
nanofin
nanofina
nanometer
nanómetro
nantradol
nantradol
napactadine
napactadina
napadisilate
napadisilato
napalm
napalm
napelline
napelina
naphazoline
nafazolina
naphtha
nafta
naphtha, solvent
nafta disolvente
naphthacene
naftaceno, tetraceno,
rubeno
naphthalene
naftaleno, naftalina,
alcanfor de alquitrán
1-naphthalene acetic
acid
ácido 1-naftalen-
acético
naphthalene diamine
naftalendiamina
1,8-naphthalene-
diamine
1,8-naftalendiamina
1,6-naphthalene-
disulfonic acid
ácido 1,6-naftalen-
disulfónico
1-naphthalenesulfonic
acid
ácido 1-naftalen-
sulfónico
1-naphthalenethiol
1-naftalentiol

naphthalic acid
ácido naftálico
naphthenate
naftenato
naphthene
nafteno
naphthenic acid
ácido nafténico
naphthenoic acid
ácido naftenoico
naphthionic acid
ácido naftiónico
naphthite
naftita
naphthoic acid
ácido naftoico
α-naphthol
α-naftol
ß-naphthol
ß-naftol
ß-naphthol benzoate
benzoato de ß-naftol
naphthol Green B
verde B de naftol
ß-naphthol methyl
ether
ß-naftol metil éter, éter
ß-naftol metílico
ß-naphthol sodium
ß-naftol sódico
naphthol yellow S
amarillo naftol S
1-naphthol-8-amino-
3,6-disulfonic acid
ácido 1-naftol-8-
amino-3,6-disulfónico
naphtholate
naftolato
3-naphthol-2-
carboxylic acid
ácido 3-naftol-2-
carboxílico
1-naphthol-3,6-
disulfonic acid
ácido 1-naftol-3,6-
disulfónico
2-naphthol-3,6-
disulfonic acid,
disodium salt
sal disódica del ácido
2-naftol-3,6-
disulfónico
α-naphtholphthalein
α-naftolftaleína

1-naphthol-2-sulfonic
acid
ácido 1-naftol-2-
sulfónico
α-naphtholsulfonic
acids
ácidos α-naftol-
sulfónicos
1-naphthol-4-sulfonic
acid, sodium salt
sal sódica del ácido 1-
naftol-4-sulfónico
naphthonone
naftonona
1,2-naphthoquinone
1,2-naftoquinona
naphthoquinone
oxime
naftoquinonoxima
1,2-naphthoquinone-4-
sulfonic acid
ácido 1,2
naftoquinona-4-
sulfónico
naphthoresorcinol
naftorresorcinol
ß-naphtoxyacetic acid
ácido ß-naftoxiacético
naphthyl
naftilo
ß-naphthyl benzoate
ß-naftilbenzoato,
benzoato de ß-naftilo
ß-naphthyl ethyl ether
etil éter ß-naftílico,
éter etil ß-naftílico
2-naphthyl lactate
lactato de 2-naftilo
1-naphthyl salicylate
salicilato de 1-naftilo
1-naphthylacetic
acid
ácido 1-naftilacético
α-naphthylamine
α-naftilamina
ß-naphthylamine
ß-naftilamina
α-naphthylamine
hydrochloride
clorhidrato de
α-naftilamina
1-naphthylamine-3,8-
disulfonic acid
ácido 1-naftilamino-
3,8-disulfónico
naphthylamine-
sulfonic acid
ácido naftil-
aminasulfónico

1-naphthylamine-3,6,8-
trisulfonic acid
ácido 1-naftilamina-
3,6,8-trisulfónico
o-2-naphthyl-m-N-
dimethyl-
thiocarbanilate
o-2-naftil-m-N-
dimetiltiocarbanilato
1,5-naphthylene-
diamine
1,5-naftilendiamina
N-α-naphthylene-
diamine
dihydrochloride
diclorhidrato de N-α-
naftilendiamina
N-(1-naphthyl)
ethylenediamine
N-(1-naftil)
etilendiamina
1-naphthylisocyanate
1-naftilisocianato
1-naphthyliso-
thiocyanate
1-naftilisotiocianato
1-naphthyl-N-methyl
carbamate
carbamato de 1-naftil-
N-metilo
α-naphthylmethyl
chloride
cloruro de α-
naftilmetilo
ß-naphthylmethyl
ether
éter ß-naftilmetilo
2-(2-naphthyloxy)
ethanol
2-(2-naftiloxi)etanol
α-naphthylphenyl-
oxazole
α-naftilfeniloxazol
N-1-naphtyl-
phthalamic acid
ácido N-1-
naftilftalámico
α-naphthylthiourea
α-naftiltiourea
naphtite
naftita
Naples yellow
amarillo de Nápoles
naprodoxime
naprodoxima
napropamide
napropamida
naproxen
naproxeno

naproxol
naproxol
napsilate
napsilato
naptalam
naptalán, ácido α-
naftilftalámico
naranol
naranol
narasin
narasino
narbomycin
narbomicina
narceine
narceína
narcobarbital
narcobarbital
narcosine
narcosina
narcotic
narcótico
1-α-narcotine
1-α-narcotina
narcotoline
narcotolina
naringenin
naringenina
naringin
naringina
nascent
naciente
natamycin
natamicina
natrolite
natrolita
natron
natrón
Natta catalysts
catalizadores Natta
natural gas
gas natural
natural gasoline
gasolina natural
natural product
producto natural
natural rubber
caucho natural
Nauheim salts
(artificial)
sales de Nauheim
(artificiales)
Nazarov cyclization
reaction
reacción de ciclización
de Nazarov
nealbarbital
nealbarbital
neamine
neamina

neatsfoot oil
aceite de pata de buey
Neber rearrangement
transposición de Neber
nebramycin
nebramicina
nebularine
nebularina
neburon
neburón
nedocromil sodium
nedocromil sódico
nefazodone
hydrochloride
clorhidrato de
nefazodona
nefopam
nefopán
Nef reaction
reacción de Nef
Nef synthesis
síntesis de Nef
negamycin
negamicina
negative valence
valencia negativa
negatol
negatol
nelfinavir mesylate
mesilato de
nelfinaviro
nematocide
nematocida
Nencki reaction
reacción de Nencki
Nenitzescu indole
synthesis
síntesis de indoles de
Nenitzescu
neoarsphenamine
neoarsenofenilamina
neocembrene
neocembreno
neocinchophen
neocincófeno
neo-cupferron
neocupferrona
neodecanoic acid
ácido neodecanoico
neodymia
neodimia
neodymium
neodimio
neodymium acetate
acetato de neodimio
neodymium
ammonium nitrate
nitrato de neodimio y
amonio

neodymium carbonate
carbonato de neodimio
neodymium chloride
cloruro de neodimio
neodymium fluoride
floruro de neodimio
neodymium nitrate
nitrato de neodimio
neodymium oxalate
oxalato de neodimio
neodymium oxide
óxido de neodimio
neodymium sulfate
sulfato de neodimio
neoergosterol
neoergosterol
neohesperidin
dihydrochalcone
neohesperidina
dihidrocalcona
neohexane
neohexano
neomethymycin
neometimicina
neomycin
neomicina
neomycin sulfate
sulfato de neomicina
neomycin undecylenate
undecilenato de
neomicina
neon
neón
neonicotine
neonicotina
neopentane
neopentano,
tetrametilmetano
neopentanoic acid
ácido neopentanoico
neopentyl alcohol
alcohol neopentílico
neopentyl glycol
glicolneopentílico,
neopentilglicol
neophyl chloride
cloruro de neofilo
neopine
neopina
neoplasm
neoplasma
neoprene
neopreno
neopyrithiamine
neopiritiamina
neopterin
neopterina
neoquassin
neocuasina

neostigmine
neoestigmina
neostigmine bromide
bromuro de
neoestigmina
neostigmine
methylsulfate
metilsulfato de
neoestigmina
neotetrazolium
chloride
cloruro de
neotetrazolio
neotridecanoic acid
ácido neotridecanoico
neovitamin A
neovitamina A
nepetalactone
nepetalactona
nephelite
nefelita
nephelometry
nefelometría
neptamustine
neptamustina
neptunium
neptunio
neptunium dioxide
dióxido de neptunio
nequinate
nequinato,
metilbenzocuato
neriifolin
neriifolina
nerol
nerol
neroli oil
esencia (aceite) de
nerolí
nerolidol
nerolidol, 3,7,11-
trimetil-1,6,10-
dodecatrien-3-ol
nerolin
nerolina, (éter etil ß-
naftílico)
Nessler cylinder
bureta de Nessler
Nessler's reagent
reactivo de
Nessler
netilmicin
netilmicina
netobimin
netobimina
netropsin
netropsina
net weight
peso neto

Neuberg blue
azul de Neuberg
neuraminic acid
ácido neuramínico
neurine
neurina, hidróxido de
trimetilvinilamonio
neurotensin
neurotensina
neutral
neutral
neutral red
rojo neutral
neutral magnesium
phosphate
fosfato magnésico
neutro
neutral oil
aceite neutro
neutral red
rojo neutro
neutralization
neutralización
neutralization number
índice de
neutralización
neutramycin
neutramicina
neutron
neutrón
neutron activation
analysis
análisis de activación
por neutrón
neutron diffraction
difracción de neutrón
Neville-Winter acid
ácido de Neville y
Winter
nevirapine
nevirapina
newtonian flow
flujo newtoniano
newtonian liquid
líquido newtoniano
nexeridine
nexeridina
niacin
niacina
niacinamide
niacinamida
niacinamide
ascorbate
ascorbato de
niacinamida
nialamide
nialamida
niaprazine
niapracina, niaprazina

nibroxane
nibroxano
nicarbazin
nicarbacina,
nicarbazina
nicafenine
nicafenina
nicainoprol
nicainoprol
nicametate
nicametato
nicardipine
nicardipina
nicardipine
hydrochloride
clorhidrato de
nicardipina
niccolite
nicolita, niquenita
nicergoline
nicergolina
niceritrol
niceritrol
nicethamide
nicetamida
niceverine
niceverina
nickel
níquel
nickel acetate
acetato de níquel
nickel acetylacetonate
acetilacetonato de
níquel
nickel ammonium
chloride
cloruro de níquel y
amonio
nickel ammonium
sulfate
sulfato de níquel y
amonio
nickel arsenate
arseniato de níquel
nickel bromide
bromuro de níquel
nickel carbonate, basic
carbonato básico de
níquel
nickel carbonyl
carbonil níquel
nickel chloride
cloruro de níquel
nickel cyanide
cianuro de níquel
nickel dibutyldithio-
carbamate
dibutilditiocarbamato
de níquel

nickel dimethyl-
glyoxime
dimetilglioxima de
níquel
nickel fluoride
fluoruro de níquel
nickel formate
formiato de níquel
nickel hydroxide
hidróxido de níquel
nickel iodide
yoduro de níquel
nickel matte
mata de níquel
nickel monoxide
monóxido de níquel
nickel nitrate
nitrato de níquel
nickel nitrate,
ammoniated
nitrato amoniacal de
níquel
nickel oxide
óxido de níquel
nickel oxide, black
óxido negro de níquel
nickel oxide, green
óxido verde de
níquel
nickel peroxide
peróxido de níquel
nickel phosphate
fosfato de níquel
nickel potassium
sulfate
sulfato de níquel y
potasio
nickel protoxide
protóxido de niquel
nickel salt, double
sal doble de níquel
nickel salt, single
sal única de níquel
nickel sesquioxide
sesquióxido de níquel
nickel silver
metal blanco, plata
alemana
nickel stannate
estannato de níquel
nickel steel
aceroníquel (aleación
de acero y níquel)
nickel sulfate
sulfato de níquel
nickel titanate
titanato de níquel
nickelic
niquélico

nickelic hydroxide
hidróxido niquélico
nickelic oxide
óxido niquélico
nickel-iron alloys
aleaciones de níquel y
hierro
nickelocene
niqueloceno
nickelous arsenate
arseniato niqueloso
nickelous bromide
bromuro niqueloso
nickelous chloride
cloruro niqueloso
nickelous hydroxide
hidróxido niqueloso
nickelous iodide
yoduro niqueloso
nickelous nitrate
nitrato niqueloso
nickelous phosphate
fosfato niqueloso
nickel-rhodium
níquel y rodio
niclofolan
niclofolano
niclosamide
niclosamida
nicoboxil
nicoboxilo
nicoclonate
nicoclonato
nicocodine
nicocodina
nicocortonide
nicocortonida
nicodicodine
nicodicodina
nicofibrate
nicofibrato
nicofuranose
nicofuranosa
nicofurate
nicofurato
nicomol
nicomol
nicomorphine
nicomorfina
nicopholine
nicofolina
nicosulfuron
nicosulfurona
nicorandil
nicorandil
nicothiazone
nicotiazona
nicotinamide
nicotinamida

nicotinamide adenine
dinucleotide
dinucleótido de
nicotinamida y adenina
nicotinamide ascorbate
ascorbato de
nicotinamida
nicotine
nicotina
nicotine sulfate
sulfato de nicotina
nicotine salts
sales de nicotina
nicotinic acid
ácido nicotínico
nicotinic acid amide
amida del ácido
nicotínico
nicotinic acid benzyl
ester
éster bencílico del
ácido nicotínico
nicotinic acid mono-
ethanolamine salt
sal monoetanol-
amínica del ácido
nicotínico
nicotinyl alcohol
alcohol nicotinílico
nicotinyl tartrate
tartrato de nicotinilo
nicoxamat
nicoxamato
nictindole
nictindol
nidroxyzone
nidroxizona
Niementowski
quinazoline synthesis
síntesis de quinazolinas
de Niementowski
Niementowski
quinoline synthesis
síntesis de quinolinas
de Niementowski
Nierenstein reaction
reacción de Nierenstein
nifedipine
nifedipina
nifenalol
nifenalol
nifenazone
nifenazona
niflumic acid
ácido niflúmico
nifungin
nifungina
nifuradene
nifuradeno

nifuraldezone
nifuraldezona
nifuralide
nifuralida
nifuratel
nifuratel
nifuratrone
nifuratrona
nifurdazil
nifurdacilo
nifurethazone
nifuretazona
nifurfoline
nifurfolina
nifurimide
nifurimida
nifurizone
nifurizona
nifurmazole
nifurmazol
nifurmerone
nifurmerona
nifuroquine
nifuroquina
nifuroxazide
nifuroxazida
nifuroxime
nifuroxima
nifurpipone
nifurpipona
nifurpirinol
nifurpirinol
nifurprazine
nifurpracina,
nifurprazina
nifurquinazol
nifurquinazol
nifursemizone
nifursemizona
nifursol
nifursol
nifurthiazole
nifurtiazol
nifurtimox
nifurtimox
nifurtoinol
nifurtoinol
nifurvidine
nifurvidina
nifurzide
nifurzida
nigericin
nigericina
nigre
solución de
jabón con
impurezas
nigrosine
nigrosina

nihydrazone
nihidrazona
nikethamide
nicetamida
nileprost
nileprost
nilestriol
nilestriol
nilprazole
nilprazol
niludipine
niludipina
nilutamide
nilutamida
nilvadipine
nilvadipina
nimazone
nimazona
nimbin
nimbina
nimbiol
nimbiol
nimesulide
nimesulida
nimetazepam
nimetacepán,
nimetazepam
nimidane
nimidano
nimodipine
nimodipina
nimorazole
nimorazol
nimustine
nimustina
ninhydrin
ninhidrina, hidrato de
tricetohidrindeno
ninopterin
ninopterina
niobe oil
aceite de niobe,
esencia de niobe,
benzoato de
metilo
niobic
nióbico
niobic acid
ácido nióbico
niobite
niobita
niobium
niobio
niobium carbide
carburo de niobio
niobium chloride
cloruro de niobio
niobium diselenide
diseleniuro de niobio

niobium oxalate
oxalato de niobio
niobium oxide
óxido de niobio
niobium
pentachloride
pentacloruro de niobio
niobium pentafluoride
pentafluoruro de niobio
niobium pentoxide
pentóxido de niobio
niobium potassium
oxyfluoride
oxifluoruro de niobio y
potasio
niobium silicide
siliciuro de niobio
niobium-tin
niobio y estaño
niobium-titanium
niobio y titanio
niobium-uranium
niobio y uranio
niometacin
niometacina
nipecotic acid
ácido nipecótico
nipradilol
nipradilol
niprofazone
niprofazona
niridazole
niridazol
nisbuterol
nisbuterol
nisin
nisina
nisobamate
nisobamato
nisoldipine
nisoldipina
nisoxetine
nisoxetina
nisterine
nisterina
nitarsone
nitarsona
nitazoxanide
nitazoxanida
nitenpyram
nitempirán
niter
nitro
niter, Chile
nitro de Chile
nithiazide
nitiazida
niton
nitón, radón

nitracrine
nitracrina
nitralin
nitralina
nitralloy
aleación nitrada
nitramide
nitramida
nitramine
nitramina
nitramisole
nitramisol
nitranilic acid
ácido nitranílico
nitraniline
nitroanilina
nitrapyrin
nitrapirina
nitrate
nitrato
nitrated
nitrado
nitrating acid
ácido nitrante
nitration
nitración
nitrazepam
nitracepán, nitrazepam
nitre
nitro
nitrefazole
nitrefazol
nitrendipine
nitrendipino
nitrenes
nitrenos
nitric
nítrico
nitric acid
ácido nítrico, agua
fuerte
nitric acid, fuming
ácido nítrico fumante
nitric anhydride
anhídrido nítrico
nitric ester
éster nitrico
nitric oxide
óxido nítrico
nitricholine
perchlorate
perclorato de
nitricolina
nitride
nitruro
nitriding
nitruración
nitriding steel
acero nitrurado

nitrification
nitrificación
nitrile
nitrilo
nitrile rubber
caucho nitrilo
nitrile-silicon
rubber
caucho de nitrilo y
silicona
nitrilotriacetic acid
ácido nitrilotriacético
nitrin(e)
nitrina
nitrite
nitrito
nitro-
nitro-
nitro carbon nitrate
nitrocarbonitrato
nitro compounds
compuesto nitro
p-nitro sodium
phenolate
fenolato de sodio p-
nitro
nitroacetanilide
nitroacetanilida
nitroamine
nitroamina
p-nitro-o-amino-
phenol
p-nitro-o-aminofenol
m,o,p-nitroaniline
m,o,p-nitroanilina
o,p-nitroanisole
o, p-nitroanisol
5-nitrobarbituric
acid
ácido 5-nitro-
barbitúrico
3-nitrobenzaldehyde
3-nitrobenzaldehído
nitrobenzene
nitrobenceno
p-nitrobenzene-
azoresorcinol
p-nitrobenceno-
azorresorcinol
m-nitrobenzene-
sulfonic acid
ácido m-nitro-
bencenosulfónico
nitrobenzimidazole
nitrobencimidazol
nitrobenzoic acid
ácido nitrobenzoico
nitrobenzol
nitrobenzol

m-nitrobenzo-
trifluoride
m-nitrobenzo-
trifluoruro
m-nitrobenzoyl
chloride
cloruro de m-
nitrobenzoílo
p-nitrobenzoyl chloride
cloruro de p-
nitrobenzoílo
p-nitrobenzyl cyanide
cianuro de p-
nitrobencilo
o-nitrobiphenyl
o-nitrobifenilo
nitrobromoform
nitrobromoformo
2-nitro-1-butanol
2-nitro-1-butanol
nitrocellulose
nitrocelulosa
nitrocellulose lacquer
laca de nitrocelulosa
nitrochlorobenzene
nitroclorobenceno
nitrochloroform
nitrocloroformo
p-nitro-o-chloro-
phenyldimethyl
thionophosphate
dimetiltionofosfato de
p-nitro-o-clorofenilo
2-nitro-1,1-bis(p-
chlorophenyl)propane
2-nitro-1,1-bis(p-
clorofenil)propano
m-nitrocinnamic acid
ácido m-nitrocinámico
nitroclofene
nitroclofeno
nitrocobalamin
nitrocobalamina
nitrocotton
nitroalgodón
2-nitro-p-cresol
2-nitro-p-cresol
nitrodan
nitrodano
nitrodichloro
derivative
derivado
nitrodiclorado
nitrodichlorobenzene
nitrodiclorobenceno
o-nitrodiphenyl
o-nitrodifenilo
o-nitrodiphenylamine
o-nitrodifenilamina

nitrodracylic acid
ácido nitrodracílico
nitroethane
nitroetano
2-nitro-2-ethyl-1,3-
propanediol
2-nitro-2-etil-1,3-
propanodiol
nitrofen
nitrofeno
nitrofural
nitrofural
nitrofuran
nitrofurano
nitrofurantoin
nitrofurantoína
nitrofurazone
nitrofurazona
nitrogen
nitrógeno
nitrogen-15
nitrógeno 15
nitrogen chloride
cloruro de nitrógeno
nitrogen compounds
compuestos de
nitrógeno
nitrogen dioxide
dióxido de nitrógeno
nitrogen fixation
fijación del nitrógeno
nitrogen fluoride
fluoruro de nitrógeno
nitrogen monoxide
monóxido de nitrógeno
nitrogen mustard
mostaza de nitrógeno
nitrogen oxides
óxidos de nitrógeno
nitrogen peroxide
peróxido de hidrógeno,
agua oxigenada
nitrogen selenide
seleniuro de nitrógeno
nitrogen sesquioxide
sesquióxido de
nitrógeno
nitrogen solution
solución de nitrógeno
nitrogen tetroxide
tetróxido de nitrógeno
nitrogen trichloride
tricloruro de nitrógeno
nitrogen trifluoride
trifluoruro de nitrógeno
nitrogen triiodide
triyoduro de nitrógeno
nitrogen trioxide
trióxido de nitrógeno

nitrogenase
nitrogenasa
nitrogenous
nitrogenado, azoado
nitroglycerin(e)
nitroglicerina
nitroglycol
nitroglicol
nitroguanidine
nitroguanidina
nitrohydrochloric
acid
ácido nitroclorhídrico
3-nitro-2-hydro-
benzoic acid
ácido 3-nitro-2-
hidroxibenzoico
4-nitro-3-hydroxy-
mercuri-o-cresol
anhydride
anhídrido del 4-nitro-3-
hidroximercuri-o-
cresol
3-nitro-4-hydroxy-
phenylarsonic acid
ácido 3-nitro-4-
hidroxifenilarsónico
nitrolic
nitrólico
nitromersol
nitromersol
nitrometer
nitrómetro
nitromethane
nitrometano
2-nitro-4-methoxy-
aniline
2-nitro-4-metoxi-
anilina
2-nitro-2-methyl-1,3-
propanediol
2-nitro-2-metil-1,3-
propanodiol
nitromide
nitromida
nitromifene
nitromifeno
nitron
nitrón
α-nitronaphthalene
α-nitronaftaleno
1-nitronaphthalene-5-
sulfonic acid
ácido 1-nitro-
naftaleno-5-sulfónico
1-nitro-2-naphthol
1-nitro-2-naphthol
nitronium perchlorate
perclorato de nitronio

nitroparaffin
nitroparafina
3-nitropentane
3-nitropentano
5-nitro-o-phenetidine
5-nitro-o-fenetidina
p-nitrophenetole
p-nitrofenetol
nitrophenide
nitrofenida
m-nitrophenol
m-nitrofenol
p-nitrophenol sodium
salt
sal sódica de p-
nitrofenol
p-nitrophenylacetic
acid
ácido p-nitrofenil-
acético
4-nitrophenylarsonic
acid
ácido nitrofenil-
arsónico
p-nitrophenylazo-
salycilate sodium
p-nitrofenilazo-
salicilato sódico
4-nitro-o-phenylene-
diamine
4-nitro-o-fenilen-
diamina
p-nitrophenyl-
hydrazine
p-nitrofenilhidracina
o-nitrophenyl-
propionic acid
ácido o-nitrofenil-
propiónico
(4-nitrophenyl)urea
(4-nitrofenil)urea
nitrophosphate
nitrofosfato
1-nitropropane
1-nitropropano
5'-nitro-2'-propoxy-
acetanilide
5'-nitro-2'-propoxi-
acetanilida
5-nitro-2-propoxy-
aniline
5-nitro-2-
propoxianilina
5-nitroquinaldic
acid
ácido 5-nitro-
quináldico
m-nitrosalicylic acid
ácido m-nitrosalicílico

nitrosamine
nitrosamina
nitroscanate
nitroscanato
nitroso dyes
colorantes nitrosos
nitroso ester
terpolymer
terpolímero de éster
nitroso
nitroso polymer
polímero nitroso
N-nitrosodiethanol-
amine
nitrosodietanolamina
N-nitrosodiethylamine
N-nitrosodietilamina
N-nitrosodimethyl-
amine
N-nitrosodimetilamina
p-nitrosodiphenyl-
amine
p-nitrosodifenil-
amina
nitrosoguanidine
nitrosoguanidina
nitrosomethylurethane
nitrosometiluretano
N-nitrosomorpholine
N-nitrosomorfolina
1-nitroso-2-naphtol
1-nitroso-2-naftol
p-nitrosophenol
p-nitrosofenol
nitrosophenyl-
hydroxilamine
nitrosofenil-
hidroxilamina
N-nitrosopyrrolidine
N-nitrosopirrolidina
nitrostarch
nitroalmidón
ß-nitrostyrene
ß-nitroestireno
nitrosulfathiazole
nitrosulfatiazol
nitrosyl chloride
cloruro de nitrosilo
nitrosyl fluoride
fluoruro de nitrosilo
nitrosyl sulfuric acid
ácido nitrosil-
sulfúrico
nitrosyl tetra-
fluoroborate
tetrafluoroborato de
nitrosilo
m,o,p-nitrotoluene
m,o,p-nitrotolueno

p,m-nitro-α-toluic acid
ácido p,m-nitro-α-
toluico
p-nitro-o-toluidine
p-nitro-o-toluidina
p-nitro-α-tolunitrile
p-nitro-α-tolunitrilo
nitrotrichloromethane
nitrotriclorometano
m-nitrotrifluoro-
methylbenzene
m-nitrotrifluoro-
metilbenceno
2-nitro-4-trifluoro-
methylbenzonitrile
2-nitro-4-trifluoro-
metilbenzonitrilo
2-nitro-4-trifluoro-
methylchlorobenzene
2-nitro-4-trifluoro-
metilclorobenceno
nitrourea
nitrourea
nitrous
nitroso
nitrous acid
ácido nitroso
nitrous diphenyl-
amide
difenilamida del ácido
nitroso
nitrous ester
éster nitroso
nitrous ether
éter nitroso
nitrous oxide
óxido nitroso
nitrous polymer
polímero nitroso
nitrovin
nitrovina
nitroxanthic acid
ácido nitroxántico
nitroxinil
nitroxinilo
nitroxoline
nitroxolina
nitroxylene
nitroxileno
nitroxylol
nitroxilol
nitroxynil
titroxinilo
nitryl chloride
cloruro nitrílico
nitryl fluoride
fluoruro nitrílico
nivacortol
nivacortol

nivalenol
nivalenol
nivimedone
nivimedona
nizatidine
nizatidina
nizofenone
nizofenona
no leakage
sin pérdida
nobelium
nobelio
noble
noble
noble gas
gas noble
noble metal
metal noble
nocardamin
nocardamina
nocardicin
nocardicina
nocodazole
nocodazol
nodakenin
nodaquenina
nodal
nodal
nodular iron
fundición nodular
nodulisporic acid
ácido nodulispórico
nofecainide
nofecainida
noformicin
noformicina
nogalamycin
nogalamicina
noise level
ruido de fondo
nolinium
bromide
bromuro de nolinio
nomelidine
nomelidina
nomenclature
nomenclatura
nomifensine
nomifensina
nomilin
nomilina
nomograph
nomógrafo
non aqueous
no acuoso
nonabine
nonabina
nonactin
nonactino

non-actinic
no actínico
nonadecane
nonadecano
n-nonadecanoic acid
ácido n-nona-
decanoico
Υ-nonalactose
Υ-nonalactosa
nonallyl chloride
cloruro de nonalilo
nonanal
nonanal
nonane
nonano
nonanedioic acid
ácido nonanodioico
nonane-1,3-diol
monoacetate
monoacetato de
nonano 1,3-diol
n-nonanoic acid
ácido n-nonanoico
nonaperone
nonaperona
nonapyrimine
nonapirimina
noncombustible
material
material no
combustible
nondestructive testing
prueba no destructiva
nondrying oil
aceite no secante
nonelectrolyte
no electrólito
nonene
noneno
nonfammable material
material no inflamable
non-geminate
no geminado
non-glycosylated
no glucosilado
non-ideal
no ideal
nonionic
no iónico
nonivamide
nonivamida
nonmetal
metaloide, no metal
non-newtonian
behavior
comportamiento no
newtoniano
n-nonoic acid
ácido n-nonoico

nonoic acid
ácido nonoico
nonoxynol
nonoxinol
non-pareil seeds
semillas Non-Pareil,
microgránulos de
sucrosa y almidón
nonpolar
apolar
nonvolatile
no volátil
nonviscous neutral oil
aceite neutro no
viscoso
n-nonyl acetate
acetato de n-nonilo
n-nonyl alcohol
alcohol n-nonílico
nonyl bromide
bromuro de nonilo
nonyl chloride
cloruro de nonilo
nonyl hydride
hidruro de nonilo
Υ-nonyl lactone
Υ-nonil lactona
nonyl nonanoate
nonanoato de nonilo
nonyl thiocyanate
tiocianato de nonilo
n-nonylamine
n-nonilamina
tert-nonylamine
terc-nonilamina
nonylbenzene
nonilbenceno
1-nonylene
1-nonileno
n-nonylic acid
ácido n-nonílico
nonylphenol
nonilfenol
nonylphenoxyacetic
acid
ácido nonil-
fenoxiacético
nonyltrichlorosilane
noniltriclorosilano
nopinene
nopineno
noprylsulfamide
noprilsulfamida
noracymethadol
noracimetadol
norbolethone
norboletona
norbormide
norbormida

5-norbornene-2-
methanol
5-norborneno-2-
metanol
5-norbornene-2-methyl
acrylate
acrilato de 5-
norborneno-2-metilo
norbudrine
norbudrina
norcarane
norcarano
norcholanic acid
ácido norcolánico
norclostebol
norclostebol
norcodeine
norcodeina
nor compounds
compuestos nor
nordazepam
nordacepán,
nordazepam
nordefrin
hydrochloride
clorhidrato de
nordefrina
nordhausen acid
ácido nordhausen
nordihydroguaiaretic
acid
ácido nordihidro-
guayarético
nordinone
nordinona
norea
norea
norephedrine
hydrochloride
clorhidrato de
norefedrina
norepinephrine
norepinefrina
norethandrolone
noretandrolona
norethindrone
noretindrona
norethindrone acetate
acetato de noretindrona
norethisterone
noretisterona
norethynodrel
noretinodrel
noreximide
noreximida
norfenefrine
norfenefrina
norfloxacin
norfloxacino

norflurane
norflurano
norflurazon
norflurazona
Norge niter
nitro de Noruega
norgesterone
norgesterona
norgestimate
norgestimato
norgestomet
norgestomet
norgestrel
norgestrel
norgestrienone
norgestrienona
norhyoscyamine
norhiosciamina
norletimol
norletimol
norleucine
norleucina
norleusactide
norleusáctido
norlevorphanol
norlevorfanol
norlobelanine
norlobelanina
normal
normal
normal chain
cadena normal
normal pentane
pentano normal
normal solution
solución normal
normal valence
valencia normal
normality
normalidad
normalization
normalización
normalize
normalizar
normalized
normalizado
Normant reagents
reactivos de
Normant
normetanephrine
normetanefrina
normethadone
normetadona
normethandrone
normetandrona
normorphine
normorfina
nornicotine
nornicotina

norphenazone
norfenazona
norpipanone
norpipanona
norphytane
norfitano
norpseudoephedrine
norpseudoefedrina
nortetrazepam
nortetracepán,
nortetrazepam
nortriptyline
nortriptilina
nortriptyline
hyrochloride
clorhidrato de
nortriptilina
norvaline
norvalina
norvinisterone
norvinisterona
Norway saltpeter
salitre de Noruega
Norwegian saltpeter
salitre noruego
noscapine
noscapina
nosepiece
porta objeto
nosiheptide
nosiheptida
novembichin
novembiquina
novobiocin
novobiocina
novolak
novolaca
novoldiamine
novoldiamina
novonal
novonal
noxious
nocivo
noxious gas
gas nocivo
noxiptilin
noxiptilina
noxythiolin
noxitiolina
NQR spectroscopy
espectroscopia MNC
(momento nuclear
cuadrípolo, resonancia
nuclear cuadrípola)
nuclear chain reaction
reacción nuclear en
cadena
nuclear chemistry
química nuclear

nuclear energy
energía nuclear
nuclear fission
fisión nuclear
nuclear fuel
combustible nuclear
nuclear fuel element
elemento de combustible nuclear
nuclear fusion
fusión nuclear
nuclear magnetic resonance (NMR)
resonancia magnética nuclear (RMN)
nuclear quadrupole resonance
resonancia nuclear cuadrípola
nuclear reaction
reacción nuclear
nuclear reactor
reactor nuclear
Nuclear Regulatory Commission
Comisión de Regulación Nuclear

nuclear waste
desechos nucleares
nucleases
nucleasas
nucleation
nucleación
nucleic acid
ácido nucleico
nucleocidin
nucleocidina
nucleogenesis
nucleogénesis
nucleon
nucleón
nucleophile
nucleófilo
nucleophilic
nucleofílico
nucleoprotein
nucleoproteína
nucleoside
nucleósido
nucleotide
nucleótido
nucleus
núcleo
nuclide
núclido

nuclotixene
nuclotixeno
nudic acid
ácido núdico
nufenoxole
nufenoxol
nuisance p articulate
partículas molestas
Nujol
nujol
numerals
números
nupharidine
nufaridina
Nusselt number
número de Nusselt
nutgall
cecidia
nutmeg
nuez moscada
nutmeg oil
aceite de nuez moscada
nutrient
nutriente, agentes nutritivos
nutrient solution
solución nutriente

nutrification
nutrificación
nutrition
nutrición
nut shells
cáscara de almendra o avellana
nux vomic(a)
nuez vómica
NW acid
ácido NW (ácido de Nevie y Winter)
nybomycin
nibomicina
Nylander's reagent
reactivo de Nylander
nylidrin
nilidrín
nylidrin hydrochloride
clorhidrato de nilidrín
nylon
nilón
nylon 46
nilón 46
nystatin
nistatina

O

oakmoss resin
resina de musgo de
encina
oakum
estopa
Obermayer's reagent
reactivo de Obermayer
obidoxime chloride
cloruro de obidoxima
ocher, ochre
ocre
ochratoxins
ocratoxinas
occlude
obstruir
occlusion
oclusión
occlusion compound
compuesto de oclusión
occur
suceder, encontrar,
producir
ocimene
ocimeno
ocrase
ocraso
ocrilate
ocrilato
octabenzone
octabenzona
octacaine
octacaína
octacosanol
octacosanol
octadecadienoic acid
ácido
octadecadienoico
n-octadecane
n-octadecano
1,12-octadecanediol
1,12-octadecanodiol
n-octadecanoic acid
ácido n-octadecanoico
1-octadecanol
1-octadecanol
n-octadecanoyl chloride
cloruro de n-
octadecanoílo
octadecatrienol
octadecatrienol
9-octadecen-1,12-diol
9-octadecen-1,12-diol
1-octadecene
1-octadeceno

octadecene-
octadecadieneamine
octadeceno-
octadecadienamina
cis-9-octadecenoic acid
ácido cis-9-
octadecenoico
octadecenol
octadecenol
cis-octadecenoyl
chloride
cloruro de cis-
octadecenoílo
octadecenyl aldehyde
aldehído octadecenílico
octadecyl alcohol
alcohol octadecílico
octadecyl isocyanate
isocianato de
octadecilo
octadecyl mercaptan
octadecilmercaptano
octadecyldimethyl-
benzyl ammonium
chloride
cloruro de
octadecildimetil-
bencilamonio
octadecylen
octadecileno
octadecyltrichloro-
silane
octadeciltriclorosilano
octadecyltri-
methylammonium
pentachlorophenate
pentaclorofenato de
octadeciltrimetil-
amonio
octafluoro-2-butene
octafluoro-2-buteno
octafluorocyclo-
butane
octafluorociclo-
butano
2,2,3,3,4,4,5,5-
octafluoro-1-
pentanol
2,2,3,3,4,4,5,5-
octafluoro-1-pentanol
octafluoro-propane
octafluoropropano
octafonium chloride
cloruro de octafonio

octakis(2-hydroxy-
propyl)sucrose
octaquis(2-hidroxi-
propil)sucrosa
octamethyl pyro-
phosphoramide
octametilpiro-
fosforamida
octamethylcyclo-
tetrasiloxane
octametilciclo-
tetrasiloxano
octamethyltrisiloxane
octametiltrisiloxano
octamoxin
octamoxina
octamylamine
octamilamina
1-octanal
1-octanal
n-octane
n-octano
octane number
índice de octano
1,8-octanedicarboxylic
acid
ácido 1,8-octano-
dicarboxílico
octanedioic acid
ácido octanodioico
octanoic acid
ácido octanoico
octanohydroxamic
acid
ácido octano-
hidroxámico
octanol
octanol
2-octanone
2-octanona
octanoyl chloride
cloruro de octanoílo
octapinol
octapinol
octastine
octastina
octatropine
methylbromide
metilbromuro de
octatropina
octavalent
octavalente
octaverine
octaverina

octazamide
octazamida
1-octene
1-octeno
octenidine
octenidina
octhilinone
octilinona
octoic acid
ácido octoico
octocrilene
octocrileno
octodrine
octodrina
octopamine
octopamina
octotiamine
octotiamina
octoxynol
octoxinol
octreotide
octreotida
octriptyline
octriptilina
octrizole
octrizol
octyl
octilo
n-octyl acetate
acetato de n-octilo,
acetato n-octílico
n-octyl alcohol,
primary
alcohol n-octílico
primario
sec-n-octyl alcohol
alcohol sec-n-
octílico
octyl aldehyde
aldehído octílico
n-octyl bromide
bromuro de n-octilo,
bromuro n-octílico
octyl carbinol
octilcarbinol
n-octyl chloride
cloruro de n-octilo,
cloruro n-octílico
octyl formate
formiato de octilo,
formiato octílico
2-octyl iodide
yoduro de 2-octilo,
yoduro 2-octílico

n-octyl mercaptan
n-octilmercaptano
tert-octyl mercaptan
terc-octilmercaptano
n-octyl methacrylate
metacrilato de n-octilo,
metacrilato n-octílico
octyl methoxy-
cinnamate
metoxicinamato de
octilo, metoxi-
cinamato octílico
octyl peroxide
peróxido de octilo,
peróxido octílico
octyl phenol
octilfenol
octyl phosphate
fosfato de octilo,
fosfato octílico
n-octyl sulfoxide
isosafrole
n-octilsulfóxido
isosafrol
octyl trichlorosilane
octiltriclorosilano
octylamine
octilamina
tert-octylamine
terc-octilamina
n-octylbicycloheptene
dicarboximide
n-octilbiciclohepten-
dicarboximida
n-octyl-n-
decyl adipate
adipato de n-octil-n-
decilo, adipato n-octil-
n-decílico
n-octyl-decyl alcohol
alcohol n-octildecílico
n-octyl-n-decyl
phthalate
ftalato de n-octil-n-
decilo, ftalato n-octil-
n-decílico
octyldodecyl
neopentanoate
neopentanoato de
octildodecilo,
neopentanoato
octildodecílico
octylene
octileno
octylene
glycol titanate
titanato de
octilenglicol, titanato
de glicoloctilénico

octylene oxide
óxido de octileno,
óxido octilénico
octylic acid
ácido octílico
octylmagnesium
chloride
cloruro de
octilmagnesio
p-tert-octylphenoxy
polyethoxyethanol
p-terc-octilfenoxi-
polietoxietanol
p-octylphenyl salycilate
salicilato de p-
octilfenilo
odor
olor
odorant
odorante
odorless
inodoro
oenanthic acid
ácido enántico
oenanthic aldehyde
aldehído enántico
oenology
enología
ofloxacin
ofloxacina
oftasceine
oftasceína
off-line
desconectado
off-white
blanco crema, blanco
grisáceo
oil
aceite
oil black
negro de petróleo
oil cake
torta de aceite
oil, chloronaphthalene
aceite de
cloronaftaleno
oil gas
gas de petróleo
oil shale
esquisto aceitoso,
esquisto bituminoso
oil varnish
barniz de aceite
oil white
blanco de aceite
oiliness
oleoginosidad
oily
aceitoso

ointment
ungüento
okadaic acid
ácido okadaico
olaflur
olaflur
olamine
olamina
olanzapine
olanzapina
olaquindox
olaquindox
old yellow enzime
enzima color amarillo
antiguo
oleamide
oleamida
oleandomycin
oleandomicina
oleandomycin
phosphate
fosfato de
oleandomicina
oleandrin
oleandrina
oleanolic acid
ácido oleanólico
olefin
olefina
olefinic
olefínico
oleic acid
ácido oleico
oleic acid nitrile
nitrilo del ácido oleico
oleic alcohol
alcohol oleico
olein(e)
oleína
oleoresin
oleorresina
oleoresin of aspidium
oleorresina de helecho
macho
oleoyl chloride
cloruro de oleoílo
n-oleoylsarcosine
n-oleoilsarcosina
oletimol
oletimol
oleuropein
oleuropeína
oleyl alcohol
alcohol oleílico
oleyl aldehyde
aldehído oleílico
oleyl methyl
tauride
oleilmetiltaurida

oleylhydroxamic
acid
ácido oleil-
hidroxámico
oleyl-linoleylamine
oleil linoleilamina,
linoleilamina oleílica
olibanum
olíbano
olibanum oil
aceite de olíbano
oligodynamic
oligodinámica
oligomer
oligómero
oligomycins
oligomicinas
oligopeptide
oligopéptido
oligosaccharide
oligosacárido
olivacine
olivacina
olivanic acids
ácidos olivánicos
olive oil
aceite de oliva
olivetol
olivetol
olivil
olivil
olivomycin
olivomicina
olmidine
olmidina
olsalazine
olsalacina
olsalazine sodium
olsalacina sódica
oltipraz
oltipraz
omeprazole
omeprazol
omidoline
omidolina
omoconazole
omoconazol
omonasteine
omonasteína
ondansetron
ondansetrona
one mark pipette
pipeta de aforo
one-step resin
resina de un paso
on-going
en progreso
onion oil
aceite de cebolla

ontianil
ontianil

oosporein
oosporeína

opacity
opacidad

open-chain compound
compuesto de cadena abierta

operating conditions
condiciones de operación

opianic acid
ácido opiánico

opiniazide
opiniazida

opipramol
opipramol

opium
opio

Oppenauer oxidation
oxidación de Oppenauer

opromazine
opromacina, opromazina

opsins
opsinas

optical activity
actividad óptica

optical brightener
abrillantador óptico

optical crystals
cristales ópticos

optical isomer
isómero óptico

optical isomerism
isomerismo óptico

optical microscope
microscopio óptico

optical rotation
rotación óptica

optical spectroscopy
espectroscopía óptica

oral contraceptive
anticonceptivo oral

orange I
anaranjado I

orange B
anaranjado B

orange cadmium
cadmio anaranjado

orange flowers oil
esencia (aceite) floral de azahar

orange mineral
mineral anaranjado

orange oil
esencia (aceite) de naranja dulce

orange peel bitter oil
esencia (aceite) de corteza de naranja amarga

orange peel sweet oil
esencia (aceite) de corteza de naranja dulce

orazamide
orazamida

orbital theory
teoría orbital

orcein
orceína

orcin
orcina

orcinol
orcinol

orciprenaline
orciprenalina

orconazole
orconazol

order of magnitude
orden de magnitud

ore
mena, mineral

ore flotation
flotación de mineral

orestrate
orestrato

organic
orgánico

organic chemistry
química orgánica

organic compound
compuesto orgánico

organic matter
materia orgánica

organic sulfur
azufre orgánico

organoborane
organoborano

organoclay
organoarcilla

organoleptic
organoléptico

organometallic compound
compuesto organometálico

organophosphorus compound
compuesto de organofósforo

organopolysilicate
organopolisilicato

organosilane
organosilano

organosilicon
organosilício

organosol
organosol

organotin compound
compuesto organoestaño

orgotein
orgoteína

origanum oil
esencia (aceite) de mejorana silvestre

oripavine
oripavina

ormetoprim
ormetoprima

ormosinine
ormosinina

ornidazole
ornidazol

ornipressin
ornipresina

ornithine
ornitina

ornoprostil
ornoprostil

orotic acid
ácido orótico, ácido uracil-6-carboxílico

orotidine
orotidina

oroxylin A
oroxilina A

orpanoxin
orpanoxina

orphenadrine
orfenadrina

orphenadrine citrate
citrato de orfenadrina

orpiment
oropimente, oropimento, trisulfuro de arsénico

orris
lirio de Florencia

orris oil
aceite de lirio de Florencia

o-orsellinic acid
ácido o-orselínico

ortetamine
ortetamina

orthamine
ortamina

orthanilic acid
ácido ortanílico

ortho-
orto-

orthoarsenic acid
ácido ortoarsénico

orthoboric acid
ácido ortobórico

orthocaine
ortocaína

orthoformic acid
ácido ortofórmico

orthophosphate
ortofosfato

orthovaleric acid
ácido ortovalérico

oryzacidin
orizacidina

oryzalin
orizalina

Υ-oryzanol
Υ-orizanol

osajin
osajina

osalmid
osalmida

osmadizone
osmadizona

osmaron B
osmaron B

osmic acid
ácido ósmico

osmiridium
osmiridio

osmium
osmio

osmium ammonium chloride
cloruro de osmio y amonio

osmmium chloride
cloruro de osmio

osmium dichloride
dicloruro de osmio

osmium hexafluoride
hexafluoruro de osmio

osmium sodium chloride
cloruro de osmio y sodio

osmium tetrachloride
tetracloruro de osmio

osmium tetroxide
tetróxido de osmio

osmometer
osmómetro

osmometry
osmometría

osmose
someter a ósmosis

osmosis
ósmosis
osmotic pressure
presión osmótica
osmotically
por ósmosis
osmous,osmious
ósmico
osthole
ostol
ostreogrycin
ostreogricina
Ostromyslenskii
reaction
reacción de
Ostromyslenskii
ostruthin
ostrutina
ostruthol
ostrutol
otilonium bromide
bromuro de
otilonio
otobain
otobaína
ouabagenin
ouabagenina, ouabain
ouabaína
outgassing
desgasificación
outline
sinopsis
ovalbumin
ovalbúmina
overfill
sobrecargado
overlay
cubrir, extender
overstimate
calcular en exceso
overview
panorama,
generalidades
oven
horno
oxa-
oxa-
oxabrexine
oxabrexina
oxaceprol
oxaceprol
oxacid
oxácido
oxacillin
oxacilina
oxadiargyl
oxadiargil
1,3,4-oxadiazole
1,3,4-oxadiazol

oxadiazon
oxadiazona
oxadimedine
oxadimedina
oxadixyl
oxadixilo
oxaflozane
oxaflozano
oxaflumazine
ozaflumacina,
oxaflumazina
oxagrel
oxagrel
oxagrelate
oxagrelato
oxalacetic acid
ácido oxalacético
oxalate
oxalato
oxaldehyde
oxaldehído
oxalenedi-
uramidoxime
oxalendiuramidoxima
oxalic
oxálico
oxalic acid
ácido oxálico
7-oxalobicyclo-(2,2,1)
heptane-2,3-
dicarboxylic acid
ácido 7-oxalobiciclo-
(2,2,1)-heptano-2,3-
dicarboxílico
oxalomolybdic acid
ácido oxalomolíbdico
oxalonitrile
oxalonitrilo
oxalyl chloride
cloruro de oxalilo
oxamarin
oxamarina
oxametacin(e)
oxametacina
oxamic acid
ácido oxámico
oxamide
oxamida
oxammonium
oxamonio,
hidroxilamina
oxamniquine
oxamniquina
oxamycin
oxamicina
oxamyl
oxamilo
oxanamide
oxanamida

oxandrolone
oxandrolona
oxantel
oxantel
oxapadol
oxapadol
oxapium iodide
yoduro de oxapio
oxapropanium iodide
yoduro de
oxapropanio
oxaprotiline
oxaprotilina
oxaprozin
oxaprocina
oxarbazole
oxarbazol
oxatomide
oxatomida
oxazafone
oxazafona
oxazepam
oxacepán, oxazepam
oxazidione
oxacidiona
oxazolam
oxazolán, oxazolam
oxazoline wax
cera de oxazolina
oxazorone
oxazorona
oxcarbazepine
oxcarbacepina
ox bile extract
extracto de la bilis
de buey
oxdralazine
oxdralacina,
oxdralazina
oxeladin
oxeladina
oxendolone
oxendolona
oxenin
oxenina
oxepinac
oxepinaco
oxetacaine
oxetacaína
oxetacillin
oxetacilina
oxetane
oxetano
oxethazaine
oxetazaína
oxetorone
oxetorona
oxfendazole
oxfendazol

oxfenicine
oxfenicina
oxibendazole
oxibendazol
oxibetaine
oxibetaína
oxiconazole
oxiconazol
oxiconazole nitrate
nitrato de oxiconazol
oxidable
oxidable
oxidant
oxidante
oxidase
oxidasa
oxidation
oxidación
oxidation number
índice de oxidación
oxidation process
proceso de oxidación
oxidation-reduction
oxidación-reducción
oxidation-reduction
indicator
indicador de
oxidación-reducción
oxidation-reduction
potential
potencial de óxido-
reducción, potencial
red-ox
oxidative
oxidante
oxidative coupling
asociación oxidante
oxide
óxido
oxidimethiin
oxidimetiína
oxiding material
material oxidante
oxidize
oxidar, oxidarse
oxidized cellulose
celulosa oxidada
oxidizer
oxidante
oxidopamine
oxidopamina
oxidoreductase
oxidorreductasa
oxidronic acid
ácido oxidrónico
oxifentorex
oxifentorex
oxifungin
oxifungina

oxilorphan
oxilorfano
oximes
oximas
oxindoles
oxindolas
oxine
oxina
oxiniacic acid
ácido oxiniácico
oxiperomide
oxiperomida
oxipurinol
oxipurinol
oxiracetam
oxiracetán,
oxiracetam
oxiramide
oxiramida
oxirane
oxirano
oxirane process
proceso oxirano
oxirene
oxireno
oxisopred
oxisopred
oxisuran
oxisurano
oxitriptan
oxitriptano
oxitriptyline
oxitriptilina
oxitropium bromide
bromuro de oxitropio
oxmetidine
oxmetidina
oxogestone
oxogestona
oxoglurate
oxoglurato
**2-oxohexamethylen-
imine**
2-oxohexametilen-
imina
oxolamine
oxolamina
oxolinic acid
ácido oxolínico
oxomemazine
oxomemacina,
oxomemazina
oxonazine
oxonacina,
oxonazina
oxonic acid
ácido oxónico

oxonium ion
ion oxonio
2-oxopentanedioic acid
ácido 2-oxopentano-
dioico
4-oxopentanoic acid
ácido 4-oxo-
pentanoico
oxophenarsine
oxofenarsina
**oxophenarsine
hydrochloride**
clorhidrato de
oxofenarsina
oxophenylarsine
oxofenilarsina
oxoprostol
oxoprostol
oxosilane
oxosilano
oxotremorine
oxotremorina
oxpheneridine
oxofeneridina
oxprenolol
oxprenolol
oxy-
oxi-
oxyacanthine
oxiacantina
oxyacetylene
oxiacetileno
oxyacid
oxiácido, oxácido
oxybenzoic acid
ácido oxibenzoico
oxybenzone
oxibenzona
**p,p'-oxybis(benzene-
sulfonylhydrazide)**
p,p'-oxibis(benceno-
sulfonilhidrazida)
oxybromide
oxibromuro
oxybuprocaine
oxibuprocaina
oxybutynin
oxibutinina
oxybutynin chloride
cloruro de
oxibutinina
oxychloride
oxicloruro
oxychlorosene
oxicloroseno
oxycinchophen
oxicincófeno

oxyclipine
oxiclipina
oxyclozanide
oxyclozanida
oxycodone
oxicodona
oxyconiine
oxiconiína
4,4'-oxydi-2-butanol
4,4'-oxidi-2-butanol
**oxydipentonium
chloride**
cloruro de
oxidipentonio
**10,10-oxydipheno-
xarsine**
10,10-oxidifeno-
xarsina
**ß,ß'-oxydipropio-
nitrile**
ß,ß'-oxidipropio-
nitrilo
oxyfedrine
oxifedrina
oxyfenamate
oxifenamato
oxyfluorfen
oxifluorfeno
oxygen
oxígeno
oxygen 18
oxígeno 18
oxygen fluoride
fluoruro de oxígeno,
difluoruro de oxígeno
oxygen liquid
oxígeno líquido
oxygenate
oxigenar
oxygenation
oxigenación
oxygen consumed
oxígeno consumido
oxygenase
oxigenasa
oxigenize
oxigenar
oxyhemoglobin
oxihemoglobina
oxyluminescence
oxiluminiscencia
oxymesterone
oximesterona
oxymetazoline
oximetazolina
oxymetholone
oximetolona

oxymethurea
oximeturea
oxymethylene
oximetileno
oxymorphone
oximorfona
ß-oxynaphthoic acid
ácido ß-oxi-
naftoico
oxyneurine
oxineurina
oxypendyl
oxipendilo
oxypertine
oxipertina
oxyphenbutazone
oxifembutazona
oxyphencyclimine
oxifenciclimina
oxyphenisatin
oxifenisatina
**oxyphenisatin(e)
acetate**
acetato de oxifenisatina
**oxyphenonium
bromide**
bromuro de oxifenonio
oxyphosphorane
oxifosforano
oxypinocamphone
oxipinoalcanfor
oxypolygelatin
oxipoligelatina
**oxypyrronium
bromide**
bromuro de oxipirronio
oxyquinoline
oxiquinolina
oxyridazine
oxiridacina,
oxiridazina oxisal
oxysonium iodide
yoduro de oxisonio
oxysulfide
oxisulfuro
oxytetracycline
oxitetraciclina
oxythiamine
oxitiamina
oxythioquinox
oxitioquinox
oxytocin
oxitocina
ozocerite
ozocerita
ozolinone
ozolinona

ozonation
ozonización

ozone
ozono

ozonic
de ozono, ozonizado

ozonic ether
éter ozonizado

ozonide
ozónido, ozonuro

ozonization
ozonización

ozonizer
ozonizador

ozonolysis
ozonólisis

ozonometer
ozonómetro

P

Paal-Knorr pyrrole
synthesis
  síntesis de pirroles de
  Paal y Knorr
PABA
  PABA, ácido p-amino
  benzoico
PABA, sodium
  PABA sódico, p-
  aminobenzoato sódico
pack, to
  empaquetar, empacar
packed column
  columna empacada
packing
  empaque, embalaje
paclitaxel
  paclitaxel
paclobutrazol
  paclobutrazol
pacrinolol
  pacrinolol
pactamycin
  pactamicina
paddle stirrer
  agitador de paleta
padimate
  padimato
pafenolol
  pafenolol
paint
  pintura
paint, emulsion
  pintura en emulsión
paint, inorganic
  pintura inorgánica
paint, metallic
  pintura metálica
paint, water-based
  pintura con base
  acuosa
pair ion
chromatography
  cromatografía iónica
  pareada
palitantin
  palitantina
palladic
  paládico
palladium
  paladio
palladium
chloride
  cloruro de paladio

palladium diacetate
  diacetato de paladio
palladium dichloride
  dicloruro de paladio
palladium iodide
  yoduro de paladio
palladium monoxide
  monóxido de paladio
palladium nitrate
  nitrato de paladio
palladium oxide
  óxido de paladio
palladium potassium
chloride
  cloruro de paladio y
  potasio
palladium sodium
chloride
  cloruro de paladio y
  sodio
palladous chloride
  cloruro paladioso
palladous iodide
  yoduro paladioso
palladous nitrate
  nitrato paladioso
palladous potassium
chloride
  cloruro paladioso
  potásico
palladous sodium
chloride
  cloruro paladioso
  sódico
palm butter
  manteca de palma
palm nut cake
  torta de nuez de
  palma
palm oil, from fruit
  aceite del fruto de la
  palma, mantequilla de
  palma
palm oil, from seed
  aceite de la semilla de
  la palma
palmatine
  palmatina
palmidrol
  palmidrol
palmitate
  palmitato
palmitic
  palmítico

palmitic acid
  ácido palmítico
palmitic acid cetyl
ester
  éster cetílico del ácido
  palmítico
palmitin
  palmitina
palmitoleic acid
  ácido palmitoleico
palmitoyl chloride
  cloruro de palmitoílo
palmityl alcohol
  alcohol palmítico
palustric acid
  ácido palústrico
palytoxin
  palitoxina
pamabrom
  pamabrón
pamaquine
  pamaquina
pamaquine naphtoate
  naftoato de pamaquina
pamatolol
  pamatolol
pamidronate disodium
  pamidronato disódico
pamidronic acid
  ácido pamidrónico
pamoic acid
  ácido pamoico
pancreatic dornase
  dornasa pancreática
pancreatin(e)
  pancreatina
pancrelipase
  pancrelipasa
pancuronium bromide
  bromuro de pancuronio
pangamic acid
  ácido pangámico
panidazole
  panidazol
pankrin
  pancrina
pantetheine
  panteteína
panthetine
  pantetina
panthenol
  pantenol
pantocaine
  pantocaína

pantolactone
  pantolactona
pantothenate
  pantotenato
pantothenic acid
  ácido pantoténico
pantothenol
  pantotenol
papain
  papaína
papaveraldine
  papaveraldina
papaveretum
  papavereto
papaverine
  papaverina
papaveroline
  papaverolina
papaya
  papaya
paper
  papel
paper, artificial
  papel artificial
paper chromatography
  cromatografía de papel
paper, coated
  papel revestido
paper, synthetic
  papel sintético
para-
  para-
parabanic acid
  ácido parabánico
paracasein
  paracaseína
paracetaldehyde
  paracetaldehído
paracetamol
  paracetamol
paracymene
  paracimeno
paradichlorobenzene
  paradiclorobenceno
paraffin
  parafina
paraffin chlorinated
  parafina clorada
paraffin distillate
  destilado de parafina
paraffin oil
  aceite de parafina
paraffin series
  serie parafínica

paraffin wax
cera de parafina
paraflutizide
paraflutizida
paraformaldehyde
paraformaldehído
paraherquamide
paraherquamida
paraldehyde
paraldehído
parallel columns
columnas en paralelo
paramethadione
parametadiona
paramethasone
parametasona
paramorphism
paramorfismo
paranitraniline red
rojo de paranitranilina
paranyline
paranilina
paraoxon
paraoxón
parapenzolate bromide
bromuro de
parapenzolato
parapropamol
parapropamol
paraquat
paraquat
pararosaniline
pararrosanilina
pararosaniline
embonate
embonato de
pararrosanilina
parasorbic acid
ácido parasórbico
parathiazine
paratiacina, paratiazina
parathion
paratión
parathyroid hormone
hormona paratiroidea
paraxazone
paraxazona
parbendazole
parbendazol
parconazole
parconazol
paregoric
paregórico
pareira
pareira, pareira brava
pareptide
pareptida
parethoxycaine
paretoxicaína

parethoxycaine
hydrochloride
clorhidrato de
paretoxicaína
pargeverine
pargeverina
pargolol
pargolol
pargyline
pargilina
paricalcitol
paricalcitol
paridocaine
paridocaína
Paris green
verde de Schweinfurt,
verde París
Paris white
blanco de París
Parkes process
proceso de Parkes
paromomycin
paromomicina
paromomycin sulfate
sulfato de
paromomicina
parotin
parotina
paroxetine
paroxetina
paroxypropione
paroxipropiona
parsalmide
parsalmida
parsley oil
esencia (aceite) de
semilla de perejil
parsley seed
semilla de perejil
parthenin
partenina
parthenolide
partenolida
partial
pressure
presión parcial
particle
partícula
particle accelerator
acelerador de
partículas
particle size
tamaño de la
partícula
particulate matter
material en
partículas
parting agent
agente de partición

partition
chromatography
cromatografía de
partición
partition column
columna de
fraccionamiento
partricin
partricina
parvaquone
parvacuona
parylene
parileno
pasiniazid(e)
pasiniazida
Passerini reaction
reacción de
Passerini
passiflora
pasiflora
passivity
inactividad
pasteurization
pasteurización
patchouli alcohol
alcohol de pachuli,
alcohol de pachulí
patchouli oil
esencia (aceite) de
pachuli, esencia
(aceite) de pachulí
patentability
patentabilidad
patent alum
alumbre patente
patent leather
charol
path
senda
path length
longitud de trayectoria
pathfinder element
elemento trazador
pathway
ruta
patina
pátina
patronite
patronita
Pattinson process
proceso Pattison
patulin
patulina
Pauli exclusion
principle
principio de exclusión
de Pauli
paulomycin
paulomicina

pavoninin-5
pavoninina-5
paxamate
paxamato
pazoxide
pazóxido
peach oil
aceite de durazno,
aceite pérsico
peacock blue
azul pavo real
peak
pico
peak area
área del pico
peak shape
forma del pico
pearl ash
cenizas de perla,
carbonato de potasio
pearl pigment
pigmento de
perla,pigmento
nacarado
pearl white
blanco perla
peanut
cacahuete, maní
peanut oil
aceite de maní, aceite
de cacahuete
pebulate
pebulato
pecazine
pecacina, pecazina
Pechmann pyrazole
synthesis
síntesis de pirazoles de
Pechmann
pecilocin
pecilocina
pecocycline
pecociclina
pectate
pectato
pectic
péctico
pectic acid
ácido péctico
pectin
pectina
pectin sugar
azúcar de pectina
pectinase
pectinasa
pectolinarigerin
pectolinarigerina
pederin
pederina

pefloxacin(e)
pefloxacino
pegaspargase
pegaspargasa
pegoterate
pegoterato
pelargonic acid
ácido pelargónico
pelargonic alcohol
alcohol pelargónico
pelargonic aldehyde
aldehído pelargónico
pelargonidin
pelargonidina
pelargonyl chloride
cloruro de pelargonilo
pelargonyl peroxide
peróxido de
pelargonilo
Peligot's salt
sal de Peligot
peliomycin
peliomicina
pellet
gránulo
pelletierine
peletierina
pelletierine tannate
tanato de peletierina
pelleting
formando gránulos
pellitorine
pelitorina
pellotine
pelotina
peltatin
peltatina
pemerid
pemerida
pemoline
pemolina
pempidine
pempidina
penamecillin
penamecilina
penbutolol
pembutolol
penbutolol sulfate
sulfato de
pembutolol
pendecamaine
pendecamaína
pendimethalin
pendimetalina
penethamate
hydriodide
penetamato yohidrado
penetrant
penetrante

penetrability
penetrabilidad
penfluridol
penfluridol
penflutizide
penflutizida
pengitoxin
pengitoxina
penicillamine
penicilamina
penicillamine cysteine
disulfide
disulfuro de
penicilamina y cisteína
penicillamine disulfide
disulfuro de
penicilamina
penicillanic acid
ácido penicilánico
penicillic acid
ácido penicílico
penicillin
penicilina
penicillin BT
BT penicilina,
butilmercaptometil-
penicilina
penicillin G
benethamine
penicilina G
benetamina
penicillin G
benzathine
penicilina G benzatina
penicillin G
benzhydrylamine
penicilina G
bencidrilamina
penicillin G calcium
penicilina G cálcica
penicillin G
hydrabamine
penicilina G
hidrabamina
penicillin G potassium
penicilina G potásica
penicillin G procaine
penicilina G con
procaína
penicillin N
penicilina N
penicillin O
penicilina O
penicillin S potassium
penicilina S potásica
penicillin V
penicilina V
penicillin V benzathine
penicilina V benzatina

penicillin V
hydrabamine
penicilina V
hidrabamina
penicillinase
penicilinasa
penicilloic acids
ácidos peniciloicos
penicilloyl polylysine
peniciloil polilisina
penimepicycline
penimepiciclina
penimocycline
penimociclina
penirolol
penirrolol
penmesterol
penmesterol
pennyroyal
poleo
pennyroyal oil-
american
esencia (aceite) de
poleo americano,
esencia (aceite) de
hedeoma
pennyroyal oil-
european
esencia (aceite) de
poleo europeo
penoctonium bromide
bromuro de penoctonio
penprostene
pemprosteno
penta resin
resina penta
pentabamate
pentabamato
pentaborane
pentaborano
pentabromoacetone
pentabromoacetona
pentacene
pentaceno
pentachloroethane
pentacloroetano
pentachloro-
naphthalene
pentacloronaftaleno
pentachloro-
nitrobenzene
pentacloronitro-
benceno
pentachlorophenol
pentaclorofenol
pentachlorothiophenol
pentaclorotiofenol
pentacynium
bis(methylsulfate)

bis(metilsulfato) de
pentacinio
pentacynium chloride
cloruro de pentacinio
pentadecalactone
pentadecalactona
pentadecane
pentadecano
n-pentadecanoic acid
ácido n-penta-
decanoico
pentadecanolide
pentadecanólido
pentadecenyl phenol
pentadecenilfenol
3-pentadecylcatechol
3-pentadecilcatecol
pentadecylic acid
ácido pentadecílico
1,3-pentadiene
1,3-pentadieno
pentaerythrite
pentaeritrita
pentaerythrite
tetranitrate
tetranitrato de
pentaeritrita
pentaerythritol
pentaeritrita
pentaerythritol chloral
pentaeritrita cloral
pentaerythritol
dichlorohydrin
pentaeritrita diclorhidrina
pentaerythritol
tetraacetate
tetraacetato de
pentaeritrita
pentaerythritol tetrakis
(diphenyl phosphite)
tetraquis (difenil-
fosfito) de pentaeritrita
pentaerythritol tetra(3-
mercapto propionate)
tetra(3-mercapto-
propionato) de
pentaeritrita
pentaerythritol
tetranitrate
tetranitrato de
pentaeritrita
pentaerythritol
tetrastearate
tetraestearato de
pentaeritrita
pentaerythritol
tetrathioglycolate
tetratioglicolato de
pentaeritrita

pentaerythrityl
tetranitrate
  tetranitrato de
  pentaeritritilo
pentafluranol
  pentafluranol
pentagastrin
  pentagastrina
pentagestrone
  pentagestrona
pentaglycerine
  pentaglicerina
pentahomoserine
  pentahomoserina
pentahydroxy-
cyclohexane
  pentahidroxi-
  ciclohexano
2',3',4',5',7'-
pentahydroxy-
flavone
  2',3',4',5',7'-penta-
  hidroxiflavona
pentalamide
  pentalamida
pentalin
  pentalina
pentamethonium
bromide
  bromuro de
  pentametonio
1,1,3,3,5-pentamethyl-
4,6-dinitroindane
  1,1,3,3,5-pentametil-
  4,6-dinitroindano
pentamethylene
  pentametileno
pentamethylene
dibromide
  dibromuro de
  pentametileno
pentamethylene
glycol
  pentametilenglicol,
  glicol penta-
  metilénico
pentamethylene
tetrazole
  pentametilentetrazol
pentamethyleneamine
  pentametilenamina
pentamethylene-1,1-
bis(1-methyl-
pyrrolidinium
bitartrate)
  bitartrato de
  pentametileno-1,1-
  bis(1-metil-
  pirrolidinio)

pentamethylene-
diamine
  pentametilendiamina
pentamethyl-
pararosaniline chloride
  cloruro de penta-
  metilpararrosanilina
pentamidine
  pentamidina
pentamoxane
  pentamoxano
pentanal
  pentanal
n-pentane
  n-pentano
pentanedinitrile
  pentanodinitrilo
pentanedioic acid
  ácido pentanodioico
pentanedioic acid
anhydride
  anhídrido del ácido
  pentanodioico
1,5-pentanediol
  1,5-pentanodiol
2,3-pentanedione
  2,3-pentanodiona
pentanethiol
  pentanotiol
pentanoic acid
  ácido pentanoico
1-pentanol
  1-pentanol
3-pentanone
  3-pentanona
pentapiperide
  pentapiperida
pentapiperium
metilsulfate
  metilsulfato de
  pentapiperio
pentaquine
  pentaquina
pentasodium
diethylenetriamine
pentaacetate
  dietilentriamina
  pentaacetato
  pentasódico
pentasodium
triphosphate
  trifosfato
  pentasódico
n-pentatriacontane
  n-pentatriacontano
pentavalent
  pentavalente
pentazocine
  pentazocina

pentazocine
hydrochloride
  clorhidrato de
  pentazocina
1-pentene
  1-penteno
pentetrazol
  pentetrazol
2-pentenylpenicillin
sodium
  2-pentenilpenicilina
  sódica
pentetate calcium
trisodium
  pentetato de calcio
  trisódico
pentetic acid
  ácido pentético
penthienate bromide
  bromuro de pentienato
penthrichloral
  pentricloral
pentifylline
  pentifilina
pentigetide
  pentigetida
pentisomicin
  pentisomicina
pentizidone
  penticidona
pentlandite
  pentlandita
pentobarbital
  pentobarbital
pentobarbital sodium
  pentobarbital sódico
1-pentol
  1-pentol
pentolinium tartrate
  tartrato de pentolinio
pentolite
  pentolita
pentolonium tartrate
  tartrato de pentolonio
pentomone
  pentomona
pentorex
  pentorex
pentosan
  pentosana
pentosan polysulfate
  polisulfato de
  pentosana
pentose
  pentosa
pentoside
  pentosida
pentostatin
  pentostatina

pentothal
  tiopental sódico
pentoxifylline
  pentoxifilina
pentoxyl
  pentoxilo
pentoxyverine
  pentoxiverina
pentrinitrol
  pentrinitrol
pentyl
  pentilo
pentyl acetate
  acetato de pentilo
tert-pentyl alcohol
  alcohol terc-pentilo,
  terc-pentanol
pentylamine
  pentilamina
α-pentylcinnam-
aldehyde
  α-pentilcinam-
  aldehído
pentylenetetrazole
  pentilentetrazol
p-tert-penthylphenol
  p-terc-pentilfenol
Penzold's reagent
  reactivo de Penzold
peonidin
  peonidina
peplomycin
  peplomicina
pepper
  pimienta
pepper oil
  esencia (aceite) de
  pimienta negra
peppermint
  menta piperita
peppermint oil
  aceite de menta
  piperita
pepsin
  pepsina
pepsinogen
  pepsinógeno
pepstatin
  pepestatina
peptidase
  peptidasa
peptide
  péptido
peptization
  peptización
peptone
  peptona
peptonic
  peptónico

peptonization
peptonización
peptonized iron
hierro peptonizado
peracetic acid
ácido peracético
per-acids
perácidos
peradoxime
peradoxima
perafensine
perafensina
peralopride
peraloprida
peraquinsin
peraquinsin
perastine
perastina
peratizole
peratizol
perazine
peracina, perazina
perbenzoic acid
ácido
perbenzoico
perborate
perborato
perboric acid
ácido perbórico
percarbamide
percarbamida
perchlorate
perclorato
perchloric acid
ácido perclórico
perchloride
percloruro
perchlorobenzene
perclorobenceno
perchlorocyclo-
pentadiene
perclorociclo-
pentadieno
perchloroethane
percloroetano
perchloroethylene
percloroetileno
perchloromethane
perclorometano
perchloromethyl
mercaptan
perclorometil-
mercaptano
perchloropenta-
cyclodecane
percloropentaciclo-
decano
perchloropropylene
percloropropileno

perchloryl fluoride
fluoruro de
perclorilo
perchromic acid
ácido percrómico
percolate, to
colar, filtrar
percolation
percolación
perezone
perezona
perfect gas
gas perfecto
perfluamine
perfluamina
perfluidone
perfluidona
perflunafene
perflunafeno
perfluoro-2-butene
perfluor-2-buteno
perfluorobutyric acid
ácido perfluorbutírico
perfluorocarbon
compound
compuesto
perfluorcarbonado
perfluorocyclobutane
perfluorciclobutano
perfluorodimethyl-
cyclobutane
perfluordimetil-
ciclobutano
perfluoroethylene
perfluoretileno
perfluoropropane
perfluorpropano
perfluoropropene
perfluorpropeno
perfluorosulfonic acid
ácido perfluor-
sulfónico
performance
comportamiento,
funcionamiento
performic acid
ácido perfórmico
perfume
perfume
pergolide
pergolida
perhexiline
perhexilina
perhydrosqualene
perhidroscualeno
peri acid
ácido peri
pericyazine
periciacina, periciazina

periclase
periclasa
perilla ketona
perilla cetona
perillaldehyde
perillaldehído
perilla oil
aceite de perilla
perimethazine
perimetacina,
perimetazina
perimycin
perimicina
perindopril
perindopril
period
período, tiempo
periodate
periodato
periodic acid
ácido periódico
periodic law
ley periódica
periodic table
tabla periódica,
clasificación periódica
de los elementos
periodic system
sistema periódico
periodide
peryoduro
periodyl
peryodil
periplanones
periplanonas
periplocin
periplocina
periplocymarin
periplocimarina
periplogenin
periplogenina
perisoxal
perisoxal
perivine
perivina
Perkin alicyclic
synthesis
síntesis alicíclica de
Perkin
Perkin reaction
reacción de Perkin
Perkin rearrangement
transposición de Perkin
Perkow reaction
reacción de Perkow
perlapine
perlapina
permanent magnet
imán permanente

permanent orange
anaranjado permanente
permanent-press resin
resina de planchado
permanente
permanent red 2B
amine
amina de rojo
permanente 2B
permanent set
permanente
permanent yellow
amarillo permanente
permanganate
permanganato
permanganic
permangánico
permanganic acid
ácido permangánico
permeability
permeabilidad
permethrin
permetrina
pernambuco
pernambuco
peronine
peronina
perosmic acid
ácido perósmico
perospirone
perospirona
peroxidase
peroxidasa
peroxide
peróxido
peroxyacetic acid
ácido peroxiacético
peroxybenzoyl nitrate
nitrato de
peroxibenzoílo
peroxyformic acid
ácido peroxifórmico
peroxysulfuric acid
ácido peroxisulfúrico
perphenazine
perfenacina,
perfenazina
persalt
persal
persic oil
aceite pérsico
persulfuric acid
ácido persulfúrico
Peru balsam
bálsamo del Perú
Peruvian bark
quina, cincona
perylene
perileno

213

pesticide
pesticida
pestle
mano
petalite
petalita
Peterson reaction
(olefination)
reacción de Peterson
(olefinación)
pethidine
petidina
Petrensko-Kristchenko
piperidone synthesis
síntesis de piperidonas
de Petrensko y
Kristchenko
petri dish
placa de petri
petricloral
petricloral
petrochemical
producto químico del
petroleo
petrolatum
petrolato
petrolatum, liquid
petrolato líquido, aceite
mineral
petroleum
petróleo
petroleum benzin(e)
bencina de petróleo
petroleum ether
éter de petróleo
petroleum gas, liquefied
gas de petróleo licuado
petroleum jelly
vaselina, petrolato
petroleum spirits
alcoholes de petróleo
petroleum, synthetic
petróleo sintético
petroleum thinner
diluyente del petróleo
petunidin
petunidina
peucedanin
peucedanina
pewter
peltre
pexantel
penxantel
pexiganan
pexiganan
peyonine
peyonina
peyote
peyote

Pfau-Plattner azulene
synthesis
síntesis de azuleno de
Pfau y Plattner
Pfeiffer's substance
sustancia de Pfeiffer
Pfitzinger reaction
reacción de Pfitzinger
Pfitzner-Moffatt
oxidation
oxidación de Ptizner y
Moffatt
pH
pH
phalloidin
faloidina
phanquinone
fanquinona
pharmaceutical
farmacéutico, fármaco
phase
fase, etapa
phase diagram
diagrama de fases
phase rule
regla de la fase
phaseolin
faseolina
phasin
fasina
α-phellandrene
α-felandreno
phenacaine
fenacaína
phenacaine
hydrochloride
clorhidrato de
fenacaína
phenacemide
fenacemida
phenacetin
fenacetina
phenacetolin
fenacetolina
phenacridane
chloride
cloruro de fenacridano
phenactropinium
chloride
cloruro de
fenantropinio
phenacyclamine
fenaciclamina
phenacyl chloride
cloruro de fenacilo
phenacylamine
fenacilamina
phenadoxone
fenadoxona

phenadoxone
hydrochloride
clorhidrato de
fenadoxona
phenaglycodol
fenaglicodol
phenallymal
fenalimal
phenamazoline
fenamazolina
phenamet
fenamet
phenamidine
fenamidina
phenampromid(e)
fenampromida
phenanthraquinone
fenantraquinona
phenanthrene
fenantreno
phenanthrenequinone
fenantrenoquinona
o-phenanthroline
o-fenantrolina
phenarsazine chloride
cloruro de fenarsazina
phenarsone
sulfoxylate
sulfoxilato de
fenarsona
phenatine
fenatina
phenazine
fenacina, fenazina
phenazocine
fenazocina
phenazone
fenazona
phenazopyridine
fenazopiridina
phenazopyridine
hydrochloride
cloruro de
fenazopiridina
phenbutamide
fembutamida
phencarbamide
fencarbamida
phencyclidine
fenciclidina
phendimetrazine
fendimetrazina
phendimetrazine
tartrate
tartrato de
fendimetracina, tartrato
de fendimetrazina
phenelzine
fenelcina, fenelzina

phenelzine sulfate
sulfato de fenelcina,
sulfato de fenelzina
pheneridine
feneridina
phenesterine
fenesterina
phenetharbital
fenetarbital
phenethicillin
feneticilina
phenethicillin
potassium
feneticilina pótasica
phenethyl acetate
acetato de fenetilo
phenethyl alcohol
alcohol fenetílico
sec-phenethyl alcohol
alcohol sec-fenetílico
phenethyl anthranilate
antranilato de fenetilo
phenethyl
isobutyrate
isobutirato de fenetilo
phenethyl
phenylacetate
fenilacetato de fenetilo
phenethyl propionate
propionato de fenetilo
phenethyl salicylate
salicilato de fenetilo
phenethylamine
fenetilamina, amina
fenetílica
o-phenetidine
o-fenetidina
p-phenetidine
p-fenetidina
phenetole
fenetol
pheneturide
feneturida
phenformin
fenformina
phenglutarimide
fenglutarimida
phenic acid
ácido fénico
phenicarbazide
fenicarbazida
phenicin
fenicina
phenindamine
fenindamina
phenindamine tartrate
tartrato de fenindamina
phenindione
fenindiona

214

pheniodol sodium
feniodol sódico
pheniprazine
fenipracina,
feniprazina
pheniramine
feniramina
pheniramine
maleate
maleato de feniramina
phenmedipham
fenmedifán
phenmetrazine
fenmetrazina
phenobarbital
fenobarbital
phenobarbital sodium
fenobarbital sódico
phenobutiodil
fenobutiodilo
phenocoll
fenocol
phenocoll
hydrochloride
clorhidrato de fenocol
phenoctide
fenoctida
phenol
fenol
phenol coefficient
coeficiente de fenol
phenol red
rojo de fenol
phenol trinitrate
trinitrato de fenol
phenolate
fenolato
phenolate process
método del fenolato
phenoldisulfonic acid
ácido fenol-
disulfónico
phenol-formaldehyde
resin
resina de fenol y
formaldehído
phenolic
fenólico
phenolic resin
resina fenólica
phenolphthalein
fenolftaleína
phenolphthalein
sodium
fenoftaleína sódica
phenolphthalin
fenolftalina, ftalina
phenolphthalol
fenolftalol

phenolsulfone-
phthalein
fenolsulfonftaleína
phenolsulfonic acid
ácido fenolsulfónico
phenolsulfonphthalein
fenolsulfonftaleína
phenoltetrachloro-
phthalein
fenoltetracloroftaleína
phenomorphan
fenomorfano
phenoperidine
fenoperidina
phenosafranin
fenosafranina
phenosulfazole
fenosulfazol
phenothiazine
fenotiazina,
tiodifenilamina
phenothrin
fenotrina
phenoxazine
fenoxazina
phenoxazole
fenoxazol
phenoxy resin
resina fenóxido
phenoxyacetic acid
ácido fenoxiacético
phenoxyacetyl
cellulose
celulosa fenoxiacetílica
phenoxybenzamine
fenoxibenzamina
phenoxybenzamine
hydrochloride
clorhidrato de
fenoxibenzamina
phenoxydihydroxy-
propane
fenoxidihidroxi-
propano
2-phenoxyethanol
2-fenoxietanol
α-phenoxyethyl-
penicillin
α-fenoxietilpenicilina
phenoxymethyl-
penicillin
fenoximetilpenicilina
phenoxypropanediol
fenoxipropanodiol
phenoxypropilene
oxide
óxido de
fenoxipropileno, óxido
fenoxipropilénico

phenoxypropazine
fenoxipropacina,
fenoxipropazina
phenpentermine
fempentermina,
fenilpentermina
phenprobamate
femprobamato,
fenilprobamato
phenprocoumon
femprocumona,
fenilprocumona
phenpromethamine
femprometamina,
fenilprometamina
phensuximide
fensuximida
phentermine
hydrochloride
clorhidrato de
fentermina
phentermine resin
resina de fentermina
phentetiothalein
sodium
fentetiotaleína sódica
phentolamine
fentolamina
phentolamine mesylate
mesilato de
fentolamina
phentydrone
fentidrona
phenyl
fenilo
phenyl acetate
acetato de fenilo
phenyl acetylsalicylate
acetilsalicilato fenílico
phenyl acrylyl chloride
cloruro de fenilacrililo
phenyl amino-
salicylate
aminosalicilato fenílico
phenyl arsonic acid
ácido fenilarsónico
phenyl benzoate
benzoato de fenilo
phenyl biguanide
biguanida fenílica
phenyl bromide
bromuro de fenilo
phenyl carbimide
fenilcarbimida,
carbimida fenílica
phenyl carbonate
carbonato de fenilo
phenyl chloride
cloruro de fenilo

phenyl chloromethyl
ketone
fenilclorometil cetona,
clorometilcetona
fenílica
phenyl cinnamic acid
ácido fenilcinámico
phenyl cyanide
cianuro de fenilo
phenyl diethanolamine
fenildietanolamina
phenyl diglycol
carbonate
carbonato
fenildiglicólico
phenyl ether
éter fenílico
phenyl ethyl ether
éter feniletílico
phenyl ferrocenyl
ketone
fenilferrocenil cetona
phenyl fluoride
fluoruro de fenilo
phenyl fluoromethyl
ketone
fenilfluorometil cetona
phenyl isocyanate
isocianato de fenilo
phenyl isothio-
cyanate
isotiocianato de fenilo
phenyl J acid
ácido fenil J (ácido
fenil-2-amino-5-naftol-
7-sulfónico)
phenyl mercaptan
fenilmercaptano
phenyl mustard oil
aceite de fenilmostaza,
isotiocianato de fenilo
N-phenyl ß-naphthyl-
amine
N-fenil ß-naftilamina
N-phenyl 1-naphthyl-
amine-8-sulfonic
acid
ácido N-fenil 1-
naftilamina-8-sulfónico
phenyl phthalate
ftalato de fenilo
phenyl salicylate
salicilato de fenilo
phenyl sulfide
sulfuro fenílico
phenylacetaldehyde
fenilacetaldehído,
acetaldehídofenílico,
aldehído α-toluico

phenylacetaldehyde
dimethylacetal
dimetilacetal de
fenilacetaldehído
phenylacetamide
fenilacetamida
N-phenylacetamide
N-fenilacetamida
phenylacetic acid
ácido fenilacético
phenylacetone
acetona fenílica,
fenilacetona
phenylacetonitrile
fenilacetonitrilo
α-phenylacetophenone
α-fenilacetofenona
phenylacetyl chloride
cloruro de fenilacetilo
phenylacetylurea
fenilacetilurea
ß-phenylacrylic acid
ácido ß-fenilacrílico
phenylalanine
fenilalanina
phenylallylic alcohol
alcohol fenilalílico
phenylamine
fenilamina
phenylamino cadmiun
dilactate
dilactato fenilamino-
cádmico
phenyl-2-amino-5-
naphtol-7-sulfonic-
acid
ácido fenil-2-
amino-5-naftol-7-
sulfónico
1-phenyl-2-amino-
propane
1-fenil-2-amino-
propano
N-phenylaniline
N-fenilanilina
N-phenylanthranilic
acid
ácido N-fenil-
antranílico
phenylazoaniline
fenilazoanilina
1-(phenylazo)-2-
naphthylamine
1-(fenilazo)-2-
naftilamina
phenylbarbital
fenilbarbital
phenylbenzamide
fenilbenzamida

2-phenyl-1H-
benzimidazole
1H-bencimidazol 2-
fenílico
3-phenyl-3-
benzoborepin
3-fenil-3-
benzoborepino
phenylbiphenyl-
oxadiazole
fenilbifeniloxa-
diazol
phenylbis [1-(2-
methyl)aziridinyl]
phosphine oxide
óxido de fenilbis [1-(2-
metil) aziridinil]-
fosfina
1-phenylbutane
1-fenilbutano
phenylbutazone
fenilbutazona
1-phenylbutene
1-fenilbuteno
phenylbutynol
fenilbutinol
phenylbutyramide
butiramida fenílica,
fenilbutiramida
2-phenylbutyric acid
ácido 2-fenilbutírico
1-phenyl-3-carbethoxy-
pyrazolone
1-fenil-3-carbetoxi-
pirazolona
phenylcarbinol
fenilcarbinol
phenylcarbylamine
chloride
cloruro de
fenilcarbilamina
phenylchloroform
fenilcloroformo
1-phenyl-3-chloro-
propane
1-fenil-3-cloropropano
2-phenyl-6-
chlorophenol
2-fenil-6-clorofenol
α-phenylcinnamic acid
ácido α-fenilcinámico
phenylcyclohexane
fenilciclohexano
2-phenylcyclohexanol
2-fenilciclohexanol
N-phenyl-N'-
cyclohexyl-p-
phenylenediamine
N-fenil-N'-ciclohexil-

p-fenilendiamina
phenylcyclydene
hydrochloride
clorhidrato de
fenilciclideno
phenyldichloroarsine
fenildicloroarsina
phenyldidecyl
phosphite
fosfito de fenildidecilo
N-phenyl-N'-(1,3-
dimethyl butyl)-p-
phenylenediamine
N-fenil-N'-(1,3-
dimetilbutil)-p-
fenilendiamina
3-phenyl-1,1-
dimethylurea
3-fenil-1,1-dimetilurea
phenylenediamine
fenilendiamina
phenylephrine
fenilefrina
phenylephrine
hydrochloride
clorhidrato de
fenilefrina
phenylethane
feniletano
2-phenylethanol
2-feniletanol
phenylethanolamine
feniletanolamina
2-phenylethyl acetate
acetato de 2-feniletilo
sec-phenylethyl
acetate
acetato de sec-
feniletilo
2-phenylethyl
anthranilate
antranilato de 2-
feniletilo
2-phenylethyl
alcohol
alcohol 2-feniletílico
phenylethyl carbinol
feniletilcarbinol
2-phenylethyl
isobutyrate
isobutirato de 2-
feniletilo
2-phenylethyl
mercaptan
2-feniletilmercaptano
2-phenylethyl
phenylacetate
fenilacetato de 2-
feniletilo

2-phenylethyl
propionate
propionato de 2-
feniletilo
2-phenylethyl
salicylate
salicilato de 2-
feniletilo
phenylethylacetic acid
ácido feniletilacético
2-phenylethylamine
2-feniletilamina
phenylethylene
feniletileno
phenylethylene glycol
glicol feniletilénico,
feniletilenglicol
N-phenylethyl-
ethanolamine
N-feniletiletanolamina
5-phenyl-5-ethyl-
hydantoin
5-fenil-5-etil-
hidantoína
phenylethylmalonyl-
urea
feniletilmalonilurea
5-(α-phenylethyl)
semioxamazide
5-(α-feniletil)
semioxamazida
phenylformamide
fenilformamida
phenylformic acid
ácido fenilfórmico
phenylglyceryl ether
éter fenilglicerílico
phenylglycidyl ether
éter fenilglicidílico
N-phenylglycine
N-fenilglicina
phenylglycol
fenilglicol
phenylglycolic acid
ácido fenilglicólico
α-phenylglycine
α-fenilglicina
C-phenylglycine
C-fenilglicina, α-
fenilglicina
phenylhydrazine
fenilhidracina,
fenilhidrazina
phenylhydrazine
hydrochloride
clorhidrato de
fenilhidracina,
clorhidrato de
fenilhidrazina

α-phenylhydroxy-
acetic acid
ácido α-fenil-
hidroxiacético
phenylhydroxylamine
fenilhidroxilamina
phenylic acid
ácido fenílico
phenylmagnesium
bromide
bromuro de
fenilmagnesio
phenylmagnesium
chloride
cloruro de
fenilmagnesio
N-phenylmaleimide
N-fenilmaleimida
phenylmercuric
acetate
acetato fenilmercúrico
phenylmercuric
benzoate
benzoato fenil-
mercúrico
phenylmercuric borate
borato fenilmercúrico
phenylmercuric
chloride
cloruro fenilmercúrico
phenylmercuric
compounds
compuestos de
fenilmercurio
phenylmercuric
hydroxide
hidróxido
fenilmercúrico
phenylmercuric
lactate
lactato fenilmercúrico
phenylmercuric
naphthenate
naftenato
fenilmercúrico
phenylmercuric
nitrate, basic
nitrato fenilmercúrico
básico
phenylmercuric oleate
oleato fenilmercúrico
phenylmercuric
propionate
propionato
fenilmercúrico
phenylmercuric
salycilate
salicilato
fenilmercúrico

phenylmercuri-
ethanolammonium
acetate
acetato de fenilmercuri-
etanolamonio
phenylmercuri-
triethanilammonium
lactate
lactato de fenil-
mercuritrietanil-
amonio
phenylmercury borate
borato fenilmercúrico
phenylmercury
formamide
formamida
fenilmercúrica
phenylmercury urea
urea fenilmercúrica
phenylmethane
fenilmetano
phenylmethanol
fenilmetanol
phenylmethyl acetate
acetato de fenilmetilo
phenylmethyl ketona
fenilmetil cetona,
cetona fenilmetílica
phenylmethyl-
barbituric acid
ácido fenilmetil-
barbitúrico
phenylmethylcarbinol
fenilmetilcarbinol
phenylmethylcarbinyl
acetate
acetato de
fenilmetilcarbinilo
N-phenylmethyl-
ethanolamine
N-fenilmetil-
etanolamina
1-phenyl-3-methyl-5-
pyrazolone
1-fenil-3-metil-5-
pirazolona
phenyl α-methylstyryl
ketone
fenil α-metilestiril
cetona
N-phenylmorpholine
N-fenilmorfolina
N-phenyl α-naphthyl-
amine
N-fenil α-naftilamina
phenylneopentyl
phosphite
fosfito de
fenilneopentilo

1-phenylnonane
1-fenilnonano
2-phenylpentane
2-fenilpentano
o-phenylphenol
o-fenilfenol
N-phenyl-p-phenylene-
diamine
N-fenil-p-fenilen-
diamina
phenylphosphine
fenilfosfina
phenylphosphinic acid
ácido fenilfosfínico
phenylphosphonic acid
ácido fenilfosfónico
N-phenylpiperazine
N-fenilpiperazina
phenylpropane
fenilpropano
3-phenyl-1-propanol
3-fenil-1-propanol
phenylpropanolamine
hydrochloride
clorhidrato de
fenilpropanolamina
1-phenylpropanone
1-fenilpropanona
phenylstearic acid
3-phenylpropenal
3-fenilpropenal
3-phenylpropenoic acid
ácido 3-fenil-
propenoico
3-phenylpropenol
3-fenilpropenol
1(α-phenyl)-
propenylveratrole
1(α-fenil)-
propenilveratrol
3-phenylpropion-
aldehyde
3-fenilpropion-
aldehído
3-phenylpropionic
acid
ácido 3-fenil-
propiónico
phenylpropyl acetate
acetato de fenilpropilo
phenylpropyl alcohol
alcohol fenilpropílico
phenylpropyl aldehyde
aldehído fenilpropílico
phenylpropyl chloride
cloruro de fenilpropilo
phenylpropylmethyl-
amine
fenilpropilmetilamina

4-phenylpropyl-
pyridine
4-fenilpropilpiridina
1-phenyl-3-
pyrazolidinone
1-fenil-3-
pirazolidinona
1-phenyl-3-
pyrazolidone
1-fenil-3-pirazolidona
4-phenylpropyl-
pyridine
4-fenilpropilpiridina
phenylsemicarbazide
fenilsemicarbazida
phenylstearic acid
ácido fenilesteárico
phenylsulfanilic acid
ácido fenilsulfanílico
phenylsulfohydrazide
fenilsulfohidrazida
phenylsulfonic acid
ácido fenilsulfónico
4-phenyl-1,4-
thiazane
4-fenil-1,4-tiazano
phenylthio-
carbonimide
feniltiocarbonimida
phenylthiourea
feniltiourea
phenyltoloxamine
feniltoloxamina
phenyltoloxamine
citrate
citrato de
feniltoloxamina
phenyltolyl ketone
feniltolil cetona
phenyltrichlorosilane
feniltriclorosilano
phenyltrimethyl-
ammonium iodide
yoduro de
feniltrimetilamonio
1-phenyltridecane
1-feniltridecano
phenyltrimetoxysilane
feniltrimetoxisilano
phenylurea
urea fenílica
phenylurethan(e)
feniluretano
phenyracillin
feniracilina
phenyramidol
feniramidol
phenythilone
fenitilona

phenytoin
fenitoína

phenytoin sodium
fenitoína sódica

pheromones
feromonas

phetharbital
fetarbital

phethenylate sodium
fetenilato de sodio

phial
ampolla, ampolleta

phillyrin
filirina

phlogistic
flogístico

phlogiston
flogisto

phloionic acid
ácido floiónico

phloretin
floretina

phloridzin, phlorizin
floricina

phloroglucinol
floriglucinol

phlorol
florol

phloxine
floxina

pholcodine
folcodina

pholedrine
foledrino

phorate
forato

phorbol
forbol

phorone
forona

phosalone
fosalona

phosfolan
fosfolano

phosgene
fosgeno

phosmet
fosmet

phosphamidon
fosfamidón

phosphatase, alkaline
fosfatasa alcalina

phosphates, condensed
fosfatos condensados

phosphate glass
vidrio fosfatado

phosphate rock
roca de fosfato

phosphate slag
escoria de fosfato

phosphatide
fosfátido

phosphatidyl choline
fosfatidilcolina

phosphatidyl ethanolamine
fosfatidiletanolamina

phosphatidyl serine
fosfatidilserina

phosphatize
fosfatar, reducir a fosfato

phosphazene
fosfaceno

phosphene
fosfeno

phosphide
fosfuro

phosphinate
fosfinato

phosphine
fosfina

phosphinothricin
fosfinotricina

phosphite
fosfito

phosphocreatine
fosfocreatina

phosphodiesterase
fosfodiesterasa

2-phosphoglyceric acid
ácido 2-fosfoglicérico

phosphoglyceride
fosfoglicérido

phospholipid
fosfolípido

phosphomolybdate
fosfomolibdato

phosphomolybdic acid
ácido fosfomolíbdico

phosphomolybdic pigment
pigmento fosfomolíbdico

phosphonate
fosfonato

phosphonitrile
fosfonitrilo

phosphonitrilic polymer
polímero fosfonitrílico

phosphonium
fosfonio

phosphonium iodide
yoduro de fosfonio

phosphor
fosforescente

phosphor bronze
bronce fosforado

phosphorescence
fosforescencia

phosphoric acid
ácido fosfórico

phosphoric acid, anhydrous
ácido fosfórico anhidro

phosphoric acid, meta
ácido metafosfórico

o-phosphoric acid
ácido o-fosfórico

phosphoric acid, anhydrous
ácido fosfórico anhidro

phosphoric anhydride
anhídrido fosfórico

phosphoric bromide
bromuro fosfórico

phosphoric chloride
cloruro fosfórico

phosphoric oxide
óxido fosfórico

phosphoric perbromide
perbromuro fosfórico

phosphoric perchloride
percloruro fosfórico

phosphoric sulfide
sulfuro fosfórico

phosphorous acid, ortho
ácido ortofosforoso

phosphorus
fósforo

phosphorus chloride
cloruro de fósforo

phosphorus hemitriselenide
hemitriseleniuro de fósforo

phosphorus heptasulfide
heptasulfuro de fósforo

phosphorus nitride
nitruro de fósforo

phosphorus oxybromide
oxibromuro de fósforo

phosphorus oxychloride
oxicloruro de fósforo

phosphorus pentabromide
pentabromuro de fósforo

phosphorus pentachloride
pentacloruro de fósforo

phosphorus pentafluoride
pentafluoruro de fósforo

phosphorus pentaselenide
pentaseleniuro de fósforo

phosphorus pentasulfide
pentasulfuro de fósforo

phosphorus pentoxide
pentóxido de fósforo

phosphorus persulfide
persulfuro de fósforo

phosphorus salt
sal de fósforo

phosphorus sesquisulfide
sesquisulfuro de fósforo

phosphorus sulfide
sulfuro de fósforo

phosphorus sulfochloride
sulfocloruro de fósforo

phosphorus tribromide
tribromuro de fósforo

phosphorus trichloride
tricloruro de fósforo

phosphorus triiodide
triyoduro de fósforo

phosporus trioxide
trióxido de fósforo

phosphorus triselenide
triseleniuro de fósforo

phosphorus trisulfide
trisulfuro de fósforo

phosphorylase
fosforilasa

phosphorylated cellulose
celulosa fosforilada

phosphorylation
fosforilación

phosphoryl chloride
cloruro de fosforilo

phosphorylcholine
fosforilcolina

phosphoserine
fosfoserina

phosphotungstic acid
ácido fosfotúngstico

phosphotungstic acid, sodium salt
sal sódica del ácido fosfotúngstico

phosphotungstic
pigment
  pigmento
  fosfotúngstico
phosvitin
  fosvitina
photocatalysis
  fotocatálisis
photochemistry
  fotoquímica
photochromism
  fotocromía
photodecomposition
  fotodescomposición
photo-glycin
  fotoglicina
photographic chemistry
  química fotográfica
photolysis
  fotólisis
photometer
  fotómetro
photometric analysis
  análisis fotométrico
photon
  fotón
photophor
  fotóforo
photopolymer
  fotopolímero
photosynthesis
  fotosíntesis
phototropism
  fototropía
photovoltaic cell
  célula fotovoltaica
phoxim
  foxima
phrenosin
  frenosina
phthalamide
  ftalamida
phthalazine
  ftalacina, ftalazina
phthalein
  ftaleína
phthalic
  ftálico
phthalic acid
  ácido ftálico
phthalic anhydride
  anhídrido ftálico
phthalimide
  ftalimida
phthalocyanine
  ftalocianina
phthalocyanine colorant
  colorante de
  ftalocianina

phthalofyne
  ftalofina
phthalonitrile
  ftalonitrilo
phthaloyl chloride
  cloruro de
  ftaloílo
phthalylsulfacetamide
  ftalilsulfacetamida
phthalylsulfa-
methizole
  ftalilsulfametizol
phthalylsulfathiazole
  ftalilsulfatiazol
phthiocol
  ftiocol
phycobiliproteins
  ficobiliproteínas
phylloquinone
  filoquinona
physalaemin
  fisalaemina,
  fisalamina
physical chemistry
  fisicoquímica
physiological salt
solution
  solución salina
  fisiológica
physodic acid
  ácido fisódico
physostigma
  fisostigma
physostigmine
  fisostigmina
physovenine
  fisovenina
phytane
  fitano
phytic acid
  ácido fítico
phytochemistry
  fitoquímica
phytochlorin
  fitoclorina
phytofluene
  fitoflueno
phytol
  fitol
phytolacca
  fitolaca
phytomenadione
  fitomenadiona
phytonadiol sodiun
diphosphate
  difosfato sódico de
  fitonadiol
phytonadione
  fitonadiona

phytosterol
  fitosterol
pi bond
  enlace pi
pibecarb
  pibecarbo
piberaline
  piberalina
picadex
  picadex
picafibrate
  picafibrato
picein
  piceína
picenadol
  picenadol
picene
  piceno
picilorex
  picilorex
piclonidine
  piclonidina
piclopastine
  piclopastina
picloram
  piclorán
pickle alum
  alumbre de curtido
picloxydine
  picloxidina
picobenzide
  picobenzida
picodralazine
  picodralacina,
  picodralazina
picolamine
  picolamina
α-picoline
  α-picolina
picoline-N-oxide
  N-óxido de picolina
picolinic acid
  ácido picolínico
picoperine
  picoperina
picoprazole
  picoprazol
picosulfate sodium
  picosulfato de sodio
picotamide
  picotamida
picotrin
  picotrino
picramic acid
  ácido picrámico
picrasmin
  picrasmina
picrate
  picrato

picric acid
  ácido pícrico, 2,4,6-
  trinitrofenol
picrocrocin(e)
  picrocrocina
picrolonic acid
  ácido picrolónico
picromycin
  picromicina
picronitric acid
  ácido picronítrico,
  ácido pícrico
picropodophyllin
  picropodofilina
picrorrhiza
  picrorhiza
picrotin
  picrotina
picrotol
  picrotol
picrotoxin
  picrotoxina
picrotoxinin
  picrotoxinina
picryl chloride
  cloruro de picrilo
Pictet-Gams
isoquinoline synthesis
  síntesis de isoquinolina
  de Pictet y Gams
Pictet-Hubert reaction
  reacción de Pictet y
  Hubert
Pictet-Splenger
isoquinoline synthesis
  síntesis de isoquinolina
  de Pictet y Splenger
picumast
  picumast
pidorubicin
  pidorrubicina
piezochemistry
  piezoquímica
pifarnine
  pifarnina
pifenate
  pifenato
pifexole
  pifexol
piflutixol
  piflutixol
pifoxime
  pifoxima
pig iron
  hierro en lingotes
pigment
  pigmento
pigment blue
  pigmento azul

pigment E
pigmento E, pigmento
de cromato bárico
potásico
pigment, plant
pigmento vegetal
pigment, precipitated
pigmento precipitado
**pigment volume
concentration**
concentración de
volumen de pigmento
piketoprofen
picetoprofeno
pilchard oil
aceite de sardina
pildralazine
pildralacina,
pildralazina
pill
pastilla
pilocarpine
pilocarpina
pilocarpus
pilocarpo
pilocereine
pilocereína
pilot plant
planta piloto
**Piloty-Robinson
synthesis**
síntesis de Piloty y
Robinson
pimaric acid
ácido pimárico
pimeclone
pimeclona
pimefylline
pimefilina
pimelic acid
ácido pimélico
pimelic ketone
cetona pimélica
pimenta
pimienta
pimento oil
esencia (aceite)
de amomo, esencia
(aceite) de pimienta
pimetacin
pimetacina
pimethixene
pimetixeno
pimetine
pimetina
pimetremide
pimetremida
piminodine
piminodina

pimobendan
pimobendano,
pimobendán
pimozide
pimocida, pimozida
pimpinella
pimpinela
pimpinellin
pimpinelina
pinacidil
pinacidil
pinacol
pinacol
**Pinacol
rearranagement**
transposición de
Pinacol
pinacolone
pinacolona
pinafide
pinafida
pinaverium bromide
bromuro de pinaverio
pinazepam
pinacepán, pinazepam
pindolol
pindolol
pindone
pindona
pine oil
aceite de pino
pine tar
alquitrán de pino
pine tar oil
aceite de alquitrán de
pino
pine tar pitch
pez de alquitrán de
pino
α-pinene
α-pineno
pinene hydrochloride
clorhidrato de pineno
pinguinain
pinguinaína
Pinner reaction
reacción de Pinner
**Pinner triazine
synthesis**
síntesis de triazina de
Pinner
pinolcaine
pinolcaína
pinosylvin
pinosilvina
pinoxepin
pinoxepina
pioglitazone
pioglitazona

pipacycline
pipaciclina
pipamazine
pipamacina,
pipamazina
pipamperone
pipamperona
pipazethate
pipazetato
pipebuzone
pipebuzona
pipecolic acid
ácido pipecólico
pipecoline
pipecolina, 2-
metilpiperidina
pipecurium bromide
bromuro de pipecurio
pipemidic acid
ácido pipemídico
pipenzolate bromide
bromuro de
pipenzolato
piperacetazine
piperacetacina,
piperacetazina
piperacillin
piperacilina
piperacillin sodium
piperacilina sódica
piperalin
piperalina
piperamide
piperamida
piperazidine
piperazidina, piperazina
piperazine
piperacina, piperazina
piperazine adipate
adipato de piperazina
**piperazine calcium
edetate**
edetato de piperazina y
calcio
piperazine citrate
citrato de piperazina
**piperazine
dihydrochloride**
diclorhidrato de
piperazina
piperazine hexahydrate
hexahidrato de
piperazina
piperazine tartrate
tartrato de piperazina
2,5-piperazinedione
2,5-piperazinadiona
piperic acid
ácido pipérico

piperidine
piperidina
**piperidine
pentamethylene
dithiocarbamate**
pentametilen-
ditiocarbamato de
piperidina
2-piperidinoethanol
2-piperidinoetanol
piperidione
piperidiona
piperidolate
piperidolato
piperilate
piperilato
piperine
piperina
piperitone
piperitona
piperocaine
piperocaína
**piperocaine
hydrochloride**
clorhidrato de
piperocaína
piperonal
piperonal
piperonyl butoxide
butóxido de piperonilo
piperonylic acid
ácido piperonílico
piperoxan
piperoxano
piperylene
piperileno
piperylone
piperilona
PIPES
ácido 1,4-piperazina-
dietanosulfónico
pipethanate
pipetanato
pipette
pipeta
pipobroman
pipobromano
pipoctanone
pipoctanona
pipofezine
pipofecina, pipofezina
piposulfan
piposulfano
pipotiazine
pipotiacina, pipotiazina
pipoxizine
pipoxizina
pipoxolan
pipoxolán

220

pipoxolan hydrochloride
cloruro de pipoxolán
pipradimadol
pipradimadol
pipradrol
pipradrol
pipramadol
pipramadol
pipratecol
pipratecol
piprinhydrinate
piprinhidrinato
piprocurarium iodide
yoduro de piprocurario
piprofurol
piprofurol
piprozolin
piprozolina
pipsyl chloride
cloruro de pipsilo
piquizil
piquicilo
piracetam
piracetán, piracetam
pirandamine
pirandamina
pirarubicin
pirarrubicina
pirazofurin
pirazofurina
pirazolac
pirazolaco
pirbencillin
pirbencilina
pirbuterol
pirbuterol
pirbuterol acetate
acetato de pirbuterol
pirdonium bromide
bromuro de pirdonio
pirenoxine
pirenoxina
pirenperone
piremperona
pirenzepine
pirencepina
piretanide
piretanida
pirfenidone
pirfenidona
Piria reaction
reacción de Piria
piribedil
piribedil
piridicillin
piridicilina
piridocaine
piridocaína

piridoxilate
piridoxilato
pirifibrate
pirifibrato
pirimicarb
pirimicarbo
pirimiphos-ethyl
etilpirimifós
pirinidazole
pirinidazol
pirinixic acid
ácido piriníxico
pirinixil
pirinixilo
piriqualone
piricualona
pirisudanol
pirisudanol
piritramide
piritramida
pirlimycin
pirlimicina
pirlindole
pirlindol
pirmenol
pirmenol
pirnabin
pirnabino
piroctone
piroctona
pirogliride
piroglirida
piroheptine
piroheptina
pirolate
pirolato
pirolazamide
pirolazamida
piromen
piromen
piromidic acid
ácido piromídico
piroxicam
piroxicán,
piroxicam
pirozadil
pirozadil
pirprofen
pirprofeno
pirquinozol
pirquinozol
pirralkonium bromide
bromuro de pirralconio
piscidin
piscidina
pitch
pez
pitenodil
pitenodilo

pithecolobine
pitecolobina
pitofenone
pitofenona
pituitary, posterior
pituitaria posterior
pituitrin
pituitrina
pituxate
pituxato
pivalate
pivalato
pivalic acid
ácido piválico, ácido trimetilacético
2-pivaloyl-1,3-indandione
2-pivaloil-1,3-indandiona
pivalylbenzhydrazine
pivalilbencidracina, pivalilbencidrazina
pivampicillin
pivampicilina
pivcefalexin
pivcefalexina
pivenfrine
pivenfrina
pivmecillinam
pivmencilinamo ·
pivoxazepam
pivoxacepán, pivoxazepam
pivoxil
pivoxil
pizotifen
pizotifeno
pizotyline
pizotilina
placenta
placenta
plafibride
plafibrida
planetology, chemical
planetología química
plant
planta
plant hormone
hormona vegetal
plant growth regulator
regulador del crecimiento de las plantas
plant location
situación de fábricas
plantago seed
semilla de plátano
plantisul
plantisul

plasma
plasma
plasma volume expander
expansor de volumen de plasma
plasmalogens
plasmalógenos
plasmid
plásmido
plasmin
plasmina
plasminogen
plasminógeno
plasmocid
plasmócido
plasmoquin
plasmoquina
plaster of Paris
yeso de París
plastic
plástico
plastic coating
revestimiento plástico
plastic flow
flujo plástico
plastic foam
espuma de plástico
plastic reinforced
plástico reforzado
plastic pipe
tubería de plástico
plasticity
plasticidad
plasticizer
plastificante
plastisol
plastisol
plate
lámina, placa, plato
platelet activating factor
factor activador de plaquetas
platelet-derived growth factor
factor de crecimiento derivado de plaquetas
platinic
platínico
platinic ammonium chloride
cloruro platínico amónico
platinic chloride
cloruro platínico
platinic iodide
yoduro platínico

platinic oxide
óxido de platino
platinic salt ammoniac
sal platínica amoniacal
platinic sodium
chloride
cloruro platínico
sódico
platinic sulfate
sulfato platínico
platinous chloride
cloruro platinoso
platinous iodide
yoduro platinoso
platinum
platino
platinum ammoniun
chloride
cloruro de platino y
amonio
platinum barium
cyanide
cianuro de platino
y bario
platinum black
negro de platino
platinum chloride
cloruro de platino
platinum dichloride
dicloruro de platino
platinum dioxide
dióxido de platino
platinum iodide
yoduro de platino
platinum metal
metal de platino
platinum potassium
chloride
cloruro de platino
y potasio
platinum sponge
esponja de platino
platinum sulfate
sulfato de platino
platinum
tetrachloride
tetracloruro de platino
platinum-cobalt alloy
aleación de platino
y cobalto
platinum-iridium alloy
aleación de platino
e iridio
platinum-lithium
platino y litio
platinum-rhodium
alloys
aleaciones de platino y
rodio

platinum-sodium
chloride
cloruro de platino y
sodio
platonin
platonina
platyphylline
platifilina
plaunotol
plaunotol
plauracin
plauracina
pleconaril
pleconaril
pleuromulin
pleuromulina
pleuromutilin
pleuromutilina
pleurotin(e)
pleurotina
plicamycin
plicamicina
plot, to
trazar
plug
clavija, tapón
plumbagin
plumbagina
plumbic acid,
anhydrous
ácido plúmbico anhidro
plumbous oxide
óxido plumboso
plumbous sulfide
sulfuro plumboso
plumericin
plumericina
plumieride
plumierida
plunge, to
sumergir
plutonium
plutonio
podilfen
podilfeno
podocarpic acid
ácido podocárpico
pododacric acid
ácido pododácrico
podofilox
podofilox
podophyllic acids
ácidos podofílicos
podophyllinic acid
2-ethylhydrazide
ácido podofilínico 2-
etilhidrazida,
2-etilhidrazida
del ácido podofilínico

podophyllin
podofilina
podophyllotoxin
podofilotoxina
podophyllum
podofilo, raiz de
mandrágora
podophyllum, indian
podofilo de la India
podophyllum, resina
resina de podofilo,
podofilina
point of intersection
punto de intersección
poise
poise, unidad de
viscosidad dinámica
poison
veneno
poison gas
gas venenoso
poison ivy
hiedra venenosa
poison oak
zumaque venenoso
polaprezinc
polaprecinc
polar
polar
polar valence
electrovalencia
polarimeter
polarímetro
polarimetry
polarimetría
polarized light
luz polarizada
polarograph
polarógrafo
poldine methysulfate
metilsulfato de poldina
policapram
policaprán, policapram
policresule
policresul
polidexide
polidexido
polidexide sulfate
sulfato de polidexido
polidocanol
polidocanol
polifeprofan
polifeprofano
poligeenan
poligeenano
polihexanide
polihexanido
polisaponin
polisaponina

politef
politefo
pollucite
polucita
pollution
contaminación
polonium
polonio
polonium dioxide
dióxido de polonio
polonium tetrachloride
tetracloruro de polonio
Polonovski reaction
reacción de
Polonovski
poloxalene
poloxaleno
poloxamer
poloxamero
poly⁻
poli⁻
poly cetal
poliacetal
polyacetylene
poliacetileno
polyacrylamide
poliacrilamida
polyacrylate
poliacrilato
polyacrylic acid
ácido poliacrílico
polyacrylonitrile
poliacrilonitrilo
polyalcohol
polialcohol
polyallomer
polialómero
polyamide
poliamida
polyaminemethylene
resin
resina poliamin-
metilénica
polyaminotriazole
poliaminotriazol
polybasic
polibásico
polybenzarsol
polibenzarsol
polybenzimidazole
polibencimidazol
polybrominated
biphenyls
bifenilos
polibrominados
polybutadiene
polibutadieno
polybutene
polibuteno

polybutylene
terephthalate
tereftalato de
polibutileno
polycarbonate
policarbonato
polycarbophil
policarbofila
polycarboxylic acid
ácido policarboxílico
polychlor
policloro
polychlorinated
biphenyls
bifenilos policlorinados
polychloroethylene
sulfonyl chloride
cloruro de
policloroetilen-
sulfonilo
polychloroprene
policloropreno,
neopreno
polychlorotrifluoro-
ethylene
policlorotri-
fluoretileno
polycondensation
policondensación
polycoumarone resin
resina de policumarona
polycyclic
policíclico
poly(1,4-cyclo-
hexylenedimethylene)
terephthalate
tereftalato de poli(1,4-
ciclohexilendi-
metileno)
polydatin
polidatina
polidextrose
polidextrosa
poly-1,1-dihydro-
perfluorobutyl acrylate
acrilato de poli-1,1-
dihidroperfluorbutilo
polydimethylsiloxane
polidimetilsiloxano
poly-p-dinitroso-
benzene
poli-p-dinitroso-
benceno
polyelectrolyte
polielectrólito
polyene
polieno
polyester fiber
fibra de poliéster

polyester film
película de poliéster
polyester resin
resina de poliéster
polyestradiol
phosphate
fosfato de poliestradiol
polyetadene
polietadeno
polyethenoid
polietenoide
polyether
poliéter
polyether, chlorinated
poliéter clorado
polyether cyclic
poliéter cíclico
polyether glycol
glicol de poliéter
polyethylene
polietileno
polyethylene cross-
linked
polietileno
entrecruzado
polyethylene glycol
glicol polietilénico,
polietilenglicol
polyethylene glycol
chloride
cloruro de glicol
polietilénico,
cloruro de
polietilenglicol
polyethylene glycol
ester
éster de glicol
polietilénico, éster de
polietilenglicol
polyethylene imine
polietilenimina
polyethylene linear
polietileno lineal
polyethylene low
molecular weight
polietileno de bajo
peso molecular
polyethylene oxide
óxido de polietileno
polyethylene oxide
sorbitan fatty acid
esters
ésteres de ácidos
grasos de sorbitán y
óxido de polietileno
polyethylene
terephthalate
tereftalato de
polietileno

polyferose
poliferoso
polyformaldehyde
poliformaldehído
polyfurfuryl alcohol
alcohol polifurfurílico
polygeline
poligelina
polyglycerol
poliglicerol,
poliglicerina
polyglycerol ester
éster de poliglicerol,
éster de poliglicerina
polyglycol
poliglicol
polyglycol diestearate
diestearato de
poliglicol
polygodial
poligodial
polyhalite
polihalita
polyhexamethylene-
dipamide
polihexametilen-
dipamida
polyhydric alcohol
alcohol polihídrico
polyimide
polimida
polyisobutene
polisobuteno
polyisobutylene
polisobutileno
polyisotopic
polisótopo
polylysine
polilisina
polyisoprene
polisopreno
polymer
polímero
polymer, addition
polímero de adición
polymer, high
polímero alto
polymer, inorganic
polímero inorgánico
polymer, ladder
polímero escalonado
polymer, natural
polímero natural
polymer, synthetic
polímero sintético
polymer water-soluble
polímero hidrosoluble
polymerase
polimerasa

polymeric
polimérico
polymerism
polimerismo
polymerization
polimerización
polymerize
polimerizar(se)
polymethylbenzene
polimetilbenceno
polymethylene
polifenilisocyanate
polyphenylisocyanate
polifenilisocianato de
polimetileno
polymethylene wax
cera de polimetileno
polymorphism
polimorfismo
polymyxin
polimixina
polymyxin B-methane-
sulfonic acid
ácido polimixin B-
metanesulfónico
polynoxylin
polinoxilina
polynuclear
polinuclear
polyol
poliol
polyolefin
poliolefina
polyoxadiazole
polioxadiazol
polyoxamide
polioxamida
polyoxins
polioxinas
polyoxyethane
polioxietano
polyoxyethylene
polioxietileno
polyoxyethylene
alcohol
alcohol polioxietilénico
polyoxyethylene
fatty acid ester
éster del ácido
graso de polioxietileno
polyoxyl 8 stearate
estearato de polioxilo 8
polyoxyl 40 stearate
estearato de
polioxietileno (40)
polyoxymethylene
polioximetileno
polyoxypropylene
ester
éster de polioxipropileno

polyoxypropylene
diamine
polioxipropilendiamina
polypeptide
polipéptido
polyphenylene oxide
óxido de polifenileno
polyphenylene triazole
polifenilentriazol
polyphosphazenes
polifosfacenos
polyphosphoric acid
ácido polifosfórico
polypropylene
polipropileno
polypropylene,
chlorinated
polipropileno clorado
polypropylene glycol
ester
éster de
polipropilenglicol,
éster de glicol
polipropilénico
polypropylene glycol
monobutyl ester
éster monobutílico de
glicol polipropilénico
polypropylene oxide
óxido de polipropileno
polypropylenebenzene
polipropilenbenceno
polypropyleneimine
polipropilenimina
polypirrolydone
polipirrolidona
polysaccharide
polisacárido
polysiloxane
polisiloxano
polysorbate
polisorbato
polystyrene
poliestireno
polysulfide
polisulfuro
polysulfide elastomer
elastómero polisulfuro
polysulfone
polisulfona
polyterpene resin
resina de politerpeno
polytetrafluoro-
ethylene
politetrafluoretileno
polytetraethylene ether
glycol
éter de glicol
politetraetilénico

polythene
politeno, polietileno
polythiadiazole
politiadiazol
polythiazide
politiazida
polytrifluoro-
chloroethylene
politrifluorcloro-
etileno
polytrifluoro-
chloroethyleneresin
resina de poli-
trifluorcloroetileno
polyunsaturated fat
grasa rica en enlaces
no saturados
polyurethan(e)
poliuretano
polyvalence
polivalencia
polyvalent
polivalente
polividone
polividona
polyvinyl
polivinilo
polyvinyl acetate
acetato de polivinilo
polyvinyl alcohol
alcohol polivinílico
polyvinyl carbazole
carbazol polivinílico
polyvinyl chloride
cloruro de polivinilo
polyvinyl dichloride
dicloruro de
polivinilo
polyvinyl ether
éter polivinílico
polyvinyl fluoride
fluoruro de polivinilo
polyvinyl isobutyl
ether
éter isobutil-
polivinílico
polyvinyl methyl
ether
éter metilpolivinílico
polyvinyl resin
resina polivinílica
polyvinylpyrrolidone
polivinilpirrolidona
Pomeranz-Fritsch
reaction
reacción de Pomeranz
y Fritsch
pomegranate
granado

ponasterone A
ponasterona A
Ponceau 3R
punzó 3R
Ponceau SX
punzó SX
ponfibrate
ponfibrato
Ponzio reaction
reacción de Ponzio
poppy capsules
cápsulas de
adormidera
poppy oil
aceite de adormidera
populin
populina
porcelain
porcelana
porcelain enamel
esmalte de porcelana
porfiromycin
porfiromicina
porosity
porosidad
porous
poroso
porphine
porfina
porphobilinogen
porfobilinógeno
porphyrillic acid
ácido porfírico
porphyrin
porfirina
porphyropsin
porfiropsina
porpoise oil
aceite de marsopa
positive charge
carga positiva
positive valence
valencia positiva
positron
positrón
poskine
posquina
potash
potasa, potasa cáustica,
potasio
potash alum
alumbre de potasa
potash, caustic
potasa cáustica
potash chrome alum
alumbre de potasa y
cromo
potash feldspat
feldespato de potasa

potash magnesia
double salt
sal doble de potasa y
magnesia
potash sulfurated
potasa sulfurada
potassic
potásico
potassium
potasio
potassium abietate
abietato de potasio
potassium acetate
acetato de potasio
potassium alginate
alginato de potasio
potassium
aluminate
aluminato de potasio
potassium
aluminosilicate
aluminosilicato de
potasio
potassium aluminun
fluoride
fluoruro de potasio y
aluminio
potassium p-
aminobenzoate
p-aminobenzoato de
potasio
potassium antimonyl
tartrate
tartrato de potasio y
antimonilo
potassium
argentocyanide
argentocianuro de
potasio
potassium arsenate
arseniato de potasio
potassium arsenite
arsenito de potasio
potassium arsenite
solution
solución de arsenito de
potasio, solución de
Fowler, solución
arsenical
potassium aurate
aurato de potasio
potassium beryllium
fluoride
fluoruro de potasio
y berilio
potassium bicarbonate
bicarbonato de potasio,
carbonato ácido de
potasio

potassium bichromate
bicromato de potasio
potassium bifluoride
bifluoruro de potasio,
fluoruro ácido de
potasio
potassium binoxalate
binoxalato de potasio,
oxalato ácido de
potasio, sal de acederas
potassium biphthalate
biftalato de potasio,
ftalato ácido de potasio
potassiun biselenite
biselenita potásica
potassium bismuth
tartrate
tartrato de potasio y
bismuto
potassium bisulfate
bisulfato de potasio,
sulfato ácido de potasio
potassium bisulfide
bisulfuro de potasio
potassium bisulfite
bisulfito de potasio,
sulfito ácido de potasio
potassium bitartrate
bitartrato de potasio
potassium borate
borato de potasio
potassium borofluoride
borofluoruro de potasio
potassium borohydride
borohidruro de potasio
potassium bromate
bromato de potasio
potassium bromide
bromuro de potasio
potassium tert-
butoxide
terc-butóxido de
potasio
potassium tert-
butylate
terc-butilato de potasio
potassium carbacrylic
resin
resina carbacrílica de
potasio
potassium carbonate
carbonato de potasio
potassium chlorate
clorato de potasio
potassium chloride
cloruro de potasio
potassium
chloroaurate
cloroaurato de potasio

potassium
chlorochromate
clorocromato de
potasio
potassium
chloroiridate
cloroiridato de potasio
potassium
chloroplatinate
cloroplatinato de
potasio
potassium chromate
cromato de potasio
potassium chromate
red
cromato rojo de potasio
potassium chromium
sulfate
sulfato de potasio y
cromo
potassium citrate
citrato de potasio
potassium
cobaltinitrite
cobaltonitrito de
potasio
potassium cobaltous
selenate
seleniato cobaltoso de
potasio
potassium columbate
columbato de potasio
potassium copper
cyanide
cianuro de potasio y
cobre
potassium copper
ferrocyanide
ferrocianuro de potasio
y cobre
potassium cupric
ferrocyanide
ferrocianuro de potasio
cúprico
potassium
cuprocyanide
cuprocianuro de
potasio
potassium cyanate
cianato de potasio
potassium cyanide
cianuro de potasio
potassium
cyanoargentate
cianargentato de
potasio
potassium
cyclamate
ciclamato de potasio

potassium di-n-butyl
dithiocarbamate
di-n-butilditio-
carbamato de potasio
potassium dichloro-
isocyanurate
dicloroisocianurato de
potasio
potassium dichromate
dicromato de potasio
potassium dihydrogen
phosphate
fosfato ácido de
potasio
potassium
dicyanoaurate (I)
cianuro de potasio y
oro, aurocianuro de
potasio
potassium
dimethyldithio-
carbamate
dimetilditiocarbamato
de potasio
potassium diphosphate
difosfato de potasio
potassium dithionate
ditionato de potasio
potassium ethyldithio-
carbonate
etilditiocarbonato de
potasio
potassium ethyl sulfate
etilsulfato de potasio
potassium
ethylxanthate
etilxantato de potasio
potassium
ethylxanthogenate
etilxantogenato de
potasio
potassium feldspar
feldespato de potasio
potassium ferric
oxalate
oxalato potásico férrico
potassium ferricyanide
ferricianuro de potasio
potassium ferrocyanide
ferrocianuro de potasio
potassium fluoborate
fluoborato de potasio
potassium fluoride
fluoruro de potasio
potassium
fluosilicate
fluosilicato de potasio
potassium formate
formiato de potasio

potassium germanium
fluoride
fluoruro de potasio y
germanio
potassium gibberellate
giberelato de potasio
potassium gluconate
gluconato de potasio
potassium glutamate
glutamato de potasio
potassium
glycerophosphate
glicerofosfato de
potasio
potassium gold
chloride
cloruro de potasio y oro
potassium gold
cyanide
cianuro de potasio
y oro
potassium guaiacol-
sulfonate
sulfonato de potasio y
guayacol
potassium hexa-
chloroosmate (IV)
hexaclorosmiato (IV)
de potasio
potassium hexa-
chloroplatinate (IV)
hexacloroplatinato (IV)
de potasio, cloruro
potásico platínico
potassium hexa-
cyanocobaltate (III)
hexacianocobaltato
(III) de potasio,
cianuro de potasio y
cobalto
potassium -2,4-
hexadienoate
2,4-hexadienoato de
potasio, sorbato de
potasio
potassium hexa-
fluoromanganate (IV)
hexafluoromanganato
(IV) de potasio, hexa-
fluoruro de manganeso
y potasio
potassium hexa-
fluoromanganite
hexafluoromanganito
de potasio
potassium hexa-
fluorophosphate
hexafluorofostato
de potasio

potassium hexa-
fluorosilicate
hexafluorosilicato de
potasio, fluosilicato de
potasio
potassium hexa-
fluorozirconate (IV)
hexafluorocirconato
(IV) de potasio,
fluoruro de potasio y
circonio
potassium hexanitro-
cobaltate (III)
hexanitrocobaltato (III)
de potasio, nitrito de
cobalto y potasio, sal
de Fischer
potassium hexathio-
cyanateplatinate (IV)
hexatiocianato-
platinato (IV) de
potasio, tiocianato
platínico potásico
potassium hydrate
hidrato de potasio
potassium hydride
hidruro de potasio
potassium hydrogen
phosphate
fosfato dibásico de
potasio
potassium hydrogen
sulfate
sulfato ácido de
potasio, bisulfato de
potasio
potassium
hydrosulfide
hidrosulfuro de potasio
potassium hydroxide
hidróxido de potasio
potassium
hypophosphite
hipofosfito de potasio
potassium hyposulfate
hiposulfato de potasio
potassium hyposulfite
hiposulfito de potasio,
tiosulfato de potasio
potassium iodate
yodato de potasio
potassium iodide
yoduro de potasio
potassium iridium
chloride
cloruro de iridio y
potasio
potassium laurate
laurato de potasio

potassium linoleate
linoleato de potasio
potasium manganate
(IV)
manganato (IV)
de potasio
potassium mercuric
iodide
yoduro de potasio
y mercurio
potassium
metabisulfite
metabisulfito de
potasio, pirosulfito de
potasio
potassium
metaphosphate
metafosfato de
potasio
potassium methyl
sulfate
metilsulfato de potasio
potassium molybdate
molibdato de potasio
potassium
naphthenate
naftenato de potasio
potassium nickel
sulfate
sulfato de potasio y
niquel
potassium nitrate
nitrato de potasio
potassium nitrite
nitrito de potasio
potassium oleate
oleato de potasio
potassium osmate
osmiato de potasio
potassium oxalate
oxalato de potasio
potassium oxide
óxido de potasio
potassium palladium
chloride
cloruro de potasio y
paladio
potassium penicillin G
penicilina G potásica
potassium penicillin V
penicilina V potásica
potassium
percarbonate
percarbonato de
potasio
potassium perchlorate
perclorato de potasio
potassium periodate
peryodato de potasio

potassium
permanganate
permanganato de
potasio
potassium peroxide
peróxido de potasio
potassium persulfate
persulfato de potasio
potassium
phenolsulfate
fenolsulfato de
potasio, sulfocarbolato
de potasio
potassium phenoxide
fenóxido de potasio,
carbolato de potasio
potassium α-
phenoxyethyl-
penicillin
α-fenoxietilpenicilina
potásica
potassium phenoxy-
methylpenicillin
fenoximetilpenicilina
potásica
potassium phosphate,
dibasic
fosfato de potasio
dibásico
potassium phosphate,
monobasic
fosfato de potasio
monobásico
potassium phosphate,
tribasic
fosfato de potasio
tribásico
potassium phosphite
fosfito de potasio
potassium picrate
picrato de potasio,
trinitrofenolato de
potasio
potassium polysulfide
polisulfuro de potasio
potassium prussiate,
red
prusiato de potasio rojo
potassium prussiate,
yellow
prusiato de potasio
amarillo
potassium
pyroantimonate
piroantimoniato de
potasio
potassium
pyrophosphate
pirofosfato de potasio

potassium
pyrosulfate
pirosulfato de potasio,
sulfato ácido de
potasio
potassium rhodanide
rodanuro de potasio,
tiocianato de potasio
potassium ricinoleate
ricinoleato de potasio
potassium salycilate
salicilato de potasio
potassium selenate
seleniato de potasio
potassium selenide
seleniuro de potasio
potassium silicate
silicato de potasio
potassium silver
cyanide
cianuro de potasio y
plata
potassium sodium
carbonate
carbonato de potasio y
sodio
potassium sodium
ferricyanide
ferricianuro de potasio
y sodio
potassium sodium
phosphate
fosfato de potasio y
sodio
potassium sodium
tartrate
tartrato de potasio y
sodio, sal de Rochell
potassium sorbate
sorbato de potasio
potassium stannate
estannato de potasio
potasium
stannosulfate
estannosulfato de
potasio, sal de
Marignac
potassium stearate
estearato de potasio
potassium sulfate
sulfato de potasio
potassium sulfide
sulfuro de potasio
potassium sulfite
sulfito de potasio
potassium
sulfobenzoate
sulfobenzoato de
potasio

potassium
sulfocarbonate
sulfocarbonato de
potasio
potassium sulfocyanate
sulfocianato de potasio,
tiocianato de potasio
potassium sulfurate
potasio sulfurado
potassium tartrate
tartrato de potasio
potassium tellurate
telurato de potasio
potassium tellurite
telurito de potasio
potassium
tetraborate
tetraborato de potasio
potassium tetra-
bromoaurate (III)
tetrabromoaurato (III)
de potasio
potassium tetra-
chloroaurate (III)
tetracloroaurato (III) de
potasio
potassium tetra-
chloroplatinate (II)
tetracloroplatinato (II)
de potasio
potassium tetra-
cyanomercurate (II)
tetraciano-
mercuriato (II) de
potasio
potassium tetra-
cyanonickelate (II)
tetracianoniquelato (II)
de potasio
potassium tetra-
cyanoplatinate(II)
tetracianoplatinato (II)
de potasio
potassium tetra-
cyanozincate
tetracianocincato de
potasio
potassium tetra-
fluoroborate
tetrafluoroborato de
potasio
potassiun tetra-
iodoaurate (III)
tetrayodoaurato (III) de
potasio
potassium tetra-
iodocadmate
tetrayodocadmato de
potasio

potassium tetra-
iodomercurate (II)
tetrayodomercuriato de
potasio (II)
potassium tetroxalate
tetroxalato de potasio
potassium thio-
antimonate (V)
tioantimoniato (V) de
potasio
potassium
thiocarbonate
tiocarbonato de potasio
potassium
thiocyanate
tiocianato de potasio
potassium thiosulfate
tiosulfato de potasio
potassium titanate
titanato de potasio
potassium titanyl
oxalate
titaniloxalato de
potasio
potassium tri-
chlorophenate
triclorofenato de
potasio
potassium triiodide
triyoduro de potasio
potassium triiodo-
mercurate (II)
solutión
solución de triyodo-
mecuriato (II) de
potasio
potassium
triiodozincate
triyodocincato de
potasio
potassium tungstate
tungstato de potasio
potassium
undecylenate
undecilenato de
potasio
potassium uranate
(VI)
uranato (VI) de
potasio
potassium uranyl
nitrate
nitrato uranílico de
potasio, uranilnitrato
de potasio
potassium wolframate
wolframato de potasio
potassium xanthate
xantato de potasio

potassium
xanthogenate
xantogenato de potasio
potassium zinc sulfate
sulfato de potasio y
cinc
potassium zirconium
chloride
cloruro de potasio y
circonio
potassium zirconium
sulfate
sulfato de potasio y
circonio
pot clay
arcillas para crisol
potency
potencia
potentiator
potenciador
potentiometer
potenciómetro
Pounceau 3R
Punzó 3R
pour point depressant
reductor del punto de
goteo
povidone
povidona
powder
polvo
practolol
practolol
prajmaline
prajmalina
prajmalium bitartrate
bitartrato de prajmalio
pralidoxime chloride
cloruro de pralidoxima
pralidoxime iodide
yoduro de pralidoxima
pramiracetam
pramiracetán
pramiverin(e)
pramiverina
pramocaine
pramocaína
pramoxine
pramoxina
pramoxine
hydrochloride
clorhidrato de
pramoxina
prampine
prampina
pranolium chloride
cloruro de pranolio
pranoprofen
pranoprofeno

pranosal
pranosal
praseodymium
praseodimio
praseodymium oxalate
oxalato de praseodimio
praseodymium oxide
óxido de praseodimio
prasterone
prasterona
pratensein
pratenseína
pravastatin sodium
pravastatina sódica
praxadine
praxadina
prazepam
pracepán, prazepam
prazepine
pracepina,
prazepina
praziquantel
praciquantel
prazitone
pracitona
prazocillin
prazocilina
prazosin
prazosina
prazosin
hydrochloride
clorhidrato de
prazosina
precipitate
precipitado
precipitator,
electrostatic
precipitador
electrostático
precocenes
precocenos
precursor
precursor
prednazate
prednazato
prednazoline
prednazolina
prednicarbate
prednicarbato
prednimustine
prednimustina
prednisolamate
prednisolamato
prednisolone
prednisolona
prednisolone 21-
diethylaminoacetate
21-dietilaminoacetato
de prednisolona

227

prednisolone steaglate
  esteaglato de
  prednisolona
prednisolone sodium
phosphate
  fosfato sódico de
  prednisolona
prednisolone sodium
succinate
  succinato sódico de
  prednisolona
prednisolone sodium
21-m-sulfobenzoate
  21-m-sulfobenzoato
  sódico de
  prednisolona
prednisolone 21-
stearoylglycolate
  21-estearoilglucolato
  de prednisolona
prednisolone tebutate
  tebutato de
  prednisolona
prednisolone 21-
trimethylacetate
  21-trilmetilacetato de
  prednisolona
prednisone
  prednisona
prednival
  prednival
prednylidene
  prednilideno
prednylidene 21-
diethylaminoacetate
  21-dietilaminoacetato
  de prednilideno
predominant
  predominante
prefenamate
  prefenamato
preferential
  preferencial
pregnane
  pregnano
pregnanediol
  pregnanodiol
3,20-pregnanedione
  3,20-pregnanodiona
pregnan-3-α-ol-20-one
  pregnan-3-α-ol-20-ona
pregnenedione
  pregnenodiona
pregneninolone
  pregneninolona
4-pregnen-21-ol-3,20-
dione
  4-pregneno-21-ol-3,20-
  diona

4-pregnene-20,21-diol-
3,11-dione
  4-pregneno-20,21-diol-
  3,11-diona
pregnenolone
  pregnenolona
pregnenolone methyl
ether
  éter metílico de
  pregnenolona
premazepam
  premacepán,
  premazepam
premise
  local
prenalterol
  prenalterol
prenisteine
  prenisteína
prenitene
  preniteno
prenoverine
  prenoverina
prenoxdiazine
hydrochloride
  cloruro de
  prenoxdiazina
prenylamine
  prenilamina
prephenic acid
  ácido prefénico
presenilins
  presenilinas
preservative
  conservador
pressure
  presión
pretamazium iodide
  yoduro de pretamacio
pretiadil
  pretiadil
pretilachlor
  pretilaclor
pribecaine
  pribecaína
pridefine
  pridefina
pridinol
  pridinol
prifinium bromide
  bromuro de prifinio
prifuroline
  prifurolina
prilocaine
  prilocaína
primaperone
  primaperona
primaquine
  primaquina

primary
  primario
primary azo dyes
  colorantes azoicos
  primarios
primary calcium
phosphate
  fosfato de calcio
  primario
primeverose
  primeverosa
primidolol
  primidolol
primidone
  primidona
primocarcin
  primocarcina
primulaverin
  primulaverina
primuline dye
  colorante de
  primulina
primycin
  primicina
prinomastat
  prinomastat
printing ink
  tinta de imprenta
pristane
  pristano
pristinamycin
  pristinamicina
prizidilol
  prizidilol
proadifen
  proadifeno
probarbital
  probarbital
probarbital sodium
  probarbital sódico
probenecid
  probenecida
probucol
  probucol
procainamide
  procainamida
procainamide
hydrochloride
  cloruro de
  procainamida
procaine
  procaína
procaine penicillin G
  penicilina G procaína
procarbazine
  procarbacina,
  procarbazina
procaterol
  procaterol

process
  proceso
process industry
  proceso industrial
prochloraz
  procloraz
prochlorperazine
  proclorperacina,
  proclorperazina,
prochlorperazine
edisylate
  edisilato de
  proclorperacina,
  edisilato de
  proclorperazina
prochlorperazine
maleate
  maleato de
  proclorperacina,
  maleato de
  proclorperazina
procinolol
  procinolol
procinonide
  procinonida
proclonol
  proclonol
procodazole
  procodazol
procyclidine
  prociclidina
procymate
  procimato
procymidone
  procimidona
prodeconium
bromide
  bromuro de
  prodeconio
prodiamine
  prodiamina
prodigiosin
  prodigiosina
prodilidine
  prodilidina
prodipine
  prodipina
prodlure
  prodlura
producer gas
  gas de generador
profadol
  profadol
profenamine
  profenamina
profexalone
  profexalona
proflavine
  proflavina

proflavine sulfate
sulfato de proflavina
proflazepam
proflacepán,
proflazepam
profluralin
profluralina
progabide
progabida
progesterone
progesterona
proglumetacin
proglumetacina
proglumide
proglumida
proguanil
proguanil
proheptazine
proheptazina
proinsulin
proinsulina
prolactin
prolactina
prolamin
prolamina
prolan
prolan
proligestone
proligestona
proline
prolina
prolintane
prolintano
prolonium iodide
yoduro de prolonio
promazine
promacina, promazina
promazine
hydrochloride
clorhidrato de
promacina, clorhidrato
de promazina
promecarb
promecarb
promedol
promedol
promegestone
promegestona
promethazine
prometacina,
prometazina
promethazine teoclate
teoclato de
prometacina, teoclato
de prometazina
promethium
prometio
prometon
prometona

prometryn
prometrina
promolate
promolato
promoxolane
promoxolano
pronethalol
pronetalol
proof
graduación de
alcohol
pro-opiomelanocortin
proopiomelanocortina
propacetamol
propacetamol
propachlor
propacloro
propadiene
propadieno
propafenone
propafenona
propallylonal
propalilonal
propamidine
propamidina
propanal
propanal, aldehído
propílico
propane
propano
1-propanearsonic
acid
ácido 1-propano-
arsónico
1,3-.propanediamine
1,3-propanodiamina
1,2-propanediol
1,2-propanodiol
1,3-propanedithiol
1,3-propanoditiol
propanethial S-oxide
S-óxido de
propanotial
1-propanethiol
1-propanotiol
propanidid
propanidido
propanil
propanilo
propanocaine
propanocaína
propanoic acid
ácido propanoico
propanol
propanol
propanolamine
propanolamina
2-propanolpyridine
2-propanolpiridina

2-propanone
2-propanona, acetona,
cetona dimetílica
2-propanone oxime
oxima de 2-propanona,
acetoxima
propantheline bromide
bromuro de
propantelina
proparacaine
proparacaína
propanoyl chloride
cloruro de propanoílo
propargite
propargita
propargyl alcohol
alcohol propargílico
propargyl bromide
bromuro de propargilo
propargyl chloride
cloruro de propargilo
propatyl nitrate
nitrato de propatilo,
propatilnitrato
propazine
propacina, propazina
propazolamide
propazolamida
propellant
propulsor
2-propenal
2-propenal, acroleína,
aldehído acrílico
propene
propeno
2-propene-1-thiol
2-propeno-1-tiol
propene-1,2,3-
tricarboxylic acid
ácido propeno-1,2,3-
tricarboxílico
propenidazole
propenidazol
2-propenoic acid
ácido 2-
propenoico,
ácido acrílico
propentofylline
propentofilina
propenyl guaiacol
propenilguayacol
2-propenyl
hexanoate
hexanoato de 2-
propenilo
2-propenyl
isothiocyanate
isotiocianato de 2-
propenilo

2-propenylamine
2-propenilamina
propenzolate
propenzolato
properdin
properdina
properidine
properidina
propetamide
propetamida
propetamphos
propetanfós
propetandrol
propetandrol
propham
profán
propicillin
propicilina
propiconazole
propiconazol
propikacin
propikacina,
propicacina
propineb
propineb
propinetidine
propinetidina
propiodal
propiodal
ß-propiolactone
ß-propiolactona
propiolic acid
ácido propiólico
propiomazine
propiomazina
propionaldehyde
aldehído
propiónico,
propionaldehído,
propanal
propionamide
propionamida, amida
del ácido propiónico,
propanamida
propionamide nitrile
nitrilpropionamida
propione
propiona, dietilacetona
propranolol
propionic acid
ácido propiónico
propionic aldehyde
aldehído propiónico
propionic anhydride
anhídrido propiónico
propionitrile
propionitrilo
propionyl benzene
propionilbenceno,

propiofenona,
feniletilcetona
propionyl chloride
cloruro de propionilo
propionylpromazine
propionilpromacina,
propionilpromazina
propiophenone
propiofenona
propipocaine
propipocaína
propiram
propiramo
propisergide
propisergida
propiverine
propiverina
propizepine
propicepina
propofol
propofol
propolis
propolis
propoxate
propoxato
propoxicaine
propoxicaína
propoxycaine hydrochloride
cloruro de propoxicaína
n-propoxypropanol
n-propoxipropanol
propoxur
propoxur
propoxyphene
propoxifeno
propoxyphene hydrochloride
clorhidrato de propoxifeno
propoxyphene napsylate
napsilato de propoxifeno
n-propoxypropanol
n-propoxipropanol
propranolol
propranolol
propyl acetate
acetato de propilo
propyl acetone
acetona propílica, propilacetona
propyl alcohol
alcohol propílico
sec-propyl alcohol
alcohol sec-propílico
propyl aldehyde
aldehído propílico

propyl bromide
bromuro de propilo
propyl butyrate
butirato de propilo
propyl chloride
cloruro de propilo
propyl chloro-carbonate
clorocarbonato de propilo
propyl chlorosulfonate
clorosulfonato de propilo
propyl docetrizoate
docetrizoato de propilo
propyl ether
éter propílico
n-propyl furoate
furoato de n-propilo
propyl gallate
galato de propilo
propyl p-hydroxy-benzoate
p-hidroxibenzoato de propilo, propilparabeno
propyl iodide
yoduro de propilo
propyl magnesium bromide
bromuro de propilmagnesio
propyl malonic acid diethyl ester
éster dietílico del ácido propilmalónico
propyl pelargonate
pelargonato de propilo
propyl propionate
propionato de propilo
n-propyl nitrate
nitrato de n-propilo
n-propyl nitrite
nitrito de n-propilo
n-propylamine
n-propilamina
n-propylbenzene
n-propilbenceno
propylene
propileno
propylene carbonate
carbonato de propileno
propylene chloride
cloruro de propileno
propylene chlorohydrin
clorohidrina propilénica
propylene dibromide
dibromuro de propileno

propylene dichloride
dicloruro de propileno
propylene disulfate
disulfato de propileno
propylene glycol
glicol propilénico, propilenglicol
propylene glycol alginate
alginato de glicol propilénico
propylene glycol distearate
diestearato de glicol propilénico
propylene glycol disulfate
disulfato de glicol propilénico
propylene glycol monomethyl ether
monometil éter de glicol propilénico
propylene glycol monoricinoleate
monorricinoleato de glicol propilénico
propylene glycol monostearate
monoestearato de glicol propilénico
propylene glycol phenyl ether
éter fenílico de glicol propilénico
propylene imine
imina propilénica
propylene oxide
óxido de propileno
propylenediamine
propilendiamina
propylhexedrine
propilhexedrina
propylidene chloride
cloruro de propilideno
propyliodone
propilyodona
n-propylmercaptan
n-propilmercaptano
propylparaben
propilparabeno, p-hidroxibenzoato de propilo
propylthiouracil
propiltiouracilo
propylure
propiluro
propyperone
propiperona

propyphenazone
propifenazona
propyromazine
propiromazina
propyromazine bromide
bromuro de propiromazina
propyzamide
propizamida
proquazone
procuazona
proquinolate
proquinolato
prorenoate potassium
prorrenoato de potasio
proroxan
proroxan
proscillaridin
proscilaridina
prospidium chloride
cloruro de prospidio
prostacyclin(e)
prostaciclina, epoprosterol
prostaglandin
prostaglandina
prostalene
prostaleno
prosthetic group
grupo prostético
prosulpride
prosulprida
prosultiamine
prosultiamina
protactinium
protactinio
protamine sulfate
sulfato de protamina
protamine zinc insuline suspension
suspensión de protamina cinc insulina
protamines
protaminas
protease
proteasa
protective coating
revestimiento protector
protein
proteína
protein hydrolysates
hidrolisados de proteína
proteolysis
proteólisis
protheobromine
proteobromina

prothipendyl
protipendilo
prothixene
protixeno
prothrombin
protrombina
protiofate
protiofato
protionamide
protionamida
protirelin
protirelina
protizinic acid
ácido proticínico
protoanemonin
protoanemonina
protocatechualdehyde
aldehído
protocatéquico
protocatechuic acid
ácido protocatéquico
protokosin
protocosina
protokylol
protoquilol
proton
protón
protopine
protopina
protoplasm
protoplasma
protoporphyrin IX
protoporfirina IX
protostephanine
protoestefanina
protoveratrines
protoveratrinas
protoverine
protoverina
protriptyline
protriptilina
protriptyline
hydrochloride
clorhidrato de
protriptilina
pro-urokinase
prourocinasa
provitamin
provitamina
proxazole
proxazol
proxibarbal
proxibarbal
proxibutene
proxibuteno
proxicromil
proxicromilo
proxifezone
proxifezona

proxorphan
proxorfano
proxymetacaine
proximetacaína
proxyphilline
proxifilina
prozapine
prozapina
prunetin
prunetina
Prussian blue
azul de Prusia
prussiate
prusiato
prussic acid
ácido prúsico, ácido
cianhídrico
Pschorr reaction
reacción de Pschorr
pseudoaconitine
pseudoaconitina
pseudobaptigen
pseudobaptígeno
pseudobutylene
glycol
glicol pseudo-
butilénico
pseudococaine
pseudococaína
pseudocodeine
pseudocodeína
pseudoconhydrine
pseudoconhidrina
pseudocumene
pseudocumeno
pseudocumidine
pseudocumidina
pseudoephedrine
pseudoefedrina
pseudohecogenin
pseudohecogenina
pseudoionone
pseudoionona
pseudomonic acids
ácidos pseudomónicos
pseudomorphine
pseudomorfina
pseudopederin
pseudopederina
pseudopelletierine
pseudopeletierina
pseudotropine
pseudotropina
pseudoyohimbine
pseudoyohimbina
psicofuranine
psicofuranina
psilocin
psilocina

psilocybin(e)
psilocibina
psoralen
psoraleno
psychotrine
psicotrina
psyllium
zaragatona
ptaquiloside
ptaquilósido
pteridine
pteridina
pterocarpin
pterocarpina
pteroic acid
ácido pteroico
pteropterin
pteropterina
pteroylhexa-
glutamylglutamic acid
ácido pteroilhexa-
glutamilglutámico
pteroylglutamic acid
ácido pteroilglutámico
ptomaine
ptomaína, tomaína
ptyalin
ptialina, tialina
pukateine
pucateína
pulegium oil
aceite de poleo
pulegone
pulegona
pulsatilla
pulsatilla
pumactant
pumactant
pumice
piedra pomez
pumpkin seeds
semillas de calabaza
purification
purificación
1H-purine
1H-purina
purity, chemical
pureza química
puromycin
puromicina
purothionin
purotionina
purple of Cassius
púrpura de Cassius,
precipitado de oro y
estaño
purpurin
purpurina, 1,2,4-
trihidroxiantraquinona

purpurin red
rojo purpurina,
antrapurpurina
purpurogallin
purpurogalina
putrescine
putrescina
putty
masilla
putty powder
polvo de masilla
pyocyanine
piocianina
pyracarbolid
piracarbólido
pyran
pirano
pyrantel
pirantel
pyrathiazine
piratiacina, piratiazina
pyrazinamide
piracinamida,
pirazinamida
pyrazine
piracina,
pirazina
pyrazine
hexahydride
hexahidruro de
piracina, hexahidruro
de pirazina
2,3-pyrazinedi-
carboxilic acid
ácido 2,3-piracin-
dicarboxílico,
ácido 2,3-pirazin-
dicarboxílico
pyrazinoic acid
ácido piracinoico
pyrazole
pirazol
pyrazoline
pirazolina
pyrazolone dye
colorante de
pirazolona
pyrazophos
pirazofós
pyrene
pireno
pyrethrins
piretrinas
pyrethroid
piretroide
pyrethrum
piretro, pelitre
pyrethrum extract
extracto de piretro

pyrethrum flowers
flores de piretro
pyricarbate
piricarbato
pyridarone
piridarona
pyridate
piridato
pyridic
pirídico
pyridine
piridina
2-pyridine aldoxime
methiodide
metyoduro de 2-
piridinaldoxima
pyridine-3-carboxylic
acid
ácido piridin-3-
carboxílico
3-pyridine-
diazonium fluoborate
fluoborato de 3-
piridindiazonio
2,5-pyridinedi-
carboxylic acid
ácido 2,5-piridin-
dicarboxílico
pyridinemethanol
piridinmetanol
pyridine-1-oxide
óxido de 1-piridina
pyridine polymer
polímero de piridina
2-pyridinethiol-1-oxide
1-óxido de 2-
piridinatiol
pyridinium bromide
perbromide
perbromuro bromuro
de piridinio
pyridinium
chlorochromate
clorocromato de
piridinio
pyridinol carbamate
carbamato de piridinol
pyridofylline
piridofilina
pyridomycin
piridomicina
pyridostigmine
bromide
bromuro de
piridoestigmina
pyridoxal
hydrochloride
clorhidrato de
piridoxal

pyridoxal phosphate
fosfato de piridoxal
pyridoxamine
dihydrochloride
diclorhidrato de
piridoxamina
4-pyridoxic acid
ácido 4-piridóxico
pyridoxine
piridoxina
piridoxine
hydrochloride
clorhidrato de
piridoxina
pyridylamine
piridilamina
pyrilamine
pirilamina
pyrimethamine
pirimetamina
pyrimidine
pirimidina
pyriminil
piriminilo
pyrimithate
pirimitato
pyrinoline
pirinolina
pyrisuccideanol
pirisuccideanol
pyrite
pirita
pyrithiamine
piritiamina
pyrithione
piritiona
pyrithyldione
piritildiona
pyrithidium bromide
bromuro de piritidio
pyritinol
piritinol
pyro-
piro-
pyroboric acid
ácido pirobórico
pyrocalciferol
pirocalciferol
pyrocarbonic acid
diethyl ester
éster dietílico del ácido
pirocarbónico
pyrocatechol,
pyrocatechin
pirocatequina
pyrocatechol dimethyl
ether
éter dimetílico de
pirocatequina

pyrocatechol methyl
ester
éster metílico de
pirocatequina,
metilpirocatequina
pyrochemical
piroquímico
pyrogallate
pirogalato
pyrogallic acid
ácido pirogálico,
pirogalol, 1,2,3-
trihidroxibenceno,
pyrogallol
pirogalol, 1,2,3-
trihidroxibenceno,
ácido pirogálico
pyrogen
pirógeno
pyroglutamic acid
ácido piroglutámico
pyrolygneous acid
ácido piroleñoso
pyrolignic
piroleñoso
pyrolysis
pirólisis
pyrolusite
pirolusita
pyromellitic acid
ácido piromelítico
pyromellitic
dianhydride
dianhídrido piromelítico
pyromucic acid
ácido piromúcico,
acido furoico
pyromucic aldehyde
aldehído piromúcico,
furfural
pirone
pirona
pyronine B
pironina B
phyrophendane
pirofendano
pyrophoric
pirofórico
pyrophoric material
material pirofórico
pyrophorus
piróforo
pyrophosphate
pirofosfato
pyrophosphoric acid
ácido pirofosfórico
pyroracemic acid
ácido pirorracémico,
ácido pirúvico

pyrosulfate
pirosulfato
pyrosulfuric acid
ácido pirosulfúrico
pyrosulfuryl chloride
cloruro de pirosulfurilo
pyrotartaric acid
ácido pirotartárico
pyrovalerone
pirovalerona
pyrovanadic acid
ácido pirovanádico
pyroxamine
piroxamina
pyroxylin(e)
piroxilina
pyrrobutamine
pirrobutamina
pyrrobutamine
phosphate
fosfato de
pirrobutamina
pyrrocaine
pirrocaína
pyrrole
pirrol
pyrrolidine
pirrolidina
2-pyrrolidine-
carboxylic acid
ácido 2-pirrolidin-
carboxílico
2-pyrrolidone
2-pirrolidona
pyrrolifene
pirrolifeno
pyrroline
pirrolina
pyrrolnitrin
pirrolnitrina
pyrrone
pirrona
pyruvaldehyde
piruvaldehído
pyruvate
decarboxylase
piruvato descarboxilado
pyruvic acid
ácido pirúvico
pyruvic alcohol
alcohol pirúvico
pyruvic aldehide
aldehído pirúvico
pyrvinium chloride
cloruro de pirvinio
pyrvinium pamoate
pamoato de pirvinio
pytamine
pitamina

Q

quad
quad (unidad de energía)
quadrivalent
cuadrivalente, tetravalente
quadrosilan
quadrosilán
quadrupole resonance
resonancia cuadrípola
qualitative analysis
análisis cualitativo
quality
calidad
quality assesment
valoración de la calidad
Quality Assurance
Seguridad Cualitativa
quality control
control de calidad
quantify
cuantificar, determinar cuantitativamente
quantitation
determinación cuantitativa
quantitative analysis
análisis cuantitativo
quantivalence
cuantivalencia
quantum number
número cuántico
quartz
cuarzo
quartz, fused
cuarzo fundido
quartz glass
cristal de cuarzo
quassia
cuasia
quassin, quassiun
cuasina
quatacaine
cuatacaína
quaternary
cuaternario
quatrimycin
cuatrimicina
quazepam
quacepán, quazepam
quazodine
cuazodina

quebrachamine
quebrachamina
quebrachine
quebrachina
quebracho colorado
quebracho rojo
quebracho extract
extracto de quebracho
queen substance
sustancia de la reina
Quelet reaction
reacción de Quelet
quenched
detener la reacción
quercetagetin
quercetagetina
quercetic
quercético
quercetin
quercetina
quercimeritrin
quercimeritrina
quercin
quercina, cuercina
d-quercitol
d-quercitol
quercitrin
quercitrina
quercus
roble blanco
quetiapine
quetiapina
quetiapine fumarate
fumarato de quetiapina
quick aging
envejencimiento rápido
quicksilver
azogue, mercurio
quifenadine
quifenadino
quillaic acid
ácido de quillay
quillaja
corteza de quillay
quillaja saponin
saponina de corteza de quillay
quillifoline
quilifolina
quina
quina
quinacillin
quinacilina

quinacridone
quinacridona
quinacridone hydrochloride
clorhidrato de quinacridona
quinacrine
quinacrina
quinacrine hydrochloride
clorhidrato de quinacrina
quinhydrone
quinhidrona
quinaldic acid
ácido quináldico
quinaldine
quinaldina, 2-metilquinolina
quinaldine blue
azul de quinaldina
quinaldine red
rojo de quinaldina
quinaldine sulfate
sulfato de quinaldina
quinalizarin
quinalizarina
quinamine
quinamina
quinaphthol
quinaftol
quinapril hydrochloride
clorhidrato de quinapril
quinapyramine
quinapiramina
quinaquina
quinaquina, quina
quinate
quinato
quinazoline
quinazolina
quinazosin
quinazosina
quinazosin hydrochloride
clorhidrato de quinazosina
quinbolone
quimbolona
quincarbate
quincarbato
quince seed
semilla de membrillo

quindecamine
quindecamina
quindecamine acetate
acetato de quindecamina
quindonium bromide
bromuro de quindonio
quindoxin
quindoxina
quinestradiol, quinestradol
quinestradiol, quinestradol
quinestrol
quinestrol
quinetalate
quinetalato
quinethazone
quinetazona
quinfamide
quinfamida
quingestanol
quingestanol
quingestanol acetate
acetato de quingestanol
quingestrone
quingestrona
quinhydrone
quinhidrona
quinic acid
ácido químico
quinidine
quinidina
quinidine glucolate
glucolato de quinidina
quinidine poly-galacturonate
poligalacturonato de quinidina
quinidine sulfate
sulfato de quinidina
quinine
quinina
quinine acid sulfate
sulfato ácido de quinina
quinine ascorbate
ascorbato de quinina
quinine bisulfate
bisulfato de quinina
quinine carbacrylic resin
resina de quinina carbacrílica

quinine carbonate
  carbonato de quinina
quinine dihydro-
bromide
  dibromhidrato de
  quinina
quinine dihydro-
chloride
  diclorhidrato de
  quinina
quinine ethyl-
carbonate
  etilcarbonato de
  quinina
quinine formate
  formiato de quinina
quinine gluconate
  gluconato de quinina
quinine hydrate
  hidrato de quinina
quinine hydriodide
  yodohidrato de quinina
quinine hydro-
bromide
  bromhidrato de quinina
quinine hydrochloride
  clorhidrato de quinina
quinine hypo-
phosphite
  hipofosfito de quinina
quinine iodosulfate
  yodosulfato de
  quinina
quinine oleate
  oleato de quinina
quinine phosphate
  fosfato de quinina
quinine salicylate
  salicilato de quinina
quinine sulfate
  sulfato de quinina

quinine tannate
  tanato de quinina
quinine urea
hydrochloride
  clorhidrato de
  urea y quinina
quininic acid
  ácido quinínico
quininone
  quininona
quinisocaine
  quinisocaína
quinizarin
  quinizarina
quinizarin green SS
  verde SS de
  quinizarina
quinocide
  quinocida
quinocide hydro-
chloride
  clorhidrato de
  quinocida
quinoidine, chinoidine
  quinoidina
quinol
  hidroquinona, quinol
quinoline
  quinolina, quinoleína
8-quinoline boronic
acid
  ácido 8-quinolin
  borónico
quinoline dye
  colorante de quinolina
quinoline yellow
  amarillo de quinolina
8-quinolinecarboxylic
acid
  ácido 8-quinolin-
  carboxílico

quinolinic acid
  ácido quinolínico
8-quinolinol
  8-quinoleinol,
  8-hidroxi-
  quinoleína
8-quinolinol-7-
iodo-5-sulfonic acid
  ácido 8-quinoleinol-
  7-yodo-5-
  sulfónico
quinolones
  quinolonas
quinomethionate
  quinometionato
quinonaphtholic dye
  colorante
  quinonaftólico
quinone
  quinona
quinone oxime dye
  colorante de
  quinonoxima
p-quinonedioxime
  p-quinonadioxima
quinophan
  quinofano
quinopyrine
  quinopirina
quinosol
  quinosol
quinotoxin(e)
  quinotoxina
quinovic acid
  ácido quinóvico
quinovin
  quinovina
quinovose
  quinovosa
quinoxaline
  quinoxalina

quinoxalinedithiol
cyclic trithio-
carbonate
  tritiocarbonato
  cíclico de
  quinoxalinditiol
quinprenaline
  quinprenalina
quinquevalence
  pentavalencia
quinquevalent
  quinquevalente
quinterenol sulfate
  sulfato de quinterenol
quintiofos
  quintiofós
quintozene
  quintoceno
quinuclidine
  quinuclidina
3-quinuclidinol
  3-quinuclidinol
quinuclium
bromide
  bromuro de quinuclio
quinupramine
  quinupramina
quipazine
  quipacina, quipazina
quipazine maleate
  maleato de quipazina
quisqualic acid
  ácido quiscuálico
quisultazine
  quisultazina
quisultidine
  quisultidina
quitenidine
  quitenidina
quizalofop-ethyl
  etilquizalofop

R

rac⁻
rac⁻
R-acid
ácido R (ácido 2-naftol 3,6-disulfónico)
racefemine
racefemina
racefenicol
racefenicol
racemate
racemato
racemethionine
racemetionina
racemethorphan
racemetorfano
racemetirosine
racemetirosina
racemic
racémico
racemic acid
ácido racémico
racemization
racemización
racemoramide
racemoramida
racemorphan
racemorfano
racephedrine
racefedrina, efedrina racémica
racephenicol
racefenicol
racepinephrine
racepinefrina
racepinephrine hydrochloride
clorhidrato de racepinefrina
rack
rejilla, soporte para tubos de ensayo
radiation
radiación
radiation biochemistry
bioquímica de radiación
radical
radical
radicinin
redicinina
radioactive isotope
isótopo radioactivo
radioactive waste
residuos radioactivos

radioactivity
radioactividad
radiocarbon
radiocarbono
radiochemistry
radioquímica
radioisotope
isótopo radioactivo
radiolabeled
radiomarcado
radium
radio
radium bromide
bromuro de radio
radium carbonate
carbonato de radio
radium chloride
cloruro de radio
radium sulfate
sulfuro de radio
radon
radón
raffinose
rafinosa
rafoxanide
rafoxanida
ralitoline
ralitolina
raloxifene
raloxifeno
raloxifene hydrochloride
clorhidrato de raloxifeno
Raman spectroscopy
espectroscopía Raman
rambufaside
rambufasida
ramie
ramio
ramiferazone
ramiferazona
ramipril
ramipril
ramiprilat
ramiprilat
ramixotidine
ramixotidina
ramnodigin
ramnodigina
ramoplanin
ramoplanina

ramycin
ramicina, ácido fusídico
random
azar, aleatorio
randomized
al azar, aleatorio
Raney nickel
niquel Raney
range
límites
ranimustine
ranimustina
ranimycin
ranimicina
ranitidine
ranitidina
ranitidine hydrochloride
clorhidrato de ranitidina
Raoult's law
ley de Raoult
rapeseed oil
aceite de colza
rare earth
tierras raras
rare earth elements
elementos de tierras raras
rare metal
metal raro
Raschip phenol process
método del fenol de Raschig
Raschig rings
anillos de Raschig
raspberry
frambuesa
rate
tasa, velocidad
rathyronine
ratironina
ratio
proporción
rational
razonalización
ratsbane
arsénico blanco, trióxido de arsénico
raubasine
raubasina
rauhimbine
rauhimbina

rauwolfia
rauwolfia
rauwolfia serpentina
rauwolfia serpentina
raw material
materia prima
rayon
rayón
rayon, purified
rayón purificado
razinodil
racinodil, razinodil
razobazam
razobazán
razoxane
razoxana
react
reaccionar
reactant
reactante, reaccionante
reactant molecule
molécula reaccionante
reaction
reacción
reaction, chemical
reacción química
reaction, nuclear
reacción nuclear
reactivity
reactividad
reactor
reactor
reagent
reactivo
reagent bottles
frascos para reactivos
rearrangement
transposición
reboxetine
reboxetina
recainam hydrochloride
clorhidrato de recainán
recainam tosylate
tosilato de recainán
recipe
receta
reclaiming
recuperación
reclazepam
reclacepán, reclacepam
recombinant DNA
ADN recombinante

reconstitution
reconstitución
recorder
registrador
recover
recobrar, recuperar
rectification
rectificación
rectify
rectificar, purificar
recycle
reciclaje
recycling
reciclado
red lake C
laca roja C
red precipitate
precipitado rojo
redox
redox
redox reaction
reacción de oxidación
y reducción
redox system
sistema redox
reduce
reducir
reducer
reductor
reduction in size of
ring
regresión del núcleo
Reed reaction
reacción de Reed
re-evaporate
reevaporar, volver a
evaporar
refine
purificar, refinar
refinery gas
gas de refinería
reflux
reflujo
refractivity
refractividad,
refracción específica
refractive index
índice de refracción
refractory
refractario
refrigerant
mezcla refrigerante
regeneration
regeneración
regression equation
ecuación de
regresión
regression plot
curva de regresión

regulating agent
agente estabilizante
Regulatory Affairs
Asuntos
Reglamentarios
rehydration
rehidratación
Reichert-Meissl
number
índice de Reichert y
Meissl
Reich process
método Reich
Reinecke salt
sal de Reinecke
reinforced plastic
plástico reforzado
reinforcing agent
agente de refuerzo
Reissert compounds
compuestos de Reissert
Reissert indole
synthesis
síntesis de indoles de
Reissert
relative humidity
humedad relativa
relaxin
relaxina
release
liberación, aprobación
remifentanil
hydrochloride
clorhidrato de
remifentanilo
relomycin
relomicina
remove
extraer, sacar
renanolone
renanolona
renewable resources
recursos renovables
renin
renin
rennet
cuajo
rennin
renina, quimosina
rentiapril
rentiapril
renytoline
renitolina
renytoline
hydrochloride
clorhidrato de
renitolina
repaglinide
repaglinida

repellent
repelente
Repipet dispenser
dispensadores de
solución como
Repipets
repirinast
repirinast
replicate tubes
tubos de repetición
report
informe
Reppe process
proceso de Reppe
reprocessing
reprocesado
reproducibility
facilidad o posibilidad
de reproducir
reproducibility of test
precisión de la prueba
repromicin
repromicina
reproterol
reproterol
reproterol
hydrochloride
clorhidrato de
reproterol
requirements
exigencias, requisitos
resacetophenone
resacetofenona
resazurin
resazurina
rescimetol
rescimetol
rescinnamine
rescinamina
research
laboratory
laboratorio de
investigación
resene
reseno
reserpic acid
ácido resérpico
reserpiline
reserpilina
reserpine
reserpina
reserpinine
reserpinina
reserpinolic acid
ácido reserpinólico
resibufogenin
resibufogenina
residual
residuo

residual oil
aceite residual
residue
residuo
resilin
resilina
resin
resina
resin acids
ácidos resínicos
resin, ion exchange
resina de intercambio
de iones
resin ipomea
resina de ipomea
resin jalap
resina de jalapa
resin, natural
resina natural
resin, scammony
resina de escamonea
resin, synthetic
resina sintética
resinol
resinol
resistomycin
resistomicina
resodec
resodec
resolution
resolución
resolving power
poder de resolución
resonance
resonancia
resorantel
resorantel
resorcinol
resorcinol, resorcina
resorcinol acetate
acetato de resorcina
resorcinol blue
azul de resorcina
resorcinol diglycidyl
ether
éter diglicidílico de
resorcina
resorcinol dimethyl
ether
éter dimetílico de
resorcina
resorcinol-
formaldehyde resin
resina de resorcina y
formaldehído
resorcinol
monoacetate
monoacetato de
resorcina

resorcinol
monobenzoate
monobenzoato de
resorcina
resorcinolphthalein
resorcinftaleína
ß-resorcylaldehyde
aldehído ß-resorcílico
ß-resorcylic acid
ácido ß-resorcílico
resultants
productos de una
reacción
resuspend
volver a suspender
retamine
retamina
retarder
retardador
retene
reteno
retention
retención
retest
repetir la prueba
retesting
repetición de la prueba
reticulin (the protein)
reticulina (la proteína)
reticuline
reticulina
retinal
retinal
retine
retino
retinene
retineno, retinal
retinoic acid
ácido retinoico
retinol
retinol
retronecine
retronecina
retropinacol
rearrangement
transposición del
retropinacol
retrorsine
retrorsina
retrosynthesis
retrosíntesis
revatrine
revatrina
reverse osmosis
ósmosis inversa
reversible
reversible
reversion
reversión

review
examinar
revise
alterar, cambiar
rhamnetin
ramnetina
rhamnose
ramnosa
rhapontin
rapontina
rheadine
readina
rhein
reín, ácido reínico
rhenium
renio
renium heptasulfide
heptasulfuro de renio
rhenium heptoxide
heptóxido de renio
rhenium
hexafluoride
hexafluoruro de renio
rhenium
oxychloride
oxicloruro de renio
rhenium
pentachloride
pentacloruro de renio
rhenium trichloride
tricloruro de renio
rhenium trioxide
trióxido de renio
rheology
reología
rheometer
reómetro
rhesus factor
factor rhesus
rhizobitoxin
rizobitoxina
rho acid
ácido rho (ácido 1,5-
disulfónico)
rhodamine B
rodamina B
rhodanilic acid
ácido rodanílico
rhodanine
rodanina, 2-tio-4-
cetotiazolidina
rhodinal
rodinal
rhodinol
rodinol
rhodinyl acetate
acetato de rodinilo
rhodium
rodio

rhodium carbonyl
chloride
cloruro carbonílico de
rodio
rhodium
chloride
cloruro de rodio
rhododendrin
rododendrina
rhodomycins
rodomicinas
rhodonite
rodonita
rhodopin
rodopina
rhodopsin
rodopsina
rhodoquinone
rodoquinona
rhodoviolascin
rodoviolascina
rhodoxanthin
rodoxantina
rhubarb
ruibarbo
rhyncophylline
rincofilina
ribaminol
ribaminol
ribavirin
ribavirina
α-ribazole
α-ribazol
riboflavin(e)
riboflavina
riboflavine phosphate
(sodium)
fosfato sódico de
riboflavina
9-ß-D-ribofuranosyl-
adenine
9-ß-D-ribofuranosil-
adenina
ribonuclease
ribonucleasa
ribonucleic acid
ácido ribonucleico
riboprine
riboprina
D-ribose
D-ribosa
D-ribose-5-phosphoric
acid
ácido D-ribosa-5-
fosfórico
ribostamycin
ribostamicina
ribosome
ribosoma

D-ribosyl uracil
D-ribosil uracilo
D-ribulose
D-ribulosa
ricin
ricina
ricinine
ricinina
ricinoleate
ricinoleato
ricinoleic acid
ácido ricinoleico
ricinoleyl alcohol
alcohol ricinoleílico
ricinus oil
aceite de ricino
ridazolol
ridazolol
ridiflone
ridiflona
Riehm quinoline
synthesis
síntesis de quinolinas
de Riehm
Riemschneider
thiocarbamate
synthesis
síntesis de
tiocarbamato
Riemschhneider
rifabutin
rifabutina
rifamide
rifamida
rifampicin
rifampicina, rifampina
rifampin
rifampina,
rifampicina
rifamycin
rifamicina
rifapentine
rifapentina
rifaximin
rifaximina
rifoçamycin
rifocamicina
Riley oxidations
oxidaciones de Riley
rilmazafone
rilmazafona
rilmenidine
rilmenidino
rilopirox
rilopirox
rilozarone
rilozarona
riluzole
riluzol

rimantadine
rimantadina

**rimantadine
hydrochloride**
clorhidrato de
rimantadina

**rimazolium
methylsulfate**
metilsulfato de
rimazolio

rimexolone
rimezolona

rimiterol
rimiterol

**rimiterol
hydrobromide**
bromhidrato de
rimiterol

rimocidin
rimocidina

ring
anillo

ring compound
compuesto cíclico

ring rupture
ruptura del núcleo

ring-opening
ruptura del anillo

Ringer's injection
inyección de Ringer

riodipine
riodipina

rioprostil
rioprostil

ripazepam
ripacepán, ripazepam

ripening
maduración

risedronate sodium
risedronato sódico

risocaine
risocaína

risperidone
risperidona

ristocetin
ristocetina

Ritter reaction
reacción de Ritter

Rittinger´s law
ley de Rittinger

ritiometan
ritiometano

ritodrine
ritodrina

ritonavir
ritonavir

**ritropirronium
bromide**
bromuro de ritropirronio

ritrosulfan
ritrosulfano

rituximab
rituximab

RNA polimerase
ARN polimerasa

rizatriptan benzoate
benzoato de
rizatriptano

rizolipase
rizolipasa

roasting
tostar

robenidine
robenidina

**robenidine
hydrochloride**
clorhidrato de
robenidina

robinin
robinina

roccellic acid
ácido rocélico

Rochelle powder
polvo de la Rochela,
polvos de Seidlitz

Rochelle salt
sal de la Rochela,
tartrato de potasio y
sodio

rociverine
rociverina

rock crystal
cristal de roca

Rockwell hardness
dureza Rockwell

rocuronium bromide
bromuro de rocuronio

rod
varilla

rodocaine
rodocaína

rodorubucin
rodorrubucina

rofelodine
rofelodina

roflurane
roflurano

rokitamycin
rokitamicina,
rikamicina

roletamide
roletamida

rolicyclidine
roliciclidina

rolicyprine
roliciprina

rolipram
roliprán, rolipram

rolitetracycline
rolitetraciclina

rolitetracycline nitrate
nitrato de
rolitetraciclina

roller bottle
frasco rodante, botella
rodante

roll mill
triturador de rodillo

rolodine
rolodina

rolziracetam
rolciracetán

romifenone
romifenona

romifidine
romifidina

ronidazole
ronidazol

ronifibrate
ronifibrato

ronipamil
ronipamil

ronnel
ronel, ácido
fósforotioico

room temperature
temperatura ambiente

**ropinirole
hydrochloride**
clorhidrato de ropinirol

ropitoin
ropitoína

**ropitoin
hydrochloride**
clorhidrato de
ropitoína

ropivacaine
ropivacaína

**ropivacaine
hydrochloride**
clorhidrato de
ropivacaína

ropizine
ropicina, ropizina

roquinimex
roquinimex

rosamicin
rosamicina

rosanilin(e)
rosanilina

rosaprostol
rosaprostol

rosaramicin
rosaramicina

rosaramicin butyrate
butirato de
rosaramicina

**rosaramicin
propionate**
propionato de
rosaramicina

**rosaramicin sodium
phosphate**
fosfato sódico de
rosaramicina

rosaramicin stearate
estearato de
rosaramicina

rose Bengal
rosa de Bengala

rose hip
escaramujo

rosemary
romero

**Rosenmund-von Braun
synthesis**
síntesis de
Rosenmund-von
Braund

rose oil
aceite (esencia) de
rosas

rose water ointment
ungüento de agua de
rosas

rose water, stronger
agua de rosas fuerte

rosein
roseína, fucsina

rosin
colofonia

rosin oil
aceite de colofonia

rosin soap
jabón de colofonia

rosoxacin
rosoxacina

rotamicillin
rotamicilina

rotation
rotación

rotenone
rotenona

rotoxamine
rotoxamina

rotoxamine tartrate
tartrato de
rotoxamina

rotraxate
rotraxato

rottlerin
rotlerina

Rowe rearramgement
transposición de Rowe

roxarsone
roxarsón

roxatidine
roxatidina
roxatidine acetate
acetato de roxatidina
roxibolone
roxibolona
roxithromycin
roxitromicina
roxolonium
metilsulfate
metilsulfato de
roxolonio
roxoperone
roxoperón
royal jelly
jalea real
RR acid
ácido RR (ácido 2-
amino-8-naftol-3,6-
disulfónico
rubber
caucho
rubber bulb
pera de goma
rubber cement
pegamento de caucho
rubeanic acid
ácido rubeánico

ruberythric acid
ácido ruberítrico
rubiadin
rubiadina
rubidium
rubidio
rubidium bromide
bromuro de
rubidio
rubidium chloride
cloruro de rubidio
rubidium
hydroxide
hidróxido de rubidio
rubidium iodide
yoduro de rubidio
rubijervine
rubijervina
rubixanthin
rubixantina
rubus
corteza de zarzamora
ruby
rubí
rue oil
aceite de ruda
rufigallol
rufigalol

rufocromomycin
rufocromomicina
ruggedness
robustez
rugulovasines
rugulovasinas
run
procesar, tanda, poner
en funcionamiento
run a test
efectuar una prueba
running buffer
tampón del análisis
rutamycin
rutamicina
rutecarpine
rutecarpina
ruthenic
ruténico
ruthenious
rutenioso
ruthenium
rutenio
ruthenium
chloride
cloruro de rutenio
ruthenium red
rojo rutenio

ruthenium
tetroxide
tretróxido de rutenio
ruthenium
trichloride
tricloruro de rutenio
ruthenocene
rutenoceno
rutherfordium
ruterfordio
rutile
rutilo
rutin
rutino, rutósido
rutinose
rutinosa
rutoside
rutosido
ruvazone
ruvazón
Ruzicka large ring
synthesis
síntesis de anillos
grandes de Ruzicka
ryania
riania
ryanodine
rianodina

S

sabadilla
sabadilla
sabadine
sabadina, cevadina
Sabatier-Senderens
reduction
reducción de Sabatier
y Senderens
saccharate
sacarato
d-saccharic acid
ácido d-sacárico
saccharide
sacárido
saccharin
sacarina
saccharolactic acid
ácido sacaroláctico
L-saccharopine
L-sacaropina
saccharose
sacarosa
Sachsse process
método de
Sachsse
safety
seguridad
safety device
dispositivo de
seguridad
safety factor
factor de seguridad
safety glass
vidrio de seguridad
safety valve
válvula de
seguridad
safflower oil
aceite de cártamo
saffron
azafrán
safranal
safranal
safranine
safranina
safrol(e)
safrol
sage oil
aceite de salvia
sakuranetin
sacuranetina
sal ammoniac
sal amoníaco, sal
amoniaco

sal soda
sal de sosa, soda
cáustica
salacetamide
salacetamida
salafibrate
salafibrato
salicin
salicina
salantel
salantel
salatrim
salatrima
salazodine
salazodino
salazosulfadimidine
salazosulfadimidina
salazosulfadimine
salazosulfadimina
salazosulfamide
salazosulfamida
salazosulfapyridine
salazosulfapiridina
salazosulfathiazole
salazosulfatiazol
salbutamol
salbutamol
salcolex
salcolex
salep
salep
saletamide
saletamida
salfluverine
salfluverina
salicin
salicina
salicyl alcohol
alcohol salicílico
salicylaldehyde
salicilaldehído,
aldehído salicílico
salicylaldoxime
salicilaldoxima
salicylamide
salicilamida
salicylamide o-acetic
acid
ácido salicilamida o-
acético
salicylanilide
salicilanilida
salicylate
salicilato

salicylhydroxamic acid
ácido
salicilhidroxámico
salicylic
salicílico
salicylic acid
ácido salicílico
salicylic acid
dipropylene glycol
monoester
monoéster
dipropilenglicólico del
ácido salicílico
salicylic aldehyde
aldehído salicílico
4-salicyloyl-
morpholine
4-saliciloilmorfolina
salicylsalicylic acid
ácido salicilsalicílico
salicylsulfuric acid
ácido salicilsulfúrico
salify
salificar
salification
salificación
saligenin
saligenina
salinazid
salinazida
saline solution
solución salina
saline water
agua salina
salinomycin
salinomicina
salinity
salinidad
salipyrin(e)
salipirina
salmefanol
salmefanol
salmeterol xinafoate
xinafoato de salmeterol
salmine sulfate
sulfato de salmina
salmon oil
aceite de salmón
salol
salol, salicilato de
fenilo
saloquinine
saloquinina, quinina
salicílica

salprotoside
salprotosida
salsalate
salsalato
salsoline
salsolina
salt
sal
salt bath
baño de sal
salts, Epsom
sales de Epsom,
sal inglesa
saltpeter,
saltpetre
salitre, nitrato de
potasio
salutaridine
salutaridina
salverine
salverina
salvia
salvia
salvia oil
aceite de salvia
samaderins
samaderinas
samandarine
samandarina
samandarone
samandarona
samarium
samario
samariun chloride
cloruro de samario
samarium oxide
óxido de samario
samarium sulfate
sulfato de samario
sambucus
sambuco
sampatrilat
sampatrilat
sample
muestra
sampler
inyector automático de
muestras
sampling
obtención de muestras,
muestreo
sampling nozzle
inyector para sacar
muestras

sancycline
sanciclina
sand
arena
sandalwood oil
esencia (aceite) de
sándalo, esencia
(aceite) de sándalo de
las Indias Orientales
sandalwood, white
sándalo blanco
sandarac
sandáraca
Sandmeyer, reaction
reacción de Sandmeyer
sandstone
arenisca
sandwich molecule
molécula emparedada
sanguinaria
sanguinaria
sanguinarine
sanguinarina
santal oil
esencia (aceite) de
sándalo, esencia
(aceite) de sándalo de
las Indias Orientales
ß-santalol
ß-santalol
santalyl acetate
acetato de santalilo
santonica
santónica,
santónico
santonic acid
ácido santónico
α-santonin
α-santonina
saperconazole
saperconazol
saponaria
saponaria
saponarin
saponarina
saponifiable
saponificable
saponification
saponificación
saponification
number
número de
saponificación
saponify
saponificar
saponins
saponinas
sapphire
zafiro

saquinavir
saquinavir
saquinavir mesylate
mesilato de saquinavir
saralasin
saralasina
saran
sarán, cloruro de
polivinilideno
sarcolactic acid
ácido sarcoláctico
sarcolactate
sarcolactato
sarcolysin
sarcolisina
sarcosine
sarcosina
Sarett oxidation
oxidación de
Sarett
sarin
sarina
sarkomycin
sarcomicina
sarmentogenin
sarmentogenina
sarmentose
sarmentosa
sarmoxillin
sarmoxilina
sarpagine
sarpagina
sarpicillin
sarpicilina
sarraceniaceae
sarraceniacea
sarsaparrilla
zarzaparrilla
sarsasapogenin
zarzasapogenina
sassafras
sasafrás
sassafras oil
esencia (aceite) de
sasafrás
satigrel
satigrel
saturated
saturado
saturated
hydrocarbons
hidrocarburos
saturados
saturation
saturación
saturation point
punto de saturación
saturator
saturador (aparato)

saunders, red
sándalo rojo
savin
sabina
savin oil
esencia (aceite) de
sabina
savory oil
aceite de ajedrea
saxitoxin
saxitoxina
Saybolt color
color de Saybolt
Saybolt Universal
viscosity
viscosidad universal
Saybolt
Saytzeff (Zaitsev)
rule
regla de Saytzeff
(Zaitsev)
scabiolide
escabiolida
scale
balanza, escala
scale-up
llevado a escala,
escala total
scammony root
raíz de escamonea
scan, to
examinar,
explorar
scandium
escandio
scandium fluoride
fluoruro de escandio
scandium oxide
óxido de escandio
scanning
exploración
scandium
escandio
scarlet red
rojo escarlata
scattering
dispersión, disperso
scavenger
eliminador,
depurador
SCFU
pie cúbico estándar por
hora
Schaeffer acid
ácido de Schaeffer
(ácido 2-naftol-6-
sulfónico)
Schaeffer's salt
sal de Schaeffer (sal

sódica del ácido 2-
naftol-6-sulfónico)
schedule
horario, programa, plan
Scheele's green
verde de Scheele
(arseniato de cobre)
scheelite
scheelita, esquelita
scheme
esquema, diagrama
Schmidlin ketene
synthesis
síntesis de cetenos de
Schmidlin
Schmidt reaction
reacción de Schmidt
Scholler
saccharification
process
método de
sacarificación de
Scholler
Schweizer's reagent
reactivo de Schweizer
scientist
científico
scillaren
escilareno
scillarenin
escilarenina
scilliroside
escilirosida
scintillation
centelleo
scintillation counter
contador de
centelleo
sclerometer
esclerómetro
scleroprotein
escleroproteína
scoparin
escoparina
scoparone
escoparona
scope
objeto
scopolamime
escopolamina
scopolamine
hydrobromide
bromhidrato de
escopolamina
scopolamine N-oxide
N-óxido de
escopolamina
scopoletin
escopoletina

scopolin
escopolín
scopoline
escopolina
scorch, to
chamuscar, arder
score, to
marcar, rayar
scored
marcado, rayado
score mark
con ranura
scotophobin
escotofobina
screen
tamiz, criba
screening formulation
clasificación o estudio
de la fórmula
scrubbing
depuración
scutellarein
escutelareína
scutellaria
escutelaria
SDS gel electrophoresis
electroforesis de gel
SDS
seaboard process
método Seaboard
sealing gaskets
guarniciones sellantes
sealing wax
lacre
sebacic acid
ácido sebácico
sebacil
sebacilo
sebacoin
sebacoína
sebacoyl chloride
cloruro de sebacoílo
sebacylic acid
ácido sebacílico, ácido
sebácico
secalonic acids
ácidos secalónicos
secbutabarbital
secbutabarbital
seclazone
seclazona
secnidazole
secnidazol
secobarbital
secobarbital
secobarbital sodium
secobarbital sódico
seconal sodium
seconal sódico

secondary alcohol
alcohol secundario
secondary reaction
reacción secundaria
secondary valence
valencia secundaria
secoverine
secoverina
secretin
secretina
secure, to
proteger, asegurar
securinine
securinina
sedanolic acid
ácido sedanólico
sedanolide
sedanólido
sedative
sedante
sedecamycin
sedecamicina
sediment
sedimento
sedimentation
sedimentación
seed
sembrado
seed crystal
siembra, germen
cristalino
segment
segmento
Seidlitz mixture
mezcla de Seidlitz
selagine
selagenina
selection
selección
selective solvent
solvente selectivo
selegiline
selegilina
selegiline
hydrochloride
clorhidrato de
selegilina
selenate
seleniato
selenic acid
ácido selénico
selenide
seleniuro
seleniferous
selenífero
selenious acid
ácido selenioso
selenite
selenita

selenium
selenio
selenium bromide
bromuro de selenio
selenium chloride
cloruro de selenio
selenium dioxide
dióxido de selenio
selenium hexafluoride
hexafluoruro de
selenio
selenium oxide
óxido de selenio
selenium oxybromide
oxibromuro de selenio
selenium oxychloride
oxicloruro de selenio
selenium oxyfluoride
oxifluoruro de selenio
selenium sulfide
sulfuro de selenio
selenium tetrabromide
tetrabromuro de
selenio
selenium tetrachloride
tetracloruro de selenio
selenium
tetrafluoride
tetrafluoruro de selenio
selenocysteine
selenocisteína
selenomethionine
selenometionina
selenous acid
ácido selenioso
selenous acid
anhydride
anhídrido del
ácido selenioso
self acting
automático
self exclusion
autoexclusión
self preserved
se mantiene sin
contaminación
self sealability
autosellado
semicarbazide
hydrochloride
clorhidrato de
semicarbazida
semiconductor
semiconductor
semifinished product
producto
semiterminado
semioxamazide
semioxamizida

semipermeable
membrane
membrana
semipermeable
semisolid
semisólido
semisynthetic
semisintético
semivalent
semivalente
Semmler-Wolf reaction
reacción de Semmler y
Wolf
semotiadil
semotiadilo
sempervirine
sempervirina
semustine
semustina
senecialdehyde
senecialdehído,
senecioaldehído
senecic acid
ácido senécico
senecio
senecio
senecionine
senecionina
seneciphylline
senecifilina
senega
sénega
senna
sen, sena
sennoside A & B
senosida A y B
senociclin
senociclina
sensibility
sensibilidad, precisión
sensible
susceptible
sensitive to heat
sensible al calor
sensitivity
sensibilidad,
susceptividad
sensitizer
sensibilizador
separation
separación
separation process
proceso de separación
separatory funnel
embudo separador,
embudo de separación
sepazonium chloride
cloruro de
sepazonio

sepia
sepia
sepimostat
sepimostat
sepiomelanin
sepiomelanina
septiphene
septifeno, clorofeno, o-bencil-p-clorofenol
septivalent
septivalente
sequence
secuencia
seractide
seractida
serfibrate
serfibrato
serial 2-fold dilution
dilución seriada doble
sericin
sericina
serine
serina
Serini reaction
reacción de Serini
sermetacin
sermetacina
sermorelin
sermorelina
sermorelin acetate
acetato de sermorelina
serotonin
serotonina
serpentaria
serpentaria
serpentine (alkaloid)
serpentina (alcaloide)
serrapeptase
serrapeptasa
sertaconazole
sertaconazol
sertindole
sertindol
sertraline
sertralina
sertraline hydrochloride
clorhidrato de sertralina
serum
suero
serum albumin
albúmina sérica
sesame oil
aceite de sésamo
sesamex
sesamex
sesamin
sesamina

sesamolin
sesamolina
sesin
sesina
sesone
sesona
sesqui..
sesqui..
sesquicarbonate
sesquicarbonato
sesquioxide
sesquióxido
sesquisulfate
sesquisulfato
sesquisulfide
sesquisulfuro
sesquiterpene
sesquiterpeno
set
juego, equipo
set up, to
montar
setastine
setastina
setastine hydrochloride
clorhidrato de setastina
setazindol
setazindol
sethoxydim
setoxidín
setting time
tiempo de corrección
settled
asentado, asentarse
settler
decantador
sevoflurane
sevoflurano
sexivalent
sexivalente
sfericase
esfericasa
shade
tono
shake
agitación, sacudimiento
shaker
agitador
shaking
agitación
shape
forma
shark liver oil
aceite de hígado de tiburón
sharp
bien definida, fuerte

shear resistant
resistencia al desgarre
shelf-life
tiempo de almacenamiento autorizado
shell
cáscara, corteza
shellac
goma laca
shellolic acid
ácido de goma laca
shield
protección
shift
cambio, sustitución
shionone
shionona
shipping
envío
shikimic acid
ácido shikímico
shortstopping agent
agente de terminación
shoulder
hombro
showdomycin
showdomicina
shut-down
apagado
shutter
obturador
sialic acids
ácidos sialicos
sibutramine hydrochloride monohydrate
clorhidrato de sibutramina monohidratado
siccanin
sicanina
side by side
lado a lado, paralelo
side chain
cadena lateral
side reaction
reacción secundaria
side stream
corrientes residuales de extracción
siderite
siderita
siduron
sidurona
sienna
siena
sieve
criba, tamiz

sieromicin
sieromicina
sigma bond
enlace sigma
silandrone
silandrona
silane
silano, tetrahidruro de silicio
silane compounds
compuestos de silano
sildenafil citrate
citrato de sildenafil
silibinin
silibinina
silica
sílice, óxido de silicio
silica fused
sílice fundida
silica gel
gel de sílice
silicate
silicato
silicic acid
ácido silícico
silicide
siliciuro
silicochloroform
silicocloroformo, triclorosilano
silicomolybdic acid
ácido silicomolíbdico, ácido 12-molibdosilícico
silicon
silicio
silicon, amorphous
silicio amorfo
silicon bromide
bromuro de silicio, tetrabromuro de silicio
silicon carbide
carburo de silicio
silicon chloride
cloruro de silicio, tetracloruro de silicio
silicon compounds
compuestos de silicio
silicon-copper
aleación de silicio y cobre, siliciuro de cobre
silicon dioxide
dióxido de silicio, sílice
silicon disulfide
disulfuro de silicio

243

silicon fluoride
fluoruro de silicio,
tetrafluoruro de silicio
silicon monoxide
monóxido de silicio
silicon nitride
nitruro de silicio
silicon tetraacetate
tetraacetato de silicio
silicon tetrabromide
tetrabromuro de silicio,
bromuro de silicio
silicon tetrachloride
tetracloruro de silicio,
cloruro de silicio
silicon tetrafluoride
tetrafloruro de silicio,
fluoruro de silicio
silicon tetrahydride
tetrahidruro de silicio,
silano
silicon tetraiodide
tetrayoduro de silicio
silicon-gold alloy
aleación de silicio y
oro
silicones
siliconas
silicone oil
aceite de silicona
silicotungstic acid
ácido silicotúngstico,
ácido tungstosilícico
silicowolframic acid
ácido silico-
wolfrámico
silicristin
silicristina
silidianin
silidianina
silk
seda
sillimanite
silimanita (silicato de
aluminio)
siloxane
siloxano
silver
plata
silver acetate
acetato de plata
silver arsphenamine
arsfenamina de plata
silver bromate
bromato de plata
silver bromide
bromuro de plata
silver carbonate
carbonato de plata

silver chlorate
clorato de plata, clorato
argentoso
silver chloride
cloruro de plata
silver chromate
cromato de plata
silver citrate
citrato de plata
silver cyanide
cianuro de plata
silver dichromate
dicromato de plata,
bicromato de plata
silver difluoride
difluoruro de plata
silver fluoride
fluoruro de plata
silver iodate
yodato de plata
silver iodide
yoduro de plata
silver lactate
lactato de plata
silver litharge
litargirio de plata
silver mercury iodide
yoduro de plata y
mercurio, yoduro
mercúrico argéntico
silver methylarsonate
metilarsonato de plata
silver nitrate
nitrato de plata
silver nitrate
toughened
nitrato de plata
endurecido, nitrato de
plata moldeado
silver nitride
nitruro de plata
silver nitrite
nitrito de plata
silver orthophosphate
ortofosfato de plata,
fosfato de plata
silver oxalate
oxalato de plata
silver oxide
óxido de plata, óxido
argentoso
silver (II) oxide
óxido de plata (II),
oxido argéntico,
peróxido de plata
silver perchlorate
perclorato de plata
silver permanganate
permanganato de plata

silver peroxide
peróxido de plata,
óxido de plata (II),
oxido argéntico
silver phosphate
fosfato de plata,
ortofosfato de plata
silver picrate
picrato de plata
silver potassium
cyanide
cianuro de plata y
potasio
silver protein, mild
proteína de plata ligera
silver protein, strong
proteína de plata fuerte
silver selenate
seleniato de plata
silver selenide
seleniuro de plata
silver selenite
selenito de plata
silver sodium chloride
cloruro de plata y
sodio
silver sodium
thiosulfate
tiosulfato de plata y
sodio
silver staining
pigmento de plata
silver, sterling
plata esterlina
silver subfluoride
subfluoruro de plata
silver sulfate
sulfato de plata
silver sulfide
sulfuro de plata
silver tetraiodo-
mercurate(II)
tetrayodomercuriato
(II) de plata, yoduro
de plata y mercurio
silvex
silvex
silylene
silileno
silymarin
silimarina
simaldrate
simaldrato
simazine
simacina, simazina
simethicone
simeticona
simetride
simetrida

simfibrate
sinfibrato
similar
similar
Simmons-Smith
reaction
reacción de Simmons y
Smith
simple distillation
destilación simple
simtrazene
sintraceno
simvastatin
sinvastatina
sinalbin
sinalbina
sinapine
sinapina
sincalide
sincalida
sinefungin
sinefungina
single
individual, simple,
único
single crystal x-ray
análisis radiográfico de
un solo cristal
single stage
de un solo paso
sinigrin
sinigrina
sink
descenso
sinomenine
sinomenina
sintered glass funnel
embudo de vidrio
sinterizado
sintering
sinterización
sintropium bromide
bromuro de
sintropio
sisal
sisal
sisomicin
sisomicina
sisomicin sulfate
sulfato de
sisomicina
site
lugar
sitofibrate
sitofibrato
sitogluside
sitoglúsido
ß-sitosterol
ß-sistosterol

size
tamaño, medida,
dimensión
sizofiran
sizofirano
skatole
escatol
skimmianine
esquimianina
skimmin
esquimina
Skraup synthesis
síntesis de Skraup
slab gel electrophoresis
apparatus
aparato de
electroforesis para
placa de gel
slant
cultivo de plano
inclinado
slate black
negro de pizarra
slide
platina, portaobjeto
slope
inclinación,
pendiente
sludge
sedimentos
slurry
suspensión
smalt
esmaltín
smaltite
esmaltita
smelting
fusión
smilagenin
esmilagenina
smoke black
negro de humo
soaking
remojo
soap bark
palo de jabón
sobrerol
sobrerol
soda
sosa, soda
soda alum
alumbre de soda
soda ash
ceniza de sosa, sosa
comercial
soda caustic
sosa cáustica
soda crystals
cristales de sosa

soda monohydrate
monohidrato de
sosa
soda, natural
sosa natural
soda niter
nitro de sosa,
nitrato de sodio
soda, washing
sosa para lavar
sodalite
sodalita, zeolita
sodamide
sodamida, amida
sódica
sodium
sodio
sodium abietate
abietato de sodio
sodium acetate
acetato de sodio
sodium acetazolamide
acetazolamida de sodio
sodium N-acetoacetyl-
p-sulfanilate
N-acetoacetil-p-
sulfanilato de sodio
sodium acetone
bisulfate
bisulfato de sodio y
acetona
sodium acetyl formate
acetilformiato de sodio
sodium acid carbonate
carbonato ácido de
sodio, bicarbonato de
sodio
sodium acid
phosphate
fosfato ácido de sodio,
fosfato de sodio
monobásico
sodium acid
pyrophosphate
pirofosfato ácido de
sodio
sodium acid sulfate
sulfato ácido de sodio,
bisulfato de sodio
sodium acid sulfite
sulfito ácido de sodio,
bisulfito de sodio
sodium acid tartrate
tartrato ácido de sodio,
bitartrato de sodio
sodium alizarine-
sulfonate
alizarinsulfonato de
sodio

sodium alginate
alginato de sodio
sodium aluminate
aluminato de sodio
sodium alumino-
silicate
aluminosilicato de
sodio
sodium aluminum
hydride
hidruro de sodio y
aluminio
sodium aluminum
phosphate
fosfato de sodio y
aluminio
sodium aluminum
silicofluoride
silicofluoruro de sodio
y aluminio
sodium aluminum
sulfate
sulfato de sodio y
aluminio
sodium amalgam
amalgama de sodio
sodium amide
amida sódica
sodium p-
aminobenzoate
p-aminobenzoato de
sodio
sodium aminophenyl-
arsonate
aminofenilarsonato de
sodio
sodium p-
aminosalicylate
p-aminosalicilato de
sodio
sodium amidotrizoate
amidotrizoato de
sodio
sodium ammonium
hydrogen phosphate
hidrofosfato de sodio
y amonio
sodium amylosulfate
amilosulfato de
sodio
sodium amytal
amital sódico
sodium antimonate
antimoniato de
sodio
sodium apolate
apolato de sodio
sodium arsanilate
arsanilato de sodio

sodium arsenate,
dibasic
arseniato de sodio
dibásico
sodium arsenite
arsenito de sodio
sodium
arsphenamine
arsfenamina de sodio
sodium ascorbate
ascorbato de sodio
sodium auro-
thiomalate
aurotiomalato de sodio
sodium auro-
thiosulfate
aurotiosulfato de sodio
sodium azide
azida sódica
sodium bacitracín
methylene
disalicylate
metilendisalicilato
de sodio y bacitracina
sodium barbital
barbital sódico
sodium barbiturate
barbiturato de sodio
sodium benzoate
benzoato de sodio
sodium benzyl-
penicillin
bencilpenicilina sódica
sodium benzyl-
succinate
bencilsuccinato
de sodio
sodium beryllium
fluoride
fluoruro de sodio y
berilio
sodium bicarbonate
bicarbonato de sodio,
carbonato ácido de
sodio
sodium bichromate
bicromato de sodio
sodium bifluoride
bifluoruro de sodio
sodium biphosphate
bifosfato de sodio
fosfato ácido de sodio
sodium bismuthate
bismutato de sodio
sodium bisulfate
bisulfato de sodio,
sulfato ácido de sodio
sodium bisulfide
bisulfuro de sodio

sodium bisulfite
bisulfito de sodio,
sulfito ácido de sodio
sodium bitartrate
bitartrato de sodio,
tartrato ácido de sodio
sodium bithionolate
bitionolato de sodio
sodium borate
borato de sodio
sodium borate
anhydrous
borato de sodio
anhídro
sodium borate solution
compound
compuesto de solución
de borato de sodio
sodium boroformate
boroformiato de sodio
sodium borohydride
borohidruro de sodio
sodium bromate
bromato de sodio
sodium bromide
bromuro de sodio
sodium bromite
bromito de sodio
sodium cacodylate
cacodilato de sodio
sodium carbolate
carbolato de sodio,
fenolato de sodio
sodiun carbonate
carbonato de sodio
sodium carbonate
monohydrate
carbonato de sodio
monohidratado
sodium carboxy-
methyl cellulose
carboximetilcelulosa
sódica
sodium caseinate
caseinato de sodio
sodium chlorate
clorato de sodio
sodiun chloride
cloruro de sodio
sodium chlorite
clorito de sodio
sodium chloroacetate
cloroacetato de sodio
sodium chloro-
aluminate
cloroaluminato de
sodio
sodium chloroaurate
cloroaurato de sodio

sodium p-chloro-m-
cresolate
p-cloro-m-cresolato de
sodio
sodium 6-chloro-5-
nitrotoluene-3-
sulfonate
6-cloro-5-nitrotolueno-
3-sulfonato de sodio
sodium-4-chloro-
phthalate
4-cloroftalato de sodio
sodium chloro-
platinate
cloroplatinato de
sodio,cloruro de
platino y sodio,
sodium-o-
chlorotoluene-p-
sulfonate
o-clorotoluen-p-
sulfonato de sodio
sodium chromate
sodium chromate
cromato de sodio
sodium chromate,
tetrahydrate
cromato de sodio
tetrahidratado
sodium chromate,
radioactive
cromato de sodio
radioactivo
sodium citrate
citrato de sodio
sodium citrate, acid
citrato ácido de sodio
sodium cobaltinitrite
cobaltinitrito de sodio
sodium copper chloride
cloruro de sodio y
cobre
sodium copper cyanide
cianuro de sodio y
cobre
sodium cyanate
cianato de sodio
sodium cyanide
cianuro de sodio
sodium cyano-
borohydride
cianoborohidruro
de sodio
sodium cyanocuprate
cianocuprato de sodio
sodium cyclamate
ciclamato de sodio
sodium dehydrocholate
dehidrocolato de sodio

sodium deoxycholate
deoxicolato de sodio
sodium dextran
sulfate
sulfato de sodio y
dextrano
sodium diacetate
diacetato de sodio
sodiumn 1-diazo-2-
naphthol-4-sulfonate
1-diazo-2-naftol-4-
sulfonato de sodio
sodium dibunate
dibunato de sodio
sodium dibutyldithio-
carbamate
dibutilditiocarbamato
de sodio
sodium dibutyl
naphthalene
sulfonate
dibutilnaftalen-
sulfonato de sodio
sodium-α,ß-dichloro-
isobutyrate
α,ß-dichloroiso-
butirato de sodio
sodium dichloroiso-
cyanurate
dicloroisocianurato de
sodio
sodium 2,4-dichloro-
phenoxyacetate
2,4-diclorofenoxi-
acetato de sodio
sodium 2,4-dichloro-
phenoxyethyl sulfate
2,4-diclorofenoxi-
etilsulfato de sodio
sodium 2,2-dichloro-
propionate
2,2-dicloropropionato
de sodio
sodium dichromate
dicromato de sodio
sodium
dicyanoaurate
dicianoaurato de sodio
sodium diethyldithio
carbamate
dietilditiocarbamato
de sodio
sodium dihydrogen
phosphate
fosfato ácido de sodio
sodium dihydroxy-
ethylglycine
dihidroxietilglicina
sódica

sodium dimethyl-
arsenate
dimetilarseniato de
sodio
sodium dimethyl-
dithiocarbamate
dimetilditiocarbamato
de sodio
sodium dinitro-o-
cresylate
dinitro-o-cresilato de
sodio
sodium dioctyl
sulfosuccinate
dioctilsulfosuccinato
de sodio
sodium dioxide
dióxido de sodio
sodium
diprotizoate
diprotizoato de sodio
sodium dispersion
dispersión de sodio
sodium dithionate
ditionato de sodio
sodium dithionite
ditionito de sodio
sodium dodecyl-
benzenesulfonate
dodecilbenceno-
sulfonato de sodio
sodium dodecyl
diphenyl oxide
disulfonate
dodecildifenil-
oxidodisulfonato de
sodio
sodium edetate
edetato de sodio
sodium etasulfate
etasulfato de sodio
sodium ethoxide
etóxido de sodio
sodium ethylate
etilato de sodio
sodium ethylenebis-
dithiocarbamate
etilenbisditio-
carbamato de sodio
sodium 2-ethylhexyl-
sulfoacetate
2-etilhexilsulfo-
acetato de sodio
sodium ethyl
oxalacetate
etiloxalacetato
de sodio
sodium ethyl sulfate
etilsulfato de sodio

sodium ethylxanthate
etilxantato de sodio
sodium feredetate
feredetato de sodio
sodium ferricyanide
ferricianuro de sodio
sodium ferrocyanide
ferrocianuro de sodio
sodium fluoborate
fluoborato de sodio
sodium fluophosphate
fluofosfato de sodio
sodium fluoride
fluoruro de sodio
sodium fluoroacetate
fluoacetato de sodio
sodium fluoroborate
fluoborato de sodio
sodium
fluorophosphate
fluofosfato de sodio
sodium fluorosilicate
fluosilicato de sodio
sodium folate
folato de sodio, sal
sódica del ácido fólico
sodium formaldehyde
bisulfite
formaldehído bisulfito
de sodio
sodium formaldehyde
hydrosulfite
formaldehído
hidrosulfito de sodio
sodium formaldehyde
sulfoxylate
formaldehído
sulfoxilato de sodio
sodium formate
formiato de sodio
sodium gentisate
gentisato de sodio
sodium glucaspaldrate
glucaspaldrato de sodio
sodium
glucoheptonate
glucoheptonato
de sodio
sodium gluconate
gluconato de sodio
sodium glucosulfone
glucosulfona sódica
sodium glutamate
glutamato de sodio
sodium glycero-
phosphate
glicerofosfato de sodio
sodium glycolate
glicolato de sodio

sodium gold chloride
cloruro de sodio y oro
sodium gold cyanide
cianuro de sodio y oro
sodium gualenate
gualenato de sodio
sodium guanylate
guanilato de sodio
sodium gynocardate
ginocardato de sodio
sodium heparin
heparina sódica
sodium heptameta-
phosphate
heptametafosfato de
sodio
sodium hexachloro-
osmate
hexaclorosmiato de
sodio
sodium hexachloro-
platinate
hexacloroplatinato de
sodio
sodium hexacyclonate
hexaciclonato de sodio
sodium hexafluoro-
silicate
hexafluorosilicato de
sodio
sodium hexameta-
phosphate
hexametafosfato de
sodio
sodium hexylene glycol
monoborate
hexilenglicol
monoborato de sodio
sodium hyaluronate
hialuronato de sodio
sodium
hydnocarpate
hipnocarpato de sodio
sodium hydrate
hidrato de sodio
sodium hydride
hidruro de sodio
sodium hydrogen
sulfide
sulfuro ácido de sodio
sodium hydrosulfide
hidrosulfuro de sodio,
bisulfuro de sodio
sodium hydrosulfite
hidrosulfito de sodio
sodium hydroxide
hidróxido de sodio
sodium hypochlorite
hipoclorito de sodio

sodium hypochlorite
solution, alkaline
solución alcalina de
hipoclorito de sodio
sodium hypochlorite
solution, diluted
solución diluida de
hipoclorito de sodio
sodium hypophosphate
hipofosfato de sodio
sodium hypophosphite
hipofosfito de sodio
sodium hyposulfate
hiposulfato de sodio
sodium hyposulfite
hiposulfito de sodio
sodium inosinate
inosinato de sodio
sodium iodate
yodato de sodio
sodium iodide
yoduro de sodio
sodium iodide,
radioactive
yoduro de sodio
radioactivo
sodium iodipamide
yodipamida sódica
sodium
iodohippurate
yodohipurato de sodio
sodium iodo-
methamate
yodometamato de
sodio
sodium iodo-
methane sulfonate
yodometanosulfonato
de sodio
sodium iothalamate
yodotalamato de sodio
sodium ipodate
ipodato de sodio
sodium iron
pyrophosphate
pirofosfato de sodio y
hierro
sodium isethionate
isetionato de sodio
sodium isoascorbate
isoascorbato de sodio
sodium isobutyl-
xanthate
isobutilxantato de
sodio
sodium isopropyl
xanthate
isopropilxantato de
sodio

sodium isovalerate
isovalerato de sodio
sodium lactate
lactato de sodio
sodium n-lauroyl
sarcinate
n-lauroil sarcosinato
de sodio
sodium lauryl sulfate
sulfato laurílico de
sodio, sulfato
dodecílico de sodio
sodium lauryl
sulfoacetate
sulfoacetato laurílico
de sodio
sodium-lead alloy
aleación de sodio y
plomo
sodium lead
hyposulfite
hiposulfito de sodio y
plomo
sodium lead thiosulfate
tiosulfato de sodio y
plomo
sodium lignosulfate
lignosulfato de sodio
sodium liothyronine
liotironina sódica
sodium MBT
MBT sódico (solución
acuosa al 50% de
mercaptobenzotiazol
sódico)
sodium mercapto-
acetate
mercaptoacetato de
sodio
sodium 2-mercapto-
benzothiazole
2-mercapto-
benzotiazol sódico
sodium metabisulfite
metabisulfito de sodio
sodium metaborate
metaborato de sodio
sodium metanilate
metanilato de sodio
sodium
metaperiodate
metaperiodato de sodio
sodium meta-
phosphate
metafosfato de sodio
sodium metasilicate
metasilicato de sodio
sodium metavanadate
metavanadato de sodio

sodium methacrylate
metacrilato de sodio
**sodium methane-
arsonate**
metanoarsoniato
de sodio
sodium methiodal
metiodal sódico
sodium methoxide
metóxido de sodio
sodium methylate
metilato de sodio
**sodium methyl
carbonate**
metilcarbonato de
sodio
**sodium N-methyl-
dithiocarbamate
dihydrate**
N-metilditiocarbamato
de sodio dihidratado
**sodium methyl-N-
oleoyl taurate**
metil-N-oleoiltaurato
de sodio
**sodium methyl
siliconate**
metilsiliconato de
sodio
sodium methyl sulfate
metilsulfato de sodio
**sodium N-methyl-
taurate**
N-metiltaurato de sodio
sodium metrizoate
metrizoato de sodio
**sodium miristyl
sulfate**
miristilsulfato de sodio
sodium molybdate
molibdato de sodio
**sodium-12-molybdo-
phosphate**
12-molibdofosfato de
sodio
**sodium-12-molybdo-
silicate**
12-molibdosilicato de
sodio
sodium monobasic
sodio monobásico
**sodium monofluoro-
phosphate**
monofluorofosfato de
sodio
sodium monoxide
monóxido de sodio
sodium morrhuate
morruato de sodio

**sodium naphthalene
sulfonate**
naftalensulfonato de
sodio
sodium naphthenate
naftenato de sodio
sodium naphthionate
naftionato de sodio
**sodium naphthol-
sulfonates**
naftolsulfonatos de
sodio
**sodium ß-naphtho-
quinone-4-sulfonate**
ß-naftoquinona-4-
sulfonato de sodio
**sodium naphthyl-
aminesulfonate**
naftilaminsulfonato de
sodio
sodium nitrate
nitrato de sodio
**sodium nitrilo-
triacetate**
nitrilotriacetato de
sodio
sodium nitrite
nitrito de sodio
**sodium nitro-
ferricyanide**
nitroferricianuro
de sodio
**sodium p-nitro-
phenolate**
p-nitrofenolato de
sodio
**sodium
nitroprusside**
nitroprusiato de sodio
sodium novobiocin
novobiocina sódica
sodium octyl sulfate
octilsulfato de sodio
sodium oleate
oleato de sodio
**sodium ortho-
phosphate**
ortofosfato de sodio
**sodium
orthosilicate**
ortosilicato de sodio
sodium oxalate
oxalato de sodio
sodium oxide
óxido de sodio
sodium oxybate
oxibato de sodio
sodium palconate
palconato de sodio

**sodium palladium
chloride**
cloruro de sodio
y paladio
sodium palmitate
palmitato de sodio
sodium paraperiodate
paraperyodato de sodio
**sodium pentaborate
decahydrate**
pentaborato de
sodio decahidratado
**sodium penta-
chlorophenate**
pentaclorofenato de
sodio
sodium pentobarbital
pentobarbital sódico
sodium "penthotal"
"pentotal" sódico,
tiopental sódico
sodium perborate
perborato de sodio
sodium perchlorate
perclorato de sodio
sodium periodate
periodato de sodio
sodium permanganate
permanganato de sodio
sodium peroxide
peróxido de sodio
sodium persulfate
persulfato de sodio
sodium pertechnetate
pertecnetato de sodio
sodium phenate
fenato de sodio,
carbolato de sodio,
fenolato de sodio
sodium phenobarbital
fenobarbital sódico
sodium phenolate
fenolato de sodio,
fenato de sodio
**sodium phenol-
sulfonate**
fenolsulfonato de
sodio, sulfocarbolato
de sodio
sodium phenoxide
fenóxido de sodio
sodium phenylacetate
fenilacetato de sodio,
α-toluato de sodio
**sodium N-phenyl-
glycinamide-p-
arsonate**
N-fenilglicinamida-p-
arsoniato de sodio

**sodium o-phenyl-
phenate**
o-fenilfenato de sodio
**sodium phenyl-
phosphinate**
fenilfosfinato de sodio
sodium phosphate
fosfato de sodio
**sodium phosphate,
dibasic**
fosfato de sodio
dibásico
**sodium phosphate,
monobasic**
fosfato de sodio
monobásico
**sodium phosphate,
radioactive**
fosfato de sodio
radioactivo
**sodium phosphate,
tribasic**
fosfato de sodio
tribásico, fosfato
trisódico
sodium phosphide
fosfuro de sodio
sodium phosphite
fosfito de sodio
**sodium phospho-
aluminate**
fosfoaluminato de
sodio
**sodium phospho-
molybdate**
fosfomolibdato de
sodio
**sodium phospho-
tungstate**
fosfotungstato de sodio
sodium phytate
fitato de sodio
sodium picofosfate
picofosfato de sodio
sodium picosulfate
picosulfato de sodio
sodium picramate
picramato de sodio
**sodium
platinichloride**
platinocloruro de
sodio, cloroplatinato
de sodio
sodium plumbate
plumbato de sodio
**sodium polyanethole-
sulfonate**
polianetolsulfonato de
sodio

sodium poly-
metaphosphate
polimetafosfato de
sodio
sodium polyphosphate
polifosfato de sodio
sodium polysulfide
polisulfuro de sodio
sodium polystyrene
sulfonate
poliestirensulfonato de
sodio
sodium-potassium
alloy
aleación de sodio y
potasio
sodium potasium
carbonate
carbonato de sodio y
potasio
sodium potasium
phosphate
fosfato de sodio y
potasio
sodium potasium
tartrate
tartrato de sodio y
potasio
sodium propionate
propionato de sodio
sodium prussiate, red
prusiato de sodio rojo
sodium prussiate,
yellow
prusiato de sodio
amarillo, ferrocianuro
de sodio
sodium pyro-
antimonate
piroantimoniato de
sodio
sodium pyro-
phosphate
pirofosfato de sodio
sodium pyro-
phosphate acid
pirofosfato ácido de
sodio
sodium
pyroracemate
pirorracemato de sodio
sodium pyrosulfite
pirosulfito de sodio
sodium pyrovanadate
pirovanadato de sodio
sodium pyruvate
piruvato de sodio
sodium resinate
resinato de sodio

sodium rhodanate
rodanato de sodio,
tiocianato de sodio
sodium rhodanide
rodanuro de sodio
sodium rhodizonate
rodizonato de sodio
sodium ricinoleate
ricinoleato de sodio
sodium saccharin
sacarina sódica
sodium salicylate
salicilato de sodio
sodium sarcosinate
sarcosinato de sodio
sodium secobarbital
secobarbital sódico
sodium selenate
seleniato de sodio
sodium selenide
seleniuro de sodio
sodium selenite
selenita sódica
sodium sesqui-
carbonate
sesquicarbonato de
sodio
sodium sesquisilicate
sesquisilicato de sodio
sodium silicate
silicato de sodio
sodium silicate
solution
solución de
silicato de sodio
sodium silico-
aluminate
silicoaluminato de
sodio
sodium silicofluoride
silicofluoruro de sodio
sodium silico-12-
molybdate
silico-12-molibdato de
sodio
sodium 12-silico-
tungstate
12-silicotungstato
de sodio
sodium silver chloride
cloruro de sodio y plata
sodium silver
thiosulfate
tiosulfato de sodio
y plata
sodium sorbate
sorbato de sodio
sodium stannate
estannato de sodio

sodium stearate
estearato de sodio
sodium stearoyl-2-
lactylate
estearoil-2-lactilato de
sodio
sodium stibocaptate
estibocaptato de sodio
sodium stibogluconate
estibogluconato de
sodio
sodium succinate
succinato de sodio
sodium succinate
sulfacetamide
sulfacetamida sódica
sodium sulfanilate
sulfanilato de sodio
sodium sulfapyridine
sulfapiridina sódica
sodium sulfate
sulfato de sodio
sodium sulfate
anhydrous
sulfato de sodio anhidro
sodium sulfate
decahydrate
sulfato de sodio
decahidratado
sodium sulfide
sulfuro de sodio
sodium sulfite
sulfito de sodio
sodium sulfo-
bromophthalein
sulfobromoftaleína
sódica
sodium sulfocarbolate
sulfocarbolato de
sodio, fenolsulfonato
de sodio
sodium sulfocyanate
sulfocianato de sodio,
tiocianato de sodio
sodium sulfocyanide
sulfocianuro de sodio
sodium ß-sulfo-
propionitrile
ß-sulfopropionitrilo de
sodio
sodium sulfo-
ricinoleate
sulforricinoleato de
sodio
sodium tartrate
tartrato de sodio
sodium tartrate acid
tartrato ácido de sodio,
bitartrato de sodio

sodium tellurate
telurato de sodio
sodium tellurite
telurito de sodio
sodium tetraborate
tetraborato de sodio
sodium tetrachloro-
aluminate
tetracloroaluminato de
sodio
sodium tetrachloro-
aurate(III)
tetracloroaurato (III) de
sodio
sodium 2,3,4,6-
tetrachlorophenate
2,3,4,6-tetracloro-
fenato de sodio
sodium tetradecyl
sulfate
sulfato tetradecílico de
sodio, tetradecilsulfato
de sodio
sodium tetraphenyl-
borate
tetrafenilborato de
sodio
sodium tetrasulfide
tetrasulfuro de sodio
sodium tetrathionate
tetrationato de sodio
sodium thimerfonate
timerfonato de sodio
sodium thiocarbonate
tiocarbonato de sodio
sodium thiocyanate
tiocianato de sodio,
rodanato de sodio
sodium thioglycolate
tioglucolato de sodio
sodium thiophosphate
tiofosfato de sodio
sodium thiopental
tiopental sódico,
pentotal sódico
sodium thiosulfate
tiosulfato de sodio
sodium titanate
titanato de sodio
sodium α-toluate
α-toluato de sodio,
fenilacetato de sodio
sodium toluene-
sulfonate
toluensulfonato de
sodio
sodium trichloro-
acetate
tricloroacetato de sodio

sodium 2,4,5-trichlorophenate
2,4,5-triclorofenato de sodio

sodium trimetaphosphate
trimetafosfato de sodio

sodium tri-p-periodate
tri-p-peryodato de sodio

sodium triphenyl-p-rosaniline sulfonate
trifenil-p-rosanilin-sulfonato de sodio

sodium triphosphate
trifosfato de sodio

sodium tripolyphosphate
tripolifosfato de sodio

sodium trititanate
trititanato de sodio

sodium tungstate
tungstato de sodio

sodium 12-tungstophosphate
12-tungstofosfato de sodio

sodium 12-tungstosilicate
12-tungstosilicato de sodio

sodium tyropanoate
tiropanoato de sodio

sodium undecylenate
undecilenato de sodio

sodium uranate
uranato de sodio

sodium valproate
valproato de sodio

sodium vanadate
vanadato de sodio

sodium-p-vinylbenzene sulfonate
p-vinilbenceno-sulfonato de sodio

sodium xanthate
xantato de sodio‾

sodium xanthogenate
xantogenato de sodio

sodium xylenesulfonate
xilenosulfonato de sodio

sodium zinc hexamethaphosphate
hexametafosfato de sodio y cinc

sodium zirconium glycolate
glicolato de sodio y circonio

sodium zirconium lactate
lactato de sodio y circonio

sodiumacetic acid sodium salt
sal de sodio del ácido sodioacético

sofalcone
sofalcona

soft porcelain
porcelana porosa

soft water
agua tratada

softener
ablandador

softening agent
agente suavizador, agente suavizante

software
programa

sol
sol, solución coloidal

solan
solana

solanidine
solanidina

solanine
solanina

solanocapsine
solanocapsina

solanone
solanona

solanum
solano

solar energy
energía solar

solasodine
solasodina

solasonine
solasonina

solasulfone
solasulfona

solid
sólido

solidification
solidificación

solid state chemistry
química del estado sólido

solidification point
temperatura de solidificación

solidify, to
solidificar

solubility
solubilidad

solubilize
solubilizar

soluble
soluble

soluble oil
aceite soluble

soluble starch
almidón soluble

solute
soluto

solution
solución

solution, colloidal
solución coloidal

solution, saturated
solución saturada

solution, true
solución verdadera

solvability
solubilidad

solvate
solvato, solvatación

solvated
solvatado

solvation
solvatación

Solvay process
procedimiento de Solvay

solvent
solvente, disolvente

solvolysis
solvolisis

soman
somán

somatoliberin
somatoliberina

somatomedins
somatomedinas

somatostatin
somatostatina

somatotropin
somatotropina

somatrem
somatren

somatropin
somatropina

Sommelet reaction
reacción de Sommelet

Sommelet-Hauser rearrangement
transposición de Sommelet y Hausen

songorine
songorina

sonicating
ultrasonido

sonication
poner en el baño de ultrasonido, mediante ultrasonido

Sonn-Muller method
método de Sonn y Muller

sonolysis
sonolisis

SOP
procedimiento operativo estándar

sophorabioside
soforabiosida

sophoricoside
soforicosida

sophorose
soforosa

sopitazine
sopitacina, sopitazina

soporific
soporífico

sopromidine
sopromidina

soquinolol
soquinolol

sorbic acid
ácido sórbico

sorbic alcohol
alcohol sórbico

sorbides
sórbidos

sorbinicate
sorbinicato

sorbinil
sorbinil

sorbitan
sorbitán

sorbitan fatty acid ester
éster graso de sorbitán

sorbitan laurate
laurato de sorbitán

sorbitan oleate
oleato de sorbitán

sorbitan palmitate
palmitato de sorbitán

sorbitan polyexyethylene fatty acid esters
ésteres grasos de sorbitan y poliexietileno

sorbitan sesquioleate
sesquioleato de sorbitán

sorbitan stearate
estearato de sorbitán

sorbitan trioleate
trioleato de sorbitán

sorbitan tristearate
triestearato de sorbitán

sorbite
sorbita, sorbitol

sorbose
sorbosa,sorbitosa, sorbín

sorbitol
sorbitol, sorbita

sorption
absorción, adsorción

sorrel salt
sal de acederas
(bioxalato de potasio)

sorting
clasificación

sotalol
sotalol

sotalol hydrochloride
clorhidrato de sotalol

soterenol
soterenol

source
origen

soybean
soya, soja

soybean flour
harina de soya o soja

soybean oil
aceite de soya o soja

soy sauce
salsa de soja

sozoiodolic acid
ácido sozoyodólico

space, chemistry
química del espacio

space velocity
velocidad espacial

spaglumic acid
ácido espaglúmico

spandex
espandex

Spanish white
blanco de España

spar
espato

spar, Greenland
espato de Groenlandia

sparassol
esparasol

sparfloxacin
esparfloxacina

sparfosic acid
ácido esparfósico

sparge
rociar

sparger
roceador

sparging
burbujeando

sparingly
escasamente

sparking metal
metal centelleante

sparsiflorine
esparsiflorina

sparsomycin
esparsomicina

spartein(e)
esparteína

spasmolytol
espasmolitol

spatula
espátula

spearmint
menta

spearmint oil
esencia (aceite) de
menta

specific gravity
peso específico,
gravedad específica

specific heat
calor específico

specific reaction ratio
velocidad de reacción
específica

specific weight
peso específico

specifications
especificaciones

specificity
especifidad

specimen
muestra, espécimen

spectinomycin
espectinomicina

spectrin
espectrina

spectrograph
espectrógrafo

spectrography
espectrografía

spectrometer
espectrómetro

spectrometry
espectrometría

spectrophotometry
espectrofotometría

spectropolarimeter
espectropolarímetro

spectroscope
espectroscopio

spectroscopic
espectroscópico

spectroscopy
espectroscopía

spectrum
espectro

spectrum analysis
análisis del espectro

spelter
peltre,cinc

spermaceti
espermaceti, esperma o
blanco de ballena

spermidine
espermidina

spermine
espermina

sperm oil
aceite de esperma

Sperry process
método de Sperry

sphalerite
esfalerita

spherophysine
esferofisina

sphingomyelins
esfingomielinas

sphingosine
esfingosina

spiclomazine
espiclomacina,
espiclomazina

spigelia
espigelia

spike (graphic)
pico, punta

spiked with
enriquecido

spike oil
aceite de espigas

α-spinasterol
α-espinasterol

spin
rotación, giro
rápido

spindle
vástago

spindle oil
aceite para husos

spinulosin
espinulosina

spiperone
espiperona

spiramide
espiramida

spiramycin
espiramicina

spirazine
espiracina, espirazina

spirendolol
espirendolol

spirgetine
espirgetina

spirilene
espirileno

**spirit of ammonia,
aromatic**
tintura amoniacal
aromática

spirit of camphor
tintura de alcanfor

spirit of chloroform
tintura de
cloroformo

spirit of ether
tintura de éter

**spirit of ether
compound**
compuesto de espíritu
de éter

spirit of ethylnitrite
tintura de nitrito de
etilo

spirit of formic acid
tintura de ácido
fórmico

**spirit of glyceryl
trinitrate**
tintura de trinitrato de
glicerilo

spirit of peppermint
tintura de menta

spirit of spearmint
tintura de
yerbabuena

spirits of terpentine
esencia (aceite) de
trementina

spiro system
sistema espiro

spirogermanium
espirogermanio

spiromustine
espiromustina

spironolactone
espironolactona

spiropentane
espiropentano

spirorenone
espirorenona

spiroxasone
espiroxasona

spiroxatrine
espiroxatrina

spiroxepin
espiroxepina

spizofurone
espizofurona

splenin
esplenina

split into
desdoblar, hidrolizar

split up
desdoblar

splitting
desdoblamiento,
hidrólisis, eliminación

spodumene
espodúmeno

spontaneous
combustion
combustión espontánea

sporidesmins
esporidesminas

sporidesmolides
esporidesmolidas

spot
mancha

spotter
marcador

spray dried
secado al rocío

spray nozzle
boquilla
pulverizadora

spraying
rociado

spread
extender

sprinkle, to
rociar

squalane
escualano

squalene
escualeno

squill
escila

stability
estabilidad

stabilizer
estabilizador

stable
estable

stable isotope
isótopo estable

stachydrine
estaquidrina

stage
etapa

stain
colorante

stainless steel
acero inoxidable

stallimycin
estalimicina

standard
estándar

standard deviatión
desviación del
estándar

standard equipment
equipo estándar

standard solution
solución estándar

standardization
valoración,
normalización

standardize
valorar, normalizar

stannate
estannato

stannic
estánnico

stannic anhydride
anhídrido estánnico,
óxido estánnico

stannic bromide
bromuro estánnico

stannic chloride
cloruro estánnico

stannic chloride
pentahydrate
cloruro estánnico
pentahidratado

stannic chromate
cromato estánnico

stannic fluoride
fluoruro estánnico

stannic iodide
yoduro estánnico

stannic oxide
óxido estánnico

stannic selenide
seleniuro estánnico

stannic selenite
selenita estánnica

stannic sulfide
sulfuro estánnico

stannite
estanita

stannous
estannoso

stannous acetate
acetato estannoso

stannous bromide
bromuro estannoso

stannous chloride
cloruro estannoso

stannous chromate
cromato estannoso

stannous fluoride
fluoruro estannoso

stannous hexafluoro
zirconate
hexafluorocirconato
estannoso

stannous iodide
yoduro estannoso

stannous octoate
octoato estannoso

stannous oleate
oleato estannoso

stannous oxalate
oxalato estannoso

stannous oxide
óxido estannoso

stannous
pyrophosphate
pirofosfato estannoso

stannous selenide
seleniuro estannoso

stannous sulfate
sulfato estannoso

stannous sulfide
sulfuro estannoso

stannous tartrate
tartrato estannoso

stannum
estaño

stanolone
estanolona

stanozolol
estanozolol

staphisagria
estafisagria

staphylokinase
estafilocinasa

star anise
anís estrellado

starch
almidón

starch, modified
almidón modificado

starch, soluble
almidón soluble

starting material
materia prima

start-up
poner en marcha

state of equilibrium
estado de equilibrio

statine
estatina

statolon
estatolona

stavudine
estavudina

steaglate
esteaglato

steam
vapor de agua

steam distillation
destilación al vapor

stearate
estearato

stearic acid
ácido esteárico

stearin(e)
estearina

stearone
estearona

N-stearoyl-p-
aminophenol
N-estearoil-p-
aminofenol

stearoyl chloride
cloruro de estearoílo

stearyl
estearilo

stearyl alcohol
alcohol estearílico

stearyl-amine
estearilamina

stearyl mercaptan
estearilmercaptano

stearyl mono-
glyceridyl citrate
citrato de estearilmono-
gliceridilo

stearyl sulfamide
estearilsulfamida

steel
acero

steffimycin
estefimicina

Steinbuhl yellow
amarillo Steinbuhl,
cromato de bario

stem
vástago

stenbolone
estembolona

step
etapa, paso

Stephen aldehyde
synthesis
síntesis de aldehídos de
Stephen

stepronin
estepronina

stercuronium iodide
yoduro de
estercuronio

stereochemistry
estereoquímica

stereoformula
estereofórmula

stereoisomer
estereoisómero

stereospecific catalyst
catalizador
estereoespecífico

steric
estérico

steric hindrance
impedimento estérico
sterile
estéril
sterilization
esterilización
sterilizer
esterilizador
sterling silver
plata esterlina
steroid
esteroide
sterol
esterol
stevaladil
estevaladilo
Stevens rearrangement
transposición de
Stevens
steviol
esteviol
stevioside
esteviosida
stibamine glucoside
glucósido estibamina
stibic anhydride
anhídrido estíbico,
pentóxido de antimonio
stibine
estibina
stibiun
estibio, antimonio
stibnite
estibinita
stibocaptate
estibocaptato
stibophen
estibofeno
stibosamine
estibosamina
stifoben
estifobeno
stigmastanol
estigmastanol
stigmasterol
estigmasterol
stilbamidine
estilbamidina
stilbamidine isetionate
isetionato de
estilbamidina
stilbazium iodide
yoduro de estilbacio
stilbene
estilbeno
stilbene dye
colorantes del estilbeno
stilbestrol
estilbestrol

stillingia
estilingia
stillonium iodide
yoduro de estilonio
stir, to
agitar
stirimazole
estirimazol
stiripentol
estiripentol
stirocainide
estirocainida
stirofos
estirofós
stock solution
solución madre
stoichiometry
estequiometría
Stoke's law
ley de Stoke
stop
detener, interrumpir
stopcork
llave
stopper
tapón
stopwatch
cronómetro
storage conditions
condiciones de
almacenamiento
storage tank
tanque de
almacenamiento
storax
estoraque
straight chain
cadena recta o lineal
straight chain
hydrocarbons
hidrocarburos de
cadena recta
straight run
destilación directa
strain
cepa
strainer
tamiz, filtro
stramonium
estramonio
streak
raya, línea
streaming potential
potencial de flujo
Strecker amino acid
synthesis
síntesis de
aminoácidos
de Strecker

strength
potencia,
concentración
strepogenin
estrepogenina
streptidine
estreptidina
streptobiosamine
estreptobiosamina
streptodornase
estreptodornasa
streptogramin
estreptogramina
streptokinase
estreptoquinasa
streptolin
estreptolina
streptolydigin
estreptolidigina
streptomycin
estreptomicina
streptomycin B
estreptomicina B
streptomycin sulfate
sulfato de
estreptomicina
streptoniazid
estreptoniazida
streptonicozid
estreptonicozida
streptonigrin
estreptonigrina
L-streptose
L-estreptosa
streptothricins
estreptotricinas
streptovaricin
estreptovaricina
streptovirudin
estreptovirudina
streptozocin
estreptozocina
stress
estrés
stretch (spectroscopy)
tramo
strigol
estrigol
strinoline
estrinolina
strong solution
solución concentrada
strontia
óxido de estroncio,
estronciana
strontianite
estroncianita
strontium
estroncio

strontium acetate
acetato de estroncio
strontium arsenite
arsenito de estroncio
strontium bromate
bromato de estroncio
strontium bromide
bromuro de estroncio
strontium carbonate
carbonato de estroncio
strontium chlorate
clorato de estroncio
strontium chloride
cloruro de estroncio
strontium chromate
cromato de estroncio
strontium dioxide
dióxido de estroncio
strontium fluoride
fluoruro de estroncio
strontium formate
formiato de estroncio
strontium hydrate
hidrato de estroncio
strontium hydroxide
hidróxido de estroncio
strontium hyposulfite
hiposulfito de
estroncio
strontium iodide
yoduro de estroncio
strontium lactate
lactato de estroncio
strontium molybdate
molibdato de estroncio
strontium
monosulfide
monosulfuro de
estroncio
strontium nitrate
nitrato de estroncio
strontium nitrite
nitrito de estroncio
strontium oxalate
oxalato de estroncio
strontium oxide
óxido de estroncio
strontium perchlorate
perclorato de estroncio
strontium peroxide
peróxido de estroncio
strontium-potassium
chloride
cloruro de estroncio y
potasio
strontium phosphate,
tribasic
fosfato de estroncio
tribásico

strontium salycilate
salicilato de estroncio
strontium selenate
seleniato de estroncio
strontium stearate
estearato de estroncio
strontium sulfate
sulfato de estroncio
strontium sulfide
sulfuro de estroncio
strontium tartrate
tartrato de estroncio
strontium thiosulfate
tiosulfato de estroncio
strontium titanate
titanato de estroncio
strontium zirconate
circonato de estroncio
strophanthidin
estrofantidina
strophanthin
estrofantina
strophanthobiose
estrofantobioso
strophanthus
estrofanto
structural formula
fórmula estructural
structure
estructura
strychnidine
estricnidina
strychnine
estricnina
strychnine nitrate
nitrato de estricnina
strychnine N⁶-oxide
N^6-óxido de
estricnina
strychnine phosphate
fosfato de estricnina
strychnine sulfate
sulfato de estricnina
stuff
pasta papelera
stylopine
estilopina
styphnic acid
ácido estífnico
styracyn
estiracina
styramate
estiramato
styrax
estoraque
styrene
estireno, vinilbenceno
styrene glycol
glicol estirénico

styrene oxide
óxido de estireno
styrene resins
resinas de estireno
styrolene bromide
bromuro de estireno,
bromuro de estiroleno
subacetate
subacetato
subathizone
subatizona
subcarbonate
subcarbonato
subchloride
subcloruro
subendazole
subendazol
suberane
suberano, cicloheptano
suberic
subérico
suberic acid
ácido subérico
suberin
suberina
suberone
suberona,
cicloheptanona
subgallate
subgalato
sublimation
sublimación
subnitrate
subnitrato
subnuclear particle
partícula subnuclear
suboxide
subóxido
subsalt
subsal, sal básica
substance
sustancia, substancia
substantive dye
colorantes
sustantivos
substituent
sustituyente
substitution
sustitución
substrate, substratum
sustrato
subtilin
subtilina
succimer
succimero
succinaldehyde
succinaldehído
succinamide
succinamida

succinanil
succinanilo
succinanilic acid
ácido succinanílico
succinate
succinato
succinic acid
ácido succínico
succinic acid-2,2-
dimethylhydrazide
2,2-dimetilhidrazida
del ácido succínico
succinic acid peroxide
peróxido del ácido
succínico
succinic anhydride
anhídrido succínico
succinimide
succinimida
succinonitrile
succinonitrilo
succinoresinol
succinorresinol
succinyl chloride
cloruro de succinilo
succinylcholine
bromide
bromuro de
succinilcolina
succinylcholine chloride
cloruro de
succinilcolina
succinylcholine iodide
yoduro de
succinilcolina
succinyl peroxide
peróxido de succinilo
succinylsalicylic acid
ácido succinil-
salicílico
succinylsulfathiazole
succinilsulfatiazol
succisulfone
succisulfona
suclofenide
suclofenida
sucralfate
sucralfato
sucralose
sucralosa
sucralox
sucralox
sucrate
sucrato
sucrose
sacarosa, sucrosa
sucrose monosteatate
monoestearato de
sacarosa

sucrose octaacetate
octaacetato de sacarosa
sucrose polyester
poliéster de sacarosa
sudan III
sudán III
sudexanox
sudexanox
sudoxicam
sudoxicán
suet, prepared
sebo preparado
sufentanil
sufentanilo
sufentanil citrate
citrato de sufentanilo
sufosfamide
sufosfamida
sugar
azúcar
sugar, corn
azúcar de cereales
sugar, grape
azúcar de uva
sugar, invert
azúcar invertido
sugar of lead
azúcar de plomo,
sal de plomo, sal
de saturno
sugar of milk
azúcar de leche
sugar, reducing
azúcar reductor
sugar substitute
sustituto de azúcar
sugar-cane wax
cera de caña de
azúcar
sulazepam
sulacepán, sulazepam
sulbactam
sulbactán, sulbactam
sulbenicillin
sulbenicilina
sulbenox
sulbenox
sulbentine
sulbentina
sulbutiamine
sulbutiamina
sulclamide
sulclamida
sulconazole
sulconazol
sulesomab
sulesomab
sulfa
sulfa

sulfabenz
sulfabenzo
sulfabenzamide
sulfabenzamida
sulfabromomethazine
sulfabromometacina,
sulfabromometazina
sulfacarbamide
sulfacarbamida
sulfacecole
sulfacecol
sulfacetamide
sulfacetamida
sulfachlorpyridazine
sulfaclorpiridacina,
sulfaclorpiridazina
sulfachrysoidine
sulfacrisoidina
sulfacitine
sulfacitina
sulfaclomide
sulfaclomida
sulfaclorazole
sulfaclorazol
sulfaclozine
sulfaclocina,
sulfaclozina
sulfacytine
sulfacitina
sulfadiazine
sulfadiazina
sulfadiazine sodium
sulfadiazina sódica
sulfadicramide
sulfadicramida
sulfadimethoxine
sulfadimetoxina
sulfadimidine
sulfadimidina
sulfadoxine
sulfadoxina
sulfaethidole
sulfaetidol
sulfafurazole
sulfafurazol
sulfaguanidine
sulfaguanidina
sulfaguanole
sulfaguanol
sulfaldehyde
sulfaldehído
sulfaguanole
sulfaguanola
sulfalene
sulfaleno
sulfallate
sulfalato
sulfaloxic acid
ácido sulfalóxico

sulfamazone
sulfamazona
sulfamerazine
sulfameracina,
sulfamerazina
sulfamerazine sodium
sulfamerazina sódica
sulfamethazine
sulfametacina,
sulfametazina
sulfamethizole
sulfametizol
sulfamethomidine
sulfametomidina
sulfamethoxazole
sulfametoxazól
sulfamethoxydiazine
sulfametoxidiacina,
sulfametoxidiazina
**sulfamethoxy-
pyridazine**
sulfametoxipiridacina,
sulfametoxipiridazina
sulfamethylthiazole
sulfametiltiazol
sulfametrole
sulfametrol
sulfamic acid
ácido sulfámico
sulfamide
sulfamida
sulfamidochrysoidine
sulfamidocrisoidina
sulfamine
sulfamina
sulfamonomethoxine
sulfamonometoxina
sulfamoxole
sulfamoxol
sulfanilamide
sulfanilamida
**sulfanilamido-
methanesulfonic acid
triethanolamine salt**
sal trietanolamínica del
ácido sulfanil-
amidometano sulfónico
**4-sulfanilamido-
salicylic acid**
ácido 4-sulfanil-
amidosalicílico
sulfanilate
sulfanilato
sulfanilic acid
ácido sulfanílico
**2-p-sulfanilyl-
anilinoethanol**
2-p-sulfanilil-
anilinetanol

**p-sulfanilylbenzyl-
amine**
p-sulfanililbencil-
amina
sulfanilylbutylurea
sulfanililbutilurea
sulfanilyl fluoride
fluoruro de sulfanililo
N^4-**sulfanilylsulfanil-
amide**
N^4-sulfanililsulfanil-
amida
sulfanilylurea
sulfanililurea
N-**sulfanilyl-3,4-
xylamide**
N-sulfanilil-3,4-
xilamida
sulfanitran
sulfanitrano
sulfaperine
sulfaperina
sulfaphenazole
sulfafenazol
sulfaproxyline
sulfaproxilina
sulfapyrazine
sulfapiracina,
sulfapirazina
sulfapyrazole
sulfapirazol
sulfapyridine
sulfapiridina
sulfaquinoxaline
sulfaquinoxalina
**sulfaquinoxaline
sodium salt**
sal de sodio de
sulfaquinoxalina
sulfarside
sulfarsida
sulfarsphenamine
sulfaresfenamina
sulfasalazine
sulfasalazina
sulfasomizole
sulfasomizol
sulfasuccinamide
sulfasuccinamida
sulfasymazine
sulfasimazina
sulfate
sulfato
sulfathiazole
sulfatiazol
sulfathiourea
sulfatiourea
sulfation
sulfatación

sulfatolamide
sulfatolamida
sulfatroxazole
sulfatroxazol
sulfatrozole
sulfatrozol
sulfazamet
sulfazameto
sulfazecin
sulfacecina
sulfhydryl
sulfhidrilo
sulfide
sulfuro
sulfide dye
colorante al
sulfuro, colorante
al azufre
sulfinalol
sulfinalol
**sulfinalol
hydrochloride**
clorhidrato de
sulfinalol
sulfinpyrazone
sulfinpirazona
sulfinyl
sulfinilo
sulfinyldianiline
sulfinildianilina
sulfiram
sulfirán
sulfisomidine
sulfisomidina
sulfisoxazole
sulfisoxazol
sulfite
sulfito
sulfite acid liquor
licor ácido de sulfito
sulfite paper
papel sulfito
sulfitocobalamine
sulfitocobalamina
sulfo-
sulfo-
sulfoacetic acid
ácido sulfoacético
sulfobenzoic acid
ácido sulfobenzoico
sulfobenzoic anhydride
anhídrido
sulfobenzoico
**sulfobromophthalein
sodium**
sulfobromoftaleína
sódica
sulfocarbanilide
sulfocarbanilida,

tiocarbanilida, N,N'-difeniltiourea
sulfocarbolate
sulfocarbolato
sulfocarbolic acid
ácido sulfocarbólico
sulfocyanate
sulfocianato
sulfocyanic acid
ácido sulfociánico,
ácido tiociánico
sulfocyanide
sulfocianuro
1-(4-sulfo-2,3-dichlorophenyl)-3-methylpyrazolone
1-(4-sulfo-2,3-diclorofenil-3-metilpirazolona
sulfogaiacol
sulfoguayacol
sulfogel
sulfogel
sulfoichtyolate
sulfoictiolato
sulfolane
sulfolane
3-sulfolene
3-sulfoleno
sulfometuron methyl
sulfometurón metílico, metilsulfometurón
sulfomyxin
sulfomixina
sulfonal
sulfonal
sulfonamide
sulfonamida
sulfonate
sulfonato
sulfonated castor oil
aceite de ricino sulfonado
sulfonation
sulfonación
p-sulfondichloro-aminobenzoic acid
ácido p-sulfon-dicloroamino-benzoico
sulfone
sulfona
sulfonethylmethane
sulfonetilmetano, metilsulfonal
sulfoniazide
sulfoniazida
sulfonic
sulfónico

sulfonic ácid
ácido sulfónico
sulfonium
sulfonio
sulfonmethane
sulfonmetano
sulfonterol
sulfonterol
sulfonyl
sulfonilo, sulfurilo
sulfonyl chloride
cloruro de sulfonilo
sulfonyldiacetic acid
ácido sulfonildiacético
4,4-sulfonyldianiline
4,4-sulfonildianilina
p,p'-sulfonyldianiline-N,N'-digalactoside
p,p'-sulfonildianilina-N,N-digalactósida
4,4-sulfonyldiphenol
4,4-sulfonildifenol
p-1-sulfophenyl-3-methyl-5-pyrazolone
p-1-sulfofenil-3-metil-5-pirazolona
4-sulfophthalic anhydride
anhídrido 4-sulfoftálico
sulforaphen
sulforafeno
sulforidazine
sulforidacina, sulforidazina
sulfosalicylic acid
ácido sulfosalicílico
sulfosalt
sulfosal
sulfotep
sulfotep
sulfoxide
sulfóxido
sulfoxone sodium
sulfoxona sódica
sulfur
azufre
sulfur bromide
bromuro de azufre
sulfur chloride
cloruro de azufre
sulfur compound
compuesto de azufre
sulfur dichloride
dicloruro de azufre
sulfur dioxide
anhidrido sulfuroso, dióxido de azufre

sulfur flowers
flores de azufre
sulfur hexafluoride
hexafluoruro de azufre
sulfur iodide
yoduro de azufre
sulfur, pharmaceutical
azufre farmacéutico
sulfur tetrachloride
tetracloruro de azufre
sulfur tetrafluoride
tetrafluoruro de azufre
sulfur trioxide
trióxido de azufre
sulfurate
sulfurado
sulfuration
sulfuración
sulfureous
sulfúreo, sulfuroso
sulfuret
sulfurar
sulfuretin
sulfuretina
sulfuric
sulfúrico
sulfuric acid
ácido sulfúrico, aceite de vitriolo
sulfuric anhydride
anhídrido sulfúrico
sulfuric chloride
cloruro sulfúrico
sulfuric ester
éster sulfúrico
sulfuric ether
éter sulfúrico
sulfuric oxichloride
oxicloruro sulfúrico
sulfurization
sulfurización
sulfurous
sulfuroso, sulfúreo
sulfurous acid
ácido sulfuroso
sulfurous oxychloride
oxicloruro sulfuroso
sulfuryl
sulfurilo
sulfuryl chloride
cloruro de sulfurilo
sulfuryl fluoride
fluoruro de sulfurilo
sulglicotide
sulglicótido
sulindac
sulindaco

sulisatin
sulisatina
sulisobenzone
sulisobenzona
sulmarin
sulmarina
sulmazole
sulmazol
sulmepride
sulmeprida
sulnidazole
sulnidazol
sulocarbilate
sulocarbilato
suloctidil
suloctidil
sulodexide
sulodexido
suloxifen
suloxifen
sulphan blue
azul sulfano, azul ácido IC (Índice de color)
sulpiride
sulpirida
sulprofos
sulprofós
sulprostone
sulprostona
sultamicillin
sultamicilina
sulthiame
sultiamo
sultopride
sultoprida
sultopride hydrochloride
clorhidrato de sultoprida
sultosilic acid
ácido sultosílico
sultosilic acid, piperazine salt
sal de piperazina del ácido sultosílico
sultroponium
sultroponio
sulverapride
sulveraprida
sumach
hoja del zumaque
sumatriptan
sumatriptano
sumatriptan succinate
succinato de sumatriptano
sumbul
raiz del almizcle

sumetizide
sumetizida

summarize
resumir, hacer un
resumen

summary report
informe resumido

summation
recapitular

suncillin
suncilina

sunflower meal
harina de girasol

sunflower oil
aceite de girasol

supercalender
supercalandria

supercalender paper
papel supercalandria

supercarbonate
supercarbonato

superconductivity
superconductividad

superficial layer
capa superficial

supernatant
sobrenadante

supersaturated
sobresaturado

supersaturation
supersaturación

supersede
reemplazar

supidimide
supidimida

supplement
suplemento

supplier
abastecedor

supply
suministrar, abastecer

supply vessel
tanque de alimentación

supportive data
datos para respaldar o
apoyar

suprasterol II
suprasterol II

suproclone
suproclona

suprofen
suprofeno

suppress
suprimir

suramin sodium
suramina sódica

surfactant
agente tensioactivo,
surfactante

surface
superficie

surface area
área de superficie

surface chemistry
química de superficie

surface tension
tensión superficial

surface unit
unidad de superficie

surfomer
surfomer

suriclone
suriclona

surinamine
surinamina

susceptibility
susceptibilidad

suspending agent
agente de
suspensión

suspension
suspensión

suspensoid
suspensoide

sustained release
liberación constante

sustituent
sustituyente

sustitution
sustitución

sustrate
sustrato

sutilains
sutilaínas

suxamethonium
chloride
cloruro de
suxametonio

suxemerid
suxemerido

suxethonium
bromide
bromuro de
suxetonio

suxethonium chloride
cloruro de suxetonio

suxibuzone
suxibuzona

Swarts reaction
reacción de Swarts

sweet almond oil
aceite de almendras
dulces

sweet bay oil
esencia (aceite) de
laurel

sweet oil
aceite dulce

sweeten
endulzar

swertiamarin
swertiamarina

switch
interruptor

swirl
arremolinar,
remolinear

sydnones
sidnonas

sylvic acid
ácido sílvico, ácido
abiético

sylvite
silvita

sym-
sim- (prefijo en
nomenclatura que
significa simétrico)

symbol
símbolo

symclosene
sincloseno

symetine
simetina

symmetrical
compound
compueto
simétrico

symmetry
simetría

synchronism
sincronismo

synephrine
sinefrina

synephrine tartrate
tartrato de sinefrina

synhexyl
sinhexilo

synthesis
síntesis

synthetic resin
resina sintética

synthetic rubber
caucho sintético

syringaldehyde
siringaldehído

syringe
jeringa,
jeringuilla

syringeability
inyectabilidad

syringin
siringina

syrosingopine
sirosingopina

syrup
jarabe

systematically
sistemáticamente

system priming
cebado del sistema

system suitability
pertinencia del
sistema

T

tabbleting machine
máquina tableteadora
tabernanthine
tabernantina
table of contents
índice general o de
materias
tablet
tableta
tabun
tabún
tachysterol
taquisterol
tackiness
pegajosidad
tacalcitol
tacalcitol
taclamine
taclamina
tacrine
tacrina
Tafel rearrangement
transposición de Tafel
D-tagatose
D-tagatosa
tagged atom
átomo marcado
tagged compound
compuesto marcado
taglutimide
taglutimida
tail gas
gas de cola
tailing factor
factor de cola
talampicillin
talampicilina
talastine
talastina
talbutal
talbutal
talc
talco
taleranol
taleranol
talinolol
talinolol
talisomycin,
tallysomycin
talisomicina
tallow
sebo
tallow alcohol
alcohol de sebo

tallysomycin,
talisomycin
talisomicina
talmetacin
talmetacina
talmetoprim
talmetoprima
talniflumate
talniflumato
talopram
taloprán
talosalate
talosalato
taloximine
taloximina
talsupram
talsuprán, talsupram
tamarind
tamarindo
tameticillin
tameticilina
tametraline
tametralina
tamitinol
tamitinol
tamoxifen
tamoxifeno
tamoxifen citrate
citrato de
tamoxifeno
tamsulosin
hydrochloride
clorhidrato de
tansulosina
tanacetin
tanacetina
tandamine
tandamina
tandospirone
tandospirona
tangerine oil
aceite de mandarina,
aceite de naranja
tangerina
tanghinine
tanginina
tannate
tanato
tannic acid
ácido tánico
tannin
tanino
tannoform
tanoformo

tannyl acetate
acetato de tanilo, ácido
acetiltánico
tansy oil
esencia (aceite) de
tanaceto
tantalate
tantalato
tantalic
tantálico
tantalic acid anhydride
anhídrido tantálico,
pentóxido de tantalio
tantalum
tantalio
tantalum chloride
cloruro de tantalio
tantalum pentachloride
pentacloruro de
tantalio
tantalum pentafluoride
pentafluoruro de
tantalio
tantalum pentoxide
pentóxido de tantalio
tapioca
tapioca
tar
alquitrán, brea
tar camphor
naftaleno, naftalina
tar oil
aceite de alquitrán
tar oil rectified
aceite de alquitrán
rectificado
tar, refined
alquitrán refinado
taraxacum
amargón, diente de
león
taraxasterol
taraxasterol
taraxein
taraxeína
taraxerol
taraxerol
tare
tara
target weight
peso propuesto
tarnish
deslustre,
descoloramiento

tarragon oil
aceite de tárrago
tartar, cream of
crémor tártaro
tartar emetic
tártaro emético
tartaric acid
ácido tartárico
tartarize
tartarizar
tartarous
tartaroso
tartrate
tartrato
tartrated
tártrico
tartrazine
tartracina, tartrazina
tartronic acid
ácido tartrónico
taurine
taurina
taurocholic acid
ácido taurocólico
taurolidine
taurolidina
taurultam
taurultán, taurultam
tautomer
tautómero
tautomeric
tautómero
taxicins
taxicinos
taxine
taxina
taxine A
taxina A
taxodione
taxidiona
taxol A
taxol A
tazarotene
tazaroteno
taziprinone
hydrochloride
clorhidrato de
taciprinona
tazobactam sodium
tazobactán sódico
tazolol
tazolol
tebatizole
tebatizola

tebutate
tebutato
tebuthiuron
tebutiurona
technetium
tecnecio
technical
técnico
teclothiazide
teclotiazida
teclozan
teclozán
tecomanine
tecomanina
tecoplanin
tecoplanina
tectorigenin
tectorigenina
tedisamil
tedisamil
tefazoline
tefazolina
tefenperate
tefemperato
teflurane
teflurano
teflutixol
teflutixol
tegafur
tegafur
teichoic acids
ácidos teicoicos
teicoplanin
teicoplanina
tellurate
telurato
telluric acid
ácido telúrico
telluric bromide
bromuro telúrico,
tetrabromuro de telurio
telluride
telururo
tellurite
telurito
tellurium
telurio
tellurium dibromide
dibromuro de telurio,
bromuro teluroso
tellurium dichloride
dicloruro de telurio,
cloruro teluroso
tellurium dioxide
dióxido de telurio
tellurium hexafluoride
hexafluoruro de telurio
tellurium tetrabromide
tetrabromuro de

telurio, bromuro
telúrico
tellurium tetrachloride
tetracloruro de
telurio,cloruro telúrico
tellurium tetraiodide
tetrayoduro de telurio
telllurous
teluroso
tellurous acid
ácido teluroso
tellurous bromide
bromuro teluroso,
dibromuro de telurio
tellurous chloride
cloruro teluroso,
dicloruro de telurio
telomerization
telomerización
telomycin
telomicina
temazepam
temacepán, temazepam
temefos
temefós
temephos
temefós
temocillin
temocilina
temodox
temodox
temperature
temperatura
temperature coefficient
coeficiente de
temperatura
template
patrón, solera
tendamistat
tendamistat
tenderization
ablandamiento
teniloxazine
teniloxazina
teniposide
tenipósido
tenocyclidine
tenociclidina
tenonitrozole
tenonitrozol
tenoxicam
tenoxicán,
tenoxicam
tension test
prueba de ruptura
tenuazonic acid
ácido tenuazónico
tenylidone
tenilidona

teoclate
teoclato
teoprolol
teoprolol
tephrosin
tefrosina
teprenone
teprenona
teprosilate
teprosilato
teprotide
teprótido
terazosin
terazosina
terazocin
hydrochloride
clorhidrato de
terazocina
terbacil
terbacil
terbia
óxido de terbio
terbinafine
terbinafina
terbium
terbio
terbium chloride,
hexahydrate
cloruro de terbio
hexahidratado
terbium nitrate
nitrato de terbio
terbium oxide
óxido de terbio, terbia
terbium sulfate
sulfato de terbio
terbucromil
terbucromil
terbufibrol
terbufibrol
terbuficin
terbuficino
terbufos
terbufós
terbuprol
terbuprol
terbutaline
terbutalina
terbutaline sulfate
sulfato de terbutalina
terciprazine
tercipracina,
terciprazina
terconazole
terconazol
terebene
terebeno
terebic acid
ácido terébico

terebinth
terebinto, cornicabra
terebinthic
relativo a la trementina
terephthalic acid
ácido tereftálico
2-terephthaloyl-
benzoic acid
ácido 2-tereftaloil-
benzoico
terephthaloyl chloride
cloruro de tereftaloílo
terfenadine
terfenadine
terfenadine
terfenadina
terfluranol
terfluranol
terguride
tergúrida
teriparatide acetate
acetato de teriparátido
terizidone
tericidona
terlipressin
terlipresina
termonuclear
termonuclear
ternary
ternario
ternidazole
ternidazol
terodiline
terodilina
terofenamate
terofenamato
teroxalene
teroxaleno
teroxirone
teroxirona
1,4(8)-terpadiene
1,4(8)-terpadieno,
terpinoleno
terpene
terpeno
terpenic
terpénico
terpenylic acid
ácido terpenílico, ácido
terpenólico
terpin
terpino
terpinene
terpineno
α-terpineol
α-terpinol, α-terpineol
terpinolene
terpinoleno
terpinyl acetate
acetato de terpinilo

terreic acid
ácido terreico
terramycin
terramicina
terramycin
terc
tertatolol
tertatolol
tertiary
terciario
α-tertienyl
α-tertienilo
tertiomycins
tertiomicinas
tervalent
trivalente
tesicam
tesicán, tesicam
tesimide
tesimida
test
prueba, ensayo
test kits
juegos de pruebas
tester
probador, ensayador;
reactivo
testing, chemicals
ensayos químicos
testing, physicals
ensayos físicos
testolactone
testolactona
testosterone
testosterona
testosterone 17-chloral
hemiacetal
17-cloral
hemiacetal testosterona
testosterone 17ß-
cypionate
17ß-cipionato de
testosterona
testosterone
enanthate
enantato de
testosterona
testosterone
ketolaurate
cetolaurato de
testosterona
testosterone
nicotinate
nicotinato de
testosterona
testosterone
phenylacetate
fenilacetato de
testosterona

testosterone propionate
propionato de
testosterona
test paper
papel indicador, papel
reactivo
test tube
tubo de ensayo
test tube rack
portatubos
tetraamineditolyl-
methane
tetraaminoditolil-
metano
tetraamylbenzene
tetraamilbenceno
tetrabarbital
tetrabarbital
tetrabasic
tetrabásico
tetrabenazine
tetrabenazina
tetraborate
tetraborato
tetraborane
tetraborano
tetraboric acid
ácido tetrabórico
tetrabromide
tetrabromuro
tetrabromo-o-cresol
tetrabromo-o-cresol
tetrabromoethane
tetrabromoetano
tetrabromoethylene
tetrabromoetileno
tetrabromofluorescein
tetrabromo-
fluoresceína, eosina
tetrabromo-
phenolphthalein
tetrabromo-
fenoftaleína
tetrabromophthalic
anhydride
anhídrido
tetrabromoftálico
tetra-n-butyl-
ammonium chloride
cloruro de tetra-n-
butilamonio
tetrabutyltin
tetrabutil estaño
tetrabutyl titanate
titanato de tetrabutilo
tetrachlorothiophene
tetracaine
tetracaína
tetracaine

hydrocloride
clorhidrato de
tetracaína
tetrachloride
tetracloruro
tetrachlormethiazide
tetraclorometiazida
1,2,3,4-tetrachloro-
benzene
1,2,3,4-tetra-
clorobenceno
tetrachloro-p-
benzoquinone
tetracloro-p-
benzoquinona,
cloranil
sym-tetrachloro-
difluoroethane
sim-tetracloro-
difluoroetano
tetrachloro-
dinitroethane
tetraclorodinitroetano
tetrachloroethane
tetracloroetano
tetrachloroethylene
tetracloroetileno
tetrachloromethane
tetraclorometano,
tetracloruro de
carbono
2,3,4,6-tetrachloro-
phenol
2,3,4,6-tetraclorofenol
tetrachlorophthalic
acid
ácido tetracloroftálico
tetrachlorophthalic
anhydride
anhídrido
tetracloroftálico
tetrachloroquinone
tetracloroquinona,
cloranil
tetrachloro-
salicylanilide
tetraclorosalicilanilida
tetrachlorothiophene
tetraclorotiofeno
tetracid
tetrácido
tetracosactide
tetracosactida
tetracosamethyl-
hendecasiloxane
tetracosametil-
hendecasiloxano
tetracosane
tetracosano

tetracosanoic acid
ácido tetracosanoico,
ácido lignocérico
tetracyanoethylene
tetracianoetileno
tetracycline
tetraciclina
tetracycline
hydrochloride
clorhidrato de
tetraciclina
tetrad
átomo o elemento
tetravalente
tetradecamethyl-
hexasiloxane
tetradecametil-
hexasiloxano
n-tetradecane
n-tetradecano
tetradecanoic acid
ácido tetradecanoico,
ácido mirístico
1-tetradecanol
1-tetradecanol, alcohol
mirístico, alcohol
tetradecílico
tetradecyl alcohol
alcohol tetradecílico,
alcohol mirístico
tetradecyl chloride
cloruro de tetradecilo
tetradecylamine
tetradecilamina
α-tetradecylene
α-tetradecileno, 1-
tetradeceno
tetradecylmercaptan
tetradecilmercaptano
tetradifon
tetradifón
tetradonium bromide
bromuro de tetradonio
1,1,3,3-tetraethoxy-
propane
1,1,3,3-tetraetoxi-
propano
tetraethyl dithiono-
pyrophosphate
ditionopirofosfato de
tetraetilo
tetraethyl lead
tetraetilplomo
tetraethyl
pyrophosphate
pirofosfato de
tetraetilo
tetraethyl tin
tetraetilestaño

tetraethylammonium
bromide
bromuro de
tetraetilamonio
tetraethylammonium
chloride
cloruro de
tetraetilamonio
tetraethylammonium
hydroxide
hidróxido de
tetraetilamonio
tetra-(2-ethylbutyl)
silicate
silicato de tetra-(2-
etilbutilo)
tetraethylene glycol
glicol tetraetilénico,
tetraetilenglicol
tetraethylene glycol
dibutyl ether
dibutil éter de glicol
tetraetilénico,
dibutoxitetraglicol
tetraethylene glycol
dimethacrylate
dimetacrilato de
glicol tetra-
etilénico
tetraethylene glycol
dimethyl ether
dimetil éter de glicol
tetraetilénico,
dimetoxitetraglicol
tetraethylene
pentamine
tetraetilenpentamina
tetra-(2-ethylhexyl)
silicate
silicato tetra-(2-
etilhexílico)
N,N,N',N'-tetra-
ethylphthalamide
N,N,N',N'-tetra-
etilftalamida
tetrafluoride
tetrafluoruro
tetrafluorodichloro-
ethane
tetrafluorodi-
cloroetano
tetrafluorohydrazine
tetrafluorohidracina
tetrafluoromethane
tetrafluorometano
tetrafluoro-1-
propanol
tetrafluoro-1-
propanol

tetraglycine
hydroperiodide
peryodhidrato de
tetraglicina
tetraglycol dichloride
dicloruro de
tetraglicol
tetraglyme
tetraglima
tetrahydro cannabinol
tetrahidrocannabinol
tetrahydrocortisone
tetrahidrocortisona
tetrahydrofuran
tetrahidrofurano
2,5-tetrahydro-
furandimethanol
2,5-tetrahidro-
furanodimetanol
tetrahydrofurfuryl
acetate
acetato de
tetrahidrofurfurilo
tetrahydrofurfuryl
alcohol
alcohol tetrahidro-
furfurílico
tetrahydrofurfuryl
benzoate
benzoato de
tetrahidrofurfurilo
tetrahydrofurfuryl
laurate
laurato de
tetrahidrofurfurilo
tetrahydrofurfuryl
levulinate
levulinato de
tetrahidrofurfurilo
tetrahydrofurfuryl
oleate
oleato de
tetrahidrofurfurilo
tetrahydrofurfuryl
phthalate
ftalato de
tetrahidrofurfurilo
tetrahydro-
furfurylamine
tetrahidro-
furfurilamina
tetrahydrogeraniol
tetrahidrogeraniol
tetrahydrolinalol
tetrahidrolinalol
1,2,3,4-tetrahydro-6-
methylquinoline
1,2,3,4-tetrahidro-6-
metilquinoleína

tetrahydro-
naphthalene
tetrahidronaftaleno
tetrahydropalmatine
tetrahidropalmatina
tetrahydro-
papaveroline
tetrahidropapaverolina
tetrahydropyran
tetrahidropirano
tetrahydropyran-2-
methanol
tetrahidropirán-2-
metanol
1,2,5,6-tetrahydro-
pyridine
1,2,5,6-tetrahidro-
piridina
tetrahydro thiophene
tetrahidrotiofeno
tetrahydroxybutane
tetrahidroxibutano,
eritritol, eritrol
tetrahydroxydiphenyl
tetrahidroxidifenilo
tetrahydroxy-
ethylethylenediamine
tetrahidroxietil-
etilendiamina
tetrahydrozoline
tetrahidrozolina
tetraiodoethylene
tetrayodoetileno
tetraiodofluorescein
tetrayodofluoresceína
tetraiodopyrrole
tetrayodopirrol
tetraisopropyl titanate
titanato de
tetraisopropilo
tetraisopropyl
zirconate
circonato de
tetraisopropilo,
zirconato de
tetraisopropilo
tetrakis(hydroxy-
methyl) phosphonium
chloride
cloruro de tetraquis
(hidroximetil) fosfonio
tetralol
tetralol
1-tetralone
1-tetralona
1,1,3,3-tetramethoxy-
propane
1,1,3,3-tetra-
metoxipropano

tetramethrin
tetrametrina
tetramethyl-
ammonium chloride
cloruro de
tetrametilamonio
tetramethyl-
ammonium hydroxide
hidróxido de
tetrametilamonio
tetramethyl-
ammonium iodide
yoduro de
tetrametilamonio
1,2,3,5-tetramethyl-
benzene
1,2,3,5-tetra-
metilbenceno
2,2,4,4-tetramethyl-1,3-
cyclobutanediol
2,2,4,4-tetrametil-1,3-
ciclobutanodiol
tetramethyl-
diaminobutane
tetrametildi-
aminobutano
tetramethyldiamino
phosphoric
fluoride
fluoruro
tetrametildiamino
fosfórico
tetramethyldiamino-
benzhydrol
tetrametildiamino-
benzohidrol
tetramethyl-
diaminobenzo-
phenone
tetrametildiamino-
benzofenona
tetramethyl-
diaminodiphenyl
methane
tetrametildiamino-
difenilmetano
tetramethyl-
diaminodiphenyl-
sulfone
tetrametildi-
aminodifenilsulfona
tetramethylene
tetrametileno,
ciclobutano
tetramethylene
bismethane
sulfonate
bismetanosulfonato de
tetrametileno

tetramethylene
dichloride
dicloruro de
tetrametileno
tetramethylene glycol
glicol tetrametilénico,
tetrametilenglicol
tetramethylene sulfone
tetrametilensulfona
tetramethylene-
diamine
tetrametilendiamina
tetramethylene-
disulfotetramine
tetrametilen-
disulfotetramina
tetramethylethylene-
diamine
tetrametiletilen-
diamina
tetramethylmethane
tetrametilmetano,
neopentano
3,3'-tetramethylnonyl
thiodipropionate
tiodipropionato de 3,3'-
tetrametilnonilo
tetramethyl-p-
phenylenediamine
tetrametil-p-
fenilendiamina
tetramethylsilane
tetrametilsilano
tetramethylurea
tetrametilurea
tetramisole
tetramisol
tetrandrine
tetrandrina
tetranectin
tetranectina
tetranitroaniline
tetranitroanilina
tetranitromethane
tetranitrometano
tetrantoin
tetrantoína
tetraphenylarsonium
bromide
bromuro de
tetrafenilarsonio
tetraphenylarsonium
chloride
cloruro de
tetrafenilarsonio
tetraphenylsilane
tetrafenilsilano
tetraphenyltin
tetrafenilestaño

tetraphosphorus
trisulfide
trisulfuro de
tetrafósforo
tetrasilane
tetrasilano
tetrasodium
diphosphate
difosfato de tetrasodio
tetrasodium etidronate
etidronato de tetrasodio
tetrasodium EDTA
edetato (EDTA) de
tetrasodio
tetrasodium
monopotassium
tripolyphosphate
tripolifosfato
tetrasódico
monopotásico
tetrasodium
pyrophosphate
pirofosfato tetrasódico
tetrastearyl titanate
titanato de
tetraestearilo
tetrasulfur
tetranitride
tetranitruro de
tretraazufre
tetratomic
tetratómico,
tetraatómico
tetravalent
tetravalente
tetrazene
tetraceno
tetrazepam
tetrazepam
tetrazolium blue
azul de tetrazolio
tetrazolium chloride
cloruro de tetrazolio
tetridamine
tetridamina
tetrin
tetrina
tetriprofen
tetriprofen
tetrodotoxin
tetrodotoxina
tetrol
tetrol
tetronal
tetronal
tetronasin
tetronasina
tetroquinone
tetroquinona

tetroxoprim
tetroxoprima
tetryl
tetrilo, butilo, tetril
tetryl ammonium
bromide
bromuro de
tetrilamonio
tetryzoline
tetrizolina
textured protein
proteína con textura
thacapzol
tacapzol
thalicarpine
talicarpina
thalictrine
talictrina
thalidomide
talidomida
thallic oxide
óxido tálico
thallium
talio
thallium acetate
acetato de talio
thallium bromide
bromuro de talio
thallium carbonate
carbonato de talio
thallium chloride
cloruro de talio
thallium cyanide
cianuro de talio
thallium fluoride
fluoruro de talio
thallium hydroxide
hidróxido de talio
thallium iodide
yoduro de talio
thallium-mercury alloy
aleación de talio y
mercurio
thallium nitrate
nitrato de talio
thallium oxide
óxido de talio
thallium selenate
seleniato de talio
thallium selenide
seleniuro de talio
thallium sesquioxide
sesquióxido de talio
thallium sulfate
sulfato de talio
thallium sulfide
sulfuro de talio
thallium trifluoride
trifluoruro de talio

thallous
talioso
thaumatin
taumatina
thaw, to
descongelar
theaflavine
teaflavina
thebacon
tebacona
thebain(e)
tebaína
thebainone
tebainona
theine
teína
thenalidine
tenalidina
Thenard's blue
azul de Thenard, azul
de cobalto
thenium closylate
closilato de tenio
3-thenoic acid
ácido 3-tenoico
thenyldiamine
tenildiamina
theobroma oil
aceite de teobroma
theobromine
teobromina
1-theobromine acetic
acid
ácido acético 1-
teobromina
theobromine-sodium
salicylate
salicilato de
teobromina y sodio
theodrenaline
teodrenalina
theofibrate
teofibrato
theophylline
teofilina
theophylline ephedrine
teofilina efedrina
therm
termia
thermal
decomposition
descomposición
térmica
thermal expansion
coefficient
coeficiente de
dilatación térmica
thermal neutron
neutrón térmico

thermal pollution
contaminación
térmica
thermal stability
estabilidad térmica
thermatomic process
método termatómico
thermit(e)
termita
thermochemistry
termoquímica
thermolabile
termolábil
thermolysin
termolisina
thermolysis
termólisis
thermolityc
termolítico
thermometer
termómetro
thermonuclear
reaction
reacción
termonuclear
thermoplastic
termoplástico
thermorubin
termorrubina
thevetin A
tevetina A
thevetose
tevetosa
thia-
tia-
thiabendazole
tiabendazol
thiacetarsamide
sodium
tiacetarsamida sódica
thiacetazone
tiacetazona
thialbarbital
tialbarbital
thiamazole
tiamazol
thiambutene
tiambuteno
thiambutosine
tiambutosina
thiamine
tiamina
thiamine disulfide
disulfuro de tiamina
thiamine
hydrochloride
clorhidrato de tiamina
thiamine mononitrate
mononitrato de tiamina

thiamine phosphoric
acid ester chloride
cloruro de tiamina del
éster de ácido fosfórico
thiamine phosphoric
acid ester phosphate
salt
sal de fosfato de
tiamina del éster del
ácido fosfórico
thiamine 1,5-salt
1,5-sal de tiamina
thiamine triphosphoric
acid ester
éster del ácido
trifosfórico tiamina
thiamiprine
tiamiprina
thiamorpholine
tiamorfolina
thiamphenicol
tianfenicol
thiamylal
tiamilal
thianaphthene
tianafteno
1,4-thiazane
1,4-tiazano
thiazesim
tiacesima
thiazinamium
methylsulfate
metilsulfato de
tiazinamio
thiazin(e)
tiazina
thiazosulfone
tiazosulfona
thiazole
tiazol
thiazole dye
colorantes de tiazol
thiazole yellow G
amarillo G de
tiazol
thiazolinobutazole
tiazolinobutazol
thiazolsulfone
tiazolsulfona
thibenzazoline
tibenzazolina
thickener
espesante
thickening agent
agente espesante
Thiele reaction
reacción de Thiele
thienamycin
tienamicina

thiethylperazine
tietilperacina,
tietilperazina
thiethylperazine
maleate
maleato de
tietilperacina, maleato
de tietilperazina
thihexinol
tihexinol
thihexinol
methylbromide
metilbromuro de
tihexinol
thimerfonate
sodium
timerfonato sódico
thimerosal
timerosal
thin-layer
chromatography
cromatografía en capa
delgada
thinner
disolvente, diluyente,
diluente
thio-
tio-
thioacetaldehyde
tioacetaldehído
thioacetamide
tioacetamida
thioacetic acid
ácido tioacético
thioacetazone
tioacetazona
thioallyl ether
éter tioalílico, sulfuro
de alilo
thioanisole
tioanisol
thioarsenate
tioarseniato
thioarsenite
tioarsenito
thiobarbital
tiobarbital
thiobenzoic acid
ácido tiobenzoico
thiobenzyl alcohol
alcohol tiobencílico
thiobutabarbital
tiobutabarbital
thiocarbamide
tiocarbamida, tiourea
thiocarbamizine
tiocarbamizina
thiocarbanil
tiocarbanilo

thiocarbanilide
tiocarbanilida, N,N'-
difeniltiourea,
sulfocarbanilida
thiocarbarsone
tiocarbarsona
thiocarbonyl chloride
cloruro de tiocarbonilo
thiocolchicine
tiocolchicina
thiocolchicoside
tiocolchicósido
thiocresol
tiocresol
thioctic acid
ácido tióctico
thiocyanate
tiocianato
thiocyanate sodium
tiocianato sódico
thiocyanic acid
ácido tiociánico
thiodicarb
thiodicarb
2,2'-thiodiethanol
2,2'-tiodietanol
thiodiethylene glycol
glicol tiodietilénico
thiodiglycol
tiodiglicol
thiodiglycolic acid
ácido tiodiglicólico
thiodiphenylamine
tiodifenilamina,
fenotiacina
thiodipropionic acid
ácido tiodipropiónico
ß,ß-thiodipropionitrile
ß,ß-tiodipropionitrilo
thioethanolamina
tioetanolamina
thioflavine T
tioflavina T
thioformamide
tioformamida
thiofuradene
tiofuradeno
thiofuran
tiofurano, tiofeno
5-thio-D-glucose
5-tio-D-glucosa
thioglycerol
tioglicerol
thioglycolic acid
ácido tioglicólico
thioguanine
tioguanina
thioguanosine
tioguanosina

thiohexamide
tiohexamida
2-thiohydantoin
2-tiohidantoína
2-thio-4-keto-
thiazolidine
2-tio-4-ceto-
tiazolidina,
rodanina
thiol
tiol
thiolactic acid
ácido tioláctico
2-thiolhistidine
2-tiolhistidina
thiolutin
tiolutina
thiomalic acid
ácido tiomálico
thiomersal
tiomersal
thionalide
tionalida
thionate
tionato
thionaphthen-2-
carboxylic acid
ácido tionaften-2-
carboxílico
thionazin
tionazina
thionic
tiónico
thionic acid
ácido tiónico
thionine
tionina
thionyl bromide
bromuro de tionilo
thionyl chloride
cloruro de tionilo
thionyl fluoride
fluoruro de tionilo
thiopental sodium
tiopental sódico
thiopeptin
tiopeptina
thiophanate
tiofanato
thiophane
tiofano
thiophene
tiofeno, tiofurano
α-thiophenealdehyde
α-tiofenaldehído
2-thiophenecarboxylic
acid
ácido 2-tiofeno-
carboxílico

thiophenol
tiofenol
thiophosgene
tiofosgeno
thiophosphoric acid
ácido tiofosfórico
thiopropazate
tiopropazato
thioproperazine
tioproperacina,
tioproperazina
thioquinox
tioquinox
thioredoxin
tiorredoxina
thioridazine
tioridacina, tioridazina
thiosalicylic acid
ácido tiosalicílico
thiosemicarbazide
tiosemicarbacida
thiosinamine
tiosinamina
thiosorbitol
tiosorbitol
thiostrepton
tioestreptona
thiosulfate
tiosulfato
thiosulfuric
tiosulfúrico
thiotepa
tiotepa
thiotetrabarbital
tiotetrabarbital
thiothixene
tiotixeno
thiothixene
hydrochloride
clorhidrato de tiotixeno
thiouracil
tiouracil
thiourea
tiourea, tiocarbamida
thioxanthene
* tioxanteno
thioxanthone
tioxantona
thioxolone
tioxolona
thiphenamil
tifenamil
thiram
tiramo, disulfuro de
tetrametiltiuramo
thiuranide
tiuránido
thixotropy
tixotropía

Thomas phosphate
fosfato de Thomas,
fosfato de calcio
tetrabásico
thonzonium bromide
bromuro de tonzonio
thonzylamine
toncilamina
thonzylamine
hydrochloride
clorhidrato de
toncilamina
thoria
toria, dióxido de torio,
óxido de torio
thorin
torina
thorite
torita
thorium
torio
thorium
acetylacetonate
acetilacetonato de torio
thorium chloride
cloruro de torio,
tetracloruro de torio
thorium decay series
serie de desintegración
de torio
thorium dioxide
dióxido de torio, óxido
de torio, toria
thorium disulfide
disulfuro de torio
thorium fluoride
fluoruro de torio
thorium iodide
yoduro de torio
thorium nitrate
nitrato de torio
thorium oxalate
oxalato de torio
thorium oxide
óxido de torio, di-
óxido de torio, toria
thorium sulfate
sulfato de torio
thorium tetrachloride
tetracloruro de torio,
cloruro de torio
thorium tetracyano-
platinate (II)
tetracianoplatinato de
torio (II)
thozalinone
tozalinona
three neck flask
balón de tres bocas

threonine
treonina
threose
treosa
D-threose triacetate
triacetato de D-treosa
thrombin
trombina
thrombin, topical
trombina tópica
thomboplastin
tromboplastina
thrombospondin
trombospondina
thromboxane
tromboxano
thuja
tuya, árbol de la vida
thuja oil
aceite de tuya
thujic acid
ácido túyico
thujone
tuyona
thujopsene
tuyopseno
thulia
óxido de tulio
thulium
tulio
thulium chloride
cloruro de tulio
thulium oxalate
oxalato de tulio
thulium oxide
óxido de tulio, tulia
thurfyl nicotinate
nicotinato turfílico
thyme
tomillo
thyme oil
esencia (aceite) de
tomillo
thymidine
timidina, timina-2-
desoxirribósido
thymine
timina
thymine-2-
desoxyriboside
timina-2-
desoxirribósido,
timidina
thymol
timol
thymol acetate
acetato de timol
thymol blue
azul de timol

thymol iodide
yoduro de timol
thymolphthalein
timolftaleína
thymolsulfone-
phthalein
timolsulfonftaleína
thymomodulin
timomodulina,
leucotrofina
thymopentin
timopentina
thymopoietin
timopoietina
p-thymoquinone
p-timoquinona
thymosin
timosina
thymostatin
timostatina
thymostimulin
timoestimulina
o-thymotic acid
ácido o-timótico
thymyl N-
isoamylcarbamate
N-isoamilcarbamato de
timilo
thyrocalcitonin
tirocalcitonina
thyroglobulin
tiroglobulina
thyroid
tiroide
thyroidin
tiroidina,
yodotirina
thyronine
tironina
thyropropic acid
ácido tiroprópico
thyroprotein
tiroproteína
thyrotrophin
tirotrofina
thyroxine
tiroxina
tiabendazole
tiabendazol
tiadenol
tiadenol
tiafibrate
tiafibrato
tiagabine
hydrochloride
clorhidrato de
tiagabina
tiamenidine
tiamenidina

tiametonium iodide
yoduro de
tiametonio
tiamiprine
tiamiprina
tiamizide
tiamizida
tiamulin
tiamulina
tianafac
tianafaco
tianeptine
tianeptina
tiapamil
tiapamilo
tiapirinol
tiapirinol
tiapride
tiaprida
tiaprofenic acid
ácido tiaprofénico
tiaprost
tiaprost
tiaramide
tiaramida
tiazesim
tiacesima
tiazuril
tiazuril
tibenzate
tibenzato
tibezonium iodide
yoduro de tibezonio
tibolone
tibolona
tibric acid
ácido tíbrico
tibrofan
tibrofano
ticarbodine
ticarbodina
ticarcillin
ticarcilina
ticarcillin disodium
ticarcilina disódica
ticlatone
ticlatona
ticlopidine
ticlopidina
ticrynafen
ticrinafeno
tidiacic
tidiácico
Tiemann
rearrangement
transposición de
Tiemann
tiemonium iodide
yoduro de tiemonio

tienilic acid
ácido tienílico
tienocarbine
tienocarbino
tienopramine
tienopramina
tifemoxone
tifemoxona
tifenamil
tifenamil
tifencillin
tifencilina
Tiffeneau-Denjanov
ring expansion
expansión de anillo de
Tiffeneau y Denjanov
tiflamizole
tiflamizol
tiflorex
tiflorex
tiformin
tiformina
tigemonam
tigemonán
tigestol
tigestol
tiglic acid
ácido tíglico
tiglium oil
aceite de tiglio, aceite
de crotón
tigloidine
tigloidina
tigogenin
tigogenina
tigonin
tigonina
tilbroquinol
tilbroquinol
tiletamine
tiletamina
tiliacorine
tiliacorina
tilidine
tilidino
tiliquinol
tiliquinol
tilorone
tilorona
tilozepine
tilocepina
tiludronate disodium
tiludronato disódico
time points
intervalos
timegadine
timegadina
timepidium bromide
bromuro de timepidio

timiperone
timiperona
timofibrate
timofibrato
timolol
timolol
timolol maleate
maleato de timolol
timonacic
timonácico,
tiazolidina
timoprazole
timoprazol
tin
estaño
tin chloride
cloruro de estaño
tin dichloride
dicloruro de estaño
tin oxide
óxido de estaño
tin phosphides
fosfuros de estaño
tin salt
sal de estaño
tin tetrabromide
tetrabromuro de estaño,
bromuro estánnico
tin tetrachloride
tetracloruro de estaño,
cloruro estánnico
tinazoline
tinazolina
tincture
tintura
tinidazole
tinidazol
tinisulpride
tinisulprida
tinofedrine
tinofedrina
tinoridine
tiroridino
tinplate
hojalata
tiocarlide
tiocarlida
tioclomarol
tioclomarol
tioconazole
tioconazol
tioctilate
tioctilato
tiodazosin
tiodazosina
tiodonium chloride
cloruro de tiodonio
tioguanine
tioguanina

tiomesterone
tiomesterona

tioperidone
tioperidona

tiopinac
tiopinaco

tiopronin
tiopronina

tiopropamine
tiopropamina

tiosalan
tiosalán

tiosinamine
tiosinamina

tiotidine
tiotidina

tiotixene
tiotixeno

tioxacin
tioxacino

tioxaprofen
tioxaprofeno

tioxidazole
tioxidazol

tioxolone
tioxolona

tipepidine
tipepidina

tipetropium bromide
bromuro de tipetropio

tipindole
tipindol

tiprenolol
tiprenolol

tipropidil
tipropidil

tiquinamide
tiquinamida

tiquizium bromide
bromuro de tiquicio

tiratricol
tiratricol

tirofiban
hydrochloride
clorhidrato de
tirofibano

tiropramide
tiropramida

Tishchenko reaction
reacción de
Tishchenko

tisocromide
tisocromida

tisopurine
tisopurina

tisoquone
tisocuona

titanate
titanato

titanic acid
ácido titánico

titaniferous
titanífero

titanium
titanio

titanium chelate
quelato de titanio

titanium dichloride
dicloruro de titanio

titanium dioxide
dióxido de titanio

titanium disulfide
disulfuro de titanio

titanium hydride
hidruro de titanio

titanium isopropylate
isopropilato de titanio

titanium peroxide
peróxido de titanio

titanium potassium
fluoride
fluoruro de titanio y
potasio

titanium potassium
oxalate
oxalato de titanio y
potasio

titanium sesquioxide
sesquióxido de titanio

titanium sponge
esponja de titanio

titanium steel
acero al titanio

titanium sulfate
sulfato de titanio

titanium tetrabromide
tetrabromuro de titanio

titanium tetrachloride
tetracloruro de titanio

titanium tetrafluoride
tetrafluoruro de titanio

titanium trichloride
tricloruro de titanio

titanium trioxide
trióxido de titanio

titanium white
blanco de titanio

titanocene dichloride
dicloruro de titanoceno

titanous chloride
cloruro titanoso

titanous sulfate
sulfato titanoso

titanyl sulfate
sulfato de titanilo

titanylacetylacetonate
acetilacetonato de
titanilo

titer
título

titrant
titulador

titration
titulación, valoración

titrimetric
por titulación

tixadil
tixadil

tixanox
tixanox

tixocortol
toxocortol

tizanidine
tizanidina

tizanidine
hydrochloride
clorhidrato de
tizanidina

tizolemide
tizolemida

tizoprolic acid
ácido tizoprólico

tobacco mosaic virus
virus del mosaico de
tabaco

Tobias acid
ácido de Tobías, ácido
2-naftilamina-1-
sulfónico

tobramycin
tobramicina

tobramycin sulfate
sulfato de tobramicina

tobuterol
tobuterol

tocainide
tocainida

tocamphyl
tocanfil

tocofenoxate
tocofenoxato

tocofersolan
tocofersolano

tocofibrate
tocofibrato

tocol
tocol

tocopherol
tocoferol

α-tocopherol succinate
succinato de
α-tocoferol

tocophersolan
tocofersolano

todralazine
todralacina,
todralazina

tofenacin
tofenacina

tofesilate
tofesilato

tofetridine
tofetridina

tofisopam
tofisopán, tofisopam

tolan(e)
tolano

tolamolol
tolamolol

tolazamide
tolazamida

tolazoline
tolazolina

tolboxane
tolboxano

tolbutamide
tolbutamida

tolcapone
tolcapona

tolciclate
tolciclato

tolcyclamide
tolciclamida

toldimfos
toldinfós

toldimfos sodium
toldinfós sódico

tolfamide
tolfamida

tolfenamic acid
ácido tolfenámico

o-tolidine
o-tolidina

tolimidone
tolimidona

tolindate
tolindato

toliodium chloride
cloruro de toliodio

toliprolol
toliprolol

Tollens' reagent
reactivo de Tollens

tolmesoxide
tolmesóxido

tolmetin
tolmetina

tolmetin sodium
tolmetina sódica

tolnaftate
tolfnaftato

tolnidamine
tolnidamino

toloconium metilsulfate
metilsulfato de
toloconio

tolonidine
tolonidina
tolonium chloride
cloruro de tolonio
toloxatone
toloxatona
toloxychlorinol
toloxiclorinol
tolpentamide
tolpentamida
tolperisone
tolperisona
tolpiprazole
tolpiprazol
tolpovidone
tolpovidona
tolpronine
tolpronina
tolpropamine
tolpropamina
tolpyrramide
tolpirramida
tolquinzole
tolquinzol
tolrestat
tolrestat, tolrestatina
tolterodine tartrate
tartrato de tolterodina
toltrazuril
toltrazuril
tolu
bálsamo de Tolú
o-tolualdehyde
o-tolualdehído
o-toluamide
o-toluamida
toluate
toluato
toluazotoluidine
toluazotoluidina,
o-aminoazotolueno
toluene
tolueno
toluene 2,4-diamine
toluen-2,4-diamina
**toluene 2,4-
diisocyanate**
2,4-diisocianato de
tolueno
toluene trichloride
tricloruro de tolueno,
tricloruro bencénico
toluene trifluoride
trifluoruro de tolueno
toluene-3,4-dithiol
toluen-3,4-ditiol
p-toluenesulfinic acid
ácido p-toluen-
sulfínico

**p-toluenesulfonic
acid**
ácido p-toluen-
sulfónico
**o-toluenesulfonyl
chloride**
cloruro de o-
toluensulfonilo
toluic acid
ácido toluico
α-toluic aldehyde
aldehído α-toluico,
fenilacetaldehído
toluidine
toluidina
toluidine blue
azul de toluidina
toluidine red
rojo de toluidina
o-tolunitrile
o-tolunitrilo
p-tolunitrile
p-tolunitrilo
toluol
toluol, tolueno,
metilbenceno
**2-(p-toluyl) benzoic
acid**
ácido 2-(p-toluil)
benzoico
toluylene
toluileno
toluylene blue
azul de toluileno
m-, o-, p-toluylic acid
ácido m-, o- y
p-toluílico
tolycaine
tolicaína
tolyl
tolilo
tolyl acetate
acetato de tolilo
o-tolyl biguanide
o-tolilbiguanida
p-tolyl isobutyrate
isobutirato de p-tolilo
**p-tolyldiethanol-
amine**
p-tolildietanolamina
tolylhydrazine
tolilhidracina
**p-tolyl-1-naphthyl-
amine-8-sulfonic acid**
ácido p-tolil-1-
naftilamina-8-
sulfónico
p-tolylphenylacetate
fenilacetato de p-tolilo

**p-tolylsulfonyl-
methylnitrosamide**
p-tolilsulfonilmetil-
nitrosamida
tomatidine
tomatidina
tomatine
tomatina
tonazocine
tonazocina
toner
matizador
tonic
tónico
tonin
tonina
tonka bean
haba tonca
tonzonium bromide
bromuro de tonzonio
**topochemical
reaction**
reacción topoquímica
**topotecan
hydrochloride**
clorhidrato de
topotecano
toprilidine
toprilidina
topterone
topterona
toquizine
toquicina
torasemide
torasemida. torsemida
toremifene
toremifeno
toril oil
aceite de torilo
torasemide
torasemida
torsemide
torsemida
torula yeast
levadura de tórula
torularhodin
torularrodina
tosactide
tosactida
tosifen
tosifeno
tosilate, tosylate
tosilato
tosufloxacin
tosufloxacina
**tosufloxacin
hydrochloride**
clorhidrato de
tosufloxacina

tosyl
tosilo
**tosylchloramide
sodium**
tosilcloramida sódica
tourmalina
turmalina
toxaphene
toxafeno
toxic substances
sustancias tóxicas
toxicity
toxicidad
toxiferine I
toxiferina I
toxoflavin
toxoflavina
toxohormone
toxohormona
toxopyrimidine
toxopirimidina
toyocamycin
toyocamicina
tozalinone
tozalinona
tracazolate
tracazolato
trace
trazas
trace element
oligoelemento
tracer
trazador
trade mark
marca registrada
trade name
nombre comercial
tragacanth gum
goma tragacanto
tralomethrin
tralometrina
tralonide
tralonida
tramadol
tramadol
**tramadol
hydrochloride**
clorhidrato de tramadol
tramazoline
tramazolina
trandolapril
trandolapril
tranexamic acid
ácido tranexámico
tranilast
tranilast, tranilasto
tranquilizer
tranquilizador,
tranquilizante

trans-
trans-
transfer mold
molde de transferencia
transfer RNA
ARN (ácido
ribonucleico) de
transferencia
transferase
transferasa
transference number
número de
transferencia
transferrins
transferrinas
transition element
elemento de transición
transmutation
transmutación
transportation label
etiqueta de transporte
transuranic element
elemento transuránico
trantelinium bromide
bromuro de trantelinio
tranylcypromine
tranilcipromina
**tranylcypromine
sulfate**
sulfato de
tranilcipromina
trapidil
trapidil
traumatic acid
ácido traumático
traxanox
traxanox
trazitiline
tracitilina
trazodone
trazodona
**trazodone
hydrochloride**
clorhidrato de
trazodona
**Traube purine
synthesis**
síntesis de purinas de
Traube
trebenzomine
trebenzomina
trehalose
trehalosa
treloxinate
treloxinato
tremetone
tremetona
tremorine
tremorina

trenbolone
trembolona
trengestone
trengestona
treosulfan
treosulfano
trepibutone
trepibutona
trepipam
trepipán,
trepipam
trepirium iodide
yoduro de trepirio
treptilamine
treptilamina
trequinsin
trequinsina
trestolone
trestolona
tretamine
tretamina
trethinium
tosilate
tosilato de tretinio
tretinoin
tretinoino
trethocanic acid
ácido tretocánico
tretoquinol
tretoquinol
triacetate fiber
fibra de triacetato
triacetic acid
ácido triacético
triacetin
triacetina, tri-
acetato de glicerilo
triacid
triácido
1-triacontanol
1-triacontanol
triad, triadic
trivalente
triadimefon
triadimefona
triadimenol
triadimenol
triafur
triafur
triafungin
triafungina
triallate
trialato
triamcinolone
triancinolona
**triamcinolone
acetonide**
acetónido de
triancinolona

**triamcinolone
benetonide**
triancinolona
benetónido
**triamcinolone
diacetate**
diacetato de
triancinolona
**triamcinolone
furetonide**
triancinolona
furetónido
**triamcilonone
hexacetonide**
hexacetónido de
triancinolona.
1,3,5-triaminobenzene
1,3,5-triaminobenceno
**2,4,6-triaminotoluene
trihydrochloride**
triclorhidrato de 2,4,6-
triaminotolueno
**2,4, 6-triamino-sym-
triazine**
2,4,6-triamino-
sim-triacina,
2,4,6-triamino-
sim-triazina, melamina
triampyzine
triampicina,
triampizina
triamterene
trianterena
triamylamine
triamilamina
triamylbenzene
triamilbenceno
triamyl borate
borato de triamilo
**tri-p-anisyl chloro-
ethylene**
tri-p-anisil-
cloroetileno,
clorotrianiseno
**triarylmethane
dye**
colorantes de
triarilmetano
triasulfuron
triasulfurona
triazine
triazina
**s-triazine-3,5-
(2H, 4H)dione riboside**
ribósido de s-triazina-
3,5-(2H, 4H)diona,
6-azauridina
triaziquone
triacicuona

triazolam
triazolán, triazolam
1H-1,2,4-triazole
1H-1,2,4-triazol,
pirrodiazol
tribasic
tribásico
tribenoside
tribenósido
tribromide
tribromuro
tribromoacetaldehyde
tribromo-
acetaldehído
tribromoacetic acid
ácido tribromoacético
2,4,6-tribromoaniline
2,4,6-tribromoanilina
**tribromo-tert-butyl
alcohol**
alcohol tribromo-terc-
butílico
**2,4,6-tribromo-m-
cresol**
2,4,6-tribromo-m-
cresol
tribromoethanol
tribromoetanol
tribromomethane
tribromometano,
bromoformo
**1,1,1-tribromo-2-
methyl-2-propanol**
1,1,1-tribromo-2-metil-
2-propanol
tribromonitromethane
tribromonitrometano
2,4,6-tribromophenol
2,4,6-tribromofenol,
bromol
**1,2,3-tribromo-
propane**
1,2,3-tribromo-
propano
**3,4',5-tribromo-
salicylanilide**
3,4',5-tribromo-
salicilanilida
tribromosilane
tribromosilano
tribromsalan
tribromosalán
tributylamine
tributilamina
tributyltin acetate
acetato de
tributilestaño
tributyltin oxide
óxido de tributilestaño

tributyrin
tributirina
tribuzone
tribuzona
tricaine
tricaína
tricarballylic acid
ácido tricarbalílico
tricetamide
tricetamida
trichlorfon
triclorfón, metrifonato
trichloride
tricloruro
trichlormethiazide
triclormetiazida
trichlormethine
triclormetina
trichloro acetaldehyde
tricloroacetaldehído
trichloroacetic acid
ácido tricloroacético
trichloroacetonitrile
tricloroacetonitrilo
S-2,3,3-trichloroallyl-
N,N-diisopropyl-
thiolcarbamate
N,N-diisopropil-
tiolcarbamato de S-
2,3,3-tricloroalilo
2,4,6-trichloroanisole
2,4,6-tricloroanisol
1,2,3-trichloro-
benzene
1,2,3-triclorobenceno,
vec- triclorobenceno
1,2,4-trichloro-
benzene
1,2,4-triclorobenceno,
asim- triclorobenceno
1,3,5-trichloro-
benzene
1,3,5-triclorobenceno,
sim-triclorobenceno
2,3,6-trichloro-
benzyloxy-propanol
2,3,6-tricloro-
benciloxipropanol
1,1,1-trichloro-2,2-
bis(p-methoxyphenyl)
ethane
1,1,1-tricloro-
2,2-bis(p-metoxifenil)
etano, metoxicloro
ß-trichloroborazole
ß-tricloroborazol
trichlorobromo-
methane
triclorobromometano

α,α,ß--trichloro-n-
butyraldehide
α,α,ß--tricloro-n-
butiraldehído
3,4,4-trichloro-
carbanilide
3,4,4-tricloro-
carbanilida
2,3,6-trichloro-p-cresol
2,3,6-tricloro-p-cresol
2,4,6-trichloro-m-
cresol
2,4,6-tricloro-m-cresol
4,5,6-trichloro-o-
cresol
4,5,6-tricloro-o-cresol
1,1,1-trichloroethane
1,1,1-tricloroetano
2,2,2-trichloro-
ethanol
2,2,2-tricloroetanol
trichloroethylene
triocloroetileno
trichlorofluoro-
methane
triclorofluormetano
trichloroisocyanuric
acid
ácido tricloroiso-
cianúrico
trichloromelamine
tricloromelamina
trichloromethane
tricorometano,
cloroformo
α-(trichloromethyl)
benzyl acetate
acetato de α-(tri-
clorometil) bencilo
trichlorosilane
trichloromethyl
chloroformate
cloroformiato de
triclorometilo
trichloromethyl-
phenylcarbinyl
acetate
acetato de
triclorometil-
fenilcarbinilo
trichloromethyl-
phosphoric acid
ácido triclorometil-
fosfórico
1,1,1-trichloro-
2-methyl-2-propanol
1,1,1-tricloro-2-metil-
2-propanol,
clorobutanol

trichloromethyl-
sulfenyl chloride
cloruro de tricloro-
metilsulfenilo
trichloronitro-
methane
tricloronitro-
metano, cloropicrina
3,4,6-trichloro-2-
nitrophenol
3,4,6-tricloro-
nitrofenol
trichloronitroso-
methane
tricloronitrosometano
2,4,5-trichlorophenol
2,4,5-triclorofenol
2,4,5-trichloro-
phenoxy acetic acid
ácido 2,4,5-
triclorofenoxiacético
1,1,1-trichloro-2-
propanol
1,1,1-tricloro-2-
propanol
3',4',5-trichloro-
salicylanilide
3',4',5-triclor-
salicilanilida
trichlorosilane
triclorosilano
N,N',N''-trichloro-
2,4,6-triamine-1,3,5-
triazine
N,N',N''-tricloro-
2,4,6-triamina-1,3,5-
triazina
2,2',2''-trichloro-
triethylamine
2,2',2''-tricloro-
trietilamina
trichlorotrifluoro-
acetone
triclorotrifluoro-
acetona
trichodermin
tricodermina
tricholine citrate
citrato de tricolina
trichosanthin
tricosantina
trichostatin
tricostanina
trichothecin
tricotecina
tricine
tricina
triciribine
triciribina

triclabendazole
triclabendazol
triclacetamol
triclacetamol
triclazate
triclazato
triclobisonium
chloride
cloruro de triclobisonio
triclocarban
triclocarbán
triclodazol
triclodazol
triclofenate
triclofenato
triclofenol piperazine
triclofenol piperazina
triclofos
triclofós, fosfato de
tricloroetilo
triclonide
triclonida
triclopyr
triclopir
triclophylline
triclofilina
triclosan
triclosán
tricosactide
tricosactida
tricosane
tricosano
α-tricosanoic acid
ácido α-tricosanoico
tricresyl phosphate
fosfato de tricresilo
tricromyl
tricromilo
tricyanic acid
ácido triciánico
tricyclamol
chloride
cloruro de triciclamol
tricyclic
tricíclico
n-tridecanoic acid
ácido n-tridecanoico
tridecylbenzene
tridecilbenceno
tri(decyl)
orthoformate
ortoformiato de
tri(decilo)
tridemorph
tridemorfo
tridihexethyl chloride
cloruro de tridihexetilo
tridihexethyl iodide
yoduro de tridihexetilo

269

tri(dimethylamino-
methyl)phenol
tri(dimetilamino-
metil)fenol
tridiphane
tridifano
tridodecyl amine
tridodecilamina
trientine
trientina
trietazine
trietacina, trietazina
triethanolamine
trietanolamina
triethanolamine lauryl
sulfate
laurilsulfato de
trietanolamina
triethoxymethane
trietoximetano
triethyl phosphate
fosfato de trietilo
triethyl phosphine
trietilfosfina,
tietilfosfamina
triethylaluminum
trietilaluminio
triethylamine
trietilamina
triethylammonium
formate
formiato de
trietilamonio
triethylene glycol
glicol trietilénico
triethylene glycol
dichloride
dicloruro de glicol
trietilénico
triethylene glycol
dimethyl ether
éter dimetilílico de
glicol trietilénico
triethylenediamine
trietilendiamina
triethylenemelamine
trietilenmelamina,
2,4,6-tris-(1-etilen-
imino)s-triazina
triethylene-
phosphoramide
trietilenfosforamida,
óxido de tris(1-
aciridinil)fosfina
triethylenetetramine
trietilentetramida
triethylenethio-
phosphoramide
trietilentiofosforamida

triethylorthoformate
ortoformiato de trietilo
trifenmorph
trifenmorfo
trifezolac
trifezolaco
triflocin
triflocino
triflubazam
triflubazán
triflumidate
triflumidato
trifluomeprazine
trifluoromepracina,
trifluoromeprazina
triflumuron
triflumurón
trifluoperazine
trifluoperacina,
trifluoperazina
trifluoracetic acid
ácido trifluoracético
trifluperidol
trifluperidol
triflupromazine
triflupromacina,
triflupromazina
triflupromazine
hydrochloride
clorhidrato de
triflupromazina
trifluralin
trifluralina
trifluridine
trifluridina
triflusal
triflusal
trifolium
trifolio
triforine
triforina
triglycerides
triglicéridos
triglyme
triglima
tri-n-hexylaluminum
tri-n-hexilaluminio
trihexyphenidyl
trihexifenidilo
trihexyphenidyl
hydrochloride
clorhidrato de
trihexifenidilo
trihydrate
trihidrato
trihydrazine
dihydriodide
diyohidrato de
trihidracina,

diyohidrato de
trihidrazina
1,2,4-trihydroxy-
anthraquinone
1,2,4-trihidroxi-
antraquinona,
purpurina
1,2,3-trihydroxy-
benzene
1,2,3-trihidroxi-
benceno, pirogalol,
ácido pirogálico
3,4,5-trihydroxy-
benzoic acid
ácido 3,4,5-trihidroxi-
benzoico, ácido gálico
2,4,5-trihydroxy-
butyrophenone
2,4,5-trihidroxi-
butirofenona
tri-hydroxyethylamine
oleate
oleato de trihidroxi-
etilamina
tri-hydroxyethylamine
stearate
estearato de tri-
hidroxietilamina
2,3,5-triiodobenzoic
acid
ácido 2,3,5-
triyodobenzoico
triiodomethane
triyodometano,
yodoformo
triiodothyronine
triyodotironina
triisobutylaluminum
triisobutilaluminio
triisopropanolamine
triisopropanolamina
triketohydrinden
hydrate
hidrato de
tricetohidrindeno,
ninhidrina
trilaurylamine
trilaurilamina
trilauryl phosphite
fosfito de trilaurilo
trilobine
trilobino
trilostane
trilostano
trimagnesium
phosphate
fosfato de trimagnesio
trimazosin
trimazosino

trimebutine
trimebutina
trimecaine
trimecaína
trimedlure
trimedluro
trimedoxine bromide
bromuro de
trimedoxina
trimellitic acid
ácido trimelítico
trimellitic anhydride
anhídrido trimelítico
trimeperidine
trimeperidina
trimeprazine
trimepracina,
trimeprazina
trimer
trímero
trimetamide
trimetamida
trimetazidine
trimetacidina
trimethadione
trimetadiona
trimethaphan
camsylate
cansilato de
trimetafano
trimethidinium
methosulfate
metosulfato de
trimetidinio
trimethobenzamide
trimetobenzamida
trimethobenzamide
hydrochloride
clorhidrato de
trimetobenzamida
trimethoprim
trimetoprima
trimethoprim sulfate
sulfato de
trimetoprima
3,4,5-trimethoxy-
phenethylamine
3,4,5-trimetoxi-
fenetilamina,
mescalina
trimethyl borate
borato de trimetilo
trimethyl carbinol
trimetilcarbinol,
alcohol terc-butílico
trimethyl nitrilo-
tripropionate
nitrilotripropionato de
trimetilo

trimethylacet-
hydrazide ammonium
chloride
cloruro de trimetil-
acethidrazida amonio
trimethylacetic acid
ácido trimetilacético,
ácido piválico
trimethylamine
trimetilamina
2,2,3-trimethylbutane
2,2,3-trimetilbutano
N,N,1-trimethyl-3,3-
diphenylpropyl-amine
N,N,1-trimetil-3,3-
difenilpropilamina
3,7,11-trimethyl-1,6,10-
dodeca-trien-3-ol
3,7,11-trimetil-1,6,10-
dodecatrien-3-ol,
nerolidol
trimethylene
trimetileno,
ciclopropano
trimethylene bromide
bromuro de trimetileno
2,2,5-trimethylhexane
2,2,5-trimetilhexano
trimethylmethane
trimetilmetano
2,6,8-trimethyl-4-
nonanone
2,6,8-trimetil-4-
nonanona
2,6,8-trimethylnonyl-4-
alcohol
4-alcohol 2,6,8-
trimetilnonílico
trimethylol-
melamine
trimetilolmelamina
trimethylol propane
trimetilolpropano
3,5,5-trimethyl-2,4-
oxazolidinedione
3,5,5-trimetil-2,4-
oxazolidindiona,
trimetadiona
2,2,4-trimethyl-
pentane
2,2,4-trimetilpentano,
isooctano
2,2,4-trimethyl-1,3-
pentanediol
2,2,4-trimetil-1,3-
pentanodiol
2,4,4-trimethyl-
pentene-1
2,4,4-trimetilpenteno-1

tri-2-methylpenthyl-
aluminium
tri-2-metilpentil-
aluminio
N-α,α-trimethyl-
phenethylamine
N-α,α-trimetil-
fenetilamina,
mefentermina
trimethylpropyl-
methane
trimetilpropilmetano
2,4,6-trimethyl-
pyridine
2,4,6-trimetilpiridina
trimethylsilyl
triflate
triflato de trimetilsililo
trimethylvinyl-
ammonium hydroxide
hidróxido de
trimetilvinilamonio,
neurina
trimethylxanthine
trimetilxantina,
cafeína
trimetozine
trimetocina,
trimetozina
trimetrexate
trimetrexato
trimexiline
trimexilina
trimipramine
trimipramina
trimipramine maleate
maleato de
trimipramina
trimoprostil
trimoprostilo
trimoxamine
trimoxamina
trimyristin
trimiristina
sym-trinitrobenzene
sim-trinitrobenceno
2,4,7-trinitro-
fluorenone
2,4,7-trinitro-
fluorenona
trinitromethane
trinitrometano
2,4,6-trinitrophenol
2,4,6-trinitrofenol,
ácido pícrico
2,4,6-trinitrotoluene
2,4,6-trinitrotolueno
trioctadecylphosphite
fosfito de trioctadecilo

trioctyl phosphate
fosfato de trioctilo
trioctyl phosphite
fosfito de trioctilo
tri-n-octylaluminun
tri-n-octilaluminio
triolein
trioleína
triostins
triostinas
s-trioxane
s-trioxano
trioxide
trióxido
trioxifene
trioxifeno
trioxsalen
trioxsaleno,
trioxisaleno
trioxysalen
trioxisaleno,
trioxsaleno
2,6,8-trioxypurine
2,6,8-trioxipurina,
ácido úrico
tripalmitin
tripalmitina
tripamide
tripamida
triparanol
triparanol
tripelennamine
tripelenamina
tripelennamine
citrate
citrato de
tripelenamina
tripentaerythritol
tripentaeritrita
triphenyl phosphate
fosfato de trifenilo
triphenyl phosphite
fosfito de trifenilo
triphenylantimony
trifenilantimonio
triphenylcarbinol
trifenilcarbinol
triphenylguanidine
trifenilguanidina
triphenylene
trifenileno
triphenylmethane
trifenilmetano
triphenylphosphine
trifenilfosfina
triphenyltetrazolium
chloride
cloruro de
trifeniltetrazolio

triphenyltin
hydroxide
hidróxido de
trifenilestaño
triple bond
enlace triple
triple point
punto triple
triprolidine
triprolidina
tripolidine oxalate
oxalato de
tripolidina
tri-n-propyl-
aluminium
tri-n-propil-
aluminio
tripropylene glycol
glicol tripropilénico,
tripropilenglicol
triptane
triptano, 2,2,3-
trimetilbutano
triptorelin
triptorelina
triptycene
tripticeno
2,4,6-tripyridil s-
triazine
2,4,6-tripiridil s-
triacina, 2,4,6-
tripiridil
s-triazina
tris-
tris-
tris(1-aziridinyl)
phosphine oxide
óxido de tris(1-
aciridinil)fosfina,
trietilenfosforamida
2,4,6-tris-(1-
aziridinyl)s-
triazine
2,4,6-tris-(1-
aciridinil)s-triazina,
trietilenmelamina
trisaccharide
trisacárido
trisazo dye
colorante triazoico
tris(2-chloroethyl)
phosphite
fosfito de tris(2-
cloroetilo)
tris(ethylenediamine)
cadmium dihydroxide
dihidróxido de
tris(etilendiamina)
cadmio

tris(diethylene gycol
monoethyl ether)
citrate
  citrato de tris
  (monoetiléter de glicol
  dietílico)
2,4,6-tris-
(ethyleneimino) s-
triazine
  2,4,6-tris (etilenimino)-
  s-triazina, trietilen-
  melamina
tris(hydroxymethyl)
aminomethane
  tris(hidroximetil)
  aminometano
tris(hydroxy-
methyl) nitromethane
  tris(hidroximetil)
  nitrometano
1,1,3-tris(hydroxy-
phenyl) propane
  1,1,3-tris-
  (hidroxifenil)
  propano
trisilane
  trisilano
trisodium citrate
  citrato trisódico, citrato
  de sodio
trisodium EDTA
  edetato (EDTA)
  trisódico
  (etilendiamino-
  tetracetato trisódico)
trisodium phosphate
  fosfato trisódico,
  fosfato de sodio
  tribásico
tristearin
  tristearina
tris(tetrahydro-
furfuryl) phosphate
  fosfato de tris
  (tetrahidrofurfurilo)
trisulfide
  trisulfuro
trithiocarbonic acid
  ácido tritiocarbónico
trithiozine, tritiozine
  tritiozina
triticum
  grama, gramilla
  colorada
tritium
  tritio, triterio
tritolyl phosphate
  fosfato de tritolilo,
  fosfato de tricresilo

tri-o-tolyl phosphate
  fosfato de tri-o-tolilo,
  fosfato de tri-o-cresilo
tritopine
  tritopina, laudanidina
tritoqualine
  tritocualina
triturate
  triturar
triuret
  carbonildiurea
trivalence
  trivalencia
trivalent
  trivalente
trivial name
  nombre trivial
trixolane
  trixolán
trizoxime
  trizoxima
trocimine
  trocimina
troclosene
potassium
  trocloseno potásico
trofosfamide
  trofosfamida
troglitazone
  troglitazona
troleandromycin
  troleandromicina
trolnitrate
  trolnitrato
trolnitrate
phosphate
  fosfato de trolnitrato
tromantadine
  tromantadina
trometamol
  trometamol
tromethamine
  trometamina
tropabazate
  tropabazato
tropacine
  tropacina
tropacocaine
  tropacocaína
tropacocaine
hydrochloride
  clorhidrato de
  tropacocaína
tropane
  tropano
3-tropanol
  3-tropanol
tropatepine
  tropatepina

tropenziline bromide
  bromuro de
  tropenzilina
tropesin
  tropesina
tropic acid
  ácido trópico
tropicamide
  tropicamida
tropigline
  tropliglina
tropine
  tropina
tropine benzylate
  bencilato de tropina
tropirine
  tropirina
tropisetron
  tropisetrona
tropodifene
  tropodifeno
tropomyosins
  tropomiosinas
tropylium bromide
  bromuro de tropilio
trospectomycin
  trospectomicina
trospium chloride
  cloruro de trospio
Trouton's rule
  regla de Trouton
trovafloxacin mesylate
  mesilato de
  trovafloxacina
troxerutin
  troxerrutina
troxipide
  troxípido
troxonium tosilate
  tosilato de troxonio
truxillic acid
  ácido truxílico
toxypyrrolium tosilate
  tosilato de toxipirrolio
truttine
  trutina
truxicurium iodide
  yoduro de truxicurio
truxipicurium iodide
  yoduro de truxipicurio
trypan blue
  azul trípano, azul
  diamina, azul congo
trypan red
  rojo trípano
tryparsamide
  triparsamida
trypsin
  tripsina

trypsinogen
  tripsinógeno
tryptamine
  triptamina
tryptazan
  triptazano
tryptophan
  triptófano
tryptophol
  triptofol
tsuduranine
  tsuduranina, tuduranina
tuaminoheptane
  tuaminoheptano
tuaminoheptane sulfate
  sulfato de
  tuaminoheptano
tube mill
  molino tubular
tuberactinomycin
  tuberactinomicina
tuberose oil
  aceite de tuberosa
tubercidin
  tubercidina
tuberculin
  tuberculina
tuberin
  tuberina
tubocurarine chloride
  cloruro de tubocurarina
tubulin
  tubulina
tuclazepam
  tuclazepán, tuclazepam
tuftsin
  tuftsina
tulobuterol
  tulobuterol
tumbler blender
  mezcladora de tambor
tung oil
  aceite de madera de
  China, aceite de palo
tungstate
  tungstato
tungstate white
  blanco de tungstato
tungsten
  tungsteno, wolframio
tungsten boride
  boruro de tungsteno
tungsten
hexafluoride
  hexafluoruro de
  tungsteno
tungsten oxychloride
  oxicloruro de
  tungsteno

tungsten trioxide
  trióxido de tungsteno,
  anhídrido túngstico
tungstic acid
  ácido túngstico
tungstic anhydride
  anhídrido túngstico,
  trióxido de tungsteno
tunicamycin
  tunicamicina
tunichrome B1
  tunicromo B1
turanose
  turanosa
turicine
  turicino
Turkey red oil
  aceite rojo de Turquía,
  aceite de castor
  sulfatado, aceite rojo

Turks Island salt
  sal de isla turca
turmeric
  cúrcuma, batatilla
turmeric paper
  papel de cúrcuma
ar-turmerone
  ar-turmerona
turpentine
  aguarrás,
  trementina
turpentine oil
  esencia (aceite) de
  trementina
tutin
  tutina
tutocaine
hydrochloride
  clorhidrato de
  tutocaína

twistane
  triciclo [4.4.0.0,^{3,8}]
  decano
Twitchell
reagent
  reactivo de
  Twitchell
tybamate
  tibamato
Tyer sulfonation
  sulfonación de
  Tyer
tylocrebrine
  tilocrebrina
tylophorine
  tiloforina
tylosin
  tilosina
tyloxapol
  tiloxapol

tyloxin
  tiloxina
tymazoline
  timazolina
Tyndall effect
  efecto Tyndall
tyramine
  tiramina
tyrocidine
  tirocidina
tyromedan
  tiromedano
tyropanoate sodium
  tiropanoato sódico
tyrosinase
  tirosinasa
tyrosine
  tirosina
tyrothricin
  tirotricina

U

ubenimex
ubenimex
ubiquinones
ubiquinonas
ubiquitin
ubiquitina
ubisindine
ubisindina
Udex process
método Udex
Uglow black silver
plata negra de Uglow
uldazepam
uldacepán, uldazepam
ulexite
ulexita
uliginosins
uliginosinas
ultimate state of
reaction
última etapa de la
reacción
ultimate stress
tensión de ruptura
ultracentrifuge
ultracentrífuga
ultrafilter
ultrafiltro
ultrafiltration
ultrafiltración
ultramarine
azul de ultramar, azul
ultramarino
ultramicron
ultramicrón, partícula
ultramicroscópica
ultramicroscope
ultramicroscopio
ultraviolet
ultravioleta
umbellifore
umbelifora
unctuousness
untuosidad
γ-undecalactone
γ-undecalactona
undecanal
undecanal
n-undecane
n-undecano
undecanoic acid
ácido undecanoico
1-undecanol
1-undecanol

2-undecanone
2-undecanona
undecenal
undecenal, aldehído
undecílénico
undecoylium chloride
cloruro de undecoilio
n-undecyl alcohol
alcohol n-undecílico
undecylenic acetate
acetato undecilénico
undecylenic acid
ácido undecilénico
undecylenic alcohol
alcohol undecilénico
undecylenic aldehyde
aldehído undecilénico,
undecenal
n-undecylic acid
ácido n-undecílico
uniform
uniforme
uniformity
uniformidad
unit
unidad
univalence
univalencia
univalent
univalente
universal indicator
indicador universal
unknown
incógnita, desconocido
uns⁻; unsym⁻
asim⁻ (prefijo en
nomenclatura que
significa asimétrico)
unsaponifiable
matter
material no
saponificable
unsaturate
no saturado
unsaturated
hydrocabon
hidrocarburo no
saturado
unstable
inestable
unsymmetric
asimétrico
updated
actualizada

upper
superior
upright
vertical, derecho
uracil
uracilo
uracil-6-carboxylic
acid
ácido uracil-6-
carboxílico, ácido
orótico
uramil
uramilo
uramustine
uramustina
uranate
uranato
uranediol
uranediol
uranic
uránico
uranic chloride
cloruro uránico
uranic oxide
óxido uránico
uranine
uranina
uraninite
uraninita
uranium
uranio
uranium acetate
acetato de uranio
uranium carbide
carburo de uranio
uranium compounds
compuestos de uranio
uranium decay series
serie de desintegración
de uranio
uranium dicarbide
dicarburo de uranio
uranium dioxide
dióxido de uranio
uranium disulfide
disulfuro de uranio
uranium enriched
uranium enriquecido
uranium hexafluoride
hexafluoruro de uranio
uranium hydride
hidruro de uranio
uranium nitride
nitruro de uranio

uranium peroxide
peróxido de uranio
uranium tetrachloride
tetracloruro de uranio
uranium tetra fluoride
tetrafluoruro de uranio
uranium trichloride
tricloruro de uranio
uranium trioxide
trióxido de uranio
uranium-radium
series
serie de uranio y radio
uranyl acetate
acetato de uranilo
uranyl chloride
cloruro de uranilo
uranyl nitrate
nitrato de uranilo
uranyl phosphate
fosfato de uranilo
uranyl sulfate
sulfato de uranilo
urapidil
urapidil
urate
urato
urazole
urazol
urea
urea
urea ammonia liquor
licor de urea y
amoníaco
urea half-chloride
semicloruro de
urea
urea hydrochloride
clorhidrato de urea
urea nitrate
nitrato de urea
urea peroxide
peróxido de urea
urea-formaldehyde
resin
resina de urea y
aldehído fórmico
urease
ureasa
Urech cyanohydrin
method
método de la
cianohidrina de
Urech

Urech hydantoin synthesis
síntesis de hidantoína de Urech

uredepa
uredepa

uredofos
uredofós

urefibrate
urefibrato

ureide
ureído

p-ureidobenzene arsonic acid
ácido p-ureidobenceno arsónico, carbarsona

urena
urena

urethan(e)
uretano

uric acid
ácido úrico, 2,6,8-trioxipurina

uricase
uricasa

uridine
uridina

uridine 5'-diphosphate
5'-difosfato de uridina

uridine diphosphate glucose
difosfato de uridina y glucosa

uridine mono-phosphate
monofosfato de uridina, ácido uridílico

uridine phosphoric acid
ácido uridina fosfórico, ácido uridílico

uridine 5'-triphosphate
5'-trifosfato de uridina

5'-uridylic acid
ácido 5'-uridílico, monofosfato de uridina

urobilins
urobilinas

urochloralic acid
ácido uroclorálico

urofollitropin
urofolitropina

urokinase
urocinasa

urothion
urotión

ursin
ursina, arbutina

ursodiol
ursodiol

ursolic acid
ácido ursólico

urylon
urilón

uscharidin
uscaridina

usnic acid
ácido úsnico

ustilagic acid
ácido ustilágico

u-tube
tubo en u

uva ursi
gayuba,uva ursi

uzarin
uzarina

V

vaccenic acid
ácido vacénico
vaccum
vacío
vaccum distillation
destilación al vacío
vaccum filter
filtro al vacío
vaccum forming
formación al vacío
valacidin
valacidina
valacyclovir
hydrochloride
clorhidrato de
valaciclovir
valconazole
valconazol
valdetamide
valdetamida
valdipromide
valdipromida
valence
valencia
valentinite
valentinita
valeral
valeral, aldehído
valérico
n-valeraldehyde
n-valeraldehído,
valeral, aldehído
valérico
valerate
valerato, valerianato
valerian
valeriana
valerianate
valerianato, valerato
valerianic acid
ácido valeriánico
valerian oil
aceite de valeriana
valeric acid
ácido valérico
valeric aldehyde
aldehído valérico,
valeral
valeridin
valeridina
γ-valerolactone
γ-valerolactona
valethamate bromide
bromuro de valetamato

validamycins
validamicinas
validation
validación
valine
valina
valinomycin
valinomicina
valofane
valofana
valperinol
valperinol
valproate sodium
valproato sódico
valproic acid
ácido valproico
valpromide
valpromida
valsartan
valsartán
valtrate
valtrato
vanadate
vanadato
vanadic acid
ácido vanádico
vanadic acid anhydride
anhídrido vanádico,
pentóxido de vanadio
vanadic oxide
óxido vanádico,
sesquióxido de
vanadio, trióxido de
vanadio
vanadic sulfate
sulfato vanádico
vanadic sulfide
sulfuro vanádico,
sulfuro de vanadio
vanadinite
vanadinita
vanadium
vanadio
vanadium
acetylacetonate
acetilacetonato de
vanadio
vanadium carbide
carburo de vanadio
vanadium carbonyl
carbonilvanadio,
vanadio hexacarbonilo
vanadium dichloride
dicloruro de vanadio

vanadium disulfide
disulfuro de vanadio
vanadium ethylate
etilato de vanadio
vanadium
hexacarbonyl, sodium
salt
sal de sodio del
vanadio hexacarbonilo
vanadium nitride
nitruro de vanadio
vanadium
oxydichloride
oxidicloruro de
vanadio, dicloruro de
vanadilo
vanadium
oxytrichloride
oxitricloruro de
vanadio
vanadium
pentafluoride
pentafluoruro de
vanadio
vanadium pentoxide
pentóxido de vanadio,
anhídrido vanádico
vanadium sesquioxide
sesquióxido de
vanadio, trióxido de
vanadio, óxido
vanádico
vanadium sulfate
sulfato de vanadio
vanadium sulfide
sulfuro de vanadio
vanadium
tetrachloride
tetracloruro de vanadio
vanadium
tetrafluoride
tetrafluoruro de
vanadio
vanadium tetraoxide
tetróxido de vanadio
vanadium trichloride
tricloruro de vanadio
vanadium trifluoride
trifluoruro de vanadio
vanadium trioxide
trióxido de vanadio,
sesquióxido de
vanadio, óxido
vanádico

vanadium trisulfate
trisulfato de vanadio
vanadium trisulfide
trisulfuro de vanadio
vanadous chloride
cloruro vanadioso
vanadyl dichloride
dicloruro de vanadilo,
oxidicloruro de
vanadio
vanadyl sulfate
sulfato de vanadilo
vanadyl trichloride
tricloruro de vanadilo
vanaspati
vanaspati
vancomycin
vancomicina
vancomycin
hydrochloride
clorhidrato de
vancomicina
van der Waals' forces
fuerzas de van de
Waals
Van Dyke red
rojo de Van Dyke
vanilla
vainilla
vanillic acid
ácido vainillínico
vanillic aldehyde
aldehído vainíllico,
vainillina
vanillin
vainillina, aldehído
vainíllico
vanilmandelic acid
ácido vainil-
mandélico
vanitiolide
vainitiolida
vanyldisulfamide
vanildisulfamida
vapor
vapor
vapor phase
cromatography
cromatografía de fase
de vapor
vapor pressure
presión de vapor
varnish
barniz

276

varnish remover
eliminador de barniz
vaseline
vaselina
vasicine
vasicina
vasopressin
vasopresina
veatchine
veatchina
vector
vector
vecuronium bromide
bromuro de
vecuronio
vedaprofen
vedaprofeno
vegetable black
negro vegetal
vegetable dye
colorante vegetal
vegetable gum
resina vegetal
vegetable oil
aceite vegetal
vehicle
vehículo
vellosimine
vellosimina
venetian red
rojo veneciano, óxido
de hierro rojo
Venice turpentine
aguarrás de Venecia,
aguarrás de alerce
venlafaxine
hydrochloride
clorhidrato de
venlafaxina
venturicidins
venturicidinas
veradoline
veradolina
veralipride
veraliprida
veralkamine
veralcamina
verapamil
verapamilo
verapamil
hydrochloride
clorhidrato de
verapamilo
veratraldehyde
veratraldehído
veratramine
veratramina
veratric acid
ácido verátrico

veratridine
veratridina
veratrine
veratrina
veratrole
veratrol
veratrum
veratro
veratrum viride
veratro americano,
veratro verde
verazide
verazida
verbascose
verbascosa
verbenalin
verbenalina
d-verbenone
d-verbenona
verilopam
verilopán,
verilopam
vermiculite
vermiculita (silicato de
hierro, aluminio y
magnesio, hidratado)
vermifuge
vermífugo
vermilion natural
bermellón natural,
cinabrio natural
vernadigin
vernadigina
vernamycin B
vernamicina B
vernolate
vernolato
vernolepin
vernolepina
vernolic acid
ácido vernólico
verofylline
verofilina
verrucarins
verrucarinas
verticillins
verticilinas
verticine
verticina
vetiver oil
aceite de vetiver
α-vetivone
α-vetivona
vetivones
vetivonas
vessel
recipiente, vaso
vetrabutine
vetrabutina

vic-
vec- (prefijo en
nomenclatura que
significa vecino,
adyacente)
vicianose
vicianosa
vicine
vicina
Victoria blue
azul Victoria
Victoria green
verde Victoria, verde
malaquita, verde de
benzaldehído
vidarabine
vidarabina
vigabatrin
vigabatrina
villikinin
villiquinin
viloxazine
viloxazina
viminol
viminol
vinal fiber
fibra vinal
vinbarbital
vimbarbital
vinbarbital sodium
vimbarbital sódico
vinblastine
vimblastina
vinblastine sulfate
sulfato de vimblastina
vinburnine
vimburnina
vincamine
vincamina
vincanol
vincanol
vinclozolin
vinclozolina
vincofos
vincofós
vinconate
vinconato
vincristine
vincristina
vincristine sulfate
sulfato de vincristina
vindesine
vindesina
vindoline
vindolina
vinegar
vinagre
vinetine
vinetina, oxiacantina

vinformide
vinformida
vinglycinate
vinglicinato
vinic ether
éter vínico
vinleurosine
vinleurosina
vinorelbine
vinorelbina
vinorelbine tartrate
tartrato de vinorelbina
vinpocetine
vimpocetina
vinpoline
vimpolina
vinrosidine
vinrosidina
vintiamol
vintiamol
vinyl
vinilo
vinyl acetate
acetato de vinilo
vinyl acetate ethylene
copolymer
copolímero de etileno y
acetato de vinilo
vinyl alcohol
alcohol vinílico
vinyl bromide
bromuro de vinilo
vinyl n-butyl ether
éter n-butilvinilo
vinyl butyrate
butirato de vinilo
vinyl cetyl ether
éter cetilvinílico
vinyl chloride
cloruro de vinilo
vinyl 2-chloroethyl
ether
éter 2-cloroetilvinilo
vinyl compounds
compuestos vinílicos
vinyl cyanide
cianuro de vinilo,
acrilonitrilo
vinyl ether
éter de vinilo, éter
vinílico
vinyl ethyl ether
éter etilvinílico
vinyl 2-ethyl hexyl
ether
éter 2-etilhexil-
vinílico
vinyl fluoride
fluoruro de vinilo

vinyl methyl ether
éter vinilmetílico
vinyl methyl
ketone
vinilmetilcetona
vinyl plastics
plásticos de vinilo
vinyl propionate
propionato de vinilo
vinyl resin
resina de vinilo
vinyl stabilizers
estabilizadores de
vinilo
vinyl stearate
estearato de vinilo
vinyl trichloride
tricloruro de vinilo
vinylacetonitrilo
vinilacetonitrilo,
cianuro de alilo
vinylbenzene
vinilbenceno,
estireno
vinylbital
bitalvinilo, vinilbital
vinylcyclohexene
dioxide
dióxido de
vinilciclohexeno
vinylcyclohexene
monoxide
monóxido de
vinilciclohexeno
vinylethylene
viniletileno, 1,3-
butadieno, eritreno
2-vinyl-5-ethyl-
pyridine
2-vinil-5-etilpiridina
vinylmagnesium
chloride
cloruro de
vinilmagnesio

vinylpyridine
vinilpiridina
n-vinyl-2-pyrrolidone
n-vinil-2-pirrolidona
vinylation
vinilación
vinylic
vinílico
vinylidene chloride
cloruro de vinilideno
vinylidene fluoride
fluoruro de
vinilideno
vinylisobutyl ether
éter vinilisobutílico,
éter isobutilvinílico
vinylstyrene
vinilestireno
vinyltoluene
viniltolueno
vinzolidine
vinzolidina
violacein
violaceína
violanthrone
violantrona,
violaxanthin
violaxantina
viologen
viológeno
violuric acid
ácido violúrico
viomycin
viomicina
viomycin
pantothenate
pantotenato de
viomicina
viosterol
viosterol
viqualine
viqualina
viquidil
viquidil

virginiamycin
virginiamicina
viridicatin
viridicatina
viridin
viridina
viridofulvin
viridofulvina
virus
virus
viscometer
viscosímetro
viscose
viscosa
viscosin
viscosina
viscosity
viscosidad
visnadine
visnadina
visnafylline
visnafilina
visnagin
visnagina
vistatolon
vistatolona
visual purple
púrpura visual
vital red
rojo vital
vitamin
vitamina
vitamin A
vitamina A
vitamin B complex
complejo de
vitamina B
vitamin B_{12} radioactive
vitamina B_{12}
radioactiva
vitamin B_{12} -zinc
tannate complex
complejo de tanato de
vitamin B_{12} y cinc

vitamin E acetate
acetato de
vitamina E
vitamin K_1 oxide
óxido de vitamina K_1
vitrification
vitrificación
vitriol
vitriolo
vitronectin
vitronectina
voacamine
voacamina
vodka
vodka
voglibose
voglibosa
void volume
volumen nulo
volatility
volatilidad
volazocine
volazocina
volume
volumen
volumetric analysis
análisis
volumétrico
volumetric flash
matraz aforado
vomicine
vomicina
vomitoxin
vomitoxina
von Richter
reaction
reacción de von
Richter
vortex mixer
mezcladora
a vórtice
vs.
comparado con, en
función de

W

Wacker reaction
reacción de Wacker
warburganal
warburganal
warfarin
warfarina
warfarin sodium
warfarina sódica
washing soda
sosa de lavado, sal de
soda
waste bottle
frasco de desechos o
desperdicios
waste, chemical
residuos químicos
waste disposal
eliminación de
desperdicios
waste hazardous
desperdicios peligrosos
waste, radioactive
residuos radioactivos
water
agua
water base paint
pintura con base de
agua
water conditioner
acondicionador de
agua
water gas
gas de agua
water glass
vidrio acuoso, vidrio
soluble
watermelon
sandía, melón de agua
**water of
crystallization**
agua de cristalización
waterproofing agent
agente
impermeabilizante
water purification
purificación del agua
water-soluble oil
aceite soluble en agua
water-soluble resin
resina soluble en agua
watt
vatio horas, vatiohora

wattle bark
corteza de acacia
wax
cera
wax, microcrystalline
cera microcristalina
wax tailings
residuos de cera
Weerman degradation
degradación de
Weerman
weighing bottle
frasco de pesada
weight
peso
welding
soldadura
wetting agent
agente humectante
whale oil
aceite de ballena
Wharton reaction
reacción de Wharton
wheat germ oil
aceite de germen de
trigo
whiskey, whisky
whisky
white acid
ácido blanco
white alloy
metal blanco
white antimony
antimonio blanco
white arsenic
arsénico blanco
white copperas
caparrosa blanca
white dye
colorante blanco
white gasoline
gasolina blanca
white iron
hierro con estaño,
hojalata
white lead
blanco de plomo,
albayalde
white gold
oro blanco
white liquor
licor blanco

white metal
metal blanco
white oil
aceite blanco
white petrolatum
petrolato blanco
white pine
pino blanco
white precipitate
precipitado blanco,
mercurio amoniacal
white vitriol
vitriolo blanco, sulfato
de cinc, vitriolo de cinc
white wash
lechada de cal
white wax
cera blanca
whiten
blanquear
whitener
blanqueador
whiting
blanco de España
Whiting reaction
reacción de Whiting
**Wieland-Gumlich
aldehyde**
aldehido de Wieland y
Gumlich
wild cherry
cereza silvestre
Williamson synthesis
síntesis de Williamson
wine
vino
wine ether
éter de vino,
pelargonato de etilo
wintergreen oil
esencia de gaulteria
wipes
pañuelos de celulosa
de laboratorio
withaferin A
witaferina A
witherite
witerita
Witting reaction
reacción de Witting
Wolff rearrangement
transposición de Wolff

wolframite
volframita,
wolframita
wolfram white
blanco de volframio
wollastonite
wolastonita
wood alcohol
alcohol de madera
woodruff
asperilla, rubilla,
hepática estrellada
wood flour
harina de madera
Wood's metal
metal de Wood
wood pulpe
pulpa de madera
wood spirit
metanol, alcohol
metílico, alcohol de
madera
wood tar
alquitrán de madera,
alquitrán vegetal
**Woodward's
reagent K**
reactivo K de
Woodward
wool alcohols
alcoholes de lana
wool fat
grasa de lana,
lanolina
wormseed oil
aceite de hierba de
zorrillo
wormwood
ajenjo, absintio
wort
mosto
wortmannin
wortmannin
writing ink
tinta
wulfenite
wulfenita
Wulff process
método de Wulff
Wurtz reaction
reacción de
Wurtz

X

xaliproden
xaliprodeno
xamoterol
xamoterol
xanthan
xantan
xanthan gum
goma xantan
xanthathe
xantato
xanthatin
xantatina
xanthene
xanteno
xanthene dye
colorante de xanteno
xanthic
xántico
xanthin
xantina
xanthine
xantina
xanthine oxidase
xantina oxidasa
xanthinol niacinate
niacinato de xantinol
xanthiol
xantiol
xanthocillin
xantocilina
xanthogen
xantógeno
xanthogenic
xantogénico
xanthogenic acid
ácido xantogénico
xanthone
xantona
xanthophyll
xantófila

xanthopterin
xantopterina
xanthosine
xantosina
xanthoxyletin
xantoxiletina
xanthoxylin
xantoxilina
xanthurenic acid
ácido xanturénico
xanthydrol
xantidrol
xanthyletin
xantiletina
xantifibrate
xantifibrato
xantinol nicotinate
nicotinato de xantinol
xantocillin
xantocilina
xantofyl palmitate
palmitato de xantófila
xenazoic acid
ácido xenazoico
xenbucin
xenbucino
xenon
xenón
xenon compounds
compuestos de xenón
xenon difluoride
difluoruro de xenón
xenon tetrafluoride
tetrafluoruro de xenón
xenon trioxide
trióxido de xenón
xenthiorate
xentiorato
xenygloxal
xenigloxal

p-xenylcarbimide
p-xenilcarbimida
xenysalate
xenisalato
xenytropiun bromide
bromuro de xenitropio
xibenolol
xibenolol
xibornol
xibornol
xilobam
xilobán, xilobam
ximoprofen
ximoprofeno
xinidamine
xinidamine
xinomiline
xinomilina
xipamide
xipamida
xipranolol
xipranolol
X-linked
cruzamiento X
X-radiation
radiación X
X-ray
rayos X
X-ray análisis
análisis radiográfico
X-ray spectroscopy
espectroscopía
radiográfica
xylamidine tosilate
tosilato de
xilamidina
xylan
xilana, xilano
xylazine
xilacina, xilazina

xylene
xileno
xylenol
xilenol
xylenol blue
xilenol azul
xylic
xílico
xylic acid
ácido xílico
xylidine
xilidina
xylitol
xilitol
xylocoumarol
xilocumarol
xyloidin
xiloidina
xylol
xilol, xileno
xylometazoline
xilometazolina
xylopyranose
xilopiranosa
xylose
xilosa
xylotile
xilotila
xyloxemine
xiloxemina
xylulose
xilulosa
xylyl bromide
bromuro de xililo
xylyl chloride
cloruro de xililo
1-xylylazo-2-naphthol
1-xililazo-2-naftol
p-xylylene
p-xilileno

Y

Yam, mexican
boniato mejicano,
boniato gigante
yangonin
yangonina
Y-axis
ordenadas
yeast
levadura
yellow AB
amarillo AB;
FD y C amarillo
número 3,
[1-fenilazo)-
2-naftilamina]
yellow gentian
genciana amarilla,
genciana
yellow lake
laca amarilla
yellow OB
amarillo OB;
FD y C amarillo
número 4, 1-[(2-metil-
fenil)azo]-2-
naftalenamina

yellow phenophthalein
fenolftaleína amarilla
yellow precipitate
precipitado amarillo
yield
rendimiento,
producción
yield point
límite de resistencia
yig
óxido de itrio y hierro
yingzhaosu
yinghzhaosu
ylang ylang oil
esencia,(aceite) de
ilang ilang, esencia
(aceite) de cananga
ylangene
ilangeno
ylem
protilo, plasma
primordial
yogurt, yoghurt
yogur, yogurt
yohimbenine
yohimbenina

yohimbic acid
ácido yohímbico
yohimbine
yohimbina
**yohimbine
hydrochoride**
clorhidrato de
yohimbina
Young's modulus
módulo de
Young
yperite
iperita, gas
mostaza
ytterbia
iterbina
ytterbium
iterbio
ytterbium chloride
cloruro de iterbio
ytterbium fluoride
fluoruro de iterbio
ytterbium oxide
óxido de iterbio
ytterbium sulfate
sulfato de iterbio

yttria
itria
yttric
ítrico
yttrium
itrio
yttrium acetate
acetato de itrio
yttrium antimonide
antimoniuro de itrio
yttrium arsenide
arseniuro de itrio
yttrium bromide
bromuro de itrio
yttrium chloride
cloruro de itrio
yttrium nitrate
nitrato de itrio
yttrium oxide
óxido de itrio
yttrium phosphide
fosfuro de itrio
yttrium sulfate
sulfato de itrio
yttrium vanadate
vanadato de itrio

Z

zafirlukast
zafirlucast
zalcitabine
zalcitabina
Zanzibar gum
goma de Zanzíbar
zapizolam
zapizolam,
zapinolán
zaprinast
zaprinast
zea (corn silk)
zea
zearalenone
cearalenona
zeatin
ceatina
zeaxanthin
ceaxantina
zein
ceína, zeína
Zeisel
determination
determinación de
Zeisel
Zeise's salt
sal de Zeise
zeolites
ceolitas, zeolitas
zeolitic catalysts
catalizador ceolítico
zepastine
cepastina, zepastina
zeranol
ceranol, zeranol
Zerewitinoff
determination
determinación de
Zerewitinoff
zeta potential
potencial zeta
zetidoline
cetidolina, zetidolina
zidometacin
cidometacina,
zidometacina
zidovudine
cidovudina
zilantel
cilantela, zilantela
zileuton
cileutón
zimeldine
cimeldina, zimeldina

Zimmermann reaction
reacción de
Zimmermann
zinc
cinc
zinc abietate
abietato de cinc
zinc acetate
acetato de cinc
zinc acetylacetonate
acetilacetonato de cinc
zinc ammonium
chloride
cloruro de cinc y
amonio
zinc ammonium nitrite
nitrito de cinc y
amonio
zinc antimonide
antimoniuro de cinc
zinc arsenate
arseniato de cinc
zinc arsenite
arsenito de cinc
zinc bacitricin
bacitricina de cinc
zinc borate
borato de cinc
zinc bromate
bromato de cinc
zinc bromide
bromuro de cinc
zinc butylxanthathe
butilxantato de cinc
zinc cadmium
sulfide
sulfuro de cinc y
cadmio
zinc caprylate
caprilato de cinc
zinc carbonate
carbonato de cinc
zinc chlorate
clorato de cinc
zinc chloride
cloruro de cinc
zinc chloroiodide
cloroyoduro de cinc
zinc chromate
cromato de cinc
zinc citrate
citrato de cinc
zinc coated
recubrimiento de cinc

zinc cyanide
cianuro de cinc
zinc dialkyldithio-
phosphate
dialquilditiofosfato de
cinc
zinc dibenzyldithio-
carbamate
dibencilditio-
carbamato de cinc
zinc dibutyldithio-
carbamate
dibutilditiocarbamato
de cinc
zinc dichromate
dicromato de cinc
zinc diethyldithio-
carbamate
dietilditiocarbamato
de cinc
zinc dimethyldithio-
carbamate
dimetilditiocarbamato
de cinc
zinc ethylenebis-
dithiocarbamate
etilenbisditio-
carbamato de cinc
zinc-2-ethylexoate
2-etilexoato de cinc
zinc ethylsulfate
etilsulfato de cinc
zinc fluoride
fluoruro de cinc
zinc fluoroborate
fluoroborato de cinc
zinc fluorosilicate
fluorosilicato de cinc
zinc formate
formiato de cinc
zinc gluconate
gluconato de cinc
zinc glycerophosphate
glicerofosfato de cinc
zinc hexafluoro-
silicate
hexafluorosilicato de
cinc
zinc hydroxide
hidróxido de cinc
zinc iodate
yodato de cinc
zinc iodide
yoduro de cinc

zinc iodide-starch
yoduro de cinc y
almidón
zinc lactate
lactato de cinc
zinc laurate
laurato de cinc
zinc linoleate
linoleato de cinc
zinc malate
malato de cinc
zinc meta-arsenite
meta-arsenito de cinc
zinc molibdate
molibdato de cinc
zinc nitrate
nitrato de cinc
zinc nitride
nitruro de cinc
zinc nitrite
nitrito de cinc
zinc oleate
oleato de cinc
zinc orthoarsenate
ortoarseniato de cinc
zinc orthophosphate
ortofosfato de zinc
zinc orthosilicate
ortosilicato de cinc
zinc oinment
ungüento de cinc
zinc oxalate
oxalato de cinc
zinc oxide
óxido de cinc,
flores de cinc
zinc palmitate
palmitato de cinc
zinc perborate
perborato de cinc
zinc perchlorate
perclorato de cinc
zinc permanganate
permanganato de cinc
zinc peroxide
peróxido de cinc
zinc phenate
fenato de cinc
zinc-p-phenol-
sulfonate
p-fenolsulfonato de
cinc
zinc phosphate
fosfato de cinc

zinc phosphide
fosfuro de cinc
zinc potassiun
chromate
cromato de cinc y
potasio
zinc potassium
iodide
yoduro de cinc y
potasio
zinc propionate
propionato de cinc
zinc
pyrophosphate
pirofosfato de cinc
zinc resinate
resinato de cinc
zinc rhodanide
rodanuro de cinc
zinc ricinoleate
ricinoleato de cinc
zinc salicylate
salicilato de cinc
zinc selenate
seleniato de cinc
zinc selenide
seleniuro de cinc
zinc silicate
silicato de cinc
zinc silicofluoride
silicofluoruro de cinc
zinc stearate
estearato de cinc
zinc subcarbonate
subcarbonato de cinc
zinc sulfate
sulfato de cinc,
vitriolo de cinc
zinc sulfate
monohydrate
sulfato de cinc
monohidratado
zinc sulfide
sulfuro de cinc
zinc sulfite
sulfito de cinc
zinc sulfocyanate
sulfocianato de
cinc
zinc sulfoxylate
sulfoxilato de cinc
zinc tannate
tanato de cinc
zinc tartrate
tartrato de cinc
zinc telluride
telururo de cinc
zinc thiocyanate
tiocianato de cinc

zinc undecylenate
undecilenato de cinc
zinc valerate
valerato de cinc
zinc white
blanco de cinc
zinc yellow
amarillo de cinc
zincate
cincato
zincite
cincita
zincous
cíncico, de cinc
zineb
zineb (etilenbis-
ditiocarbamato
de cinc)
zingerone
cingerona
zinostatin
cinostatino,
zinostatino
zinterol
cinterol, zinterol
zinviroxime
cinviroxima,
zinviroxima
zipeprol
cipeprol, zipeprol
zip-lock
cierre a presión
ziram
ciram (dimetil-
ditiocarbamato
de cinc)
zircon
circón, zircón
zirconate
circonato
zirconia
circona
zirconic
circónico
zirconic anhydride
anhídrido
circónico
zirconium
circonio, zirconio
zirconium acetate
acetato de circonio
zirconium
acetylacetonate
acetilacetonato de
circonio
zirconium ammonium
chloride
cloruro de circonio y
amonio

zirconium boride
boruro de circonio
zirconium carbonate
basic
carbonato básico de
circonio
zirconium chloride
cloruro de circonio
zirconium chloride,
basic
cloruro básico de
circonio
zirconium diboride
diboruro de circonio
zirconium dioxide
dióxido de circonio
zirconium disilicide
disiliciuro de circonio
zirconium disulfide
disulfuro de circonio
zirconium fluoride
fluoruro de circonio
zirconium glycolate
glicolato de circonio
zirconium hydride
hidruro de circonio
zirconium hydroxide
hidróxido de circonio
zirconium iodide
yoduro de circonio
zirconium lactate
lactato de circonio
zirconium naphthenate
naftenato de circonio
zirconium nitrate
nitrato de circonio
zirconium nitride
nitruro de circonio
zirconium
orthophosphate
ortofosfato de circonio
zirconium oxide
circona, óxido de
circonio
zirconium
oxychloride
oxicloruro de circonio
zirconium phosphate
fosfato de circonio
zirconium picramate
picramato de circonio
zirconium potassium
chloride
cloruro de circonio y
potasio
zirconium potassium
fluoride
fluoruro de circonio y
potasio

zirconium potassium
sulfate
sulfato de circonio y
potasio
zirconium pyrophos-
phate
pirofosfato de circonio
zirconium silicate
silicato de circonio
zirconium silicide
siliciuro de circonio
zirconium sulfate
sulfato de circonio
zirconium sulfate,
basic
sulfato básico de
circonio
zirconium tetra-
acetylacetonate
tetraacetilacetonato de
circonio
zirconium tetrafluoride
tetrafluoruro de
circonio
zirconyl acetate
acetato de circonilo
zirconyl carbonate
carbonato de circonilo
zirconyl chloride
cloruro de circonilo
zirconyl nitrate
nitrato de circonilo
zirconyl sulfate
sulfato de circonilo
zoapatanol
zoapatanol
zocainone
zocainona
zoficonazole
zoficonazol
zolamine
zolamina
zolazepam
zolacepán,
zolazepam
zolertine
zolertina
zolimidine
zolimidina
zolmitriptan
zolmitriptano
zoloperone
zoloperona
zolpidem
zolpidén
zomepirac
zomepirac
zonisamide
zonisamida

zopolrestat
zopolrestat
zopiclone
zopiclona
zorubicin
zorrubicina

zotepine
zotepina
zoxazolamine
zoxazolamina
zuclomifene
zuclomifeno

zwitterion
ión
anfotérico
zygadenine
cigadenina,
zigadenina

zylofuramine
cilofuramina,
zilofuramina
zymase
cimasa, zimasa
zymosan
cimosán, zimozán